Fundamentals of Management

ESSENTIAL CONCEPTS AND APPLICATIONS

Fundamentals of Management

ESSENTIAL CONCEPTS AND APPLICATIONS

FOURTH EDITION

Stephen P. Robbins
San Diego State University

David A. DeCenzo
Coastal Carolina University

Upper Saddle River, New Jersey 07458

Library of Congress Cataloging-in-Publication Data

Robbins, Stephen P.
Fundamentals of management: essential concepts and applications/
Stephen P. Robbins, David A. DeCenzo.—4th ed.
p. cm.
Includes bibliographical references and index.
ISBN 0-13-101964-3 (pbk.: alk. paper)
1. Management. I. DeCenzo, David A. II. Title.

HD31.R5643 2003
658—dc21 2003042953

Acquisitions Editor: Michael Ablassmeir
Vice President/Editor-in-Chief: Jeff Shelstad
Assistant Editor: Melanie Olsen
Media Project Manager: Jessica Sabloff
AVP/Executive Marketing Manager: Shannon Moore
Marketing Assistant: Patrick Danzuso
Senior Managing Editor (Production): Judy Leale
Production Assistant: Joe DeProspero
Permissions Supervisor: Suzanne Grappi
Associate Director, Manufacturing: Vincent Scelta
Production Manager: Arnold Vila
Manufacturing Buyer: Diane Peirano
Design Manager: Maria Lange
Art Director: Janet Slowik
Interior Design: Liz Harasymczuk
Cover Design: Joseph DePinho
Cover Illustration: Jerry McDaniel
Illustrator (interior): ElectrGraphics
Photo Researcher: Teri Stratford
Image Permission Coordinator: Carolyn Gauntt
Manager, Print Production: Christy Mahon
Composition: Preparé Inc.
Full-Service Project Management: Preparé Inc.
Printer/Binder: Von Hoffmann

Credits and acknowledgments borrowed from other sources and reproduced, with permission, in this textbook appear on the appropriate page within text and on page 449.

Pearson Education Ltd.
Pearson Education Singapore, Pte. Ltd
Pearson Education, Canada, Ltd
Pearson Education—Japan
Pearson Education Australia PTY, Ltd.
Pearson Education North Asia Ltd.
Pearson Educación de Mexico, S.A. de C.V.
Pearson Education Malaysia, Pte. Ltd.

10 9 8 7 6 5 4 3 2
ISBN 0-13-101964-3

Brief Contents

Contents

Preface

A SHORT NOTE TO STUDENTS

Steve

Dave

Now that our writing chores are over, we can put our feet up on the table and offer a few brief comments to those of you who will be reading and studying this book. First, this text provides exposure to the fundamentals of management. As you'll see in our first chapter, fundamentals implies coverage of the basic functions of management. We've made every effort to give you the essential information a student will need to solidly build a knowledge foundation. A knowledge base, however, is not easily attained unless you have a text that is straightforward, timely, and interesting to read. We have made every effort to achieve those goals with a writing style that tries to capture the conversational tone that you would get if you were personally attending one of our lectures. That means logical reasoning, clear explanations, and lots of examples to illustrate concepts.

A book, in addition to being enjoyable to read and understand, should help you learn. Reading for reading's sake, without comprehension, is a waste of your time and effort. So, we've done a couple of things in this book to assist your learning. We've introduced major topic headings in each chapter. These green underlined heads provide exposure to a broad management concept. Most of these leading heads are followed by questions. Each question heading was carefully chosen to reinforce understanding of very specific information. Accordingly, as you read each of these sections, material presented will address the question posed. Thus, after reading a chapter (or a section for that matter), you should be able to return to these headings and respond to the question. If you can't answer a question or are unsure of your response, you'll know exactly what sections you need to reread or where more of your effort needs to be placed. All in all, this format provides a self-check on your reading comprehension.

We've added other check points that you should find useful. Our review and discussion questions (called Reading for Comprehension and Linking Concepts to Practice, respectively) are designed to reinforce the chapter outcomes from two perspectives. First, review questions focus on material covered in the chapter. These are another way to reinforce your comprehension of the important concepts in the chapter. The discussion questions require you to go one step further. Rather than asking you to recite facts, discussion questions require you to integrate, synthesize, or apply a management concept. True understanding of the material is revealed when you can apply these more complex issues to a variety of situations.

There is another element of this text that we hope you'll enjoy. These are the "Management Workshop" sections at the end of each chapter. Managing today requires sound competencies—competencies that can be translated into specific skills. These sections are designed to help you enhance your analytical, diagnostic, investigative, team-building, Internet, and writing skills. We hope that you find them useful and use them as a source of self-development. You'll also find step-by-step skill guidance to help you learn such skills as how to build a power base, interview candidates, build trust, and provide performance feedback. We encourage you to carefully review each of these, practice the behaviors, and keep them handy for later reference.

We conclude by extending an open invitation to you. If you'd like to give us some feedback, we encourage you to write. Send your correspondence to Dave DeCenzo, Dean, Wall College of Business, Coastal Carolina University, P. O. Box 261954, Conway, SC 29528-6054. Dave is also available on e-mail ddecenzo@coastal.edu.

Good luck this semester and we hope you enjoy reading this book as much as we did preparing it for you.

Steve Robbins   Dave DeCenzo

Welcome to the fourth edition of *Fundamentals of Management.* We have continued the tradition started with the first edition of this book: covering the essential concepts in management; providing a sound foundation for understanding the key issues; offering a strong practical focus, including the latest research studies in the field; and achieving these ends through a writing style that readers will find interesting and straightforward. By keeping the length around 500 pages, the book is designed to be completed in a one-term course.

We want to use this preface to address three critical questions: (1) What assumptions guided the development of this book? (2) What's new in this revision? and (3) how does the book encourage learning?

WHAT WERE OUR ASSUMPTIONS IN WRITING THIS BOOK?

Every author who sits down to write a book has a set of assumptions—either explicit or implicit—that guides what is included and what is excluded. We want to state ours up front. Management is an exciting field. The subject matter encompassed in an introductory management text is inherently exciting. We're talking about the real world. We're talking about why StrawberryFrog is revolutionizing the international advertising industry; how an entrepreneurial venture, Zane's Cycles, competes so effectively against large retail chains; why companies like Cincinnati Milacron and British Airways have achieved ISO 9000 certification to demonstrate their commitment to quality; how Trufresh LLC operates a virtual organization; how the leadership of Rudy Giuliani comforted a nation; and how a lack of control mechanisms and ethics led to the fall of corporate giants like Enron, Adelphia, and WorldCom. A good management text should capture this excitement. How? Through a crisp and conversational writing style, elimination of nonessential details, a focus on issues that are relevant to the reader, and inclusion of examples and visual stimuli to make concepts come alive.

It's our belief that management shouldn't be studied solely from the perspective of "top management," "billion-dollar companies," or "U.S. corporations." The subject matter in management encompasses everyone from the lowest supervisor to the chief executive officer. The content should give as much attention to the challenges and opportunities in supervising a team of five, some of whom may be telecommuting, as those in directing a staff of MBA-educated vice presidents. Similarly, not everyone wants to work for a *Fortune* 500 company. Readers who are interested in working in small businesses, entrepreneurial ventures, or not-for-profit organizations should find the descriptions of management concepts applicable to their needs. Finally, organizations operate today in a global village. Readers must understand how to adjust their practices to reflect differing cultures. Our book addresses each of these concerns.

Before we committed anything to paper and included it in this book, we made sure it met our "so what?" test. Why would someone need to know this fact? If the relevance isn't overtly clear, either the item should be omitted or its relevance should be directly explained. In addition, content must be timely. We live in dynamic times. Changes are taking place at an unprecedented pace. A textbook in a dynamic field such as management must reflect this fact by including the latest concepts and practices. Ours does!

Have you ever walked into someone's office—or house for that matter—and seen piles of clutter? Is the adage "a cluttered desk is a sign of a cluttered mind" accurate? Of course that's debatable, but for Garrett Boone and Kip Tindell, it really doesn't matter. That's because they have a solution to the disorganization.[1]

In 1978, Boone and Tindell founded The Container Store. The Container Store is a business that sells "boxes, bottles, jars, trunks, racks, baskets, dividers, and much, much more." It's an organization that sells storage products for businesses and homes. Based in Dallas, Texas, The Container Store now has annual revenues exceeding $230 million, and employs more than 1,600 individuals in 26 stores located in 11 states. And since its inception, the company has enjoyed a sales growth of more than 20 percent each year. What's interesting about The Container Store is not its phenomenal growth. Rather, it's the entrepreneurial spirit of Tindell and Boone in creating the organization mind-set that's a testament to sound management practice-with customer service as the driving force.

Customer service is a term that neither of these founding members takes lightly. They recognize that customer service is more than lip service—it's establishing a supportive atmosphere in the organization where employees can truly understand and resolve customer issues. Rather than simply "making the sale at all costs," it is these founders' mission to fully recognize customer needs and recommend appropriate solutions. For example, they invest heavily in employee training to ensure that each employee has thorough product knowledge as well as customer service and selling skills. This training involves 235 hours of instruction in the first year, and more than 160 training hours annually thereafter for each employee. Employees meet daily, in what are called team huddles (see photo), to discuss goals for the day. As a result, sales associates are able to listen to a customer's problems and recommend "tailor-made" solutions. For instance, one associate creatively determined, for a customer who wanted to store and ship videocassettes, that men's shoeboxes will snugly and securely hold 11 videotapes. That employee's insight became one of the topics of the following day's team huddle!

To ensure that each trained employee stays with the company, Tindell and Boone make every effort to pay above-average salaries and benefits. In fact, for the past several years, The Container Store has been recognized by *Fortune* magazine as one of the best companies to work in. But these two founders aren't sitting back and congratulating each other for their success. Although they have clearly differentiated their organization from the competition, they know they won't enjoy that position for long. Major discount stores, like Target, have seen the success of The Container Store, and are beginning to replicate some of their activities. As Garrett Boone says, "we welcome these challenges as it keeps us constantly focused on bettering our services to keep us unique. Being complacent in an ever-changing world is simply unacceptable."

Management Workshop

Team Skill-Building Exercise

Understanding Cultural Differences

Workforce diversity has become a major issue for managers. Although there are often similarities among individuals, obvious differences do exist. A means of identifying some of those differences is to get to know individuals from the diverse groups. For this exercise, you will need to contact people from a different country. If you don't know any, the office of your college that is responsible for coordinating international students may be able to give you a list of names. Interview at least three people to get responses to such questions as:

- What country do you come from?
- What is your first language?
- Describe your country's culture in terms of, for example, form of government, emphasis on individual versus group, role of women in the workforce, benefits provided to employees, and how managers treat their employees.
- What were the greatest difficulties in adapting to your new culture?
- What advice would you give me if I had a management position in your country?

In groups of three to five class members, discuss your findings. Are there similarities in what each of you found? If so, what are they? Are there differences? Describe them. What implications for managing in the global village has this exercise generated for you and your group?

Understanding Yourself

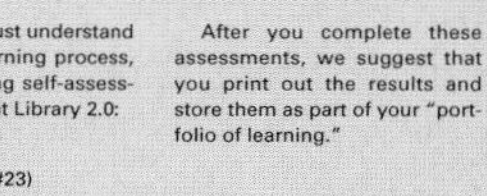

Before you can develop other people, you must understand your present strengths. To assist in this learning process, we encourage you to complete the following self-assessments from the Prentice-Hall Self-Assessment Library 2.0:

- How Do My Ethics Rate? (#19)
- Am I Likely to Become an Entrepreneur? (#23)

After you complete these assessments, we suggest that you print out the results and store them as part of your "portfolio of learning."

Developing Your Ethics Skill

Guidelines for Acting Ethically

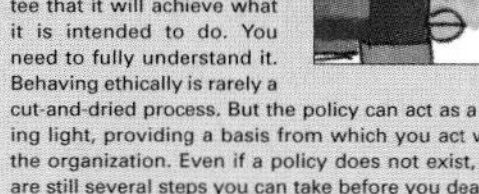

About the Skill

Making ethical choices can often be difficult for managers. Obeying the law is mandatory, but acting ethically goes beyond mere compliance with the law. It means acting responsibly in those gray areas, where right and wrong are not defined. What can you do to enhance your managerial abilities in acting ethically? We offer some guidelines.

Steps in Practicing the Skill

1. **Know your organization's policy on ethics.** Company policies on ethics, if they exist, describe what the organization perceives as ethical behavior and what it expects you to do. This policy will help you to clarify what is permissible and the managerial discretion you will have. This becomes your code of ethics!
2. **Understand the ethics policy.** Just having the policy in your hand does not guarantee that it will achieve what it is intended to do. You need to fully understand it. Behaving ethically is rarely a cut-and-dried process. But the policy can act as a guiding light, providing a basis from which you act within the organization. Even if a policy does not exist, there are still several steps you can take before you deal with the difficult situation.
3. **Think before you act.** Ask yourself, "Why am I going to do what I'm about to do? What led up to the problem? What is my true intention in taking this action? Is my reason valid? Or are there ulterior motives behind it—such

as demonstrating organizational loyalty? Will my action injure someone? Would I disclose to my boss or my family what I'm going to do?" Remember, it's your behavior and your actions. You need to make sure that you are not doing something that will jeopardize your role as a manager, your organization, or your reputation.
4. **Ask yourself what-if questions.** If you are thinking about why you are going to do something, you should also be asking yourself what-if questions. For example, the following questions may help you shape your actions: "What if I make the wrong decision? What will happen to me? To my job? What if my actions were described, in detail, on the local TV news show or in the newspaper? Would it bother or embarrass me or those around me? What if I get caught doing something unethical? Am I prepared to deal with the consequences?"
5. **Seek opinions from others.** If it is something major that you must do, and about which you are uncertain, ask for advice from other managers. Maybe they have been in a similar situation and can give you the benefit of their experience. Or maybe they can just listen and act as a sounding board for you.
6. **Do what you truly believe is right.** You have a conscience, and you are responsible for your behavior. Whatever you do, if you truly believe it was the right action to take, then what others say or what the Monday morning quarterbacks say is immaterial. You need to be true to your own internal ethical standards. Ask yourself: Can I live with what I've done?

Practicing the Skill

Find a copy of your school's code of conduct or the code of ethics of any organization to which you belong. Or, obtain a copy of the code of ethics for a professional organization you hope to join after graduating. Evaluate the code's provisions and policies. Are there any that you are uncomfortable with? Why? Are there any that are routinely violated? Why do you think this is happening? What are the usual consequences of such violations? Do you think they are appropriate?

If you had trouble obtaining the code of conduct, find out why. Under what circumstances is it normally distributed, posted, or otherwise made available to members?

Developing Your Diagnostic and Analytical Skills

Pets.com

Pets.com was one of the most visible of the thousands of e-commerce firms that sprouted up in the late 1990s. It had a clever slogan—"Because Pets Can't Drive"—and its ad agency created a charming sock puppet to act as the company's "spokesperson." Unfortunately, buying pet supplies over the Internet didn't prove to be a profitable business model. In retrospect, the business model's basic flaw was that the company's primary product—pet food—tends to be modestly priced and expensive to ship. It's also readily available in most supermarkets and retail stores like Wal-Mart and Target. As a result, Pets.com went out of business in the summer of 2000—selling most of its assets to Petco.[84]

In contrast, Dell Computer has become a large and profitable company by selling computers online. Dell's success is attributed to a carefully developed and executed business model that allows customers to custom design computers online, initiate the order, and have the products built and shipped within three business days. While competitors have attempted to copy many of Dell's Web site features and internal systems, Dell's continual efforts at improving customer service, minimizing costs, and passing its cost reductions on to customers through lower prices has kept its sales and profits growing.

Why the dramatic difference between these two organizations? Although a number of factors may enter into the equation, one critical component is that managing in an "electronic" environment is significantly different from managing in traditional organizations. Companies like Dell that understand this difference position themselves better to succeed. Those that don't, well, their businesses may go to the dogs!

Questions

1. Describe how technology has assisted a company like Dell Computers. What managerial changes do you believe are necessary to ensure that the full benefits of technology are reaped.
2. Do you believe a company like Pets.com was simply a "flash in the PAN," going out of business when the realities of dot-coms hit? Or do you believe that the demise of Pets.com might be attributable to poor management of the company? Defend your position.
3. Do you believe a company like Dell Computer is customer-responsive? Cite examples to support your position.

This book is organized around the four traditional functions of management—planning, organizing, leading, and controlling. It is supplemented with material that addresses current issues affecting managers. For example, we take the reader through "Managing in Today's World" (Chapter 2), "Understanding Work Teams" (Chapter 9), "Leadership and Trust" (Chapter 11), and "Value Chain Management" (Chapter 14). We also integrate throughout the text such contemporary topics as technology, entrepreneurship, empowerment, diversity, and continuous improvements. There are a total of 14 chapters, plus 3 modules that describe the evolution of management thought, focus on popular quantitative techniques used in business today, and provide some special information to students regarding how to build their management careers.

Fundamentals of Management, Fourth Edition, is lean and focused. Since the last edition, there have been a number of topics that needed to be included. But we didn't want to simply add pages to cover the new material. Rather, to keep the book at 14 chapters, we had to make some difficult decisions regarding the cutting and reshaping of material. We were greatly assisted in this process by feedback from previous users. The result, we believe, is a text that identifies the essential elements students' need in an introductory management course.

It's not enough, however, to simply know about management. Today's students need the skills and competencies to succeed in management. So we enhanced our "Management Workshop" section at the end of each chapter. The "Management Workshop" is designed to help students build analytical, diagnostic, team-building, investigative, and writing skills. We address these skill areas in several ways. For example, we include experiential exercises to develop team-building skills; cases to build diagnostic, analytical, and decision-making skills; and suggested topical writing assignments to enhance writing skills.

Learning from Experience: One Manager's Reflection

D. J. Hanlon Operations Manager, Tiger Woods Foundation, Inc.

HOW DO WE MAKE MANAGERS MORE SENSITIVE TO DIFFERENCES?

Describe the situation you faced. The Tiger Woods Foundation, Inc. coordinates several events annually to raise money for charities designed to assist underprivileged youth. As operations manager, one of my responsibilities was to coordinate volunteers for the events. I quickly discovered that part of the challenge of coordinating volunteers is convincing them that they are a crucial link in the larger good. This problem was compounded by the fact that I was relatively young, and was trying to convince people who were older than me that a menial task such as standing in a parking lot holding a sign that reads "EVENT HERE" was a valuable service. The key issues here were first, convincing them that they were vital players for the greater good and, second, matching them with jobs that best suited their skills and personalities.

What action did you take? I took various approaches to handling these issues. But, most importantly, I learned to read the subtle signs of resistance; only then could I nip problems in the bud. For instance, if it became clear that someone was irreconcilably unhappy with a job, I would try to offer that person another position. In planning events there is always a lot to do, and offering someone a respectable way out helped to prevent many mild disgruntlements from growing into something more problematic. Reading people was a key in this: If someone felt they were more valuable moving heavy objects than handing out programs, I would go along with that. From a management standpoint, you have to be willing to respect genuine issues. And yet, sometimes there were no other positions to offer, so I learned a second art of management: subtle coaxing. Reminding them that they were part of a larger activity that had ultimately a greater good was a key here. If that didn't work I knew I had to develop other techniques.

What results occurred? During the years I worked at the Tiger Woods Foundation, Inc., I developed several different management techniques. For instance, for some volunteers I developed a technique that relied on direct, straightforward orders. For others, I would more gently rationalize the importance of their actions. And for still others, I learned to bring in other people from within the Foundation if I felt my personality didn't effectively "click" with one of the volunteers. Here again, reading personalities is a key to managing a diverse group.

The results were mostly positive. During my years with Tiger Woods Foundation, I developed techniques that helped me to manage a diverse group of workers and to prevent many management problems from getting bigger.

WHAT'S NEW IN THIS FOURTH EDITION?

Previous editions of this book have always contained the latest research and practices in management. In this edition, we raised the ante. A brief review of the end notes will reveal that most are from references dated 2000 or later. In addition, we've included recent events that have reshaped the world of organizations and management—specifically; the terrorist attacks on the World Trade Towers and the Pentagon, and the corporate scandals at companies like Enron, WorldCom, Adelphia, and Tyco International.

We continued with our practical perspective in this edition. Our experience has led us to conclude that students like to see and read about people who have made a contribution to their organization and use the management techniques we discuss. Sometimes that contribution is attributable to learning from a previous situation, so we've added "Learning from Experience: One Manager's Reflection" boxes. These vignettes are designed to talk about a "mistake" a manager made, how he or she addressed the mistake, and the outcome of their actions.

SEVERAL CONTENT TOPICS HAVE BEEN ADDED OR EXPANDED IN THIS REVISION

We continue to present material that is current and relevant. The more prominent of these include the following:

- Entrepreneurial ventures (Chapter 2)
- Customer responsive culture (Chapter 2)
- Work/family balances (Chapter 2)
- The coming labor shortage (Chapter 2)
- The fall of dot-coms (Chapter 2)
- E-business, e-commerce, and e-organizations (Chapter 2)
- Entrepreneurs and establishing competitive advantages (Chapter 3)
- Creativity and the rational decision-making model (Chapter 4)
- The learning organization (Chapter 5)
- Entrepreneurial change and innovation (Chapter 7)
- Emotional intelligence (Chapter 8)
- Teams and entrepreneurs (Chapter 9)
- The ethics of stock options (Chapter 10)
- Information technology and communications (Chapter 12)
- Employee theft (Chapter 13)
- Value change management (Chapter 14)

HOW DO WE ENCOURAGE LEARNING?

Just what do students need to facilitate their learning? We began to answer that question by thinking through some fundamental issues: Could we make this book both "fun" to read and pedagogically sound? Could it motivate students to read on and facilitate learning? Our conclusion was that an effective textbook could and should teach, as well as present ideas. Toward that end, we designed this book to be an effective learning tool. Let's specifically describe some of the pedagogical features—in addition to what we've mentioned previously—that we included to help students better assimilate the material.

LEARNING OUTCOMES. Before you start a trip, it's valuable to know where you're headed. That way, you can minimize detours. The same holds true in reading a text. To make learning more efficient, we open each chapter of this book with a list of outcomes that describes what the student should be able to do after reading the chapter. These outcomes are designed to focus students' attention on the major issues within each chapter. Each outcome is a key learning element for readers.

CHAPTER SUMMARIES. Just as outcomes clarify where one is going, chapter summaries remind you where you have been. Each chapter of this book concludes with a concise summary directly linked to the opening learning outcomes.

REVIEW AND DISCUSSION QUESTIONS. Every chapter in this book ends with a set of review and discussion questions. If students have read and understood the contents of a chapter, they should be able to answer the review questions. These "Reading for Comprehension" review questions are drawn directly from the material in the chapter. The discussion questions go beyond comprehending chapter content. They're designed to foster higher order thinking skills. That is, they require the reader to apply, integrate, synthesize, or evaluate management concepts. The "Linking Concepts to Practice" discussion questions will allow students to demonstrate that they not only know the facts in the chapter but also can use those facts to deal with more complex issues.

A TEACHING AND LEARNING PACKAGE

Fundamentals of Management, Fourth Edition comes with a complete, high-tech support package for faculty and students. This includes a comprehensive instructor's manual and test bank; a dedicated Web site (www.prenhall.com/robbins); inclusion on myCW (Companion Website), a faculty support Website featuring Instructor's Manual, PowerPoint slides, and test item file; an online student study guide; and the Robbins Self-Assessment Library, which provides students with insights into their skills, abilities, and interests. The updated supplements package also includes BusinessNow videos, each corresponding to one of the chapters in the text.

- ***Instructor's Manual with Video Guide***—Designed to guide the educator through the text, each chapter in the instructor's manual includes learning objectives, a detailed lecture outline, teaching tips for boxed features, teaching notes for the "Management Workshop," and answers for all end-of-chapter materials.
- ***Instructor's Resource CD ROM***—All of the resources for your text are available in one place! On the IRCD, you will find the electronic files for the instructor's manual, the TestGen software, and the complete set of PowerPoints.

- ***Test Item File***—Each chapter contains true/false, multiple-choice, short answer/essay questions, and situation-based questions. Together the questions cover the content of each chapter in a variety of ways providing flexibility in testing the students' knowledge of the text.

- ***TestGenEQ Test Generating Software***—The print Test Banks are designed for use with the TestGen-EQ test generating software. This computerized package allows instructors to custom design, save, and generate classroom tests. The test program permits instructors to edit, add, or delete questions from the test banks; edit existing graphics and create new graphics; analyze test results; and organize a database of tests and student results. This new software allows for greater flexibility and ease of use. It provides many options for organizing and displaying tests, along with a search and sort feature.
- ***PowerPoint Electronic Transparencies***—A comprehensive package, these PowerPoint transparencies are designed to aid the educator and supplement in class lectures. They are available both online at (www.prenhall.com/robbins) or on the Instructor's Resource CD-ROM.
- ***The Video Package***—We offer two different options for enhanced learning.
  1. **Skills Videos**. Five videos (one for each part of the text) offer dramatizations that highlight various management skills. The videos provide excellent starting points for classroom discussion and debate. These videos are available on VHS for classroom presentation.
  2. ***BusinessNow* Videos**. New to this edition, Prentice Hall is pleased to offer exciting *BusinessNOW* video cases. *BusinessNOW* is a fast-paced television news magazine that takes viewers on location and behind closed doors to look at America's most interesting companies and the corporate executives who run them. These videos offer interesting, up-to-date content pertaining to the topics raised in *Fundamentals of Management*, and there is one video segment to accompany each of the chapters in the book. Some of the companies featured on the *BusinessNOW* video include Beyond Components and NLX Corporation, and some of the topics featured include types of training, social responsibility, teamwork, and employee motivation.

- ***MyCW Companion Website***—The format of our Website has been updated, and includes the same great features in a more user-friendly format. Here you will find password-protected instructor's resources, as well as a student section, which features sample true/false, multiple-choice, and Internet essay questions. The Website for Robbins/DeCenzo *Fundamentals of Management, Fourth Edition* can be found at **www.prenhall.com/robbins**.
- ***Self-Assessment Library 2.0 CDROM***—Free as a value pack, this valuable tool includes 49 individual self-assessment exercises, organized around individuals, groups, and organizations. Each exercise can be taken electronically and scored immediately, giving students individual feedback.

- ***WebCT Course***—Developed by educators, WebCT provides faculty with easy-to-use Internet tools to create online courses. Prentice Hall provides the content and enhanced features to help instructors create a complete online course. Please visit our Web site **http://www.prenhall.com/webct** for more information.

- ***Bloackboard***—Easy to use, Blackboard's single template and tools make it easy to create, manage, and use online course materials. Instructors can create online courses using the Blackboard tools, which include design, communication, testing, and course management tools. For more information, please visit our Web site **http://www.prenhall.com/blackboard**.

- ***Course Compass***—This customizable, interactive online course management tool powered by Blackboard provides the most intuitive teaching and learning environment available. Instructors can communicate with students, distribute course material, and access student progress online. For further information, please visit our Web site **http://www.prenhall.com/coursecompass**.

ACKNOWLEDGMENTS

Writing and publishing a textbook requires the talents of a number of people whose names never appear on the cover. We'd like to recognize some special people who gave so unselfishly in making this book a reality.

First are our friends at Prentice Hall. Specifically, we want to thank our editor Michael Ablassmeir along with Melanie Olsen, Shannon Moore, Jeff Shelstad, and Jerome Grant. From the production side: Judy Leale, Janet Slowik, Teri Stratford, and Diane Peirano. We appreciate their support and efforts to make this book successful.

We also want to thank our previous users and students who provided us with a number of suggestions for this revision. We also recognize the assistance our reviewers provided. Their constructive comments and suggestions have made this a much better book.

Lorraine P. Anderson, Marshall University

Kenneth R. Tillery, Middle Tennessee State University

Debora Gilliard, Metropolitan State College, Denver

Marca Marie Bear, University of Tampa

Christine Miller, Tennessee Technological University

Elena Capella, University of San Francisco

Mantha Vlahos Mehallis, Florida Atlantic University

Barbara Ann Boyington, Brookdale Community College

Gary Greene, Manatee Community College, Venice Campus

Edward A. Johnson, University of North Florida

Pollis Robertson, Kellogg Community College

Leroy Plumlee, Western Washington University

Finally, we'd like to add a personal note. Each of us has some special people we'd like to recognize.

From Steve's corner: I want to acknowledge my wife, Laura, for her love and support.

From Dave's: Wow, it feels just like yesterday that I was writing this section for the first edition of Fundamentals of Management. In the past decade a lot has transpired. But through it all, one thing has remained–our commitment to family. Thanks to each of you—Terri, Mark, Meredith, Gabriella, and Natalie—for being the best part of my life. Thanks again to all of you for making me who I am.

PART 1

Introduction

CHAPTER 1

Managers and Management

LEARNING OUTCOMES

After reading this chapter, I will be able to:

1 Describe the difference between managers and operative employees.

2 Explain what is meant by the term *management*.

3 Differentiate between efficiency and effectiveness.

4 Describe the four primary processes of management.

5 Classify the three levels of managers and identify the primary responsibility of each group.

6 Summarize the essential roles performed by managers.

7 Discuss whether the manager's job is generic.

8 Describe the four general skills necessary for becoming a successful manager.

9 Describe the value of studying management.

10 Identify the relevance of popular humanities and social science courses to management practices.

MEET A REAL MANAGER!

"One Manager's Reflection" page 13

James C. Ray Jr., Court Administrator, Hamilton County Juvenille Court

In today's fiercely competitive marketplace, an organization can fail at a moment's notice. What distinguishes those organizations that succeed from those that don't succeed? Good managers, and their ability to adapt to the ever-changing environment around them. Managers come from all walks of life; they differ in terms of shape, color, age, nationality, and gender. They work to produce a profit, or to achieve some social good. Yet, managers don't accomplish these goals by themselves; they are achieved through and with the efforts of others. Managers make sure plans are laid out, activities are kept on track, and the environment is conducive to productive work. And they do all of this while the world around them undergoes constant change. Take the case of Hiroshi Okuda, Chairman of Toyota.[1] (See photo.)

For years, Toyota was regarded as one of the premier auto companies worldwide. To continue its tradition of outstanding shareholder return, Okuda and company officials set out to develop a multipart strategy that would make Toyota the envy of the world. Their goals included growing Toyota steadily in Japan, making significant inroads into the U.S. auto market, expanding market share in the European market, and becoming the automotive market leader in Southeast Asia. Challenging goals for any organization, especially one with sales of $108 billion and profits of $4.2 billion. Yet Okuda was not pleased, because the goals of Toyota had not been met.

During the past several years, Toyota's world has changed. The Japanese market for Toyota automobiles has shrunk significantly. Plans to forge ahead in Europe have been put on hold; and sales in the Southeast Asia market have come to a grinding halt. Without the U.S. market, Toyota would be in trouble; Toyota USA sold more than 1.7 million vehicles in 2001. It employs more than 123,000 Americans—more than Coca-Cola, Microsoft, and Oracle combined—and of its $4.2 billion in profits in 2001, more than two-thirds came from the U.S. market. Toyota, for all intents and purposes, has become Americanized.

With Toyota's increased reliance on the United States for its sales and profits, its executives decided to focus on local hires in their U.S. management positions. In doing so, they have significantly reduced the Japanese influence on the day-to-day operations of Toyota USA. This has led to conflicts between the "American Way" and the focus created by Toyota's founder, Kiirchiro Toyota, regarding consensus decision making, cost cutting, and the company's concern for quality and customer service. Conflicts over color schemes, design, and product offerings have also been a source of contention. For example, Toyota U.S. executives wanted to enter the expanding U.S. market for full-size pickup trucks, and they wanted to do it immediately. Toyota Japan thought differently, and consistent with consensus decision making, wanted to research the idea further and get a full range of input. U.S. executives wouldn't take "slow down" as an option. To make their point, they invited Toyota executives from Japan to a Dallas Cowboys' football game. There the Japanese executives saw a parking lot filled with pickup trucks and sport utility vehicles, and they got the message. They gave the go ahead for Toyota U.S. to produce the Tundra pickup, and the Sequoia and Highlander sport utility vehicles. These three models have become market leaders for Toyota, and they are its fastest-growing product line.

The message in this story is that Okuda and Toyota were willing to adapt to a changing environment. While the company plans were important, Okuda was not so wedded to them that the company would flounder just to reach their goals. Instead, Okuda recognized where Toyota's growth potential was and shifted resources to grow the expanding U.S. market.

HIROSHI OKUDA PROVIDES A GOOD EXAMPLE OF WHAT A successful manager does. The key word, however, is example. There is no universally accepted model of what a successful manager looks like. Managers today can be under age 18 or over 80. Nowadays, they are as likely to be women as they are to be men.[2] They manage large corporations, small businesses, government agencies, hospitals, museums, schools, and such nontraditional organizations as cooperatives. Some hold positions at the top of their organizations, some are middle managers, and others are first-line supervisors who directly oversee employees. And today's managers can be found in every country on the globe.

This book is about the work activities of Hiroshi Okuda and the tens of millions of other managers like him. In this chapter, we introduce you to managers and management by answering, or at least beginning to answer, these questions: Who are managers, and where do they work? What is management, and what do managers do? And why should you spend your time studying management?

How does an organization like the Anaheim Angels become successful? By having in place a systematic arrangement of quality people—both on and off the field—focusing their efforts on achieving some goal. For them, that's winning baseball's coveted fall classic honor, the World Series.

WHO ARE MANAGERS AND WHERE DO THEY WORK?

Managers work in organizations. Therefore, before we identify who managers are and what they do, we must clarify what we mean by the term *organization.*

An **organization** is a systematic arrangement of people brought together to accomplish some specific purpose. Your college or university is an organization. So are sororities, the United Way, churches, your neighborhood convenience store, the Anaheim Angels baseball team, the Sprint Corporation, as well as the globally based Sony and Unilever corporations.[3] These are all organizations because each has three common characteristics.

organization
A systematic arrangement of people brought together to accomplish some specific purpose

WHAT THREE COMMON CHARACTERISTICS DO ALL ORGANIZATIONS SHARE?

Every organization has a purpose and is made up of people who are grouped in some fashion (see Exhibit 1–1). The distinct purpose of an organization is typically expressed in terms of a goal or set of goals. For example, the president of 7-Eleven stores has set his sights on "reinvigorating the merchandise mix by aggressively branding fresh foods." Second, no purpose or goal can be achieved without people making decisions to establish the purpose and performing a variety of activities to make the goal a reality. Third, all organizations develop a systematic structure that defines and limits the behavior of its members. Developing structure may include, for example, creating rules and regulations, giving some members supervisory control over other members, forming work teams, or writing job descriptions so that organizational members know what they are supposed to do. The term *organization,* therefore, refers to an entity that has a distinct purpose, has people or members, and has a systematic structure.

HOW ARE MANAGERS DIFFERENT FROM OPERATIVE EMPLOYEES?

operatives
People who work directly on a job or task and have no responsibility for overseeing the work of others

managers
Individuals in an organization who direct the activities of others

Managers work in organizations, but not everyone who works in an organization is a manager. For simplicity's sake, we can divide organizational members into two categories: operatives and managers. **Operatives** are people who work directly on a job or task and have no responsibility for overseeing the work of others. The people at Covisint who operate the information system for Ford, those who ring up your sale at Foot Locker, or individuals who process your course registration in your college's registrar's office are all operatives. In contrast, **managers** direct the activities of

EXHIBIT 1–1
Common Characteristics of Organizations

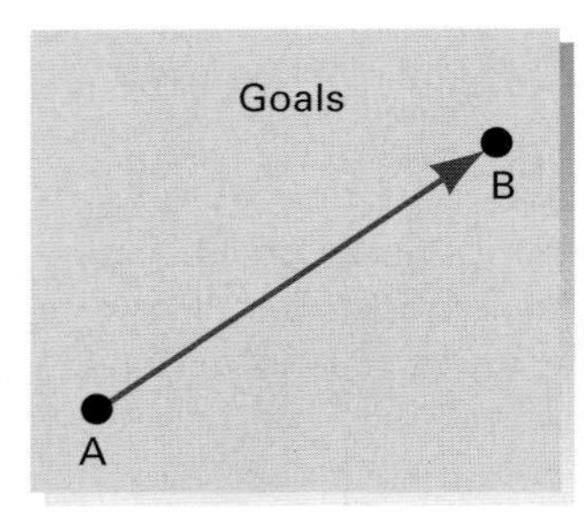

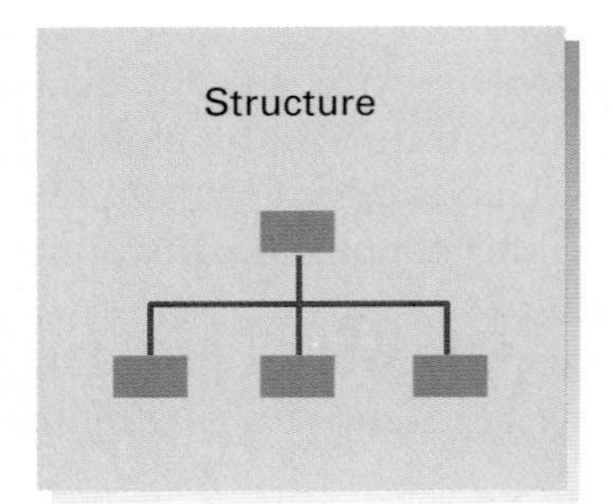

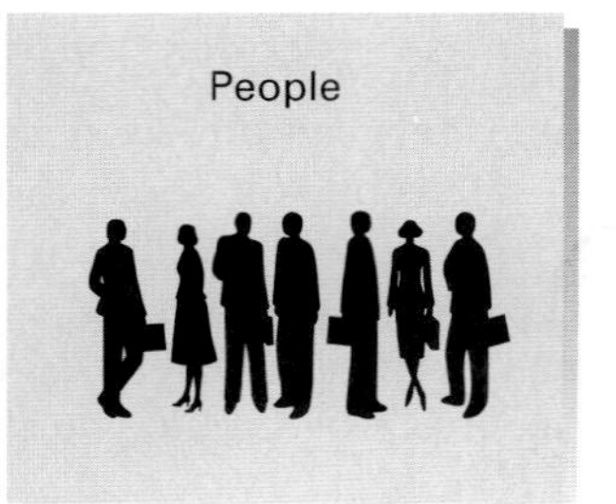

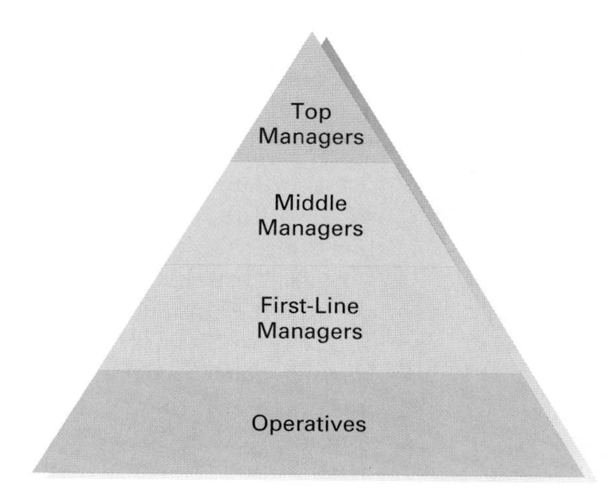

EXHIBIT 1–2
Organizational Levels

other people in the organization. Customarily classified as top, middle, or first-line managers, these individuals supervise both operative employees and lower-level managers (see Exhibit 1–2). That does not mean, however, that managers don't work directly on tasks. Some managers also have operative responsibilities themselves. For example, regional sales managers for GS Metals Corporation also have basic responsibilities of servicing some accounts, in addition to overseeing the activities of the other sales associates in their territories. The distinction, then, between the two groups—operatives and managers—is that managers have employees who report directly to them.

first-line managers
Supervisors responsible for directing the day-to-day activities of operative employees

middle managers
Individuals at leaves of management between the first-line manager and top management

WHAT TITLES DO MANAGERS HAVE IN ORGANIZATIONS?

Identifying exactly who managers are in an organization is often not a difficult task, although you should be aware that management positions come with a variety of titles. **First-line managers** are usually called supervisors. They may also be called team leaders, coaches, or unit coordinators. They are responsible for directing the day-to-day activities of operative employees. In your college, for example, the department chair would be a first-line supervisor overseeing the activities of the departmental faculty (the operatives). **Middle managers** represent levels of management between the first-line manager (the supervisor) and top management. These individuals manage other managers—and possibly some operative employees—and are typically responsible for translating the goals set by top management into specific details that lower-level managers can perform. In organizations, middle managers may have such titles as department or agency head, project leader, unit chief, district manager, dean, bishop, or division manager.

At or near the top of an organization are **top managers**. These individuals, like Oracle's Lawrence Ellison, Hewlett-Packard's Carly Fiorina, and KB Home's Daniel Warmenhoven,[4] are responsible for making decisions about the direction of the organization and establishing policies that affect all organizational members. Top managers typically have titles such as vice president, president, chancellor, managing director, chief operating officer, chief executive officer, or chairperson of the board.

Not all organizational members have management responsibilities. Some are operative employees—responsible for working directly on a job or providing direct service to customers like this salesman at Foot Locker. Although there are specific job responsibilities, this Foot Locker employee does not oversee the work of others.

An organization is defined as a systematic arrangement of people brought together to accomplish some specific purpose. That definition applies to all organizations—for-profit as well as not-for-profit organizations like the United Way.

WHAT IS MANAGEMENT AND WHAT DO MANAGERS DO?

Just as organizations have common characteristics, so, too, do managers. Despite the fact that their titles vary widely, there are several common elements to their jobs—regardless of whether the manager is a head nurse in the cardiac surgery unit of Sinai Hospital who oversees a staff of critical care specialists, or the president of the 360,000-plus-member General Motors Corporation.[5] In this section we will look at these commonalities as we define management, present the classical management functions, review recent research on managerial roles, and consider the universal applicability of managerial concepts.

HOW DO WE DEFINE MANAGEMENT?

The term **management** refers to the process of getting things done, effectively and efficiently, through and with other people. Several components in this definition warrant discussion. These are the terms *process*, *effectively*, and *efficiently*.

The term *process* in the definition of management represents the primary activities managers perform. We explore these in the next section.

Effectiveness and efficiency deal with what we are doing and how we are doing it. **Efficiency** means doing the task correctly and refers to the relationship between inputs and outputs. For instance, if you get more output for a given input, you have increased efficiency. So, too, do you increase efficiency when you get the same output with fewer resources. Since managers deal with input resources that are scarce—money, people, equipment—they are concerned with the efficient use of those resources. Management, therefore, is concerned with minimizing resource costs.

top managers
Individuals who are responsible for making decisions about the direction of the organization and establishing policies that affect all organizational members

management
The process of getting things done, effectively and efficiently, through and with other people

efficiency
Means doing the task correctly; refers to the relationship between inputs and outputs; seeks to minimize resource costs

effectiveness
Means doing the right tasks; goal attainment

Although minimizing resource costs is important, it is not enough simply to be efficient. Management is also concerned with completing activities. In management terms, we call this ability **effectiveness**. Effectiveness means doing the right task. In an organization, that translates into goal attainment (see Exhibit 1–3).

Although efficiency and effectiveness are different terms, they are interrelated; for instance, it's easier to be effective if one ignores efficiency. Hewlett-Packard, for example, could produce more sophisticated and longer-lasting toner cartridges for its laser printers if it disregarded labor and material input costs. Similarly, some government agencies have been regularly attacked on the grounds that they are reasonably effective but extremely inefficient. That is, they accomplish their goals but do so at a very high cost. Our conclusion: Good management is concerned with both attaining goals (effectiveness) and doing so as efficiently as possible.

Can organizations be efficient and yet not be effective? Yes, by doing the wrong things well! A number of colleges have become highly efficient in processing students. Through the use of computer-assisted learning, distance-learning programs, or a heavy reliance on part-time faculty, administrators may have significantly cut the cost of educating each student. Yet some of these colleges have been criticized by students, alumni, and accrediting agencies for failing to educate students properly. Of course, high efficiency is associated more typically with high effectiveness. And poor management is most often due to both inefficiency and ineffectiveness or to effectiveness achieved through inefficiency.

"Good management is concerned with both attaining goals and doing so as efficiently as possible."

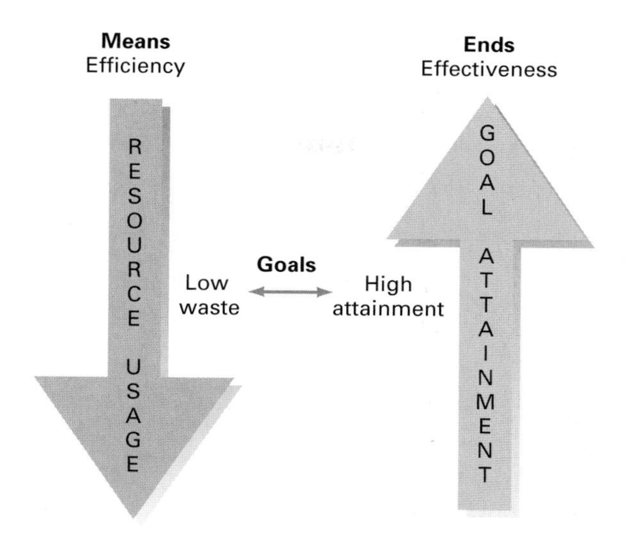

EXHIBIT 1–3
Efficiency and Effectiveness

WHAT ARE THE MANAGEMENT PROCESSES?

In the early part of this century, the French industrialist Henri Fayol wrote that all managers perform five management activities referred to as the "management process". They plan, organize, command, coordinate, and control.[6] In the mid-1950s, two professors at UCLA used the terms *planning, organizing, staffing, directing,* and *controlling* as the framework for a textbook on management that for 20 years was unquestionably the most widely sold text on the subject.[7] The most popular textbooks still continue to be organized around the **management processes**, though these have generally been condensed to the basic four: planning, organizing, leading, and controlling (see Exhibit 1–4). Let us briefly define what each of these encompasses. Keep in mind before we begin, however, that, although we will look at each as an independent task, managers must be able to perform all four activities simultaneously and realize that each has an effect on the others; that is, these processes are interrelated and interdependent. "If you don't much care where you want to get to, then it doesn't matter which way you go," the Cheshire cat said in Alice in Wonderland. Since organizations exist to achieve some purpose, someone has to define that purpose and the means for its achievement. A manager is that someone. The **planning** component encompasses defining an organization's goals, establishing an overall strategy for achieving those goals, and developing a comprehensive hierarchy of plans to integrate and coordinate activities. Setting goals keeps the work to be done in its proper focus and helps organizational members keep their attention on what is most important.

management processes
Planning, organizing, leading, and controlling

planning
Includes defining goals, establishing strategy, and developing plans to coordinate activities

Managers like Hiroshi Okuda are also responsible for designing an organization's structure. We call this management activity **organizing**. Organizing includes determining what tasks are to be done, who is to do them, how the tasks are to be grouped, who reports to whom, and where decisions are to be made.

organizing
Includes determining what tasks are to be done, who is to do them, how the tasks are to be grouped, who reports to whom, and where decisions are to be made

We know that every organization contains people. And it is part of a manager's job to direct and coordinate those people. Performing this activity is the **leading** component of management. When managers motivate employees, direct the activities of others, select the most effective communication channel, or resolve conflicts among members, they are leading.

leading
Includes motivating employees, directing the activities of others, selecting the most effective communication channel, and resolving conflicts

The final activity managers perform is **controlling**. After the goals are set, the plans formulated, the structural arrangements determined, and the people hired, trained, and motivated, something may still go amiss. To ensure that things are going as they should, a manager must monitor the organization's performance. Actual performance must be compared with the previously set goals. If there are any significant deviations, it is the manager's responsibility to get the organization back on track. This method of monitoring, comparing, and correcting is what we mean when we refer to the controlling process.

controlling
The process of monitoring performance, comparing it with goals, and correcting any significant deviations

EXHIBIT 1–4
Management Process Activities

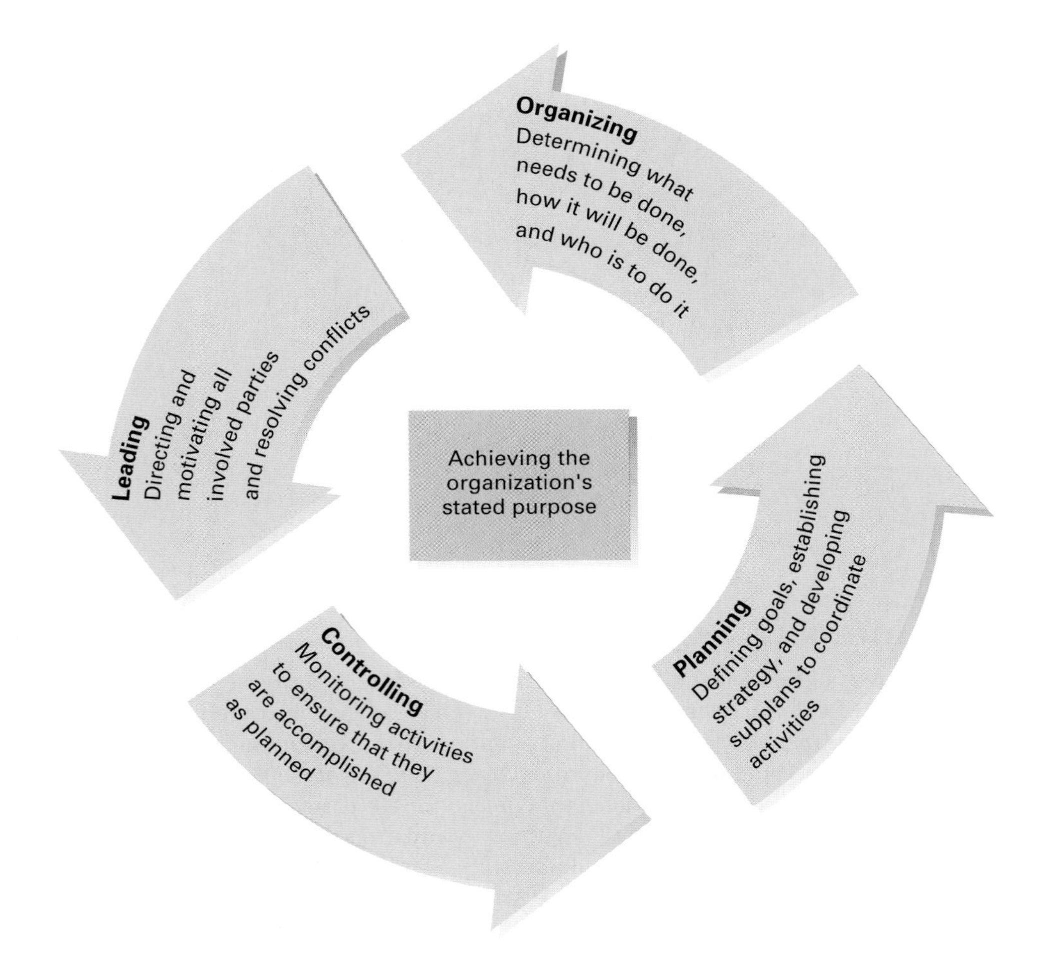

The continued popularity of the process approach is a tribute to its clarity and simplicity. But is it an accurate description of what manager's actually do? Do they actually plan, organize, lead, and control? Fayol's original analysis was not derived from careful survey of thousands of managers in hundreds of organizations. Rather, it merely represented observations from his experience in the French mining industry. In the late 1960s, Henry Mintzberg provided empirical insights into the manager's job.[8]

WHAT ARE MANAGEMENT ROLES?

Henry Mintzberg undertook a careful study of five chief executives at work. What he discovered challenged several long-held notions about the manager's job. For instance, in contrast to the predominant views at the time that managers were reflective thinkers who carefully and systematically processed information before making decisions, Mintzberg found that the managers he studied engaged in a large number of varied, unpatterned, and short-duration activities. There was little time for reflective thinking because the managers encountered constant interruptions. Half of these managers' activities lasted less than nine minutes. But in addition to these insights, Mintzberg provided a categorization scheme for defining what managers do on the basis of actual managers on the job. These are commonly referred to as Mintzberg's **managerial roles**.

managerial roles
Specific categories of managerial behavior; often grouped under three primary headings: interpersonal relationships, transfer of information, and decision making

Mintzberg concluded that managers perform 10 different but highly interrelated roles. The term *managerial roles* refers to specific categories of managerial behavior. These 10 roles, as shown in Exhibit 1–5, can be grouped under three primary headings—interpersonal relationships, the transfer of information, and decision making.

EXHIBIT 1-5 **Mintzberg's Managerial Roles**

ROLE	DESCRIPTION	IDENTIFIABLE ACTIVITIES
Interpersonal		
Figurehead	Symbolic head; obliged to perform a number of routine duties of a legal or social nature	Greeting visitors; signing legal documents
Leader	Responsible for the motivation and activation of employees; responsible for staffing, training, and associated duties	Performing virtually all activities that involve employees
Liaison	Maintains self-developed network of outside contacts and informers who provide favors and information	Acknowledging mail; doing external board work; performing other activities that involve outsiders
Informational		
Monitor	Seeks and receives wide variety of special information (much of it current) to develop thorough understanding of organization and environment; emerges as nerve center of internal and external information about the organization	Reading periodicals and reports; maintaining personal contacts
Disseminator	Transmits information received from other employees to members of the organization—some information is factual, some involves interpretation and integration of diverse value positions of organizational influences	Holding informational meetings; making phone calls to relay information
Spokesperson	Transmits information to outsiders on organization's plans, policies, actions, results, etc.; serves as expert on organization's industry	Holding board meetings; giving information to the media
Decisional		
Entrepreneur	Searches organization and its environment for opportunities and initiates "improvement projects" to bring about change; supervises design of certain projects as well	Organizing strategy and review sessions to develop new programs
Disturbance hander	Responsible for corrective action when organization faces important disturbances	Organizing strategy and review sessions that involve disturbances and crises
Resource allocator	Responsible for the allocation of organizational resources of all kinds—in effect, the making or approval of all significant organizational decisions	Scheduling; requesting authorization; performing any activity that involves budgeting and the programming of employees' work
Negotiator	Responsible for representing the organization at major negotiations	Participating in union contract negotiations or in those with suppliers

Source: *The Nature of Managerial Work* (paperback) by H. Mintzberg, Table 2, pp. 92–93. Reprinted by permission of Pearson Education Inc., Upper Saddle River, New Jersey.

IS THE MANAGER'S JOB UNIVERSAL?

Previously, we mentioned the universal applicability of management activities. So far, we have discussed management as if it were a generic activity. That is, a manager is a manager regardless of where he or she manages. If management is truly a generic discipline,

Whenever a manager like Michael Miller of Goodwill Industries represents his organization to the community at large, he is performing the management role of spokesperson.

then what a manager does should be essentially the same regardless of whether he or she is a top-level executive or a first-line supervisor; in a business firm or a government agency; in a large corporation or a small business; or located in Paris, France, or Paris, Texas. Let's take a closer look at the generic issue.

Level in the organization We have already acknowledged that the importance of managerial roles varies depending on the manager's level in the organization. But the fact that a supervisor in a research laboratory at Abbott Laboratories doesn't do exactly the same things that the president of Abbott does should not be interpreted to mean that their jobs are inherently different. The differences are of degree and emphasis but not of activity.

As managers move up in the organization, they do more planning and less direct overseeing of others. This distinction is visually depicted in Exhibit 1–6. All managers, regardless of level, make decisions. They perform planning, organizing, leading, and controlling activities, but the amount of time they give to each activity is not necessarily constant. In addition, the content of the managerial activities changes with the manager's level. For example, as we will demonstrate in Chapter 5, top managers are concerned with designing the overall organization's structure, whereas lower-level managers focus on designing the jobs of individuals and work groups.

Profit versus not-for-profit Does a manager who works for the U.S. Census Bureau,the Scotland Yard Police, or Goodwill Industries do the same things that a manager in a business firm does?[9] Put another way, is the manager's job the same in both profit and not-for-profit organizations? The answer is, for the most part, yes. Regardless of the type of organization a manager works in, the job has commonalities with all other managerial positions. All managers make decisions, set objectives, create workable organization structures, hire and motivate employees, secure legitimacy for their organization's existence, and develop internal political support in order to implement programs. Of course, there are some noteworthy differences. The most important is measuring performance. Profit, or the "bottom line," acts as an unambiguous measure of the effectiveness of a business organization. There is no such universal measure in not-for-profit organizations. Measuring the performance of schools, museums, government agencies, or charitable organizations, therefore, is more difficult. But don't interpret this difference to mean that managers in those organizations can ignore the financial side of their operations. Even not-for-profit organizations need to make money to survive. It's just that making a profit for the "owners" of not-for-profit organizations is not the primary focus. Consequently, managers in these organizations generally do not face a profit-maximizing market test for performance.

EXHIBIT 1–6

Distribution of Time per Activity by Organizational Level

Source:Adapted from T. A. Mahoney, T. H. Jerdee, and S. J. Carroll, "The Job(s) of Management," *Industrial Relations* 4, no. 2 (1965), p. 103.

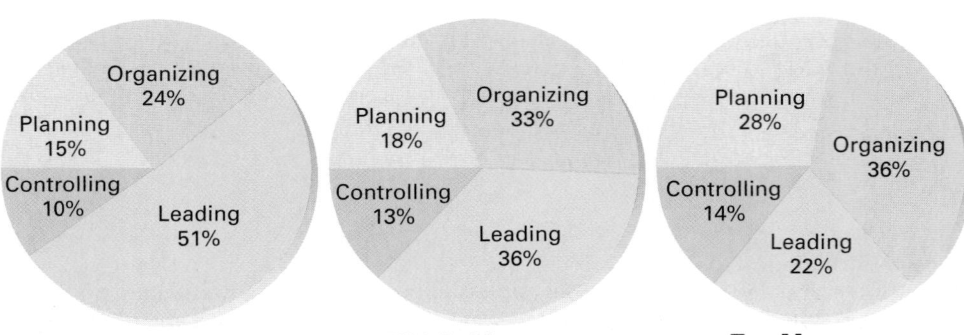

Our conclusion is that, while there are distinctions between the management of profit and not-for-profit organizations, the two are far more alike than they are different. Managers in both are similarly concerned with planning, organizing, leading, and controlling.

Size of organization Would you expect the job of a manager in a print shop that employs 12 people to be different from that of a manager who runs a 1,200-person printing plant for *USA Today*? This question is best answered by looking at the job of managers in small business firms and comparing them with our previous discussion of managerial roles. First, however, let's define small business and the part it plays in our society.

There is no commonly agreed upon definition of a small business because of different criteria used to define *small*. For example, an organization can be classified as a small business using such criteria as number of employees, annual sales, or total assets. For our purposes, we will call a **small business** any independently owned and operated profit-seeking enterprise that has fewer than 500 employees. Small businesses may be little in size, but they have a major effect on the world economy. Small Business Administration statistics tell us that small businesses account for about 98 percent of all nonfarm businesses in the United States; they employ over 60 percent of the private workforce; they dominate such industries as retailing and construction; and they will generate half of all new jobs during the next decade. Moreover, small businesses are where the job growth has been in recent years. Between 1980 and 2002, for example, Fortune 1000 companies eliminated millions of jobs. Yet, companies with fewer than 500 employees have created more than 2 million jobs annually.[10] This phenomenon is not confined solely to the United States. Similar small business start-ups have been witnessed in such countries as China, Japan, Korea, Taiwan, and Great Britain.[11]

small business
Any independently owned and operated profit-seeking enterprise that has fewer than 500 employees

Now to the question at hand: Is the job of managing a small business different from that of managing a large one? Some differences appear to exist. For example, as illustrated in Exhibit 1–7, the small business manager's most important role is that of spokesperson. The small business manager spends a large amount of time performing outwardly directed actions such as meeting with customers, arranging financing with bankers, searching for new opportunities, and stimulating change. In contrast, the most important concerns of a manager in a large organization are directed internally—deciding which organizational units get what available resources and how much of them. Accordingly, the entrepreneurial role—looking for business opportunities and planning activities for performance improvement—appears to be least important to managers in large firms, especially among first-level and middle managers.

Compared with a manager in a large organization, a small business manager is more likely to be a generalist. His or her job will combine the activities of a large corporation's chief executive with many of the day-to-day activities undertaken by a first-line supervisor. Moreover, the structure and formality that characterize a manager's job in a large organization tend to give way to informality in small firms. Planning is less likely to be a carefully orchestrated ritual. The organization's design will be less complex and structured, and control in the small business will rely more on direct observation than on sophisticated, computerized monitoring systems. Again, as with organizational level, we see differences in degree and emphasis but not in activities. Managers in both small and large organizations perform essentially the same activities; only how they go about them and the proportion of time they spend on each are different.

Earth Treks, Inc. is an example of a small business. With a staff of nine people, companies like Earth Treks account for the majority of all businesses in the global economy. Moreover, these businesses have represented most of the job growth for employees in recent years.

Management concepts and national borders The last generic issue concerns whether management concepts are transferable across national borders. If managerial concepts were completely generic, they would also apply universally in any country in the world, regardless of economic, social, political, or cultural differences. Studies that have compared

EXHIBIT 1–7

Importance of Managerial Roles in Small and Large Businesses

Source: Adapted from J. G. P. Paolillo, "The Manager's Self Assessments of Managerial Roles: Small vs. Large Firms," *American Journals of Small Business*, January–March 1984, pp. 61–62.

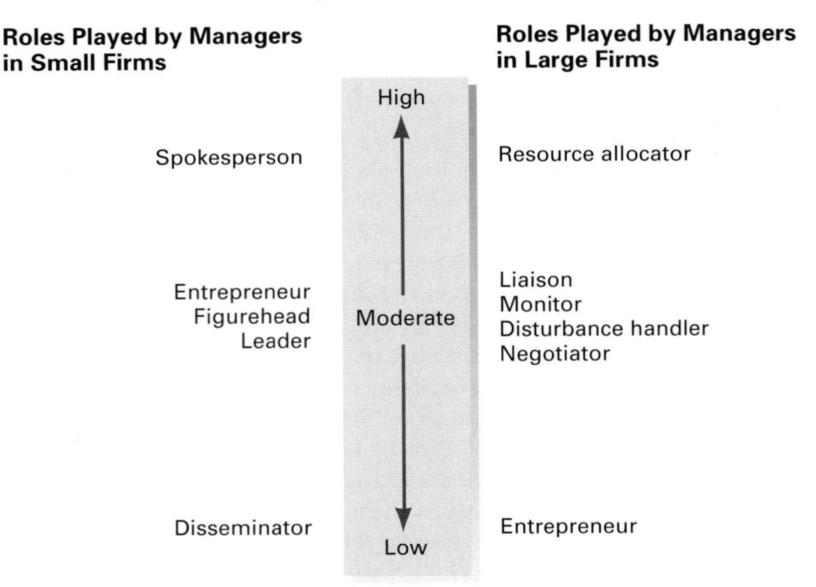

managerial practices between countries have not generally supported the universality of management concepts.[12] In Chapter 2, we will examine some specific differences between countries and describe their effect on managing. At this point, it is sufficient to say that most of the concepts we will be discussing in future chapters primarily apply to the United States, Canada, Great Britain, Australia, and other English-speaking countries. We should be prepared to modify these concepts if we want to apply them in India, China, Chile, or other countries whose economic, political, social, or cultural environments differ greatly from that of the so-called free-market democracies.

Making decisions and dealing with change Two final points of view need to be considered regarding what managers do. Managers make decisions, and managers are agents of change. Almost everything managers do requires them to make decisions. Whether it involves setting goals in the organization, deciding how to structure jobs, determining how to motivate and reward employees, or determining where significant performance variances exist, a manager must make a decision. The best managers, then, are the ones who can identify critical problems, assimilate the appropriate data, make sense of the information, and choose the best course of action to take for resolving the problem. We'll address the proper way to make decisions in Chapter 4.

Organizations today also operate in a world of dynamic change. Managing in chaos has become the rule, not the exception. Successful managers acknowledge the rapid changes around them and are flexible in adapting their practices to deal with those changes. For instance, successful managers recognize the potential effect of technological improvements on a work unit's performance, but they also realize that people often resist change. Accordingly, managers need to be in a position to "sell" the benefits of the change while simultaneously helping their employees deal with the uncertainty and anxiety that the changes may bring. This example illustrates how managers act as agents of change. We'll look at this change phenomenon in greater detail in Chapter 7.

WHAT SKILLS AND COMPETENCIES DO SUCCESSFUL MANAGERS POSSESS?

In addition to recognizing that all managers—regardless of level, organization size, profit or nonprofit enterprise—perform the four basic activities of management, we also need to determine what the critical skills are that are related to

Learning from Experience: One Manager's Reflection

James C. Ray Jr. Ohio Court Administrator, Hamilton County Juvenile Court, Cincinnati, OH

DEALING WITH CHANGE

Describe the situation you faced. I was new to the organization and, like many governmental agencies, this one did not weigh or evaluate fiscal impacts when making decisions. My job was to interject financial considerations into the decision-making process and to see that the organization became more responsive and more accountable to the taxpayer. Since I had come from a business and accounting background I was highly motivated to fulfill my task.

What action(s) did you take? The mistake I made was in not accurately assessing the financial skills of an organization that was primarily made up of attorneys, social workers, and criminal justice professionals.

What results occurred? The result of my attempt to quickly achieve an outcome was that many people become confused and alienated, and developed the impression that dollars were now the only criterion for making a decision.

What did/should you have done differently? Initially, what I should have done was slow down and establish smaller, more achievable goals in helping the managers to understand the financial aspects of the decision-making process.

If you took a corrective action, what were the results? I took corrective action by changing my approach, slowing the pace, and implementing a more gradual process of building the awareness that was necessary for the managers to effectively address organizational decision making. Once they were able to see the importance of the bottom line, and appropriately weigh financial issues in the decision-making process, it became easier to achieve the overall goal, even for people who were not particularly business-minded.

managerial competence. In the 1970s, management researcher Robert L. Katz attempted to answer that question.[13] What Katz and others have found is that managers must possess four critical management skills.[14] Management skills identify those abilities or behaviors that are crucial to success in a managerial position. These skills can be viewed on two levels—general skills a manager must possess, and the specific skills that are related to managerial success. Let's look at these two categories.

conceptual skills
A manager's mental ability to coordinate all of the organization's interests and activities

Interpersonal skills
A manager's ability to work with, understand, mentor, and motivate others, both individually and in groups

General skills There seems to be overall agreement that effective managers must be proficient in four general skill areas. These are conceptual, interpersonal, technical, and political skills.

"There seems to be overall agreement that effective managers must be proficient in conceptual, interpersonal, technical, and political skills."

Conceptual skills refer to the mental ability to analyze and diagnose complex situations. They help managers see how things fit together and facilitate making good decisions. **Interpersonal skills** encompass the ability to work with, understand, mentor, and motivate other people, both individually and in groups (see Developing Your Mentoring Skill on p. 23). Since managers get things done through other people, they must have good interpersonal skills to communicate, motivate, and delegate. Additionally, all managers need **technical skills**. These are abilities to apply specialized knowledge or expertise. For top-level managers, these abilities tend to be related to knowledge of the industry and a general understanding of the organization's processes and products. For middle- and lower-level managers, they are related to the specialized knowledge required in the areas with which they work—finance, human resources, information technology,

technical skills
A manager's ability to use the tools, procedures, and techniques of a specialized field

manufacturing, computer systems, law, marketing, and the like. Finally, managers need **political skills**. This area is related to the ability to enhance one's position, build a power base, and establish the right connections. Organizations are political arenas in which people compete for resources. Managers with good political skills tend to be better at getting resources for their groups than are managers with poor political skills, and they also appear to receive higher evaluations and get more promotions.

Debra Stark, founder of Debra's Natural Gourmet in Concord, Massachusetts, is an epitome of today's small business manager. She spends a considerable amount of time as spokesperson and entrepreneur for her company, which she finds helpful in aiding her business growth.

Specific skills Research has also identified six sets of behaviors that explain a little bit more than 50 percent of a manager's effectiveness.[15]

- ***Controlling the organization's environment and its resources.*** This includes demonstrating, in planning and allocation meetings as well as in on-the-spot decision making, the ability to be proactive and stay ahead of environmental changes. It also involves basing resource decisions on clear, up-to-date, accurate knowledge of the organization's objectives.
- ***Organizing and coordinating.*** In this skill, managers organize around tasks and then coordinate interdependent relationships among tasks wherever they exist.
- ***Handling information.*** This set of behaviors comprises using information and communication channels for identifying problems, understanding a changing environment, and making effective decisions.
- ***Providing for growth and development.*** Managers provide for their own personal growth and development, as well as for the personal growth and development of their employees, through continual learning on the job.
- ***Motivating employees and handling conflicts.*** Managers enhance the positive aspects of motivation so that employees feel impelled to perform their work and eliminate those conflicts that may inhibit employees' motivation.
- ***Strategic problem solving.*** Managers take responsibility for their own decisions and ensure that subordinates effectively use their decision-making skills.

political skills
A manager's ability to build a power base and establish the right connections

management competencies
A cluster of knowledge, skills, and attitudes related to effective managerial performance

Management competencies The most recent approach to defining the manager's job focuses on **management competencies**.[16] These are defined as a cluster of knowledge, skills, and attitudes related to effective managerial performance. One of the most comprehensive competency studies has come out of the United Kingdom.[17] It's called the management charter initiative (MCI). Based on an analysis of management activities and focusing on what effective managers should be able to do rather than on what they know, the MCI sets generic standards of management competence. Currently, there are several sets of standards for first-line supervisors, middle managers, and top management.

Exhibit 1–8 lists standards for middle management. For each area of competence there is a set of specific related elements that defines effectiveness in that area. For instance, one area of competence is recruiting and selecting personnel. Successful development of this competency area requires that managers be able to define future personnel requirements, determine specifications to secure quality people, and assess and select candidates against team and organizational requirements.

The MCI standards are attracting global interest. The Australian Institute of Management, for example, has already started using the standards, and the Management Development Center of Hong Kong is considering introducing them to help managers become more mobile after China's recent takeover of Hong Kong.

EXHIBIT 1–8 Management Charter Initiative Competencies for Middle Managers

BASIC COMPETENCE	SPECIFIC ASSOCIATED ELEMENTS (SAMPLE)
1. Initiate and implement change and improvement in services, products, and systems	Identify opportunities for improvement in services, products, and systems Negotiate and agree on the introduction of change
2. Monitor, maintain, and improve service and product delivery	Establish and maintain the supply of resources into the organization/department Establish and agree on customer requirements
3. Monitor, and control the use of resources	Control costs and enhance value Monitor and control activities against budgets
4. Secure effective resource allocation for activities and projects	Justify proposals for expenditures on projects Negotiate and agree on budget
5. Recruit and select personnel	Define future personnel requirements Determine specifications to secure quality people
6. Develop teams, individuals, and self to enhance performance	Develop and improve teams through planning and activities Identify, review, and improve developmental activities for indivuduals
7. Plan, allocate, and evaluate work carried out by teams, individuals, and self	Set and update work objective for teams and individuals Allocate work and evaluate teams, individuals, and self against objectives
8. Create, maintain, and enhance effective working relationships	Establish and maintain trust and support of one's employees Identify and minimize interpersonal conflict
9. Seek, evaluate, and organize information for action	Obtain and evaluate information to aid decision making Record and store information
10. Exchange information to solve problems and make decisions	Lead meetings and group discussions Advise and inform others

HOW MUCH IMPORTANCE DOES THE MARKETPLACE PUT ON MANAGERS?

Good managers can turn straw into gold. Poor managers can do the reverse. This realization has not been lost on those who design compensation systems for organizations. Managers tend to be more highly paid than operatives. As a manager's authority and responsibility expand, so typically does his or her pay. Moreover, many organizations willingly offer extremely lucrative compensation packages to get and keep good managers.

If you were privy to the compensation paid to employees at large toy manufacturing firms such as Mattel and Fisher Price, you would discover an interesting fact. Their best sales associates rarely earn more than $95,000 a year. In contrast, the annual income of their most senior managers is typically in excess of $300,000, and, in some cases, it can exceed $900,000. The fact that these firms pay managers considerably more than nonmanagers is a measure of the importance placed on effective management skills. What is true at these toy manufacturing firms is true in most organizations. Good managerial skills are a scarce commodity, and compensation packages are one measure of the value that organizations place on them.

However, realize that not all managers make six-figure incomes. Such salaries are usually reserved for senior executives. What, then, could you expect to earn as a manager? The answer depends on your level in the organization, your education and experience, the type of business the organization is in, comparable pay standards in the community, and how effective a manager you are. Most first-line supervisors earn between $30,000 and $55,000 a year. Middle managers often start near $45,000 and top out at around $120,000. Senior managers in large corporations can earn $1 million a year or more. In 2001, for instance, the average cash compensation (salary plus annual bonus) for 727 of the top two executives at the 363 largest U.S. corporations was well over $2 million.[18] The top 20 of these individuals (CEOs from Oracle, Lehman Brothers, Coca-Cola, and Citigroup) averaged more than $112 million in total compensation (including their stock options).[19] Management compensation reflects the market forces of supply and demand. Management superstars, like superstar athletes in professional sports, are wooed with signing bonuses, interest-free loans, performance incentive packages, and guaranteed contracts. Of course, as in the case of athletes, some controversy surrounds the large dollar amounts paid to these executives[20] (see Ethical Dilemma in Management).

WHY STUDY MANAGEMENT?

Management as an academic field of study offers a number of insights into many organizational aspects of our daily lives. Consequently, there are several reasons why we may want to study this topic.

The first reason for studying management is that we all have a vested interest in improving the way organizations are managed. Why? Because we interact with them every day of our lives. Does it frustrate you when you have to spend a couple of hours in a Department of Motor Vehicles office to get your driver's license renewed? Are you perplexed when none of the salespeople in a department store seem interested in helping you? Does it surprise you when a major corporation that everyone thought was thriving suddenly declares bankruptcy? Are you angered when you call an airline three times and its representatives quote you three different prices for the same trip? As a taxpayer, doesn't it seem as if something is wrong when you read about companies that have overbilled the federal government for defense-related equipment? These are all examples of problems that can largely be attributed to poor management. Organizations that are well managed—such as Wal-Mart, General Electric, Siemens, Southwest Airlines, Merck Pharmaceuticals, and Ssangyong Investment and Securities Company—develop a loyal constituency, grow, and prosper.[21] Those that are poorly managed often find themselves with a declining customer base and reduced revenues. Eventually, the survival of poorly managed organizations becomes threatened. For instance, Gimbel's, W.T. Grant, Smith Corona, Eastern Airlines, and Enron were once thriving corporations. They employed tens of thousands of people and provided goods and services on a daily basis to hundreds of thousands of customers. But weak management did them in. Today those companies no longer exist.

The second reason for studying management is that once you graduate from college and begin your career, you will either manage or be managed. For those who plan on careers in management, an understanding of the management process forms the foundation upon which to build their management skills, but it would be naive to assume that everyone who studies management is planning a career in management. A course in management may only be a requirement for a desired degree, but that needn't make the study of management irrelevant. Assuming that you will have to work for a living and that you will almost certainly work in an organization, you will be a manager or work for a manager. You can

Ethical Dilemma in Management

Are U.S. Executives Overpaid?

Are we paying U.S. executives too much? Is an average salary in excess of $60 million justifiable? In any debate, there are two sides to the issue. One thing that supports paying this amount is the fact that these executives have tremendous organizational responsibilities. They not only have to manage the organization in today's environment; they must keep it moving into the future. Their jobs are not 9-to-5 jobs, but rather six to seven days a week, often ten to fourteen hours a day. If jobs are evaluated on the basis of skills, knowledge, abilities, and responsibilities, executives should be highly paid.[22] Furthermore, there is the issue of motivation and retention. If you want these individuals to succeed and stay with the company, you must provide a compensation package that motivates them to stay. Incentives based on various measures also provide the impetus for them to excel.

On the other hand, most of the research done on executive salaries questions the linkage to performance. Even when profits are down, many executives are paid handsomely. In fact, American corporate executives are thought to be some of the highest paid people in the world. Additionally, when performance problems lead to dismissal, some executives are paid phenomenal severance packages. For example, ousted CEOs of both Mattel and Conseco were given $50 and $49 million, respectively, as severance pay.[23] U.S. executives make two to five times the salaries of their foreign counterparts—even though some executives in Japan-based organizations perform better. Finally, the U.S. CEOs make more than 500 times as much as the average employees.[24]

Do you believe that U.S. executives are overpaid? What's your opinion?

Why do organizations pay CEOs millions of dollars, as they do at Coca-Cola? Douglas Daft, as Chairman and CEO of Coca-Cola, earned $5.8 million total pay in 2002. This represents compensation for the organizational responsibilties he has and the extreme requirements imposed on him, as well as a sum that provides motivation and retention incentives.

gain a great deal of insight into the way your boss behaves and the internal workings of organizations by studying management. The point is that you needn't aspire to be a manager to gain something valuable from a course in management.

Before we leave this chapter, it's important to put this whole topic of studying management into a proper perspective. That's because management as a field doesn't exist in isolation. Rather, it embodies the work and practices of individuals from a wide variety of disciplines. In the next section, we'll look at some of these linkages.

HOW DOES MANAGEMENT RELATE TO OTHER DISCIPLINES?

College courses frequently appear to be independent bodies of knowledge. Too often, little of what is taught in one course is linked to past or future courses. As a result, many students don't believe that they should retain what they've previously learned. This has been especially true in most business curriculums. There is typically a lack of connectedness between core business courses and between courses in business and the liberal arts. Accounting classes, for instance, make little reference to marketing; and marketing

"College curriculums often resemble a group of silos, with each silo representing a separate and distinct discipline."

classes typically make little reference to courses in economics or political science. College curriculums often resemble a group of silos, with each silo representing a separate and distinct discipline.

A number of management educators have begun to recognize the need to build bridges between these silos by integrating courses across the college curriculum. Toward this end, we offer the following interdisciplinary overview.

We've integrated topics around some of the humanities and social science courses you may have taken as part of your general education requirements. This is designed to help you see how courses in disciplines such as economics, psychology, sociology, political science, and philosophy relate to topics in management.

The big picture is often lost when management concepts are studied in isolation. By adding this cross-disciplinary perspective, you'll gain a greater appreciation of how general education courses are useful to students of management. This, in turn, can help you to be a more effective manager.

WHAT CAN STUDENTS OF MANAGEMENT GAIN FROM HUMANITIES AND SOCIAL SCIENCE COURSES?

Let's briefly look at the disciplines in popular humanities and social science courses that directly affect management practices.

Anthropology Anthropology is the study of societies, which helps us learn about human beings and their activities. Anthropologists' work on cultures and environments, for instance, has helped managers to better understand differences in fundamental values, attitudes, and behavior between people in different countries and within different organizations.

Economics Economics is concerned with the allocation and distribution of scarce resources. It provides us with an understanding of the changing economy as well as the role of competition and free markets in a global context. For example, why are most athletic shoes made in Asia? Or why does Mexico now have more automobile plants than Detroit? Economists provide the answer to these questions when they discuss comparative advantage. Similarly, an understanding of free trade and protectionist policies is absolutely essential to any manager operating in the global marketplace, and these topics are addressed by economists.

Philosophy Philosophy courses inquire into the nature of things, particularly values and ethics. Ethics are standards that govern human conduct. Ethical concerns go directly to the existence of organizations and what constitutes proper behavior within them. For instance, the liberty ethic (John Locke) proposes that freedom, equality, justice, and private property were legal rights; the Protestant ethic (John Calvin) encourages individuals to be frugal, work hard, and attain success; and the market ethic (Adam Smith) argues that the market and competition, not government, should be the sole regulators of economic activity. These ethics have shaped today's organizations by providing a basis for legitimate authority, linking rewards to performance and justifying the existence of business and the corporate form.

Political Science Political science is the study of the behavior of individuals and groups within a political environment. Specific topics of concern to political scientists include structuring of conflict, allocating power, and manipulating power for individual self-interest.

Capitalism is just one economic system. The economies of the former Soviet Union and much of Eastern Europe, for example, were based on socialist concepts.

Planned economies were not free markets; rather, governments owned most of the goods-producing businesses. And organizational decision makers essentially carried out the dictates of government policies. Efficiency had little meaning in such economies, and there was no competition in most of the basic industries because they were government controlled. In many cases, effectiveness was defined by how many people a plant employed rather than by basic financial criteria.

Management is affected by a nation's form of government—by whether it allows its citizens to hold property, by its citizens' ability to engage in and enforce contracts, and by the appeal mechanisms available to redress grievances. In a democracy, for instance, people typically have the right to private property, the freedom to enter or not enter into contracts, and an appeal system for justice. A nation's stand on property, contracts, and justice, in turn, shapes the type, form, and policies of its organizations.

Psychology Psychology is the science that seeks to measure, explain, and sometimes change the behavior of humans and other animals. Psychologists concern themselves with studying and attempting to understand individual behavior. The field of psychology is leading the way in providing managers with insights into human diversity. Today's managers confront both a diverse customer base and a diverse set of employees. Psychologists' efforts to understand gender and cultural diversity provide managers with a better perception of the needs of their changing customer and employee populations. Psychology courses are also relevant to managers in terms of gaining a better understanding of motivation, leadership, trust, employee selection, performance appraisals, and training techniques.

Learning from the humanities and business core concepts has helped an individual like Meredith Keiser, executive director of FIRST, the Philadelphia-based organization that urges voter registration. By having a broader perspective, Keiser is better able to understand cultures, the political environment, and the needs and wants of people.

Sociology Sociology is the study of people in relation to their fellow human beings. What are some of the sociological issues that have relevance to managers? Here are a few. How are societal changes such as globalization, increasing cultural diversity, changing gender roles, and varying forms of family life affecting organizational practices? What are the implications of schooling practices and education trends on future employees' skills and abilities? How are changing demographics altering customer and employment markets? What will the information age society look like 10 years from now? Answers to questions such as these have a major effect on how managers operate their businesses.

A CONCLUDING REMARK

We've attempted to provide some insight into the need to integrate the college courses you have taken. That's because what you learn in humanities and social science courses can assist you in becoming better prepared to manage in today's dynamic marketplace.

Review, Comprehension, Application

CHAPTER SUMMARY

How will you know if you fulfilled the Learning Outcomes on page 2? You will have fulfilled the Learning Outcomes if you are able to:

1. **Describe the difference between managers and operative employees.** Managers direct the activities of others in an organization. They have such titles as supervisor, department head, dean, division manager, vice president, president, and chief executive officer. Operatives are nonmanagerial personnel. They work directly on a job or task and have no responsibility for overseeing the work of others.
2. **Explain what is meant by the term *management*.** Management refers to the process of getting activities completed efficiently with and through other people. The process represents the primary activities of planning, organizing, leading, and controlling.
3. **Differentiate between efficiency and effectiveness.** Efficiency is concerned with minimizing resource costs in the completion of activities. Effectiveness is concerned with getting activities successfully completed—that is, goal attainment.
4. **Describe the four primary processes of management.** The four primary processes of management are planning (setting goals), organizing (determining how to achieve the goals), leading (motivating employees), and controlling (monitoring activities).
5. **Classify the three levels of managers and identify the primary responsibility of each group.** The three levels of management are first-line supervisors, middle managers, and top managers. First-line supervisors are the lowest level of management and are typically responsible for directing the day-to-day activities of operative employees. Middle managers represent the levels of management between the first-line supervisor and top management. These individuals—who manage other managers and possibly some operative employees—are primarily responsible for translating the goals set by top management into specific details that lower-level managers can perform. Top managers, at or near the pinnacle of the organization, are responsible for making decisions about the direction of the organization and establishing policies that affect all organizational members.
6. **Summarize the essential roles performed by managers.** Henry Mintzberg concluded that managers perform 10 different roles or behaviors. He classified them into three sets. One set is concerned with interpersonal relationships (figurehead, leader, liaison). The second set is related to the transfer of information (monitor, disseminator, spokesperson). The third set deals with decision making (entrepreneur, disturbance handler, resource allocator, negotiator).
7. **Discuss whether the manager's job is generic.** Management has several generic properties. Regardless of level in an organization, all managers perform the same four activities; however, the emphasis given to each function varies with the manager's position in the hierarchy. Similarly, for the most part, the manager's job is the same regardless of the type of organization he or she is in. The generic properties of management are found mainly in the world's democracies. One should be careful in assuming that management practices are universally transferable outside so-called free-market democracies.
8. **Describe the four general skills necessary for becoming a successful manager.** The four critical types of skills necessary for becoming a successful manager are conceptual (the ability to analyze and diagnose complex situations); interpersonal (the ability to work with and understand others); technical (applying specialized knowledge); and political (enhancing one's position and building a power base).
9. **Describe the value of studying management.** People in all walks of life have come to recognize the important role that good management plays in our society. For those who aspire to managerial positions, the study of management provides the body of knowledge that will help them to be effective managers. For those who do not plan on careers as managers, the study of management can give them considerable insight into the way their bosses behave and into the internal activities of organizations.
10. **Identify the relevance of popular humanities and social science courses to management practices.** Management does not exist in isolation. Rather, management practices are directly influenced by research and practices in such fields as anthropology (learning about individuals and their activities); economics (understanding allocation and distribution of resources); philosophy (developing values and ethics); political science (understanding behavior of individuals and groups in a political setting); psychology (learning about individual behavior); and sociology (understanding relationships among people).

COMPANION WEBSITE

We invite you to visit the Robbins/DeCenzo companion Website at **www.prenhall.com/robbins** for this chapter's Internet resources, including an online study guide, Internet exercises, and "In the News" with full text articles provided by XanEdu.

READING FOR COMPREHENSION

1. What is an organization? Why are managers important to an organization's success?
2. What four common activities comprise the process approach to management? Briefly describe each of them.
3. What are the four general skills and the six specific skills that affect managerial effectiveness?
4. How does a manager's job change with his or her level in the organization?
5. What value do courses in anthropology, economics, philosophy, political science, psychology, and sociology have for managers? Give an example of one application to management practice from each of these disciplines.

LINKING CONCEPTS TO PRACTICE

1. Are all effective organizations also efficient? Discuss. If you had to choose between being effective or being efficient, which one would you say is more important? Why?
2. Contrast planning, organizing, leading, and controlling with Henry Mintzberg's 10 roles.
3. Is your college instructor a manager? Discuss in terms of planning, organizing, leading, and controlling, and of Mintzberg's managerial roles.
4. In what ways would the job activities of an owner of an automotive repair shop that employs two people and the president of the Ford Motor Company be similar? In what ways would they be different?
5. Some individuals today have the title of project leader. They manage projects of various sizes and durations and must coordinate the talents of many people to accomplish their goals, but none of the workers on their projects report directly to them. Can these project leaders really be considered managers if they have no employees over whom they have direct authority? Discuss.

VIDEO CASE APPLICATION

Deploy Solutions: Meeting the Human Resources Needs of Tomorrow

When Nicole Strata, CEO of Deploy Solutions, speaks, corporate heads in the emerging biotechnology, technology, and service sectors listen. In 1997, just six years after earning a business degree from the University of Vermont, Nicole Strata founded Deploy Solutions.[25] Even then, she was convinced that the Web could be a powerful tool for workforce management. Today, Strata claims, "Deploy Solutions' Web-based software is turning customers into their own best recruiters."

Her Boston area company "looks at the internal population of an organization as a viable and strong resource for filling mission-critical jobs," says Strata. This philosophy, coupled with technical expertise, has enabled Deploy Solutions to retain its entire staff throughout economic downturns. Employ!, the same software package developed during the dot-com boom, when talent was scarce, still works today. Now that downsizing has become commonplace, human resources managers are often overwhelmed with hundreds of résumés for a single opening. This easy-to-use, e-mail-based application can literally turn businesses around.

Deploy Solutions has done just that for Micron PC. According to Chris Gebhardt, director of corporate staffing, MicronPC, Employ! enabled the Idaho-based company to leverage its existing staff in order to meet the challenge of ambitious expansion plans. Moreover, it was able to lower the cost of attrition and vastly reduce the cycle time for hiring. Perhaps most importantly, "implementing the software showed we valued our employees," Gebhardt says.

Rather than letting technology obstruct personal communication, Employ! helps to facilitate it. The human element is at the core of everything Deploy Solutions stands for. "People and their intellectual capital are the most important asset a company has," is a point Nicole Strata fires home again and again. Her entire staff has a profound knowledge of the human resources management process and a dedication to its clients on a personal level. "We really believe that we're not successful unless our customers are successful," says Terrie Perella, who is vice president of marketing and business development at Deploy Solutions. The company invests a lot of time in gathering feedback to form a true partnership with its clients for the long term. It provides job applicants around the world with a program that can be easily loaded onto a laptop and quickly processed across time zones. It also gives employees a chance to take a proactive role in managing their own careers by creating a profile to be matched to current and future job opportunities.

Behind the scenes, the best minds in the field are at work, refining Deploy Solutions' approach to the predicted shortage of skilled labor that will most likely affect us by 2010. Professor Foulkes, director of Human Resources Policy Institute and professor of management policy at Boston University's School of Management, chairs Deploy Solutions' advisory board. He lends his expertise and thought leadership in human resources management and corporate strategy.[26]

Any time the United States prepares for possible conflict in other parts of the world, the American business community finds itself facing a challenge of its own, here at home. According to Nicole Strata, there is a "talent war to be waged and won by those companies who hire or promote the right people first." Clients like FleetBoston Bank, FedEx, and MicronPC would, no doubt, concur.

Questions

1. As an account supervisor at a large advertising agency, how might Employ! software give *you* a competitive advantage? As a vice president of human resources at the same agency, how might Employ! software give *you* a competitive advantage? As CEO of a small entrepreneurial mail-order business, would *you* invest in Employ! software? Explain your responses.
2. What general and specific managerial skills should a sales representative at Deploy Solutions possess in order to be successful? Why?
3. In what ways do you think a global corporation could benefit from using a Deploy Solutions program such as Employ!? Consider the information in your text on the management charter initiative (MCI) in your answer.
4. According to Vice President Terrie Perella, executive account managers at Deploy Solutions "really understand how human resources and the business can better collaborate to do the things that need to be done." What do you think she means by this? Why is familiarity with the hiring process important for managers in all areas of a corporation?

Management Workshop

Team Skill-Building Exercise

A New Beginning

One of the more unnerving aspects of beginning a new semester is gaining an understanding of what is expected in each class. By now, your instructor has probably provided you with a course syllabus, which gives you some necessary information about how the class will function. Understandably, this information is important to you. But your instructor would also value learning what you want from the class. This information can be useful for providing insight into this class. To collect these data, you will need to answer some questions. First, take out a piece of paper and place your name at the top; then respond to the following:

1. What do I want from this course?
2. Why is this class important to me?
3. How does this course fit into my career plans?
4. How do I like an instructor to "run" the class?
5. What do I think is my greatest challenge in taking this class?

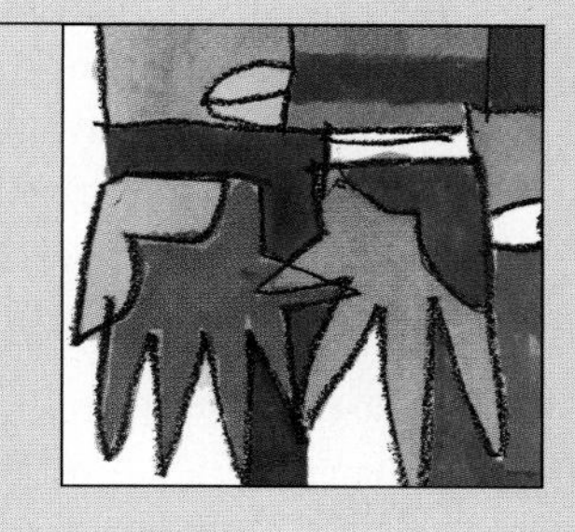

When you have finished answering these questions, pair up with another class member (preferably someone you do not already know) and exchange papers. Get to know one another (using the information on these sheets as a starting point). Prepare an introduction of your partner, and share your partner's responses to the five questions with the class and your instructor.

Understanding Yourself

Before you can develop other people, you need to understand your present strengths. To assist in this learning process, we encourage you to complete the following self-assessments from the Prentice-Hall Self-Assessment Library 2.0:

- How Motivated Am I to Manage? (#45)
- Am I Well Suited for a Career as a Global Manager? (#46)

After you complete these assessments, we suggest that you print out the results and store them as part of your "portfolio of learning."

Developing Your Mentoring Skill

Guidelines for Mentoring Others

About the Skill

A mentor is usually someone in the organization who is more experienced and in a higher-level position, and sponsors or supports another employee (frequently called a protégé). A mentor can teach, guide, and encourage. Some organizations have formal mentoring programs, but even if your organization does not, mentoring should be an important skill for you to develop.

Steps in Practicing the Skill

1. **Communicate honestly and openly with your protege.** If that person is going to learn from you and benefit from your experience, you're going to have to be open and honest as you talk about what you've done. Bring up the failures as well as the successes. Remember that mentoring is a learning process and, in order for learning to take place, you're going to have to "tell it like it is."

2. **Encourage honest and open communication from your protégé.** You need to know what that person hopes to gain from this relationship. You should encourage the protégé to ask for information and to be specific about what he or she wants to gain.
3. **Treat the relationship with the protégé as a learning opportunity.** Don't pretend to have all the answers and all the knowledge, but do share what you've learned through your experiences. And in your conversations

and interactions with your protégé, you may be able to learn as much from that person as he or she does from you. So listen to what your protégé is saying.

4. **Take the time to get to know your protégé.** As a mentor, you should be willing to take the time to get to learn about his or her interests. If you're not willing to spend extra time, you should probably not embark on a mentoring relationship.

Practicing the Skill

Select a relative, neighbor, or friend and spend an hour teaching that individual a new skill that you've mastered—such as playing a musical instrument, rollerblading, cooking a meal, playing a video game, singing a song in a foreign language, or balancing a checkbook.

Write a brief set of notes about each mentoring experience. Be sure to record what you learned from your protégé and how you might have improved your own learning opportunity. Could you have prepared ahead of time? How would that have helped you learn better? In assessing your performance as a mentor, evaluate your skill in organizing and presenting the necessary information. Did your protégé ask questions you could not immediately answer? How did you handle these? How do you think you could have done better?

Developing Your Diagnostic and Analytical Skills

Managing Macronix International

Miin Wu was educated in the United States at MIT and Stanford University. He began his career in California at Intel. After several years of working at this high-tech company, he felt that he was ready to move on. He had a vision of how to make better computer chips, and he felt that he could make this vision a reality if he had his own company. Wu made that vision a reality in 1989 when he founded Macronix International, Ltd., in Taiwan's Hsinchu Science Park. Macronix designs, develops, manufacturers, and sells such products as integrated circuits, flash memory, and several logic products.[27]

From the beginning, Wu understood the value of good management. As the founder of the company, he knew that to fulfill his mission he needed to surround himself with high-quality people. He did this by offering several workers an opportunity to join him in Taiwan—giving them a chance to return home and to have a "piece" of the company. Many of these individuals gave up comfortable and stable jobs in the U.S. "chip" industry for a chance to help Wu succeed.

Wu also realized that no organization could remain complacent in the volatile microchip market and survive. He knew that long-term success came from identifying opportunities and staking out a growth plan, so he created alliances with other companies and invested heavily in research and development, spending nearly 16 percent of the company's revenues on product development.

While making decisions about the company, its directions, and how its money would be spent, Wu never overlooks the role of the human factor. He constantly seeks ways to re-create the organization, making it possible for employees to do the best job they can while facing the fewest obstacles. He fosters a work environment that promotes enthusiasm—one where employees look forward to coming to work. And Wu knows that he must "grow and nurture" his people, providing them opportunities to develop so they'll stay knowledgeable and able to respond to change.

Have Miin Wu's efforts proven successful for Macronix International? The answer appears to be yes. Company sales in 2001 exceeded $825 million, with gross profits nearing $212 million—better than a 25 percent gross margin. These results, and Miin Wu's positioning of the company to reach $1 billion in sales in the next few years, have earned Macronix the honor of being one of Taiwan's thriving hi-tech companies and recipient of the 2001 Golden Silicon Award.

Questions

1. Describe how Miin Wu performs planning, organizing, leading, and controlling activities in managing Macronix International.
2. What management roles does Miin Wu demonstrate in dealing (1) with other companies and (2) with his employees? Cite examples.
3. Describe how lessons learned from such disciplines as economics, philosophy, and sociology could be of benefit to Miin Wu.

Enhancing Your Communication Skills

1. Develop a response to the following question: "Are U.S. executives overpaid?" Present both sides of the argument and include supporting data. Conclude your discussion by defending and supporting one of the two arguments you've presented.
2. Describe how the president of your college fulfills the 10 managerial roles identified by Henry Mintzberg (refer to Exhibit 1–5). In your discussion, provide specific references to actual activities by the president of your college—not just the "identifiable activities" we've listed in the exhibit.
3. Schedule a meeting with three faculty members—one who teaches economics, one who teaches psychology, and one who teaches political science. Ask each of them how their respective courses relate to today's business environment, and what are the most critical elements from their courses that a business student should understand. Present your findings.

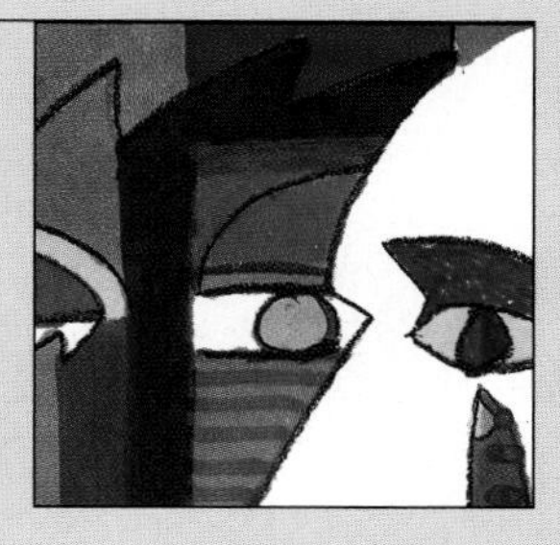

HISTORY MODULE

The Historical Roots of Contemporary Management Practices

THIS MODULE WILL DEMONSTRATE THAT A KNOWLEDGE OF management history can help you understand contemporary management theory and practice. We'll introduce you to the origins of many contemporary management concepts and show how they evolved to reflect the changing needs of organizations and society as a whole.

THE PRE-MODERN ERA

Organized activities and management have existed for thousands of years. The Egyptian pyramids and the Great Wall of China are evidence that projects of tremendous scope, employing tens of thousands of people, were undertaken well before modern times. The pyramids are a particularly interesting example. The construction of a single pyramid occupied thousands of people for several decades. Who told each worker what he or she was supposed to do? Who ensured that there would be enough stones at the site to keep workers busy? The answer to such questions is management. Regardless of what managers were called at the time, someone had to plan what was to be done, organize people and materials to do it, and provide direction for the workers.

When you hear the name Michelangelo, what comes to your mind? Renaissance artist? Genius? How about manager? Recent evidence tells us that the traditional image of Michelangelo—the lonely genius trapped between agony and ecstasy, isolated on his back on a scaffold, single-handedly painting the ceiling of the Sistine Chapel—is a myth.[1] Some 480 years ago, Michelangelo was actually running a medium-sized business. Thirteen people helped him paint the Sistine Chapel ceiling, about 20 helped carve the marble tombs in the Medici Chapel in Florence, and at least 200 men, under his supervision, built the Laurentian Library in Florence. Michelangelo personally selected his workers, trained them, assigned them to one or more teams, and kept detailed employment records. For example, he recorded the names, days worked, and wages of every employee, every week. Meanwhile, Michelangelo played the role of the trouble-shooting manager. Each day he would dart in and out of the various work areas under his supervision, check on workers' progress, and handle any problems that arose.

These historical examples demonstrate that organized activities and managers have been with us since before the Industrial Revolution. However, it has been only in the past several hundred years, particularly in the twentieth century, that management has undergone systematic investigation, acquired a common body of knowledge, and become a formal discipline.

WHAT WAS ADAM SMITH'S CONTRIBUTION TO THE FIELD OF MANAGEMENT?

Adam Smith's name is typically cited in economics courses for his contributions to classical economic doctrine, but his discussion in *Wealth of Nations* (1776) included a brilliant argument on the economic advantages that organizations and society would reap from the **division of labor**.[2] He used the pin manufacturing industry for his examples. Smith noted that 10 individuals, each doing a specialized task, could produce about 48,000 pins a day. However, if each worked separately and independently, those 10 workers would be lucky to make 200—or even 10—pins in one day.

Smith concluded that division of labor increased productivity by increasing each worker's skill and dexterity, by saving time that is commonly lost in changing tasks, and by the creation of labor-saving inventions and machinery. Today the general popularity of job specialization—in service jobs such as teaching and medicine as well as on assembly lines in automobile plants—is undoubtedly due to the economic advantages cited over 200 years ago by Adam Smith.

Was Michelangelo a manager? While most individuals regard him as a lonely painter, he actually ran a medium-sized business. Many employees helped him paint the Sistine Chapel as well as carve the marble tombs in the Medici Chapel. In selecting workers, training them, assigning them to jobs, and keeping employment records, Michelangelo was, in fact, acting as a manager.

HOW DID THE INDUSTRIAL REVOLUTION INFLUENCE MANAGEMENT PRACTICES?

Possibly the most important pre-twentieth-century influence on management was the **Industrial Revolution**. Originating in late-eighteenth-century Great Britain, the Revolution had crossed the Atlantic to America by the end of the Civil War. Machine power was rapidly substituted for human power. Using machines, in turn, made it economical to manufacture goods in factories.

The advent of machine power, mass production, the reduced transportation costs that followed the rapid expansion of the railroads, and lack of governmental regulation also fostered the development of big organizations. John D. Rockefeller was putting together the Standard Oil monopoly, Andrew Carnegie was gaining control of two-thirds of the steel industry, and similar entrepreneurs were creating other large businesses that would require formalized management practices. A formal theory to guide managers in running their organizations was needed. However, it was not until the early 1900s that the first major step toward developing such a theory was taken.

CLASSICAL CONTRIBUTIONS

The roots of modern management lie with a group of practitioners and writers who sought to formulate rational principles that would make organizations more efficient. Because they set the theoretical foundations for a discipline called management, we call their contributions the **classical approach** to management. We can break the classical approach into two subcategories: scientific management and general administrative theory. Scientific management theorists looked at the field from the perspective of how to improve the productivity of operative personnel. The general administrative theorists, on the other hand, were concerned with the overall organization and how to make it more effective.

WHAT CONTRIBUTIONS DID FREDERICK TAYLOR MAKE?

If one had to pinpoint the year that modern management theory was born, one could make a strong case for 1911, the year that Frederick Winslow Taylor's *The Principles of Scientific Management* was published.[3] Its contents would become widely accepted by managers throughout the world. The book described the theory of **scientific management**—

division of labor
The breakdown of jobs into narrow, repetitive tasks

Industrial Revolution
The advent of machine power, mass production, and efficient transportation begun in the late eighteenth century in Great Britain

classical approach
The term used to describe the hypotheses of the scientific management theorists and the general administrative theorists

scientific management
The use of the scientific method to define the one best way for a job to be done

Frederick Taylor is regarded as the "Father of Scientific Management." His book, *the Principles of Scientific Management* introduced concepts of the "one best way" for promoting efficiency for each worker in the organization. His recommendations, provided nearly 100 years ago, still hold true today.

the use of the scientific method to define the "one best way" for a job to be done. The studies conducted before and after the book's publication would establish Taylor as the father of scientific management. Frederick Taylor did most of his work at the Midvale and Bethlehem Steel companies in Pennsylvania (see Details on a Management Classic). As a mechanical engineer with a Quaker/Puritan background, he was consistently appalled at the inefficiency of workers. Employees used vastly different techniques to do the same job. They were prone to "taking it easy" on the job. Taylor believed that worker output was only about one-third of what was possible. Therefore, he set out to correct the situation by applying the scientific method to jobs on the shop floor. He spent more than two decades pursuing with a passion the "one best way" for each job to be done.

Taylor sought to create a mental revolution among both the workers and management by creating clear guidelines for improving production efficiency. He defined four principles of management (see Exhibit HM–1). He argued that following these principles would result in the prosperity of both management and workers. Workers would earn more pay and management more profits.

Using scientific management techniques, Taylor was able to define the one best way of doing each job. He could then select the right people for the job and train them to do it precisely in this one best way. To motivate workers, he favored incentive wage plans. Overall, Taylor achieved consistent improvements in productivity in the range of 200 percent or more, and he reaffirmed the function of managers to plan and control, and that of workers to perform as instructed.

The impact of Taylor's work cannot be overstated.[4] During the first decade of the century, he delivered numerous public lectures to teach scientific management to interested industrialists. Between 1901 and 1911, at least 18 firms adopted some variation of scientific management. In 1908, the Harvard Business School declared Taylor's approach the standard for modern management and adopted it as the core around which all courses were to be organized. Taylor, himself, began lecturing at Harvard in 1909. Between 1910 and 1912, two events catapulted scientific management into the limelight. In 1910, the Eastern Railroad requested a rate increase from the Interstate Commerce Commission. Appearing before the commission, an efficiency expert claimed that railroads could save $1 million a day (equivalent to about $17 million today) through the application of scientific management. This assertion became the centerpiece of the hearings and created a national audience for Taylor's ideas. Then in 1911, *The Principles of Scientific Management* became an instant best-seller. By 1914, Taylor's principles had become so popular that an efficiency exposition held in New York City, with Taylor as the keynote speaker, drew a crowd estimated at 69,000. Although Taylor spread his ideas not only in the United States but also in France,

EXHIBIT HM–1

Taylor's Four Principles of Management

1. Develop a science for each element of an individual's work, which replaces the old rule-of-thumb method.
2. Scientifically select and then train, teach, and develop the worker. (Previously, workers chose their own work and trained themselves as best they could.)
3. Heartily cooperate with the workers so as to ensure that all work is done in accordance with the principles of the science that has been developed.
4. Divide work and responsibility almost equally between management and workers. Management takes over all work for which it is better fitted than the workers. (Previously, almost all the work and the greater part of the responsibility were thrown upon the workers).

Details on a Management Classic

Frederick Taylor

Probably the most widely cited example of scientific management is Taylor's pig iron experiment. Workers loaded "pigs" of iron weighing 92 pounds onto rails cars. Their average daily output was 12.5 tons. Taylor beleived that if the job was scientifically analyzed to determine the one best way to load pig iron, the output could be increased to 47 or 48 tons per day.

Taylor began his experiment by looking for a physically strong subject who placed a high value on the dollar. The individual Taylor chose was a big, strong Dutch immigrant, whom he called "Schmidt," Schmidt, like the other loaders, earned $1.15 a day, which even at the turn of the century was barely a subsistence wage. Taylor offered Schmidt $1.85 a day if he would do what Taylor asked.

Using money to motivate Schmidt, Taylor asked him to load the pig irons, alternating various job factors to see what impact the changes had on Schmidt's daily output. For instance, on some days, Schmidt would lift the pig irons by bending his knees; on other days, he would keep his legs straight and use his back. Taylor experimented with rest periods, walking speed, carrying positions, and other variables. After a long period of methodically trying various combinations of procedures, techniques, and tools, Taylor obtained the level of productivity he thought possible. By putting the right person on the job with the correct tools and equipment, by having the worker follow his instructions exactly, and by motivating the worker with a significantly higher daily wage, Taylor was able to reach his 48-ton objective.

It's important to understand what Taylor saw at Midvale Steel that aroused his determination to improve the way things were done in the plant. At the time, there were no clear concepts of worker and management responsibilities. Virtually no effective work standards existed. Workers purposely worked at a slow pace. Management decisions were of the "seat-of-the-pants" variety, based on hunch and intuition. Workers were placed on jobs with little or no concern for matching their abilities and aptitudes with the tasks required. Most important, management and workers considered themselves to be in continual conflict. Rather than cooperating to their mutual benefit, they perceived their relationship as a zero-sum game—any gain by one would be at the expense of the other.

Germany, Russia, and Japan, his greatest influence was on U.S. manufacturing. His method gave U.S. companies a comparative advantage over foreign firms that made U.S. manufacturing efficiency the envy of the world—at least for 50 years or so.

WHO WERE THE OTHER MAJOR CONTRIBUTORS TO SCIENTIFIC MANAGEMENT?

Taylor's ideas inspired others to study and develop methods of scientific management. His most prominent disciples were Frank and Lillian Gilbreth,[5] and Henry Gantt.

A construction contractor by background, Frank Gilbreth gave up his contracting career in 1912 to study scientific management, after hearing Taylor speak at a professional meeting. Along with his wife Lillian, a psychologist, he studied work arrangements to eliminate wasteful hand and body motions. The Gilbreths also experimented with the design and use of the proper tools and equipment for optimizing work performance.[6] Frank Gilbreth is probably best known for his experiments in reducing the number of motions in bricklaying.

The Gilbreths were among the first to use motion picture films to study hand and body motions. They devised a microchronometer that recorded time to 1/2,000 of a second, placed it in the field of study being photographed, and thus determined how long a worker spent enacting each motion. Wasted motions missed by the naked eye could be identified and eliminated. The Gilbreths also devised a classification scheme to label 17 basic hand motions—such as "search," "select," "grasp," and "hold" —which they called **therbligs** (Gilbreth spelled backward with the th transposed). This scheme allowed the Gilbreths to more precisely analyze the exact elements of workers' hand movements.

therbligs
The Gilberths' classification scheme for labeling 17 basic hand motions

Another associate of Taylor's at Midvale and Bethlehem Steel was a young engineer named Henry L. Gantt. Like Taylor and the Gilbreths, Gantt sought to increase worker efficiency through scientific investigation. He extended some of Taylor's original ideas and added a few of his own. For instance, Gantt devised an incentive system that gave workers a bonus for completing their jobs in less time than the allowed standard. He also introduced a bonus for a foreman to be paid for each worker who made the standard plus an extra bonus if all of that foreman's workers made it. In so doing, Gantt expanded the scope of scientific management to encompass the work of managers as well as that of operatives. Gantt is probably most noted for creating a graphic bar chart that could be used by managers as a scheduling device for planning and controlling work. We'll look at the Gantt Chart in more detail in Chapter 14.

WHY DID SCIENTIFIC MANAGEMENT RECEIVE SO MUCH ATTENTION?

Many of the guidelines Taylor and others devised for improving production efficiency appear today to be common sense. For instance, one can say that it should have been obvious to managers in those days that workers should be carefully screened, selected, and trained before being put into a job.

To understand the importance of scientific management, you have to understand the times in which Taylor, the Gilbreths, and Gantt lived. The standard of living was low. Production was highly labor intensive. Midvale Steel, at the turn of the century, may have employed 20 or 30 workers who did nothing but load pig iron onto rail cars. Today, their entire daily production could probably be done in several hours by one person with a hydraulic lift truck, but they didn't have such mechanical devices. Similarly, the breakthroughs Frank Gilbreth achieved in bricklaying are meaningful only when you recognize that most quality buildings at that time were constructed of brick, that land was cheap, and that the major cost of a plant or home was the cost of the materials (bricks) and the labor cost to lay them.

WHAT DID HENRI FAYOL AND MAX WEBER CONTRIBUTE TO MANAGEMENT THEORY?

Henri Fayol and Max Weber were two important individuals who helped to develop general administrative theory. We mentioned Henri Fayol in Chapter 1 as having designated management as a universal set of activities—specifically, planning, organizing, commanding, coordinating, and controlling. Because his writings were important, let's take a more careful look at what he had to say.[7]

Fayol wrote during the same period that Taylor did. However, whereas Taylor was concerned with management at the shop level (or what we today would describe as the job of a supervisor) and used the scientific method, Fayol's attention was directed at the activities of all managers, and he wrote from personal experience. Taylor was a scientist; Fayol, the managing director of a large French coal mining firm, was a practitioner.

Fayol described the practice of management as distinct from accounting, finance, production, distribution, and other typical business functions. He argued that management was an activity common to all human undertakings in business, in government, and even in the home. He then proceeded to state 14 **principles of management**—fundamental or universal truths—that could be taught in schools and universities. These principles are listed in Exhibit HM–2.

principles of management
Fayol's fundamental or universal principles of management practice

bureaucracy
Weber's ideal type of organization characterized by division of labor, a clearly defined hierarchy, detailed rules and regulations, and impersonal relationships

Max Weber was a German sociologist. Writing in the early part of this century, he developed a theory of authority structures and described organizational activity on the basis of authority relations.[8] He described an ideal type of organization that he called a **bureaucracy**, characterized by division of labor, a clearly defined hierarchy, detailed rules and regulations, and impersonal relationships. Weber recognized that

EXHIBIT HM-2

Fayol's Fourteen Principles of Management

1. **Division of Work** This principle is the same as Adam Smith's "division of labor." Specialization increases output by making employees more efficient.
2. **Authority** Managers must be able to give orders. Authority gives them this right. Along with authority, however, goes responsibility. Whenever authority is exercised, responsibility arises.
3. **Discipline** Employees must obey and respect the rules that govern the organization. Good discipline is the result of effective leadership, a clear understanding between management and workers regarding the organization's rules, and the judicious use of penalties for infractions of the rules.
4. **Unity of Command** Every employee should receive orders from only one superior.
5. **Unity of Direction** Each group of organizational activities that have the same objective should be directed by one manager using one plan.
6. **Subordination of Individual Interests to the General Interest** The interests of any one employee or group of employees should not take precedence over the interests of the organization as a whole.
7. **Remuneration** Workers must be paid a fair wage for their services.
8. **Centralization** Centralization refers to the degree to which subordinates are involved in decision making. Whether decision making is centralized (to management) or decentralized (to subordinates) is a question of proper proportion. The task is to find the optimum degree of centralization for each situation.
9. **Scalar Chain** The line of authority from top management to the lowest ranks represents the scalar chain. Communications should follow this chain. However, if following the chain creates delays, cross-communications can be allowed if agreed to by all parties and if superiors are kept informed.
10. **Order** People and materials should be in the right place at the right time.
11. **Equity** Managers should be kind and fair to their subordinates.
12. **Stability of Tenure of Personnel** High employee turnover is inefficient. Management should provide orderly personnel planning and ensure that replacements are available to fill vacancies.
13. **Initiative** Employees who are allowed to originate and carry out plans will exert high levels of effort.
14. **Esprit de Corps** Promoting team spirit will build harmony and unity within the organization.

this ideal bureaucracy didn't exist in reality but, rather, represented a selective reconstruction of the real world. He used it as a basis for theorizing about work and the way that work could be done in large groups. His theory became the design prototype for many of today's large organizations. The features of Weber's ideal bureaucratic structure are outlined in Exhibit HM–3.

HOW DO WE SEE SOME CLASSICAL WRITINGS APPLIED TODAY?

One of the benefits of studying history is the opportunity to learn from the past. A number of our current ideas and practices in management can be directly traced to the contributions of the classical management writers.

For example, matching people to their jobs and training them in how to be more effective on these jobs is just one way we see the "one best way" being applied. The

EXHIBIT HM-3
Weber's Ideal Bureaucracy

1. **Division of Labor** Jobs are broken down into simple, routine, and well-defined tasks.
2. **Authority Hierarchy** Offices or positions are organized in a hierarchy, each lower one being controlled and supervised by a higher one.
3. **Formal Selection** All organizational members are to be selected on the basis of technical qualifications demonstrated by training, education, or formal examination.
4. **Formal Rules and Regulations** To ensure uniformity and to regulate the actions of employees, managers must depend heavily on formal organizational rules.
5. **Impersonality** Rules and controls are applied uniformly, avoiding involvement with personalities and personal preferences of employees.
6. **Career Orientation** Managers are professional officials rather than owners of the units they manage. They work for fixed salaries and pursue their careers within the organization.

field of industrial engineering, which looks at the minutiae in processing work, also has its roots in scientific management. Furthermore, the concern today of fitting the workplace to the worker, creating a work environment that is conducive to productive work, can be traced back to scientific management principles, as can the emphasis today on project management, scheduling, and so on. The use of videotape to enhance productivity—either at work or in the case of athletics—has its roots in the work of Frank and Lillian Gilbreth.

The functional view of the manager's job originated with Henri Fayol. Although many of his principles may not be applicable to the wide variety of organizations that exist today, they were a frame of reference for many current concepts. Weber's bureaucracy was an attempt to formulate an ideal model for organization design and a response to the abuses that Weber observed within organizations. Weber believed that his model could remove the ambiguity, inefficiencies, and patronage that characterized most organizations at that time. Weber's bureaucracy is not as popular as it was a decade or two ago, but many of its components are still inherent in large organizations. When we see organizations laying off significant numbers of workers, restructuring the organization, shifting long-term goals and the like, the **general administrative theorists'** principles are at work. And today's emphasis on team-building has a strong "esprit de corp" element embedded in it.[9]

general administrative theorists
Writers who developed general theories of what managers do and what constitutes good management practice

HUMAN RESOURCES APPROACH

Managers get things done by working with people, which explains why some writers and researchers have chosen to look at management by focusing on the organization's human resources. Much of what currently makes up the field of personnel or human resources management, as well as contemporary views on motivation and leadership, has come out of the work of theorists we have categorized as part of the human resources approach to management.

WHO WERE SOME EARLY ADVOCATES OF THE HUMAN RESOURCES APPROACH?

Undoubtedly, many people in the nineteenth and the early part of the twentieth century recognized the importance of the human factor to an organization's success, but five individuals stand out as early advocates of the human resources approach. They are Robert Owen, Hugo Munsterberg, Mary Parker Follett, Chester Barnard, and Elton Mayo.

What claim to fame does Robert Owen hold? Robert Owen was a successful Scottish businessman who bought his first factory in 1789 when he was just eighteen. Repulsed by the harsh practices he saw in factories across Scotland—such as the employment of young children (many under the age of 10), 13-hour workdays, and miserable working conditions—Owen became a reformer. He chided factory owners for treating their equipment better than their employees. He said that they would buy the best machines but then buy the cheapest labor to run them. Owen argued that money spent on improving laboring conditions was one of the best investments that business executives could make. He claimed that a concern for employees was highly profitable for management and would relieve human misery.

Owen proposed a utopian workplace; he is not remembered in management history for his successes but rather for his courage and commitment to reducing the suffering of the working class. He was more than a hundred years ahead of his time when he argued, in 1825, for regulated hours of work for all, child labor laws, public education, company-furnished tools and equipment, and business involvement in community projects.[10]

For what is Hugo Munsterberg best known? Hugo Munsterberg created the field of industrial psychology—the scientific study of individuals at work to maximize their productivity and adjustment. In his text *Psychology and Industrial Efficiency* (1913),[11] he argued for the scientific study of human behavior to identify general patterns and to explain individual differences. Munsterberg suggested the use of psychological tests to improve employee selection, the value of learning theory in the development of training methods, and the study of human behavior to determine what techniques are most effective for motivating workers. Interestingly, he saw a link between scientific management and industrial psychology: Both sought increased efficiency through scientific work analyses and through better alignment of individual skills and abilities with the demands of various jobs. Much of our current knowledge of selection techniques, employee training, job design, and motivation is built on the work of Munsterberg.

What contributions did Mary Parker Follett make to management? One of the earliest writers to recognize that organizations could be viewed from the perspective of individual and group behavior was Mary Parker Follett.[12] A transitional figure who wrote during the time of scientific management but proposed more people-oriented ideas, Follett was a social philosopher whose ideas had clear implications for management practice. She thought that organizations should be based on a group ethic rather than on individualism. Individual potential, she argued, remained as potential until released through group association. The manager's job was to harmonize and coordinate group efforts—the notion of "power with" versus "power over" employees. Managers and workers should view themselves as partners—as part of a common group. As such, managers should rely more on their expertise and knowledge to lead employees

One of the earliest writers to focus on individual and group behaviors was Mary Parker Follett. Suggesting that organizations should be based on group ethics, she believed that individual potential would only be released by group association. Her writings still have influence today when you talk about motivation, leadership, and power.

than on the formal authority of their position. Follett's humanistic ideas influenced the way we look at motivation, leadership, power, and authority.

Who was Chester Barnard? A transitional figure like Follett, Chester Barnard proposed ideas that bridged classical and human resources viewpoints. Like Fayol, Barnard was a practitioner—he was the president of New Jersey Bell Telephone Company. He had read Weber and was influenced by his work; but unlike Weber, who had an impersonal view of organizations, Barnard saw organizations as social systems that require human cooperation. He expressed his views in his book *The Functions of the Executive* (1938).[13]

Barnard believed that organizations were made up of people with interacting social relationships. The manager's major functions were to communicate and stimulate subordinates to high levels of effort. A major part of an organization's success, as Barnard saw it, depended on the cooperation of its employees and their acceptance of authority. Barnard also argued that success depended on maintaining good relations with the people and institutions with whom the organization regularly interacted. By recognizing the organization's dependence on investors, suppliers, customers, and other external stakeholders, Barnard introduced the idea that managers had to examine the external environment and then adjust the organization to maintain a state of equilibrium. Regardless of how efficient an organization's production might be, if management failed to ensure a continuous input of materials and supplies or to find markets for its output, then the organization's survival would be threatened.

The current interest in building cooperative work groups, making business firms more socially responsible, and matching organizational strategies to opportunities in the environment can be traced to ideas originally proposed by both Follett and Barnard.

Hawthorne studies
A series of studies done during the 1920s and 1930s that provided new insights into group norms and behaviors

What were the Hawthorne Studies? Without question, the most important contribution to the human resources approach to management came out of the **Hawthorne studies** undertaken at the Western Electric Company's Hawthorne Works in Cicero, Illinois.[14] The Hawthorne studies, begun in 1924 but expanded and continued through the early 1930s, were initially devised by Western Electric industrial engineers to examine the effect of different illumination levels on worker productivity. Control and experimental groups were established. The experimental group was presented with different levels of illumination intensity, and the control group worked under a constant intensity. The engineers expected individual output to be directly related to the intensity of light. However, they found that as the light level was increased in the experimental group, output for both groups rose. To the surprise of the engineers, as the light level was dropped in the experimental group, productivity continued to increase in both groups. In fact, productivity decreased in the experimental group only after the light intensity had been reduced to that of moonlight. The engineers concluded that illumination intensity was not directly related to group productivity, but they could not explain the behavior they had witnessed.

In 1927, the Western Electric engineers asked Harvard Professor Elton Mayo and his associates to join the study as consultants, a relationship that would last through 1932 and encompass numerous experiments covering the redesign of jobs, changes in the lengths of the workday and workweek, the introduction of rest periods, and individual versus group wage plans.[15] For example, one experiment evaluated the effect of a piecework incentive pay system on group productivity. The results indicated that the incentive plan had less effect on workers' output than did group pressure and acceptance and the concomitant security. Social norms or standards of the group, therefore, were concluded to be the key determinants of individual work behavior.

Scholars generally agree that the Hawthorne studies, under the leadership of Elton Mayo, had a dramatic impact on the direction of management thought. Mayo concluded that behavior and sentiments are closely related, that group influences significantly affect individual behavior, that group standards establish individual worker output, and that money is less a factor in determining output than are group standards, group sentiments, and security—called the Hawthorne Effect. These conclusions led to a new emphasis on the human factor in the functioning of organizations and the attainment of their goals. They also led to increased paternalism by management.

The Hawthorne studies, however, have not been without critics. Attacks have been made on procedures, analyses of the findings, and the conclusions drawn.[16] From a historical standpoint, it is of little importance whether the studies were academically sound or their conclusions justified. What is important is that they stimulated an interest in human factors. The Hawthorne studies went a long way in changing the prevalent view of the time that people were no different than machines; that is, you put them on the shop floor, cranked in the inputs, and caused them to produce a known quantity of outputs. Furthermore, the legacy of Hawthorne is still with us today.

Why was the Human Relations Movement important to management history? Another group within the human resources approach is important to management history for its unflinching commitment to making management practices more humane. Members of the human relations movement uniformly believed in the importance of employee satisfaction—a satisfied worker was believed to be a productive worker. For the most part, the people associated with this movement—Dale Carnegie, Abraham Maslow, and Douglas McGregor—were individuals whose views were shaped more by their personal philosophies than by substantive research evidence.

Dale Carnegie is often overlooked by management scholars, but his ideas and teachings have had an enormous effect on management practice. His book *How to Win Friends and Influence People*[17] was read by millions in the 1930s, 1940s, and 1950s. In addition, during this same period, thousands of managers and aspiring managers attended his management speeches and seminars. What was the theme of Carnegie's book and lectures? Essentially, he said that the way to succeed was to (1) make others feel important through a sincere appreciation of their efforts; (2) make a good first impression; (3) win people over to your way of thinking by letting others do the talking, being sympathetic, and "never telling a man he is wrong;" and (4) change people by praising good traits and giving the offender the opportunity to save face.

Abraham Maslow, a humanistic psychologist, proposed a hierarchy of five needs: physiological, safety, social, esteem, and self-actualization.[18] In terms of motivation, Maslow argued that each step in the hierarchy must be satisfied before the next level can be activated and that once a need was substantially satisfied, it no longer motivated behavior.

The needs hierarchy is arguably still the best-known theory of general motivation, despite the fact that continued research does not support the Maslow theory to any significant degree. However, even today, no author of an introductory textbook in management, organizational behavior, human relations, supervision, psychology, or marketing is likely to omit a discussion of the needs hierarchy.

Douglas McGregor is best known for his formulation of two sets of assumptions—Theory X and Theory Y—about human nature.[19] Theory X presents an essentially negative view of people. It assumes that they have little ambition, dislike work, want to avoid responsibility, and need to be closely supervised to work effectively. On the other hand, Theory Y offers a positive view, assuming that people can exercise self-direction, accept responsibility, and consider work to be as natural as rest or play. McGregor believed that Theory Y assumptions best captured the true nature of workers and should guide management practice.

A story about McGregor effectively captures the essence of the human relations perspective. McGregor had taught for a dozen years at the Massachusetts Institute of Technology (MIT) before he became president of Antioch College. After six years at Antioch, he seemed to recognize that his philosophy had failed to cope with the realities of organizational life.

> I believed, for example, that a leader could operate successfully as a kind of advisor to his organization. I thought I could avoid being a "boss." Unconsciously, I suspect, I hoped to duck the unpleasant necessity of making difficult decisions, of taking the responsibility for one course of action, among many uncertain alternatives, of making mistakes and taking the consequences. I thought that maybe I could operate so that everyone would like me—that "good human relations" would eliminate all discord and disagreement. I couldn't have been more wrong. It took a couple of years but I finally began to realize that a leader cannot avoid the exercise of authority any more than he can avoid responsibility for what happens to his organization.[20]

The irony in McGregor's case was that he went back to MIT and began preaching his humanistic doctrine again. And he continued to do so until his death. Like Maslow's, McGregor's beliefs about human nature have had a strong following among management academics and practitioners.

What common thread linked the advocates of the human relations movement? The thing that united human relations supporters, including Carnegie, Maslow, and McGregor, was an unshakable optimism about people's capabilities. They believed strongly in their cause and were inflexible in their beliefs, even when faced with contradictory evidence. No amount of contrary experience or research evidence would alter their views. Despite this lack of objectivity, advocates of the human relations movement had a definite influence on management theory and practice.

Who were the behavioral science theorists? One final category within the human resources approach encompasses a group of psychologists and sociologists who relied on the scientific method for the study of organizational behavior. Unlike the theorists of the human relations movement, behavioral science theorists engaged in objective research on human behavior in organizations. They carefully attempted to keep their personal beliefs out of their work. They sought to develop rigorous research designs that could be replicated by other behavioral scientists. In so doing, they hoped to build a science of organizational behavior.

How is the human resources approach applied today? A list of important human resources approaches would number into the hundreds. But beginning after World War II and continuing today, the work of these individuals has created a wealth of studies that allows us to make fairly accurate predictions about behavior in organizations. Our current understanding of such issues as leadership, employee motivation, personality differences, the design of jobs and organizations, organizational cultures, high-performance teams, performance appraisals, conflict management, attitude surveys, employee counseling, management training, participative decision making, team-based compensation systems, and negotiation techniques are largely due to the contributions of scholars from the human resource focus.

THE QUANTITATIVE APPROACH

The quantitative approach to management, sometimes referred to as operations research (OR) or management science, evolved out of the development of mathematical and statistical solutions to military problems during World War II. For instance, when the British had to get the maximum effectiveness from their limited aircraft capability against the massive forces of the Germans, they asked their mathematicians to devise an optimum allocation model. Similarly, U.S. antisubmarine warfare teams used operations research (OR) techniques to improve the odds of survival for Allied convoys crossing the North Atlantic and for selecting the optimal depth charge patterns for aircraft and surface vessel attacks on German U-boats.

After the war, many of the quantitative techniques that had been applied to military problems were moved into the business sector.[21] One group of military officers, labeled the "Whiz Kids," joined Ford Motor Company in the mid-1940s and immediately began using statistical methods to improve decision making at Ford. Two of the most famous Whiz Kids were Robert McNamara and Charles "Tex" Thornton. McNamara rose to the presidency of Ford and then became U.S. Secretary of Defense. At the Department of Defense, he sought to quantify resource allocation decisions in the Pentagon through cost–benefit analyses. He concluded his career as head of the World Bank. Tex Thornton founded the billion-dollar conglomerate Litton Industries, again relying on quantitative techniques to make acquisition and allocation decisions. Dozens of other operations researchers from the military went into consulting. The consulting firm of Arthur D. Little, for instance, began applying OR techniques to management problems in the early 1950s. By the mid-1950s, many firms had established formal OR groups, employing hundreds of OR analysts in industry.

The genesis of the quantitative approach to management can be traced to World War II. These operations research techniques looked at developing mathematical and statistical solutions to military problems. For example, U.S. warfare teams used operations research methods to improve the odds of surviving naval crossings of the North Atlantic, as well as determining optimal depth-charge patterns for aircraft attack on enemy vessels.

What are quantitative techniques, and how have they contributed to current management practice? The quantitative approach to management includes applications of statistics, optimization models, information models, and computer simulations. Linear programming, for instance, is a technique that managers can use to improve resource allocation. Work scheduling can become more efficient as a result of critical path scheduling analysis. Decisions on determining optimum inventory levels have been significantly influenced by the economic order quantity model. In general, the quantitative approaches have contributed directly to management decision making, particularly to planning and control decisions.

ANALYSIS: HOW SOCIAL EVENTS SHAPE MANAGEMENT APPROACHES

We conclude this historical review by showing you how social events shape what theorists write about and what practicing managers focus on. Although some management historians may quarrel with the following cause–effect analysis, few would disagree that societal conditions are the primary driving forces behind the emergence of the different management approaches.

WHAT STIMULATED THE CLASSICAL APPROACH?

The common thread in the ideas offered by people like Taylor, the Gilbreths, Fayol, and Weber was increased efficiency. The world of the late nineteenth and early twentieth century was highly inefficient. Most organizational activities were unplanned and unorganized. Job responsibilities were vague and ambiguous. Managers, when they existed, had no clear notion of what they were supposed to do. There was a crying need for ideas that could bring order out of this chaos and improve productivity. And the standardized practices offered by the classicists were a means to increase productivity. Take the specific case of scientific management. At the turn of the twentieth century, the standard of living was low; wages were modest, and few workers owned their own homes. Production was highly labor intensive. It wasn't unusual, for instance, for hundreds of people to be doing the same repetitive, backbreaking job, hour after hour, day after day. So Taylor could justify spending six months or more studying one job and perfecting a standardized "one best way" to do it because the labor-intensive procedures of the time had so many people performing the same task. And the efficiencies on the production floor could be passed on in lower prices for steel, thus expanding markets, creating more jobs, and making products such as stoves and refrigerators more accessible to working families. Similarly, Frank Gilbreth's breakthroughs in improving the efficiency of bricklayers and standardizing those techniques meant lower costs for putting up buildings and, thus, more buildings being constructed. The cost of putting up factories and homes dropped significantly, so more factories could be built, and more people could own their own homes. The end result: The application of scientific management principles contributed to raising the standard of living of entire countries.

WHAT STIMULATED THE HUMAN RESOURCES APPROACH?

The human resources approach really began to roll in the 1930s when two related forces were instrumental in fostering this interest. First was a backlash to the overly mechanistic view of employees held by the classicists. Second was the Great Depression.

The classical view treated organizations and people as machines. Managers were the engineers who ensured that the inputs were available and that the machines were properly maintained. Any failure by the employee to generate the desired output was viewed as an engineering problem: It was time to redesign the job or grease the machine by offering the employee an incentive wage plan. Unfortunately, this kind of thinking created an alienated workforce. Human beings were not machines and did not necessarily respond positively to the cold and regimented work environment of the classicists' perfectly designed organization. The human resources approach offered managers solutions for decreasing this alienation and for improving worker productivity.

The Great Depression swept the globe in the 1930s and dramatically increased the role of government in individual and business affairs. For instance, in the United States, Franklin D. Roosevelt's New Deal sought to restore confidence to a stricken nation. Between 1935 and 1938 alone, the Social Security Act was created to provide old-age assistance; the National Labor Relations Act was passed to legitimize the rights of labor unions; the Fair Labor Standards Act introduced the guaranteed hourly wage; and the Railroad Unemployment Insurance Act established the first national unemployment protection. This New Deal climate increased the importance of the worker. Humanizing the workplace had become congruent with society's concerns.

WHAT STIMULATED THE QUANTITATIVE APPROACHES?

The major impetus to the quantitative approaches was World War II. Government-funded research programs were created to develop mathematical and statistical aids for solving military problems. The success of these operations research techniques in the military was impressive. After the war, business executives became more open to applying these techniques to their organizational decision making. And, of course, as these techniques improved the quality of decisions and increased profits in those firms that used them, managers in competing firms were forced to adopt these same techniques.

New organizations were created to disseminate information to managers on these quantitative techniques. The Operations Research Society of America was founded in 1952 and began publishing its journal, *Operations Research.* In 1953, the Institute of Management Science stated its objectives were "to identify, extend, and unify scientific knowledge that contributes to the understanding of the practice of management" and began publishing the journal *Management Science.*[22]

By the late 1960s, courses in mathematics, statistics, and operations management had become required components of most business school curriculums. The quality focus of such individuals as Joseph Juran and W. Edwards Deming were beginning to change the way people looked at business.[23] As a result, a new generation of managers was knowledgeable in such techniques as probability theory, linear programming, queuing theory, games theory, and total quality management.[24]

BUILDING ON HISTORY: STUDYING MANAGEMENT TODAY

The material in this module has focused on very specific schools of management thought. Although each school of management was formed in response to the social climate of the period, each stood in isolation of the others. However, three integrative frameworks have evolved that can help you organize and better understand the subject matter of management. These are the process, systems, and contingency approaches.

WHAT IS THE PROCESS APPROACH?

In December 1961, Harold Koontz published an article in which he carefully detailed the diversity of approaches to the study of management—functions, quantitative emphasis, human relations approaches—and concluded that there existed a "management theory jungle." [25] Koontz conceded that each of the diverse approaches had something to offer management theory, but he then proceeded to demonstrate that many were only managerial tools. He felt that a process approach could encompass and synthesize the diversity of the day. The **process approach**, originally introduced by Henri Fayol, is based on the management activities discussed in Chapter 1. The performance of these activities—planning, organizing, leading, and controlling—is seen as circular and continuous (refer to Exhibit HM-4).

process approach
The performance of planning, leading, and controlling activities is seen as circular and continuous

Although Koontz's article stimulated considerable debate, most management teachers and practitioners held fast to their own individual perspectives.[26] But Koontz had made a mark. The fact that most current management textbooks employ the process approach is evidence that it continues to be a viable integrative framework.

EXHIBIT HM-4
The Organization and Its Environment

HOW CAN A SYSTEMS APPROACH INTEGRATE MANAGEMENT CONCEPTS?

systems approach
Defines a system as a set of interrelated and interdependent parts arranged in a manner that produces a unified whole

closed system
A system that is not influenced by and does not interact with its environment

open system
A system that dynamically interacts with its environment

stakeholders
Any group that is affected by organizational decisions and policies

The mid-1960s began a decade in which the idea that organizations could be analyzed in a systems framework gained a strong following. The **systems approach** defines a system as a set of interrelated and interdependent parts arranged in a manner that produces a unified whole. Societies are systems and so, too, are computers, automobiles, organizations, and animal and human bodies.

There are two basic types of systems: closed and open. **Closed systems** are not influenced by and do not interact with their environment. In contrast, an **open systems** approach recognizes the dynamic interaction of the system with its environment (see Exhibit 1–4). Today, when we talk of organizations as systems, we mean open systems. That is, we acknowledge the organization's constant interaction with its environment.

An organization (and its management) is a system that interacts with and depends on its environment. In management terms, we call this relationship dealing with the organization's stakeholders. **Stakeholders** are any group that is affected by organizational decisions and policies, including government agencies, labor unions, competing organizations, employees, suppliers, customers and clients, local community leaders, or public interest groups. The manager's job is to coordinate all these parts to achieve the organization's goals. Most organizational members realize that customers are the lifelines of organizations, and bringing a new product to market without first ensuring that it is needed, and desired, by customers could lead to disaster. If failing to anticipate what customers want leads to a reduction in revenues, there may be less financial resources to pay wages and taxes, buy new equipment, or repay loans. The systems approach recognizes that such relationships exist and that management must understand them and the potential constraints that they may impose. This is also true regarding managerial ethics. The questionable actions of executives at such companies as Enron, Arthur Anderson, WorldCom, ImClone, and Adelphia are likely to lead to new laws and regulations regarding accounting practices. Furthermore, these actions are also generating a renewed concern by the public for ethical practices in contemporary organizations.

The systems approach also recognizes that organizations do not operate in isolation. Organizational survival often depends on successful interactions with the external environment, which encompasses economic conditions, the global marketplace, political activities, technological advancements, and social customs. Ignoring any of these over a long period of time can have a detrimental effect on the organization.

How do we see an open system of management operating in today's dynamic world of work? We simply need to look at a company like ImClone. Because of ImClone executives' questionable actions, and similar actions by other companies, public interest in managerial ethics is being renewed. Furthermore, such actions may result in U.S. companies facing new laws regulating how they account for their finances.

Just how relevant is the systems approach for a manager? It appears to be quite relevant, particularly because a manager's job entails coordinating and integrating various work activities so that the system of interrelated and interdependent parts (the organization) meets its goals. Although the systems perspective does not provide specific descriptions of what managers do, it does provide a broader picture than the process approach does. Moreover, viewing the manager's job as linking the organization to its environment makes the organization more sensitive and responsive to key stakeholders such as customers, suppliers, government agencies, and the community in which it operates.

WHAT IS A CONTINGENCY APPROACH TO THE STUDY OF MANAGEMENT?

Management, like life itself, is not based on simplistic principles.[27] Insurance companies know that not all people have the same probability of becoming seriously ill. Factors such as age, fitness, and the use of alcohol or tobacco are contingencies that influence one's health. Similarly, you cannot say that students always learn less in a distance learning course than in one in which a professor is physically present. An extensive body of research tells us that contingency factors such as course content and the way in which individuals learn influence learning effectiveness.

The **contingency approach** (sometimes called the situational approach) has been used to replace simplistic principles of management and to integrate much of management theory. A contingency approach to the study of management is logical. Because organizations are diverse—in size, objectives, tasks being done, and the like—it would be surprising to find universally applicable principles that would work in all situations. In other words, managing Oracle's software design engineers would be different from managing sales clerks at Nordstrom and would even be different from managing Oracle's own marketing staff. But, of course, it is one thing to say "It all depends," and another to say what it depends on. Advocates of the contingency approach—a group that includes most management researchers and practitioners—have been trying to identify the "what" variables. Exhibit HM–5 describes four popular contingency variables. This list is not comprehensive—at least 100 different variables have been identified—but it represents those most widely used and gives you an idea of what we mean by the term *contingency variable*.[28] As you can see from the list, the contingency variables can have a significant effect on what managers do, that is, on the way work activities are coordinated and integrated.

contingency approach
The situational approach to management that replaces more simplistic systems and integrates much of management theory

EXHIBIT HM–5
Four Popular Contingency Variables

Organization Size The number of people in an organization is a major influence on what mangers do. As size increases, so do the problems of coordination. For instance, the type of organization structure appropriate for an organization of 50,000 employees is likely to be inefficient for an organization of 50 employees.

Routineness of Task Technology In order for an organization to achieve its purpose, it uses technology; that is, it engages in the process of transforming inputs into outputs. Routine technologies require organizational structures, leadership styles, and control systems that differ from those required by customized or nonroutine technologies.

Environmental Uncertainty The degree of uncertainty caused by political, technological, sociocultural, and economic changes influences the management process. What works best in a stable and predictable environment may be totally inappropriate in a rapidly changing and unpredictable environment.

Individual Differences Individuals differ in terms of their desire for growth, autonomy, tolerance for ambiguity, and expectations. These and other individual differences are particularly important when managers select motivational techniques, leadership styles, and job designs.

CHAPTER 2

Managing in a Contemporary World

LEARNING OUTCOMES

After reading this chapter, I will be able to:

1. Describe the three waves in modern social history and their implications for organizations.
2. Explain the importance of viewing management from a global perspective.
3. Identify the ways in which technology is changing the manager's job.
4. Describe the difference between an e-business, e-commerce, and an e-organization.
5. Define social responsibility and ethics.
6. Explain what is meant by the term *entrepreneurship* and identify the components of the entrepreneurial venture.
7. Describe the management implications of a diversified workforce.
8. Identify which work/life concepts are affecting employees.
9. Explain why many corporations have downsized.
10. Describe the key variables for creating a customer-responsive culture.
11. Explain why companies focus on quality and continuous improvement.

MEET A REAL MANAGER!

"One Manager's Reflection" page 58

D. J. Hanlon, Operations Manager, Tiger Woods Foundation, Inc.

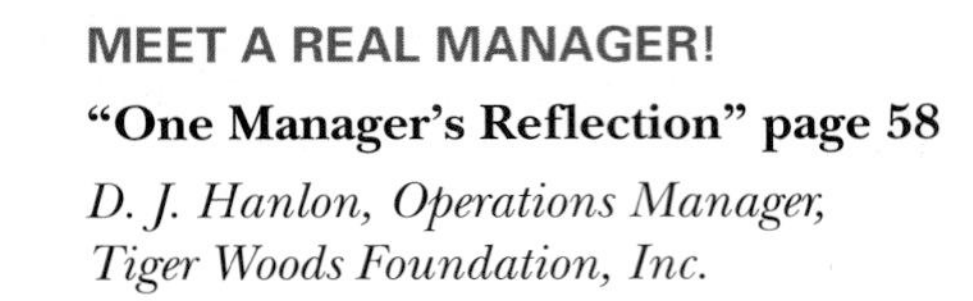

Have you ever walked into someone's office—or house for that matter—and seen piles of clutter? Is the adage "a cluttered desk is a sign of a cluttered mind" accurate? Of course that's debatable, but for Garrett Boone and Kip Tindell, it really doesn't matter. That's because they have a solution to the disorganization.[1]

In 1978, Boone and Tindell founded The Container Store. The Container Store is a business that sells "boxes, bottles, jars, trunks, racks, baskets, dividers, and much, much more." It's an organization that sells storage products for businesses and homes. Based in Dallas, Texas, The Container Store now has annual revenues exceeding $230 million, and employs more than 1,600 individuals in 26 stores located in 11 states. And since its inception, the company has enjoyed a sales growth of more than 20 percent each year. What's interesting about The Container Store is not its phenomenal growth. Rather, it's the entrepreneurial spirit of Tindell and Boone in creating the organization mind-set that's a testament to sound management practice-with customer service as the driving force.

Customer service is a term that neither of these founding members takes lightly. They recognize that customer service is more than lip service—it's establishing a supportive atmosphere in the organization where employees can truly understand and resolve customer issues. Rather than simply "making the sale at all costs," it is these founders' mission to fully recognize customer needs and recommend appropriate solutions. For example, they invest heavily in employee training to ensure that each employee has thorough product knowledge as well as customer service and selling skills. This training involves 235 hours of instruction in the first year, and more than 160 training hours annually thereafter for each employee. Employees meet daily, in what are called team huddles (see photo), to discuss goals for the day. As a result, sales associates are able to listen to a customer's problems and recommend "tailor-made" solutions. For instance, one associate creatively determined, for a customer who wanted to store and ship videocassettes, that men's shoeboxes will snugly and securely hold 11 videotapes. That employee's insight became one of the topics of the following day's team huddle!

To ensure that each trained employee stays with the company, Tindell and Boone make every effort to pay above-average salaries and benefits. In fact, for the past several years, The Container Store has been recognized by *Fortune* magazine as one of the best companies to work in. But these two founders aren't sitting back and congratulating each other for their success. Although they have clearly differentiated their organization from the competition, they know they won't enjoy that position for long. Major discount stores, like Target, have seen the success of The Container Store, and are beginning to replicate some of their activities. As Garrett Boone says, "we welcome these challenges as it keeps us constantly focused on bettering our services to keep us unique. Being complacent in an ever-changing world is simply unacceptable."

A GENERATION AGO, SUCCESSFUL MANAGERS VALUED STABILITY, predictability, and efficiency achieved through economies of large size. But many of yesterdays stars—for instance, Pan Am and Bell & Howell—have faded because they did not adapt to what was happening around them. Strong companies today—companies like Southwest Airlines, Wal-Mart, FedEx, and Intel—succeed because they are lean, fast, and flexible. They are dedicated to quality; they organize work around teams, create ethical work environments, minimize hierarchical overhead, and exhibit entrepreneurial skills when facing change.

In this chapter, we will establish a foundation for understanding this changing world of work. No successful organization, or its management, can operate without understanding and dealing with the dynamic environment that surrounds it. We will look at the forces that are causing organizations to change, what contemporary organizations are like, and how managers in these organizations are responding.

THE CHANGING ECONOMY

The realization today is that organizations that are stagnant and bound by tradition are increasingly fading from the limelight. Why? Because one of the biggest problems in managing an organization today is failing to adapt to the changing world.

Economies throughout the world are going through turbulent change. To better understand this, let's look back on the road we've taken.

It's easy to forget that just 25 years ago no one had a fax machine, a cellular phone, or a notebook computer. Terms we now use in our everyday vocabulary, like e-mail and Internet, were known to maybe, at best, a few hundred people. Computers often took up considerable space, quite unlike today's four-pound laptops. Moreover, if you were to talk about networks 25 years ago, people would have assumed you were talking about ABC, CBS, or NBC—the major television networks.

The silicon chip and other advances in technology have permanently altered the economies of the world, and as we'll show momentarily, the way people work. Digital electronics, optical data storage, more powerful and portable computers, and the ability of computers to communicate with each other are changing the way information is created, stored, used, and shared. One individual who has studied these changes and predicted some of their implications is futurist Alvin Toffler, who has written extensively about social change.[2] Classifying each period of social history, Toffler argues that modern civilization has evolved over three "waves." With each wave came a new way of doing things. Some groups of people gained from the new way; others lost.

The first wave was driven by *agriculture.* Until the late nineteenth century, all economies were agrarian. For instance, in the 1890s, approximately 90 percent of people were employed in agriculture-related jobs. These individuals were typically their own bosses and were responsible for performing a variety of tasks. Their success, or failure, was contingent on how well they produced. Since the 1890s, the proportion of the population engaged in farming has consistently dropped. Now less than five percent of the global workforce is needed to provide our food; in the United States, it's under 3 percent.

The second wave was *industrialization.* From the late 1800s until the 1960s, most developed countries moved from agrarian societies to industrial societies. In doing so, work left the fields and moved into formal organizations. The industrial wave forever changed the lives of skilled craftsmen. No longer did they grow something or produce a product in its entirety. Instead, workers were hired into tightly structured and formal workplaces. Mass production, specialized jobs, and authority relationships became the mode of operation. It gave rise to a new group of workers—the blue-collar industrial workers—individuals who were paid for performing routine work that relied almost exclusively on physical stamina. By the 1950s, industrial workers had become the largest single group in every developed country. They made products such as steel, automobiles, rubber, and industrial equipment. Ironically, no class in history has ever risen faster than the blue-collar worker. And no class in history has ever fallen faster. Today, blue-collar industrial workers account for less than 30 percent of the U.S. workforce and will be less than half of that in just a few years.[3] The shift since World War II has been away from manufacturing work and toward service jobs. Manufacturing jobs, as a proportion of the total civilian workforce, today are highest in Japan at just over 20 percent. In the United States, manufacturing jobs make up about 15 percent of the civilian workforce. In contrast, services make up about half of the jobs in Italy (the lowest percentage of any industrialized country) and more than three-fourths of the jobs in the United States and Canada.[4]

Individuals such as this computer systems analyst represent one of the fastest-growing worker populations in the global economy. These are people who work with their hands and theoretical knowledge in jobs that are designed around the acquisition and application of information.

By the start of the 1970s a new age, the information age, was gaining momentum. Technological advancements were eliminating many low-skilled, blue-collar jobs. Moreover, the *information* wave was transforming society from its manufacturing focus to one of service. People were increasingly moving from jobs on the production floor to clerical, technical, and professional jobs. Job growth in the past 20 years has been in low-skilled service work (such as fast-food employees, clerks, and home health aides) and knowledge work. This latter group includes professionals such as registered nurses, accountants, teachers, lawyers, and engineers. It also includes technologists—people who work with their hands and with theoretical knowledge—commonly referred to as information technologists.[5] Computer programmers, software designers, and systems analysts are examples of jobs in this category. **Knowledge workers** as a group currently make up about one-third of the U.S. workforce—individuals in jobs that are designed around the acquisition and application of information.

"Knowledge-work jobs are designed around the acquisition and application of information."

knowledge workers
Workers whose jobs are designed around the acquisition and application of information

The most powerful technological innovation to influence business in the past decade has been the rise of the dot-com business. Through the use of the Internet, the impact of dot-coms is unlike anything seen in the past century.[6] Just as railroads, automobiles, and computers each created entire new markets and industries, the Internet is doing the same. It is completely changing the "rules of business." We'll come back to this phenomenon shortly.

As these waves influenced society, so too have they affected how we do business (see Exhibit 2–1). International markets, technological improvements, e-commerce, changes in workforce composition, and the like are giving rise to new organizational issues. In the following section, as well as throughout this chapter, we will explore some of the more important forces that are creating challenges for contemporary managers.

A GLOBAL MARKETPLACE

Part of the rapidly changing environment that managers face is the globalization of business. Management is no longer constrained by national borders. BMW, a German-owned firm, builds cars in South Carolina. Similarly, McDonald's sells hamburgers in China. Exxon, a so-called American company, receives more than three-fourths of its revenues from sales outside the United States. Toyota makes cars in Kentucky; General Motors makes cars in Brazil; and Mercedes sport utility vehicles are made in Alabama.[7] Parts for Ford Motor Company's Crown Victoria come from all over the world: Mexico (seats, windshields, and fuel tanks), Japan (shock absorbers), Spain (electronic engine controls), Germany (anti-lock brake systems), and England (key axle parts). These examples illustrate that the world has become a **global village**. To be effective in this boundaryless world, managers need to adapt to cultures, systems, and techniques that are different from their own.

global village
Refers to the concept of a boundaryless world; the production and marketing of goods and services worldwide

EXHIBIT 2–1 The Changing Economy

OLD ECONOMY	NEW ECONOMY
National borders limit competition	National borders are nearly meaningless in defining an organization's operating boundaries
Technology reinforces rigid hierarchies and limits access to information	Technology changes in the way information is created, stored, used, and shared have made it more accessible
Job opportunities are for blue-collar industrial workers	Job opportunities are for knowledge workers
Population is relatively homogeneous	Population is characterized by cultural diversity
Business is estranged from its environment	Business accepts its social responsibilities
Economy is driven by large corporations	Economy is driven by small entrepreneurial firms
Customers get what business chooses to give them	Customer needs drive business

National boundaries no longer confine today's contemporary organizations. The global village enables companies like Wal-Mart to sell products anywhere in the world. This mega-retailer's store in Europe is just one of the 95 Wal-Marts opened in Germany. As a result of moving into the global village, Wal-Mart's annual revenues have increased by more than $3 billion from the German operations alone.

In the 1960s, Canada's prime minister described his country's proximity to the United States as analogous to sleeping with an elephant, "You feel every twitch the animal makes." In the 2000s, we can generalize this analogy to the entire world. A rise in interest rates in Japan, for example, instantly affects managers and organizations throughout the world. The fall of communism in Eastern Europe and the collapse of the Soviet Union created exciting opportunities for business firms throughout the free world.

International businesses have been with us for a long time. For instance, Siemens, Remington, and Singer were selling their products in many countries in the nineteenth century. By the 1920s, some companies, including Fiat, Ford, Unilever, and Royal Dutch/Shell, had gone multinational. But it was not until the mid-1960s that **multinational corporations (MNCs)** became commonplace. These corporations, which maintain significant operations in two or more countries simultaneously but are based in one home country, initiated the rapid growth in international trade. Today, companies such as Gillette, Wal-Mart, Coca-Cola, and Aflac are among a growing number of U.S.–based firms that realize significant portions of their annual revenues from foreign operations.[8]

The expanding global environment has extended the reach and goals of MNCs to create an even more generic global organization called the **transnational corporation (TNC)**. This type of organization does not seek to replicate its domestic successes by managing foreign operations from home. Instead, decisions in TNCs are made at the local level. Nationals (individuals born and raised in a specific country) are typically hired to run operations in each country. The products and marketing strategies for each country are tailored to that country's culture. Nestlé, for example, is a transnational corporation. With operations in almost every country on the globe, it is the world's largest food company, yet its managers match their products to their consumers. In part of Europe, Nestlé sells products that are not available in the United States or Latin America. Another example is Frito-Lay, which markets a Dorito chip in the British market that differs in both taste and texture from the U.S. and Canadian versions. Many large, well-known companies are moving to more effectively globalize their management structures by breaking down internal arrangements that impose artificial geographic barriers. This type of organization is called a **borderless organization**. For instance, IBM dropped its organizational structure based on country and reorganized into 14 industry groups. Ford merged its culturally distinct European and North American auto operations and plans to add a Latin American and an Asian-Pacific division in the future. Bristol-Myers Squibb changed its consumer business to become more aggressive in international sales and installed a new executive in charge of worldwide consumer medicines such as Bufferin and Excedrin. The move to borderless management is an attempt by organizations to increase efficiency and effectiveness in a competitive global marketplace.

multinational corporations (MNCs)
Companies that maintain significant operations in two or more countries simultaneously but are based in one home country

transnational corporation (TNC)
A company that maintains significant operations in more than one country simultaneously and decentralizes decision making in each operation to the local country

borderless organization
A management structure in which internal arrangements that impose artificial geographic barriers are broken down

HOW DOES GLOBALIZATION AFFECT ORGANIZATIONS?

An Organization is mostly affected by globalization when its management decides to enter into the global marketplace. An organization going global typically proceeds through three stages, as shown in Exhibit 2–2. In Stage I, managers make the first push toward going international merely by exporting the organization's products to foreign countries. This is a passive step toward international involvement that requires minimal risk because managers make no serious effort to tap foreign

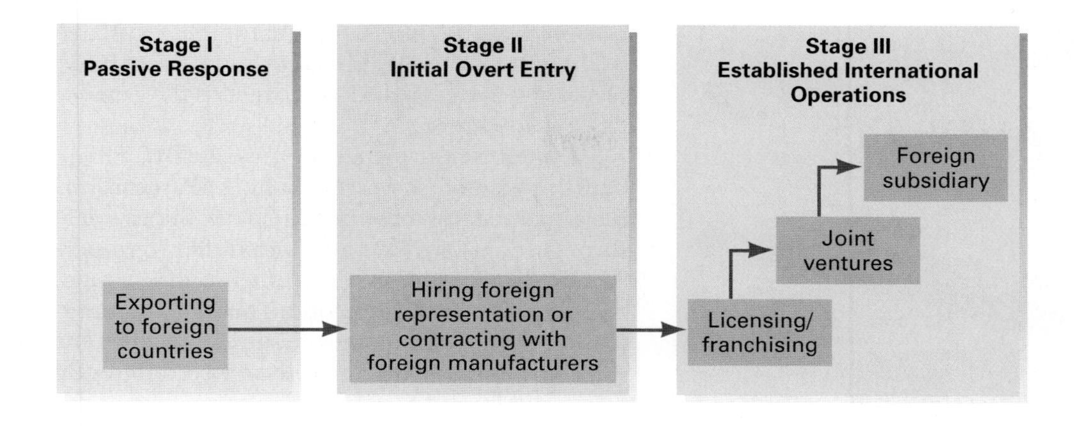

EXHIBIT 2-2
Stages of Going Global

markets. Rather, the organization fills foreign orders only when it gets them. This may be the first and only international involvement many firms in the mail-order business have.

In Stage II, managers make an overt commitment to sell products in foreign countries or to have them made in foreign factories. Yet, there is still no physical presence of company employees outside the company's home country. On the sales side, Stage II typically is done either by sending domestic employees on regular business trips to meet foreign customers or by hiring foreign agents or brokers to represent the organization's product line. On the manufacturing side, managers contract with a foreign firm to produce the organization's products.

Stage III represents a strong commitment by managers to pursue international markets aggressively.[9] As shown in Exhibit 2-2, managers can do this in different ways. They can license or franchise to another firm the right to use the organization's brand name, technology, or product specifications. This approach is used widely by pharmaceutical companies and fast-food chains such as Pizza Hut. Joint ventures involve larger commitments; a domestic and a foreign firm share the cost of developing new products or building production facilities in a foreign country. These are called **strategic alliances.**[10] These partnerships provide a faster and less expensive way for companies to compete globally than if they did it on their own. Recent cross-border alliances include British Airways and American Airlines, Polaroid and Minolta, and Nestlé and General Mills. Managers make the greatest commitment, and assume the greatest risk, when the organization sets up a foreign subsidiary. Such subsidiaries can be managed as an MNC (with domestic control), a TNC (with foreign control), or a borderless organization (with global control). Acura, a free-standing company fully owned by Honda, is an example of a foreign subsidiary.

strategic alliances
A domestic and a foreign firm share the cost of developing new products or building production facilities in a foreign country

WHAT EFFECT DOES GLOBALIZATION HAVE ON MANAGERS?

When you hear the name Whirlpool, what comes to mind? A large U.S. manufacturer of appliances such as washers, dryers, and refrigerators? That description is somewhat correct, but Whirlpool's activities are not confined to the United States. It is also the top manufacturer and distributor of appliances in Latin America, Europe, and Asia.[11]

In terms of the changing global environment, the spread of capitalism makes the world a smaller place. Business has new markets to conquer. And well-trained and reliable workers in such countries as Hungary, Slovakia, and the Czech Republic become a rich source of low-cost labor for organizations everywhere. The implementation of free markets in Eastern Europe further underscores the growing interdependence among countries and the potential for goods, labor, and capital to move easily across national borders.

A boundaryless world introduces new challenges for managers, such as managing in a country where there's a different national culture.[12] The specific challenge is

Joining forces to achieve mutually beneficial goals is one way some companies have found it efficient to compete globally. The strategic alliance between British Airways and American Airlines enables both to provide fast and cost-effective services.

parochialism
Refers to a narrow focus in which one sees things solely through one's own view and from one's own perspective

recognizing the differences that might exist and finding ways to make interactions effective. One of the first issues to deal with, then, is the perception of "foreigners."

United States managers once held a rather parochial view of the world of business. **Parochialism** is a narrow focus; these managers saw things solely through their own eyes and within their own perspectives.[13] They believed that their business practices were the best in the world. They did not recognize that people from other countries had different ways of doing things or that they lived differently from Americans. In essence, parochialism is an ethnocentric view. Of course, this view cannot succeed in a global village—nor is it the dominant view held today. But changing U.S. managers' perceptions first required understanding of the different cultures and their environments.

All countries have different values, morals, customs, political and economic systems, and laws. Traditional approaches to studying international business have sought to advance each of these topic areas. However, a strong case can be made that traditional business approaches need to be understood within their social context. That is, organizational success can come from a variety of managerial practices, each of which is derived from a different business environment. For example, status is perceived differently in different countries. In France, status is often the result of factors important to the organization, such as seniority, education, and the like. This emphasis is called ascribed status. In the United States, status is more a function of what individuals have personally accomplished (achieved status). Managers need to understand societal issues (such as status) that might affect operations in another country. Countries also have different laws. For instance, in the United States, laws guard against employers' taking action against employees solely on the basis of an employee's age. Similar laws do not exist in all other countries. One issue for organizations is that viewing the global environment from any single perspective may be too narrow and potentially problematic. A more appropriate approach is to recognize the cultural dimensions of a country's environment. An illuminating study of the differences in cultural environments was conducted by Geert Hofstede.[14]

Hofstede's framework for assessing cultures is one of the most widely referenced approaches for analyzing variations among cultures. He surveyed more than 116,000 IBM employees in 40 countries about their work-related values. He found that managers and employees vary on five value dimensions of national culture. They are listed and defined as follows:

- ***Power distance.*** The degree to which people in a country accept that power in institutions and organizations is distributed unequally. Ranges from relatively equal (low power distance) to extremely unequal (high power distance).
- ***Individualism versus collectivism.*** Individualism is the degree to which people in a country prefer to act as individuals rather than as members of groups. Collectivism is the equivalent of low individualism.[15]
- ***Quantity of life versus quality of life.*** Quantity of life is the degree to which values like assertiveness, the acquisition of money and material goods, and competition prevail. Quality of life is the degree to which people value relationships, and show sensitivity and concern for the welfare of others.[16]
- ***Uncertainty avoidance.*** The degree to which people in a country prefer structured over unstructured situations. In countries that score high on uncertainty avoidance, people have an increased level of anxiety, which manifests itself in greater nervousness, stress, and aggressiveness.

- ***Long-term versus short-term orientation.*** People in cultures with long-term orientations look to the future and value thrift and persistence. A short-term orientation values the past and present, and emphasizes respect for tradition and fulfilling social obligations.

What did Hofstede's research conclude? Here are a few highlights. China and West Africa scored high on power distance; the United States and the Netherlands scored low. Most Asian countries were more collectivist than individualistic; and the United States ranked highest among all countries on individualism. Germany and Hong Kong rated high on quantity of life; Russia and the Netherlands rated low. On uncertainty avoidance, France and Russia were high; Hong Kong and the United States were low. And China and Hong Kong had a long-term orientation, while France and the United States were low.

EMPHASIS ON TECHNOLOGY

Suppose you need information on how well your department is meeting its production standards. Thirty years ago you probably would have had to submit a requisition to the operations control department. Their response may have taken a couple of weeks, and the information would have been in whatever format the operations department dictated. Today, however, a few keystrokes on your computer will get that information almost instantaneously. Moreover, it will be precisely the information you want—which may be entirely different than the information one of your colleagues needs on a similar account.

technology
Any equipment, tools, or operating methods that are designed to make work more efficient

Since the 1970s, U.S. companies such as General Electric, Citigroup Global Technologies, Wal-Mart, and 3M have been using automated offices, robotics in manufacturing, computer-assisted design software, integrated circuits, microprocessors, and electronic meetings. These technological advances make the organizations more productive and help them create and maintain a competitive advantage.

Technology includes any equipment, tools, or operating methods that are designed to make work more efficient. Technological advances involve the integration of technology into a process for changing inputs into outputs. For example, to sell its goods or services, an organization must first take certain inputs—labor, raw materials, and the like—and transform them into outputs. In years past, many of these transforming operations were performed by human labor. Technology, however, has made it possible to enhance this production process by replacing human labor with electronic and computer equipment. For instance, assembly operations at General Motors rely heavily on robotics. Robots perform repetitive tasks, such as spot welding and painting, much more quickly than humans can. And the robots are not subject to health problems caused by exposure to chemicals or other hazardous materials. Technology is also making it possible to better serve customers. For example, Merilatt Industries, the Adrian, Michigan cabinetmaker, gives customers more than 63,000 cabinet configurations, allowing them to create customized cabinets at a fraction of the design time and cost of specially made cabinetry.[17] Technology, however, is not used only in manufacturing enterprises. The banking industry has been able to replace thousands of tellers with ATM machines and online banking systems.

Technological advancements are also used to provide better, more useful information. Most cars built today have an onboard computer circuit that a technician can plug into to determine

How has technology helped Merillat's customers? Those looking to purchase cabinetry now have the opportunity to make unique selections at a cost that is equivalent to "off-the-shelf" prices. That's made possible through a high-tech process which can configure and mass-customize more than 63,000 cabinet options.

operating problems, saving countless diagnostic hours for a mechanic. And at Wal-Mart, technology has meant getting better and more timely information. Company representatives are able to instantly obtain warehouse logistics and inventories. As a result, Wal-Mart has increased its efficiency by more than 20 percent.

HOW DOES AN ORGANIZATION BENEFIT FROM INFORMATION TECHNOLOGY?

Technological changes, especially those related to *information technology (IT)*, have had and continue to have a significant effect on the way organizations are managed. For instance, Dell Computer Corporation designed its newest factory without any space for inventory storage. General Electric, too, plans to save millions of dollars by buying spare parts for its facilities over the Internet. Both of those decisions and actions were made possible by IT. In addition, IT has created the ability to circumvent the physical confines of working only in a specified organizational location. With notebook and desktop computers, fax machines, high-speed modems, organizational Intranets, and other forms of IT, organizational members can do their work from any place, at any time.[18]

What are the implications of this vast spread of IT? One important implication is that employees' job skill requirements will increase.[19] Workers will need the ability to read and comprehend software and hardware manuals, technical journals, and detailed reports. Another implication is that IT tends to level the competitive playing field.[20] It provides organizations (no matter what their size or market power) with the ability to innovate, bring products to market rapidly, and respond to customer requests. Companies like E*TRADE and Ameritrade, for example, have made it possible for any individual to personally trade stocks online, as opposed to making similar transactions through a large brokerage house. One of the greatest phenomena we've witnessed in business today, however, is the proliferation of activities over the Internet—commonly grouped under the term of the e-organization.

WHAT IS AN E-ORGANIZATION?

e-commerce
Any computer transaction that occurs when data are processed and transmitted over the Internet

Let's begin by clarifying some concepts. Two terms that seem to cause considerable confusion are e-commerce and e-business.[21] The term **e-commerce** is becoming the standard label for the sales side of electronic business. It encompasses presenting

What does the term e-organization mean? An e-organization refers to applications of e-business concepts offered to stakeholders. For example, by providing taxpayers with access to a variety of its services over the Internet, the IRS can be considered an e-organization.

products on Web sites and filling orders. The vast majority of articles and media attention given to using the Internet in business are directed at online shopping—marketing and selling goods and services over the Internet. When you hear about the tremendous number of people who are shopping on the Internet—how businesses can set up Web sites where they can sell goods, conduct transactions, get paid, and fulfill orders—you're hearing about e-commerce. It's a dramatic change in the way a firm relates to its customers. And e-commerce is exploding. Global e-commerce spending was $132 billion in 2000. It's expected to be $6.8 trillion by the 2004.[22] You should be aware, however, that 90 percent of e-commerce sales are business-to-business transactions. The vast majority of e-commerce sales will be things like Intel chip sales to Compaq, or Goodyear sales to Ford, rather than consumers like us buying computers or sweaters for personal consumption.

In contrast, **e-business** refers to the full breadth of activities included in a successful Internet-based enterprise. It includes developing strategies for running Internet-based companies; improving communication between employees, customers, and suppliers; and collaborating with partners to electronically coordinate design and production. And the term *e-organization* (e-orgs) merely refers to applications of e-business concepts to all organizations. E-orgs include not only business firms, but also hospitals, schools, museums, government agencies, and the military. For instance, the Internal Revenue Service is an e-organization because it now provides taxpayers access over the Internet.

e-business
The full breadth of activities included in a successful Internet-based enterprise

The best way to understand the e-organization concept is to look at its three underlying concepts—the Internet, intranets, and extranets. The Internet is a worldwide network of interconnected computers; intranets are an organization's private Internet; and extranets are extended intranets, accessible only to selected employees and authorized outsiders. As Exhibit 2–3 illustrates, an e-organization is defined by the degree to which it uses global (Internet) and private (intranet and extranet) network linkages. Type As are traditional organizations such as small retailers and service firms. Most organizations today fall into this category. Type Bs are contemporary organizations with heavy reliance on intranets and extranets; Type Cs are small e-commerce firms; and finally, Type Ds are full e-organizations. They've completely integrated global and private networks. Type Ds include such firms as eBay, Cisco Systems, Amazon.com, and Wal-Mart. Note that as an organization moves from a Type A toward a Type D, it increases the degree to which it takes on e-org properties.

While there have been numerous stories of the sudden rise of e-organizations, and the unheralded wealth created by these companies, readers must recognize that many of these organizations have typically been viewed as high-reward ventures. But that's simply not the case. Many have failed miserably.[23] The Internet created

EXHIBIT 2–3
What Defines an E-Business?

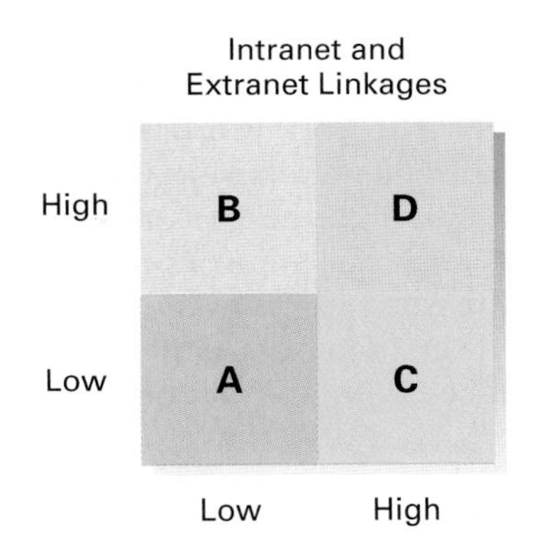

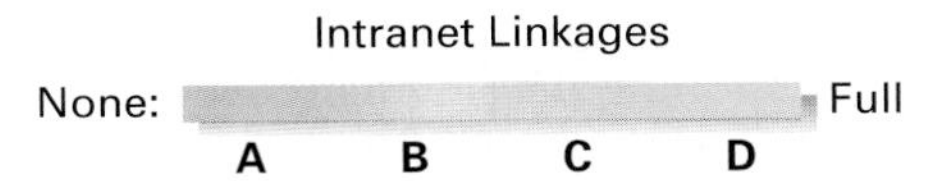

thousands of new businesses; it changed the way organizations operated. But, in retrospect, it left a lot of road kill. Yet that's not meant to paint a gloomy picture. Internet use by individuals and organizational members is growing significantly each year. As technology continues to evolve, and management learns to better manage the e-organization, we can expect a resurgence.[24]

IN WHAT WAYS DOES TECHNOLOGY ALTER A MANAGER'S JOB?

As you read through this book, we'll return to e-organizations as they affect the four components of the management process—planning, organizing, leading, and controlling. For our purposes here, let's go back to the larger picture regarding the effect of technology on a manager's job.

Technology has had a positive effect on the internal operations of organizations, but it has also changed the manager's job. Organizations today have become integrative communication centers. By linking computers, telephones, fax machines, copiers, printers, and the like, managers can get complete information quickly. With that information, managers can better formulate plans, make faster decisions, more clearly define the jobs that workers need to perform, and monitor work activities. In essence, information technology today has enhanced a manager's ability to more effectively and efficiently perform the four primary activities associated with a manager's job.

Technology is also changing how a manager's work is performed. Historically, the work site was located close to a source of skilled labor, so employees were near their bosses. Management could observe what work was being done and could easily communicate with employees face-to-face. Through the advent of technological advancements, managers are able to supervise employees in remote locations, and the need for face-to-face interaction has decreased dramatically.[25] Work, for many, occurs where their computers are. **Telecommuting** capabilities that exist today have made it possible for employees to be located anywhere on the globe.[26] With this potential, employers no longer have to consider locating a business near its workforce. Moreover, telecommuting offers an opportunity for a business in a high-labor-cost area to have its work done in an area where lower wages prevail. For example, if Progressive Auto Insurance in Omaha, Nebraska, finds that it is having problems attracting qualified local applicants for its claims-processing jobs, and a pool of qualified workers is available in Berlin, Maryland, Progressive doesn't need to establish a facility in Maryland. Rather, by providing these employees with computer equipment and appropriate ancillaries, the work can be done hundreds of miles away and then be transmitted to the home office.

telecommuting
The linking of a worker's computer and modem with those of co-workers and management at an office

Effectively communicating with individuals in remote locations and ensuring that performance objectives are being met have become two of managers' biggest challenges. In addressing these challenges, organizations will focus on training managers to establish performance standards and ensure appropriate work quality and on-time completion. Traditional "face time" is removed in decentralized work sites, and managers' need to "control" the work will have to change. Instead, there will have to be more employee involvement, allowing workers to make those decisions that affect them. For instance, although the work assigned to employees has a due date, managers must recognize that home workers will work at their own pace. Instead of an individual focusing work efforts over an eight-hour period, the individual may work two hours here, three hours at another time, and another three late at night. The emphasis, then, will be on output, not means.

WHAT DOES SOCIETY EXPECT FROM ORGANIZATIONS AND MANAGERS?

The importance of corporate social responsibility surfaced in the 1960s when the activist movement began questioning the singular economic objective of business. For instance, were large corporations irresponsible because they discriminated against

EXHIBIT 2–4 Arguments for and against Social Responsibility

The major arguments for the assumption of social responsibilities by business are:

1. **Public expectations** Social expectations of business have increased dramatically since the 1960s. Public opinion in support of business pursuing social as well as economic goals is now well solidified.
2. **Long-run profits** Socially responsible businesses tend to have more secure long-run profits. This is the normal result of the better community relations and improved business image that responsible behavior brings.
3. **Ethical obligation** A business firm can and should have a conscience. Business should be socially responsible because responsible actions are right for their own sake.
4. **Public image** Firms seek to enhance their public image to gain more customers, better employees, access to money markets, and other benefits. Since the public considers social goals to be important, business can create a favorable public image by pursuing social goals.
5. **Better environment** Involvement by business can solve difficult social problems, thus creating a better quality of life and a more desirable community in which to attract and hold skilled employees.
6. **Discouragement of further government regulation** Government regulation adds economic costs and restricts management's decision flexibility. By becoming socially responsible, business can expect less government regulation.
7. **Balance of responsibility and power** Business has a large amount of power in society. An equally large amount of responsibility is required to balance it. When power is significantly greater than responsibility, the imbalance encourages irresponsible behavior that works against the public good.
8. **Stockholder interests** Social responsibility will improve the price of a business's stock in the long run. The stock market will view the socially responsible company as less risky and open to public attack. Therefore, it will award its stock a higher price-earnings ratio.
9. **Possession of resources** Business has the financial resources, technical experts, and managerial talent to provide support to public and charitable projects that need assistance.
10. **Superiority of prevention over cures** Social problems must be dealt with at some time. Business should act on them before they become serious and costly to correct and take management's energy away from accomplishing its goal of producing goods and services.

The major arguments against the assumption of social responsibilities by business are:

1. **Violation of profit maximization** This is the essence of the classical viewpoint. Business is most socially responsible when it attends strictly to its economic interests and leaves other activities to other institutions.
2. **Dilution of purpose** The pursuit of social goals dilutes business's primary purpose: economic productivity. Society may suffer as both economic and social goals are poorly accomplished.
3. **Costs** Many socially responsible activities do not pay their own way. Someone has to pay these costs. Business must absorb these costs or pass them on to consumers in higher prices.
4. **Too much power** Business is already one of the most powerful institutions in our society. If it pursued social goals, it would have even more power. Society has given business enough power.
5. **Lack of skills** The outlook and abilities of business leaders are oriented primarily toward economics. Business people are poorly qualified to cope with social issues.
6. **Lack of accountability** Political representatives pursue social goals and are held accountable for their actions. Such is not the case with business leaders. There are no direct lines of social accountability from the business sector to the public.
7. **Lack of broad public support** There is no broad mandate from society for business to become involved in social issues. The public is divided on the issue. In fact, it is a topic that usually generates a heated debate. Actions taken under such divided support are likely to fail.

Source: Adapted from R. J. Monsen Jr., "The Social Attitudes of Management," in J. M. McGuire, ed. *Contemporary Management: Issues and Views* (Upper Saddle River, NJ: Prentice Hall, 1974), p. 616; and K. Davis and W. Frederick, *Business and Society: Management, Public Policy, Ethics*, 5th ed. (New York: McGraw-Hill, 1984), pp. 28–41.

women and minorities, as shown by the obvious absence of female and minority managers at that time? Was a company like Dow Corning ignoring its social responsibility by marketing breast implants when data indicated that leaking silicone could be a health hazard? Were tobacco companies ignoring health risks associated with nicotine and its addictive properties? Were companies like Enron and its accounting firm Arthur Anderson failing to properly protect the financial interests of their stakeholders?[27] Before the 1960s, few people asked such questions. Even today, good arguments can be made for both sides of the social responsibility issue (see Exhibit 2–4).

Arguments aside, times have changed. Managers are now regularly confronted with decisions that have a dimension of social responsibility; philanthropy, pricing, employee relations, resource conservation, product quality, and operations in countries with oppressive governments are some of the more obvious factors. They are addressing these areas by reassessing forms of packaging, recyclability of products, environmental safety practices, and the like. The idea of being environmentally friendly or green will have an effect on all aspects of business, from the conception of products and services to use and subsequent disposal by customers.[28] In a globally competitive world, few organizations can afford the bad press or potential economic ramifications of being seen as socially irresponsible.[29]

Few terms have been defined in as many different ways as social responsibility. Some of the more popular meanings include profit maximization, going beyond profit making, voluntary activities, concern for the broader social system, and social responsiveness.[30] Most of the debate has focused on the extremes. On one side, there is the classical—or purely economic—view that management's only social responsibility is to maximize profits.[31] On the other side stands the socioeconomic position, which holds that management's responsibility goes well beyond making profits to include protecting and improving society's welfare.[32]

HOW CAN ORGANIZATIONS DEMONSTRATE SOCIALLY RESPONSIBLE ACTIONS?

social responsibility
A firm's obligation, beyond that required by the law and economics, to pursue long-term goals that are beneficial to society

What do we mean when we talk about **social responsibility**? It's a business firm's obligation, beyond that required by the law and economics, to pursue long-term goals that are good for society. Note that this definition assumes that business obeys the law and pursues economic interests. We take as a given that all business firms—those that are socially responsible and those that are not—will obey all laws that society imposes. Also note that this definition views business as a moral agent. In its effort to do good for society, it must differentiate between right and wrong.

social obligation
The obligation of a business to meet its economic and legal responsibilities and no more

We can understand social responsibility better if we compare it with two similar concepts: social obligation and social responsiveness.[33] **Social obligation** is the foundation of a business's social involvement. A business has fulfilled its social obligation when it meets its economic and legal responsibilities and no more. It does the minimum that the law requires. A firm pursues social goals only to the extent that they contribute to its economic goals. In contrast to social obligation, both social responsibility and social responsiveness go beyond merely meeting basic economic and legal standards. For example, both might mean respecting the community in which the company operates, treating all employees fairly, respecting the environment, supporting career goals and special work needs of women and minorities, or not doing business in countries in which there are human rights violations.

social responsiveness
The ability of a firm to adapt to changing societal conditions

Social responsibility also adds an ethical imperative to do those things that make society better and not to do those that could make it worse. **Social responsiveness** refers to the capacity of a firm to adapt to changing societal conditions.[34] Social responsibility requires business to determine what is right or wrong and thus seek fundamental ethical truths. Social responsiveness is guided by social norms that can provide managers with a meaningful guide for decision making.[35]

HOW DO MANAGERS BECOME MORE SOCIALLY RESPONSIBLE?

ethics
A set of rules or principles that defines right and wrong conduct

Ethics commonly refers to a set of rules or principles that defines right and wrong conduct.[36] Right or wrong behavior, though, may at times be difficult to determine. Most recognize that something illegal is also unethical. But what about the questionable "legal" areas. Our literature has been filled with management practices at companies like WorldCom, Enron, and ImClone. What executives at these companies did may be questionable, and some may have been illegal; the larger issue is what implications have such actions created? For many, the aftermath of these corporate scan-

EXHIBIT 2–5 Three Views of Ethics

Utilitarian view of ethics	Refers to a situation in which decisions are made solely on the basis of their outcomes or consequences. The goal of utilitarianism is to provide the greatest good for the greatest number. On one side, utilitarianism encourages efficiency and productivity and is consistent with the goal of profit maximization. On the other side, however, it can result in biased allocations of resources, especially when some of those affected lack representation or voice.
Rights view of ethics	Refers to a situation in which the individual is concerned with respecting and protecting individual liberties and privileges, including the rights to privacy, freedom of conscience, free speech, and due process. The positive side of the rights perspective is that it protects individuals' freedom and privacy. But it has a negative side in organizations: It can present obstacles to high productivity and efficiency by creating an overly legalistic work climate.
Theory of justice view of ethics	Refers to a situation in which an individual imposes and enforces rules fairly and impartially. A manager would be using a theory of justice perspective in deciding to pay a new entry-level employee $1.50 an hour over the minimum wage because that manager believes that the minimum wage is inadequate to allow employees to meet their basic financial commitments. Imposing standards of justice also comes with pluses and minuses. It protects the interests of those stakeholders who may be underrepresented or lack power, but it can encourage a sense of entitlement that reduces risk taking, innovation, and productivity.

Source: G. F. Cavanaugh, D. J. Moberg, and M. Valasquez, "The Ethics of Organizational Politics," *Academy of Management Journal* (June 1981): 363–74.

dals has resulted in a lack of trust in management.[37] People are questioning how such unethical actions could have gone unnoticed if proper controls were in force in the organization. Moreover, the public is now examining the unethical cultures that were pervasive in these organizations.

Understanding ethics may be difficult, depending on the view that one holds of the topic (see Developing Your Ethics Skill, p. 73). Exhibit 2–5 presents three views of ethical standards. Regardless of one's own view, whether a manager acts ethically or unethically will depend on several factors. These factors include the individual's morality, values, personality, and experiences; the organization's culture; and the issue in question.[38] A recent survey, for example, indicated that 82 percent of corporate executives surveyed admitted that they cheat at golf—and 72 percent of them believe that golf and business behaviors are parallel.[39] People who lack a strong moral sense, however, are much less likely to do the wrong things if they are constrained by rules, policies, job descriptions, or strong cultural norms that discourage such behaviors. For example, someone in your class has stolen the final exam and is selling a copy for $50. You need to do well on this exam or risk failing the course. You expect some classmates have bought copies, and that could affect any possibility of the exam being curved by the professor. Do you buy a copy because you fear that without it you'll be disadvantaged, do you refuse to buy a copy and try your best, or do you report your knowledge to your instructor?

The example of the final exam illustrates how ambiguity about what is ethical can be a problem for managers. Codes of ethics are an increasingly popular tool for attempting to reduce that ambiguity.[40] A **code of ethics** is a formal document that states an organization's primary values and the ethical rules it expects managers and operative employees to follow. Ideally, these codes should be specific enough to guide organizational personnel in what they are supposed to do yet loose enough to allow for freedom of judgment. Nearly 90 percent of *Fortune* 1000 companies have a stated code of ethics,[41] and these codes extend into the global arena.[42]

code of ethics
A formal document that states an organization's primary values and the ethical rules it expects managers and operatives to follow

In isolation, ethics codes are not likely to be much more than window dressing—Enron had a code of ethics statement. Their effectiveness depends heavily on whether management supports them and ingrains them into the corporate culture, and how individuals who break the codes are treated.[43] If management considers them to be important, regularly reaffirms their content, follows the rules themselves, and publicly reprimands rule breakers, ethics codes can supply a strong foundation for an effective corporate ethics program.[44]

WHAT IS ENTREPRENEURSHIP?

entrepreneurship
The process of initiating a business venture, organizing the necessary resources, and assuming the risks and rewards

There is no shortage of definitions of **entrepreneurship**. Some, for example, apply the term to the creation of any new business. Others focus on intentions, claiming that entrepreneurs seek to create wealth, which is different from starting businesses merely as a means of income substitution (that is, working for yourself rather than working for someone else). When most people describe entrepreneurs, they use adjectives such as bold, innovative, initiative taking, venturesome, and risk taking. They also tend to associate entrepreneurs with small businesses. We will define entrepreneurship as a process where an individual or a group of individuals risk time and money in pursuit of opportunities to create value and grow through innovation regardless of the resources they control. The three important themes in this definition are (1) the pursuit of opportunities, (2) innovation, and (3) growth. Entrepreneurs are pursuing opportunities to grow a business by changing, revolutionizing, transforming, or introducing new products or services.

Many people believe that entrepreneurial activities and small business are one and the same; but they are not. There are some key differences between the two. Entrepreneurs create entrepreneurial ventures—organizations that are pursuing opportunities, are characterized by innovative practices, and have growth and profitability as their primary goals. A small business, on the other hand, is one that is independently owned, operated, and financed; has fewer than 500 employees; doesn't necessarily engage in any new or innovative practices; and usually has relatively little impact on its industry. A small business isn't necessarily entrepreneurial because it's small. To be entrepreneurial means being innovative and seeking out new opportunities. Even though entrepreneurial ventures may start small, they pursue growth. Some new small firms may grow, but many remain small businesses by choice or by default.

"People describe entrepreneurs as bold, innovative, initiative taking, venturesome, and risk taking."

IS THERE AN ENTREPRENEURIAL PROCESS?

What's involved in the entrepreneurial process?[45] There are four key steps that entrepreneurs must address as they start and manage their entrepreneurial ventures. The first of these is *exploring the entrepreneurial context.* The context includes the realities of the new economy, society's laws and regulations that compose the legal environment, and the realities of the changing world of work. It's important to look at each of these aspects of the entrepreneurial context because they determine the "rules" of the game and what decisions and actions are likely to meet with success. Also, it's through exploring the context that entrepreneurs confront that next critically important step in the entrepreneurial process—*identifying opportunities and possible competitive advantages.* We know from our definition of entrepreneurship that the pursuit of opportunities is an important aspect. Once entrepreneurs have explored the entrepreneurial context and identified opportunities and possible competitive advantages, they must look at the issues involved in actually bringing their venture to life. Therefore, the next step in the entrepreneurial process is *starting the venture.* Included in this phase are researching the feasibility of the venture and planning, organizing, and launching the venture. Finally, once the entrepreneurial venture is up and running, the last step in the process is *managing the venture,* which an entrepreneur does by managing processes, people, and growth. We'll revisit this "managing the venture" in future chapters in the text.

WHAT DO ENTREPRENEURS DO?

Describing what entrepreneurs do isn't an easy or simple task! No two entrepreneurs' work activities are exactly alike. In a general sense, entrepreneurs are creating something new, something different. They're searching for change, responding to it, and exploiting it.[46]

Initially, an entrepreneur is engaged in assessing the potential for the entrepreneurial venture and then dealing with start-up issues. In exploring the entrepreneurial context, entrepreneurs are gathering information, identifying potential opportunities, and pinpointing possible competitive advantage(s). Then, armed with this information, the entrepreneur begins researching the venture's feasibility—uncovering business ideas, looking at competitors, and exploring financing options. After looking at the potential of the proposed venture and assessing the likelihood of pursuing it successfully, the entrepreneur proceeds to planning the venture. This includes activities such as developing a viable organizational mission, exploring organizational culture issues, and creating a well-thought-out business plan (see Chapter 3). Once these planning issues have been resolved, the entrepreneur must look at organizing the venture, which involves choosing a legal form of business organization, addressing other legal issues such as patent or copyright searches, and coming up with an appropriate organizational design for structuring how work is going to be done. After these start-up activities have been completed, the entrepreneur is ready to actually launch the venture. This involves setting goals and strategies, and establishing the technology-operations methods, marketing plans, information systems, financial-accounting systems, and cash flow management systems.

Once the entrepreneurial venture is functioning, the entrepreneur's attention switches to managing it. What's involved with actually managing the entrepreneurial venture? An important activity is managing the various processes that are part of every business: making decisions, establishing action plans, analyzing external and internal environments, measuring and evaluating performance, and making needed changes. Also, the entrepreneur must perform activities associated with managing people including selecting and hiring, appraising and training, motivating, managing conflict, delegating tasks, and being an effective leader. Finally, the entrepreneur must manage the venture's growth, which includes such activities as developing and designing growth strategies, dealing with crises, exploring various avenues for financing growth, placing a value on the venture, and perhaps eventually exiting the business.

CAN LARGE ORGANIZATIONS HAVE ENTREPRENEURS?

The entrepreneurial spirit doesn't have to be limited solely to smaller, start-up businesses. Some large companies, like General Electric, are attempting to model the activities of the entrepreneur.[47] Why? In general, entrepreneurs are better able to respond to a changing environment than are managers in a traditional hierarchical organization. The owner-manager is involved in the day-to-day operations and is usually close to the customer. Furthermore, the owner-manager is the main decision maker, and all employees report to him or her. The result is a "flatter" organization—with few layers of hierarchy.

In large organizations, people who demonstrate entrepreneurial characteristics are often called **intrapreneurs**.[48] Should this imply then that entrepreneurs can exist in every large, established organization? The answer depends on one's definition of the term. The noted management guru Peter Drucker, for instance, argues that they can exist there.[49] He describes an entrepreneurial manager as someone who is confident in his or her abilities, who seizes opportunities for change, and who not only expects surprises but capitalizes on them. He contrasts this person with the traditional manager, who feels threatened by change, is bothered by uncertainty, prefers predictability, and is inclined to maintain the status quo. Drucker's use of the term *entrepreneurial*, however, is misleading. By almost any definition of good management, his entrepreneurial type would be preferred over the traditional type. Yet intrapreneurship can never capture the autonomy and riskiness

intrapreneurs
Persons within an organization who demonstrate entrepreneurial characteristics

inherent in true entrepreneurship, because intrapreneurship takes place within a larger organization. All financial risks are carried by the parent company. Rules, policies, and other constraints are imposed by the parent company; intrapreneurs report to bosses, and the payoff for success is typically career advancement rather than financial independence.

WHAT WILL THE WORKFORCE OF 2010 LOOK LIKE?

Until very recently, organizations took a "melting-pot" approach to differences in organizations. It was assumed that people who were different would somehow automatically want to assimilate. But today's managers have found that employees do not set aside their cultural values and lifestyle preferences when they come to work. The challenge for managers, therefore, is to make their organizations more accommodating to diverse groups of people by addressing different lifestyles, family needs,

Learning from Experience: One Manager's Reflection

D. J. Hanlon Operations Manager, Tiger Woods Foundation, Inc.

HOW DO WE MAKE MANAGERS MORE SENSITIVE TO DIFFERENCES?

Describe the situation you faced. The Tiger Woods Foundation, Inc. coordinates several events annually to raise money for charities designed to assist underprivileged youth. As operations manager, one of my responsibilities was to coordinate volunteers for the events. I quickly discovered that part of the challenge of coordinating volunteers is convincing them that they are a crucial link in the larger good. This problem was compounded by the fact that I was relatively young, and was trying to convince people who were older than me that a menial task such as standing in a parking lot holding a sign that reads "EVENT HERE" was a valuable service. The key issues here were first, convincing them that they were vital players for the greater good and, second, matching them with jobs that best suited their skills and personalities.

What action did you take? I took various approaches to handling these issues. But, most importantly, I learned to read the subtle signs of resistance; only then could I nip problems in the bud. For instance, if it became clear that someone was irreconcilably unhappy with a job, I would try to offer that person another position. In planning events there is always a lot to do, and offering someone a respectable way out helped to prevent many mild disgruntlements from growing into something more problematic. Reading people was a key in this: If someone felt they were more valuable moving heavy objects than handing out programs, I would go along with that. From a management standpoint, you have to be willing to respect genuine issues. And yet, sometimes there were no other positions to offer, so I learned a second art of management: subtle coaxing. Reminding them that they were part of a larger activity that had ultimately a greater good was a key here. If that didn't work I knew I had to develop other techniques.

What results occurred? During the years I worked at the Tiger Woods Foundation, Inc., I developed several different management techniques. For instance, for some volunteers I developed a technique that relied on direct, straightforward orders. For others, I would more gently rationalize the importance of their actions. And for still others, I learned to bring in other people from within the Foundation if I felt my personality didn't effectively "click" with one of the volunteers. Here again, reading personalities is a key to managing a diverse group.

The results were mostly positive. During my years with Tiger Woods Foundation, I developed techniques that helped me to manage a diverse group of workers and to prevent many management problems from getting bigger.

and work styles. The melting-pot assumption is being replaced by the recognition and celebration of differences. Interestingly, those who do celebrate the differences are finding that their organizations' profits are higher.[50]

WHAT DOES THE WORKFORCE LOOK LIKE TODAY?

Much of the change that has occurred in the workforce is attributed to the passage of U.S. federal legislation in the 1960s prohibiting employment discrimination. Based on such laws, avenues began to open up for minority and female applicants. These two groups have since become the fastest-growing segment in the workforce, and accommodating their needs has become a vital responsibility for managers. Furthermore, during this time, birthrates in the United States had begun to decline. The baby boom generation had already reached its apex in terms of employment opportunities, which meant that as hiring continued, there were fewer baby boomers left to choose. And as globalization became more pronounced, Hispanic, Asian, and other immigrants came to the United States and sought employment.

Projecting into the future is often an educated guess at best. Trying to predict the exact composition of our **workforce diversity** is no exception, even though we do know it will be heterogeneous: made up of males and females, whites and people of color, gays and straights, Hispanics, Asians, Native Americans, the disabled, and the elderly. Another group that has a significant impact on the workforce is the aging baby boom population. Commonly referred to as the "graying of the workforce," there is a steady increase in those individuals who desire to work past "retirement" age.[51] Brought about by necessity (a need to have a greater income to sustain current living standards), or desire (to remain active), more individuals over age 55 are expected to stay in the workforce, with more than 80 percent of the baby boom generation indicating that they expect to work past age 65. Couple this with the fact that the U.S. Congress passed the Senior Citizen's Freedom to Work Act, which eliminated the benefits penalty for those individuals on Social Security who earn more than $17,000 per year. In short, we can expect our workforce to continue to get older, with 70- and 80-year-old workers no longer uncommon.

workforce diversity
The varied background of organizational members in terms of gender, race, age, sexual orientation, and ethnicity

The increased participation of women and the elderly is not the only diversity issue reshaping the labor pool. Another is multiculturalism. Globalization has been reducing barriers to immigration. In the United States, the proportion of Hispanics, Asians, Pacific Islanders, and Africans origin has increased significantly over the past two decades, and the trend will continue. Moreover, multiculturalism is not just a U.S. phenomenon. Countries such as Great Brittain, Germany, and Canada are experiencing similar changes. Canada, as a case in point, has large populations of people who have recently emigrated from Hong Kong, Pakistan, Vietnam, and Middle Eastern countries. These immigrants are making Canada's population more diverse and its workforce more heterogeneous.

HOW DOES DIVERSITY AFFECT ORGANIZATIONS?

As organizations become more diverse, management has been adapting its human resource practices to reflect those changes.[52] Many organizations today, like Bank of America, have workforce diversity programs. They tend to hire, promote, and retain minorities, encourage vendor diversity, and provide diversity training for employees.[53] Some, like Coca-Cola, Motorola, and Mars, actually conduct cultural audits to ensure that diversity is pervasive in the organization (see Exhibit 2–6).[54]

The diversity that exists in the workforce requires managers to be more sensitive to the differences that each group brings to the work setting. For instance, managers may have to shift their philosophy from treating everyone alike to recognizing individual differences and responding to those differences in ways that will ensure employee retention and greater productivity. They must be in a position to recognize and deal with the different values, needs, interests, and expectations of employees.[55] They must avoid any practice or action that can be interpreted as being sexist, racist, or offensive to any particular group; and of course, at the same time they must not

EXHIBIT 2–6 Mars Incorporated Diversity Philosophy

"Distinctive voices working together within a common culture" is one of the ways we have described how we do business at Mars. We believe that the success of our business can be enhanced by having a workforce made up of associates from many different backgrounds, much as our society and consumer base consist of a wide variety of individuals. We value the talents and contributions of our diverse workforce in reaching toward our future and in playing responsible leadership roles.

Source: www.mars.com/other_policies/diversity.as

illegally discriminate against any employee. Lastly, managers must find ways to also assist employees in managing work/life issues.[56]

HOW CAN ORGANIZATIONS HELP EMPLOYEES BALANCE WORK/LIFE CONCEPTS?

The typical employee in the 1960s or 1970s showed up at the workplace Monday through Friday and did his or her job in eight- or nine-hour chunks of time. The workplace and hours were clearly specified. That's no longer true for a large segment of today's workforce. Employees are increasingly complaining that the line between work and nonwork time has become blurred, creating personal conflicts and stress.[57] A number of forces have contributed to blurring the lines between employee work and personal lives. First, the creation of global organizations means their world never sleeps. At any time and on any day, for instance, thousands of DaimlerChrysler employees are working somewhere. The need to consult with colleagues or customers 8 or 10 time zones away means that many employees of global firms are "on-call" 24 hours a day. Second, communication technology allows employees to do their work at home, in their cars, or on the beach in Tahiti. This allows many people in technical and professional jobs to do their work at any time and from any place. Third, organizations are asking employees to put in longer hours. It's not unusual for employees to work more than 45 hours a week, and some work much more than 50. Finally, fewer families have only a single breadwinner. Today's married employee is typically part of a dual-career couple.[58] This makes it increasingly difficult for married employees to find the time to fulfill commitments to home, spouse, children, parents, and friends.

Employees are increasingly recognizing that work is squeezing out their personal lives, and they're not happy about it. For example, recent studies suggest that employees want jobs that give them flexibility in their work schedules so they can better manage work/life conflicts.[59] In addition, the next generation of employees is likely to have similar concerns.[60] A majority of college and university students say that attaining a balance between personal life and work is a primary career goal. They want "a life" as well as a job! Organizations that don't help their people achieve work/life balance will find it increasingly hard to attract and retain the most capable and motivated employees.[61]

IS LABOR IN SHORT SUPPLY?

Is skilled labor in the United States abundant? Or is there a shortage? The simple answer to both of these questions is yes. Of course, simple answers don't adequately address the issue, or begin to describe how both situations (a shortage and a surplus) can exist simultaneously. In the sections that follow, we'll provide you with that explanation.

WHY DO ORGANIZATIONS LAY OFF WORKERS?

There was a time in corporate America when organizations followed a relatively simple rule: In good times you hire employees; in bad times, you fire them.[62] Since the late 1980s that "rule" no longer holds true, at least for most of the largest companies in the world. Throughout the past decade, most *Fortune* 500 companies made significant cuts in their overall staff. Thousands of employees have been cut by organizations such as IBM, AT&T, Boeing, and Sears. In fact, in February 2002 alone, more than 64,000 jobs were cut in the *Fortune* 500 companies, bringing the total in 2002 to more than 200,000.[63] This **downsizing** phenomenon is not going on just in the United States. Jobs are also being eliminated in almost all industrialized nations.[64]

downsizing
An activity in an organization designed to create a more efficient operation through extensive layoffs

Why this trend for downsizing? Organizations are attempting to increase their flexibility to better respond to change. Quality emphasis programs are creating flatter structures and redesigning work to increase efficiency. The result is a need for fewer employees. Are we implying that big companies are disappearing? Absolutely not! It is how they are operating that is changing. Big isn't necessarily inefficient. Companies such as PepsiCo and Home Depot manage to blend large size with agility by dividing their organizations into smaller, more flexible units.

Downsizing as a strategy is here to stay. It's part of a larger goal of balancing staff to meet changing needs. When organizations become overstaffed, they will likely cut jobs. At the same time, they are likely to increase staff if doing so adds value to the organization. A better term for this organizational action, then, might be **rightsizing**. Rightsizing involves linking staffing levels to organizational goals.[65] Rightsizing promotes greater use of outside firms for providing necessary products and services—called **outsourcing**—in an effort to remain flexible and responsive to the ever-changing work environment. Lucent Technologies, for example, has reached an agreement with Solectron to not only lease Solectron a plant, but to also provide Solectron with more than 400 Lucent employees to work at the plant.[66] In doing so, they are attempting to create flexible and rapid response systems.

rightsizing
Linking staffing levels to organizational goals

outsourcing
An organization's use of outside firms for providing necessary products and services

Why is there a need for flexible and rapid response systems? Thousands of organizations in the global village have decided they could save money and increase their flexibility by converting many jobs into temporary or part-time positions—giving rise to what is commonly referred to as the **contingent workforce** (see Exhibit 2–7). Today, temporary workers can be found in secretarial, nursing, accounting, assembly-line, legal, dentistry, computer programming, engineering, marketing, and even senior management positions.

contingent workforce
Part-time, temporary, and contract workers who are available for hire on an as-needed basis

Why the organizational emphasis on contingent employees? Many large companies are converting some permanent jobs into temporary ones (see Ethical Dilemma in Management). Organizations facing a rapidly changing environment must be in a

EXHIBIT 2–7 Contingent Workers

Part-time employees	Part-time employees work fewer than 40 hours a week. In general, part-timers are afforded few, if any, employee benefits. Part-time employees are generally a good source of employees for organizations to staff their peak hours. For example, the bank that expects its heaviest clientele between 10 A.M. and 2 P.M. may bring in part-time tellers for those four hours. Part-time employees may also be involved in job sharing, in which two employees split one full-time job.
Temporary employees	Temporary employees, like part-timers, are generally employed during peak production periods. Temporary workers also fill in for employees who are off work for an extended period of time. For example, a secretarial position may be filled by a "temp" while the secretary is off work during her 12-week unpaid leave of absence for the birth of her daughter. Temporary workers create a fixed cost to an employer for labor "used" during a specified period.
Contract workers	Contract workers, subcontractors, and consultants (may be referred to as freelance individuals) are hired by organizations to work on specific projects. These workers, typically very skilled, perform certain duties for an organization. Often their fee is set in the contract and is paid when the organization receives particular deliverables. Organizations use contract workers because their labor cost is fixed, and they do not incur any of the costs associated with a full-time employee population. In addition, some contract arrangements may exist because the contractor can provide virtually the same good or service in a more efficient manner than could a permanent employee.

Ethical Dilemma in Management

The Contingent Workforce

Hiring contingent workers can be a blessing for both organizations and individuals. Contingent workers provide employers with a rich set of diverse skills on an as-needed basis. In addition, hiring precisely when the specific work is to begin is very cost-effective. Moreover, individuals who desire to work less than full time are also given the opportunity to keep their skills sharp. At the same time, being contingent workers permits them to balance their commitment to personal matters and their careers. Many of the blessings for individuals, however, revolve around a central assumption: that an individual chooses to be a contingent worker. Unfortunately, that is not always the case. Jobs in the global village have shifted in terms of requisite skills and locations, and that trend is expected to continue. Consequently, the involuntary contingent workforce will be expected to grow in the years ahead.

Being part of the contingent workforce, even if not by choice, might not be so bad if employees received benefits typically offered to full-time core employees. Although hourly rates sometimes are higher for the contingent workers, these individuals have to pay themselves for the benefits that organizations typically provide to their full-time permanent employees. For instance, as a contract worker, you are required to pay all of your Social Security premiums. For core and some part-time employees, the employee and the employer share in this "tax." So some of that "extra" hourly rate of the contingent worker is taken away as an expense. Added to Social Security are such things as paying for one's health insurance. Buying health insurance through an organization that receives group rates is generally cheaper than having to buy the insurance yourself. This is yet another added expense to the contingent worker. So too is having to pay for one's office supplies and equipment. As for time off with pay benefits, forget about it. Vacation, holidays, sick leave? It's simple. Take all you want. But remember, when you don't work, you don't get paid!

Nearly two decades ago there were 619,000 temporary jobs in the United States. Today that number is over 2.5 million.[68] Similar trends have also been witnessed in Europe and Asia. How do employees feel about this growth in temporary work? While some employees appear to prefer the flexibility their contingent status affords them, it's probably accurate to say that the majority of the workforce prefers permanent, full-time employment. But in a world of rapid change, permanent employees sometimes limit management's flexibility. A large permanent workforce, for example, restricts management's options and raises costs for firms that suffer the ups and downs of market cycles. So we can expect employers to increasingly rely on temporaries to fill new and vacated positions.

Do you believe organizations that hire contingent workers who would rather have permanent employment are exploiting them? Should organizations be legally required to provide some basic level of benefits—such as health insurance, vacation, sick leave, and retirement—to contingent workers? What's your opinion?

position to adjust rapidly to those changes. Having a large number of permanent full-time employees limits management's ability to react. For example, an organization that faces significantly decreased revenues during an economic downturn may have to cut staff. Deciding who is to be laid off and what effect the layoffs will have on productivity and on the rest of the organization will be extremely complex in organizations that have a large permanent workforce. On the other hand, organizations that rely heavily on contingent workers will have greater flexibility because workers can be easily added or eliminated as needed. In addition, staffing shortages, opportunities to capitalize on new markets, obtaining someone who possesses a special skill for a particular project, and the like all point to a need for the organization to be able to rapidly adjust its staffing level.[67]

What issues do contingent workers create for managers? Temporaries and the flexibility they foster present special challenges for managers. Each contingent worker may need to be treated differently in terms of practices and policies. Managers must also make sure that contingent workers do not perceive themselves as second-class workers. Because they often do not receive many of the amenities—such as health and paid-leave benefits—that full-time **core employees** do, contingent workers may tend to view their work as not being critically important. Accordingly, they may not be as loyal, as committed to the organization, or as motivated on the job as permanent workers. That tendency may be especially relevant to those individuals

core employees
The small group of full-time employees of an organization who provide some essential job tasks for the organization

who have been forced to join the temporary workforce. Today's managers must recognize that it will be their responsibility to motivate their entire workforce, full-time and temporary employees, and to build their commitment to doing good work!

IS THERE A PENDING LABOR SHORTAGE IN THE UNITED STATES?

Cyclical labor trends are difficult to predict. The world economy in the late 1990s, for instance, was generally quite robust and labor markets were tight. For most employers it was difficult to find skilled workers to fill vacancies. Then, in 2001, most developed countries suffered an economic recession. Layoffs were widespread, and the supply of skilled workers became much more plentiful. In contrast, demographic trends are much more predictable. And we're facing one that has direct implications for management: Barring some unforeseeable economic or political calamity, there will be a labor shortage for at least another 10 to 15 years. We'll discuss the problem using U.S. statistics, but this shortage of skilled labor is also likely to be just as prevalent in most of Europe due to a graying population and a declining birthrate.

The U.S. labor shortage is a function of two factors—birthrates and labor participation rates. From the late 1960s through the late 1980s, American employers benefitted from the large number of baby boomers (those born between 1946 and 1965) entering the workforce. Specifically, there are 76 million baby boomers in the workforce. But there are 30 million fewer Gen-Xers (those born after 1965) to replace them when they retire.[69] Some boomers have already retired early. The problem will become severe in around 2010, when the major exodus of boomers from the workplace is in full force—anticipating that nearly 6 million jobs will be unfilled.[70] And this shortage will not be relegated to one or two industries. It will encompass most industries, like health care, government, construction, engineering, finance, energy, and information technology. Importantly, in spite of continued increases in immigration, new entrants to the workforce from foreign countries will not do much to correct the supply shortage. Moreover, repercussions from the events of September 11, 2001, in the United States could have the potential of reducing this immigration, further reducing the supply of skilled labor.

"By 2010, nearly 6 million jobs will be unfilled in the United States."

The labor shortage problem is compounded by the fact that the latter part of the twentieth century benefitted from a huge increase in the number of women entering the workforce. That provided a new supply of talented and skilled workers. This source has now been tapped. Moreover, there is declining interest by older workers to stay in the labor force. In 1950, nearly 80 percent of all 62-year-old men were still working. Today, only slightly more than half are. Improved pension plans, expanded Social Security benefits, and a healthy stock market has led many workers to retire early, especially those whose jobs were stressful or not challenging. So the combination of the smaller Gen-X population, the already high participation rate of women in the workforce, and early retirements will lead to a significantly smaller future labor pool from which employers can hire.

In times of labor shortage, good wages and benefits aren't going to be enough to get and keep skilled employees. Managers will need sophisticated recruitment and retention strategies, and will need to understand human behavior.[71] In tight labor markets, those managers who don't understand human behavior and fail to treat their employees properly risk having no one to manage!

HOW DO ORGANIZATIONS MAKE THE CUSTOMER KING?

Henry Ford said his customers could have any color car they wanted—as long as it was black. In contrast, Stew Leonard, Jr., CEO of the world's largest dairy store in southern Connecticut, says there are only two rules in his business. "Rule 1—the customer is always right. Rule 2—If the customer is ever wrong, reread Rule 1.

Stew Leonard's, the Norwalk, Connecticut–based "world's largest dairy store," has two simple rules for its 2,000-plus members. These rules form the basis of the company culture. And as a result, customers have responded well, spending more than $300 million annually in the three current Stew Leonard's stores.

Managers in today's organizations are being influenced by the Stew Leonards of the world. They realize that long-term success is primarily achieved by satisfying the customer, because it's the customer who ultimately pays the bills. And as we have mentioned several times so far in this chapter, customers have more choices than ever before and are therefore more difficult to please. That is, customers are demanding quicker service, higher quality, and more value for their money. Mass customization, toll-free service hotlines, the growth of e-commerce and mail order, discount superstores, and managers who have become obsessed with quality are all responses to the concept that quality is what the customer says it is. To make this theory a reality, organizations and their managers have embarked on several critical activities: creating a customer-responsive culture, continuous improvements in quality, and work process engineering.

CAN ORGANIZATIONS IMPROVE CUSTOMER SERVICE?

American Express recently turned Joan Weinbel's worst nightmare into a nonevent. At 10 P.M. Joan was home in New Jersey, packing for a week-long trip, when she suddenly realized she had left her AmEx Gold Card at a restaurant in New York City earlier in the evening. The restaurant was 30 miles away. She had a flight to catch at 7:30 A.M. the next day and she wanted her card for the trip. She called American Express. The phone was quickly answered by a courteous and helpful AmEx customer service representative. He told Ms. Weinbel not to worry. He quickly asked her a few questions and told her "help was on the way." To say she was flabbergasted would be an understatement when her doorbell rang at 11:45 P.M., less than two hours after she had called AmEx. At her door was a courier with a new card. How the company was able to produce the card and get it to her so quickly still puzzles Weinbel. But she said the experience made her a customer for life.

The majority of employees today in developed countries work in service jobs. For instance, 75 percent of all private sector jobs in the United States and Canada are in service industries. In Australia, it's 73 percent. In the United Kingdom, Germany, and Japan it's 69, 68, and 65 percent, respectively. Some examples of these service jobs include technical support representatives, fast-food counter workers, sales clerks, teachers, waiters or waitresses, consultants, credit representatives, financial planners, and flight attendants. The common characteristic of these jobs is that they require substantial interaction with an organization's customers. And since an organization can't exist without customers—whether that organization is DaimlerChrysler, Merrill Lynch, L.L. Bean, a law firm, a museum, a school, or a government agency—management needs to ensure that employees do what it takes to please its customers.

Organizations in service industries need to also include attention to customer needs and requirements in assessing their effectiveness. Why? Because in these types of businesses, there is a clear chain of cause-and-effect running from employee attitudes and behavior to customer attitudes and behavior to an organization's revenues and profits. Sears, in fact has carefully documented this chain. The company's management found that a 5 percent improvement in employee attitudes leads to a 1.3 point increase in customer satisfaction, which in turn translates into a 0.5 percent improvement in revenue growth. More specifically, Sears found that by training employees to improve the employee–customer interaction, it was able to improve customer satisfaction by 4 percent over a 12-month period, which generated an estimated $200 million in additional revenues.[72]

Except for a few researchers' interest in customer satisfaction through improvements in quality, the field of management has generally ignored the customer. Focusing on the customer was thought to be the concern of people who study and practice marketing. But the field of management can contribute to improving an organization's performance by showing managers how employee attitudes and behavior are associated with customer satisfaction. Many an organization has failed because its employees failed to please the customer. So management needs to create a customer-responsive culture—where employees are friendly and courteous, accessible, knowledgeable, prompt in responding to customer needs, and willing to do what's necessary to please the customer.

Can you create a customer-responsive culture? French retailers have a well-established reputation for indifference to customers.[73] Sales people, for instance, routinely make it clear that their phone conversations should not be interrupted. Just getting any help at all from a sales person can be a challenge. And no one in France finds it particularly surprising that the owner of a Paris store should complain that he was unable to work on his books all morning because he kept being bothered by customers!

Most organizations today are trying very hard to be un-French-like. They are attempting to create a customer-responsive culture because they recognize that this is the path to customer loyalty and long-term profitability. Companies that have created such cultures—like Southwest Air, FedEx, Johnson & Johnson, Nordstrom, and L.L. Bean—have built a strong and loyal customer base and have generally outperformed their competitors in revenue growth and financial performance. Let's look at the variables that shape customer-responsive cultures and offer some suggestions that management can follow for creating such cultures.

What are the key variables shaping customer-responsive cultures? A review of the evidence finds that several variables are routinely evident in customer-responsive cultures (see Exhibit 2–8).[74] First is the type of employees themselves. Successful, service-oriented organizations hire employees who are outgoing and friendly. Second, service employees need to have the freedom to meet changing customer-service requirements. Rigid rules, procedures, and regulations make this difficult. Third, employees need to be empowered.

Empowerment means employees have the decision discretion to do what's necessary to please the customer (we'll come back to empowerment at the end of this chapter). Fourth is good listening skills. Employees in customer-responsive cultures have the ability to listen to and understand messages sent by the customer. Finally, customer-responsive cultures have employees that exhibit organizational citizenship behavior. They are conscientious in their desire to please the customer. And they're willing to take the initiative, even when it's outside their normal job requirements, to satisfy a customer's needs.

empowerment
The redesigning of jobs in order to increase the decision-making discretion of workers

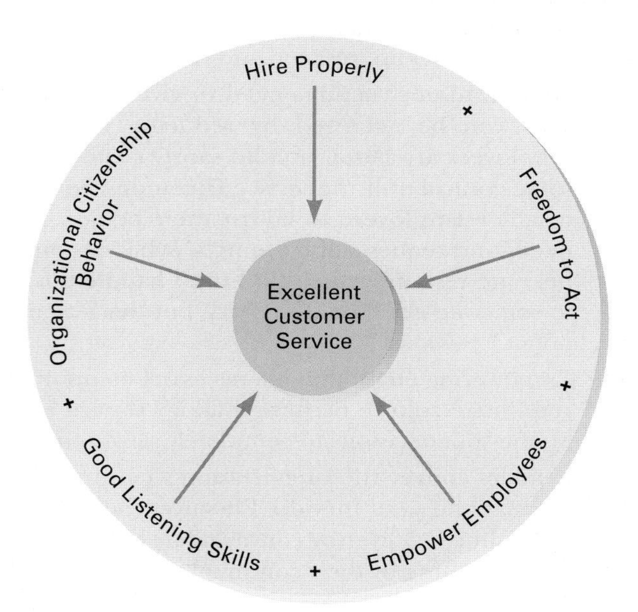

EXHIBIT 2–8
Shaping a Customer-Responsive Culture

In summary, customer-responsive cultures hire service-oriented employees with good listening skills and the willingness to go beyond the constraints of their job descriptions to do what's necessary to please the customer. It then clarifies their roles, frees them up to meet changing customer needs by minimizing rules and regulations, and provides them with a wide range of decision discretion to do their jobs as they see fit.

What managerial actions are needed? Based on the previously identified characteristics, we can suggest a number of actions that management can take if it wants to make its culture more customer-responsive. These actions are designed to create employees with the competence, ability, and willingness to solve customer problems as they arise.

- ***Selection:*** The place to start in building a customer-responsive culture is to hire service-contact people with the personality and attitudes consistent with a high service orientation. Southwest Air is a shining example of a company that has focused its hiring process on weeding out job candidates whose personalities aren't people friendly. Job applicants go through an extensive interview process at Southwest where company employees and executives carefully assess whether a candidate has the outgoing and fun-loving personality that it wants in all its employees.
- ***Training:*** Organizations that are trying to become more customer-responsive don't always have the option of hiring all new employees. More typically, management is faced with the challenge of making its current employees more customer-focused. In such cases, the emphasis will be on training rather than hiring. This describes the dilemma that senior executives at companies such as General Motors, Shell, and J.P. Morgan have faced in the past decade as they attempted to move away from their product focus. The content of these training programs will vary widely but should focus on improving product knowledge, active listening, showing patience, and displaying emotions. Additionally, even new employees who have a customer-friendly attitude may need to understand management's expectations. So all new service-contact people should be socialized into the organization's goals and values. Lastly, even the most customer-focused employees can lose direction every once in a while. This should be addressed with regular training updates where the organization's customer-focused values are restated and reinforced.
- ***Organizing:*** Organization structures need to give employees more control. This can be achieved by reducing rules and regulations. Employees are better able to satisfy customers when they have some control over the service encounter. So management needs to allow employees to adjust their behavior to the changing needs and requests of customers. What customers don't want to hear are responses such as "I can't handle this. You need to talk to someone else"; or "I'm sorry, but that's against our company policy."
- ***Empowerment:*** Empowering employees is a necessary component of a customer-responsive culture because it allows service employees to make on-the-spot decisions to completely satisfy customers.
- ***Leadership:*** Leaders convey the organization's culture through both what they say and what they do. Effective leaders in customer-responsive cultures deliver by conveying a customer-focused vision and demonstrating by their continual behavior that they are committed to customers.

- ***Evaluation:*** Employee performance needs to be evaluated based on such measures as how they behave or act—on criteria such as effort, commitment teamwork, friendliness, and the ability to solve customer problems—rather than on measurable outcomes they achieve.
- ***Rewards:*** Finally, if management wants employees to give good service, it has to reward good service. It needs to provide ongoing recognition to employees who have demonstrated extraordinary effort to please customers and who have been singled out by customers for "going the extra mile." And it needs to make pay and promotions contingent on outstanding customer service.

HOW HAVE ORGANIZATIONS SHOWN AN INCREASED CONCERN WITH QUALITY?

continuous improvement
Organizational commitment to constantly improving the quality of a product or service

kaizen
The Japanese term for an organization committed to continuous improvement

There is a quality revolution that continues to take place in both the private and public sectors. The generic term that has evolved to describe this revolution is *quality management* or **continuous improvement**. The revolution was inspired by a small group of quality experts, individuals like Joseph Juran and the late W. Edwards Deming.[75] For our discussion, we'll focus our attention primarily on Deming's work.

An American who found few managers in the United States interested in his ideas, Deming went to Japan in 1950 and began advising many top Japanese managers on ways to improve their production effectiveness. Central to his management methods was the use of statistics to analyze variability in production processes. A well-managed organization, according to Deming, was one in which statistical control reduced variability and resulted in uniform quality and predictable quantity of output. Deming developed a 14-point program for transforming organizations.[76] Today, Deming's original program has been expanded into a philosophy of management that is driven by customer needs and expectations[77] (see Exhibit 2–9). Quality management expands the term *customer* beyond the traditional definition to include everyone involved with the organization, either internally or externally, encompassing employees and suppliers as well as the people who buy the organization's products or services. The objective is to create an organization committed to continuous improvement or, as the Japanese call it, **kaizen**.[78]

Quality management is a departure from the earlier management theories that were based on the belief that low costs were the only road to increased productivity. For example, the U.S. car industry is often used as a classic example of what can go wrong when managers focus solely on trying to keep costs down. In the late 1970s, GM, Ford, and Chrysler built products that many consumers rejected. When the costs of rejects, repairing shoddy work, product recalls, and expensive controls to identify problems were considered, U.S. auto manufacturers were less productive than many foreign competitors. The Japanese, for example, demonstrated that it was possible for the highest-quality manufactures to be among the lowest-cost producers. Managers in American auto manufacturing facilities, as well as those in other industries, soon recognized the importance of quality management and implemented many of its basic components. For instance, based on a continuous improvement program—one which is heavily reliant on customer feedback—DaimlerChrysler is significantly altering the suspension of the company's Jeep Liberty sport utility vehicle after receiving considerable negative feedback from consumers.[79]

The late W. Edwards Deming, a statistician from Wyoming, has been credited with helping Japanese industries make a significant turnaround following World War II. His work on statistical methods to improve quality was but one aspect of his "movement." He also advocated extensive employee training, team work, and strong supplier relationships. His research, coupled with the efforts of others, has made quality practices the mainstay of corporate America today.

EXHIBIT 2-9 Components of Continuous Improvement

1. Intense focus on the *customer*. The customer includes not only outsiders who buy the organization's products or services but also internal customers (such as shipping or accounts payable personnel) who interact with and serve others in the organization.
2. Concern for *continuous improvement*. Continuous improvement is a commitment to never being satisfied. "Very good" is not good enough. Quality can always be improved.
3. Improvement in the *quality of everything* the organization does. Continuous improvement uses a very broad definition of quality. It is related not only to the final product but also to how the organization handles deliveries, how rapidly it responds to complaints, how politely the phones are answered, and the like.
4. Accurate *measurement*. Continuous improvement uses statistical techniques to measure every critical variable in the organization's operations. These are compared against standards, or benchmarks, to identify problems, trace them to their roots, and eliminate their causes.
5. *Empowerment of employees*. Continuous improvement involves the people on the line in the improvement process. Teams are widely used in continuous improvement programs as empowerment vehicles for finding and solving problems.

Today the term *quality management* may not be as popular as it was 15 years ago. As often happens with new business practices, they can become clichés. However, regardless of the terminology, the elements and the goals of quality management and continuous improvements are still essential characteristics in achieving an effective and lean workplace.[80]

WHEN MUST MANAGERS THINK IN TERMS OF QUANTUM CHANGES RATHER THAN CONTINUOUS IMPROVEMENT?

Although continuous improvement methods are useful innovations in many of our organizations, they generally focus on incremental change. Such action—a constant and permanent search to make things better—is intuitively appealing. Many organizations, however, operate in an environment of rapid and dynamic change. As the elements around them change so quickly, a continuous improvement process may keep them behind the times.

work process engineering
Radical or quantum change in an organization

The problem with a focus on continuous improvements is that it may provide a false sense of security. It may make managers feel as if they are actively doing something positive, which is somewhat true. Unfortunately, ongoing incremental change may allow managers to avoid facing up to the possibility that what the organization may really need is radical or quantum change, referred to as **work process engineering**.[81] Continuous change may also make managers feel as if they are taking progressive action while, at the same time, avoiding having to implement quantum changes that will threaten organizational members. The incremental approach of continuous improvement, then, may be today's version of rearranging the deck chairs on the Titanic.

If you have been reading this chapter carefully, you may be asking yourself, "Aren't these authors contradicting what they said a few paragraphs ago about quality management?" It may appear so, but consider this. Although continuous improvement can often lead to organizational improvements, it may not always be the right approach initially. That's the case if you are producing an improved version of an outdated product. Instead, a complete overhaul might be required. Once this has been done, then continuous improvement can have its rightful place. Let's see how this operates.

Assume that you are the manager responsible for implementing design changes in your electronic organizer. If you take the continuous improvement approach, your frame of reference might be an electronic search capability for names and addresses, calendar of tasks, an expanded keyboard function, and the like. Your continuous improvement program may lead you to focus on innovations such as more memory, larger storage capabilities, or longer-lasting batteries. Of course, your electronic organizer may be better than the one you previously made, but is that enough? Compare your product with that of a competitor who reengineers the design process. To begin, your competitor poses the following question: How can we design an electronic organizer that is more useful and expandable, and provides greater mobility? Starting from scratch and not being constrained by her current manufacturing process, your competitor completes her redesign with something she calls a wireless personal data assistant. Instead of larger and faster capabilities, you are now competing against a technology that may make your product obsolete.

In this theoretical example, both companies made progress. But which do you believe made the most progress given the dynamic environment they face? Our example demonstrates why companies such as Thermos, Ryder Trucks, and Casio Computer are opting for work process engineering rather than incremental change. It is imperative in today's business environment that all managers consider the challenge of work process engineering in their organizational processes. Why? Because work process engineering can lead to major gains in cost, service, or time, as well as assist an organization in preparing to meet the challenges technology changes foster.[82]

SOME CONCLUDING REMARKS

If you stop for a moment and digest what you have been reading in this chapter, you might wonder if organizations and managers as we described them in Chapter 1 still exist. They do, but with some significant modifications. Both organizations and managers need to be more flexible and able to respond to change.

Frederick Taylor, the "father of scientific management" (see History Module), argued nearly a century ago for the division of work and responsibility between management and workers. He wanted managers to do the planning and thinking. Workers were just to do what they were told. That prescription might have been good advice at the turn of the nineteenth century, but workers today are far better educated and trained than they were in Taylor's day. In fact, because of the complexity and changing nature of many jobs, today's workers may be considerably more knowledgeable than those who manage them about how best to do their jobs. This fact is not being ignored by management. Managers are transforming themselves from bosses into team leaders. Instead of telling employees what to do, an increasing number of managers are finding that they become more effective when they focus on motivating, coaching, and cheerleading. Managers also recognize that they can often improve quality, productivity, and employee commitment by redesigning jobs to increase the decision-making discretion of workers.

For much of the twentieth century, most organizations stifled the capabilities of their workforce. They overspecialized jobs and de-motivated employees by treating them like unthinking machines. Recent successes at empowering employees in companies such as Colgate-Palmolive and Fiat suggest that the future lies in expanding the worker's role in his or her job rather than in practicing Taylor's segmentation of responsibilities.

The empowerment movement is being driven by two forces. First is the need for quick decisions by those people who are most knowledgeable about the issues. That requires assigning the decision making to the individuals who are closest to the problems. If organizations are to successfully compete in a global village, they have to be able to make decisions and implement changes quickly. Second is the reality that the large layoffs in the middle-management ranks that began in the late 1980s have left many managers with considerably more people to supervise than they had in the past. And they may not have formal control over the work activities of some of these individuals.

What makes New York Jets coach Herman Edwards successful? Is it his ability to go onto the field and make the plays? Of course not. It's his ability to ready the players for the game and give them a well-developed game plan. Beyond that, his job on game day is to determine how well the game plan is working, make changes as necessary, and become one of the biggest cheerleaders for his team.

The same manager who today oversees a staff of 35 cannot micromanage in the ways that were possible when he or she supervised 10 people. Managers have to empower their people, because they can't know every job intimately, every data system, nor every policy. It has been a letting go process. That letting go and stretching process can be likened to the role of a sports team **coach**.

coach
A manager who motivates, empowers, and encourages his or her employees

Consider the job of head coach of a college football team. This individual establishes the game plan for an upcoming game and readies the players for the task. Even though the coach prepares the plans and the players, he or she cannot go out on Sunday afternoon and play the game. Instead, it is the players who execute the game plan. So what does the coach do during the game? It depends on how well the plan is working. When the competition is doing something that is counter to the game plan, the coach must quickly formulate new plans to give the players another competitive advantage. Thus, the coach deals with the exceptions. And, regardless of the game's outcome, as the players play the game, the coach becomes one of the major cheerleaders—recognizing outstanding performance toward fulfilling the plan and boosting player morale. This coaching role is increasingly becoming an accurate description of the jobs of today's managers!

Review, Comprehension, Application

CHAPTER SUMMARY

How will you know if you fulfilled the Learning Outcomes on page 42? You will have fulfilled the Learning Outcomes if you are able to:

1. **Describe the three waves in modern social history and their implications for organizations.** The first wave was agriculture (up to the 1890s). During the agricultural wave, individuals were their own bosses and were responsible for performing a variety of tasks. The second was industrialization (about 1900 to the 1960s). Work left the fields and moved into formal organizations with workers hired into tightly structured and formal workplaces dominated by mass production, specialized jobs, and authority relationships. The third wave is information technology (beginning in the 1970s). The information age has significantly reduced low-skilled, blue-collar jobs in manufacturing, but it has created abundant opportunities for educated and skilled technical specialists, professionals, and other knowledge workers.
2. **Explain the importance of viewing management from a global perspective.** Competitors are no longer defined within national borders. New competition can suddenly appear at any time, from anywhere in the world. Accordingly, managers must think globally if their organizations are to succeed over the long term. They must be prepared to deal with the changes globalization fosters, and be able to work with individuals from diverse cultures.
3. **Identify how technology is changing the manager's job.** Technology is changing the manager's job in several ways. Managers will have immediate access to information that will help them in making decisions. In addition, through the advent of technological advancements, managers may be supervising employees in remote locations, reducing the face-to-face interaction with these individuals. Consequently, effectively communicating with individuals in remote locations as well as ensuring that performance objectives are being met will become major challenges.
4. **Describe the difference between an e-business, e-commerce, and an e-organization.** The term *e-commerce* is becoming the standard label for the sales side of electronic business. It encompasses presenting products on Web sites and filling orders. E-business refers to the full breadth of activities included in a successful Internet-based enterprise. It includes developing strategies for running Internet-based companies; improving communication between employees, customers, and suppliers; and collaborating with partners to electronically coordinate design and production. And the term *e-organization* (e-orgs) refers to applications of e-business concepts to all organizations. E-orgs include not only business firms, but also hospitals, schools, museums, government agencies, and the military.
5. **Define social responsibility and ethics.** Social responsibility refers to an obligation, beyond that required by

law and economics, for a firm to pursue long-term goals that are good for society. Ethics refers to rules or principles that define right or wrong conduct.

6. **Explain what is meant by the term *entrepreneurship* and identify the components of the entrepreneurial venture.** Entrepreneurship is a process where an individual or a group of individuals risks time and money in pursuit of opportunities to create value and growth through innovation, regardless of the resources they control. The components of entrepreneurial ventures are organizations that are pursuing opportunities, that are characterized by innovative practices, and that have growth and profitability as their primary goals.
7. **Describe the management implications of a diversified workforce.** The workforce of 2010 will witness heterogeneity of gender, race, and ethnicity. It will also include the physically disabled, gays and lesbians, the elderly, and those who are significantly overweight. The most important requirement for managers is sensitivity to the differences among individuals. That means they must shift their philosophy from treating everyone alike to recognizing differences and responding to those differences in ways that will ensure employee retention and greater productivity.
8. **Identify the work/life concepts that are affecting employees.** Employees are increasingly focusing on the balance between work and personal time. Global organizations, customer responsiveness, technology, and longer work hours have all contributed to this debate. Employees are increasingly recognizing that work is squeezing out their personal lives. Employees want "a life" as well as a job! Organizations that don't help their people achieve work/life balance will find it increasingly hard to attract and retain the most capable and motivated employees.
9. **Explain why many corporations have downsized.** Many corporations have downsized in an attempt to increase their flexibility. Continuous improvements and work process engineering activities have created flatter structures and redesigned work to increase efficiency. As a result, organizations need fewer employees.
10. **Describe the key variables for creating a customer-responsive culture.** Several variables are routinely evident in customer-responsive cultures. These include hiring service-oriented, outgoing, and friendly employees; giving service employees the freedom to meet changing customer-service requirements; empowering employees, giving them decision discretion to do what's necessary to please the customer; ensuring that employees have good listening skills; ensuring that employees are conscientious in their desire to please the customer, and that they're willing to take the initiative, even when it's outside their normal job requirements, to satisfy a customer's needs.
11. **Explain why companies focus on quality and continuous improvement.** Organizations focus on quality and continuous improvement for several reasons. First, today's educated consumer demands it. Accordingly, a company that lacks quality products and services may be unsuccessful in achieving its goals. Second, quality and continuous improvements are strategic initiatives in an organization designed to make the operation more efficient and effective.

COMPANION WEBSITE

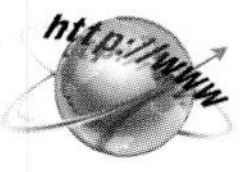

We invite you to visit the Robbins/DeCenzo companion Web site at **www.prenhall.com/robbins** for this chapter's Internet resources, including an online study guide, Internet exercises, and "In the News" with full text articles provided by XanEdu.

READING FOR COMPREHENSION

1. Describe the shifts in the types of jobs in the workforce during the past 100 years. What implications have these shifts created for today's managers?
2. Explain the managerial implications of a global village.
3. What are the managerial implications of Hofstede's research on cultural environments? The Globe Study? In what countries do you believe U.S. managers would have to make the most adjustments?
4. Describe the managerial implications of growing organizational diversity.
5. How can managers help employees deal with work/life issues?
6. Identify the characteristics and behaviors of an ethical manager.
7. Explain how organizations can create a more customer-responsive environment.
8. Explain the increased popularity of continuous improvements and work process engineering in the past 20 years.

LINKING CONCEPTS TO PRACTICE

1. Small business owners are entrepreneurs. Do you agree or disagree with this statement? Explain.
2. Continuous improvement programs include contributions from all historical management contributors. Do you agree or disagree with this statement? Discuss.
3. Customer-responsive cultures are only applicable in smaller organizations. Coordination of activities in large organizations makes it nearly impossible to implement a customer-responsive culture. Do you agree or disagree with this statement? Defend your position.
4. Coaching and empowering employees will replace the traditional management functions of planning, organizing, leading, and controlling. Do you agree or disagree with this statement? Explain.
5. Discuss the implications of hiring contingent workers from both the organizational and contingent worker perspective.

VIDEO CASE APPLICATION

Beyond Components: Altruism in the Electronics Industry

Can you imagine clicking on to your distributor's Web site to get a quote on electronic components and being greeted with free $20 gift cards to Home Depot or Victoria's Secret; or a meal at Chili's Grill & Bar? Well, if Massachusetts–based Beyond Components is your electronics distributor, *that* may be just what awaits you. And the extras don't stop there. Beyond Components has earned a reputation in the electronics industry for honesty, fairness, and attention to detail. President and CEO Lou Dinkel feels "it's doing all the little things better" that sets his company apart.

Michael McLean, senior buyer at Carlo Gavazzi Mupac, Inc., relies on Beyond Components for timely delivery of transformers, switches, and cooling fans that are essential to its assembly process. He knows that in a crunch a sales representative would be able to hop in a car and get parts to him within 15 minutes. Unlike other distributors, Beyond Components has eight strategically located, fully stocked warehouses. All that inventory translates into huge savings on both shipping costs and time for clients.

When Lou Dinkel started Beyond Components in 1987 he wasn't sure he would succeed, but he had the grit to stay true to his own beliefs and ambitions. He describes himself as having arrived in Boston from rural Minnesota as a "pie-eyed 23-year-old, fresh out of a small Catholic college and filled with big dreams." In the idealism of his youth he made many mistakes. He thought he could turn people into the right kind of employees by sheer determination. Experience taught him to hire people with "a great attitude, the willingness to make an effort, and talent, in that order." On principle, he never hires from the competition and never steals customer lists. Beyond Components is committed to promoting rank-and-file workers to management positions.

Often acting as a coach to his 75 employees, Dinkel tries to create an environment that empowers people to thrive. He acknowledges the ideas and contributions of his employees and values their time as he does his own. Ultimately, he feels it is he who must serve his workforce and not the other way around. "I've just begun to travel again, after being away from the road for five years," he says. "If my people are going to succeed, I have to go out on the road and present my vision to our customers." Even in a tough economy he has been able to avoid layoffs, turn a profit, and fulfill his pledge of gratitude to society for his good fortune. Ten percent of the organization's profits are donated to children with cancer, aids, older citizens, abused children, and unwed teen mothers.

The same core philosophy that Lou Dinkel held as a youth comprises Beyond Components' credo today. It includes being the most honest and ethical company in the industry, promoting men and women equally, encouraging employees to earn college degrees, and keeping employees until retirement.[83]

Branch manager Annette Lang says, "Things at Beyond Components roll down hill. At the top it's great. It works its way down to the employees and the customers reap the rewards." One might guess that the "it" she is referring to is a spirit of generosity and truthfulness that benefits both the company and the community at large.

Lou Dinkel has stayed true to his dream, and in so doing has surpassed it.

Questions

1. Describe the key elements at Beyond Components that make it a socially responsible organization.
2. Imagine that you are a young entrepreneur, starting out on your first business venture. What might you learn from Lou Dinkel's example?
3. What characterizes a customer-responsive culture? How did Lou Dinkel create this type of culture at Beyond Components? Be as specific as possible in your answer.
4. Would you say that Lou Dinkel thinks in terms of quantum changes or continuous improvement? Would you advise him to do anything differently in light of the predicted labor shortage? Why or why not?

Management Workshop

Team Skill-Building Exercise

Understanding Cultural Differences

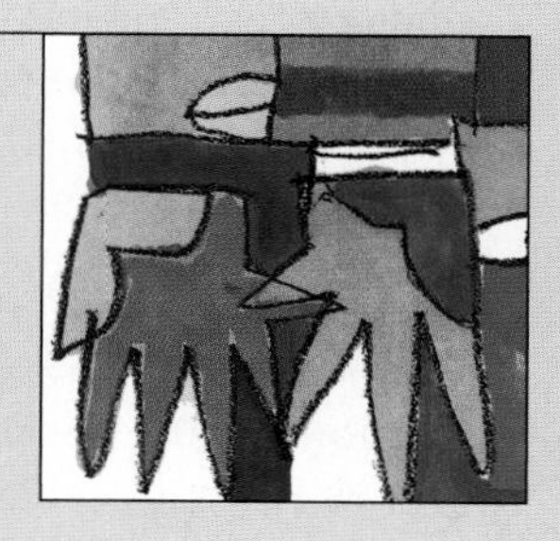

Workforce diversity has become a major issue for managers. Although there are often similarities among individuals, obvious differences do exist. A means of identifying some of those differences is to get to know individuals from the diverse groups. For this exercise, you will need to contact people from a different country. If you don't know any, the office of your college that is responsible for coordinating international students may be able to give you a list of names. Interview at least three people to get responses to such questions as:

- What country do you come from?
- What is your first language?
- Describe your country's culture in terms of, for example, form of government, emphasis on individual versus group, role of women in the workforce, benefits provided to employees, and how managers treat their employees.
- What were the greatest difficulties in adapting to your new culture?
- What advice would you give me if I had a management position in your country?

In groups of three to five class members, discuss your findings. Are there similarities in what each of you found? If so, what are they? Are there differences? Describe them. What implications for managing in the global village has this exercise generated for you and your group?

Understanding Yourself

Before you can develop other people, you must understand your present strengths. To assist in this learning process, we encourage you to complete the following self-assessments from the Prentice-Hall Self-Assessment Library 2.0:

- How Do My Ethics Rate? (#19)
- Am I Likely to Become an Entrepreneur? (#23)

After you complete these assessments, we suggest that you print out the results and store them as part of your "portfolio of learning."

Developing Your Ethics Skill

Guidelines for Acting Ethically

About the Skill

Making ethical choices can often be difficult for managers. Obeying the law is mandatory, but acting ethically goes beyond mere compliance with the law. It means acting responsibly in those gray areas, where right and wrong are not defined. What can you do to enhance your managerial abilities in acting ethically? We offer some guidelines.

Steps in Practicing the Skill

1. **Know your organization's policy on ethics.** Company policies on ethics, if they exist, describe what the organization perceives as ethical behavior and what it expects you to do. This policy will help you to clarify what is permissible and the managerial discretion you will have. This becomes your code of ethics!
2. **Understand the ethics policy.** Just having the policy in your hand does not guarantee that it will achieve what it is intended to do. You need to fully understand it. Behaving ethically is rarely a cut-and-dried process. But the policy can act as a guiding light, providing a basis from which you act within the organization. Even if a policy does not exist, there are still several steps you can take before you deal with the difficult situation.
3. **Think before you act.** Ask yourself, "Why am I going to do what I'm about to do? What led up to the problem? What is my true intention in taking this action? Is my reason valid? Or are there ulterior motives behind it—such

as demonstrating organizational loyalty? Will my action injure someone? Would I disclose to my boss or my family what I'm going to do?" Remember, it's your behavior and your actions. You need to make sure that you are not doing something that will jeopardize your role as a manager, your organization, or your reputation.

4. **Ask yourself what-if questions.** If you are thinking about why you are going to do something, you should also be asking yourself what-if questions. For example, the following questions may help you shape your actions: "What if I make the wrong decision? What will happen to me? To my job? What if my actions were described, in detail, on the local TV news show or in the newspaper? Would it bother or embarrass me or those around me? What if I get caught doing something unethical? Am I prepared to deal with the consequences?"
5. **Seek opinions from others.** If it is something major that you must do, and about which you are uncertain, ask for advice from other managers. Maybe they have been in a similar situation and can give you the benefit of their experience. Or maybe they can just listen and act as a sounding board for you.
6. **Do what you truly believe is right.** You have a conscience, and you are responsible for your behavior. Whatever you do, if you truly believe it was the right action to take, then what others say or what the Monday morning quarterbacks say is immaterial. You need to be true to your own internal ethical standards. Ask yourself: Can I live with what I've done?

Practicing the Skill

Find a copy of your school's code of conduct or the code of ethics of any organization to which you belong. Or, obtain a copy of the code of ethics for a professional organization you hope to join after graduating. Evaluate the code's provisions and policies. Are there any that you are uncomfortable with? Why? Are there any that are routinely violated? Why do you think this is happening? What are the usual consequences of such violations? Do you think they are appropriate?

If you had trouble obtaining the code of conduct, find out why. Under what circumstances is it normally distributed, posted, or otherwise made available to members?

Developing Your Diagnostic and Analytical Skills

Pets.com

Pets.com was one of the most visible of the thousands of e-commerce firms that sprouted up in the late 1990s. It had a clever slogan—"Because Pets Can't Drive"—and its ad agency created a charming sock puppet to act as the company's "spokesperson." Unfortunately, buying pet supplies over the Internet didn't prove to be a profitable business model. In retrospect, the business model's basic flaw was that the company's primary product—pet food—tends to be modestly priced and expensive to ship. It's also readily available in most supermarkets and retail stores like Wal-Mart and Target. As a result, Pets.com went out of business in the summer of 2000—selling most of its assets to Petco.[84]

In contrast, Dell Computer has become a large and profitable company by selling computers online. Dell's success is attributed to a carefully developed and executed business model that allows customers to custom design computers online, initiate the order, and have the products built and shipped within three business days. While competitors have attempted to copy many of Dell's Web site features and internal systems, Dell's continual efforts at improving customer service, minimizing costs, and passing its cost reductions on to customers through lower prices has kept its sales and profits growing.

Why the dramatic difference between these two organizations? Although a number of factors may enter into the equation, one critical component is that managing in an "electronic" environment is significantly different from managing in traditional organizations. Companies like Dell that understand this difference position themselves better to succeed. Those that don't, well, their businesses may go to the dogs!

Questions

1. Describe how technology has assisted a company like Dell Computers. What managerial changes do you believe are necessary to ensure that the full benefits of technology are reaped.
2. Do you believe a company like Pets.com was simply a "flash in the PAN," going out of business when the realities of dot-coms hit? Or do you believe that the demise of Pets.com might be attributable to poor management of the company? Defend your position.
3. Do you believe a company like Dell Computer is customer-responsive? Cite examples to support your position.

Enhancing Your Communication Skills

1. Select an industrialized country. Research information about a particular business practice in that country. For instance, you might compare U.S. employment discrimination laws with laws in your selected country and the differences that may exist. Or you may want to explore the ethics of gift-giving to political leaders.
2. Prepare a report on e-organizations. How successful have they been in the past three years? What are they doing differently than other businesses that are not "e" related?
3. Develop a report on the pros and cons of the work/life conflict. Prepare your report from either the organization's or the person's perspective. [Note: This would make for a good debate by having one individual take the organization's perspective and one person taking the individual's perspective.]

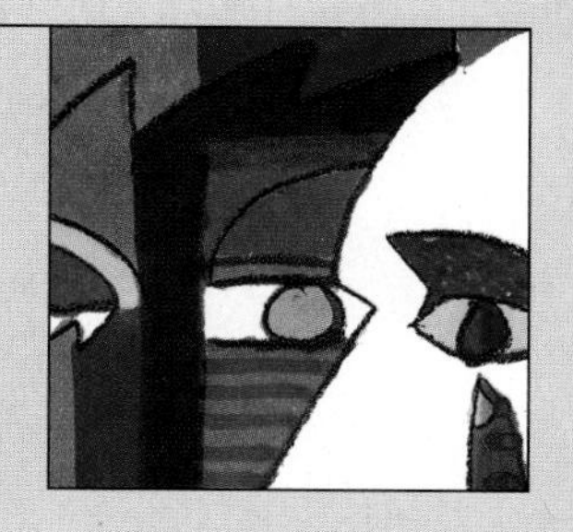

PART 2

Planning

CHAPTER 3

Foundations of Planning

LEARNING OUTCOMES

After reading this chapter, I will be able to:

1. Define planning.
2. Explain the potential benefits of planning.
3. Identify potential drawbacks to planning.
4. Distinguish between strategic and tactical plans.
5. Recognize when directional plans are preferred over specific plans.
6. Define management by objectives and identify its common elements.
7. Outline the steps in the strategic management process.
8. Describe the four grand strategies.
9. Explain SWOT analysis.
10. Describe how entrepreneurs identify a competitive advantage.

Who sells the most bikes in the Bradford, Connecticut, area? If you guessed Sears, or Wal-Mart, or any of the region's large retail outlets, you'd be wrong. The honor goes to Zane's Cycles, an independent bicycle shop run by its founder, Chris Zane (See photo.) Chris started the business nearly 20 years ago when he was a 16-year-old high school student. Is there a secret to his success? If there is, it's his ability to plan well and execute those plans.[1]

A small bike shop competing against large retailers seems an unlikely recipe for success. But Chris was resourceful. When two competitors went out of business, he negotiated a deal with the phone company. He agreed to pay the remainder of the two companies' Yellow Pages advertising. Callers to either of those numbers heard not only "The number you are calling is no longer in service," but also, "If you are in need of a bicycle dealer, Zane's Cycles will be happy to serve you." By pressing zero, the caller was automatically transferred to Chris!

As Chris's business grew, he needed to maintain his "small business" appeal, but he also needed to expand his offerings to more effectively compete against larger discount retailers and a growing bicycle mail-order business. After evaluating his company's strengths and weaknesses, Chris decided to become a distributor for premium bike manufacturer Trek. To become a distributor, Trek would require Zane's to agree to some demanding requirements. For instance, Chris would have to ship assembled bikes directly to customers. These shipments would have to be 100 percent perfect—no quality problems would be acceptable—and deliveries would have to be made in a competitive period of time. Furthermore, Zane's Cycles would be required to have ample inventory at all times.

These contractual requirements implied major changes in Chris's business. At the time, Zane's Cycles was a healthy and profitable company, selling about 3,500 bikes a year and achieving annual revenues approaching $1.75 million. Going with Trek meant significant outlays in capital expenditures—hiring more staff, implementing operating and controls systems, even investing in a new facility to handle the Trek inventory. Trek's contract also called for Zane's Cycles to sell a minimum of 125 bikes each year. Failure to do so would result in the distributorship being revoked.

Trek's requirements were demanding, but Chris felt he was up to the task. He had built a business on customer service, and he was confident that his service component would assist in this venture, too. For example, in the past, Zane provided free refreshments to customers visiting his store. He offered lifetime warranties on all bikes he sold. And for any small item, like a tire valve cap or a chain link, he simply gave the product away. In fact, he charged for nothing that normally sold for under $1.

Zane started his Trek contract with something unique in the business. He sent all ordering customers a questionnaire asking for their height, in-seam, and their bike-riding habits. He recognized that "one size fits all" didn't apply to the Trek bikes. When this information was returned, Zane Cycle employees used it for custom-building the bike and the bikes were then shipped nearly completely assembled. The few parts that needed to be assembled—like the handle bars and the pedals—were accompanied by detailed "how to install" instructions and a 24-hour 800 number to call with any questions. In its first year, Zane's Cycles achieved 184 percent of the Trek goal, and did not have one quality complaint. Shortly thereafter, Trek named Zane's Cycles as its exclusive distributorship.

Chris knew that an organization must always be looking for new ways of doing business. He also recognized that a company like his must differentiate itself to remain competitive in the premium bike market. For Chris, that differentiation comes in the form of service, speed, and quality. For example, his competitors take nearly eight weeks to ship premium bikes to customers. At Zane's, from order to customer delivery, it's two weeks.

To date, Chris Zane's plans and actions have allowed him to achieve his goal of growing the company. He now has more than 40 employees, with more than $5 million in annual revenues. His next step? Take the company to $12 million in annual revenues in the next five years.

THIS CHAPTER PRESENTS THE BASICS OF PLANNING. YOU WILL learn the difference between formal and informal planning, why managers plan, and the various types of plans managers use. We will explore the strategic planning process and look at the various strategies available to organizations and ways they can develop and maintain a competitive advantage. Finally, we will review how successful entrepreneurs like Chris Zane approach strategy.

PLANNING DEFINED

What is meant by the term *planning*? As we stated in Chapter 1, planning encompasses defining the organization's objectives or goals, establishing an overall strategy for achieving those goals, and developing a comprehensive hierarchy of plans to integrate and coordinate activities. It is concerned, then, with ends (what is to be done) as well as with means (how it is to be done).

Planning can be further defined in terms of whether it is *formal* or *informal*. All managers engage in planning, even if it is only the informal variety. In informal planning, very little, if anything, is written down. What is to be accomplished is in the heads of one or a few people. Furthermore, the organization's objectives are rarely verbalized. This generally describes planning in many smaller businesses: The owner-manager has a private vision of where he or she wants to go and how he or she expects to get there. The planning is general and lacks continuity. Of course, informal planning exists in some large organizations, while some small businesses have very sophisticated formal plans.

When we use the term *planning* in this book, however, we are implying formal planning. Specific objectives are written down and made available to organization members. This means that management clearly defines the path it wants to take to get from where it is to where it wants to be.

PLANNING IN UNCERTAIN ENVIRONMENTS

If managers performed their jobs in organizations that never faced changes in the environment, there would be little need for planning. What a manager did today, and well into the future, would be precisely the same as it was decades ago. There would be no need to think about what to do. It would be spelled out in some manual. In such a world, planning efforts would be unnecessary. But as we saw in Chapter 2, that world doesn't exist. Technological, social, political, economic, and legal changes are ever-present. The environment managers face is too dynamic and has too great an effect on an organization's survival to be left to chance. Accordingly, contemporary managers must plan—and plan effectively.

"The environment manager's face is too dynamic ... for planning to be left to chance."

WHY SHOULD MANAGERS FORMALLY PLAN?

Managers should engage in planning for at least four reasons. Planning provides direction, reduces the impact of change, minimizes waste and redundancy, and sets the standards to facilitate control (see Exhibit 3–1).

Planning establishes coordinated effort. It gives direction to managers and nonmanagers alike. When all organizational members understand where the organization is going and what they must contribute to reach the objectives, they can begin to coordinate their activities thereby fostering cooperation and teamwork. On the other hand, a lack of planning can cause various organizational members or their units to work against one another. Consequently, the organization may be prevented from moving efficiently toward its objectives.

By forcing managers to look ahead, anticipate change, consider the impact of change, and develop appropriate responses, planning reduces uncertainty. It also clarifies the consequences of the actions managers might take in response to change. Planning, then, is precisely what managers need in a chaotic environment.

Planning also reduces overlapping and wasteful activities. Coordination before the fact is likely to uncover waste and redundancy. Furthermore, when means and ends are clear, inefficiencies become obvious.

Finally, planning establishes objectives or standards that facilitate control. If organizational members are unsure of what they are attempting to achieve, how can

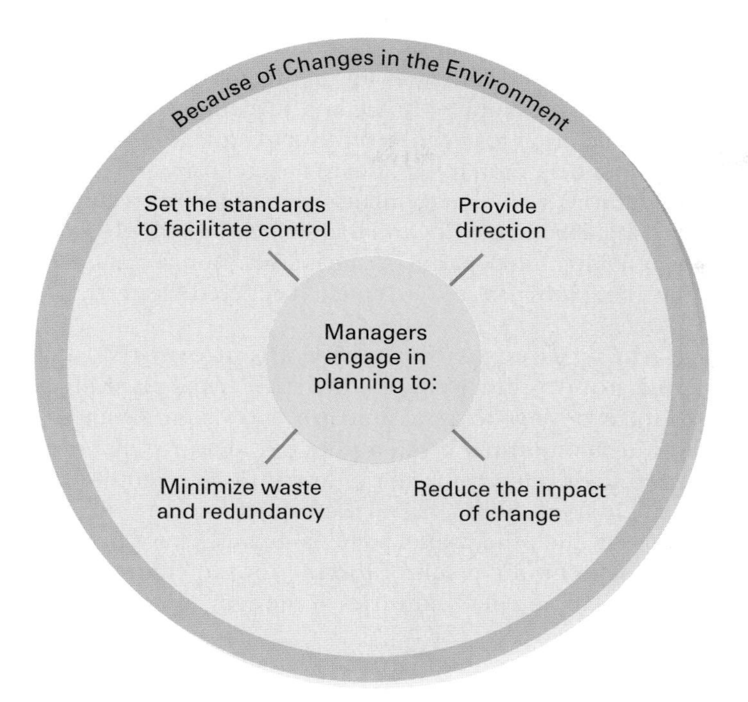

EXHIBIT 3–1
Reasons for Planning

they determine whether they have achieved it? In planning, objectives are developed. In the controlling function of management, performance is compared against the established objectives. If and when significant deviations are identified, corrective action can be taken. Without planning, then, there truly cannot be effective control.

WHAT ARE SOME CRITICISMS OF FORMAL PLANNING?

Formal planning by managers makes intuitive sense. An organization needs direction. After all, as the Cheshire Cat said to Alice, the way you ought to go "depends a good deal on where you want to get to." But critics have challenged some of the basic assumptions underlying planning. Let's look at the major arguments that have been offered against formal planning.[2]

Planning may create rigidity Formal planning efforts can lock an organization into specific goals to be achieved within specific timetables. When these objectives were set, the assumption may have been made that the environment wouldn't change during the time period the objectives cover. If that assumption is faulty, managers who follow a plan may have trouble. Rather than remaining flexible—and possibly scrapping the plan—managers who continue to do what is required to achieve the original objectives may not be able to cope with the changed environment. Forcing a course of action when the environment is fluid can be a recipe for disaster.

Plans can't be developed for a dynamic environment As we mentioned a few sentences ago, most organizations today face dynamic change in their environments. If a basic assumption in making plans—that the environment won't change—is faulty, then how can one make plans? We have described today's business environment as chaotic, by definition, that means random and unpredictable. Managing chaos and turning disasters into opportunities require flexibility, and that may mean not being tied to formal plans.

Formal plans can't replace intuition and creativity Successful organizations are typically the result of someone's vision, but these visions have a tendency to become formalized as they evolve. Formal planning efforts typically follow a methodology that includes a thorough investigation of the organization's capabilities and opportunities

Why plan? When Alice and the Cheshire Cat were at the fork in the road, and Alice asked the Cat for directions, the Cat responded, "where do you want to go?" When Alice said it didn't matter, the Cat appropriately responded, "Then either road will take you there." For organizations, the analogy is pertinent. Without knowing where one wants the organization to go, getting "there" may be impossible.

and a mechanistic analysis that reduces the vision to a programmed routine. That can spell disaster for an organization. For instance, the rapid rise of Apple Computer in the late 1970s and throughout the 1980s was attributed, in part, to the creativity and anticorporate attitudes of one of its cofounders, Steven Jobs. But as the company grew, Jobs felt a need for more formalized management—something he was uncomfortable performing. He hired a CEO, who ultimately ousted Jobs from his own company. With Jobs's departure came increased organizational formality—the very thing Jobs despised because it hampered creativity.

Planning focuses managers' attention on today's competition, not on tomorrow's survival Formal planning has a tendency to focus on how to best capitalize on existing business opportunities within the industry. It often does not allow for managers to consider creating or reinventing the industry. Consequently, formal plans may result in costly blunders and incur catch-up costs when others take the lead. On the other hand, some companies have found much of their success to be the result of forging into uncharted waters, designing and developing new industries as they go!

Formal planning reinforces success, which may lead to failure We've been taught that success breeds success. That has been an American tradition. After all, if it's not broken, don't fix it. Right? Well, maybe not! Success may, in fact, breed failure in an uncertain environment. It is hard to change or discard successful plans—to leave the comfort of what works for the anxiety of the unknown. Successful plans, however, may provide a false sense of security—generating more confidence than they deserve. Managers often won't deliberately face that unknown until they are forced to do so by changes in the environment. But by then, it may be too late.

THE BOTTOM LINE: DOES PLANNING IMPROVE ORGANIZATIONAL PERFORMANCE?

Do managers and organizations that plan outperform those that don't? Or have the critics of planning won the debate? Let's look at the evidence.

Contrary to the reasons cited by the critics of planning, the evidence generally supports the position that organizations should have formal plans. But that's not to be interpreted as a blanket endorsement of planning. It would be inaccurate to say that organizations that formally plan always outperform those that don't.

Many studies have explored the relationship between planning and performance.[3] On the basis of those studies, we can draw the following conclusions. First, formal planning in an organization generally means higher profits, higher return on assets, and other positive financial results. Second, the quality of the planning process and the appropriate implementation of the plans probably contribute more to high performance than does the extent of planning. Finally, in those organizations in which formal planning did not lead to higher performance, the environment was typically the culprit. For instance, government regulations and similar environmental constraints reduce the impact of planning on an organization's performance. Why? Because managers will have fewer viable alternatives.

TYPES OF PLANS

The most popular ways to describe plans are in terms of their *breadth* (strategic versus tactical), *time frame* (long-term versus short), *specificity* (directional versus specific), and *frequency of use* (single use versus standing). Keep in mind, however, these planning classifications are not independent of one another. For instance, there is a close relationship between the long-term time frame and the strategic focus. Exhibit 3–2 illustrates the relationship among types of plans.

Is formal planning always best? It depends. But when formal plans result in replacing the intuition and creativity that make an organization viable, they can hurt. That's precisely what Stephen Jobs, cofounder of Apple Computer found when he turned over the growing company to a "professional management team." The increased formality that "management" implemented led to a significant decrease in the same creativity that had served as the foundation of the early success of Apple Computer.

HOW DO STRATEGIC AND TACTICAL PLANNING DIFFER?

Plans that apply to the entire organization, that establish the organization's overall objectives, and that seek to position the organization in terms of its environment are **strategic plans**. Strategic plans drive the organization's efforts to achieve its goals. As these plans filter down in the organization, they serve as a basis for the tactical plans. **Tactical plans** (sometimes referred to as operational plans) specify the details of how the overall objectives are to be achieved. Strategic and tactical plans differ in three primary ways—their time frame, scope, and whether they include a known set of organizational objectives. Tactical plans tend to cover shorter periods of time. For instance, an organization's monthly, weekly, and day-to-day plans are almost all tactical. On the other hand, strategic plans tend to cover an extended time period—usually five years or more. They also cover a broader area and deal less with specifics. Finally, strategic plans include the formulation of objectives, whereas tactical plans assume the existence of objectives. Tactical plans describe how those objectives will be attained.

IN WHAT TIME FRAME DO PLANS EXIST?

Financial analysts traditionally describe investment returns as short and long term. The short term covers less than one year. Any time frame beyond five years is classified as long term. Managers have adopted the same terminology for plans. For clarity, we will emphasize **short-term plans** and **long-term plans** in this discussion.

The difference between short-and long-term plans is important given the length of future commitments and the degree of variability organizations face. For example, the more an organization's current plans affect future commitments, the longer the time frame that management should use. That is, plans should extend far enough to carry through those commitments that are made today. Planning over too long or too short a period is inefficient. With respect to the degree of variability, the greater the uncertainty, the more plans should be of the short-term variety. That is, if rapid or important technological, social, economic, legal, or other changes are taking place, well-defined and precisely chartered routes are more likely to hinder an organization's performance than to aid it. Shorter-term plans allow for more flexibility.

strategic plans
Plans that are organization-wide, establish overall objectives, and position an organization in terms of its environment

tactical plans
Plans that specify the details of how an organization's overall objectives are to be achieved

short-term plans
Plans that cover less than one year

Long-term plans
Plans that extend beyond five years

WHAT IS THE DIFFERENCE BETWEEN SPECIFIC AND DIRECTIONAL PLANS?

It appears intuitively correct that specific plans are always preferable to directional, or loosely guided, plans. **Specific plans** have clearly defined objectives. There is no ambiguity, and there are no problems with misunderstandings. For example, a

BREADTH OF USE	TIME FRAME	SPECIFICITY	FREQUENCY OF USE
Strategic	Long term	Directional	Single use
Tactical	Short term	Specific	Standing

EXHIBIT 3–2
Types of Plans

EXHIBIT 3–3 Directional versus Specific Plans

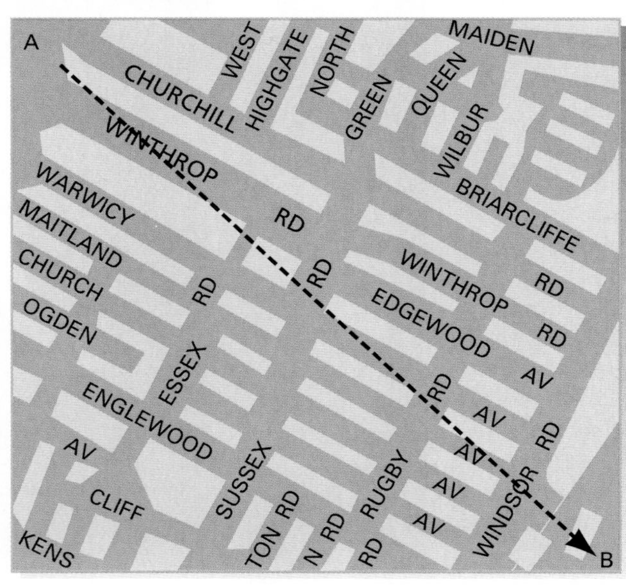

Directional plan

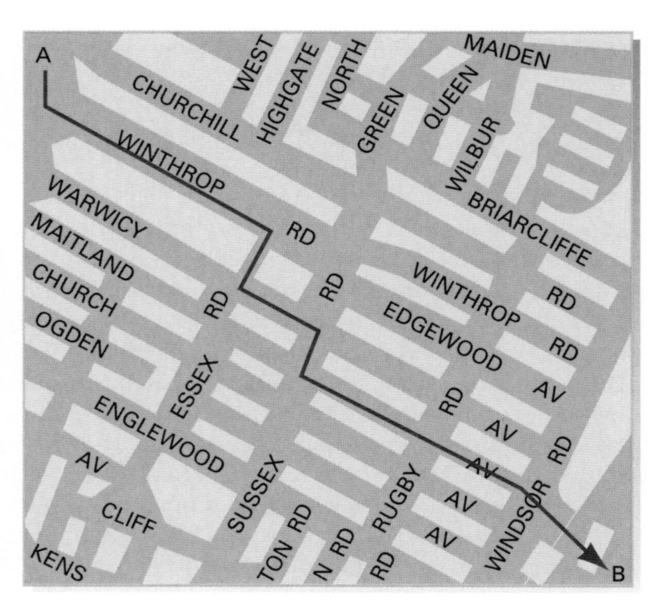

Specific plan

specific plans
Plans that have clearly defined objectives and leave no room for misinterpretation

directional plans
Flexible plans that set out general guidelines

manager who seeks to increase her firm's sales by 10 percent over a given 12-month period might establish specific procedures, budget allocations, and schedules of activities to reach that objective. These actions represent specific plans.

However, specific plans are not without drawbacks. They require a clarity and a predictability that often does not exist. When uncertainty is high and management must maintain flexibility in order to respond to unexpected changes, **directional plans** may be preferable. As shown in Exhibit 3–3, both directional and specific plans can lead you from point A to point B. If there were a detour on Sussex Road, however, the specific plans might create confusion. Directional plans, on the other hand, identify general guidelines. They provide focus but do not lock managers into specific objectives or specific courses of action. A specific plan might aim to cut costs by 10 percent and increase revenues by 8 percent in the next six months; a directional plan might aim at improving corporate profits between 6 and 12 percent during the next six months. The flexibility inherent in directional plans is obvious. This advantage must be weighed against the loss in clarity provided by specific plans.

single-use plans
A plan that is used to meet the needs of a particular or unque situation

standing plan
A plan that is ongoing and provides guidance for repeatedly performed actions in an organization

HOW DO SINGLE-USE AND STANDING PLANS DIFFER?

Some plans are meant to be used only once; others are used repeatedly. A **single-use plan** is used to meet the need of a particular or unique situation. For example, when Sears purchased apparel maker Lands' End, top managers used single-use plans to guide the acquisition, and "fold in" the activities that occurred in the Lands' End operations.[4]

Standing plans, in contrast, are ongoing. They provide guidance for repeatedly performed actions in the organization. For example, when you register for classes for the coming semester, you are using a standing registration plan at your college or university. The dates change, but the process works in the same way semester after semester.

management by objectives (MBO)
A system in which specific performance objectives are jointly determined by subordinates and their supervisors, progress toward objectives is periodically reviewed, and rewards are allocated on the basis of that progress

MANAGEMENT BY OBJECTIVES

Many organizations today are helping their employees set performance objectives in an effort to achieve organizational goals (see Details on a Management Classic). One means of doing this is through a process called **management by objectives (MBO)**, a system in which specific performance objectives are jointly determined by subordi-

Details on a Management Classic

Locke and Goal-Setting Theory

The case for the value of setting objectives in organizations was proposed 35 years ago by Edwin A. Locke.[5] Known as goal-setting theory, Locke claimed that setting specific employee goals increases performance. He suggested that difficult goals, when accepted by the employee, resulted in even higher performance than easy do goals. And, finally, Locke suggested that employee performance feedback led to higher performance than when feedback was lacking. Research in subsequent years has supported Locke's claims.

Goal-setting theory recognizes that specific hard goals produce a higher level of output than does a generalized goal of "do your best." The specificity of the goal itself seems to act as an internal stimulus and encourages employees to strive to meet the goal. If factors such as ability and acceptance of the goals were held constant, the evidence also demonstrates that the more difficult the goal, the higher the level of performance. Of course, it's logical to assume that easier goals are more likely to be accepted. But once an employee accepts a hard task, he or she will exert a higher level of effort until the goal is achieved, lowered, or abandoned. Finally, people will do better when they get feedback on how well they are progressing toward their goals because feedback helps to identify discrepancies between what they have done and what they want to do.

nates and their superiors; progress toward objectives is periodically reviewed, and rewards are allocated on the basis of that progress. Instead of using goals to control, MBO uses them to motivate.

WHAT IS MBO?

Management by objectives is not new. The concept goes back almost 50 years.[6] Its appeal lies in its emphasis on converting overall objectives into specific objectives for organizational units and individual members.

MBO makes objectives operational by a process in which they cascade down through the organization. As depicted in Exhibit 3–4, the organization's overall objectives are translated into specific objectives for each succeeding level—divisional, departmental, individual—in the organization.[7] Because lower-unit managers participate in setting their own goals, MBO works from the bottom up as well as from the top down. The result is a hierarchy that links objectives at one level to those at the next level. For the individual employee, MBO provides specific personal performance objectives. Each person, therefore, has an identified specific contribution to make to his or her unit's performance. If all the individuals achieve their goals, then the unit's goals will be attained. Subsequently, the organization's overall objectives will become a reality.

Whenever an organization faces a unique situation, it may need a single-use plan to deal with the issues. That's precisely what happened when Sears acquired apparel maker Lands' End. Bringing Lands' End operations under the Sears umbrella, and setting up mechanisms for Sears to control the newly acquired company were all made possible through the use of single-use plans.

WHAT ARE THE COMMON ELEMENTS IN AN MBO PROGRAM?

Four ingredients are common to MBO programs: goal specificity, participative decision making, an explicit time period, and performance feedback. Let's briefly look at each of these.

The objectives in MBO should be concise statements of expected accomplishments. It is not adequate, for example, merely to state a

EXHIBIT 3–4
Cascading Objectives

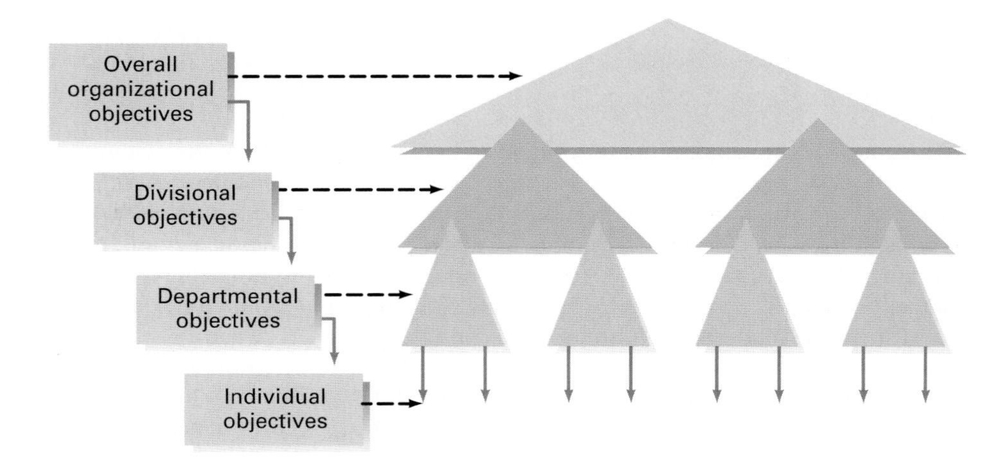

desire to cut costs, improve service, or increase quality. Such desires need to be converted into tangible objectives that can be measured and evaluated—for instance, to cut departmental costs by 8 percent, to improve service by ensuring that all insurance claims are processed within 72 hours of receipt, or to increase quality by keeping returns to less than .05 percent of sales.

In MBO, the objectives are not unilaterally set by the boss and assigned to employees, as is characteristic of traditional objective setting. Rather, MBO replaces these imposed goals with participatively determined goals. The manager and employee jointly choose the goals and agree on how they will be achieved. Each objective also has a concise time period in which it is to be completed. Typically, the time period is three months, six months, or a year.

The final ingredient in an MBO program is continuous feedback on performance and goals. Ideally, this is accomplished by giving ongoing feedback to individuals so they can monitor and correct their own actions. This is supplemented by periodic formal appraisal meetings in which superiors and subordinates can review progress toward goals and which lead to further feedback.

DOES MBO WORK?

Assessing the effectiveness of MBO is a complex task. Let's briefly review a growing body of literature on the relationship between goals and performance.[8] If factors such as a person's ability and acceptance of goals are held constant, more difficult goals lead to higher performance. Although individuals with very difficult goals achieve them far less often than those who have very easy goals, they, nevertheless, perform at a consistently higher level.

Moreover, studies consistently support the finding that specific, difficult-to-achieve goals produce a higher level of output than do no goals or generalized goals such as "do your best." Feedback also favorably affects performance. Feedback lets a person know whether his or her level of effort is sufficient or needs to be increased. It can induce a person to raise his or her goal level after attaining a previous goal and indicate ways to improve performance.

The results cited here are all consistent with MBO's emphasis on specific goals and feedback. MBO implies, rather than explicitly states, that goals must be perceived as feasible. Research on goal setting indicates that MBO is most effective if the goals are difficult enough to require some stretching.

But what about participation? MBO strongly advocates that goals be set participatively. Does the research demonstrate that participatively set goals lead to higher performance than those assigned by a manager? Somewhat surprisingly, the research comparing participatively set goals with assigned goals has not shown any strong or consistent relationship to performance.[9] When goal difficulty has been held constant, assigned goals frequently do as well as participatively determined goals, contrary to

MBO ideology. Therefore, it is not possible to argue for the superiority of participation as do MBO proponents. One major benefit from participation, however, is that it appears to induce individuals to set more difficult goals. Thus, participation may have a positive effect on performance by increasing one's goal aspiration level.

Studies of actual MBO programs confirm that MBO effectively increases employee performance and organizational productivity. One of the more critical components of this effectiveness is top management commitment to the MBO process. When top managers had a high commitment to MBO and were personally involved in its implementation, productivity gains were higher than if this commitment was lacking.[10]

HOW DO YOU SET EMPLOYEE OBJECTIVES?

Employees should have a clear understanding of what they're attempting to accomplish. Furthermore, as a manager, you have the responsibility for seeing that this task is achieved by helping your employees set work goals. Although these two statements appear to be common sense, that's not always the case. Setting objectives is a skill that every manager needs to perfect. You can better facilitate this process by following these guidelines:

- ***Identify an employee's key job tasks.*** Goal setting begins by defining what you want your employees to accomplish. The best source for this information is each employee's job description.
- ***Establish specific and challenging goals for each key task.*** Identify the level of performance expected of each employee. Specify the target for the employee to hit. Specify the deadlines for each goal. Putting deadlines on each goal reduces ambiguity. Deadlines, however, should not be set arbitrarily. Rather, they need to be realistic given the tasks to be completed.
- ***Allow the employee to actively participate.*** When employees participate in goal setting, they are more likely to accept the goals. However, it must be sincere participation. That is, employees must perceive that you are truly seeking their input, not just going through the motions.
- ***Prioritize goals.*** When you give someone more than one goal, it is important to rank the goals in order of importance. Prioritizing encourages the employee to take action and expend effort on each goal in proportion to its importance. Rate goals for difficulty and importance. Goal setting should not encourage people to choose easy goals. When goals are rated, individuals can be given credit for trying difficult goals, even if they don't fully achieve them.
- ***Build in feedback mechanisms to assess goal progress.*** Feedback lets employees know whether their level of effort is sufficient to attain the goal. Feedback should be both self and supervisor-generated. In either case, feedback should be frequent and recurrent.
- ***Link rewards to goal attainment.*** It's natural for employees to ask "What's in it for me?" Linking rewards to the achievement of goals will help answer that question.

IS THERE A DOWNSIDE TO SETTING OBJECTIVES?

Despite some strong evidence indicating that specific employee goals are linked to higher performance, not everyone supports the value of setting objectives. One of the most vocal critics of processes like MBO was the late W. Edwards Deming (of Quality Management fame, Chapter 2). Deming argued that specific goals may, in fact, do more harm than good. He felt that employees tend to focus on the goals by which they will be judged, so they may direct their efforts toward quantity of output (what's being measured) and away from quality. Specific goals also, say some critics, encourage individual achievement rather than a team focus.[11] In addition, Deming

What does this manager need to do to set employee goals? Research tells us that she must identify the employee's job tasks, establish specific and challenging goals for each key task, allow the employee to participate, help prioritize goals, build in feedback mechanisms to assess goal progress, and link employee rewards to goal attainment.

believed that, when objectives are set, employees tend to view them as ceilings rather than as floors. That is, after setting a goal and achieving it, employees will tend to relax. Consequently, specific goals may have a tendency to limit employees' potential and discourage efforts for continuous improvement.

These criticisms of specific goals are potentially correct. However, they can be overcome. One answer is for managers to ensure that employees have multiple goals and that they address quality of output as well as quantity. For instance, an insurance claims adjuster should be evaluated not only on the total number of claims processed but also on the number of errors made. Managers should treat MBO as an ongoing activity. This means that goals should be regularly reviewed and updated. Further, individuals should be rewarded for setting difficult goals even if they aren't fully achieved. Goals are more likely to limit individual effort when people believe they'll be punished for not reaching them, so employees should be encouraged to set ambitious goals that stretch their capabilities, and they should not be made to fear repercussions if they fail. Managers should regularly review goals with employees and make changes when warranted.[12]

THE IMPORTANCE OF ORGANIZATIONAL STRATEGY

Before the early 1970s, managers who made long-range plans generally assumed that better times lay ahead. Plans for the future were merely extensions of where the organization had been in the past. However, the energy crisis, deregulation, accelerating technological change, and increasing global competition as well as other environmental shocks of the 1970s and 1980s undermined this approach to long-range planning. These changes in the rules of the game forced managers to develop a systematic means of analyzing the environment, assessing their organizations' strengths and weaknesses, and identifying opportunities where the organization could have a competitive advantage. That's precisely what General Electric has been doing following the September 11, 2001 attacks in the United States. Having created the GE Global Insurance Holdings company years ago, the business unit was quite profitable. However, given significant claims from the September 11 attack and the necessity to charge customers skyrocketing insurance premiums, the business has tumbled, resulting, for example, in a $47 million loss in 2001. As a result, GE is looking to sell off this part of its holdings.[13]

The value of strategic planning appears evident. Those companies that plan strategically appear to have better financial measurements than those organizations that don't.[14] Today, strategic planning has moved beyond the private sector to include government agencies, hospitals, and educational institutions.[15] For example, the skyrocketing costs of a college education, competition from companies offering alternative educational forums, and cutbacks in federal aid for students and research have led many university administrators to assess their colleges' aspirations and identify a market niche in which they can survive, prosper, and implement an effective strategy.

A STRATEGIC FRAMEWORK: CHOOSING A NICHE

strategic management process
A nine-step process that involves strategic planning, implementation, and evaluation

When an organization attempts to develop its strategy, senior management goes through the **strategic management process** (see Exhibit 3–5), a nine-step process that involves strategic planning, implementation, and evaluation. Strategic planning encompasses the first seven steps, but even the best strategies can go awry if management fails to either implement them properly or evaluate their results. Let's look at the various steps in the strategic management process.

EXHIBIT 3–5 The Strategic Management Process

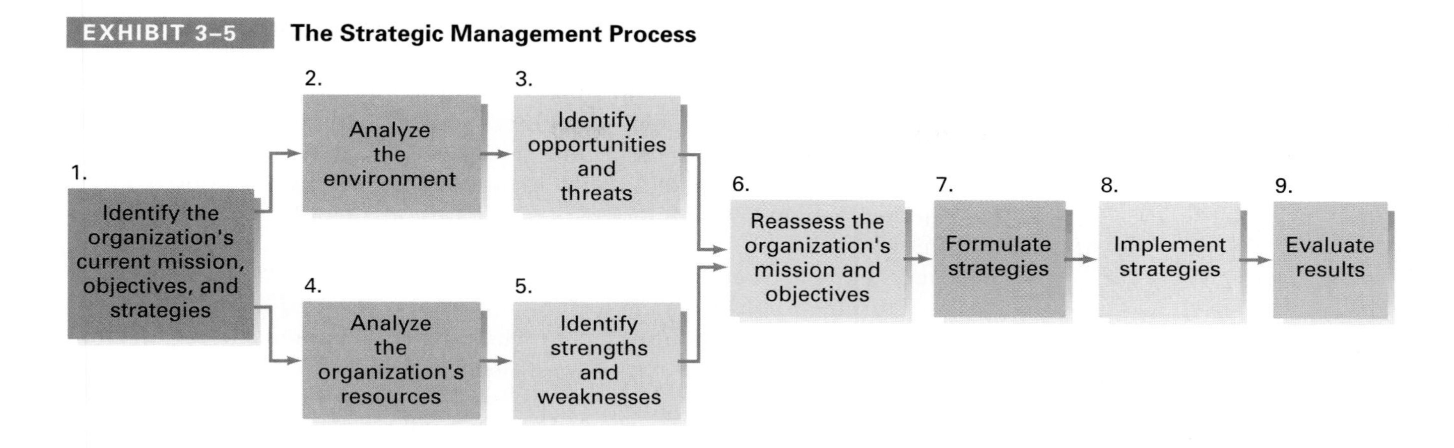

HOW DOES THE STRATEGIC MANAGEMENT PROCESS OPERATE?

In order to develop their strategy, organizational members must first identify the organization's current mission, objectives, and strategies (step 1). Every organization has a **mission statement** that defines its purpose and answers the question, "What business or businesses are we in?" Defining the organization's mission forces management to identify the scope of its products or services carefully.[16] For example, the business magazine *Fast Company* established its mission and set its sights "to chronicle the epic changes sweeping across business and to equip readers with the ideas, tools, and tactics that they need to thrive."[17]

mission statement
The purpose of an organization

Determining the nature of one's business is as important for not-for-profit organizations as it is for business firms. Hospitals, government agencies, and colleges must also identify their missions. For example, is a college training students for the professions, training students for particular jobs, or providing students with a well-rounded, liberal education? Is it seeking students from the top 5 percent of high school graduates, students with low academic grades but high aptitude test scores, or students in the vast middle ground? Answers to questions such as these clarify the organization's current purpose (see Team Skill-Building Exercise in the Management Workshop section of this chapter). Once its mission has been identified, the organization can begin to look outside the company to ensure that its strategy aligns well with the environment.[18] As a case in point, Panasonic is a major producer of home entertainment systems. But beginning in the mid-1980s, technological breakthroughs in miniaturization and the trend toward smaller homes dramatically increased the demand for powerful, but very compact, sound systems. The success of Panasonic's home audio strategy depends on understanding the technological and social changes that are taking place.

Management of every organization needs to analyze its environment (step 2). In the Netherlands, by law, proprietary information is public. But organizations in most other countries—such as the United States—must obtain that information on their own. That means that these organizations need to find out what their competition is up to, what pending legislation might affect them, what their customers desire, and what the supply of labor is like in locations where they operate. By analyzing the external environment, managers are in a better position to define the available strategies that best align with their environment. In doing so, a company like Tyco Electronics has maintained more than 18 percent of the $32 billion global connector market—and minimized its revenue losses in 2001 to 8 percent while its competition fell more than 26 percent.[19]

Step 2 of the strategy process is complete when management has an accurate grasp of what is taking place in its environment and is aware of important trends that might affect its operations. This is aided by environmental scanning activities and competitive intelligence.

environmental scanning
Screening large amounts of information to detect emerging trends and create a set of scenarios

What is environmental scanning? Managers of the Credit Union National Association (CUNA) know the importance of **environmental scanning**. Recognizing that organizational employees are turning to credit unions for more of their financial needs, CUNA directors have developed programs to meet the increased demands. Programs aimed at "determining membership trends, service opportunities, and strategic implications of technology, among others," are resulting in establishing one-step banking environments.[20] Without these, members may simply take their business elsewhere!

Managers like the directors at CUNA, in both small and large organizations, are increasingly turning to environmental scanning to anticipate and interpret changes in their environment.[21] The term refers to screening large amounts of information to detect emerging trends and create a set of scenarios.[22] There is some evidence to indicate that companies that scan the environment achieve higher profits and revenue growth than companies that don't.[23] The importance of environmental scanning was first recognized (outside of national security agencies such as the Central Intelligence Agency or National Security Agency) by firms in the life insurance industry in the late 1970s. Life insurance companies found that the demand for their products was declining even though all the key environmental signals strongly favored the sale of life insurance. The economy and population were growing. Baby boomers were finishing school, entering the labor force, and getting married. The market for life insurance should have been expanding, but it wasn't. The insurance companies had failed to recognize a fundamental change in family structure in the United States.

Young families, who represented the primary group of buyers of new insurance policies, tended to be dual-career couples who were increasingly choosing to remain childless for a longer time. The life insurance needs of a family with one income, a dependent spouse, and a houseful of kids are much greater than those of a two-income family with few, if any, children. That a multibillion-dollar industry could overlook such a fundamental social trend underscored the need to develop techniques for monitoring important environmental developments.

competitive intelligence
Accurate information about competitors that allows managers to anticipate competitors' actions rather than merely react to them

How is competitive intelligence useful? One of the fastest-growing areas of environmental scanning is **competitive intelligence**.[24] It seeks basic information about competitors: Who are they? What are they doing? How will what they are doing affect us? As managers at CUNA have recognized, accurate information about the competition can allow them to anticipate competitors' actions rather than merely react to them.

Many who study competitive intelligence suggest that nearly most of the competitor-related information an organization needs in order to make crucial strategic decisions is available and accessible to the public.[25] In other words, competitive intelligence isn't organizational espionage. Advertisements, promotional materials, press releases, reports filed with government agencies, annual reports, want ads, newspaper reports, information on the Internet, and industry studies are readily accessible sources of information. Specific information on an industry and associated organizations is increasingly available through electronic databases. Managers can literally tap into a wealth of competitive information by purchasing access to databases sold by companies such as Nexus and Knight-Ridder—or obtained free through information on corporate or the Securities and Exchange Commission Web sites. Trade shows and the debriefing of your own sales staff can be good sources of information on competitors. Many organizations even regularly buy competitors' products and ask their own employees to evaluate them to learn about new technical innovations.[26]

The techniques and sources listed above can reveal a number of issues and concerns that can affect an organization, but in a global business environment, environmental scanning and obtaining competitive intelligence are more complex. Because global scanning must gather information from around the world, many of the previously mentioned information sources may be too limited. One means of overcoming this difficulty is for management to subscribe to news services that review newspapers and magazines from around the globe and provide summaries to client companies. But even with the best information available, sometimes "intelligence" is overlooked. At AT&T, for instance, company officials' failure to truly understand the "ins and outs" of the cable industry led to the company abandoning its goal to deliver digital services over cable lines. AT&T officials were forced to sell off the AT&T Broadband division—giving up on their nearly five-year venture.[27]

What effect is information technology having on a company like FedEx? While technology is an important component of its business, this same technology is adversely affecting the company. Given its primary business of getting messages from one person to another, the technology is potentially problematic. At FedEx, this technology would be considered a "thread" in its SWOT analysis.

WHAT ARE THE PRIMARY STEPS IN THE STRATEGIC MANAGEMENT PROCESS?

After analyzing and learning about the environment, management needs to evaluate what it has learned in terms of **opportunities** (strategic) that the organization can exploit and **threats** that the organization faces (step 3). In a very simplistic way, opportunities are positive external environmental factors, and threats are negative ones.[28]

opportunities (strategic) Positive external environmental factors

threats Negative external environmental factors

Keep in mind, however, that the same environment can present opportunities to one organization and pose threats to another in the same or a similar industry because of their different resources or different focus. Take communications, for example. Telecommuting technologies have enabled organizations that sell computer modems, fax machines, and the like to prosper. But organizations such as the U.S. Postal Service, and even FedEx, have been adversely affected by this environmental change.

Next, in step 4, we move from looking outside the organization to looking inside.[29] That is, we evaluate the organization's internal resources. What skills and abilities do the organization's employees have? What is the organization's cash flow? Has it been successful at developing new and innovative products? How do customers perceive the image of the organization and the quality of its products or services?

This fourth step forces management to recognize that every organization, no matter how large and powerful, is constrained in some way by its resources and the skills it has available. An automobile manufacturer such as Ferrari cannot start making minivans simply because its management sees opportunities in that market. Ferrari does not have the resources to successfully compete against the likes of DaimlerChrysler, Ford, Toyota, and Nissan. The analysis in step 4 should lead to a clear assessment of the organization's internal resources, such as capital, worker skills, patents, and the like. It should also indicate organizational departmental abilities such as training and development, marketing, accounting, human resources, research and development, and management information systems. Internal resources or things that the organization does well are its **strengths** (strategic). And any of those strengths that represent unique skills or resources that can determine the organization's competitive edge are its **core competency**—like IBM's desire to continue to produce a personal computer and sell it at a near break-even price because it serves as a vital component of IBM's customers' information system.[30] At UAL, too, company leaders eliminated their Avolar corporate jet business so that they could return to their core business—commercial aviation.[31] That's because, in part, they lacked certain resources. When an organization lacks certain resources or identifies activities that the firm does not do well, we call them its **weaknesses**.

strengths (strategic) Internal resources that are available or things that an organization does well

core competency Any of the strengths that represent unique skills or resources that can determine the organization's competitive edge

weaknesses Resources that an organization lacks or activities that it does not do well

An understanding of the organization's culture and the strengths and weaknesses of its culture is a crucial part of step 5 that has only recently been getting the attention it deserves.[32] Specifically, managers should be aware that strong and weak cultures have different effects on strategy and that the content of a culture has a major effect on the content of the strategy.

In a strong culture, for instance, almost all employees will have a clear understanding of what the organization is about, and it should be easy for management to convey to new employees the organization's core competency. A department store chain such as Nordstrom, which has a very strong culture that embraces service and customer satisfaction, should be able to instill its cultural values in new employees in a much shorter time than can a competitor with a weak culture. The negative side of a strong culture, of course, is that it is difficult to change. A strong culture may act as a significant barrier to acceptance of a change in the organization's strategies. In fact, the strong culture at Wang Labs undoubtedly kept top management from perceiving the need to adopt a new corporate strategy in the 1980s in response to changes in the computer industry; this led, in part, to the demise of the organization. Successful organizations with strong cultures can become prisoners of their own past successes. We'll come back to organizational cultures in Chapter 5.

WHAT IS SWOT ANALYSIS?

SWOT analysis
Analysis of an organization's strengths, weaknesses, opportunities, and threats in order to identify a strategic niche that the organization can exploit

A merging of the externalities (steps 2 and 3) with the internalities (steps 4 and 5) results in an assessment of the organization's opportunities (see Exhibit 3–6). This merging is frequently called **SWOT analysis** because it brings together the organization's **S**trengths, **W**eaknesses, **O**pportunities, and **T**hreats in order to identify a strategic niche that the organization can exploit. Having completed the SWOT analysis, the organization reassesses its mission and objectives (Exhibit, step 6). In light of the SWOT analysis and identification of the organization's opportunities, management reevaluates its mission and objectives. Are they realistic? Do they need modification? If changes are needed in the organization's overall direction, this is where they are likely to originate. On the other hand, if no changes are necessary, management is ready to begin the actual formulation of strategies.

HOW DO YOU FORMULATE STRATEGIES?

grand strategies
The four primary types of strategies: growth, stability, retrenchment, and combination

Strategies need to be set for all levels in the organization (step 7). Management needs to develop and evaluate alternative strategies and then select a set that is compatible at each level and will allow the organization to best capitalize on its resources and the opportunities available in the environment. For most organizations, four primary strategies are available. Frequently called the **grand strategies**, they are growth, stability, retrenchment, and combination strategies.

EXHIBIT 3–6
SWOT: Identifying Organizational Opportunities

The growth strategy If management believes that bigger is better, then it may choose a growth strategy. A **growth strategy** is one in which an organization attempts to increase the level of the organization's operations. Growth can take the form of more sales revenues, more employees, or more market share. Many "growth" organizations achieve this objective through direct expansion, new-product development, quality improvement, or by diversifying—merging with or acquiring other firms.[33] That's been one of the primary avenues WorldCom has taken to assist in its growth plan.[34]

growth strategy
A strategy in which an organization attempts to increase the level of its operations; can take the form of increasing sales revenue, number of employees, or market share

Growth through direct expansion involves increasing company size, revenues, operations, or workforce. This effort is internally focused and does not involve other firms. For example, Subway is pursuing a growth strategy when it expands. As opposed to purchasing other fast-food stores, Subway expands by opening stores in new locations or by franchising to entrepreneurs who are willing to accept and do business the "Subway" way. Growth, too, can also come from creating businesses within the organization. When Wal-Mart entered the grocery store business with its super-centers, the company was exhibiting a growth strategy by expanding its operations to include food distribution,[35] and it caused competitors like Safeway and Kroger to make cuts to remain competitive.[36]

merger
Occurs when two companies, usually of similar size, combine their resources to form a new company

Companies may also grow by merging with other companies or acquiring similar firms. A **merger** occurs when two companies—usually of similar size—combine their resources to form a new company. For example, when the Lockheed and Martin Marietta Corporations merged to form Lockheed Martin, they did so to compete more effectively in the aerospace industry. Organizations can also acquire another firm, such as PepsiCo purchasing Quaker Oats, or Pfizer buying Pharmacia.[37] An **acquisition**, which is similar to a merger, usually happens when a larger company buys a smaller one—for a set amount of money or stocks, or both—and incorporates the acquired company's operations into its own. These acquisitions demonstrate a growth strategy whereby companies expand through diversification.

acquisition
Occurs when a larger company buys a smaller one and incorporates the acquired company's operations into its own

The stability strategy A stability strategy is best known for what it is not. That is, the **stability strategy** is characterized by an absence of significant changes. This means that an organization continues to serve its same market and customers while maintaining its market share. When is a stability strategy most appropriate? It is most appropriate when several conditions exist: a stable and unchanging environment, satisfactory organizational performance, a presence of valuable strengths and absence of critical weaknesses, and nonsignificant opportunities and threats.

stability strategy
A strategy that is characterized by an absence of significant change

Are there examples of organizations that are successfully employing a stability strategy? Yes. But most do not get the "press" that companies using other strategies get. One reason might be that no change means no news. Another might be that the company itself wants to keep a low profile; stakeholders may consider the status quo to be inappropriate, or the strategy may be an indication of rigidity of the planning process. Nonetheless, a company such as Kellogg does use the stability strategy very well. Kellogg's, intent on exploiting its unique niche, has not moved far from its breakfast food market emphasis. The company also has not demonstrated a desire to diversify into other food markets as have some of its competitors.

One means of implementing a growth strategy is to focus on new locations to establish operations. At Subway, franchised locations around the country helped the company to grow and expand.

The retrenchment strategy Before the 1980s, very few North American companies ever had to consider anything but how to grow or maintain what they currently had.[38] But, because of technological advancements, global competition, and other environmental changes, mergers and acquisitions growth and stability strategies may no longer be viable for some companies. Instead, organizations such as Sears, AT&T, General Motors, the U.S. Army, and Apple Computer have had to pursue a **retrenchment strategy**. This strategy is characteristic of an organization that is reducing its size or selling off less profitable product lines.[39]

retrenchment strategy
A strategy characteristic of a company that is reducing its size, usually in an environment of decline

The combination strategy A **combination strategy** is the simultaneous pursuit of two or more of the strategies described above. That is, one part of the organization may be pursuing a growth strategy while another is retrenching. That is precisely what happened when Procter & Gamble sold off its Jif and Crisco brands in 2002. By selling these brands to J.M. Smucker (of jam and jelly fame), Procter and Gamble was better able to concentrate on its growth strategy of consumer brands market.[40]

combination strategy
The simultaneous pursuit by an organization of two or more of growth, stability, and retrenchment strategies

Determining a competitive strategy The selection of a grand strategy sets the stage for the entire organization. Subsequently, each unit within the organization has to translate this strategy into a set of strategies that will give the organization a competitive advantage. That is, to fulfill the grand strategy, managers will seek to position their units so that they can gain a relative advantage over the company's rivals. This positioning requires a careful evaluation of the competitive forces that dictate the rules of competition within the industry in which the organization operates.

One of the leading researchers into strategy formulation is Michael Porter of Harvard's Graduate School of Business.[41] His competitive strategies framework argues that managers can choose among three generic competitive strategies.[42] According to Porter, no firm can successfully perform at an above-average profitability level by trying to be all things to all people. Rather, Porter proposed that management must select a **competitive strategy** that will give it a distinct advantage by capitalizing on the strengths of the organization and the industry it is in. These three strategies are: cost leadership, differentiation, and focus.

competitive strategy
A strategy to position an organization in such a way that it will have a distinct advantage over its competition; three types are cost leadership, differentiation, and focus strategies

According to Porter, when an organization sets out to be the low-cost producer in its industry, it is following a **cost-leadership strategy**. Success with this strategy requires that the organization be the cost leader, not merely one of the contenders for that position. In addition, the product or service being offered must be perceived as comparable to that offered by rivals or at least acceptable to buyers. How does a firm gain such a cost advantage? Typical means include efficiency of operations, economies of scale, technological innovation, low-cost labor, or preferential access to raw materials. Firms that have used this strategy include Wal-Mart, Canadian Tire, E & J Gallo Winery, and Southwest Airlines.

cost-leadership strategy
The strategy an organization follows when it wants to be the lowest-cost producer in its industry

The firm that seeks to be unique in its industry in ways that are widely valued by buyers is following a **differentiation strategy**. It might emphasize high quality, extraordinary service, innovative design, technological capability, or an unusually positive brand image. The attribute chosen must be different from those offered by rivals and significant enough to justify a price premium that exceeds the cost of differentiating. There is no shortage of firms that have found at least one attribute that allows them to differentiate themselves from competitors. Intel (technology), Maytag (reliability), Mary Kay Cosmetics (distribution), and L.L. Bean (service) are a few.

differentiation strategy
The strategy an organization follows when it wants to be unique in its industry within a broad market

The first two strategies sought a competitive advantage in a broad range of industry segments. The **focus strategy** aims at a cost advantage (cost focus) or differentiation advantage (differentiation focus) in a narrow segment. That is, management will select a segment or group of segments in an industry (such as product variety, type of end buyer, distribution channel, or geographical location of buyers) and tailor the strategy to serve them to the exclusion of others. The goal is to exploit a narrow segment of a market. Of course, whether a focus strategy is feasible depends on the size of a segment and whether it can support the additional cost of focusing. Stouffer's used a cost-focus strategy in its Lean Cuisine line to reach calorie-conscious consumers seeking both high-quality products and convenience.

focus strategy
The strategy an organization follows when it wants to establish an advantage in a narrow market segment

Which strategy management chooses depends on the organization's strengths and its competitors' weaknesses. Management should avoid a position in which it has to slug it out with everybody in the industry. Rather, the organization should put its strength where the competition isn't. Success, then, depends on selecting the right strategy, the one that fits the complete picture of the organization and the industry of which it is a part. In so doing, organizations can gain the most favorable competitive advantage.

What if an organization cannot use one of these three strategies to develop a competitive advantage? Porter uses the term *stuck in the middle* to describe that situation. Organizations that are stuck in the middle often find it difficult to achieve long-term success. When they do, it's usually the result of competing in a highly favorable market or having all their competitors similarly stuck in the middle. Porter notes, too, that successful organizations may get into trouble by reaching beyond their competitive advantage and end up stuck in the middle.

How would Porter's analysis evaluate Canadian Tire? According to his generic strategies, Canadian Tire would be viewed as emphasizing a cost-leadership strategy.By focusing on such elements as efficiency of operations and economies of scale, Canadian Tire has used this cost advantage to make the company a profitable organization.

Sustaining a competitive advantage Long-term success with any one of Porter's competitive strategies requires that the advantage be sustainable. That is, it must withstand both the actions of competitors and the evolutionary changes in the industry. That isn't easy, especially in environments as dynamic as the ones organizations face today. Technology changes. So too, do customers' product preferences. And competitors frequently try to imitate an organization's success. Managers need to create barriers that make imitation by competitors difficult or reduce the competitive opportunities. The use of patents, copyrights, or trademarks may assist in this effort. In addition, when there are strong efficiencies from economies of scale, reducing price to gain volume is a useful tactic. Organizations can also "tie up" suppliers with exclusive contracts that limit their ability to supply materials to rivals. Or organizations can encourage and lobby for government policies that impose import tariffs that are designed to limit foreign competition. The one thing management cannot do is become complacent. Resting on past successes may be the beginning of serious trouble for the organization. Sustaining a competitive advantage requires constant action by management in order to stay one step ahead of the competition.

WHAT HAPPENS AFTER STRATEGIES ARE FORMULATED?

The next-to-last step in the strategic management process is implementation (step 8). No matter how good a strategic plan is, it cannot succeed if it is not implemented properly. Top management leadership is a necessary ingredient in a successful strategy. So, too, is a motivated group of middle- and lower-level managers to carry out senior management's specific plans. Many of the issues related to implementing strategy will be discussed later in Chapters 8–12. Finally, results must be evaluated (step 9). How effective have the strategies been? What adjustments, if any, are necessary? In Chapter 13, we will review the control process. The concepts and techniques that we introduce in that chapter can be used to assess the results of strategies and to correct significant deviations.

QUALITY AS A STRATEGIC WEAPON

An increasing number of organizations are applying quality practices to build a competitive advantage.[43] To the degree that an organization can satisfy a customer's need for quality, it can differentiate itself from the competition and attract and hold a loyal customer base. Moreover, constant improvement in the quality and reliability of an organization's products or services can result in a competitive advantage others cannot steal. Product innovations, for example, offer little opportunity for sustained competitive advantage. Why? Because usually they can be quickly copied by rivals. But incremental improvement is something that becomes an integrated part of an organization's operations and can develop into a considerable cumulative advantage.

How can an organization benefit from benchmarking? A company like Ford Motors is betting a lot. By looking at the best in the field, and putting all the pieces together, Ford came to market with the 2003 Range Rover, which is touted as the benchmarked sport utility vehicle.

HOW CAN BENCHMARKING HELP PROMOTE QUALITY?

Benchmarking involves the search for the best practices among competitors or noncompetitors that lead to their superior performance.[44] The basic idea underlying benchmarking is that management can improve quality by analyzing and then copying the methods of the leaders in various fields. As such, benchmarking is a very specific form of environmental scanning.

In 1979, Xerox undertook what is widely regarded as the first benchmarking effort in the United States. Until then, the Japanese had been aggressively copying the successes of others by traveling around, watching what others were doing, and then using their new knowledge to improve their products and processes. Xerox's management couldn't figure out how Japanese manufacturers could sell midsize copiers in the United States for considerably less than Xerox's production costs. So the company's head of manufacturing took a team to Japan to make a detailed study of its competition's costs and processes. The team got most of their information from Xerox's own joint venture, Fuji-Xerox, which knew its competition well. What the team found was shocking. Their Japanese rivals were light-years ahead of Xerox in efficiency. Benchmarking these efficiencies was the beginning of Xerox's recovery in the copier field. Today, in addition to Xerox, companies such as Southwest Airlines, DuPont, Alcoa, Kraft, Ford, Eastman Kodak, and Motorola use benchmarking as a standard tool in their quest for quality improvement.

To illustrate benchmarking in practice, let's look at its application at Ford Motor Company. Ford used benchmarking in early 2000 in developing its highly promising Range Rover line. The company compiled a lengthy list of features that its customers said were the most important and then set about finding vehicles with the best of each. Then it tried to match or top the best of the competition in an effort to produce the world's best sport utility vehicle.[45]

benchmarking
The search for the best practices among competitors or noncompetitors that lead to their superior performance

WHAT IS THE ISO 9000 SERIES?

During the 1980s, there was an increasing push among global corporations to improve their quality. They knew that, to compete in the global village, they had to offer some assurances to purchasers of their products and services that what they were buying was of the quality they expected. In years past, purchasers had to accept individual "guarantees" that what was being sold met their needs and standards. Those individual guarantees changed in 1987, with the formation of the **ISO 9000 series**, designed by the International Organization for Standardization, based in Geneva, Switzerland.[46] The ISO standards reflect a process whereby independent auditors attest that a company's factory, laboratory, or office has met quality management requirements.[47] These standards, once met, assure customers that a company uses specific steps to test the products it sells; continuously trains its employees to ensure they have up-to-date skills, knowledge, and abilities; maintains satisfactory records of its operations; and corrects problems when they occur. Some of the multinational and transnational companies that have met these standards are Texas Petrochemical; British Airways; Shanghai Foxboro Company, Ltd.; Braas Company; Betz Laboratories; Hong Kong Mass Transit Railway Corporation; BP Chemicals International, Ltd.; Cincinnati Milacron's Electronic Systems Division; Borg Warner Automotive; Standard Aero Alliance; Taiwan Synthetic Rubber Corporation; and Weyerhaeuser.[48]

ISO 9000 series
Designed by the International Organization for Standardization, these standards reflect a process whereby independent auditors attest that a company's factory, laboratory, or office has met quality management standards

A company that obtains an ISO certification can boast that it has met stringent international quality standards and is one of a select group of companies worldwide to achieve that designation. Certification can be more than just a competitive advantage; it also permits entry into some markets not otherwise accessible. For example,

93 nations have adopted the ISO standards, with Japan, the United States, and Sweden having the most organizations meeting the ISO standards.[49] And more than 408,000 companies worldwide have ISO certification.[50] Uncertified organizations attempting to do business in those countries may be unable to successfully compete against certified companies. Many customers in the global village want to see the certification, and it becomes a dominant customer need. Also, in 1997, ISO 14000 went into effect. Companies achieving this certification will have demonstrated that they are environmentally responsible.[51]

Achieving ISO certification is far from cost free. Most organizations that want certification spend nearly one year and incur several hundreds of thousands of dollars in costs to achieve that goal. Many organizations are recognizing that obtaining such certification is quickly becoming a necessity to export goods to any organization in the nations that support the ISO 9000 series standards.[52] That's exactly what happened to Fris Office Outfitters in Holland, Michigan, when its biggest customer told the company it would have to be ISO 9000 certified, or it would no longer be a supplier.[53]

HOW CAN ATTAINING SIX SIGMA SIGNIFY QUALITY?

Wander around organizations like General Electric, ITT, Intel, Raytheon, or Bank of America, and you're likely to find green and black belts. Karate classes? Hardly. These green and black belts signify individuals trained in six sigma processes.[54]

Six sigma is a philosophy and measurement process developed in the 1980s at Motorola.[55] The premise behind six sigma is to design, measure, analyze, and control the input side of a production process to achieve the goal of no more than 3.4 defects per million parts or procedures.[56] That is, rather than measuring the quality of a product after it is produced, six sigma attempts to design quality in as the product is being made (see Exhibit 3–7). It is a process that uses statistical models, coupled with specific quality tools, high levels of rigor, and knowhow when improving processes.[57] How effective is six sigma at ensuring quality? Let's answer that by posing a question. In your opinion, is 99.9 percent effective enough? Consider this: At 99.9 percent effectiveness, 12 babies will be given to the wrong parents each day; 22,000 checks would be deducted from the incorrect checking accounts each hour, and 2 planes a day would fail to land safely at Chicago's O'Hare International Airport.[58] Just 10 years ago, three sigma was a fairly standard objective by most Americans which resulted in more than 66,000 defects per million.

six sigma
A philosophy and measurement process that attempts to design in quality as a product is being made. A document that explains the business founders vision and describes the strategy and operations of that business

EXHIBIT 3–7
Six Sigma 12-Process Steps

- Select the critical-to-quality characteristics.
- Define the required performance standards.
- Validate measurement system, methods, and procedures.
- Establish the current processes capability.
- Define upper and lower performance limits.
- Identify sources of variation.
- Screen potential causes of variation to identify the vital few variables needing control.
- Discover variation relationship for the vital variables.
- Establish operating tolerances on each of the vital variables.
- Validate the measurement system's ability to produce repeatable data.
- Determine the capability of the process to control the vital variables.
- Implement statistical process control on the vital variables.

Source: Cited in D. Harold and F. J. Bartos, "Optimize Existing Processes to Achieve Six Sigma Capability," reprinted from *Control Engineering Practice*, © 1998, p. 87, with permission from Elsevier Science.

Six sigma applications can also be useful on the service side of the business—especially in identifying cost savings. For example, at GE, the company is spending more than $125 million in an effort to find more than $2.5 billion in cost-cutting savings. These savings will come from reduced personnel, reduced inventories, and increased procurement and sales activities. GE is also assisting two of its customers—Wal-Mart and Dell Computer—by lending these organizations its six sigma expertise in an effort to eliminate more than $1 billion in inefficiencies in the two organizations.[59]

REVISITING ENTREPRENEURSHIP: HOW DOES THE ENTREPRENEUR IDENTIFY A COMPETITIVE ADVANTAGE?

As we discussed in the last chapter on entrepreneurship, the first thing that entrepreneurs must do is identify opportunities and possible competitive advantages. Once they've done this, they're ready to start the venture by researching its feasibility and then planning for its launch. These start-up and planning issues are what we're going to look at in the next section.

IDENTIFYING ENVIRONMENTAL OPPORTUNITIES AND COMPETITIVE ADVANTAGE

In 1994, when Jeff Bezos first saw that Internet usage was increasing by 2,300 percent a month, he knew that something dramatic was happening. "I hadn't seen growth that fast outside of a petri dish, [scientific]" he said. Bezos was determined to be a part of it. He quit his successful career as a stock market researcher and hedge fund manager on Wall Street and pursued his vision for online retailing, now the Amazon.com Web site. What would you have done if you had seen that type of number somewhere? Ignored it? Written it off as a fluke? The skyrocketing Internet usage that Bezos observed is a prime example of identifying environmental opportunities. Remember from our earlier discussion in this chapter that opportunities are positive trends in external environmental factors. These trends provide unique and distinct possibilities for innovating and creating value. Entrepreneurs need to be able to pinpoint these pockets of opportunities that a changing context provides.[60]

"Entrepreneurs need to be able to pinpoint trends that provide unique and distinct possibilities for innovating and creating value."

Peter Drucker, a well-known management author, identified seven potential sources of opportunity that entrepreneurs might look for in the external context. These include the unexpected, the incongruous, the process need, industry and market structures, demographics, changes in perception, and new knowledge.[61] Let's take a closer look at each.

- ***The unexpected.*** When situations and events are unanticipated, opportunities can be found. The event might be an unexpected success (positive news) or an unexpected failure (bad news). Either way, there can be opportunities for entrepreneurs to pursue. For instance, the well-publicized 2000 U.S. presidential vote count and recounts acquainted people with the term "chad" and all its variations (hanging, pregnant, dimpled, and so forth). Savvy entrepreneurs began fashioning jewelry, t-shirts, and other products using the chad image. And publicity surrounding the accidental skiing deaths of two well-known individuals (Sonny Bono and Michael Kennedy) proved to be a bonanza for ski helmet manufacturers as novice and seasoned skiers alike began to wear protective headgear. These events were unexpected and proved to be opportunities for entrepreneurs.
- ***The incongruous.*** When something is incongruous, there are inconsistencies and incompatibilities in the way it appears. Things "ought to be" a certain way, but aren't. When conventional wisdom about the way things should be no longer holds true, for whatever reason, there are opportunities to capture. Entrepreneurs who are willing to "think outside the box"—that is, to think beyond the traditional and conventional

approaches–may find pockets of potential profitability. Sigi Rabinowicz, CEO of Tefron, an Israeli firm, recognized incongruities in the way women's lingerie was made. His company has spent over a decade adapting a circular hosiery knitting machine to make women's underwear that is nearly seamless.[62] Another example of how the incongruous can be a potential source of entrepreneurial opportunity is Fred Smith, founder of FedEx, who recognized in the early 1970s the inefficiencies in the delivery of packages and documents. He challenged the accepted doctrine that overnight delivery was impossible. Smith's recognition of the incongruous led to the creation of FedEx, now a multibillion dollar corporation.

- ***The process need.*** What happens when technology doesn't immediately come up with the "big discovery" that's going to fundamentally change the very nature of some product or service? What happens is that there can be pockets of entrepreneurial opportunity in the various stages of the process as researchers and technicians continue to work for the monumental breakthrough. Because the full leap hasn't been possible, opportunities abound in the tiny steps. Take the medical products industry, for example. Although researchers haven't yet discovered a cure for cancer, there have been many successful entrepreneurial biotechnology ventures created as knowledge about a possible cure continues to grow, The "big breakthrough" hasn't happened, but there have been numerous entrepreneurial opportunities throughout the process of discovery.

Even the best plans for a competitive advantage can be lost if one overlooks a simple fact. In the global village, to truly understand the local area is crucial

- ***Industry and market structures.*** When changes in technology change the structure of an industry and market, existing firms can become obsolete if they're not attuned to the changes or are unwilling to change. Even changes in social values and consumer tastes can shift the structures of industries and markets. These markets and industries become open targets for nimble and smart entrepreneurs. Internet experience provides several good examples of existing industries and markets being changed by upstart entrepreneurial ventures. For instance, eBay has prospered as an online middleman to buyers and sellers. Computer giant Sun Microsystem sells up to 150 items per day on eBay, including its servers that sell for around $15,000. And Disney uses eBay to auction off authentic props from its movies.[63]
- ***Demographics.*** The characteristics of the world population are changing. These changes influence industries and markets by altering the types and quantity of products and services desired. For example, Thay Thida is one of the three individuals in Khmer Internet Development Services in Phnom Penh, Cambodia. She and her cofounders saw the opportunities in bringing the Internet to Cambodia and have profited from their entrepreneurial venture.[64]
- ***Changes in perception.*** Perception is one's reality. When changes in perception take place, facts do not vary, but their meaning does. For example, think about your perception of healthy foods. As our perception of whether or not certain groups are good for us has changed, there have been product and service opportunities for entrepreneurs to recognize and capture. For example, John Mackey started Whole Foods Market in Texas, as a place for customers to purchase food and other items free of pesticides, preservatives, sweeteners, and animal cruelty. Now, as the number-one natural foods supermarket, Mackey's entrepreneurial venture consists of about 130 stores in more than 23 states, Washington, DC, and Canada.[65]
- ***New knowledge.*** New knowledge is a significant source of entrepreneurial opportunity. For example, French scientists are using new knowledge about textiles to develop a wide array of innovative products that keeps wearers healthy and smelling good. Neyret, the Parisian lingerie maker, innovated lingerie products woven with tiny perfume microcapsules that stay in the fabric through about 10 laundry cycles. Another French company, Francital, developed a fabric that is treated with chemicals to absorb perspiration and odors.[66]

Review, Comprehension, Application

CHAPTER SUMMARY

How will you know if you fulfilled the Learning Outcomes on page 76? You will have fulfilled the Learning Outcomes if you are able to:

1. **Define planning.** Planning is the process of determining objectives and assessing the way those objectives can best be achieved.
2. **Explain the potential benefits of planning.** Planning gives direction, reduces the impact of change, minimizes waste and redundancy, and sets the standards to facilitate controlling.
3. **Identify potential drawbacks to planning.** Planning is not without its critics. Some of the more noted criticisms of planning are: It may create rigidity; plans cannot be developed for a dynamic environment; formal plans cannot replace intuition and creativity; planning focuses managers' attention on today's competition, not on tomorrow's survival; and because formal planning reinforces success, it may lead to failure.
4. **Distinguish between strategic and tactical plans.** Strategic plans cover an extensive time period (usually five or more years), encompass broad issues, and include the formulation of objectives. Tactical plans cover shorter periods of time, focus on specifics, and assume that objectives are already known.

5. **State when directional plans are preferred over specific plans.** Directional plans are preferred over specific plans when managers face uncertainty in their environments and desire to maintain flexibility in order to respond to any unexpected changes.
6. **Define management by objectives and identify its common elements.** Management by objectives (MBO) is a system in which specific performance objectives are jointly determined by employees and their bosses; progress toward objectives is periodically reviewed, and rewards are allocated on the basis of the progress. The four ingredients common to MBO programs are goal specificity, participative decision making, explicit time periods, and performance feedback.
7. **Outline the steps in the strategic management process.** The strategic management process is made up of nine steps: (1) identify the organization's current mission, objectives, and strategies; (2) analyze the environment; (3) identify opportunities and threats in the environment; (4) analyze the organization's resources; (5) identify the organization's strengths and weaknesses; (6) reassess the organization's mission and objectives on the basis of its strengths, weaknesses, opportunities, and threats; (7) formulate strategies; (8) implement strategies; and (9) evaluate results.
8. **Describe the four grand strategies.** The four grand strategies are (1) growth (increasing the level of the organization's operations), (2) stability (making no significant change in the organization), (3) retrenchment (reducing the size or variety of operations), and (4) combination (using two or more grand strategies simultaneously).
9. **Explain SWOT analysis.** SWOT analysis refers to analyzing the organization's internal strengths and weaknesses as well as external opportunities and threats in order to identify a niche that the organization can exploit.
10. **Describe how entrepreneurs identify a competitive advantage.** Opportunities are positive trends in external environmental factors. These trends provide unique and distinct possibilities for innovating and creating value. Entrepreneurs need to be able to pinpoint these pockets of opportunities that a changing context provides. Seven potential sources of opportunity that entrepreneurs might look for in the external context include: (1) the unexpected, (2) the incongruous, (3) the process need, (4) industry and market structures, (5) demographics, (6) changes in perception, and (7) new knowledge.

COMPANION WEBSITE

We invite you to visit the Robbins/DeCenzo companion Website at **www.prenhall.com/robbins** for this chapter's Internet resources, including an online study guide, Internet exercises, and "In the News" with full text articles provided by XanEdu.

READING FOR COMPREHENSION

1. Contrast formal with informal planning.
2. Under what circumstances are short-term plans preferred? Under what circumstances are specific plans preferred?
3. Compare an organization's mission with its objectives.
4. Describe the nine-step strategic management process.
5. What is a SWOT analysis?
6. How can quality provide a competitive advantage? Give an example.
7. What differentiates entrepreneurs from traditional managers in terms of developing strategy? Explain your answer.

LINKING CONCEPTS TO PRACTICE

1. Organizations that fail to plan are planning to fail. Do you agree or disagree with the statement? Explain your position.
2. Under what circumstances do you believe MBO/goal setting would be most useful? Discuss.
3. Using Michael Porter's generic strategies, describe the strategy used by each of the following companies to develop a competitive advantage in its industry: Wal-Mart, Home Depot, Nieman Marcus, Southwest Airlines. Provide specific examples.
4. "The primary means of sustaining a competitive advantage is to adjust faster to the environment than your competitors do." Do you agree or disagree with the statement? Explain your position.
5. "Benchmarking, six sigma, ISO 9000 series all have the effect of assisting a company develop a competitive advantage." Do you agree? Why or why not? Cite specific examples.

VIDEO CASE APPLICATION

Velocita Corporation: Pushing Forward at the Speed of Light

Striding across the snow-covered ground of northern Virginia, Buddy Pickle exudes energy. His excitement is palpable. The empty pipe he holds will soon be filled with high-speed fiber optical cable, linking 50 major metropolitan areas nation-wide. "As the world changes each little pipe is going to become even more valuable," he says. "We are looking at the telecommunications of the future."

Kirby G. "Buddy" Pickle is the CEO of Velocita Corporation, headquartered in Reston, Virginia. The company has just landed a plum contract with AT&T . Over the next year Velocita will lay 18,000 miles of the next-generation fiber optical cable right alongside AT&T's nearly century-old transcontinental lines. Founded in 1998 as a broadband network construction company, Velocita is now flush with monetary resources to build its own next-generation fiber optical network. This deal could turn the company into a billion-dollar business, and Velocita's management team of industry veterans is primed for action.

Up to 7,000 workers a day are busy laying Velocita's pipes in the ground. They're doing it faster and at one-fourth their competitors' costs. Not only are they utilizing AT&T's right of way, but as latecomers, they have access to cutting-edge technology that can squeeze more signals into the same fiber cables that their competitors installed several years ago. The more customers on one strand of cable, the better the company's bottom line.

"Right now," according to Robert Collett, president of Velocita," people are using an Internet whose pipes are too small and clogged with too much traffic; making Internet communication slow." Most of the warp speed service is still reserved for business-to-business connections and slows down when it reaches the bottleneck of local residences. Once Velocita connects fiber directly to individual buildings the potential for delivering voice, data, and motion pictures at rapid speed will become a reality. Not only will e-mail move faster, but you will be able to view theater-quality video in your living room. The U. S. Armed Forces are looking to the power of high-speed fiber optical cable to enable doctors to do remote control surgery by networking in the advice of medical experts around the world.

In an effort to make the joint network profitable right away, Robert Collet is working closely with AT&T to plan the installation of as much as 10,000 miles of cable this year. They are mapping out routes from California to Virginia and Illinois to Texas. Plans call for the first Velocita fiber network to be in service between Houston and Jacksonville. According to network president Don Bolar, "There will still be five conduits left that Velocita and AT&T can use to expand the network in the coming years."

No longer just a construction firm, Velocita is free to run its own network through the same buried cables AT&T is using. The company plans to offer a variety of broadband services to its customers, including private line and high-speed Internet access. According to Buddy Pickle, the demand for bandwidth is gathering momentum as people's habits change. "You're going to find that as businesses change, as streaming media and real-time video conferencing comes into play, broadband width is going to be required," he says.

Hardly strangers to reversals of fortune in the dynamic telecommunications industry, both AT&T and Velocita have been beaten before in the broadband arena. (Refer to the section on competitive intelligence in this chapter and to *www.hoovers.com/co/capsule* for more information.)

Now they are joining forces to turn adversity into advantage. As Buddy Pickle says, "competition is won by those who are quick, aggressive and willing to take risks."

It is clear that this time around Velocita is out to win.

Questions

1. At this stage of the planning process, do you think Velocita and AT&T would benefit more from the use of specific plans or directional plans? Why?
2. Write a mission statement for Velocita, taking into account what the company's goals are for the future.
3. Based on the video and on what you have learned about SWOT analysis, briefly state Velocita's Strengths, Weaknesses, Opportunities, and Threats. (If you have extensive personal knowledge of broadband width, you may want to contribute your own insight into the environment.)
4. Which of the four grand strategies would be most compatible with Velocita's priorities right now? Why?

Management Workshop

Team Skill-Building Exercise

Your College's Mission

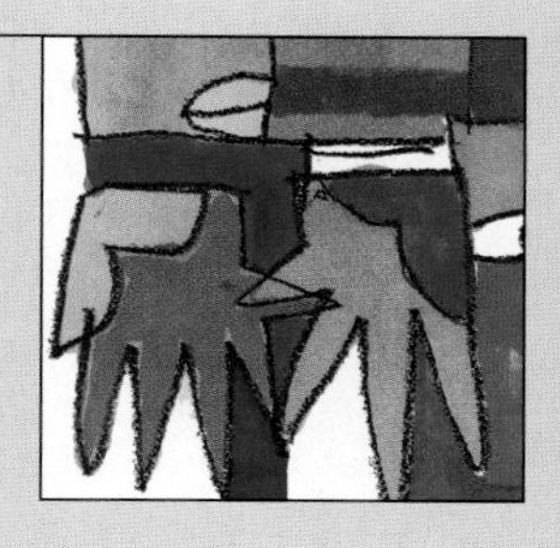

You might not pay much attention to the goals and objectives of your college because you are focusing on your studies. But your college had to carve out its niche in an effort to provide something of value to its students, and it must continue to monitor its performance.

For this exercise, break up into small groups. The charge of each small group is to prepare responses to the following questions and present its findings to the class.

1. What is your college's mission? What resources does your college have that support its mission?
2. How would you describe your college's environment in terms of technology and of government regulations?
3. What do you believe are the strengths and weaknesses of your college?
4. Which grand strategy is your college following? Which of Porter's generic strategies is evident at your college?
5. What do you believe to be your college's competitive advantage? What do you think your college should do to sustain its competitive advantage?

Understanding Yourself

Before you can develop other people, you must understand your present strengths. To assist in this learning process, we encourage you to complete the following self-assessments from the Prentice Hall Self-Assessment Library 2.0:

- What Time of the Day Am I Most Productive? (#21)
- How Good Am I at Personal Planning? (#22)

After you complete these assessments, we suggest that you print out the results and store them as part of your "portfolio of learning."

Developing Your Business Plan Skill

Writing a Business Plan

About the Skill

One of the first steps in starting a business is to prepare a business plan.[67] Not only does the business plan aid you in thinking about what you're going to do and how you're going to do it; it provides a sound basis from which you can obtain funding and resources for your organization. In fact, a well-prepared business plan can be submitted to a financial institution in its entirety as the basis for why you should get a loan to start your business.

Steps in Practicing the Skill

1. **Describe your company's background and purpose.** Provide the history of the company. Briefly describe the company's history and what this company does that's unique. Describe what your product or service will be, how you intend to market it, and what you need to bring your product or service to the market.
2. **Identify your short- and long-term objectives.** What is your intended goal for this organization? Clearly, for a new company three broad objectives are relevant—creation, survival, and profitability. Specific objectives can include such things as sales, market share, product quality, employee morale, or social responsibility. Identify how you plan to achieve each objective, how you intend to determine whether you met the objective, and when you intend the objective to be met (e.g., short or long term).
3. **Provide a thorough market analysis.** You need to convince readers that you understand what you are doing, what your market is, and what competitive pressures you'll face. In this analysis, you'll need to describe the

overall market trends, the specific market you intend to compete in, and who the competitors are. In essence, in this section you'll perform your SWOT analysis.

4. **Describe your development and production emphasis.** Explain how you are going to produce your product or service. Include time frames from start to finish. Describe the difficulties you may encounter in this stage as well as how much you believe activities in this stage will cost. Provide an explanation of what decisions (e.g., make or buy?) you will face and what you intend to do.
5. **Describe how you'll market your product or service.** What is your selling strategy? How do you intend to reach your customers? In this section, you'll want to describe your product or service in terms of your competitive advantage and demonstrate how you'll exploit your competitors' weaknesses. In addition to the market analysis, you'll also want to provide sales forecasts in terms of the size of the market, how much of the market you can realistically capture, and how you'll price your product or service.
6. **Establish your financial statements.** What is your bottom line? Investors want to know this. In the financial section, you'll need to provide projected profit-and-loss statements (income statements) for approximately three to five years. You will also need to include a cash-flow analysis as well as the company's projected balance sheets. In the financial section, you should also give thought to how much the start-up costs will be as well as to developing a financial strategy—how you intend to use funds received from a financial institution and how you'll control and monitor the financial well-being of the company.
7. **Provide an overview of the organization and its management.** Identify the key executives, summarizing their education, experience, and any relevant qualifications. Identify their positions in the organization and their job roles. Explain how much salary they intend to earn initially. Identify any others who may assist the organization's management (e.g., company lawyer, accountant, board of directors). This section should also include, if relevant, a section on how you intend to deal with employees. For example, how will employees be paid, what benefits will be offered, and how will employee performance be assessed?
8. **Describe the legal form of the business.** Identify the legal form of the business. For example, is it a sole proprietor, a partnership, a corporation? Depending on the legal form, you may need to provide information regarding equity positions, shares of stock issued, and the like.
9. **Identify the critical risks and contingencies facing the organization.** In this section you'll want to identify what you'll do if problems arise. For instance, if you don't meet sales forecasts, what will you do? Similar responses to such questions as problems with suppliers, inability to hire qualified employees, poor quality products, and so on should be addressed. Readers want to see if you've anticipated potential problems and if you have contingency plans. This is the what-if section.
10. **Put the business plan together.** Using the information you've gathered from the previous nine steps, it's now time to put the business plan together into a well-organized document. A business plan should contain a cover page that shows the company name, address, contact person, and numbers at which the individual can be reached. The cover page should also contain the date the business was established and, if one exists, the company logo. The next page of the business plan should be a table of contents. Here you'll want to list and identify the location of each major section and subsection in the business plan. Remember to use proper outlining techniques. Next comes the executive summary, the first section the readers will actually read. Accordingly, it is one of the more critical elements of the business plan because if the executive summary is poorly done, readers may not read any further. Highlight in a two- to three-page summary information about the company, its management, its market and competition, the funds requested, how the funds will be used, financial history (if available), financial projections, and when investors can expect to get their money back (called the exit). Now it's time to provide the main sections of your business plan, the material you've researched and written about in steps 1 through 9. Close out the business plan with a section that summarizes the highlights of what you've just presented. Finally, if you have charts, exhibits, photographs, tables, and the like, you may also include an appendix in the back of the business plan. If you do, remember to cross-reference this material to the relevant section of the report.

Practicing the Skill

You have come up with a great idea for a business and need to create a business plan to present to a bank. Choose one of the following products or services and draft the part of your plan that describes how you will price and market it (see step 5).

1. Haircuts at home (you make house calls)
2. Olympic snow boarding computer game
3. Online apartment rental listing
4. Ergonomic dental chair
5. Voice-activated house alarm
6. Customized running shoes

Now choose a different product or service from the list and identify critical risks and contingencies (see step 9).

Developing Your Diagnostic and Analytical Skills

On-Time Fuel

Kristen Schaffner-Irvin saw opportunities in the changing world.[68] A native of Huntington Beach, California, Schaffner-Irvin was a stay-at-home mom, but money was tight in the family, and she felt that she had to go to work. She wanted to find a job that would allow her to care for her children while simultaneously producing some extra income for the household. Having grown up in a family-owned fuel business, Kristen knew the ins and outs of the fuel delivery industry. She didn't want, however to work for her father. Instead, she wanted to "make it" on her own-fulfilling a life-long dream of being her own boss, in her own company. So with just a laptop and a telephone, she started Team Petroleum.

Having worked in the industry, Schaffner-Irvin recognized that a more efficient fuel delivery system was possible. Although the company didn't own any oil wells or even fuel trucks, Schaffner-Irvin felt that her company could be successful if she could demonstrate that Team Petroleum added value to its customers. Schaffner-Irvin envisioned this happening by buying fuel for her customers from suppliers and having it delivered to them. But delivery alone was not enough to "add value." What she did was offer her customers a special service that her competitors didn't. She linked their fuel tanks to her computer system which monitors the customer consumption and automatically notifies Team Petroleum's office when another delivery is needed. The result is a seamless "fuel procurement and management reporting" system that creates efficiencies in the fuel supply chain—saving clients like Disney, Con Edison, Frito-Lay, and Toys "R" Us upwards of 12 percent of their fuel budget.

For nearly 20 years, Team Petroleum has been a thriving business. The company has expanded, taken on several strategic alliances, and recently changed its name to TeamFuel. With revenues exceeding $60 million, the founder's dream has become a reality. She built a value-added firm, turned the management over to a new team, and now enjoys a lifestyle with her family that she always desired.

Questions:

1. What type of grand strategies do you see displayed by Kristen Schaffner-Irvin in this case? Cite specific examples.
2. Michael Porter identified three generic strategies that companies can follow to develop a competitive advantage. Which one of the three do you believe Team Petroleum/TeamFuel is primarily using? Discuss and support you choice.
3. How has TeamFuel used technology to create a competitive advantage?

Enhancing Your Communication Skills

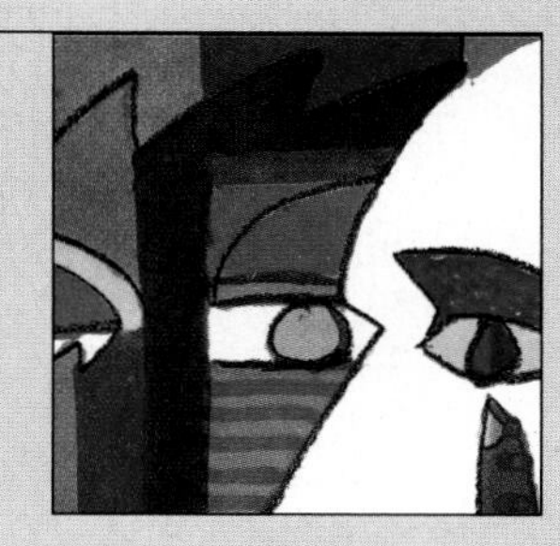

1. Develop a two- to three-page response (or three- to five-minute presentation) to the following statement: "Formal planning reduces flexibility and hinders success." Present both sides of the argument and include supporting data. Conclude your remarks by defending and supporting one of the two arguments you've presented.
2. Describe how your class syllabus is used as an objective tool. Refer to the section in the text on setting employee objectives (see pp. 85–86). In your discussion, provide specific references regarding how the guidelines we've offered apply to your class.
3. We've witnessed many corporations advocating quality programs (e.g., six sigma, ISO 9000) as part of their strategic plans. Pick one organization that has a well-publicized quality focus. Describe the strategic implications of its initiative and highlight what benefits the company expects because of this quality emphasis.

CHAPTER 4

Foundations of Decision Making

LEARNING OUTCOMES

After reading this chapter, I will be able to:

1. Describe the steps in the decision-making process.
2. Identify the assumptions of the rational decision-making model.
3. Explain the limits to rationality.
4. Define certainty, risk, and uncertainty as they relate to decision making.
5. Describe the actions of the bounded-rational decision maker.
6. Identify the two types of decision problems and the two types of decisions that are used to solve them.
7. Define heuristics and explain how they affect the decision-making process.
8. Identify four decision-making styles.
9. Describe the advantages and disadvantages of group decisions.
10. Explain three techniques for improving group decision making.

MEET A REAL MANAGER!

"One Manager's Reflection" page 121

James C. Ray Jr., Court Administrator, Hamilton County Juvenile Court

What goes into making a decision? It's lot of data, which when analyzed, point to an effective solution. There's also a significant expenditure of time and effort to mull over the options and select the best choice. Well, if you ask some researchers who study how decisions are made, they'll tell you that more than 90 percent of business decisions are made quickly and based on a "gut reaction."[1] Software maker Business Objects, located in San Jose, California, believes it has a way to help businesspeople make better decisions.

Founded in Paris in 1990, Business Objects now has more than 15,000 customers. The list includes such companies as Kraft Foods, MasterCard, PepsiCo, and General Electric. Competing with companies like Microsoft, PeopleSoft, and Oracle, Business Objects saw its revenue increase 19 percent in 2001 to more than $416 million. Let's look at how it has been used in several organizations.

One organization that attests to the usefulness of this business decision software is Owens & Minor. (Pictured are Don Stoller and Judy Springfield of O&M.) Using business intelligence software from Business Objects is revolutionizing the ways its decisions are made. Owens and Minor (O&M) sells medical supplies—about $4 billion worth a year. In 2001, it sold its products to more than 150 hospitals in the United States. In previous years, however, O&M had difficulty tracking purchases, inventory, and order backlogs. Business Objects software helped to change all that. By feeding data into a sophisticated computer database system, "neat looking tables, charts and maps" are generated that help in making a proper decision. At O&M, this has resulted in decisions that enabled the company to reduce its inventory by 14 percent, saving about $50 million annually. It also enabled O&M to recognize that about half of its product line wasn't selling, and could be eliminated.

Similar results were seen in General Electric's medical instrument business where Business Objects' software has helped track costs, maintenance, and performance of X-ray and MRI machines. Harrah's Entertainment also uses the software to accurately predict which regular casino customers would respond more favorably to a free meal, or a free room. Even the 2002 Super Bowl witnessed the benefits of Business Objects. Best Buy used the software to analyze the patterns of sport fans in the area. It predicted there would be a significant increase in television sales in Boston as a result of the game between the St. Louis Rams and the New England Patriots. Armed with this information, Best Buy shipped added inventory into the Boston area—and saw television sales increase by 26 percent.

The point of Business Objects' business intelligence software is not to suggest that a machine can make a better decision than people. Instead, Business Objects recognizes that humans have limits in processing masses of data. By giving them a "tool" that performs thousands of relational analyses in seconds, the decision maker is better able to make an informed decision with more complete information. That's precisely the foundation of decision-making theory!

MANAGERS MAKE A LOT OF DECISIONS—SOME SMALL AND SOME large. The overall quality of those decisions goes a long way in determining an organization's success or failure. In this chapter, we examine the foundations of decision making.

In the last chapter, we discussed how companies plan—for both the long-term survival of the organization and the short-term, day-to-day operations. Implied in these planning activities are the decisions managers make. Plans should not come out of thin air; they should be the result of careful analyses. After weighing the advantages and disadvantages of various alternatives, managers select the ones that will best serve the interests of the organization. This selection process is called decision making. What kinds of planning decisions do managers like those at Owens and Minor make? We have listed a few examples in Exhibit 4–1.

THE DECISION-MAKING PROCESS

Decision making is typically described as choosing among alternatives, but this view is overly simplistic. Why? Because decision making is a process rather than the simple act of choosing among alternatives. Exhibit 4–2 illustrates the **decision-making process** as a set of eight steps that begins with identifying a problem; it moves

decision-making process
A set of eight steps that includes identifying a problem, selecting a solution, and evaluating the effectiveness of the solution

EXHIBIT 4–1
Example of Planning-Function Decisions

- What are the organization's long-term objectives?
- What strategies will best achieve those objectives?
- What should the organization's short-term objectives be?
- What is the most efficient means of completing tasks?
- What might the competition be considering?
- What budgets are needed to complete department tasks?
- How difficult should individual goals be?

through selecting an alternative that can alleviate the problem, and concludes with evaluating the decision's effectiveness. This process is as applicable to your decision about what you're going to do on spring break as it was to Sears and Lands' End executives, who were considering combining companies. The process can also be used to describe both individual and group decisions. Let's take a closer look at the process in order to understand what each step encompasses.

WHAT DEFINES A DECISION PROBLEM?

problem
A discrepancy between an existing and a desired state of affairs

The decision-making process begins with the identification of a **problem** (step 1) or, more specifically, a discrepancy between an existing and a desired state of affairs.[2] Let's develop an example that illustrates this point to use throughout this section. For the sake of simplicity, we'll make the example something to which most of us can relate: the decision to buy a vehicle. Take the case of a new-product manager for the Netherlands-based food products company Unilever. The manager has spent nearly $3,000 on auto repairs over the past few years, and now the car has a blown engine. Repair estimates indicate that it is not economical to repair the car. Furthermore, convenient public transportation is unavailable.

So now we have a problem. There is a disparity between the manager's need to have a functional vehicle and the fact that her current one isn't working. Unfortunately, this example doesn't tell us much about how managers identify problems. In the real world, most problems don't come with neon signs identifying them as such. A blown engine is a clear signal to the manager that she needs a new vehicle, but few problems are so obvious. Instead, problem identification is subjective. Furthermore, the manager who mistakenly solves the wrong problem perfectly is just as likely to perform poorly as the manager who fails to identify the right problem and does nothing. Problem identification is neither a simple nor an unimportant part of the decision-making process.[3] How do managers become aware that they have a discrepancy? Managers have to make a comparison between their current state of affairs and some standard. What is that standard? It can be past performance, previously set goals, or the performance of some other unit within the organization or in other organizations. In our vehicle-buying example, the standard is a previously set goal—a vehicle that runs.

EXHIBIT 4–2 **The Decision-Making Process**

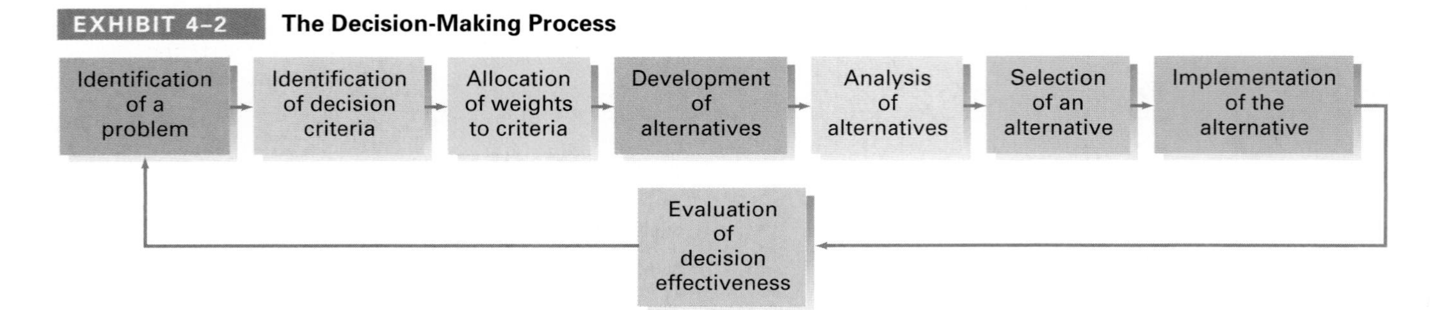

WHAT IS RELEVANT IN THE DECISION-MAKING PROCESS?

Once a manager has identified a problem that needs attention, the **decision criteria** that will be important in solving the problem must be identified (step 2).

In our vehicle-buying example, the product manager has to assess those factors that are relevant in her decision. These might include criteria such as price, model (two-door or four-door), size (compact or intermediate), manufacturer (French, German, American), optional equipment (automatic transmission, side-protection impact system, leather interior), and repair records. These criteria reflect what she thinks is relevant in her decision. Every decision maker has criteria—whether explicitly stated or not—that guide his or her decision. Note that in this step in the decision-making process, what is not identified is as important as what is. If the product manager doesn't consider fuel economy to be a criterion, then it will not influence her choice of vehicle. Thus, if a decision maker does not identify a particular factor in this second step, then it is treated as if it were irrelevant to the decision maker.

Problems in business rarely jump out at us like this one. But even here, is it a blown engine or simply a burst radiator hose? Problems may or may not be what they appear to be. Consequently, the first thing one needs to do in making a decision is to identify the problem.

decision criteria
Factors that are relevant in a decision

HOW DOES THE DECISION MAKER WEIGHT THE CRITERIA?

The criteria are not all equally important.[4] It is necessary, therefore, to allocate weights to the items listed in step 2 in order to give them their relative priority in the decision (step 3). A simple approach is merely to give the most important criterion a weight of 10 and then assign weights to the rest against that standard. Thus, in contrast to a criterion that you gave a 5, the highest-rated factor would be twice as important. The idea is to use your personal preferences to assign priorities to the relevant criteria in your decision as well as to indicate their degree of importance by assigning a weight to each. Exhibit 4–3 lists the criteria and weights that our manager developed for her vehicle replacement decision. Price is the most important criterion in her decision, with performance and handling having low weights.

Then the decision maker lists the alternatives that could succeed in resolving the problem (step 4). No attempt is made in this step to appraise these alternatives, only to list them.[5] Let's assume that our manager has identified 12 vehicles as viable choices: Jeep Cherokee, Ford Mustang, Mercedes C230, Pontiac Grand Am, Mazda Tribute, Dodge Durango, Volvo S60, Isuzu Axiom, BMW 325, Audi A6, Toyota Camry, and Volkswagen Passat.

Once the alternatives have been identified, the decision maker must critically analyze each one (step 5). The strengths and weaknesses of each alternative become evident as they are compared with the criteria and weights established in steps 2 and 3.

EXHIBIT 4–3
Criteria and Weight in Car-Buying Decision (Scale of 1 to 10)

CRITERION	WEIGHT
Price	10
Interior comfort	8
Durability	5
Repair record	5
Performance	3
Handling	1

EXHIBIT 4–4 **Assessment of Car Alternatives**

ALTERNATIVES	INITIAL PRICE	INTERIOR COMFORT	DURABILITY	REPAIR RECORD	PERFORMANCE	HANDLING	TOTAL
Jeep Cherokee	2	10	8	7	5	5	37
Ford Mustang	9	6	5	6	8	6	40
Mercedes C230	8	5	6	6	4	6	35
Pontiac Grand Am	9	5	6	7	6	5	38
Mazda Tribute	5	6	9	10	7	7	44
Dodge Durango	10	5	6	4	3	3	31
Volvo S60	4	8	7	6	8	9	42
Isuzu Axiom	7	6	8	6	5	6	38
BMW 325	9	7	6	4	4	7	37
Audi A6	5	8	5	4	10	10	42
Toyota Camry	6	5	10	10	6	6	43
Volkswagen Passat	8	6	6	5	7	8	40

Each alternative is evaluated by appraising it against the criteria. Exhibit 4–4 shows the assessed values that the manager put on each of her 12 alternatives after she had test driven each vehicle. Keep in mind that the ratings given the 12 vehicles shown in Exhibit 4–4 are based on the assessment made by the new-product manager. Again, we are using a 1-to-10 scale. Some assessments can be achieved in a relatively objective fashion. For instance, the purchase price represents the best price the manager can get from local dealers, and consumer magazines report data from owners on frequency of repairs. However, the assessment of handling is clearly a personal judgment. The point is that most decisions contain judgments. They are reflected in the criteria chosen in step 2, the weights given to the criteria, and the evaluation of alternatives. This explains why two vehicle buyers with the same amount of money may look at two totally distinct sets of alternatives or even look at the same alternatives and rate them differently.

Exhibit 4–4 is only an assessment of the 12 alternatives against the decision criteria; it does not reflect the weighting done in step 3. If one choice had scored 10 on every criterion, you wouldn't need to consider the weights. Similarly, if the weights were all equal, you could evaluate each alternative merely by summing up the appropriate lines in Exhibit 4–4. For instance, the Grand Am would have a score of 38, and the Toyota Camry a score of 43. If you multiply each alternative assessment against its weight, you get the figures in Exhibit 4–5. For instance, the Isuzu Axiom scored a 40 on durability, which was determined by multiplying the weight given to durability (5) by the manager's appraisal of Isuzu on this criterion (8). The summation of these scores represents an evaluation of each alternative against the previously established criteria and weights. Notice that the weighting of the criteria has changed the ranking of alternatives in our example. The Mazda Tribute, for example, has gone from first to third. From our analysis, both initial price and interior comfort worked against the Mazda.

WHAT DETERMINES THE BEST CHOICE?

Step 6 is the critical act of choosing the best alternative from among those enumerated and assessed. Since we determined all the pertinent factors in the decision, weighted them appropriately, and identified the viable alternatives, we merely have

EXHIBIT 4–5 **Weighting of Vehicles (Assessment Criteria X Criteria Weight)**

ALTERNATIVES	INITIAL PRICE [10]		INTERIOR COMFORT [8]		DURABILITY [5]		REPAIR RECORD [5]		PERFORMACE [3]		HANDLING [1]		TOTAL
Jeep Cherokee	2	**20**	10	**80**	8	**40**	7	**35**	5	**15**	5	**5**	**195**
Ford Mustang	9	**90**	6	**48**	5	**25**	6	**30**	8	**24**	6	**6**	**223**
Mercedes C230	8	**80**	5	**40**	6	**30**	6	**30**	4	**12**	6	**6**	**198**
Pontiac Grand Am	9	**90**	5	**40**	6	**30**	7	**35**	6	**18**	5	**5**	**218**
Mazda Tribute	5	**50**	6	**48**	9	**45**	10	**50**	7	**21**	7	**7**	**221**
Dodge Durango	10	**100**	5	**40**	6	**30**	4	**20**	3	**9**	3	**3**	**202**
Volvo S60	4	**40**	8	**64**	7	**35**	6	**30**	8	**24**	9	**9**	**202**
Isuzu Axiom	7	**70**	6	**48**	8	**40**	6	**30**	5	**15**	6	**6**	**209**
BMW 325	9	**90**	7	**56**	6	**30**	4	**20**	4	**12**	7	**7**	**215**
Audi A6	5	**50**	8	**64**	5	**25**	4	**20**	10	**30**	10	**10**	**199**
Toyota Camry	6	**60**	5	**40**	10	**50**	10	**50**	6	**18**	6	**6**	**224**
Volkswagen Passat	8	**80**	6	**48**	6	**30**	5	**25**	7	**21**	8	**8**	**212**

to choose the alternative that generated the highest score in step 5. In our vehicle example (Exhibit 4–5), the decision maker would choose the Toyota Camry. On the basis of the criteria identified, the weights given to the criteria, and the decision maker's assessment of each vehicle's achievement on the criteria, the Toyota scored highest (224 points) and thus became the best alternative.

WHAT IS DECISION IMPLEMENTATION?

Although the choice process is completed in the previous step, the decision may still fail if it is not implemented properly (step 7). Therefore, this step is concerned with putting the decision into action. **Decision implementation** includes conveying the decision to those affected and getting their commitment to it.[6] As we will demonstrate later in this chapter, groups or committees can help a manager achieve commitment. The people who must carry out a decision are most likely to enthusiastically endorse the outcome if they participate in the decision-making process.

decision implementation
Putting a decision into action; includes conveying the decision to the persons who will be affected by it and getting their commitment to it

WHAT IS THE LAST STEP IN THE DECISION PROCESS?

The last step in the decision-making process (step 8) appraises the result of the decision to see whether it has corrected the problem. Did the alternative chosen in step 6 and implemented in step 7 accomplish the desired result? The evaluation of the results of decisions is detailed in Chapter 13 where we will look at the control function.

MAKING DECISIONS: THE RATIONAL MODEL

Managerial decision making is assumed to be **rational** in that managers make consistent, value-maximizing choices within specified constraints.[7] In this section, we take a close look at the underlying assumptions of rationality, determine how valid those assumptions actually are, then review the role of creativity in decision making.

rational
Describes choices that are consistent and value-maximizing within specified constraints

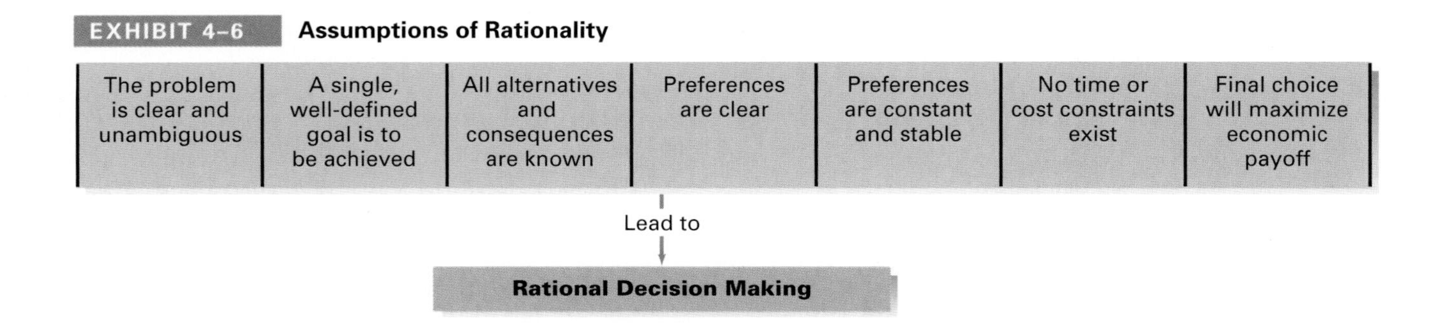

A decision maker who was perfectly rational would be fully objective and logical. He or she would define a problem carefully and would have a clear and specific goal. Moreover, the steps in the decision-making process would consistently lead toward selecting the alternative that maximizes that goal. Exhibit 4–6 summarizes the assumptions of rationality.

Remember that the assumptions of rationality often do not hold true, because the level of certainty that the rational model demands rarely exists. That is, **certainty** implies that a manager can make an accurate decision because the outcome of every alternative is known. In the real world, we know that is not the case. Most managers, then, must try to assign probabilities to outcomes that may result. We call this process dealing with **risk**. When decision makers do not have full knowledge of the problem and cannot determine even a reasonable probability of alternative outcomes, they must make their decisions under a condition of **uncertainty**.

certainty
The implication that, in making a decision, the decision maker knows the outcome of every possible alternative

risk
The probability that a particular outcome will result from a given decision creativity. The ability to produce novel and useful ideas

uncertainty
A condition in which managers do not have full knowledge of the problem they face and cannot determine even a reasonable probability of alternative outcomes

creativity
The ability to produce novel and useful ideas

WHY IS CREATIVITY IMPORTANT IN DECISION MAKING?

The rational decision maker needs **creativity**: the ability to produce novel and useful ideas. These are ideas that are different from what's been done before but that are also appropriate to the problem or opportunity presented. Why is creativity important to decision making? It allows the decision maker to appraise and understand the problem more fully, including "seeing" problems others can't see. However, creativity's most obvious value is in helping the decision maker identify all viable alternatives.[8]

WHAT IS CREATIVE POTENTIAL?

Most people have creative potential that they can use when confronted with a decision-making problem. But to unleash that potential, they have to get out of the psychological ruts most of us get into and learn how to think about a problem in divergent ways.

We can start with the obvious. People differ in their inherent creativity. Einstein, Edison, Picasso, and Mozart were individuals of exceptional creativity. Not surprisingly, exceptional creativity is scarce. A study of lifetime creativity of 461 men and women found that fewer than 1 percent were exceptionally creative. But 10 percent were highly creative, and about 60 percent were somewhat creative. This suggests that most of us have creative potential, if we can learn to unleash it.

Given that most people have the capacity to be at least moderately creative, what can individuals and organizations do to stimulate employee creativity? The best answer to this question lies in the three-component model of creativity based on an extensive body of research. This model proposes that individual creativity essentially requires expertise, creative-thinking skills, and intrinsic task motivation (see Exhibit 4–7). Studies confirm that the higher the level of each of these three components, the higher the creativity.

Expertise is the foundation of all creative work. Picasso's understanding of art and Einstein's knowledge of physics were necessary conditions for them to be able to make creative contributions to their fields. And you wouldn't expect someone with a minimal knowledge of programming to be very creative as a software engineer. The potential for creativity is enhanced when individuals have abilities, knowledge, proficiencies, and similar expertise in their fields of endeavor.

The second component is *creative-thinking skills.* This encompasses personality characteristics associated with creativity, the ability to use analogies, as well as the talent to see the familiar in a different light. For instance, the following individual traits have been found to be associated with the development of creative ideas: intelligence, independence, self-confidence, risk taking, an internal locus of control, tolerance for ambiguity, and perseverance in the face of frustration. The effective use of analogies allows decision makers to apply an idea from one context to another. One of the most famous examples in which analogy resulted in a creative breakthrough was Alexander Graham Bell's observation that it might be possible to take concepts that operate in the ear and apply them to his "talking box." He noticed that the bones in the ear are operated by a delicate, thin membrane. He wondered why, then, a thicker and stronger piece of membrane shouldn't be able to move a piece of steel. Out of that analogy the telephone was conceived. Of course, some people have developed their skill at being able to see problems a new way. They're able to make the strange familiar and the familiar strange. For instance, most of us think of hens laying eggs. But how many of us have considered that a hen is only an egg's way of making another egg?

What made an individual like Pablo Picasso creative? History tells us that he had exceptional innate creativity. This resulted from his understanding of art, his creative-thinking skills in seeing things differently than others, as well as his intrinsic task motivation for turning his creative potential into actual works of art.

The final component in our model is *intrinsic task motivation.* This is the desire to work on something because it's interesting, involving, exciting, satisfying, or personally challenging. This motivational component is what turns creativity *potential* into *actual* creative ideas. It determines the extent to which individuals fully engage their expertise and creative skills. So creative people often love their work, to the point of seeming obsessed. Importantly, an individual's work environment and the organization's culture (we'll look at organization culture in the next chapter) can have a significant effect on intrinsic motivation. Specifically, five organizational factors have been found that can impede your creativity. These are: (1) expected evaluation—focusing on how your work is going to be evaluated; (2) surveillance—being watched while you're working; (3) external motivators—emphasizing external, tangible rewards; (4) competition—facing win–lose situations with your peers; and (5) constrained choices—being given limits on how you can do your work.

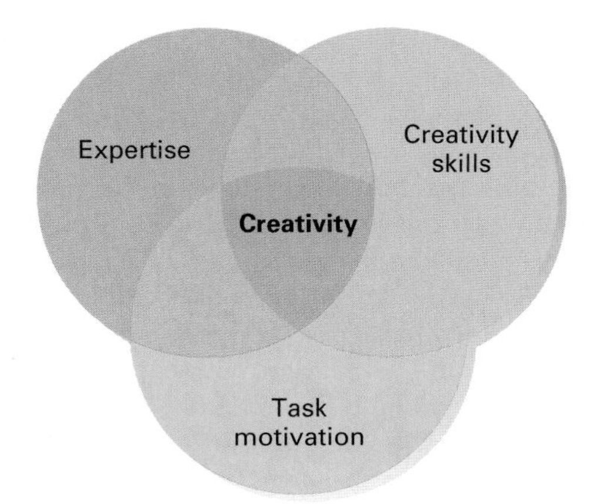

EXHIBIT 4–7

Three Elements of Creativity

Source: T. M. Amabile, "Motivating Creativity in Organizations," *California Management Review* (Fall 1997), p. 43. Copyright © 1997, by The Regents of the University of California. Reprinted by permission of the Regents.

THE REAL WORLD: MODIFICATIONS OF THE RATIONAL MODEL

When you were deciding where to attend college, did you obtain catalogs from the thousands of colleges and universities that exist throughout the world? Obviously not. Did you carefully identify all the relevant criteria—tuition costs, scholarships offered, location, majors offered, and so forth—in making your decision? Did you evaluate each potential college against these criteria in an effort to make an optimum selection? We doubt it. But don't take this as an indictment of you or your decision-making ability. Most of us make decisions on the basis of incomplete information. Why? When we are faced with complex problems, most of us respond by reducing the problem to something we can readily understand. People often have limited abilities to process and assimilate massive amounts of information to reach an optimal solution. As a result, they **satisfice**. That is, they seek solutions that are satisfactory and sufficient—or just good enough.

satisfice
Making a good enough decision

Do managers engage in satisficing behavior? Or do they act rationally by carefully assessing problems, identifying all the relevant criteria, using their creativity to identify all viable alternatives, and, after a meticulous review of each alternative, finding the optimum choice? When managers are faced with a simple problem with few alternatives, when time pressures are minimal, and when the cost of seeking out and evaluating alternatives is low, the rational model provides a good description of the decision-making process.[9] But such situations are the exception rather than the rule.

Numerous studies have added to our understanding of managerial decision making.[10] These studies often challenge one or more of the assumptions of rationality. They suggest that decision making often veers from the logical, consistent, and systematic process that rationality implies. Do these limits to rationality mean that managers ignore the eight-step decision process we described at the beginning of this chapter? Not necessarily. Why? Because despite the limits to perfect rationality, managers are expected to appear to follow the rational process.[11] They know that "good" decision makers are supposed to do certain things: identify problems, consider alternatives, gather information, behave thoughtfully, and act decisively but prudently. By doing so, managers signal to their bosses, peers, and employees that they are competent and that their decisions are the result of intelligent and rational deliberation. The process they follow is frequently referred to as bounded rationality.

WHAT IS BOUNDED RATIONALITY?

Management theory is built on the premise that individuals act rationally and that managerial jobs revolve around the rational decision-making process. However, the assumptions of rationality are rather optimistic. Few people actually behave rationally. Given this fact, how do managers make decisions if it is unlikely that they are perfectly rational? Herbert Simon, an economist and management scholar, found that within certain constraints, managers do act rationally. Because it is impossible for human beings to process and understand all the information necessary to meet the test of rationality, what they do is construct simplified models that extract the essential features from problems without capturing all of their complexities.[12] Simon called this decision-making process **bounded rationality**. Under the definition of bounded rationality, decision makers can behave rationally (the rational decision-making model) within the limits of the simplified or bounded model.[13] The result of their actions is a satisficing decision rather than a maximizing one—a decision in which "good-enough" solutions are selected. As a result, instead of optimizing a choice, decision makers select alternatives that satisfy the problem.

bounded rationality
Behavior that is rational within the parameters of a simplified model that captures the essential features of a problem

How do managers' actions within these boundaries differ from actions within the rational model? Once a problem is identified, the search for criteria and alternatives begins. But this list of criteria is generally limited to the more conspicuous choices. That is, Simon found that decision makers will often focus on easy-to-find choices, and ones that tend to be highly visible. In many instances, this means developing alternatives that vary only slightly from decisions that have been made in the past to deal with similar problems.

Once this limited set of alternatives is identified, decision makers will begin reviewing them, but that review will not be exhaustive. Rather, they will proceed to review the alternatives only until an alternative that is sufficient, or good enough, to solve the problems at hand is found. Thus, the first alternative to meet the good-enough criterion typically ends the search, and decision makers can then proceed to implement this acceptable course of action. For example, suppose as a double major in finance and e-business, you're looking for a job in a technology-based company. You would like to find employment within 75 miles of your hometown at a starting salary between $40,000 and $50,000. You accept a job offer as a cash flow manager from a midsized firm nearly 60 miles from home at a starting salary of $44,500. A more comprehensive job search would have revealed a job in cash management in a *Fortune* 1000 firm just 25 miles from your hometown and starting at $48,000. Because the first job offer was satisfactory (or good enough), you behaved in a bounded rational manner by accepting it, although, according to the assumptions of perfect rationality, you didn't maximize your decision by searching all possible alternatives.

What are the implications of bounded rationality on the manager's job? In situations in which the assumptions of perfect rationality do not apply (including many of the most important and far-reaching decisions that a manager makes), the details of the decision-making process are strongly influenced by the decision maker's self-interest, the organization's culture, internal politics, and power considerations.

Herbert Simon recognized that managerial decisions typically don't follow the assumptions of rationality. But that wasn't an indictment of the model itself. Although environmental factors may act as barriers to these assumptions, decision makers can still act in a rational but constrained way. To do so, Simon says managers make decisions in what is called *bounded rationality*.

ARE COMMON ERRORS COMMITTED IN THE DECISION-MAKING PROCESS?

When individuals make decisions, they must make choices. But doing so requires careful thought and a lot of information. Complete information, however, would overload us. Consequently, we often engage in behaviors that speed up the process. That is, in order to avoid information overload, we rely on judgmental shortcuts called **heuristics**.[14] Heuristics commonly exist in two forms—availability and representative. Both types create biases in a decision maker. Another bias is the decision maker's tendency to escalate commitment to a failing course of action.

heuristics
Judgmental shortcuts

Availability heuristic **Availability heuristic** is the tendency to base judgments on information that is readily available. Events that invoke strong emotions, are vivid to the imagination, or have recently occurred create a strong impression on us. As a result, we are likely to overestimate the frequency of the occurrence of unlikely events. For instance, many people have a fear of flying. Although traveling in commercial aircraft is statistically safer than driving a vehicle, aircraft accidents get much more attention. The media coverage of an air disaster causes individuals to overstate the risk of flying and understate the risk of driving. For managers, availability heuristic can also explain why, when conducting performance appraisals (see Chapter 6), they tend to give more weight to more recent behaviors of an employee than the behaviors of six or nine months ago.

availability heuristic
The tendency for people to base their judgments on information that is readily available to them

Representative heuristic Literally millions of recreational league players dream of becoming a professional basketball player one day. In reality, most of these youngsters have a better chance of becoming medical doctors than they do of ever playing in the

Go to any basketball court and you're likely to find one thing: Someone is playing basketball wearing the jersey of Los Angeles Laker star Kobe Bryant. Why? Because many of these players are trying to be like Kobe. Many think that wearing his jersey and playing like him will help them to go on to the NBA—after a successful college career and at least an NCAA championship. That dream is what we call the *representative heuristic.*

NBA. These dreams are examples of what we call **representative heuristic**. Representative heuristic causes individuals to match the likelihood of an occurrence with something that they are familiar with. For example, our young ballplayers may think about someone from their local league who 15 years ago went on to play in the NBA. Or they think, while watching players on television, that they could perform as well.

In organizations we can find several instances of representative heuristic. Decision makers may predict the future success of a new product by relating it to a previous product's success. Managers may also be affected by representative heuristic when they no longer hire graduates from a particular college program because the last three persons hired from that program were poor performers.

Escalation of commitment A popular strategy in playing blackjack is an effort to guarantee you can't lose. When you lose a hand, you double your next bet. This strategy, or decision rule, may appear innocent enough, but if you start with a $5 bet and lose six hands in a row (not uncommon for many of us), you will be wagering $320 on your seventh hand merely to recoup your losses and win $5.

The blackjack strategy illustrates a phenomenon called **escalation of commitment**, an increased commitment to a previous decision despite negative information. That is, the escalation of commitment represents the tendency to stay the course, despite negative data that suggest one should do otherwise.[15]

Some of the most notorious events involving escalation of commitment were decisions made by presidents of the United States. For example: Lyndon Johnson's administration increased the tonnage of bombs dropped on North Vietnam, despite constant information that bombing was not bringing the war any closer to conclusion. Richard Nixon refused to destroy his secret White House tapes. George H. W. Bush believed that, given his popularity after Operation Desert Storm and the fall of the Soviet Union, he had only to pay attention to foreign affairs to win the 1992 presidential election. History now tells us that staying the course proved detrimental to Johnson, Nixon, and Bush. In an organizational setting, similar events have occurred. For instance, at Allfirst Financial (a United States. subsidiary of Allied Irish Banks), a Baltimore trader continued to trade the yen in hopes of recouping his initial losses. When his activities were finally uncovered, his actions had led to a $691 million loss to the bank.[16]

representative heuristic
The tendency for people to base judgments of probability on things with which they are familiar

escalation of commitment
An increased commitment to a previous decision despite negative information

DECISION MAKING: A CONTINGENCY APPROACH

The types of problems managers face in decision-making situations often determine how a problem is treated. In this section, we present a categorization scheme for problems and for types of decisions. Then we show how the type of decision a manager uses should reflect the characteristics of the problem.

HOW DO PROBLEMS DIFFER?

Some problems are straightforward. The goal of the decision maker is clear, the problem familiar, and information about the problem easily defined and complete. Examples might include a supplier's tardiness with an important delivery, a customer's wanting to return an Internet purchase, a news program's having to respond to an unexpected and fast-breaking event, or a university's handling of a student who is applying for financial aid. Such situations are called **well-structured problems**. They align closely with the assumptions underlying perfect rationality.

Many situations faced by managers, however, are **ill-structured problems.** They are new or unusual. Information about such problems is ambiguous or incomplete. The decision to

well-structured problems
Straightforward, familiar, easily defined problems

ill-structured problems
New problems in which information is ambiguous or incomplete

enter a new market segment, to hire an architect to design a new office park, or to merge two organizations are all examples of an ill-structured problem. So, too, is the decision to invest in a new, unproven technology.

What would happen if while a new tire was being installed on this alloy wheel rim the rim broke? A Goodyear manager simply has to follow company policy, which may include replacing the rim at the company's expense. Following this policy is an example of a programmed decision.

HOW DOES A MANAGER MAKE PROGRAMMED DECISIONS?

Just as problems can be divided into two categories, so, too, can decisions. As we will see, programmed, or routine, decision making is the most efficient way to handle well-structured problems. However, when problems are ill structured, managers must rely on nonprogrammed decision making in order to develop unique solutions.

A Goodyear automotive mechanic breaks an alloy wheel rim while installing new tires on a vehicle. What does the manager do? There is probably some standardized method for handling this type of problem. For example, the manager may replace the rim at the company's expense. This is a **programmed decision**. Decisions are programmed to the extent that they are repetitive and routine and to the extent that a specific approach has been worked out for handling them. Because the problem is well structured, the manager does not have to go to the trouble and expense of working up an involved decision process. Programmed decision making is relatively simple and tends to rely heavily on previous solutions. The develop-the-alternatives stage in the decision-making process is either nonexistent or given little attention. Why? Because once the structured problem is defined, its solution is usually self-evident or at least reduced to a very few alternatives that are familiar and that have proved successful in the past. In many cases, programmed decision making becomes decision making by precedent. Managers simply do what they and others have done previously in the same situation. The broken wheel rim does not require the manager to identify and weight decision criteria or develop a long list of possible solutions. Rather, the manager falls back on a systematic procedure, rule, or policy.

programmed decision
A repetitive decision that can be handled by a routine approach

Procedures A **procedure** is a series of interrelated sequential steps that a manager can use when responding to a well-structured problem. The only real difficulty is identifying the problem. Once the problem is clear, so is the procedure. For instance, a purchasing manager receives a request from computing services for licensing arrangements to install 16 copies of McAfee Virus Software. The purchasing manager knows that there is a definite procedure for handling this decision. Has the requisition been properly filled out and approved? If not, one can send the requisition back with a note explaining what is deficient. If the request is complete, the approximate costs are estimated. If the total exceeds $8,500, three bids must be obtained. If the total is $8,500 or less, only one vendor need be identified and the order placed. The decision-making process is merely the execution of a simple series of sequential steps.

procedure
A series of interrelated sequential steps that can be used to respond to a well-structured problem

Rules A **rule** is an explicit statement that tells a manager what he or she ought—or ought not—to do. Rules are frequently used by managers who confront a well-structured problem because they are simple to follow and ensure consistency. In the example above, the $8,500 cutoff rule simplifies the purchasing manager's decision about when to use multiple bids.

rule
An explicit statement that tells managers what they ought or ought not to do

Policies A third guide for making programmed decisions is a **policy**. It provides guidelines to channel a manager's thinking in a specific direction. The statement that "we promote from within, whenever possible" is an example of a policy. In contrast to a rule, a policy establishes parameters for the decision maker rather than specifically stating what should or should not be done. It's at this point that one's ethical standards will come into play (See Ethical Dilemma in Management). As an analogy, think of the Ten Commandments as rules and the U.S. Constitution as policy. The latter requires judgment and interpretation; the former do not.

policy
A general guide that establishes parameters for making decisions

Ethical Dilemma in Management

Stem-Cell Research

Advanced Cell Technology is embarking on a major activity—"to produce the world's first-ever cloned human embryo . . . a microscopic version of an already living person."[17] Michael West, chief executive of Advanced Cell Technology, has begun implementation of his goal by interviewing women to serve as egg donors. Combining these eggs with a human cell produces an embryo that permits scientists at Advanced Cell to capture stem cells. As the stem cells are captured, the embryo is destroyed. Stem cells are believed to be able to develop into human tissue that could help cure a variety of diseases, or even repair a severed spinal cord.

Advanced Cell Technology's goal, of course, is facing a major debate. People supporting both sides of the issue have strongly voiced their opinions. On one hand, if such research is proven effective, many diseases as we know them today—like Parkinson's Disease and Muscular Dystrophy—could be eliminated. That could be both a major scientific breakthrough in our world, and clearly a major financial coup for Advanced Cell. Moreover, similar research is being conducted in other parts of the globe, such as Europe, where it has received support. And to assist in these endeavors in an attempt to ensure that the highest ethics enter into all decisions made, Michael West has formed an ethical board of advisors consisting of scientists and professors of religion.

But critics of such research see this differently. They view stem cell research as the next step toward cloning humans—and at times, liken it to creating a "great society." Religious groups, too, have voiced this concern over Advanced Cell's decisions, claiming that it is working in an area that it shouldn't be. They also say that making decisions regarding such research raises significant ethical issues, particularly as to how far this research can go. The federal government has also entered into the discussion, with President George W. Bush setting specific regulations on what kind of stem cell research is funded by the government. Even some Advanced Cell ethics board members have resigned, complaining that Advance Cell is more interested in "obtaining patents in the field and using the board as a rubber stamp."

Do you believe that a company like Advanced Cell Technology can make ethical decisions in this arena when so much is at stake? Should public opinion keep a company from doing something simply because it is unpopular—even though it is legal? What's your opinion.

At what cost do we perform stem-cell research? That's one of the tough questions facing Michael West, chief executive of Advanced Cell Technology. While scientific breakthroughs could eliminate such diseases as Parkinson's and Muscular Dystrophy, the research itself is charting new territories. It's become a major ethical dilemma for West, who has formed a board of ethical advisors to assist him.

IN WHAT WAYS DO NONPROGRAMMED DECISIONS DIFFER FROM PROGRAMMED DECISIONS?

nonprogrammed decisions Decisions that must be custom-made to solve unique and nonrecurring problems

Deciding whether to acquire another organization, deciding which global markets offer the most potential, engineering work processes to improve efficiency, or deciding whether to sell off an unprofitable division are examples of **nonprogrammed decisions**. Such decisions are unique and nonrecurring. When a manager confronts an ill-structured problem, there is no cut-and-dried solution. A custom-made, nonprogrammed response is required.

The creation of a new organizational strategy is a nonprogrammed decision. This decision is different from previous organizational decisions because the issue is new; a different set of environmental factors exists, and other conditions have changed. For example, Amazon.com Jeff Bezos' strategy to "get big fast" helped the company grow tremendously. But this strategy came at a cost—perennial financial losses. To turn a profit, Bezos made decisions regarding "sorting orders, anticipating demand, more efficient shipping, foreign partnerships, and opening a marketplace allowing other sellers to sell their books at Amazon." As a result, for the first time in company history, Amazon earned more than $59 million in 2001.[18]

HOW CAN YOU INTEGRATE PROBLEMS, TYPES OF DECISIONS, AND LEVEL IN THE ORGANIZATION?

Exhibit 4–8 describes the relationship among types of problems, types of decisions, and level in the organization. Well-structured problems are responded to with programmed decision making. Ill-structured problems require nonprogrammed decision making. Lower-level managers essentially confront familiar and repetitive problems; therefore, they most typically rely on programmed decisions such as standard operating procedures. However, the problems confronting managers are more likely to become ill structured as the managers move up the organizational hierarchy. Why? Because lower-level managers handle the routine decisions themselves and pass upward only decisions that they find unique or difficult. Similarly, managers pass down routine decisions to their employees in order to spend their time on more problematic issues.

Few managerial decisions in the real world are either fully programmed or fully nonprogrammed. Most decisions fall somewhere in between. Few programmed decisions are designed to eliminate individual judgment completely. At the other extreme, even the most unusual situation requiring a nonprogrammed decision can be helped by programmed routines. A final point on this topic is that organizational efficiency is facilitated by programmed decision making—a fact that may explain its wide popularity. Whenever possible, management decisions are likely to be programmed. Obviously, this approach is not too realistic at the top of the organization, because most of the problems that top management confronts are of a nonrecurring nature. However, there are strong economic incentives for top management to create policies, standard operating procedures, and rules to guide other managers.

Programmed decisions minimize the need for managers to exercise discretion. This is important because discretion costs money. The more nonprogrammed decision making a manager is required to do, the greater the judgment needed. Because sound judgment is an uncommon quality, it costs more to acquire the services of managers who possess it.

IN WHAT WAYS DOES TECHNOLOGY ASSIST DECISION MAKING?

Information technology is providing managers with a wealth of decision-making support. This includes expert systems, neural networks, groupware, and specific problem-solving software. **Expert systems** use software programs to encode the relevant experience of an expert and allow a system to act like that expert in analyzing and solving ill-structured problems. The essence of expert systems is that (1) they use specialized knowledge about a particular problem area rather than general knowledge that would apply to all problems, (2) they use qualitative reasoning rather than numerical calculations, and (3) they perform at a level of competence that is higher than that of nonexpert humans.[19] They guide users through problems by asking them a set of sequential questions about the situation and drawing conclusions based on the answers given. The conclusions are based on programmed rules that have

expert systems
Software that acts like an expert in analyzing and solving ill-structured problems

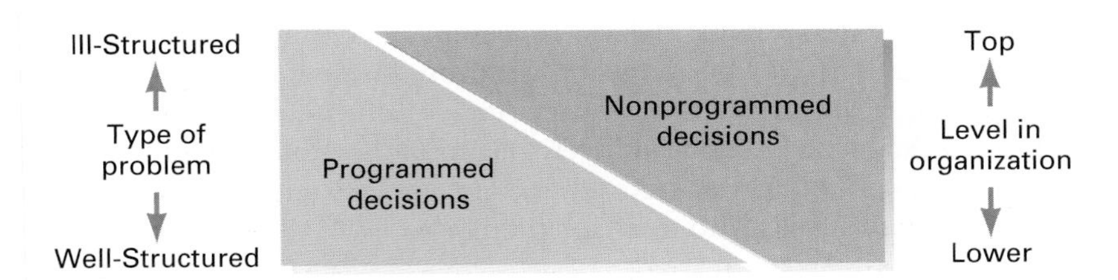

EXHIBIT 4–8
Types of Problems, Types of Decisions, and Level in the Organization

been modeled on the actual reasoning processes of experts who have confronted similar problems before. Once in place, these systems are allowing employees and lower-level managers to make high-quality decisions that previously could have been made only by senior managers.

neural networks
Software that is designed to imitate the structure of brain cells and connections among them

Neural networks are the next step beyond expert systems. They use computer software to imitate the structure of brain cells and connections among them.[20] Sophisticated robotics are using neural networks for their intelligence.[21] Neural networks have the ability to distinguish patterns and trends too subtle or complex for human beings. For instance, people can't easily assimilate more than two or three variables at once, but neural networks can perceive correlations among hundreds of variables. As a result, they can perform many operations simultaneously, recognizing patterns, making associations, generalizing about problems they haven't been exposed to before, and learning through experience. For instance, most banks today use neural networks to flag potential credit card fraud.[22] While in the past they relied on expert systems to track millions of credit card transactions, these earlier systems could look at only a few factors, such as the size of a transaction. Consequently, thousands of potential defrauding incidents were "flagged," most of which were false positives. Now with neural networks, significantly fewer numbers of cases are being identified as problematic—and it's more likely now that the majority of those identified will be actual cases of fraud. Furthermore, with the neural network system, fraudulent activities on a credit card can be uncovered in a matter of hours, rather than the two to three days it took prior to the implementation of neural networks.

DECISION-MAKING STYLES

Every decision maker brings a unique set of personal characteristics to his or her problem-solving efforts. For example, a manager who is creative and comfortable with uncertainty is likely to develop and evaluate decision alternatives differently from someone who is more conservative and less likely to accept risk. As a result of this information, researchers have sought to identify different decision-making styles.[23]

The basic premise for this decision-making model is the realization that individuals differ along two dimensions. The first is the way they think. Some decision makers are logical and rational. Being such, they process information in a sequential manner. In contrast, some individuals think creatively and use their intuition. These decision makers have a tendency to see matters from a big-picture perspective. The second dimension focuses on individuals' tolerance for ambiguity. Some individuals have a high need for consistency and order in making decisions so that ambiguity is minimized. Others, however, are able to tolerate high levels of uncertainty and can process many thoughts at the same time. When we diagram these two dimensions, four decision-making styles are formed. These styles are *directive, analytic, conceptual,* and *behavioral* (see Exhibit 4–9).

The directive style represents a decision-making style characterized by low tolerance for ambiguity and a rational way of thinking. These individuals are logical and efficient and typically make fast decisions that focus on the short term. The analytic decision-making style is characterized by high tolerance for ambiguity combined with a rational way of thinking. These individuals prefer to have complete information before making a decision. As a result, they carefully consider many alternatives. The conceptual style of decision making represents someone who tends to be very broad in outlook and to look at many alternatives. These decision makers tend to focus on the long run and often look for creative solutions. The behavioral style reflects an individual who thinks intuitively but has a low tolerance for uncertainty. These decision makers work well with others, are open to suggestions, and are concerned about the individuals who work for them.

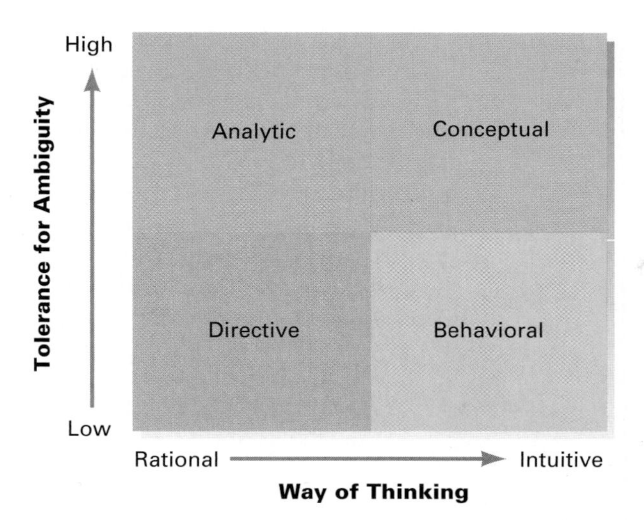

EXHIBIT 4-9
Decision-Making Styles

Although the four decision-making styles appear independent, most managers possess characteristics of more than one style. That is, although they usually have a dominant style, the other three styles can be alternatives—to be used when a situation may be best resolved by using a particular style.

MAKING DECISIONS IN GROUPS

Do managers make a lot of decisions in groups? You bet they do! Many decisions in organizations, especially important decisions that have far-reaching effects on organizational activities and personnel, are typically made in groups. It's a rare organization that doesn't at some time use committees, task forces, review panels, work teams, or similar groups as vehicles for making decisions. Why? In many cases, these groups represent the people who will be most affected by the decisions being made. Because of their expertise, these people are often best qualified to make decisions that affect them.

Studies tell us that managers spend a significant portion of their time in meetings. Undoubtedly, a large portion of that time is involved with defining problems, arriving at solutions to those problems, and determining the means for implementing the solutions. It's possible, in fact, for groups to be assigned any of the eight steps in the decision-making process.

WHAT ARE THE ADVANTAGES OF GROUP DECISION MAKING?

Individual and group decisions have their own set of strengths. Neither is ideal for all situations. Let's begin by reviewing the advantages that group decisions have over individual decisions.

Group decisions provide more complete information than do individual ones.[24] There is often truth to the saying that two heads are better than one. A group will bring a diversity of experiences and perspectives to the decision process that an individual acting alone cannot.[25] Groups also generate more alternatives. Because groups have a greater quantity and diversity of information, they can identify more alternatives than can an individual. Quantity and diversity of information are greatest when group members represent different specialties. Furthermore, group decision making increases acceptance of a solution.[26] Many decisions fail after the final choice has been made because people do not accept the solution. However, if the people who will be affected by a certain solution, and who will help implement it, participate in the decision they will be more likely to accept the decision and encourage others to accept it. And finally, this process

Will this group of individuals make the "best" decision. Research tells us that using a group to make a decision can result in more effective decisions. But, if pressure to conform is applied, a quality decision may be jeopardized. This is what Irving Janis called the "groupthink" phenomenon.

increases legitimacy. The group decision-making process is consistent with democratic ideals; therefore, decisions made by groups may be perceived as more legitimate than decisions made by a single person. The fact that the individual decision maker has complete power and has not consulted others can create a perception that a decision was made autocratically and arbitrarily.

WHAT ARE THE DISADVANTAGES OF GROUP DECISION MAKING?

If groups are so good, how did the phrase "a camel is a racehorse put together by a committee" become so popular? The answer, of course, is that group decisions are not without their drawbacks. There are several major disadvantages. First, they are *time-consuming*. It takes time to assemble a group. In addition, the interaction that takes place once the group is in place is frequently inefficient. Groups almost always take more time to reach a solution than an individual would take to make the decision alone. There may also be *minority domination*, where members of a group are never perfectly equal.[27] They may differ in rank in the organization, experience, knowledge about the problem, influence on other members, verbal skills, assertiveness, and the like. This imbalance creates the opportunity for one or more members to dominate others in the group. A minority that dominates a group frequently has an undue influence on the final decision.

groupthink
The withholding by group members of different views in order to appear to be in agreement

Another problem focuses on the *pressures to conform* in groups. For instance, have you ever been in a situation in which several people were sitting around discussing a particular item and you had something to say that ran contrary to the consensus views of the group, but you remained silent? Were you surprised to learn later that others shared your views and also had remained silent? What you experienced is what Irving Janis termed **groupthink**.[28] This is a form of conformity in which group members withhold deviant, minority, or unpopular views in order to give the appearance of agreement. As a result, groupthink undermines critical thinking in the group and eventually harms the quality of the final decision. And, finally, there is *ambiguous responsibility*. Group members share responsibility, but who is actually responsible for the final outcome?[29] In an individual decision, it is clear who is responsible. In a group decision, the responsibility of any single member is watered down.

Groupthink applies to a situation in which a group's ability to appraise alternatives objectively and arrive at a quality decision is jeopardized. Because of pressures for conformity, groups often deter individuals from critically appraising unusual, minority, or unpopular views. Consequently, an individual's mental efficiency, reality testing, and moral judgment deteriorate. How does groupthink occur? The following are examples of situations in which groupthink is evident:

- Group members rationalize any resistance to the assumptions they have made.
- Members apply direct pressures on those who momentarily express doubts about any of the group's shared views or who question the validity of arguments favored by the majority.
- Those members who have doubts or hold differing points of view seek to avoid deviating from what appears to be group consensus.

- There is an illusion of unanimity. If someone does not speak, it is assumed that he or she is in full accord.

Does groupthink really hinder decision making? Yes. Several research studies have found that groupthink symptoms were associated with poorer-quality decision outcomes. But, groupthink can be minimized if the group is cohesive, fosters open discussion, and has an impartial leader who seeks input from all members.[30]

WHEN ARE GROUPS MOST EFFECTIVE?

Whether groups are more effective than individuals depends on the criteria you use for defining effectiveness, such as accuracy, speed, creativity, and acceptance. Group decisions tend to be more accurate. On average, groups tend to make better decisions than individuals, although groupthink may occur.[31] However, if decision effectiveness is defined in terms of speed, individuals are superior. If creativity is important, groups tend to be more effective than individuals. And if effectiveness means the degree of acceptance the final solution achieves, the nod again goes to the group.

The effectiveness of group decision making is also influenced by the size of the group. The larger the group, the greater the opportunity for heterogeneous representation. On the other hand, a larger group requires more coordination and more time to allow all members to contribute. What this means is that groups probably should not be too large: A minimum of five to a maximum of about fifteen members is best. Groups of five to seven individuals appear to be the most effective. Because five and seven are odd numbers, strict deadlocks are avoided. Effectiveness

Learning from Experience: One Manager's Reflection

James C. Ray Jr. Court Administrator, Hamilton County Juvenile Court, Cincinnati, OH

USING GROUPS TO MAKE DECISIONS

Describe the situation you faced. One of the strategic goals I needed to establish when I took over as Court Administrator was to create a team environment among the Court's seven divisions. Throughout the history of the organization the divisions of the Court had evolved on their own which had led to a lot of isolation and independence. In order to collectively move the organization ahead, I had to develop a sense of teamwork among the employees.

What action did you take? My initial action was in believing that a unified sense of purpose and clearly established goals, developed jointly throughout the ranks of the organization, would create enough positive momentum to move along the naysayers, especially those in critical or management positions.

What results occurred? The general result was a wave of positive involvement and enthusiasm by the employees. However, it quickly exposed those who were not "on board" and identified which of them needed the old environment to justify their existence. They began to create setbacks in the work processes.

What did/should you have done differently? I should have been better prepared for the setbacks caused by the naysayers in order to isolate or cushion their negative impact on the positive gains.

should not be considered without also assessing efficiency. Groups almost always stack up as a poor second in efficiency to the individual decision maker. With few exceptions, group decision making consumes more work hours than does individual decision making. In deciding whether to use groups, then, primary consideration must be given to assessing whether increases in effectiveness are more than enough to offset the losses in efficiency.

HOW CAN YOU IMPROVE GROUP DECISION MAKING?

When members of a group meet face-to-face and interact with one another, they create the potential for groupthink. They can censor themselves and pressure other group members into agreement. Three ways of making group decision making more creative are brainstorming, the nominal group technique, and electronic meetings.

brainstorming
An idea-generating process that encourages alternatives while withholding criticism

What is brainstorming? **Brainstorming** is a relatively simple technique for overcoming the pressures for conformity that retard the development of creative alternatives.[32] It utilizes an idea-generating process that specifically encourages any and all alternatives while withholding any criticism of those alternatives. In a typical brainstorming session, a half-dozen to a dozen people sit around a table. Of course, technology is changing where that "table" is. The group leader states the problem in a clear manner that is understood by all participants. Members then "freewheel" as many alternatives as they can in a given time. No criticism is allowed, and all the alternatives are recorded for later discussion and analysis.[33] Brainstorming, however, is merely a process for generating ideas. The next method, the nominal group technique, helps groups arrive at a preferred solution.[34]

nominal group technique
A decision-making technique in which group members are physically present but operate independently

How does the nominal group technique work? The **nominal group technique** restricts discussion during the decision-making process, hence the term. Group members must be present, as in a traditional committee meeting, but they are required to operate independently. They secretly write a list of general problem areas or potential solutions to a problem. The chief advantage of this technique is that it permits the group to meet formally but does not restrict independent thinking, as so often happens in the traditional interacting group.[35]

electronic meeting
A type of nominal group technique in which participants are linked by computer

How can electronic meetings enhance group decision making? The most recent approach to group decision making blends the nominal group technique with sophisticated computer technology. It is called the **electronic meeting**.

Once the technology for the meeting is in place, the concept is simple. Numerous people sit around a horseshoe-shaped table that is empty except for a series of computer terminals. Issues are presented to the participants, who type their responses onto their computer screens. Individual comments, as well as aggregate votes, are displayed on a projection screen in the room.

The major advantages of electronic meetings are anonymity, honesty, and speed.[36] Participants can anonymously type any message they want, and it will flash on the screen for all to see at the push of a board key. It allows people to be brutally honest with no penalty. And it is fast—chitchat is eliminated, discussions do not digress, and many participants can "talk" at once without interrupting the others.

Electronic meetings are significantly faster and much cheaper than traditional face-to-face meetings.[37] Nestlé, for instance, continues to use the approach for many of its meetings, especially those globally focused.[38] However, there may be drawbacks to electronic meetings. Those who type quickly can outshine those who may be verbally eloquent but lousy typists; those with the best ideas don't get credit for them; and the process lacks the informational richness of face-to-face oral communication. However, as this technology continues to expand, the future of group decision making is very likely to include extensive usage of electronic meetings.[39]

A variation of the electronic meeting is the video conference. By linking together media from different locations, people can have face-to-face meetings even when they are thousands of miles apart. This has enhanced feedback among the members, saved countless hours of business travel, and ultimately saved companies like Nestlé and Colgate-Palmolive hundreds of thousands of dollars. As a result, they are more effective in their meetings and have increased the efficiency in which decisions are made.[40]

Companies such as Colgate use video conferencing as a means of bringing people from all parts of the globe together to have input into decisions that are being made. This process is quicker than bringing everyone physically together—and clearly more cost effective for companies who use this technology.

NATIONAL CULTURE AND DECISION-MAKING PRACTICES

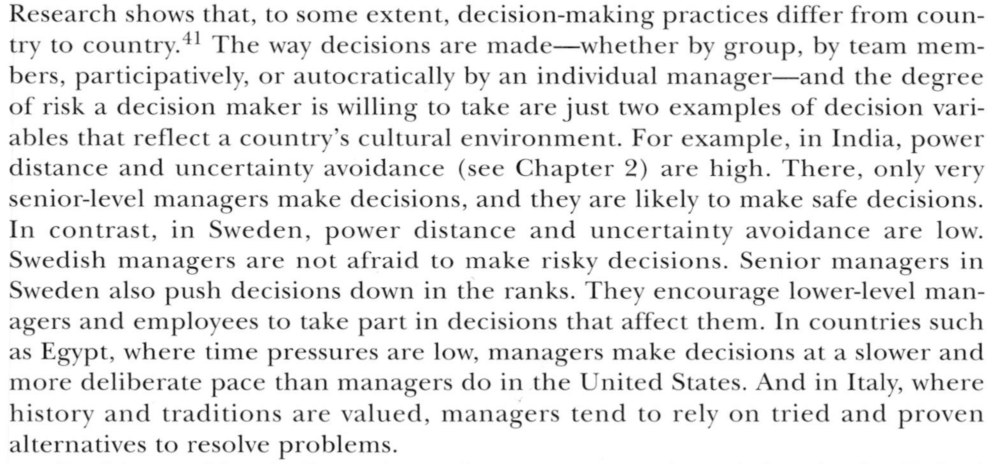

Research shows that, to some extent, decision-making practices differ from country to country.[41] The way decisions are made—whether by group, by team members, participatively, or autocratically by an individual manager—and the degree of risk a decision maker is willing to take are just two examples of decision variables that reflect a country's cultural environment. For example, in India, power distance and uncertainty avoidance (see Chapter 2) are high. There, only very senior-level managers make decisions, and they are likely to make safe decisions. In contrast, in Sweden, power distance and uncertainty avoidance are low. Swedish managers are not afraid to make risky decisions. Senior managers in Sweden also push decisions down in the ranks. They encourage lower-level managers and employees to take part in decisions that affect them. In countries such as Egypt, where time pressures are low, managers make decisions at a slower and more deliberate pace than managers do in the United States. And in Italy, where history and traditions are valued, managers tend to rely on tried and proven alternatives to resolve problems.

Decision making in Japan is much more group oriented than in the United States.[42] The Japanese value conformity and cooperation. Before making decisions, Japanese CEOs collect a large amount of information, which is then used in consensus-forming group decisions called **Ringisei**. Because employees in Japanese organizations have high job security, managerial decisions take a long-term perspective rather than focus on short-term profits, as is often the practice in the United States.

ringisei
Japanese consensus-forming group decisions

Senior managers in France and Germany also adapt their decision styles to their countries' cultures. In France, for instance, autocratic decision making is widely practiced, and managers avoid risks. Managerial styles in Germany reflect the German culture's concern for structure and order. Consequently, there are extensive rules and regulations in German organizations. Managers have well-defined responsibilities and accept that decisions must go through channels.

As managers deal with employees from diverse cultures, they need to recognize common and accepted behavior when asking them to make decisions. Some individuals may not be as comfortable as other with being closely involved in decision making, or they may not be willing to experiment with something radically different. Managers who accommodate the diversity in decision-making philosophies and practices can expect a high payoff if they capture the perspectives and strengths that a diverse workforce offers.

Review, Comprehension, Application

CHAPTER SUMMARY

How will you know if you fulfilled the Learning Outcomes on page 104? You will have fulfilled the Learning Outcomes if you are able to:

1. **Describe the steps in the decision-making process.** Decision making is an eight-step process: (1) identify a problem, (2) identify decision criteria, (3) allocate weights to the criteria, (4) develop alternatives, (5) analyze alternatives, (6) select an alternative, (7) implement the alternative, and (8) evaluate decision effectiveness.
2. **Identify the assumptions of the rational decision-making model.** The rational decision model assumes that the decision maker can identify a clear problem, has no goal conflict, knows all options, has a clear preference ordering, keeps all preferences constant, has no time or cost constraints, and selects a final choice that maximizes his or her economic payoff.
3. **Explain the limits to rationality.** Rationality assumptions do not apply in many situations because problems are not simple, goals are not clear, alternatives are many, and there are time and cost constraints. In addition, decision makers sometimes increase commitment to a previous choice to confirm its original correctness; prior decision precedents constrain current choices, and most organizational cultures discourage taking risks and searching for innovative alternatives.
4. **Define certainty, risk, and uncertainty as they relate to decision making.** Certainty implies that a manager can make an accurate decision because the outcome of every alternative is known. Because this is often not the case, risk involves assigning probabilities to outcomes that may result. When decision makers have neither full knowledge of the problem nor a reasonable probability of what may happen, they must make their decisions under a condition of uncertainty.
5. **Describe the actions of the bounded-rational decision maker.** In the bounded-rational decision-making process, decision makers construct simplified models that extract essential features from the problems they face without capturing all their complexity. They then attempt to act rationally within this simplified model.
6. **Identify the two types of decision problems and the two types of decisions that are used to solve them.** Managers face well-structured and ill-structured problems. Well-structured problems are straightforward, familiar, easily defined, and solved using programmed decisions such as procedures, rules, and policies. Ill-structured problems, on the other hand, are new or unusual, involve ambiguous or incomplete information, and are solved using nonprogrammed decisions.
7. **Define heuristics and explain how they affect the decision-making process.** Heuristics are shortcuts decision makers can take to speed up the decision-making process. Heuristics commonly exist in two forms—availability and representative. Both types create biases in a decision maker's judgment.
8. **Identify four decision-making styles.** The four decision-making styles are the directive style (characterized by low tolerance for ambiguity and a rational way of thinking), the analytic style (characterized by high tolerance for ambiguity combined with a rational way of thinking), the conceptual style (characterized by a very broad outlook and a tendency to look at many alternatives), and the behavioral style (characterized by intuitive thinking and a low tolerance for uncertainty).
9. **Describe the advantages and disadvantages of group decisions.** Groups offer certain advantages—more complete information, more alternatives, increased acceptance of a solution, and greater legitimacy. On the other hand, groups are time-consuming, can be dominated by a minority, create pressures to conform, and cloud responsibility.
10. **Explain three techniques for improving group decision making.** Three ways of improving group decision making are brainstorming (utilizing an idea-generating process that specifically encourages any and all alternatives while withholding any criticism of those alternatives), the nominal group technique (a technique that restricts discussion during the decision-making process), and electronic meetings (the most recent approach to group decision making, which blends the nominal group technique with sophisticated computer technology).

COMPANION WEBSITE

We invite you to visit the Robbins/DeCenzo companion Website at **www.prenhall.com/robbins** for this chapter's Internet resources, including an online study guide, Internet exercises, and "In the News" with full text articles provided by XanEdu.

READING FOR COMPREHENSION

1. Explain how decision making is related to the planning process.
2. How is implementation important to the decision-making process?
3. What is a satisficing decision? How does it differ from a maximizing decision?
4. How do creativity, certainty, risk, and uncertainty affect individuals when they make a decision?
5. How does escalation of commitment affect decision making?
6. What is groupthink? What are its implications for decision making?

LINKING CONCEPTS TO PRACTICE

1. Describe a decision you have made that closely aligns with the assumptions of perfect rationality. Compare this with the process you used to select your college. Is there a departure from the rational model in your college decision? Explain.
2. Is the order in which alternatives are considered more critical under assumptions of perfect rationality or bounded rationality? Why?
3. Explain how a manager might deal with making decisions under conditions of uncertainty.
4. "With more and more managers using computers, they'll be able to make more rational decisions." Do you agree or disagree with the statement? Why?
5. Why do you think organizations have increased the use of groups for making decisions during the past 20 years? When would you recommend using groups to make decisions?

VIDEO CASE APPLICATION

Mindbox: Using Technology to Make Better Decisions Faster

The product may be artificial intelligence, but the focus is on meeting human needs. At Mindbox headquarters, just 22 miles north of Califomia's Golden Gate Bridge, the goal is to turn every interface with its decision-making software into a positive experience for the consumer. Launched as an independent company in September 2000, MindBox already has 200 satisfied customers. By incorporating MindBox's artificial intelligence applications into their business operations these customers have been able to save time and money, while making optimum use of human resources.

According to MindBox president and CEO Richard Barfus, intelligent decision-making technology "is very simply the process of automating what is generally thought to be the steps people go through to make decisions." The opportunities for its use are endless. Ford Motor Company uses MindBox's decision-making software to evaluate credit applications faxed in from auto dealers and extends credit to qualifying customers in real time while they are in the showroom. Bell Atlantic uses it to guide customer service representatives through the sales process in order to correctly target specific customer requirements.

"MindBox clients are saving up to 40 percent in costs and at the same time increasing revenues close to 30 percent," says Paige Mazzoni, vice president of marketing. MindBox solutions saves Countrywide Home Loans over $5 million annually in underwriting costs, and Swiss Bank reaps a yearly payback of $2 million. Upland Mortgage recorded increased revenue within weeks of implementing MindBox's intelligent decision-making technology.

Upland Mortgage and MindBox worked together to identify many little pieces of information that needed to be analyzed in order to structure a loan option. The artificial intelligence system now analyzes credit, checks eligibility, and selects the most appropriate options to offer the applicant. Once the client has made his or her selection, the program underwrites the deal, explains policies, calculates monthly savings and other benefits of the loan, and lists the required stipulations needed to close the loan.[43] According to Milt Riseman, chairman of Upland Mortgage, the company has been able to close twice as many loan applications as before.

MindBox technology "makes it possible for us to maintain better relationships with our customers," says Riseman. "Fortunately, the information they input can be saved to start the process one day and finish it the next—or whenever it's most convenient for them," he says. "This system enables us to decrease the processing time of a loan from weeks to days. We not only save money on every loan we process, we can also process more loans. This increases profits and market share for the company, while it lowers the loans to its customers."

With over 100 years of combined experience, the management team at MindBox has engineered an artificial intelligence system that seems to be "the antidote to Web-loan phobia."[44] Customers get individually tailored, automatic interactions. Richard Barfus likens the system to putting the combined servces of the best broker and the best underwriter at the user's disposal.

MindBox applications have quelled the fear of even the most Web-averse clients. Sandra Forman, a middle-aged Philadelphia homeowner who tried Upland Mortgage's EasyLoan Advisor program for the first time, says the process was so simple that she wouldn't hesitate to go into another business venture using the Internet.

MindBox is true to Mr. Barfus's basic tenet of "ensuring the ease of the end user, the customer's customer." Training sites at corporate headquarters and in the Atlanta, Georgia, area offer clients hand-on experience as well as formal classroom instruction. Every solution melds together case-based (judgment and experience) and rules-based (business-specific regulations) reasoning. As the World Wide Web becomes an essential business channel, MindBox's decision-making systems promise users the flexibility they need to compete.

A winner of numerous awards from The American Association of Artificial Intelligence Awards, MindBox is winning the enthusiastic support of its customers and its "customers' customers" as well.

Questions

1. Did using MindBox's decision-making technology result in a maximizing decision or a satisficing decision for Sandra Forman? Why?
2. Was Upland Mortgage's decision to invest in MindBox's Web-based mortgage underwriting system a programmed decision or an unprogrammed decision? Why?
3. Would you define Sandra Forman's decision-making style as directive, analytic, conceptual or behavioral? Why?
4. BusinessNow has just taken you through a loan application process using MindBox's intelligent decision-making software. Now think of three potential uses for MindBox's decision-making technology that are *not* mentioned in the video. Try not to use the examples in your text. Be creative, think globally, and explain your choices.

Management Workshop

Team Skill-Building Exercise

Individual Versus Group Decisions

Objective To contrast individual and group decision making.

Time 15 minutes

Step 1 You have 5 minutes to read the following story and individually respond to each of the 11 statements as either true, false, or unknown. Begin.

The Story

A salesclerk had just turned off the lights in the store when a man appeared and demanded money. The owner opened a cash register. The contents of the cash register were scooped up, and the man sped away. A member of the police force was notified promptly.

Statements About the Story

1. A man appeared after the owner had turned off his store lights. True, false, or unknown?
2. The robber was a man. True, false, or unknown?
3. The man did not demand money. True, false, or unknown?
4. The man who opened the cash register was the owner. True, false, or unknown?
5. The store owner scooped up the contents of the cash register and ran away. True, false, or unknown?
6. Someone opened a cash register. True, false, or unknown?
7. After the man who demanded the money scooped up the contents of the cash register, he ran away. True, false, or unknown?

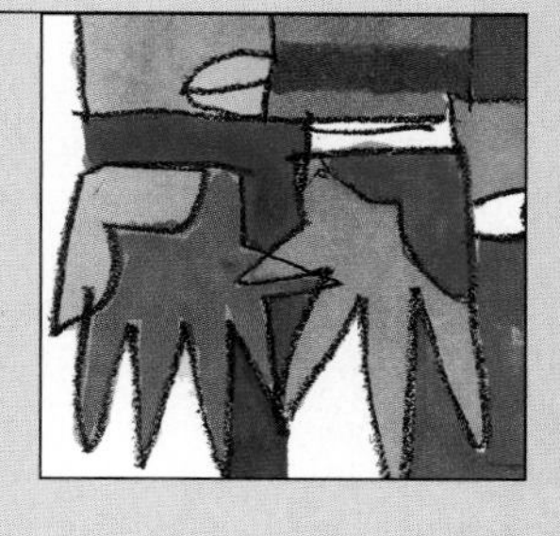

8. The cash register contained money, but the story does not state how much. True, false, or unknown?
9. The robber demanded money of the owner. True, false, or unknown?
10. The story concerns a series of events in which only three persons are referred to: the owner of the store, a man who demanded money, and a member of the police force. True, false, or unknown?
11. The following events in the story are true: Someone demanded money; a cash register was opened; its contents were scooped up; a man dashed out of the store. True, false, or unknown?

Step 2 After you have answered the 11 questions individually, form groups of 4 or 5 members each. The groups have 10 minutes to discuss their answers and agree on the correct answers to each of the 11 statements.

Step 3 Your instructor will give you the actual correct answers. How many correct answers did you get at the conclusion of step 1? How many did your group achieve at the conclusion of step 2? Did the group outperform the average individual? The best individual? Discuss the implications of these results.

Understanding Yourself

Before you can develop other people, you must understand your present strengths. To assist in this learning process, we encourage you to complete the following self-assessment from the Prentice Hall Self-Assessment Library 2.0:

- How Intuitive Am I? (#18)

After you complete this assessment, we suggest that you print out the results and store them as part of your "portfolio of learning."

Developing Your Creativity Skill

Becoming Creative

About the Skill

Creativity is a frame of mind. You need to open your mind to new ideas. Every individual has the ability to be creative, but many people simply don't try to develop that ability. In contemporary organizations, those people may have difficulty being successful. Dynamic environments and managerial chaos require that managers look for new and innovative ways to attain their goals as well as those of the organization.

Steps in Practicing the Skill

1. Think of yourself as creative. Although this is a simple suggestion, research shows that if you think you can't be creative, you won't be. Believing in yourself is the first step in becoming more creative.
2. Pay attention to your intuition. Every individual's subconscious mind works well. Sometimes answers come to you when least expected. For example, when you are about to go to sleep, your relaxed mind sometimes whispers a solution to a problem you're facing. Listen to that voice. In fact, most creative people keep a notepad near their bed and write down those great ideas when they occur. That way, they don't forget them.
3. Move away from your comfort zone. Every individual has a comfort zone in which certainty exists. But creativity and the known often do not mix. To be creative, you need to move away from the status quo and focus your mind on something new.
4. Engage in activities that put you outside your comfort zone. You not only must think differently; you need to do things differently and, thus, challenge yourself. Learning to play a musical instrument or learning a foreign language, for example, opens your mind to a new challenge.
5. Seek a change of scenery. People are often creatures of habit. Creative people force themselves out of their habits by changing their scenery. That may mean going into a quiet and serene area where you can be alone with your thoughts.
6. Find several right answers. In the discussion of bounded rationality, we said that people seek solutions that are good enough. Being creative means continuing to look for other solutions even when you think you have solved the problem. A better, more creative solution just might be found.
7. Play your own devil's advocate. Challenging yourself to defend your solutions helps you to develop confidence in your creative efforts. Second guessing yourself may also help you find more creative solutions.
8. Believe in finding a workable solution. Like believing in yourself, you also need to believe in your ideas. If you don't think you can find a solution, you probably won't.
9. Brainstorm with others. Being creative is not a solitary activity. Bouncing ideas off others creates a synergistic effect.
10. Turn creative ideas into action. Coming up with ideas is only half the process. Once the ideas are generated, they must be implemented. Keeping great ideas in your mind or on paper that no one will read does little to expand your creative abilities.

Practicing the Skill

How many words can you make using the letters in the word *brainstorm*? There are at least 95.

Developing Your Diagnostic and Analytical Skills

On the Air with Radio One

Cathy Hughes is an individual on a mission.[45] Having spent several years studying broadcasting and working as a radio broadcaster, she dreamed of one day becoming a station owner. Cathy knew that owning a radio station would not be an easy task. There's a lot of information that must be gathered and understood. For example, how does one go about getting FCC licensing? How does one obtain the necessary advertising to ensure an influx of revenues to operate the station? How does one select a program format so that a large listening audience can be generated—which in turn brings in more advertising dollars? Answers to such questions for Hughes meant dedicating herself to researching the facts, generating a database, and making appropriate decisions. Once prepared, and building on her knowledge and experience, Cathy launched Radio One, Inc.

To Cathy, building a successful company requires intuition, concrete plans, astute business savvy, and the ability to make timely and accurate decisions. She focused on one listener, one community at a time. And she has been successful. Today she owns about 30 radio stations in nine of the top 20 markets for "African-American listeners," building a $2 billion organization.

What helped her along the way? Cathy worked in almost every job in the radio business that is required to bring a radio program to life. For her, doing these jobs gave her more complete information to work from and gave her some level of confidence in running such a risky venture.

Questions

1. What decisions did Cathy Hughes make that you believe helped her build the Radio One empire?
2. What role do you believe social responsibility plays when Radio One attempts to enter into a new market?
3. How might business software, like that of Business Objects, help a company like Radio One?

Enhancing Your Communication Skills

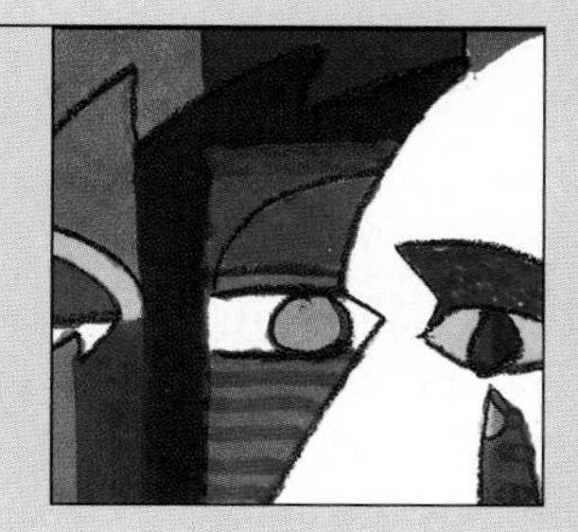

1. People often make decisions that are good enough, which may not be the best solution. Build a case that presents both sides of this argument. In your discussion, emphasize when good enough may be appropriate and when the "best solution" may be critical. Provide specific examples in your presentation.
2. Describe a situation in which a decision you made was influenced by availability or representative heuristics. In retrospect, provide an evaluation of how effective that decision was.
3. Research the question of whether there is a difference in how men and women make decisions. Present your results.

QUANTITATIVE MODULE

Quantitative Decision-Making Aids

In this module we'll look at several decision-making aids and techniques, as well as some popular tools for managing projects.[1] Specifically, we'll introduce you to payoff matrices, decision trees, break-even analysis, ratio analysis, linear programming, queuing theory, and economic order quantity. The purpose of each method is to provide managers with a tool to assist in the decision-making process and to provide more complete information to make better-informed decisions.

PAYOFF MATRICES

In Chapter 4 we introduced you to the topic of uncertainty and how it can affect decision making. Although uncertainty plays a critical role by limiting the amount of information available to managers, another factor is their psychological orientation. For instance, the optimistic manager will typically follow a *maximax* choice (maximizing the maximum possible payoff); the pessimist will often pursue a *maximin* choice (maximizing the minimum possible payoff); and the manager who desires to minimize his "regret" will opt for a *minimax* choice. Let's briefly look at these different approaches using an example.

Consider the case of a marketing manager at Visa International in New York. He has determined four possible strategies (we'll label these S1, S2, S3, and S4) for promoting the Visa card throughout the northeastern United States. However, he is also aware that one of his major competitors, American Express, has three competitive strategies (CA1, CA2, and CA3) for promoting its own card in the same region. In this case, we'll assume that the Visa executive has no previous knowledge that would allow him to place probabilities on the success of any of his four strategies. With these facts, the Visa card manager formulates the matrix in Exhibit QM–1 to show the various Visa strategies and the resulting profit to Visa, depending on the competitive action chosen by American Express.

In this example, if our Visa manager is an optimist, he'll choose S4 because that could produce the largest possible gain ($28 million). Note that this choice maxi-

EXHIBIT QM–1
Payoff Matrix for VISA

VISA MARKETING STRATEGY	AMERICAN EXPRESS'S RESPONSE (IN MILLIONS OF $)		
	CA1	*CA2*	*CA3*
S1	13	14	11
S2	9	15	18
S3	24	21	15
S4	18	14	28

EXHIBIT QM–2
Regret Matrix for VISA

VISA MARKETING STRATEGY	AMERICAN EXPRESS'S RESPONSE (IN MILLIONS OF $)		
	CA1	*CA2*	*CA3*
S1	11	7	17
S2	15	6	10
S3	0	0	13
S4	6	7	0

mizes the maximum possible gain (maximax choice). If our manager is a pessimist, he'll assume only the worst can occur. The worst outcome for each strategy is as follows: S1 = $11 million; S2 = $9 million; S3 = $15 million; and S4 = $14 million. These are the most pessimistic outcomes from each strategy. Following the maximin choice, the manager would maximize the minimum payoff—in other words, he'd select S3.

In the third approach, managers recognize that once a decision is made it will not necessarily result in the most profitable payoff. There may be a "regret" of profits foregone (given up)—regret referring to the amount of money that could have been made had a different strategy been used. Managers calculate regret by subtracting all possible payoffs in each category from the maximum possible payoff for each given—in this case, for each competitive action. For our Visa manager, the highest payoff, given that American Express engages in CA1, CA2, or CA3, is $24 million, $21 million, or $28 million, respectively (the highest number in each column). Subtracting the payoffs in Exhibit QM–1 from these figures produces the results in Exhibit QM–2.

The maximum regrets are S1 = $17 million; S2 = $15 million; S3 = $13 million; and S4 = $7 million. The minimax choice minimizes the maximum regret, so our Visa manager would choose S4. By making this choice, he'll never have a regret of profits foregone of more than $7 million. This result contrasts, for example, with a regret of $15 million had he chosen S2 and American Express had taken CA1.

DECISION TREES

decision trees
Useful quantitative tool to analyze decisions that involve a progression of decisions

Decision trees are a useful way to analyze hiring, marketing, investment, equipment purchases, pricing, and similar decisions that involve a progression of decisions. They're called decision trees because, when diagramed, they look a lot like a tree with branches. Typical decision trees encompass expected value analysis by assigning probabilities to each possible outcome and calculating payoffs for each decision path.

Exhibit QM–3 illustrates a decision facing Laurel Singleton, the midwestern region site selection supervisor for Barnes & Noble bookstores. Laurel supervises a small group of specialists who analyze potential locations and make store site recommendations to the midwestern region's director. The lease on the company's store in Cleveland, Ohio, is expiring, and the landlord has decided not to renew it. Laurel and her group have to make a relocation recommendation to the regional director.

Laurel's group has identified an excellent site in a nearby shopping mall in North Olmsted. The mall owner has offered her two comparable locations: one with 12,000 square feet (the same as she has now) and the other a larger, 20,000-square-foot space. Laurel has an initial decision to make about whether to recommend renting the larger or smaller location. If she chooses the larger space and the economy is strong, she estimates the store will make a $320,000 profit. However, if the economy is poor, the high operating costs of the larger store will mean that the profit will be only $50,000. With the smaller store, she estimates the profit at $240,000 with a good economy and $130,000 with a poor one.

EXHIBIT QM–3

Decision Tree and Expected Values for Renting a Large or Small Retail Space

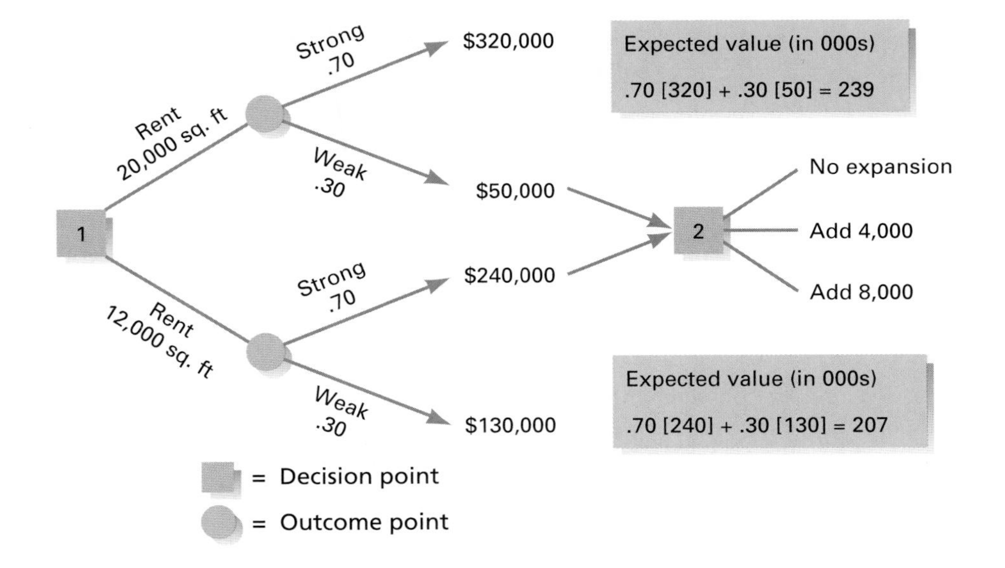

As you can see from Exhibit QM–3, the expected value for the larger store is \$239,000 [(.70 × 320) + (.30 × 50)]. The expected value for the smaller store is \$207,000 [(.70 × 240) + (.30 × 130)]. Given these projections, Laurel is planning to recommend the rental of the larger store space. What if Laurel wants to consider the implications of initially renting the smaller space and then expanding if the economy picks up? She can extend the decision tree to include this second decision point. She has calculated three options: no expansion, adding 4,000 square feet, and adding 8,000 square feet. Following the approach used for Decision Point 1, she could calculate the profit potential by extending the branches on the tree and calculating expected values for the various options.

BREAKEVEN ANALYSIS

How many units of a product must an organization sell in order to break even—that is, to have neither profit nor loss? A manager might want to know the minimum number of units that must be sold to achieve his or her profit objective or whether a current product should continue to be sold or should be dropped from the organization's product line. **Breakeven analysis** is a widely used technique for helping managers make profit projections.[2]

breakeven analysis
A technique for identifying the point at which total revenue is just sufficient to cover total costs

Breakeven analysis is a simplistic formulation, yet it is valuable to managers because it points out the relationship among revenues, costs, and profits. To compute the breakeven point (BE), the manager needs to know the unit price of the product being sold (P), the variable cost per unit (VC), and the total fixed costs (TFC).

An organization breaks even when its total revenue is just enough to equal its total costs. But total cost has two parts: a fixed component and a variable component. Fixed costs are expenses that do not change, regardless of volume, such as insurance premiums and property taxes. Fixed costs, of course, are fixed only in the short term because, in the long run, commitments terminate and are thus subject to variation. Variable costs change in proportion to output and include raw materials, labor costs, and energy costs.

The breakeven point can be computed graphically or by using the following formula:

$$BE = \left[TFC/P - VC\right]$$

This formula tells us that (1) total revenue will equal total cost when we sell enough units at a price that covers all variable unit costs, and (2) the difference

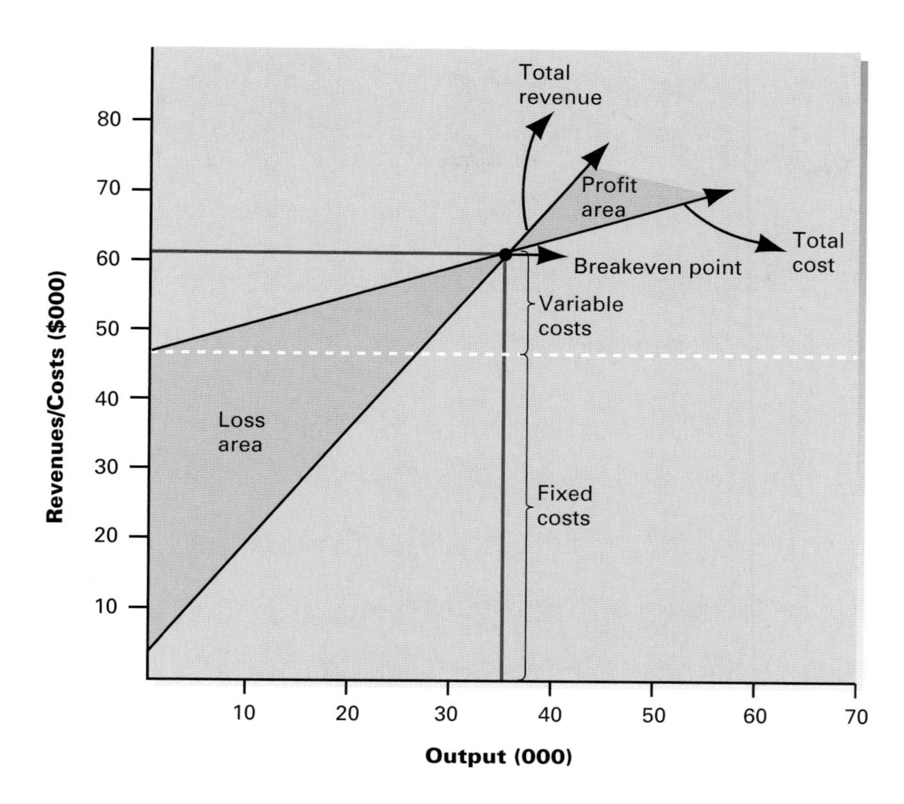

EXHIBIT QM–4
The Breakeven Analysis

between price and variable costs, when multiplied by the number of units sold, equals the fixed costs.

When is breakeven analysis useful? To demonstrate, assume that, at Wil's Atlanta Espresso, Wil charges $1.75 for an average cup of coffee. If his fixed costs (salary, insurance, etc.) are $47,000 a year and the variable costs for each cup of espresso are $0.40, Todd can compute his breakeven point as follows: $47,000/(1.75 – 0.40) = 34,815 (about 670 cups of espresso sold each week), or when annual revenues are approximately $60,926. This same relationship is shown graphically in Exhibit QM–4.

How can breakeven analysis serve as a planning and decision-making tool? As a planning tool, breakeven analysis could help Wil set his sales objective. For example, he could establish the profit he wants and then work backward to determine what sales level is needed to reach that profit. As a decision-making tool, breakeven analysis could also tell Wil how much volume has to increase in order to break even if he is currently operating at a loss, or how much volume he can afford to lose and still break even if he is currently operating profitably. In some cases, such as the management of professional sports franchises, breakeven analysis has shown the projected volume of ticket sales required to cover all costs to be so unrealistically high that management's best choice is to sell or close the business.

RATIO ANALYSIS

We know that investors and stock analysts make regular use of an organization's financial documents to assess its worth. These documents can be analyzed by managers as planning and decision-making aids.

Managers often want to examine their organization's balance and income statements to analyze key ratios, that is, to compare two significant figures from the financial statements and express them as a percentage or ratio. This practice allows managers to compare current financial performance with that of previous periods and other organizations in the same industry. Some of the more useful ratios evaluate liquidity, leverage, operations, and profitability. These are summarized in Exhibit QM–5.

EXHIBIT QM–5 Popular Financial Controls

OBJECTIVE	RATIO	CALCULATION	MEANING
Liquidity test	Current ratio	Current assets / Current liabilities	Tests the organization's ability to meet short-term obligations
	Acid test	Current assets level inventories / Current liabilities	Tests liquidity more accurately when inventories turn over slowly or are difficult to sell
Leverage test	Debt to assets	Total debt / Total assets	The higher the ratio, the more leveraged the organization
	Times interest earned	Profits before interest and taxes / Total interest charges	Measures how far profits can decline before the organization is unable to meet its interest expenses
Operations test	Inventory turnover	Cost of sales / Inventory	The higher the ratio, the more efficiently inventory assets are being used
	Total assets turnover	Revenues / Total assets	The fewer assets used to achieve a given level of sales, the more efficiently management is using the organization's total assets
Profitability	Profit margin on revenues	Net profit after taxes / Total revenues	Identifies the profits that various products are generating
	Return on investment	Net profit after taxes / Total assets	Measures the efficiency of assets to generate profits

What are liquidity ratios? *Liquidity* is a measure of the organization's ability to convert assets into cash in order that debts can be met. The most popular liquidity ratios are the current ratio and the acid test ratio.

The *current ratio* is defined as the organization's current assets divided by its current liabilities. Although there is no magic number that is considered safe, the accountant's rule of thumb for the current ratio is 2 : 1. A significantly higher ratio usually suggests that management is not getting the best return on its assets. A ratio at or below 1 : 1 indicates potential difficulty in meeting short-term obligations (accounts payable, interest payments, salaries, taxes, and so forth).

The *acid test ratio* is the same as the current ratio except that current assets are reduced by the dollar value of inventory held. When inventories turn slowly or are difficult to sell, the acid test ratio may more accurately represent the organization's true liquidity. That is, a high current ratio heavily based on an inventory that is difficult to sell overstates the organization's true liquidity. Accordingly, accountants typically consider an acid test ratio of 1 : 1 to be reasonable.

Leverage ratios refer to the use of borrowed funds to operate and expand an organization. The advantage of leverage occurs when funds can be used to earn a rate of return well above the cost of those funds. For instance, if management can borrow money at 8 percent and can earn 12 percent on it internally, it makes good sense to borrow, but there are risks to over-leveraging. The interest on the debt can be a drain on the organization's cash resources and can, in extreme cases, drive an organization into bankruptcy. The objective, therefore, is to use debt wisely. Leverage ratios such as *debt to assets ratio* (computed by dividing total debt by total assets) or the *times interest earned ratio* (computed as profits before interest and taxes divided by total interest charges) can help managers control debt levels.

Operating ratios describe how efficiently management is using the organization's resources. The most popular operating ratios are inventory turnover and total assets turnover. The *inventory turnover ratio* is defined as revenue divided by inventory. The higher the ratio, the more efficiently inventory assets are being used. Revenue divided by total assets represents an organization's *total assets turnover ratio.* It measures the level of assets needed to generate the organization's revenue. The fewer the assets used to achieve a given level of revenue, the more efficiently management is using the organization's total assets.

Profit-making organizations want to measure their effectiveness and efficiency. Profitability ratios serve such a purpose. The better known of these are profit margin-on-revenues and return-on-investment ratios.

Managers of organizations that have a variety of products want to put their efforts into those products that are most profitable. The *profit margin on revenues ratio,* computed as net profit after taxes divided by total revenues, is a measure of profits per dollar revenues.

One of the most widely used measures of a business firm's profitability is the *return on investment ratio.* It's calculated by multiplying revenues/investments by profits/revenues. This percentage recognizes that absolute profits must be placed in the context of assets required to generate those profits.

LINEAR PROGRAMMING

Maria Hernandez owns a software development company. One product line involves designing and producing software that detects and removes viruses. The software comes in two formats: Windows and MAC versions. She can sell all of these products that she can produce. That, however, is her dilemma. The two formats go through the same production departments. How many of each type should she make to maximize her profits?

A close look at Hernandez's operation tells us she can use a mathematical technique called **linear programming** to solve her resource allocation dilemma. As we will show, linear programming is applicable to her problem, but it cannot be applied to all resource allocation situations. Besides requiring limited resources and the objective of optimization, it requires that there be alternative ways of combining resources to produce a number of output mixes. There must also be a linear relationship between variables. This means that a change in one variable will be accompanied by an exactly proportional change in the other. For Hernandez's business, this condition would be met if it took exactly twice the time to produce two diskettes—irrespective of format—as it took to produce one.

linear programming
A mathematical technique that solves resource allocation problems

Many different types of problems can be solved with linear programming. Selecting transportation routes that minimize shipping costs, allocating a limited advertising budget among various product brands, making the optimum assignment of personnel among projects, and determining how much of each product to make with a limited number of resources are just a few. To give you some idea of how linear programming is useful, let's return to Hernandez's situation. Fortunately, her problem is relatively simple, so we can solve it rather quickly. For complex linear programming problems, computer software has been designed specifically to help develop solutions.

First, we need to establish some facts about the business. She has computed the profit margins to be \$18 for the Windows format and \$24 for the MAC. She can therefore express her objective function as: maximum profit = \$18 R + \$24 S, where R is the number of Windows-based CDs produced and S is the number of MAC CDs. In addition, she knows how long it takes to produce each format and the monthly production capacity for virus software [2,400 hours in design and 900 hours in production] (see Exhibit QM–6). The production capacity numbers act as constraints on her overall capacity. Now Hernandez can establish her constraint equations:

$$4R + 6S < 2{,}400$$
$$2R + 2S < 900$$

EXHIBIT QM–6 Production Data for Virus Software

	Number of Hours Required per Unit		
DEPARTMENT	**WINDOWS VERSION**	**MAC VERSION**	**MONTHLY PRODUCT CAPACITY (HOURS)**
Design	4	6	2,400
Manufacture	2.0	2.0	900
Profit per unit	$18	$24	

Of course, because a software format cannot be produced in a volume less than zero, Maria can also state that R > 0 and S > 0. She has graphed her solution as shown in Exhibit QM–7. The yellow shaded area represents the options that do not exceed the capacity of either department. What does this mean? We know that total design capacity is 2,400 hours. So if Maria decides to design only Windows format, the maximum number she can produce is 600 (2,400 hours ÷ 4 hours of design for each Windows version). If she decides to produce all MAC versions, the maximum she can produce is 400 (2,400 hours ÷ 6 hours of design for MAC). This design constraint is shown in Exhibit QM–7 as line BC. The other constraint Maria faces is that of production. The maximum of either format she can produce is 450, because each takes two hours to copy, verify, and package. This production constraint is shown in the exhibit as line DE.

Hernandez's optimal resource allocation will be defined at one of the corners of this feasibility region (area ACFD). Point F provides the maximum profits within the constraints stated. At point A, profits would be zero because neither virus software version is being produced. At points C and D, profits would be $9,600 (400 units @ $24) and $8,100 (450 units @ $18), respectively. At point F profits would be $9,900 (150 DOS units @ $18 + 300 MAC units @ $24).[3]

QUEUING THEORY

queuing theory
A technique that balances the cost of having a waiting line against the cost of service to maintain that line

You are a supervisor for a branch of Wachovia Bank outside of Charleston, SC. One of the decisions you have to make is how many of the six cashier stations to keep open at any given time. **Queuing theory**, or what is frequently referred to as waiting line theory, could help you decide.

EXHIBIT QM–7

Graphical Solution to Hernandez's Linear Programming Problem

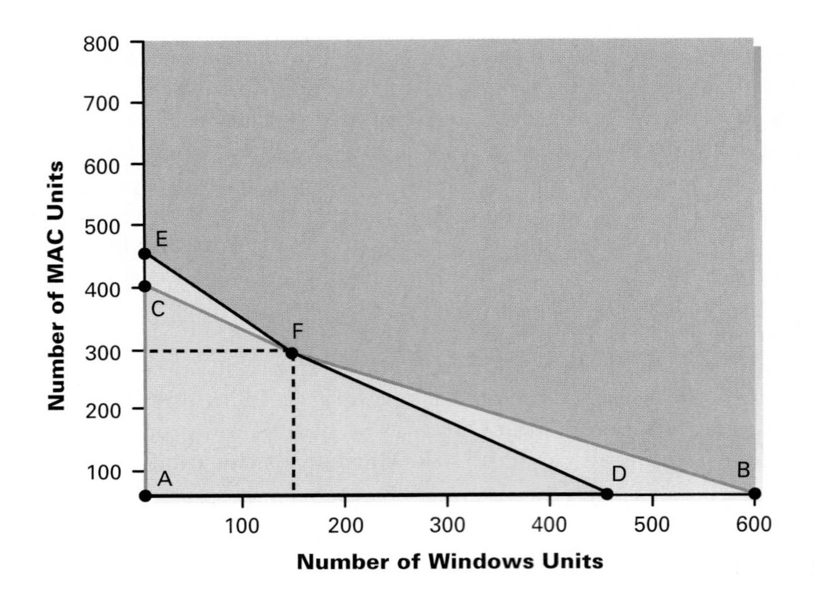

A decision that involves balancing the cost of having a waiting line against the cost of service to maintain that line can be made easier with queuing theory. This includes such common situations as determining how many gas pumps are needed at gas stations, tellers at bank windows, toll takers at toll booths, or check-in lines at airline ticket counters. In each situation, management wants to minimize cost by having as few stations open as possible yet not so few as to test the patience of customers. In our teller example, on certain days (such as the first of every month and Fridays) you could open all six windows and keep waiting time to a minimum, or you could open only one, minimize staffing costs, and risk a riot.

The mathematics underlying queuing theory is beyond the scope of this book, but you can see how the theory works in our simple example. You have six tellers working for you, but you want to know whether you can get by with only one window open during an average morning. You consider twelve minutes to be the longest you would expect any customer to wait patiently in line. If it takes four minutes, on average, to serve each customer, the line should not be permitted to get longer than three deep (12 minutes ÷ 4 minutes per customer = 3 customers). If you know from past experience that, during the morning, people arrive at the average rate of two per minute, you can calculate the probability (P) of customers waiting in line as follows:

$$P_n = \left[\frac{\text{Arrival Rate}}{1 - \text{Service Rate}}\right] \times \left[\frac{\text{Arrival Rate}}{\text{Service Rate}}\right]^n$$

where $n = 3$ customers, arrival rate = 2 per minute, and service rate = 4 minutes per customer.

Putting these numbers into the above formula generates the following:

$$P_n = [1 - 2/4] \times [2/4]^3 = (1/2) \times (8/64) = (8/128) = 0.0625$$

What does a P of 0.0625 mean? It tells you that the likelihood of having more than three customers in line during the average morning is 1 chance in 16. Are you willing to live with four or more customers in line 6 percent of the time? If so, keeping one teller window open will be enough. If not, you will have to assign more tellers to staff more windows.

ECONOMIC ORDER QUANTITY MODEL

When you order checks from a bank, have you noticed that the reorder form is placed about two-thirds of the way through your supply of checks? This is a simple example of a **fixed-point reordering system**. At some preestablished point in the process, the system is designed to "flag" the fact that the inventory needs to be replenished. The objective is to minimize inventory carrying costs while at the same time limiting the probability of *stocking out* of the inventory item. In recent years, retail stores have increasingly been using their computers to perform this reordering activity. Their cash registers are connected to their computers, and each sale automatically adjusts the store's inventory record. When the inventory of an item hits the critical point, the computer tells management to reorder.

fixed-point reordering system
A preestablished point in which inventory is replenished

One of the best known techniques for mathematically deriving the optimum quantity for a purchase order is the **economic order quantity (EOQ)** model (see Exhibit 4–8). The EOQ model seeks to balance four costs involved in ordering and carrying inventory: the purchase costs (purchase price plus delivery charges less discounts); the ordering costs (paperwork, follow-up, inspection when the item arrives, and other processing costs); carrying costs (money tied up in inventory, storage, insurance, taxes, and so forth); and stock-out costs (profits foregone from orders lost, the cost of reestablishing goodwill, and additional expenses incurred to

economic order quantity (EOQ)
A technique for balancing purchase, ordering, carrying, and stock-out costs to derive the optimum quantity for a purchase order

EXHIBIT QM–8

Determining the Most Economic Order Quantity

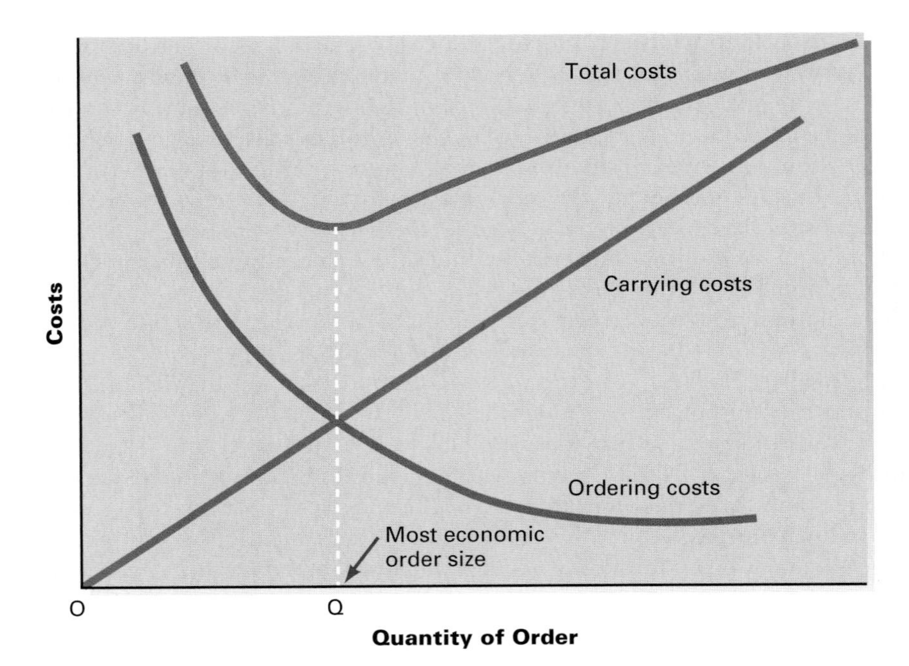

expedite late shipments). When these four costs are known, the model identifies the optimal order size for each purchase.

The objective of the economic order quantity (EOQ) model is to minimize the total costs associated with the carrying and ordering costs. As the amount ordered gets larger, average inventory increases and so do carrying costs. For example, if annual demand for an inventory item is 26,000 units, and a firm orders 500 each time, the firm will place 52 [26,000/500] orders per year. This gives the organization an average inventory of 250 [500/2] units. If the order quantity is increased to 2,000 units, there will be fewer orders (13) [26,000/2,000] placed. However, average inventory on hand will increase to 1,000 [2,000/2] units. Thus, as holding costs go up, ordering costs go down, and vice versa. The most economic order quantity is reached at the lowest point on the total cost curve. That's the point at which ordering costs equal carrying costs—or the economic order quantity (see point Q in Exhibit QM–8).

To compute this optimal order quantity, you need the following data: forecasted demand for the item during the period (D); the cost of placing each order (OC); the value or purchase price of the item (V); and the carrying cost (expressed as a percentage) of maintaining the total inventory (CC). Given these data, the formula for EOQ is as follows:

$$\text{EOQ} = \sqrt{\frac{2 \times D \times OC}{V \times CC}}$$

Let's work an example of determining the EOQ. Take, for example, Barnes Electronics, a retailer of high-quality sound and video equipment. The owner, Sam Barnes, wishes to determine the company's economic order quantities of high-quality sound and video equipment. The item in question is a Sony compact voice recorder. Barnes forecasts sales of 4,000 units a year. He believes that the cost for the sound system should be $50. Estimated costs of placing an order for these systems are $35 per order and annual insurance, taxes, and other carrying costs at 20 percent of the recorder's value. Using the EOQ formula, and the preceding information, he can calculate the EOQ as follows:

$$EOQ = \sqrt{\frac{2 \times 4,000 \times 35}{50 \times .20}}$$

$$EOQ = \sqrt{28,000}$$

$$EOQ = 167.33 \text{ or } 168 \text{ units}$$

The inventory model suggests that it's most economical to order in quantities or lots of approximately 168 recorders. Stated differently, Barnes should order about 24 [4,000/168] times a year. However, what would happen if the supplier offers Barnes a 5 percent discount on purchases if he buys in minimum quantities of 250 units? Should he now purchase in quantities of 168 or 250? Without the discount, and ordering 168 each time, the annual costs for these recorders would be as follows:

Purchase cost:	$50	×	$4,000	=	$200,000
Carrying cost (average number of inventory units times value of item times percentage:	168/2	×	$50 × 0.2	=	840
Ordering costs (number of orders times costto place order):	24	×	$35	=	840
Total Cost:				=	$201,680

With the 5 percent discount for ordering 250 units, the item cost ($50 × [$50 × 0.05]) would be $47.5. The annual inventory costs would be as follows:

Purchase cost:	$47.50	×	$4,000	=	$190,000.00
Carrying cost:	250/2	×	$47.50 × 0.2	=	1,187.50
Ordering cost:	16	×	$35	=	560.00
Total Cost:				=	$191,747.50

These calculations suggest to Barnes that he should take advantage of the 5 percent discount. Even though he now has to stock larger quantities, the annual savings amounts to nearly $10,000. A word of caution, however, needs to be added. The EOQ model assumes that demand and lead times are known and constant. If these conditions can't be met, the model shouldn't be used. For example, it generally shouldn't be used for manufactured component inventory because the components are taken out of stock all at once, in lumps, or odd lots, rather than at a constant rate. Does this mean that the EOQ model is useless when demand is variable? No. The model can still be of some use in demonstrating trade-offs in costs and the need to control lot sizes. However, there are more sophisticated lot sizing models for handling demand and special situations. The mathematics for EOQ, like the mathematics for queuing theory, go far beyond the scope of this text.

P A R T 3

Organizing

C H A P T E R 5

Basic Organization Designs

LEARNING OUTCOMES

After reading this chapter, I will be able to:

1. Identify and define the six elements of organization structure.
2. Describe the advantages and disadvantages of work specialization.
3. Contrast authority and power.
4. Identify the five different ways by which management can departmentalize.
5. Contrast mechanistic and organic organizations.
6. Summarize the effect of strategy, size, technology, and environment on organization structures.
7. Contrast the divisional and functional structures.
8. Explain the strengths of the matrix structure.
9. Describe the boundaryless organization and what elements have contributed to its development.
10. Explain what is meant by the term *learning organization.*
11. Describe what is meant by the term *organization culture.*

Trufresh LLC in Suffield, Connecticut, has a unique product and a unique organization structure for producing and delivering its products.[1] Trufresh harvests and distributes "fresh frozen" Atlantic salmon. Using a patented freezing technology, the company is able to sell salmon that is indistinguishable from fresh catch. As a case in point, when Trufresh salmon was tested against freshly caught salmon by the Culinary Institute of America, its experts couldn't tell them apart.

Trufresh farm-raises and harvests its salmon in Norway. (Pictured is the Truefresh facility in Stokmarknes, Norway.) Within hours of being plucked from the tanks, the salmon are boned, skinned, cleaned and put in airtight plastic, and then plunged into a patented cryogenic brine at –40 degrees Fahrenheit. The fish are frozen so quickly in order to lose very little moisture. The result is a product that can be served by upscale restaurants as well as institutional food service operations, such as the government-sponsored Meals-on-Wheels program.

To run this company, Trufresh's owners have chosen an unusual form of organizational design. It's sort of a "no structure" structure. There are no headquarters; there is a bare-bones sales staff and a very small set of managers spread over a five-state region. The majority owners of Trufresh, several real estate executives, oversee the company's finances from their real estate offices in New York City. A retired ocean tanker captain handles Trufresh's production in rented space in Maine that was once a sardine canning plant. The national sales manager works at home in Pittsburgh, supervising five freelance sales representatives. The only Trufresh office is in Suffield, Connecticut. It contains a couple of second-hand desks, a computer and fax machine, a telephone, and a filing cabinet. The remaining Trufresh organization is a warehouse (leased space in Massachusetts) and a distribution network that is outsourced to a small trucking company.

Trufresh's "virtual organization" enables it to focus on technology and sales without diverting resources. It also allows the company maximum flexibility while minimizing costs. In today's ever-changing business world, a lot of managers are talking about outsourcing those functions that are not part of the company's core work. A company like Trufresh is actually doing it.

THE TRUFRESH EXAMPLE DEMONSTRATES THE IMPORTANCE OF the right structure and work environment. In this chapter, we present the foundations of organization structure. We define the concept and its key components, introduce organization design options, consider contingency variables that determine when certain design options work better than others, and explore the concept of organization culture.

Once certain organizational members have made decisions regarding corporate strategies, they must develop the structure that will best facilitate the attainment of those goals. Recall from Chapter 1 that we defined organizing as the function of management that creates the organization's structure. When managers develop or change the organization's structure, they are engaging in **organization design**. This process involves making decisions about how specialized jobs should be allocated, the rules to guide employees' behaviors, and at what level decisions are to be made. Organization design decisions are typically made by senior managers. Occasionally, perhaps, they might seek input from mid-level managers, but lower-level managers and operatives rarely have an opportunity to provide input. Nonetheless, it still is important to understand the process. Why? Because each of us works in some type of organization structure, and we need to know why we are grouped as we are. In addition, given the changing environment and the need for organizations to rapidly adapt, we should begin our understanding of what tomorrow's structures may look like.

organization design
A process in which managers develop or change their organization's structure

As you read this chapter, recognize that the organization design material presented applies to any type of organization, whether it's a business enterprise interested in making profits for its owners or a not-for-profit organization that provides service to specialized customers (such as your college) or to the community at large (such as the U.S. Postal Service or your local sanitation department).

THE ELEMENTS OF STRUCTURE

The basic concepts of organization design were formulated in the early 1900s by management writers who offered a set of principles for managers to follow in organization design. More than six to eight decades have passed since most of those principles were originally proposed. Given the passing of that much time and all the changes that have taken place in our society, you might think that they would be pretty worthless today. Surprisingly, they're not. For the most part, these principles still provide valuable insights into designing effective and efficient organizations. Of course, we have also gained a great deal of knowledge over the years as to their limitations. In the following sections, we discuss the six basic elements of structure: work specialization, chain of command, span of control, authority and responsibility, centralization versus decentralization, and departmentalization.

WHAT IS WORK SPECIALIZATION?

work specialization
A component of organization structure that involves having each discrete step of a job done by a different individual rather than having one individual do the whole job

Work specialization has been around for centuries in industrialized countries. In fact, back in the 1700s when economist Adam Smith published *Wealth of Nations,* he advocated that jobs should be divided into smaller parts. In **work specialization**, a job is broken down into a number of steps, and each step is completed by a separate individual.[2] In essence, individuals specialize in doing part of an activity rather than the entire activity. Installing only the mother boards and hard-disk drives in a computer assembly line is an example of work specialization. So, too, are the specific tasks crew members perform each time they make a Whopper at Burger King.

Work specialization makes efficient use of the diversity of skills that workers hold. In most organizations, some tasks require highly developed skills; others can be performed by those who have lower skill levels. If all workers were engaged in all the steps of, say, a manufacturing process, all would have to have the skills necessary to perform both the most demanding and the least demanding jobs. Thus, except when performing the most highly skilled or highly sophisticated tasks, employees would be working below their skill levels. In addition, skilled workers are paid more than unskilled workers, and, because wages tend to reflect the highest level of skill, all workers would be paid at highly skilled rates to do easy tasks—an inefficient use of resources. That is why you rarely find a cardiac surgeon closing up a patient after surgery. Doctors doing their residencies in open-heart surgery and learning the skill usually stitch and staple the patient after the surgeon has performed bypass surgery.

Burger King employees making Whopper sandwiches reflect what is commonly referred to by management writers as work specialization. This means that each employee has a set of specific steps to accomplish before the "task" is passed on to another person.

Early proponents of work specialization believed that it could lead to great increases in productivity. At the beginning of the twentieth century and earlier, that generalization was reasonable. Because specialization was not widely practiced, its introduction almost always generated higher productivity, but a good thing can be carried too far. There is a point at which the human diseconomies from division of labor that surface as boredom, fatigue, stress, low productivity, poor quality, increased absenteeism, and high turnover exceed the economic advantages (see Exhibit 5–1).

By the 1960s, that point had been reached in a number of jobs. In such cases, productivity could be increased by enlarging, rather than narrowing, the scope of job activities.[3] For instance, successful efforts to increase

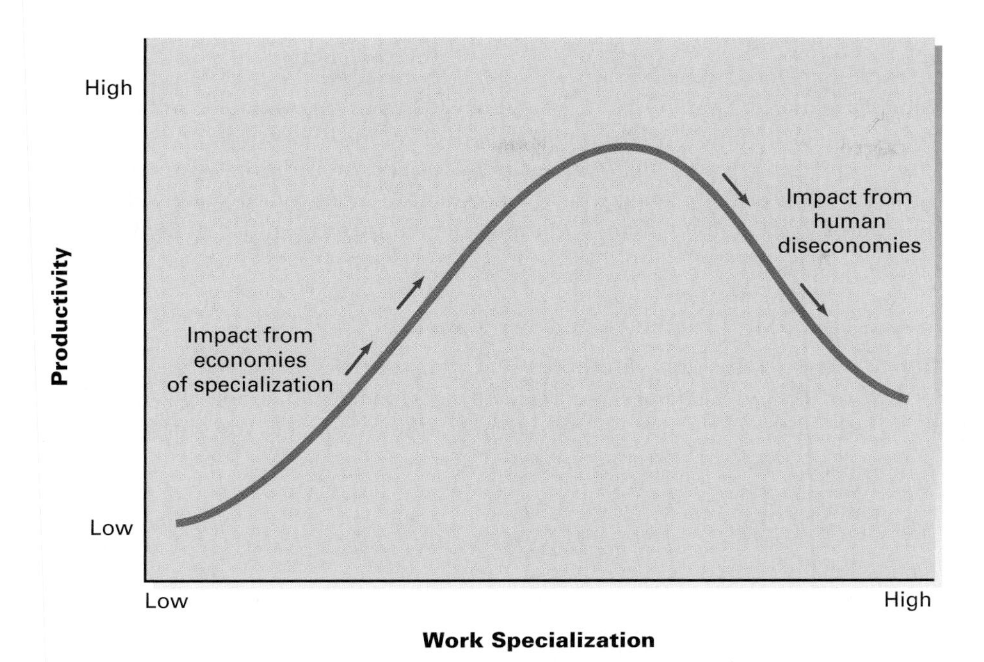

EXHIBIT 5-1
Economies and Diseconomies of Work Specialization

productivity included giving employees a variety of activities to do, allowing them to do a complete piece of work, and putting them together in teams. Each of those ideas, of course, runs counter to the work specialization concept. Yet, overall, work specialization is alive and well in most organizations today. We have to recognize the economies it provides in certain types of jobs, but we also have to recognize its limitations.

WHAT IS THE CHAIN OF COMMAND?

The early management writers argued that an employee should have one and only one superior to whom he or she is directly responsible. An employee who has to report to two or more bosses might have to cope with conflicting demands or priorities.[4] In those rare instances when the **chain of command** principle had to be violated, early management writers always explicitly designated a clear separation of activities and a supervisor responsible for each. The chain of command concept was logical when organizations were comparatively simple. Under many circumstances, it is still sound advice; many contemporary organizations continue to adhere to it. Yet there are instances, which we introduce later in this chapter, when strict adherence to the chain of command creates a degree of inflexibility that hinders an organization's performance.

chain of command
The management principle that no person should report to more than one boss

WHAT IS THE SPAN OF CONTROL?

How many employees can a manager efficiently and effectively direct? This question of **span of control** received a great deal of attention from early management writers. Although there was no consensus on a specific number, the early writers favored small spans—typically no more than six workers—in order to maintain close control.[5] However, several writers did acknowledge level in the organization as a contingency variable. They argued that as a manager rises in an organization, he or she has to deal with a greater number of ill-structured problems, so top managers need a smaller span than do middle managers, and middle managers require a smaller span than do supervisors. Over the last decade, however, we are seeing some change in theories about effective spans of control.[6]

span of control
The number of subordinates a manager can direct efficiently and effectively

Many organizations are increasing their spans of control. The span for managers at such companies as General Electric and Kaiser Aluminum has expanded significantly in the past decade. It has also expanded in the federal government, where efforts to increase the span of control are being implemented to save time in making decisions.[7] The span of control is increasingly being determined by looking at contingency variables.

It is obvious that the more training and experience employees have, the less direct supervision they need. Managers who have well-trained and experienced employees can function with a wider span. Other contingency variables that will determine the appropriate span include similarity of employee tasks, the complexity of those tasks, the physical proximity of employees, the degree to which standardized procedures are in place, the sophistication of the organization's management information system, the strength of the organization's value system, and the preferred managing style of the manager.[8]

WHAT ARE AUTHORITY AND RESPONSIBILITY?

authority
The rights inherent in a managerial position to give orders and expect them to be obeyed

Authority refers to the rights inherent in a managerial position to give orders and expect the orders to be obeyed (see Ethical Dilemma in Management). Authority was a major tenet of the early management writers; it was viewed as the glue that held the

Details on a Management Classic

Stanley Milgram

Stanley Milgram, a social psychologist at Yale University, wondered how far individuals would go in following orders.[9] If subjects were placed in the role of a teacher in a learning experiment and told by the experimenter to administer a shock each time a learner made a mistake, would the subjects follow the commands of the experimenter? Would their willingness to comply decrease as the intensity of the shock was increased?

To answer those questions, Milgram hired a set of subjects. Each was told that the experiment was to investigate the effect of punishment on memory. Their job was to act as teachers and administer punishment whenever the learner made a mistake on a learning test. Punishment in this case was an electric shock. The subject sat in front of a shock generator with 30 levels of shock—beginning at zero and progressing in 15-volt increments to a high of 450 volts. The demarcations of these positions ranged from "slight shock" at 15 volts to "danger: severe shock" at 450 volts. The subjects were able to see the learner strapped in an electric chair in an adjacent room. Of course, the learner was an actor, and the electric shocks were phony, but the subjects didn't know that.

The subjects were instructed to shock the learner each time he made a mistake and that subsequent mistakes would result in an increase in shock intensity. Throughout the experiment, the subject got verbal feedback from the learner. At 75 volts, the learner began to grunt and moan; at 150 volts, the learner demanded to be released from the experiment; at 180 volts, he cried out that he could no longer stand the pain; at 300 volts, he insisted he be released because of a heart condition. After 300 volts, the learner did not respond to further questions.

Most subjects protested and, fearful they might kill the learner if the increased shocks were to bring on a heart attack, insisted that they could not go on. The experimenter responded by saying that they had to, that was their job. Most of the subjects dissented. Dissension, however, wasn't synonymous with disobedience. Sixty-two percent of the subjects increased the shock level to the maximum of 450 volts. The average level of shock administered by the remaining 38 percent was nearly 370 volts—more than enough to kill even the strongest human!

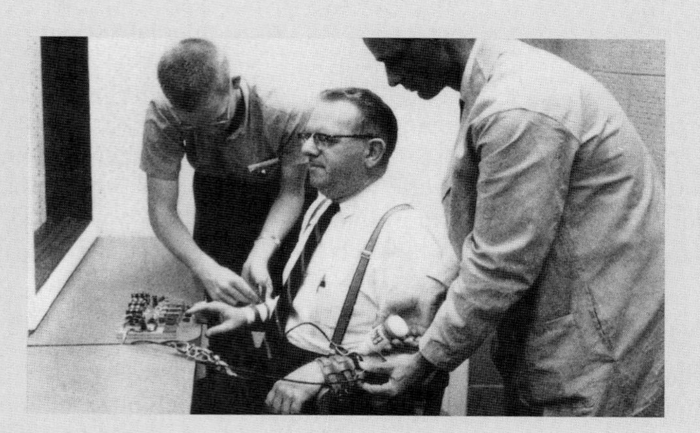

Just how far will someone go when following orders? Stanley Milgram found that people would generally do things because they were told they had to. In the Milgram experiments, this meant administering a level of shock far above what they felt comfortable giving.

What can we conclude from Milgram's results? One obvious conclusion is that authority is a potent motivation for people to do things. Subjects in Milgram's experiment administered levels of shock far above what they felt comfortable giving because they were told they had to, despite the fact that they could have walked out of the room any time they wanted.

organization together.[10] It was to be delegated downward to lower-level managers, giving them certain rights while providing certain prescribed limits within which to operate (see Details on a Management Classic). Each management position has specific inherent rights that incumbents acquire from the position's rank or title. Authority, therefore, is related to one's position within an organization and ignores the personal characteristics of the individual manager. It has nothing to do with the individual. The expression "The king is dead; long live the king" illustrates the concept. Whoever is king acquires the rights inherent in the king's position. When a position of authority is vacated, the person who has left the position no longer has any authority. The authority remains with the position and its new incumbent.

When managers delegate authority, they must allocate commensurate **responsibility**. That is, when employees are given rights, they also assume a corresponding obligation to perform. And they should be held accountable for that performance! Allocating authority without responsibility and accountability creates opportunities for abuse, and no one should be held responsible or accountable for something over which he or she has no authority.

responsibility
An obligation to perform assigned activities

Are there different types of authority relationships? The early management writers distinguished between two forms of authority: line authority and staff authority. **Line authority** entitles a manager to direct the work of an employee. It is the employer–employee authority relationship that extends from the top of the organization to the lowest echelon, according to the chain of command, as shown in Exhibit 5–2. As a link in the chain of command, a manager with line authority has the right to direct the work of employees and to make certain decisions without consulting anyone. Of course, in the chain of command, every manager is also subject to the direction of his or her superior.

line authority
The authority that entitles a manager to direct the work of an employee

Sometimes the term *line* is used to differentiate line managers from staff managers. In this context, *line* refers to managers whose organizational function contributes directly to the achievement of organizational objectives. In a manufacturing firm, line managers are typically in the production and sales functions, whereas managers in human resources and payroll are considered staff managers with staff authority. Whether a manager's function is classified as line or staff depends on the organization's objectives. For example, at Staff Builders, a supplier of temporary employees, interviewers have a line function. Similarly, at the payroll firm of ADP, payroll is a line function.

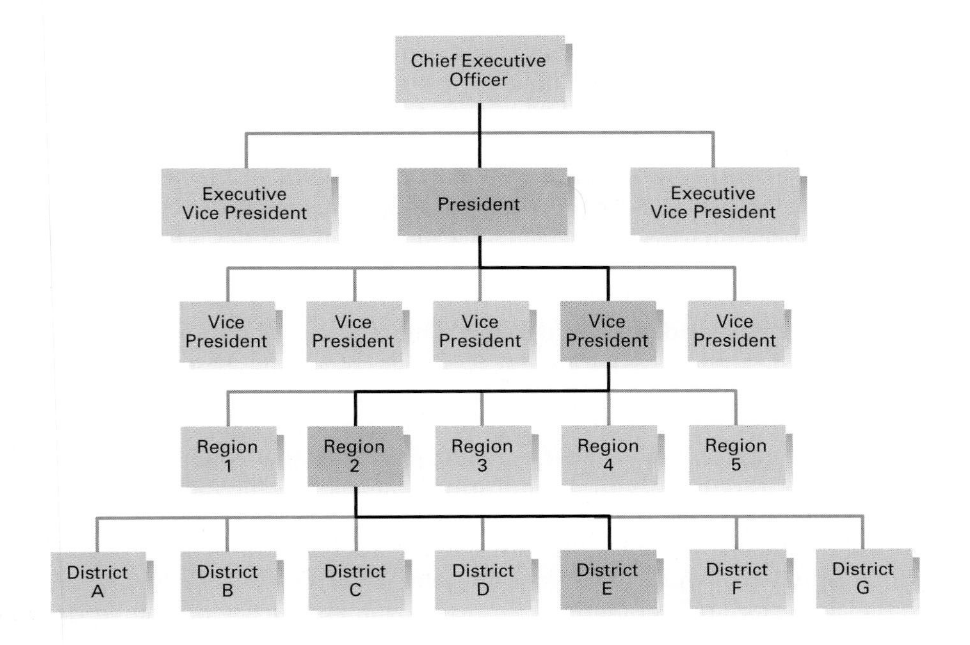

EXHIBIT 5–2
Chain of Command

EXHIBIT 5–3 **Line Versus Staff Authority**

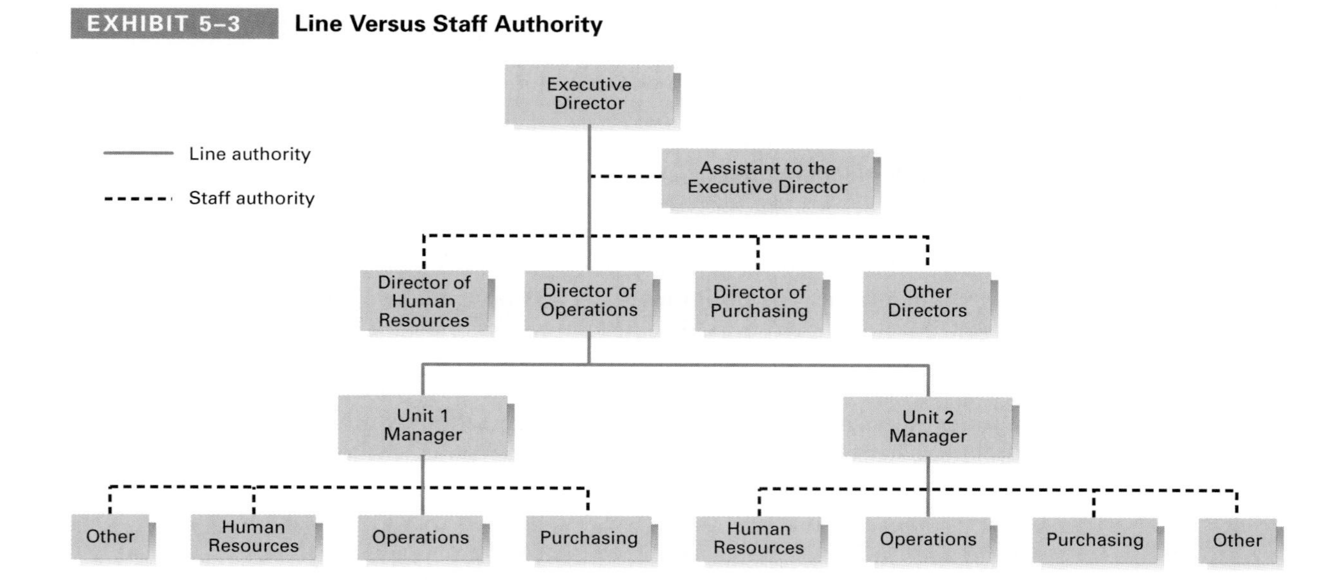

staff authority
Positions that have some authority but that are created to support, assist, and advise the holders of line authority

As organizations get larger and more complex, line managers find that they do not have the time, expertise, or resources to get their jobs done effectively. In response, they create **staff authority** functions to support, assist, advise, and generally reduce some of their informational burdens. The hospital administrator cannot effectively handle the purchasing of all the supplies the hospital needs, so she creates a purchasing department, a staff department. Of course, the head of the purchasing department has line authority over the purchasing agents who work for her. The hospital administrator might also find that she is overburdened and needs an assistant. In creating the position of her assistant, she has created a staff position. Exhibit 5–3 illustrates line and staff authority.

How does the contemporary view of authority and responsibility differ from the historical view? The early management writers were enamored of authority. They assumed that the rights inherent in one's formal position in an organization were the sole source of influence. They believed that managers were all-powerful. This might have been true 30 or 60 years ago. Organizations were simpler. Staff was less important. Managers were only minimally dependent on technical specialists. Under such conditions, influence is the same as authority. And the higher a manager's position in the organization, the more influence he or she had. However, those conditions no longer hold. Researchers and practitioners of management now recognize that you do not have to be a manager to have power and that power is not perfectly correlated with one's level in the organization (see Ethical Dilemma in Management).

Authority is an important concept in organizations, but an exclusive focus on authority produces a narrow, unrealistic view of influence. Today, we recognize that authority is but one element in the larger concept of power.

power
An individual's capacity to influence decisions

How do authority and power differ? The terms *authority* and *power* are frequently confused. Authority is a right, the legitimacy of which is based on the authority figure's position in the organization. Authority goes with the job. **Power**, on the other hand, refers to an individual's capacity to influence decisions. Authority is part of the larger concept of power. That is, the formal rights that come with an individual's position in the organization are just one means by which an individual can affect the decision process.

Exhibit 5–4 visually depicts the difference between authority and power. The two-dimensional arrangement of boxes in part A portrays authority. The area in which the authority applies is defined by the horizontal dimension. Each horizontal

Ethical Dilemma in Management

Obeying Orders

Surveys of U. S. managers have revealed significant differences in the values, attitudes, and beliefs that they personally hold and what they encounter in the workplace.[11] And this is not simply a U. S. phenomenon. Managers around the world, in such places as the Pacific Rim, Europe, and India, are all facing the same predicaments.

If you were asked to follow orders that you believed were unconscionable (for instance, if your boss asked you to destroy evidence that could by used against your company in a court proceeding), would you comply? What if you merely disagreed with the orders—say, being asked to bring him or her coffee each morning when no such task is included in your job description? What would you do in these instances? Furthermore, what effect do you feel national culture has on your complying with orders?

grouping represents a functional area. The influence one holds in the organization is defined by the vertical dimension in the structure. The higher one is in the organization, the greater one's authority.

Power, on the other hand, is a three-dimensional concept (the cone in part B of Exhibit 5–4). It includes not only the functional and hierarchical dimensions but also a third dimension called centrality. Although authority is defined by one's vertical position in the hierarchy, power is made up of both one's vertical position and one's distance from the organization's power core or center.

EXHIBIT 5–4 **Authority Versus Power**

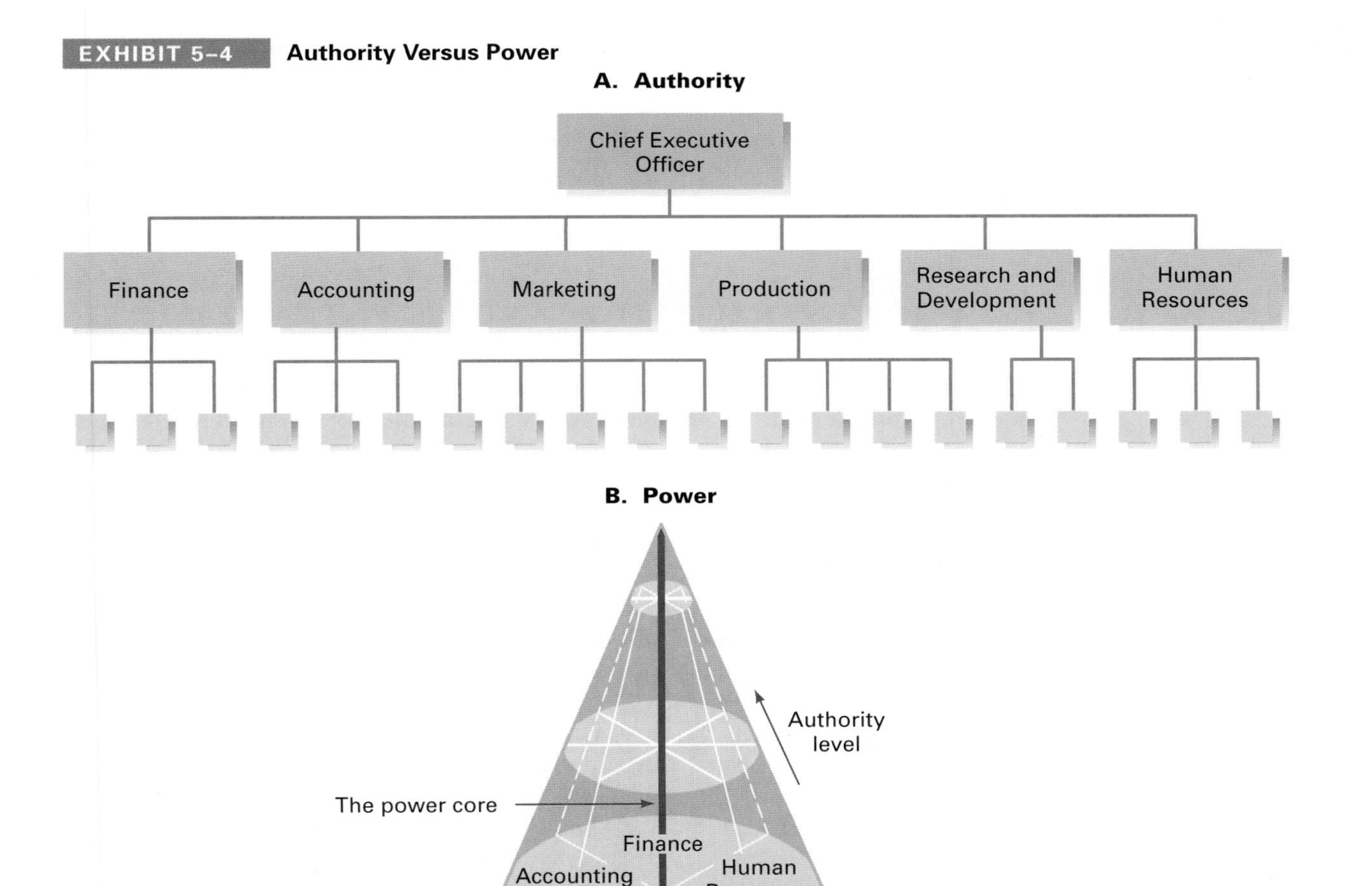

Think of the cone in Exhibit 5–4 as an organization. The center of the cone is the power core. The closer you are to the power core, the more influence you have on decisions. The existence of a power core is, in fact, the only difference between A and B in Exhibit 5–4. The vertical hierarchy dimension in A is merely one's level on the outer edge of the cone. The top of the cone corresponds to the top of the hierarchy, the middle of the cone to the middle of the hierarchy, and so on. Similarly, the functional groups in A become wedges in the cone. Each wedge represents a functional area.

The cone analogy explicitly acknowledges two facts: (1) The higher one moves in an organization (an increase in authority), the closer one moves to the power core; and (2) it is not necessary to have authority in order to wield power because one can move horizontally inward toward the power core without moving up. For instance, have you ever noticed that administrative assistants are powerful in a company even though they have little authority? Often, as gatekeepers for their bosses, these assistants have considerable influence over whom their bosses see and when they see them. Furthermore, because they are regularly relied upon to pass information on to their bosses, they have some control over what their bosses hear. It is not unusual for a $105,000-a-year middle manager to tread very carefully in order not to upset the boss's $45,000-a-year administrative assistant. Why? Because the assistant has power. This individual may be low in the authority hierarchy but close to the power core.

Low-ranking employees who have relatives, friends, or associates in high places might also be close to the power core. So, too, are employees with scarce and important skills. The lowly production engineer with 20 years of experience in a company might be the only one in the firm who knows the inner workings of all the old production machinery. When pieces of this old equipment break down, only this engineer understands how to fix them. Suddenly, the engineer's influence is much greater than it would appear from his or her level in the vertical hierarchy. What does this tell us about power? It states that power can come from different areas (see Developing Your Power Base Skill, p. 165. John French and Bertram Raven have identified five sources, or bases, of power: coercive, reward, legitimate, expert, and referent.[12] We have summarized them in Exhibit 5–5.

centralization
A function of how much decision-making authority is pushed down to lower levels in an organization; the more centralized an organization, the higher the level at which decisions are made

decentralization
The pushing down of decision-making authority to the lowest levels of an organization

HOW DO CENTRALIZATION AND DECENTRALIZATION DIFFER?

One of the questions that needs to be answered in the organizing function is "At what level are decisions made?" **Centralization** is a function of how much decision-making authority is pushed down to lower levels in the organization. Centralization-decentralization, however, is not an either-or concept. Rather, it's a degree phenomenon. By that we mean that no organization is completely centralized or completely decentralized. Few, if any, organizations could effectively function if all their decisions were made by a select few people (centralization) or if all decisions were pushed down to the level closest to the problems (**decentralization**). Let's look, then, at how the early management writers viewed centralization as well as at how it exists today.

EXHIBIT 5–5
Types of Power

Coercive power	Power based on fear.
Reward power	Power based on the ability to distribute something that others value.
Legitimate power	Power based on one's position in the formal hierarchy.
Expert power	Power based on one's expertise, special skill, or knowledge.
Referent power	Power based on identification with a person who has desirable resources or personal traits.

Decentralization means giving employees closest to the problem an opportunity to resolve the problem. This means giving them an opportunity to explore the problem and discuss what solutions are viable and can be implemented. In constrast, a centralized organization would have these decisions made by a "select few" and then have the the solution handed down to those performing the work.

Early management writers proposed that centralization in an organization depended on the situation.[13] Their objective was the optimum and efficient use of employees. Traditional organizations were structured in a pyramid, with power and authority concentrated near the top of the organization. Given this structure, historically, centralized decisions were the most prominent, but organizations today have become more complex and are responding to dynamic changes in their environments. As such, many managers believe that decisions need to be made by those individuals closest to the problems, regardless of their organizational level. In fact, the trend over the past several decades—at least in U.S. and Canadian organizations—has been a movement toward more decentralization in organizations.[14]

Today, managers often choose the amount of centralization or decentralization that will allow them to best implement their decisions and achieve organizational goals.[15] What works in one organization, however, won't necessarily work in another, so managers must determine the amount of decentralization for each organization and work units within it. You may also recall that in Chapter 2 one of the central themes of our discussion of empowering employees was to delegate to them the authority to make decisions on those things that affect their work and to change the way that they think about work. That's the issue of decentralization at work. Notice, however, that it doesn't imply that senior management no longer makes decisions.

CAN YOU IDENTIFY THE FIVE WAYS TO DEPARTMENTALIZE?

Early management writers argued that activities in the organization should be specialized and grouped into departments. Work specialization creates specialists who need coordination. This coordination is facilitated by putting specialists together in departments under the direction of a manager. These departments are typically based on the work functions performed, the product or service offered, the target customer or client, the geographic territory covered, or the process used to turn inputs into outputs. No single method of departmentalization was advocated by the early writers. The method or methods used should reflect the grouping that would best contribute to the attainment of the organization's objectives and the goals of individual units (see Exhibit 5–6).

EXHIBIT 5–6
Types of Departmentalization

■ **Functional**	Groups employees based on work performed—e.g., engineering, accounting information systems, human resources, etc.
■ **Product**	Groups employees based on major product areas in the corporation—e.g., women's footwear, men's footwear, and apparel and accessories.
■ **Customer**	Groups employees based on customers' problem and needs—wholesale, retail, government.
■ **Geographic**	Groups employees based on location served—e.g., north, south, midwest, eastern.
■ **Process**	Groups employees based on the basis of work or customer flow—testing, payment, etc.

How are activities grouped? One of the most popular ways to group activities is by functions performed or **functional departmentalization**. A manager might organize his or her plant by separating engineering, accounting, information systems, human resources, and purchasing specialists into departments. Functional departmentalization can be used in all types of organizations. Only the functions change to reflect the organization's objectives and activities. The major advantage to functional departmentalization is the achievement of economies of scale by placing people with common skills and specializations into common units.

functional departmentalization The grouping of activities by functions performed

Product departmentalization focuses attention on major product areas in the corporation. Each product is under the authority of a senior manager who is a specialist in, and is responsible for, everything having to do with his or her product line. One company that uses product departmentalization is L.A. Gear. Its structure is based on its varied product lines, which include women's footwear, men's footwear, and apparel and accessories. If an organization's activities were service related rather than product related, as are those of L.A. Gear, each service would be autonomously grouped. The advantage of product grouping is that it increases accountability for product performance, since all activities related to a specific product are under the direction of a single manager.

product departmentalization The grouping of activities by product produced

The particular type of customer the organization seeks to reach can also dictate employee grouping. The sales activities in an office supply firm, for instance, can be broken down into three departments that serve retail, wholesale, and government customers. A large law office can segment its staff on the basis of whether it serves corporate or individual clients. The assumption underlying **customer departmentalization** is that customers in each department have a common set of problems and needs that can best be met by specialists.

customer departmentalization The grouping of activities by common customers

Another way to departmentalize is on the basis of geography or territory—**geographic departmentalization**. The sales function might have western, southern, midwestern, and eastern regions. If an organization's customers are scattered over a large geographic area, this form of departmentalization can be valuable. For instance, the organization structure of Coca-Cola in the new millennium reflects the company's operations in two broad geographic areas—the North American sector and the international sector (which includes the Pacific Rim, the European Community, Northeast Europe and Africa, and Latin America).

geographic departmentalization The grouping of activities by territory

The final form of departmentalization is called **process departmentalization**, which groups activities on the basis of work or customer flow—like that found in many states' motor vehicle administrations. Units are organized around common skills needed to complete a certain process. If you have ever been to a state motor vehicle office to get a driver's license, you've probably experienced process departmentalization, where separate departments handle applications, testing, and payment collection. Since each process requires different skills, this method offers a basis for the homogeneous categorization of activities.

process departmentalization The grouping of activities by work or customer flow

Car-racing teams require split-second timing and coordination to win. Companies like Southwest Airlines and Saturn use teams to enhance productivity by "breaking the mold" of traditional bureaucracies.

How does the contemporary view differ from the historical view? Most large organizations continue to use most or all of the departmental groups suggested by the early management writers. Black & Decker, for instance, organizes each of its divisions along functional lines, its manufacturing units around processes, its sales around geographic regions, and its sales regions around customer groupings. But a recent trend needs to be mentioned; that is, rigid departmentalization is being complemented by the use of teams that cross traditional departmental lines.

Today's competitive environment has refocused the attention of management on its customers. To better monitor the needs of customers and to be able to respond to changes in those needs, many organizations have given greater emphasis to customer departmentalization. We are also seeing many more teams used as devices for accomplishing organizational objectives. Nearly all *Fortune* 500 firms are using some form of team.[16] As tasks have become more complex, and diverse skills are needed to accomplish those tasks, management has increasingly used teams and task forces. We look at the issue of teams in Chapter 9.

If we combine the basic organizational structural elements, we arrive at what most of the early writers believed to be the ideal structural design: the mechanistic or bureaucratic organization. Today we recognize that there is no single ideal organization structure for all situations.

CONTINGENCY VARIABLES AFFECTING STRUCTURE

The most appropriate structure to use will depend on contingency factors. In this section, we address two generic organization structure models and then look at the more popular contingency variables—strategy, size, technology, and environment.

HOW IS A MECHANISTIC ORGANIZATION DIFFERENT FROM AN ORGANIC ORGANIZATION?

Exhibit 5–7 describes two organizational forms.[17] The **mechanistic organization** (or bureaucracy) was the natural result of combining the six elements of structure. Adhering to the chain of command principle ensured the existence of a formal hierarchy of authority, with each person controlled and supervised by one superior. Keeping the span of control small at increasingly higher levels in the organization created tall, impersonal structures. As the distance between the top and the bottom of the organization expanded, top management would increasingly impose rules and regulations. Because top managers couldn't control lower-level activities through direct observation and ensure the use of standard practices, they substituted rules and regulations. The early management writers' belief in a high degree of work specialization created jobs that were simple, routine, and standardized. Further specialization through the use of departmentalization increased impersonality and the need for multiple layers of management to coordinate the specialized departments.

mechanistic organization
The bureaucracy; a structure that is high in specialization, formalization, and centralization

EXHIBIT 5–7
Mechanistic Versus Organic Organizations

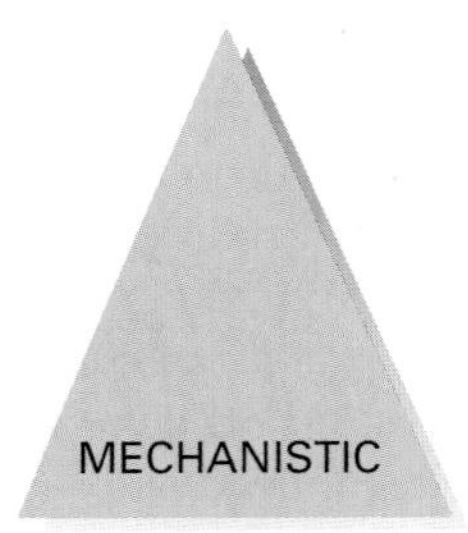

Mechanistic	Organic
☐ Rigid hierarchical relationships	☐ Collaboration (both vertical and horizontal)
☐ Fixed duties	☐ Adaptable duties
☐ Many rules	☐ Few rules
☐ Formalized communication channels	☐ Informal communication
☐ Centralized decision authority	☐ Decentralized decision authority
☐ Taller structures	☐ Flatter structures

Development of the space shuttle required significant creativity and innovation. Rockwell International, the organization in which the space shuttle was developed, found that to develop products like the space shuttle, where the technology is less routine, an organic structure works best.

The **organic organization** is a highly adaptive form that is as loose and flexible as the mechanistic organization is rigid and stable. Rather than having standardized jobs and regulations, the organic organization's loose structure allows it to change rapidly as required.[18] It has division of labor, but the jobs people do are not standardized. Employees tend to be professionals who are technically proficient and trained to handle diverse problems. They need very few formal rules and little direct supervision because their training has instilled in them standards of professional conduct. For instance, a petroleum engineer does not need to be given procedures on how to locate oil sources miles off shore. The engineer can solve most problems alone or after conferring with colleagues. Professional standards guide his or her behavior. The organic organization is low in centralization so that the professional can respond quickly to problems and because top management cannot be expected to possess the expertise to make necessary decisions.

When is each of these two models appropriate? Let's look at the contingency variables that affect organization structure.

HOW DOES STRATEGY AFFECT STRUCTURE?

An organization's structure is a means to help management achieve its objectives. Because objectives are derived from the organization's overall strategy, it is only logical that strategy and structure should be closely linked. For example, if the organization focuses on providing certain services—say, police protection in a community—its structure will be one that promotes standardized and efficient services. Similarly, if an organization is attempting to employ a growth strategy by entering into global markets, it will need a structure that is flexible, fluid, and readily adaptable to the environment. Accordingly, organization structure should follow strategy. And, if management makes a significant change in its organization's strategy, it will need to modify structure to accommodate and support that change.

organic organization
An adhocracy; a structure that is low in specialization, formalization, and centralization

The first important research on the strategy–structure relationship was Alfred Chandler's study of close to 100 large U.S. companies.[19] After tracing the development of these organizations over 50 years and compiling extensive case histories of companies such as DuPont, General Motors, Standard Oil of New Jersey, and Sears, Chandler concluded that changes in corporate strategy precede and lead to changes in an organization's structure. Specifically, he found that organizations usually begin with a single product or line. The simplicity of the strategy requires only a simple or loose form of structure to execute it. Decisions can be centralized in the hands of a single senior manager, and complexity and formalization will be low. As organizations grow, their strategies become more ambitious and elaborate. Research has generally confirmed the strategy–structure relationship using the strategy terminology presented in Chapter 3.[20] For instance, organizations pursuing a differentiation strategy (see Chapter 3) must innovate to survive. Unless they can maintain their uniqueness, they may lose their competitive advantage. An organic organization matches best with this strategy because it is flexible and maximizes adaptability. In contrast, a cost-leadership strategy seeks stability and efficiency. Stability and efficiency help to produce low-cost goods and services. This, then, can best be achieved with a mechanistic organization.

HOW DOES SIZE AFFECT STRUCTURE?

There is considerable historical evidence that an organization's size significantly affects its structure.[21] For instance, large organizations—those typically employing 2,000 or more people—tend to have more work specialization, horizontal and vertical differentiation, and rules and regulations than do small organizations. However, the relationship is not linear; size has less impact as an organization expands. Why? Essentially, once an organization has around 2,000 employees, it is already fairly mechanistic. An additional 500 employees will not have much effect. On the other hand, adding 500 employees to an organization that has only 300 members is likely to result in a shift toward a more mechanistic structure.

HOW DOES TECHNOLOGY AFFECT STRUCTURE?

Every organization uses some form of technology to convert its inputs into outputs. To attain its objectives, the organization uses equipment, materials, knowledge, and experienced individuals and puts them together into certain types and patterns of activities. For instance, workers at Maytag build washers, dryers, and other home appliances on a standardized assembly line. Employees at Kinko's produce custom copy jobs for individual customers. And employees at Bayer AG work on a continuous-flow production line for manufacturing its pharmaceuticals. Each of these organizations represents a different type of technology.

Over the years, several studies regarding the effect of technology have been conducted.[22] In one study, British scholar Joan Woodward found that distinct relationships exist between size of production runs and the structure of the firm. She also found that the effectiveness of organizations was related to the "fit" between technology and structure.[23] Most of these studies, like Woodward's, have focused on the processes or methods that transform inputs into outputs and how they differ by their degree of routineness. Three categories, representing three distinct technologies, had increasing levels of complexity and sophistication. The first category, **unit production**, described the production of items in units or small batches. The second category, **mass production**, described large-batch manufacturing. Finally, the third and most technically complex group, **process production**, included continuous-process production. The process or methods that transform an organization's inputs into outputs differ by their degree of routineness. In general, the more routine the technology, the more standardized and mechanistic the structure can be. Conversely, organizations with more nonroutine technology are more likely to have organic structures.[24]

unit production
Production in terms of units or small batches

mass production
Production in terms of large batch manufacturing

process production
Production in terms of continuous processing

HOW DOES ENVIRONMENT AFFECT STRUCTURE?

In Chapter 2, we discussed the organization's environment as a constraint on managerial discretion. It also has a major effect on the organization's structure. Essentially, mechanistic organizations are most effective in stable environments. Organic organizations are best matched with dynamic and uncertain environments.

The evidence on the environment–structure relationship helps to explain why so many managers have restructured their organizations to be lean, fast, and flexible.[25] Global competition, accelerated product innovation by all competitors, knowledge management, and increased demands from customers for higher quality and faster deliveries are examples of dynamic environmental forces.[26] Mechanistic organizations tend to be ill equipped to respond to rapid environmental change. As a result, managers, like those at Samsung Electronics, are redesigning their organizations in order to make them more organic.[27] As a result, Samsung has witnessed significant increases in sales and net profits.

ORGANIZATION DESIGN APPLICATIONS

What types of organization designs exist in small businesses or companies such as General Foods, National Cooperative Bank, and eBay? Let's look at the various types of organization designs that you might see in contemporary organizations.

A simple structure is one in which most, if not all, employees report to the owner. At this restaurant in Brooklyn, New York, workers report to the owners, who, like employees, perform many of the day-to-day activities required for quality customer service.

WHAT IS A SIMPLE STRUCTURE?

Most organizations start as an entrepreneurial venture with a simple structure. This organization design reflects the owner as president, with all employees reporting directly to her.

A **simple structure** is defined more by what it is not than by what it is. It is not an elaborate structure.[28] If you see an organization that appears to have almost no structure, it is probably of the simple variety. By that we mean that work specialization is low; few rules govern the operations and authority is centralized in a single person—the owner. The simple structure is a "flat" organization; it usually has only two or three vertical levels and a loose body of empowered employees in whom the decision-making authority is centralized.

The simple structure is most widely used in smaller businesses. The strengths of the simple structure should be obvious. It is fast, flexible, and inexpensive to maintain, and accountability is clear. However, it is effective only in small organizations. It becomes increasingly inadequate as an organization grows, because its few policies or rules to guide operations and its high centralization result in information overload at the top. As size increases, decision making becomes slower and can eventually come to a standstill as the single executive tries to continue making all the decisions. If the structure is not changed and adapted to its size, the firm is likely to lose momentum and eventually fail. The simple structure's other weakness is that it is risky: Everything depends on one person. If anything happens to the owner-manager, the organization's information and decision-making center is lost.

simple structure
An organization that is low in specialization and formalization but high in centralization

WHAT DO WE MEAN BY A BUREAUCRACY?

Many organizations do not remain simple structures. That decision is often made by choice or because structural contingency factors dictate it. For example, as production or sales increase significantly, companies generally reach a point at which more employees are needed. As the number of employees rises, informal work rules of the simple structure give way to more formal rules. Rules and regulations are implemented; departments are created; and levels of management are added to coordinate the activities of departmental people. At this point, a bureaucracy is formed. Two of the most popular bureaucratic design options grew out of the function and product departmentalizations. These are appropriately called the functional and divisional structures, respectively.

functional structure
An organization in which similar and related occupational specialties are grouped together

Why do companies implement functional structures? We introduced functional departmentalization a few pages ago. The **functional structure** merely expands the functional orientation to make it the dominant form for the entire organization. As displayed in Exhibit 5–8, management can choose to organize its structure by grouping similar and related occupational specialties. For example, Revlon, Inc. is organized around the functions of operations, finance, human resources, and product research and development. The strength of the functional structure lies in the advantages that accrue from work spe-

EXHIBIT 5–8
Functional Structure

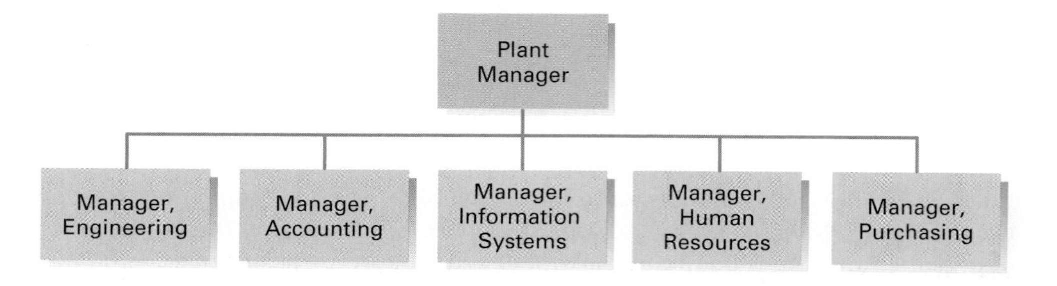

EXHIBIT 5–9 **Divisional Structure**

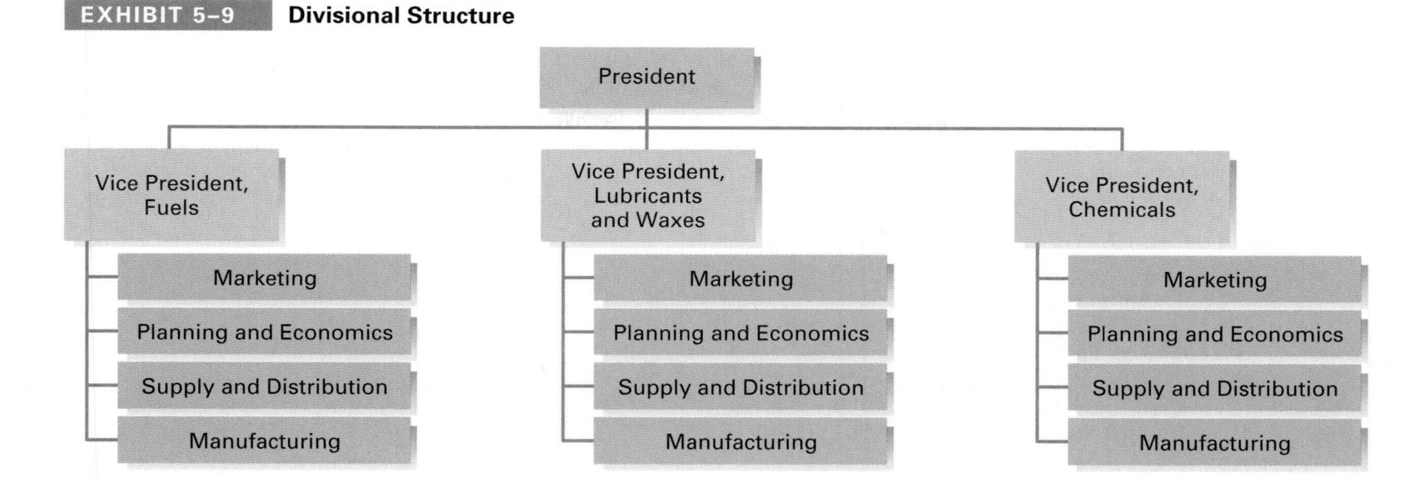

cialization. Putting like specialties together results in economies of scale, minimizes duplication of personnel and equipment, and makes employees comfortable and satisfied because it gives them the opportunity to talk the same language as their peers. The most obvious weakness of the functional structure, however, is that the organization frequently loses sight of its best interests in the pursuit of functional goals. No one function is totally responsible for results, so members within individual functions become insulated and have little understanding of what people in other functions are doing.

What is the divisional structure? The **divisional structure** is an organization design made up of self-contained units or divisions. General Foods and PepsiCo have implemented such a structure. Building on product departmentalization (see Exhibit 5–9), each division is generally autonomous, with a division manager responsible for performance and holding complete strategic and operational decision-making authority. In most divisional structures, central headquarters provides support services—such as financial and legal services—to the divisions. Of course, the headquarters also acts as an external overseer to coordinate and control the various divisions. Divisions are, therefore, autonomous within given parameters. The chief advantage of the divisional structure is that it focuses on results. Division managers have full responsibility for a product or service. The divisional structure also frees the headquarters staff from being concerned with day-to-day operating details so that they can pay attention to long-term and strategic planning. The major disadvantage of the divisional structure is duplication of activities and resources. Each division, for instance, may have a marketing research department. In the absence of autonomous divisions, all of the organization's marketing research might be centralized and done for a fraction of the cost that divisionalization requires. Thus, the divisional form's duplication of functions increases the organization's costs and reduces efficiency.

divisional structure
An organization made up of self-contained units

CAN AN ORGANIZATION DESIGN CAPTURE THE ADVANTAGES OF BUREAUCRACIES WHILE ELIMINATING THEIR DISADVANTAGES?

The functional structure offers the advantages that accrue from specialization. The divisional structure has a greater focus on results but suffers from duplication of activities and resources. Does any structure combine the advantages of functional specialization with the focus and accountability that product departmentalization provides? Yes, and it's called the **matrix structure**.[29]

Exhibit 5–10 illustrates the matrix structure of an aerospace firm. Notice that along the top of the figure are the familiar functions of engineering, accounting, human resources, manufacturing, and so forth. Along the vertical dimension, however, are the various projects on which the aerospace firm is currently working. Each

matrix structure
An organization in which specialists from functional departments are assigned to work on one or more projects led by a project manager

EXHIBIT 5–10 Sample Matrix Structure

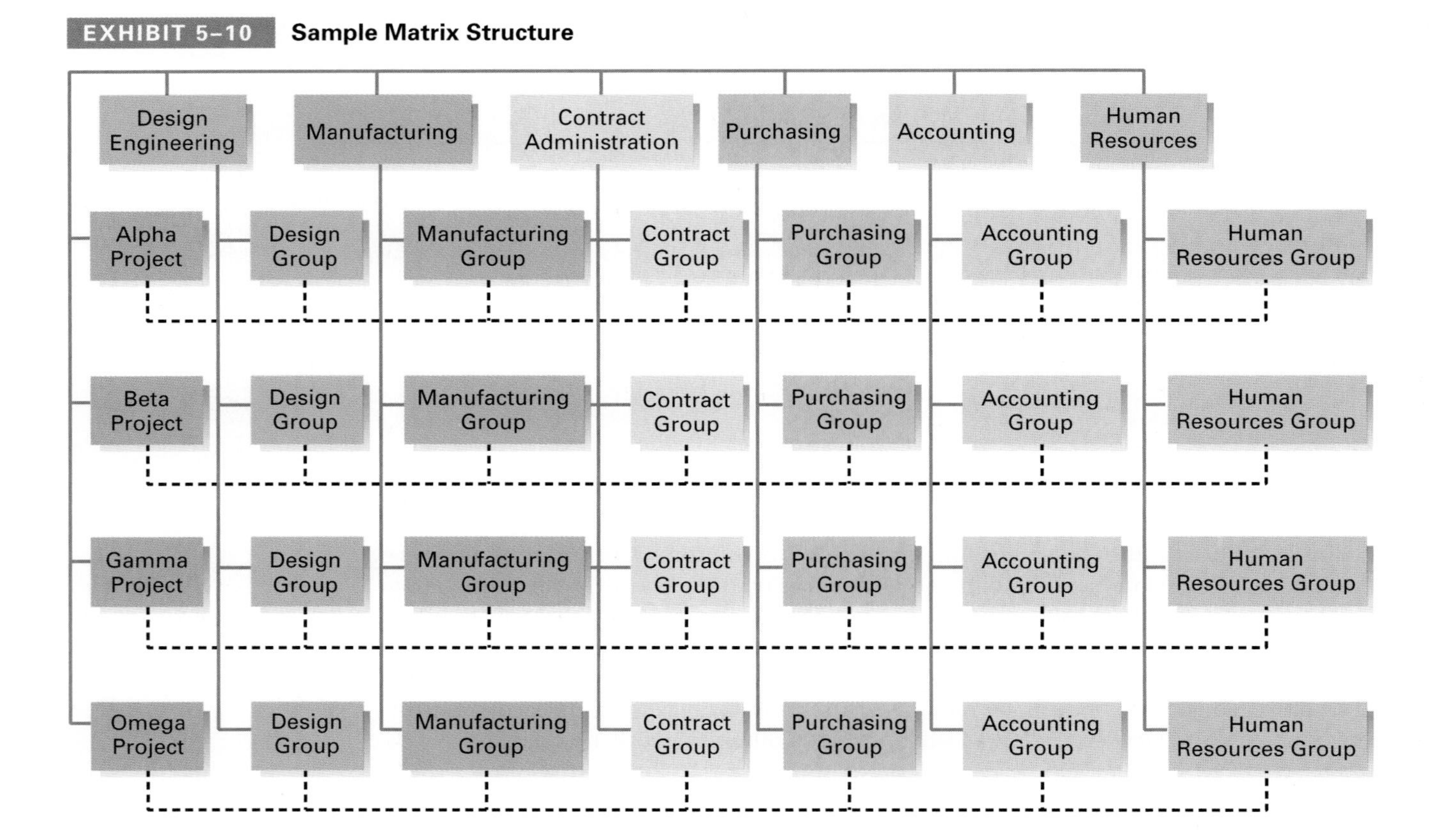

program is directed by a manager who staffs his or her project with people from the functional departments. The addition of this vertical dimension to the traditional horizontal functional departments, in effect, weaves together elements of function and product departmentalization—hence the term *matrix*.

The unique characteristic of the matrix is that employees in this structure have at least two bosses: their functional departmental manager and their product or project managers. Project managers have authority over the functional members who are part of that manager's project team, but authority is shared between the two managers. Typically, the project manager is given authority over project employees relative to the project's goals, but decisions such as promotions, salary recommendations, and annual reviews remain the functional manager's responsibility. To work effectively, project and functional managers must communicate regularly and coordinate the demands on employees, and resolve conflicts together.[30]

The primary strength of the matrix is that it can facilitate coordination of a multiple set of complex and interdependent projects while still retaining the economies that result from keeping functional specialists grouped together. The major disadvantages of the matrix are the confusion it creates and its propensity to foster power struggles. When you dispense with the chain of command principle, you significantly increase ambiguity. Confusion can arise over who reports to whom. The confusion and ambiguity, in turn, are what plants the seeds of power struggles.

WHAT ARE TEAM-BASED STRUCTURES?

team-based structure
An organization that consists entirely of work groups or teams

In a **team-based structure**, the entire organization consists of work groups or teams that perform the organization's work.[31] In such a structure, it goes without saying that team members have the authority to make decisions that affect them, because there is no rigid chain of command in these work arrangements. How can team structures benefit the organization? Let's look at what happened at The National Cooperative Bank in Washington, DC.[32]

Bank officials became aware of how their functional structure in the lending area was slowing decision making and constraining customer service—often taking as long as 20 weeks to process a loan. As a result, they restructured the bank into teams representing specific industries, such as health care, distribution, and so on, based on the special regulatory issues in each industry. In doing so, the bank witnessed significant reductions in the time spent to process a loan; customer satisfaction increased, as did employee cooperation. And at AMS Hillend's factory in Edinburgh, Scotland, a team-based structure for its circuit board production has resulted in "enhanced customer responsiveness, quality and efficiency gains, and an 88 percent increase in productivity."[33]

While team structures have been positive, simply arranging employees into teams is not enough. Employees must be trained to work on teams, receive cross-functional skills training, and must be compensated accordingly. Without a properly implemented team-based pay plan, many of the benefits of a team structure may be lost.[34]

WHY IS THERE MOVEMENT TOWARD A BOUNDARYLESS ORGANIZATION?

The last organization design application that we cover is the **boundaryless organization**. A boundaryless organization is not defined or limited by boundaries or categories imposed by traditional structures. It blurs the historical boundaries surrounding an organization by increasing its interdependence with its environment.[35] Sometimes called network organizations, learning organizations, barrier-free, modular, or virtual corporations,[36] boundaryless structures cut across all aspects of the organization. Rather than having functional specialties located in departments working on distinctive tasks, these internally boundaryless organizations group employees to accomplish some core competency (see Chapter 3). For instance, eBay has become the world's market leader in online trading—in part through its virtual corporation. That is, eBay has "no inventory, no warehouses, no sales force"—yet trades nearly $10 billion worth of goods each year![37]

boundaryless organization
An organization that is not defined or limited by boundaries or categories imposed by traditional structures

But boundaryless organizations are not merely flatter organizations. They attempt to eliminate vertical, horizontal, and interorganizational barriers. To do this, however,

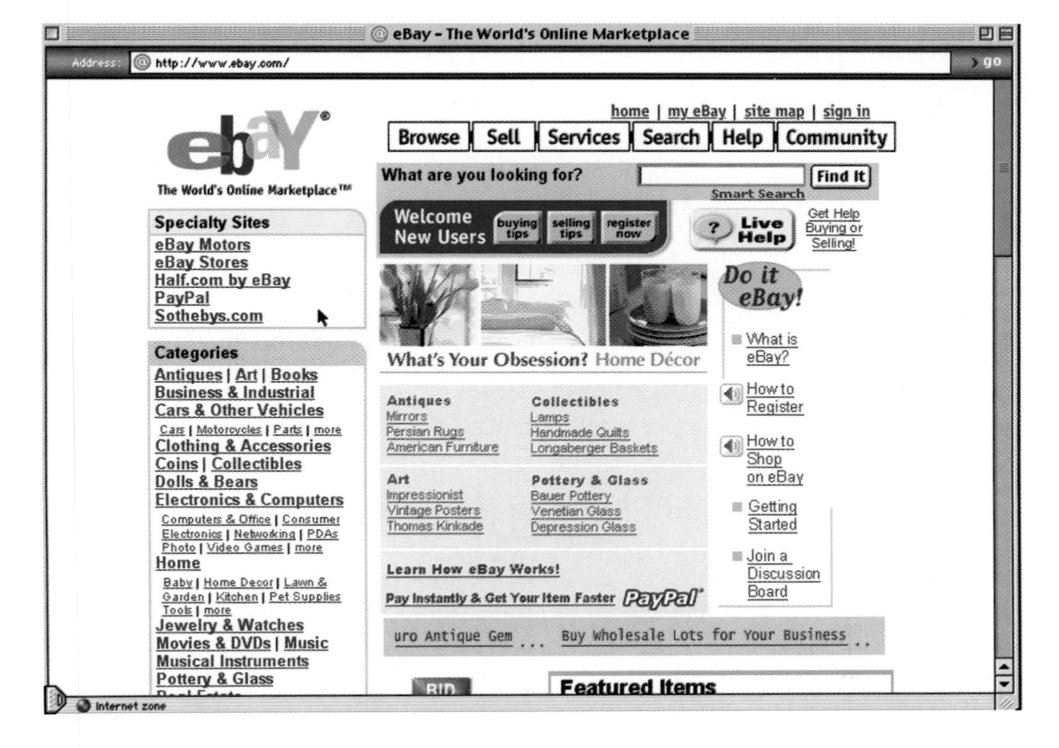

A number of organizations are recognizing the value of the virtual corporation. eBay trades nearly $10 billion in goods each year with no inventory, no warehouses, and no sales force.

frequently requires an internal revolution.[38] That is, managers must break down the traditional hierarchies that have often existed for many decades.[39] Horizontal organizations require multidisciplinary work teams who have the authority to make the necessary decisions and be held accountable for measurable outcomes. What factors have contributed to the rise of boundaryless designs in today's organizations? Undoubtedly, many of the issues we covered in Chapter 2 have had an effect. Specifically, globalization of markets and competitors has played a major role. An organization's need to respond and adapt to the complex and dynamic environment is best served by boundaryless organizations. Changes in technology have also contributed to this movement. Advances in computer power, "intelligent" software, and telecommunications enable boundaryless e-commerce organizations to exist. Each of these supports the information network that makes the virtual workplace possible.[40]

HOW DO YOU CREATE A LEARNING ORGANIZATION?

learning organization
An organization that has developed the capacity to continuously adapt and change because all members take an active role in identifying and resolving work-related issues

The concept of a learning organization doesn't involve a specific organizational design per se, but instead describes an organizational mind-set or philosophy that has significant design implications. What is a **learning organization**? It's an organization that has developed the capacity to continuously adapt and change because all members take an active role in identifying and resolving work-related issues.[41] In a learning organization, employees are practicing knowledge management by continually acquiring and sharing new knowledge and are willing to apply that knowledge in making decisions or performing their work. Some organizational design theorists even go so far as to say that an organization's ability to do this—that is, to learn and to apply that learning as they perform the organization's work—may be the only sustainable source of competitive advantage.

What would a learning organization look like? As you can see in Exhibit 5–11, the important characteristics of a learning organization revolve around organizational design, information sharing, leadership, and culture. Let's take a closer look at each.

What types of organizational design elements would be necessary for learning to take place? In a learning organization, it's critical for members to share infor-

EXHIBIT 5–11 Characteristics of a Learning Organization

THE LEARNING ORGANIZATION

Organizational Design
- Boundaryless
- Teams
- Empowerment

Information Sharing
- Open
- Timely
- Accurate

Leadership
- Shared Vision
- Collaboration

Organizational Culture
- Strong Mutual Relationships
- Sense of Community
- Caring
- Trust

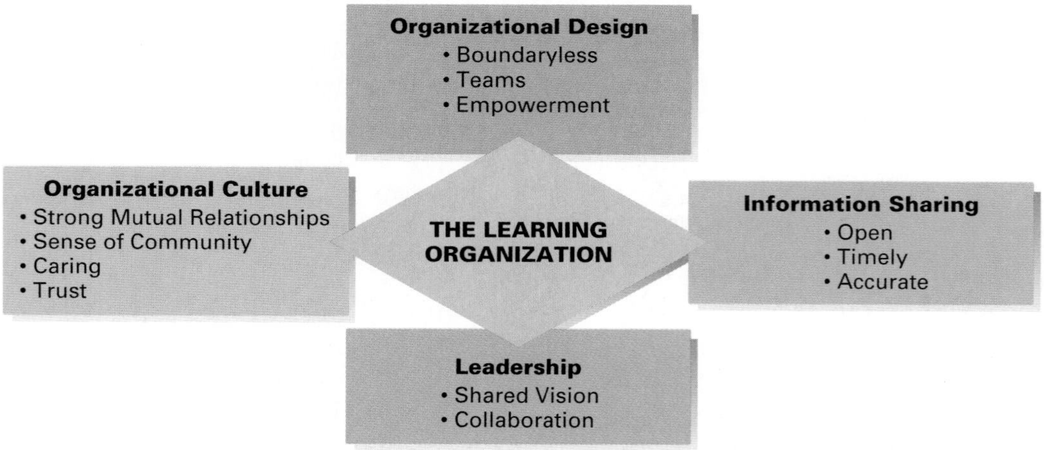

Source: Based on P. M. Senge. *The Fifth Discipline: The Art and Practice of Learning Organizations* (New York: Doubleday, 1990); and R. M. Hodgetts, F. Luthans, and S. M. Lee. "New Paradigm Organizations: From Total Quality to Learning to World Class." *Organizational Dynamics* (Winter 1994) pp. 4–19.

mation and collaborate on work activities throughout the entire organization—across different functional specialties and even at different organizational levels. This can be done by minimizing or eliminating the existing structural and physical boundaries. In this type of boundaryless environment, employees are free to work together and collaborate in doing the organization's work the best way they can, and to learn from each other. Because of this need to collaborate, teams also tend to be an important feature of a learning organization's structural design. Employees work in teams on whatever activities need to be done, and these employee teams are empowered to make decisions about doing their work or resolving issues. With empowered employees and teams, there's little need for "bosses" to direct and control. Instead, managers serve as facilitators, supporters, and advocates for employee teams.

Learning can't take place without information. For a learning organization to "learn," information must be shared among members; that is, organizational employees must engage in knowledge management. This means sharing information openly, in a timely manner, and as accurately as possible. Because there are few structural and physical barriers in a learning organization, the environment is conducive to open communication and extensive information sharing.

Leadership plays an important role as an organization moves to toward becoming a learning organization. What should leaders do in a learning organization? One of their most important functions is facilitating the creation of a shared vision for the organization's future and then keeping organizational members working toward that vision. In addition, leaders should support and encourage the collaborative environment that's critical to learning. Without strong and committed leadership throughout the organization, it would be extremely difficult to be a learning organization.

Finally, the organizational culture is an important aspect of being a learning organization. A learning organization's culture is one in which everyone agrees on a shared vision and everyone recognizes the inherent interrelationships among the organization's processes, activities, functions, and external environment. There is a strong sense of community, caring for each other, and trust. In a learning organization, employees feel free to openly communicate, share, experiment, and learn without fear of criticism or punishment.

No matter what structural design managers choose for their organizations, the design should help employees do their work in the best, most efficient, and effective way they can. The structure needs to help, not hinder, organizational members as they carry out the organization's work. After all, the structure is simply a means to an end.

ORGANIZATION CULTURE

We know that every individual has what psychologists have termed "personality," a set of relatively permanent and stable traits. When we describe someone as warm, innovative, relaxed, or conservative, we are describing personality traits. An organization, too, has a personality, which we call the organization's culture.

WHAT IS AN ORGANIZATION CULTURE?

What do we specifically mean by the term **organization culture**? We refer to a system of shared meaning.[42] Just as tribal cultures have totems and taboos that dictate how each member should act toward fellow members and outsiders, organizations have cultures that govern how their members should behave.[43] In every organization, stories, rituals, material symbols, and language have evolved over time.[44] These shared values determine, in large degree, what employees see and how they respond to their world.[45]

organization culture
A system of shared meaning within an organization that determines, to a large degree, how employees act

EXHIBIT 5–12 Ten Characteristics of Organization Culture

1. **Member identity** The degree to which employees identify with the organization as a whole rather than with their type of job or field of professional expertise.
2. **Group emphasis** The degree to which work activities are organized around groups rather than individuals.
3. **People focus** The degree to which management decisions take into consideration the effect of outcomes on people within the organization.
4. **Unit integration** The degree to which units within the organization are encouraged to operate in a coordinated or interdependent manner.
5. **Control** The degree to which rules, regulations, and direct supervision are used to oversee and control employee behavior.
6. **Risk tolerance** The degree to which employees are encouraged to be aggressive, innovative, and risk-seeking.
7. **Reward criteria** The degree to which rewards such as salary increases and promotions are allocated on employee performance criteria in contrast to seniority, favoritism, or other nonperformance factors.
8. **Conflict tolerance** The degree to which employees are encouraged to air conflicts and criticisms openly.
9. **Means-end orientation** The degree to which management focuses on results or outcomes rather than on the techniques and processes used to achieve those outcomes.
10. **Open-systems focus** The degree to which the organization monitors and responds to changes in the external environment.

HOW CAN CULTURES BE ASSESSED?

Although we currently have no definitive method for measuring an organization's culture, preliminary research suggests that cultures can be analyzed by rating an organization on 10 characteristics.[46] We have listed these characteristics in Exhibit 5–12; they are relatively stable and permanent over time. Just as an individual's personality is stable and permanent—if you were outgoing last month, you're likely to be outgoing next month—so, too, is an organization's culture.

Herb Kelleher, founder of Southwest Airlines, was instrumental in promoting a people culture in the organization. Company practices—like those in compensation and benefits—were designed to make employees happy. In turn, these happy employees could make their customers' experience on Southwest Airlines more memorable.

WHERE DOES AN ORGANIZATION'S CULTURE COME FROM?

An organization's culture usually reflects the vision or mission of the organization's founders. Because the founders had the original idea, they also have biases on how to carry out the idea. They are unconstrained by previous customs or ideologies. The founders establish the early culture by projecting an image of what the organization should be. The small size of most new organizations also helps the founders impose their vision on all organization members. An organization's culture, then, results from the interaction between (1) the founders' biases and assumptions and (2) what the first employees learn subsequently from their own experiences. For example, the founder of IBM, Thomas Watson, established a culture based on "pursuing excellence, providing the best customer service, and respect for employees." Ironically, some 75 years later, in an effort to revitalize the ailing IBM, CEO Louis Gerstner enhanced that culture with his strong, "customer-oriented sensibility," recognizing the urgency the marketplace imposes on having customers' expectations met.[47] And at Southwest Airlines, former CEO Herb Kelleher reinforced the company's "people culture" by implementing certain practices—such as compensation and benefits that are above industry averages—to make employees happy.[48]

HOW DOES CULTURE INFLUENCE STRUCTURE?

An organization's culture may have an effect on its structure, depending on how strong, or weak, the culture is.[49] For instance, in organizations that have a strong culture, the organization's culture can substitute for the rules and regulations that formally guide employees. In essence, strong cultures can create predictability, orderliness, and consistency without the need for written documentation. Therefore, the stronger an organization's culture, the less managers need to be concerned with developing formal rules and regulations.[50] Instead, those guides will be internalized in employees when they accept the organization's culture. If, on the other hand, an organization's culture is weak—if there are no dominant shared values—its effect on structure is less clear.

Review, Comprehension, Application

CHAPTER SUMMARY

How will you know if you fulfilled the Learning Outcomes on page 140? You will have fulfilled the Learning Outcomes if you are able to:

1. **Identify and define the six elements of organization structure.** The six elements of organization structure are: work specialization (having each discrete step of a job done by a different individual rather than one individual do the whole job); chain of command (management principle that no employee should report to more than one boss); span of control (the number of employees a manager can effectively and efficiently manage); authority (rights inherent in a managerial position to give orders and expect them to be followed) and responsibility (an obligation to perform assigned activities); centralization (the higher the level in which decisions are made) versus decentralization (pushing down of decision-making authority to lowest levels in an organization); and departmentalization (the grouping of activities in an organization by function, product, customer, geography, or process).
2. **Describe the advantages and disadvantages of work specialization.** The advantages of work specialization are related to economic efficiencies. It makes efficient use of the diversity of skills that workers hold. Skills are developed through repetition. Less time is wasted than when workers are generalists. Training is also easier and less costly, but work specialization can result in human diseconomies. Excessive work specialization can cause boredom, fatigue, stress, low productivity, poor quality, increased absence, and high turnover.
3. **Contrast authority and power.** Authority is related to rights inherent in a position. Power describes all means by which an individual can influence decisions, including formal authority. Authority is synonymous with legitimate power. However, a person can have coercive, reward, expert, or referent power without holding a position of authority. Thus, authority is actually a subset of power.
4. **Identify the five different ways by which management can departmentalize.** Managers can departmentalize on the basis of function (work being done), product (product or service being generated), customer (group served), geography (location of operations), or process (work flow). In practice, most large organizations use all five ways.
5. **Contrast mechanistic and organic organizations.** The mechanistic organization, or bureaucracy, rates high on worker specialization, formal work rules and regulations, and centralized decisions. Workers perform specific job duties, their actions are guided by formal work regulations, and decisions are typically made by higher levels in the organization. In the organic organization, employees are generalists and perform all parts of a job, face fewer work regulations, and oftentimes have the authority to make decisions on issues directly related to their work.
6. **Summarize the effect of strategy, size, technology, and environment on organization structures.** The strategy-determines-structure thesis argues that structure should follow strategy. As strategies move from single product, to vertical integration, to product diversification, structure must move from organic to mechanistic. As size increases, so, too, do specialization, formalization, and horizontal and vertical differentiation. But size has less of an impact on large organizations than on small ones because once an organization has around 2,000 employees, it tends to be fairly mechanistic. All other things equal, the more routine the technology, the more mechanistic the organization should be. The more nonroutine the technology, the more organic the structure should be. Finally, stable environments are better matched with mechanistic organizations, but dynamic environments fit better with organic organizations.
7. **Contrast the divisional and functional structures.** The functional structure groups similar or related occupational specialties together. It takes advantage of specialization and provides economies of scale by allowing people with common skills to work together. The divisional structure is composed of autonomous units or divisions, with managers having full responsibility for a product or service. However, these units are frequently organized as functional structures inside their divisional framework. So divisional structures typically contain functional structures within them—and they are less efficient.
8. **Explain the strengths of the matrix structure.** By assigning specialists from functional departments to work on one or more projects led by project managers, the matrix structure combines functional and product departmentalization. It thus has the advantages of both work specialization and high accountability.
9. **Describe the boundaryless organization and what elements have contributed to its development.** The boundaryless organization is a design application in which the structure is not defined by or limited to the boundaries imposed by traditional structures. It breaks down hori-

zontal, vertical, and interorganizational barriers. It's also flexible and adaptable to environmental conditions. The factors contributing to boundaryless organizations include global markets and competition, technology advancements, and the need for rapid innovation.

10. **Explain what is meant by the term *learning organization*.** A learning organization is an organization that has developed the capacity to continuously adapt and change because all members take an active role in identifying and resolving work-related issues. In a learning organization, employees are practicing knowledge management by continually acquiring and sharing new knowledge, and they are willing to apply that knowledge in making decisions or performing their work.
11. **Describe what is meant by the term *organization culture*.** Organization culture is a system of shared meaning within an organization that determines, in large degree, how employees act.

COMPANION WEBSITE

We invite you to visit the Robbins/DeCenzo companion Website at **www.prenhall.com/robbins** for this chapter's Internet resources, including an online study guide, Internet exercises, and "In the News" with full text articles provided by XanEdu.

READING FOR COMPREHENSION

1. Describe what is meant by the term *organization design*.
2. How are authority and organization structure related? Authority and power?
3. In what ways can management departmentalize? When should one method be considered over the others?
4. Why is the simple structure inadequate in large organizations?
5. Describe the characteristics of a boundaryless organization structure.
6. What is the source of an organization's culture?

LINKING CONCEPTS TO PRACTICE

1. Which do you think is more efficient—a wide or a narrow span of control? Support your decision.
2. "An organization can have no structure." Do you agree or disagree with this statement? Explain.
3. Show how both the functional and matrix structures might create conflict within an organization.
4. Do you think the concept of organizational structures, as described in this chapter, is appropriate for charitable organizations? If so, which organization design application do you believe to be most appropriate? If not, why not? Explain your position.
5. What effects do you think the characteristics of the boundaryless organization will have on employees in today's contemporary organizations?
6. Classrooms have cultures. Describe your class culture. How does it affect your instructor? You?

VIDEO CASE APPLICATION

Practicity: Keeping Track of Knowledge Work

According to David Jackson, president & CEO of Practicity, in the new economy a company's assets are people and what's inside their heads. "The day the employee you've trained, educated, and invested in walks out the foor that entire asset is lost," he says. Predictions that in our global marketplace nearly 40 percent of the workforce will be knowledge workers by 2004 means that a firm's competitive edge depends on quick access to the right information. Natural retirement greater mobility, ever-increasing geographical distances between people who work "together, and an emphasis on customer service make knowledge management the priority for survival.

In July 2000 an agile team of about 10 professional service consultants decided the time was right for a software solution that would help businesses manage knowledge in a whole new way. Within months, they transformed themselves into a software development company, moved from Buffalo Grove, Illinois to Andover, Massachusetts, and founded Practicity.[51] They were excited. Their mission was to allow organizations to create a Web-based space where people could exchange information and store it for reuse at a later time.

Not only does Practicity keep track of critical knowledge between professional service organizations and their clients; it lets all the parties collaborating on a job track comment about community documents and content. Moreover, it allows businesses to learn about the process behind the projects to develop and revamp business proctices. If an organization loses an employee, it retains access to at least some of what's inside that person's head.

Here's what happened at Final Mile Communications when Practicity came to the rescue. Final Mile found itself facing seemingly insurmountable difficulties when it was called upon to complete network infrastructure and hardwiring needs for 200 new bank branches throughout New England. Each office had to be linked to the acquiring bank's data and voice connections. The only way to meet the deadline was for crews to work seven days a week in around-the-clock shifts. The logistics of coordinating physical labor, technical planning, and communication between workers and management on both the corporate and the client side would have been impossible without Practicity.

Final Miles' Chief Financial Office Michelle Winder explained that the company had always relied on distributing documents via e-mail, fax, overnight delivery, or messenger. Sometimes project leaders would waste time working on the wrong document, updating something that had already been updated, and then spend hours on the phone straightening out mistakes. Using Practicity eliminated all that extraneous communication. Whenever a problem arose with equipment delivery or building access, the person in charge could post a description of the problem on the Web and get a response right away.[52] The seamless collaboration made timely completion of this contract possible. Now Final Mile has a satisfied client and a step-by-step record of the entire endeavor from which to learn.

The idea for Practicity was born "when it became clear that e-mail wouldn't bridge the gaps between workers who were separated geographically," says Jeff Grammer, co-founder, CTO, and executive vice president of Practicity. He likes to think of Practicity as a virtual electronic water cooler—an informal place on the Web where people can "meet" and get support or just touch base.

The need to respond and adapt to the demands of a dynamic environment make Practicity the tool of the moment. As Michelle Winder expressed it, "Nowadays you have to address client needs so rapidly that if you don't have a technological solution you're pretty much dead in the water."

Questions

1. You are a first-line supervisor at Final Mile Communications, Inc. How might your personal power base be affected now that top management has invested in Practicity's software to enhance communication capabilities both inside and outside the organization? Before answering, decide whether you are by nature an outgoing, collaborative "technology wizard, or whether you are a more reserved, independent type, inclined to work things out using a sketch pad and a pencil. Respond accordingly.
2. Based on the video, briefly describe the factors that induced Final Mile to behave like a boundaryless organization in the face of an extraordinary workload to be completed in a short amount of time.
3. Would you define Practicity as a learning organization? Explain your viewpoint.
4. How will the organizational culture at Practicity impact the likelihood of its future success in today's dynamic marketplace?

Management Workshop

Team Skill-Building Exercise

How Is Your School Organized?

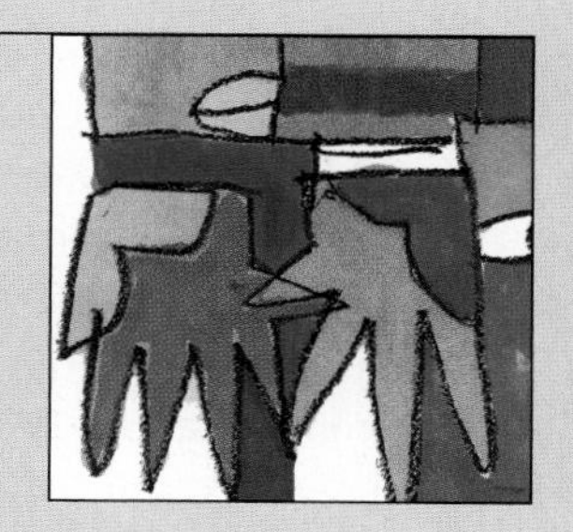

Every university or college displays a specific type of organization structure. For example, if you are a business major, your classes are often housed in a department, school, or college of business. But have you ever asked why? Or is it something you just take for granted?

In Chapter 3 you had an opportunity to assess your college's strengths, weaknesses, and comparative advantage and see how these fit into its strategy. Now, in this chapter we have built a case that structure follows strategy. Given your analysis in Chapter 3 (if you have not done so, you may want to refer to page 101 for the strategy part of this exercise), analyze your college's overall structure in terms of formalization, centralization, and complexity. Furthermore, look at the departmentalization that exists. Is your college more organic or mechanistic? Now analyze how well your college's structure fits with its strategy. Do the same thing for your college's size, technology, and environment. That is, assess its size, degree of technological routineness, and environmental uncertainty. Based on these assessments, what kind of structure would you predict your college to have? Does it have this structure now? Compare your findings with those of other classmates. Are there similarities in how each viewed the college? Differences? To what do you attribute these findings?

Understanding Yourself

Before you can develop other people, you must understand your present strengths. To assist in this learning process, we encourage you to complete the following self-assessments from the Prentice Hall Self-Assessment Library 2.0:

- How Power Oriented Am I? (#31)
- What's My Preferred Type of Power? (#32)
- What Type of Organization Structure Do I Prefer? (#39)

After you complete these assessments, we suggest that you print out the results and store them as part of your "portfolio of learning."

Developing Your Power Base Skill

Building a Power Base

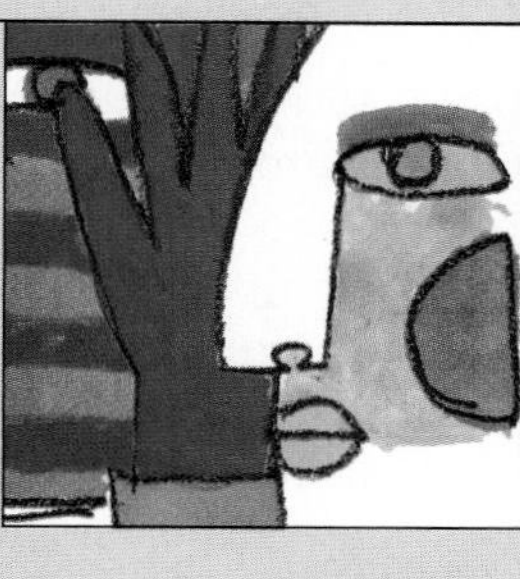

About the Skill

One of the more difficult aspects of power is acquiring it. For some individuals, power comes naturally, and, for some, it is a function of the job they hold. But what can others do to develop power? The answer is respect others, build power relationships, develop associations, control important information, gain seniority, and build power in stages.[53]

Steps in Practicing the Skill

1. **Respect others** One of the most crucial aspects of developing power is to treat others the way you would like to be treated. That sentence may be a cliche, but it holds a tremendous key. If others don't respect you, your power will generally be limited. Sure, they may do the things you ask, but only because of the authority of your position. People need to know that you're genuine, and that means respecting others. In today's world, with the great diversity that exists, you must be sensitive to others' needs. Failure to do so may only lead to problems, most of which can be avoided if you see the good in people and realize that most people try their best and want to do a good job.

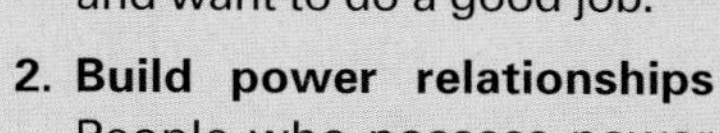

2. **Build power relationships** People who possess power often associate with others who have power. It appears to be a natural phenomenon—birds of a feather do flock together! You need to identify these people and model their behavior. The idea is that you want to make yourself visible to powerful people and let them observe you in a number of situations.

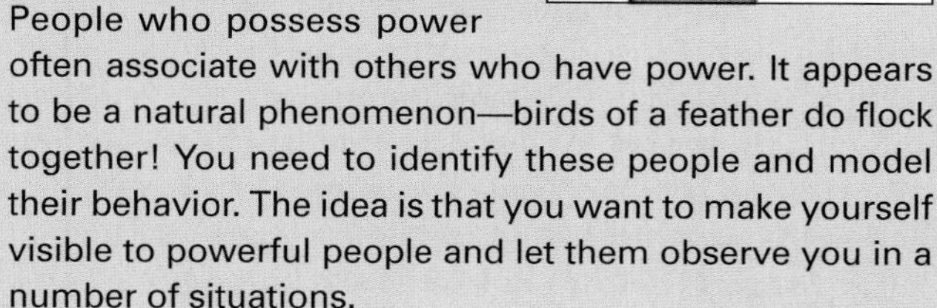

3. **Develop associations** We learn at an early age that there is strength in numbers. In the "power" world, this tenet also applies. By associating with others, you become part of a group in which all the members' energies are brought together to form one large base of power. Often called coalitions, these groups form to influence some event.

4. **Control important information** Get yourself into a position that gives you access to information other people perceive as important. Access to information is especially critical in a world where people's lives depend so much on information processing. One of the greatest means of developing this power is to continue to learn. Finding new approaches to solving old problems or creating a special process are ways of gaining a level of expertise that can make you indispensable to the organization.
5. **Gain seniority** Seniority is somewhat related to controlling information. Power can be gained by simply having been around for a long time. People will often respect individuals who have lived through the ups and downs of an organization. Their experience gives them a perspective or information that newcomers don't have.
6. **Build power in stages** No one goes from being powerless one moment to being powerful the next. That simply doesn't occur. Power comes in phases. As you build your power, remember, it will start off slowly. You will be given opportunities to demonstrate that you can handle the power. After each test you pass, you'll more than likely be given more power.

Practicing the Skill

Margaret is a supervisor in the Internet sales division of a large clothing retailer. She has let it be known that she is devoted to the firm and plans to build her career there. Margaret is hardworking and reliable, has volunteered for extra projects, has taken in-house development courses, and joined a committee dedicated to improving employee safety on the job. She undertook an assignment to research ergonomic office furniture for the head of the department and gave up several lunch hours to consult with the head of human resources about her report. Margaret filed the report late, but she excused herself by explaining that her assistant lost several pages that she had to redraft over the weekend. The report was well received, and several of Margaret's colleagues think she should be promoted when the next opening arises.

Evaluate Margaret's skill in building a power base. What actions has she taken that are helpful to her in reaching her goal? Is there anything she should have done differently?

Developing Your Diagnostic and Analytical Skills

Phone Home Nokia

Nokia, headquartered in Finland, is the world's leading maker of mobile phones and is a well-known brand. CEO Jorma Ollila isn't content with the company's current success and wants to position Nokia for the future.[54]

The company has evolved dramatically since its founding in 1865 as a wood-pulp mill. Over the years, it has moved into a number of diverse industries ranging from paper to chemicals and rubber. But during the 1990s, the company took a radically new direction as it shifted into the burgeoning field of telecommunications. Today, Nokia is a global company whose primary growth areas are in wireless and wired telecommunications. It has more than 56,000 employees worldwide, and one in every three employees works in some form of product research. Its commitment to innovation is reflected in the fact that Nokia again and again introduced better products than any of its competitors—including its new $21,000 platinum or 18k gold, crystal screen cell phone. It was also able to get its products to retailers and cellular phone companies in the right quantity and at the right time. And customers have responded, giving Nokia a 38 percent market share in the hotly contested mobile-phone global market. How has this been accomplished? Ollila says there's something about the way Nokia works that makes it more pragmatic, more focused, and more flexible than other companies. He describes it as "the way the organization creates a meeting of minds among people. How do you send a very strong signal that this is a meritocracy, and this is a place where you are allowed to have a bit of fun, to think unlike the norm, where you are allowed to make a mistake?"

Ollila has structured Nokia to be very nonhierarchical. Often, it's unclear who's in charge, although employees love the freedom once they get used to it. This kind of hands-off management encourages creativity, entrepreneurship, and personal responsibility. To balance this flexibility, rigorous financial targets keep employees focused on the organization's work. Ollila believes that Nokia could be even better if it became a learning organization.

Questions

1. Would you describe Nokia as more of a mechanistic or an organic organization? Explain and use specific examples to support your position.
2. How have technology and communications affected Nokia's organizational structure?
3. What recommendations would you make for Nokia to become a learning organization?

Enhancing Your Communication Skills

1. Visit a McDonald's on a weekday around lunch time. On your first order, ask for a Big Mac or a chicken sandwich. Record how long it takes to have your order filled. On your second order, request the Big Mac or chicken sandwich and ask for (1) no lettuce, (2) extra ketchup, and (3) extra pickles. Record how long this special order takes. Compare the two times. Discuss the time differences in terms of efficiencies of work specialization. Also note whether the second order was completed correctly. What are the implications of this simple investigation for product standardization?
2. Discuss the pros and cons of employees working on projects and reporting to several project managers. Discuss the implications you envision for violating the chain of command principle. Cite specific examples. If you were a project manager who managed project members who reported to other managers, what would you do to make sure that your project would be completed on time?

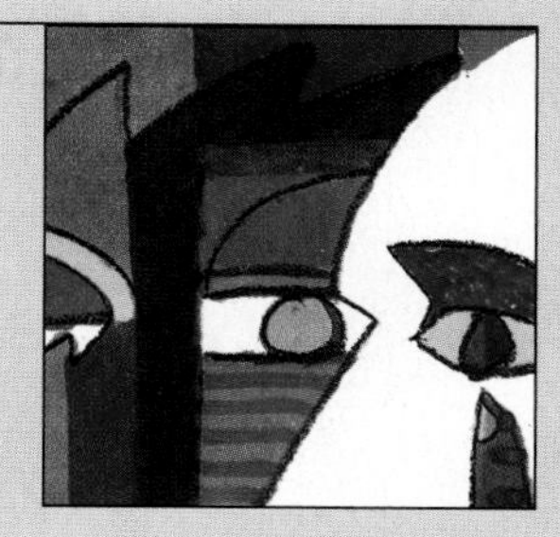

3. "Employees should follow orders and directives given to them by their managers. Those who don't are subject to being disciplined for insubordination." Develop an argument for both sides of this statement. Complete your paper by stating and supporting your position on whether employees should unquestionably follow orders given to them by their managers.

C H A P T E R 6

Staffing and Human Resource Management

LEARNING OUTCOMES

After reading this chapter, I will be able to:

1. Describe the human resource management process.
2. Identify the influence of government regulations on human resource decisions.
3. Differentiate between job descriptions and job specifications.
4. Contrast recruitment and downsizing options.
5. Explain the importance of validity and reliability in selection.
6. Describe the selection devices that work best with various kinds of jobs.
7. Identify various training methods.
8. Explain the various techniques managers can use in evaluating employee performance.
9. Describe the goals of compensation administration and factors that affect wage structures.
10. Explain what is meant by the terms *sexual harassment*, *labor-management cooperation*, *workplace violence*, and *layoff-survivor sickness*.

Imagine spending nearly $1,500 a year to maintain a daily latte and scone habit. Millions of individuals do at Starbucks. This coffee company, with more than 5,500 locations globally, plans on turning the world on to "triple-tall nonfat mochas." But it can't do that without the skilled effort of its employees.[1]

What's the secret to Starbucks' amazing success? A quality product and an organization culture focused on customer service. Every one of Starbucks's 57,000-plus employees has gone through a set of formal classes during his or her first six weeks with the company. When this socialization process is complete, it turns recruits into coffee experts. (Pictured are employees serving customers at a Starbucks' Tokyo Store.)

The Starbucks indoctrination begins with a history of the company. It's followed by a session on what customers need to know to brew a perfect cup of coffee at home. These include purchasing new beans weekly, the right type of water to use, and tips like never letting coffee sit on a hot plate for more than 20 minutes. The specific techniques for drink making are perfected in an eight-hour class on retail skills. New employees learn such varied skills as how to steam milk for latte, how to clean an espresso machine, and the proper way to fill one-pound sacks with coffee. There are also classes that teach new employees how to explain Starbucks's Italian drink names to baffled customers, and coffee-tasting classes so employees understand why Sanani is described as "winey" and Costa Rica as "tangy and bright."

Starbucks's socialization program turns out employees who are steeped in the company's culture and understand management's obsession with "elevating the coffee experience," as the company's senior vice president of marketing put it.

This comprehensive training, coupled with pay that exceeds most entry-level food service jobs and comprehensive benefits (including health insurance even for part-timers, and stock options), has produced a skilled and loyal workforce. Annual turnover among Starbucks employees, for instance, is nearly one-third less than the average within the fast-food business. This translates into good news for Starbucks's management and stockholders. Revenues now approach $2 billion a year, with profits exceeding $100 million.

MANAGERS AND THE HUMAN RESOURCE MANAGEMENT PROCESS

The quality of an organization is to a large degree determined by the quality of the people it employs. Success for most organizations depends on finding the employees with the skills to successfully perform the tasks required to attain the company's strategic goals. Staffing and human resources management decisions and methods are critical to ensuring that the organization hires and keeps the right personnel.

Some of you may be thinking, "Sure, personnel decisions are important. But aren't most of them made by people who specifically handle human resource issues?" It's true that, in many organizations, a number of the activities grouped under the label **human resource management (HRM)** are done by specialists. In other cases, HRM activities may even be outsourced to companies like HR Tech. Not all managers have HRM staff support. Many small business managers, for instance, are obvious examples of individuals who frequently must do their own hiring without the assistance of HRM specialists. Even managers in larger organizations are frequently involved in recruiting candidates, reviewing application forms, interviewing applicants, inducting new employees, making decisions about employee training, providing career advice to employees, and evaluating employees' performance. So, whether or not an organization provides HRM support activities, every manager is involved with human resource decisions in his or her unit.[2]

human resource management (HRM)
The management function that is concerned with getting, training, motivating, and keeping competent employees

Exhibit 6–1 introduces the key components of an organization's HRM process. It represents eight activities, or steps (the blue-shaded boxes), that, if properly executed, will staff an organization with competent, high-performing employees who are capable of sustaining their performance level over the long term.

EXHIBIT 6–1

The Strategic Human Resource Management Process

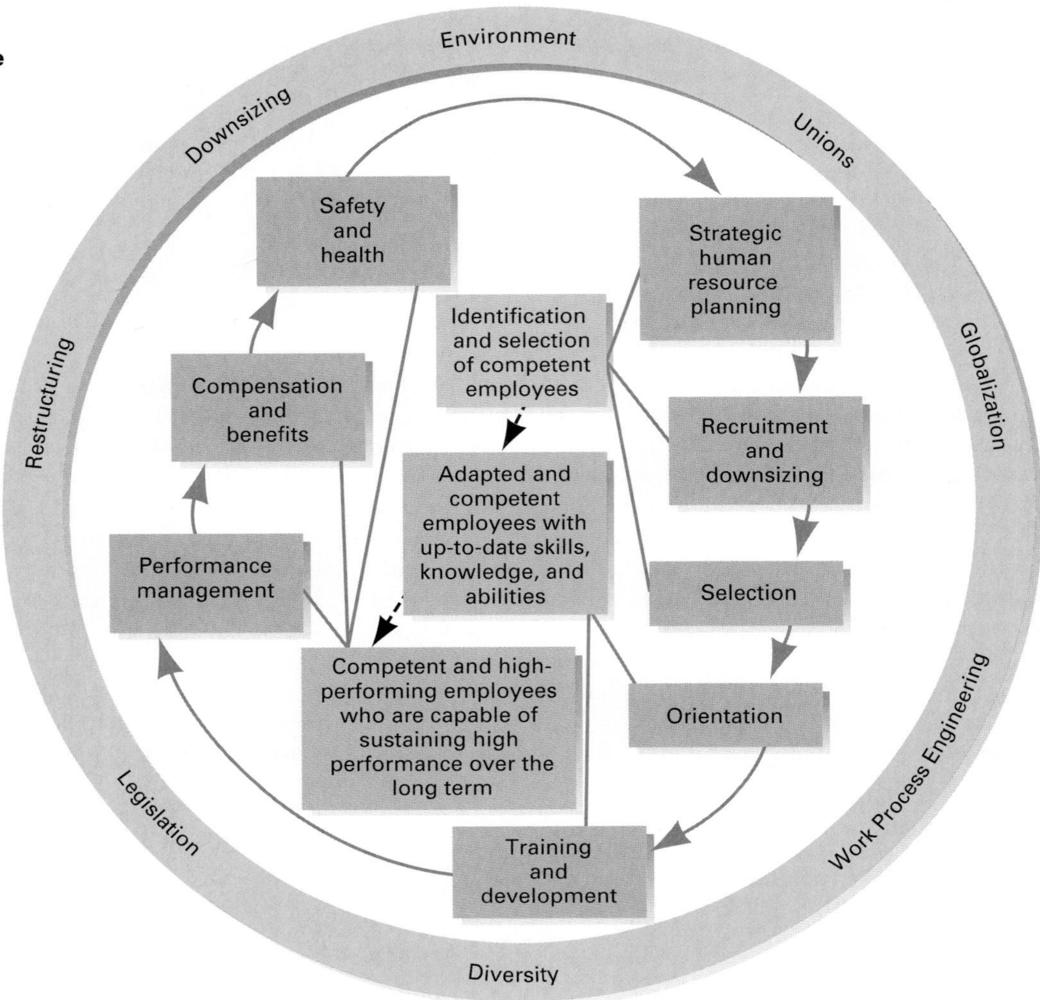

The first three steps represent employment planning, the addition of staff through recruitment and the reduction in staff through downsizing, and selection. When executed properly, these steps lead to the identification and selection of competent employees and assist organizations in achieving their strategic directions. Accordingly, once an organization's strategy has been established and the organization structure has been designed, it's now time to add the people. That's one of the most critical roles for HRM and one that has increased the importance of human resource managers to the organization.

Once you have selected competent people, you need to help them adapt to the organization and to ensure that their job skills and knowledge are kept current. You do this through orientation and training and development. The last steps in the HRM process are designed to identify performance goals, correct performance problems if necessary, and help employees sustain a high level of performance over their entire work life. The activities involved include performance appraisal, compensation and benefits, and safety and health.

Notice in Exhibit 6–1 that the entire employment process is influenced by the external environment. Many of the factors introduced in Chapter 2 (e.g., globalization, downsizing, diversity) directly affect all management practices, but their effect is probably greatest in the management of human resources, because whatever happens to an organization ultimately influences what happens to its employees. So, before we review the HRM process, let's examine one primary environmental force that affects it—employment and discrimination laws.

THE LEGAL ENVIRONMENT OF HRM

HRM practices are governed by laws of the land, and those laws vary from country to country. Within countries, there are state or provincial and local regulations that further influence specific practices. Consequently, it is impossible to provide you with a full description of the relevant regulatory environment you'll face as a manager.

WHAT ARE THE PRIMARY U.S. LAWS AFFECTING HRM?

Since the mid-1960s, the federal government in the United States has greatly expanded its influence over HRM by enacting a wealth of laws and regulations (see Exhibit 6–2 for examples). Even though we've not had a major federal employment discrimination law in a decade, don't let that lull you into the perception that discrimination laws have lost their emphasis. While at the federal level we've not seen a law enacted since 1993, many state laws have been passed which add to the provisions of the federal laws. For instance, in many states today, it is also illegal to discriminate against an individual based on sexual orientation. As a result, today's employers must ensure

EXHIBIT 6–2 Major U.S. Federal Laws and Regulations Related to HRM

YEAR	LAW OR REGULATION	DESCRIPTION
1963	Equal Pay Act	Prohibits pay differences based on sex for equal work
1964 (amended in 1972)	Civil Rights Act, Title VII	Probibits discrimination based on race, color, religion, national origin, or sex
1967 (amended in 1978)	Age Discrimination in Employment Act	Prohibits age discrimination against employees between 40 and 65 years of age
1973	Vocational Rehabilitation Act	Prohibits discrimination on the basis of physical or mental disabilities
1974	Privacy Act	Gives employees the legal right to examine letters of reference concerning them
1978	Pregnancy Discrimination Act, Title VII	Prohibits dismissal because of pregnancy alone and protects job security during maternity leaves
1978	Mandatory Retirement Act	Prohibits the forced retirement of most employees before the age of 70; later amended to eliminate upper limit.
1986	Immigration Reform and Control Act	Prohibits unlawful employment of aliens and unfair immigration-related employment practices
1988	Polygraph Protection Act	Limits an employer's ability to use lie detectors
1988	Worker Adjustment and Retraining Notification Act	Requires employers to provide 60 days' notice before a facility closing or mass layoff
1990	Americans with Disabilities Act	Prohibits employers from discriminating against and requires reasonable accommodation of essentially qualified individuals with physical or mental disabilities or the chronically ill
1991	Civil Rights Act	Reaffirms and tightens prohibition of discrimination; permits individuals to sue for punitive damages in cases of intentional discrimination
1993	Family and Medical Leave Act	Permits employees in organizations with 50 or more workers to take up to 12 weeks of unpaid leave each year for family or medical reasons

that equal employment opportunities exist for job applicants and current employees. Decisions regarding who will be hired, for example, or which employees will be chosen for a management training program must be made without regard to race, sex, religion, age, color, national origin, or disability. Exceptions can occur only when special circumstances exist. For instance, a community fire department can deny employment to a firefighter applicant who is confined to a wheelchair, but if that same individual is applying for a desk job, such as a fire department dispatcher, the disability cannot be used as a reason to deny employment. The issues involved, however, are rarely that clear-cut. For example, employment laws protect most employees whose religious beliefs require a specific style of dress—robes, long shirts, long hair, and the like. However, if the specific style of dress may be hazardous or unsafe in the work setting (e.g., when operating machinery), a company could refuse to hire a person who would not adopt a safer dress code.

affirmative action programs
Programs that ensure that decisions and practices enhance the employment, upgrading, and retention of members of protected groups

Trying to balance the "shoulds and should-nots" of these laws often falls within the realm of **affirmative action**. Many organizations operating in the United States have affirmative action programs to ensure that decisions and practices enhance the employment, upgrading, and retention of members from protected groups such as minorities and females. That is, the organization not only refrains from discrimination but actively seeks to enhance the status of members from protected groups.

American managers are not completely free to choose whom they hire, promote, or fire. Although these regulations have significantly helped to reduce employment discrimination and unfair employment practices, they have, at the same time, reduced management's discretion over human resource decisions.

DOES HRM FACE THE SAME LAWS GLOBALLY?

What we can do is remind you that you need to know the laws and regulations that apply in your locale. And to illustrate our point that laws and regulations shape HRM practices, we can highlight some of the federal legislation that influences HRM practices in countries like Canada, Mexico, Australia, and Germany.

Canadian laws pertaining to HRM practices closely parallel those in the United States. The Canadian Human Rights Act provides federal legislation that prohibits discrimination on the basis of race, religion, age, marital status, sex, physical or mental disability, or national origin. This Act governs practices throughout the country. Canada's HRM environment, however, is somewhat different from that in the United States in that there is more decentralization of lawmaking to the provincial level in Canada. For example, discrimination on the basis of language is not prohibited anywhere in Canada except in Quebec.

In Mexico, employees are more likely to be unionized than they are in the United States. Labor matters in Mexico are governed by the Mexican Federal Labor Law. One law regarding hiring states that an employer has 28 days to evaluate a new employee's work performance. After that period, the employee is granted job security and termination is quite difficult and expensive. Infractions of the Mexican Federal labor Law are subject to severe penalties, including criminal action. This means that high fines and even jail sentences can be imposed on employers who fail to pay, for example, the minimum wage.

Australia's discrimination laws were not enacted until the 1980s. The laws that do exist, however, generally apply to discrimination and affirmative action for women. Yet, gender opportunities for women in Australia appear to lag behind those in the United States. In Australia, however, a significant proportion of the workforce is unionized. The higher percentage of unionized workers has placed increased importance on industrial relations specialists in Australia, and reduced the control of line managers over workplace labor issues. However, in 1997, Australia over-

"The goal of representative participation is to redistribute power within an organization, putting labor on a more equal footing with the interests of management and stockholders."

hauled its labor and industrial land labor relations laws with the objective of increasing productivity and reducing union power. The Workplace Relations Bill gives employers greater flexibility to negotiate directly with employees on pay, hours, and benefits. It also simplifies federal regulation of labor–management relations.

Our final country, Germany, is similar to most Western European countries when it comes to HRM practices. Legislation requires companies to practice representative participation. The goal of representative participation is to redistribute power within the organization, putting labor on a more equal footing with the interests of management and stockholders. The two most common forms that representative participation takes are work councils and board representatives. **Work councils** link employees with management. They are groups of nominated or elected employees who must be consulted when management makes decisions involving personnel. **Board representatives** are employees who sit on a company's board of directors and represent the interest of the firm's employees.

work councils
Nominated or elected employees who must be consulted when management makes decisions involving personnel

board representatives
Employees who sit on a company's Board of Directors, who represent the interests of employees.

EMPLOYMENT PLANNING

Employment planning is the process by which management ensures that it has the right number and kinds of people in the right places at the right times, people who are capable of effectively and efficiently completing those tasks that will help the organization achieve its overall objectives. Employment planning, then, translates the organization's mission and objectives into a personnel plan that will allow the organization to achieve its goals. Employment planning can be condensed into two steps: (1) assessing current human resources and (2) assessing future human resources needs and developing a program to meet those needs.

employment planning
The process by which management ensures it has the right number and kinds of people in the right places at the right time, who are capable of helping the organization achieve its goals

HOW DOES AN ORGANIZATION CONDUCT AN EMPLOYEE ASSESSMENT?

Management begins by reviewing its current human resource status. This review is typically done by generating a **human resource inventory**. In an era of sophisticated computer systems, it is not too difficult a task to generate a human resource inventory report in most organizations. The input for this report is derived from forms completed by employees. Such reports might list the name, education, training, prior employment, languages spoken, capabilities, and specialized skills of each employee in the organization. This inventory allows management to assess what talents and skills are currently available in the organization.

human resource inventory report
A report listing the name, education, training, prior employer, languages spoken, and other information about each employee in the organization

Another part of the current assessment is the **job analysis**. Whereas the human resources inventory is concerned with telling management what individual employees can do, job analysis is more fundamental.[3] It is typically a lengthy process, one in which workflows are analyzed and skills and behaviors that are necessary to perform jobs are identified.[4] For instance, what does an international reporter who works for the *Wall Street Journal* do? What minimal knowledge, skills, and abilities are necessary for the adequate performance of this job? How do the job requirements for an international reporter compare with those for a domestic reporter or for a newspaper editor? These are questions that job analysis can answer. Ultimately, the purpose of job analysis is to determine the kinds of skills, knowledge, and attitudes needed to successfully perform each job. This information is then used to develop, or revise if they already exist, job descriptions and job specifications.

job analysis
An assessment of the kinds of skills, knowledge, and abilities needed to successfully perform each job in an organization

A **job description** is a written statement of what a job holder does, how it is done, and why it is done. It typically portrays job content, environment, and conditions of employment. The **job specification** states the minimum qualifications that an incumbent must possess to perform a given job successfully. It identifies the knowledge, skills, and attitudes needed to do the job effectively. The job description and specification are important documents when managers begin recruiting and selecting. For

job description
A written statement of what a job holder does, how it is done, and why it is done

job specification
A statement of the minimum acceptable qualifications that an incumbent must possess to perform a given job successfully

instance, the job description can be used to describe the job to potential candidates. The job specification keeps the manager's attention on the list of qualifications necessary for an incumbent to perform a job and assists in determining whether candidates are qualified. Furthermore, hiring individuals on the basis of the information contained in these two documents helps to ensure that the hiring process is not discriminatory.

HOW ARE FUTURE EMPLOYEE NEEDS DETERMINED?

Future human resource needs are determined by the organization's strategic direction. Demand for human resources (its employees) is a result of demand for the organization's products or services. On the basis of its estimate of total revenue, management can attempt to establish the number and mix of human resources needed to reach that revenue. In some cases, however, the situation may be reversed. When particular skills are necessary and in scarce supply, the availability of satisfactory human resources determines revenues. This might be the case for managers of an upscale chain of assisted-living retirement facilities that find themselves with more business opportunities than they can handle. The managers' primary limiting factor in building revenues is their ability to locate and hire a qualified nursing staff to fully meet the needs of the residents. In most cases, however, the overall organizational goals and the resulting revenue forecast provide the major input in determining the organization's human resource requirements.

After it has assessed both current capabilities and future needs, management is able to estimate shortages—both in number and in kind—and to highlight areas in which the organization is overstaffed. A program can then be developed that matches these estimates with forecasts of future labor supply. Employment planning not only guides current staffing needs but also projects future employee needs and availability.

RECRUITMENT AND SELECTION

Once managers know their current staffing levels—whether they are understaffed or overstaffed—they can begin to do something about it. If one or more vacancies exist, they can use the information gathered through job analysis to guide them in **recruitment**—that is, the process of locating, identifying, and attracting capable applicants. On the other hand, if employment planning indicates a surplus, management will want to reduce the labor supply within the organization and will initiate downsizing or layoff activities.

recruitment
The process of locating, identifying, and attracting capable applicants

WHERE DOES A MANAGER RECRUIT CANDIDATES?

Candidates can be found by using several sources—including the World Wide Web. Exhibit 6–3 offers some guidance. The source that is used should reflect the local labor market, the type or level of position, and the size of the organization.

Are certain recruiting sources better than others? Do certain recruiting sources produce superior candidates? The answer is generally yes. The majority of studies have found that employee referrals generally produce the best candidates.[5] The explanation for this finding is intuitively logical. First, applicants referred by current employees are prescreened by those employees. Because the recommenders know both the job and the person being recommended, they tend to refer well-qualified applicants.[6] Second, because current employees often feel that their reputation in the organization is at stake with a referral, they tend to make referrals only when they are reasonably confident that the

"Employees will make a referral when they are reasonably confident that the referral won't make them look bad."

SOURCE	ADVANTAGE	DISADVANTAGE
Internal searches	Low cost; build employee morale; candidates are familiar with organization	Limited supply; may not increase proportion of protected group employees
Advertisements	Wide distribution can be targeted to specific groups	Generate many unqualified candidates
Employee referrals	Knowledge about the organization provided by current employees; can generate strong candidates because a good referral reflects on the recommender	May not increase the diversity and mix of employees
Public employment agencies	Free or nominal cost	Candidates tend to be lower skilled, although some skilled employees available
Private employment agencies	Wide contacts; careful screening; short-term guarantees often given	High cost
School placement	Large, centralized body of candidates	Limited to entry-level positions
Temporary help services	Fill temporary needs	Expensive
Employee leasing and independent contractors	Fill temporary needs, but usually for more specific, longer-term projects	Little commitment to organization other than current project

EXHIBIT 6-3
Traditional Recruiting Sources

referral won't make them look bad. However, management should not always opt for the employee-referred candidate: Employee referrals may not increase the diversity and mix of employees.

How does a manager handle layoffs? In the past decade, most global organizations, as well as many government agencies and small businesses, have been forced to shrink the size of their workforce or restructure their skill composition. Downsizing has become a relevant means of meeting the demands of a dynamic environment.

What are a manager's downsizing options? Obviously, people can be fired, but other choices may be more beneficial to the organization. Exhibit 6–4 summarizes a manager's major downsizing options. But keep in mind, regardless of the method chosen, employees may suffer. We discuss this phenomenon for employees—both victims and survivors—later in this chapter.

IS THERE A BASIC METHOD OF SELECTING JOB CANDIDATES?

Once the recruiting effort has developed a pool of candidates, the next step in the employment process is to determine who is best qualified for the job. In essence, then, the **selection process** is a prediction exercise: It seeks to predict which applicants will be "successful" if hired, that is, which candidates will perform well on the criteria the organization uses to evaluate its employees. In filling a network administrator position, for example, the selection process should be able to predict which applicants will be capable of properly instaling, debugging, and managing the organization's computer network. For a position as a sales representative, it should

selection process
The process of screening job applicants to ensure that the most appropriate candidates are hired

EXHIBIT 6–4
Downsizing Options

OPTION	DESCRIPTION
Firing	Permanent involuntary termination
Layoffs	Temporary involuntary termination; may last only a few days or extend to years
Attrition	Not filling openings created by voluntary resignations or normal retirements
Transfers	Moving employees either laterally or downward; usually does not reduce costs but can reduce intraorganizational supply–demand imbalances
Reduced workweeks	Having employees work fewer hours per week, share jobs, or perform their jobs on a part-time basis
Early retirements	Providing incentives to older and more-senior employees for retiring before their normal retirement date
Job sharing	Having employees, typically two part-timers, share one full-time position

predict which applicants will be effective in generating high sales volumes. Consider, for a moment, that any selection decision can result in four possible outcomes. As shown in Exhibit 6–5, two of those outcomes would indicate correct decisions, and two would indicate errors.

reliability
The degree to which a selection device measures the same thing consistently

A decision is correct (1) when the applicant was predicted to be successful (was accepted) and later proved to be successful on the job, or (2) when the applicant was predicted to be unsuccessful (was rejected) and, if hired, would not have been able to do the job. In the former case, we have successfully accepted; in the latter case, we have successfully rejected. Problems occur, however, when we reject candidates who, if hired, would have performed successfully on the job (called *reject errors*) or accept those who subsequently perform poorly (*accept errors*). These problems are, unfortunately, far from insignificant. A generation ago, reject errors meant only that the costs of selection were increased because more candidates would have to be screened. Today, selection techniques that result in reject errors can open the organization to charges of employment discrimination, especially if applicants from protected groups are disproportionately rejected. Accept errors, on the other hand, have very obvious costs to the organization, including the cost of training the employee, the costs generated or profits foregone because of the employee's incompetence, and the cost of severance and the subsequent costs of additional recruiting and selection screening. The major thrust of any selection activity is, therefore, to reduce the probability of making reject errors or accept errors while increasing the probability of making correct decisions. We do this by using selection procedures that are both reliable and valid.

The selection process is somewhat like a hurdle race. You have to clear several hurdles—tests, interviews, etc.—before you actually get the job. Failing to clear any one of these hurdles means, like these runners, that you're out of the race!

What is reliability? **Reliability** addresses whether a selection device measures the same characteristic consistently. For example, if a test is reliable, any individual's score should remain fairly stable over time, assuming that the characteristics it is measuring are also stable. The importance

Later Job Performance	Reject	Accept
Successful	Reject error	Correct decision
Unsuccessful	Correct decision	Accept error
	Selection Decision	

EXHIBIT 6–5
Selection Decision Outcomes

of reliability should be self-evident. No selection device can be effective if it is low in reliability. Using such a device would be the equivalent of weighing yourself every day on an erratic scale. If the scale is unreliable—randomly fluctuating, say, 10 to 15 pounds every time you step on it—the results will not mean much. To be effective predictors, selection devices must possess an acceptable level of consistency.

What is validity? Any selection device that a manager uses—such as application forms, tests, interviews, or physical examinations—must also demonstrate **validity**. That is, there must be a proven relationship between the selection device used and some relevant measure. For example, a few pages ago, we mentioned a firefighter applicant who was wheelchair bound. Because of the physical requirements of a firefighter's job, someone confined to a wheelchair would be unable to pass the physical endurance tests. In that case, denying employment could be considered valid, but requiring the same physical endurance tests for the dispatching job would not be job related. Thus, the law prohibits management from using any selection device that cannot be shown to be directly related to successful job performance. That constraint goes for entrance tests, too; management must be able to demonstrate that, once on the job, individuals with high scores on this test outperform individuals with low scores. Consequently, the burden is on management to verify that any selection device it uses to differentiate applicants is related to job performance.

validity
The proven relationship between a selection device and some relevant criterion

"The burden is on management to verify that any selection device it uses is related to successful job performance."

HOW EFFECTIVE ARE TESTS AND INTERVIEWS AS SELECTION DEVICES?

Managers can use a number of selection devices to reduce accept and reject errors. The best known devices include written and performance-simulation tests, and interviews. Let's briefly review these devices, giving particular attention to the validity of each in predicting job performance. After we review them, we'll discuss when each should be used.

How do written tests serve a useful purpose? Typical written tests include tests of intelligence, aptitude, ability, and interest. Such tests have long been used as selection devices, although their popularity has run in cycles. Written tests were widely used for 20 years after World War II, but beginning in the late 1960s, they fell into disfavor. They were frequently characterized as discriminatory, and many organizations could not validate that their written tests were job related. But, since the late 1980s, written tests have made a comeback; many of them are Internet-based.[7] Managers have become increasingly aware that poor hiring decisions are costly and that properly designed tests could reduce the likelihood of making such decisions. In addition, the cost of developing and validating a set of written tests for a specific job has come down markedly.

How can managers at Home Depot ensure that a prospective employee can perform the job as cashier? One means is through a performance-simulation test. Using a replica of the job, candidates are evaluated on how well they can handle the actual job behaviors.

A review of the evidence finds that tests of intellectual ability, spatial and mechanical ability, perceptual accuracy, and motor ability are moderately valid predictors for many semi-skilled and unskilled operative jobs in industrial organizations.[8] However, an enduring criticism of written tests is that intelligence and other tested characteristics can be somewhat removed from the actual performance of the job itself.[9] For example, a high score on an intelligence test is not necessarily a good indicator that the applicant will perform well as a computer programmer. This criticism has led to an increased use of performance-simulation tests.

What are performance-simulation tests? What better way is there to find out whether an applicant for a technical writing position at Microsoft can write technical manuals than to ask him or her to do it? The logic of this question has led to the increasing interest in **performance-simulation tests.** Undoubtedly, the enthusiasm for these tests lies in the fact that they are based on job analysis data and, therefore, should more easily meet the requirement of job relatedness than do written tests. Performance-simulation tests are made up of actual job behaviors rather than substitutes. The best known performance-simulation tests are work sampling (a miniature replica of the job) and assessment centers (simulating real problems one may face on the job). The former is suited to persons applying for routine jobs, the latter to managerial personnel.

performance-simulation tests
Selection devices that are based on actual job behaviors; work sampling and assessment centers

The advantage of performance simulation over traditional testing methods should be obvious. Because content is essentially identical to job content, performance simulation should be a better predictor of short-term job performance and should minimize potential employment discrimination allegations. Additionally, because of the nature of their content and the methods used to determine content, well-constructed performance-simulation tests are valid predictors.

Is the interview effective? The interview, along with the application form, is an almost universal selection device. Few of us have ever gotten a job without undergoing one or more interviews (see Ethical Dilemma in Management). The irony of this fact is that the value of the interview as a selection device has been the subject of considerable debate.[10]

Interviews can be reliable and valid selection tools, but too often they are not. When interviews are structured and well organized, and when interviewers are held to relevant questioning, interviews are effective predictors.[11] But those conditions do not characterize many interviews. The typical interview in which applicants are asked a varying set of essentially random questions in an informal setting often provides little in the way of valuable information.

All kinds of potential biases can creep into interviews if they are not well structured and standardized. To illustrate, a review of the research leads us to the following conclusions:

- Prior knowledge about the applicant will bias the interviewer's evaluation.
- The interviewer tends to hold a stereotype of what represents a good applicant.
- The interviewer tends to favor applicants who share his or her own attitudes.
- The order in which applicants are interviewed will influence evaluations.
- The order in which information is elicited during the interview will influence evaluations.

Ethical Dilemma in Management

The Stress Interview

Your interview day has finally arrived. You are all dressed up to make that lasting first impression. You finally meet Mr. Abernathy, as he shakes your hand firmly and invites you to get comfortable. Your interview has started! This is the moment you've waited for.

The first few moments appear mundane enough. The questions to this point, in fact, seem easy. Your confidence is growing. That little voice in your head keeps telling you that you are doing fine—just keep on going. Suddenly, the questions get tougher. Mr. Abernathy leans back, and asks about why you want to leave your current job—the one you've been in for only 18 months. As you begin to explain that you wish to leave for personal reasons, he begins to probe more. His smile is gone and the body language is different. All right, you think, be honest. So you tell Mr. Abernathy you want to leave because you think your boss is unethical and you don't want your reputation tarnished being associated with this individual. This has led to a number of public disagreements with your boss, and you're tired of dealing with the situation any longer. Mr. Abernathy looks at you and replies: "If you ask me, that's not a valid reason for wanting to leave. Appears to me that you should be more assertive about the situation. Are you sure you're confident enough and have what it takes to make it in this company?" How dare he talk to you that way! Who does he think he is? So you respond with an angry tone in your voice. And guess what, you've just fallen victim to one of the tricks of the interviewing business—the stress interview.

Stress interviews are becoming more commonplace in today's business. Every job produces stress, and at some point in time every worker has a horrendous day. So these types of interviews become predictors of how you may react at work under less than favorable conditions. How so? Interviewers want to observe how you'll react when you are put under pressure. Those who demonstrate the resolve and strength to handle the stress indicate a level of professionalism and confidence. It's those characteristics that are being assessed. Individuals who react to the pressure interview in a more positive manner indicate that they should be more able to handle the day-to-day irritations that exist at work. Those who don't, well. . .

On the other hand, they are staged events. Interviewers deliberately lead applicants into a false sense of security—the comfortable interaction. Then suddenly and drastically, they change. They go on the attack. And it's usually a personal affront that picks on a weakness they've uncovered about the applicant. It's possibly humiliating; at the very least it's demeaning.

So, should stress interviews be used? Should interviewers be permitted to assess professionalism and confidence, and how one reacts to the everyday nuisances of work by putting applicants into a confrontational scenario? Does getting angry in an interview when pressured indicate one's propensity toward violence should things not always go smoothly at work? Should managers advocate the use of an activity that could possibly get out of control? What's your opinion?

- Negative information is given unduly high weight.
- The interviewer may make a decision concerning the applicant's suitability within the first four or five minutes of the interview.
- The interviewer may forget much of the interview's content within minutes after its conclusion.
- The interview is most valid in determining an applicant's intelligence, level of motivation, and interpersonal skills.
- Structured and well-organized interviews are more reliable than unstructured and unorganized ones.[12]

What can managers do to make interviews more valid and reliable? A number of suggestions have been made over the years. We list some in Developing Your Interviewing Skill in this chapter's Management Workshop (page 194).

How can you close the deal? Interviewers who treat the recruiting and hiring of employees as if the applicants must be sold on the job and exposed only to an organization's positive characteristics are likely to have a workforce that is dissatisfied and prone to high turnover.[13]

Every job applicant acquires, during the hiring process, a set of expectations about the company and about the job for which he or she is interviewing. When the information an applicant receives is excessively inflated, a number of things happen that have potentially negative effects on the company. First, mismatched applicants are less likely to withdraw from the search process. Second, because inflated information builds unrealistic expectations, new employees are likely to become quickly dissatisfied and to prematurely resign. Third, new hires are prone to become disillusioned and less committed to the organization when they face the unexpected harsh realities of the job. In many cases, these individuals feel that they were duped or misled during the hiring process and may become problem employees.

realistic job preview (RJP)
Providing both positive and negative information about the job and the company during the job interview

To increase job satisfaction among employees and reduce turnover, you should consider providing a **realistic job preview (RJP)**.[14] An RJP includes both positive and negative information about the job and the company. For example, in addition to the positive comments typically expressed in the interview, the candidate would be told of the less attractive aspects of the job. For instance, he or she might be told that there are limited opportunities to talk to co-workers during work hours, that promotional advancement is slim, or that work hours fluctuate so erratically that employees may be required to work during what are usually off hours (nights and weekends). Research indicates that applicants who have been given a realistic job preview hold lower and more realistic job expectations for the jobs they will be performing and are better able to cope with the frustrating elements of the job than are applicants who have been given only inflated information. The result is fewer unexpected resignations by new employees.

orientation
The introduction of a new employee to the job and the organization

For managers, realistic job previews offer a major insight into the HRM process. That is, retaining good people is as important as hiring them in the first place. Presenting only the positive aspects of a job to an applicant may initially entice him or her to join the organization, but it may be an affiliation that both parties will quickly regret.

ORIENTATION, TRAINING, AND DEVELOPMENT

If we have done our recruiting and selecting properly, we should have hired competent individuals who can perform successfully, but successful performance requires more than the possession of certain skills. New hires must be acclimated to the organization's culture and be trained to do the job in a manner consistent with the organization's objectives. To achieve these ends, HRM embarks on orientation and training.

Several years ago, employees working the registration desk at a Marriott Hotel would have received no more than a one-day orientation program. In an effort to enhance customer service, Marriott now offers new employees a 90-day new employee orientation. As such, new employees are better oriented to Marriott policies and practices, and better trained—all in an effort to offer the best customer service.

HOW DO WE INTRODUCE NEW HIRES TO THE ORGANIZATION?

Once a job candidate has been selected, he or she needs to be introduced to the job and organization. This introduction is called **orientation**.[15] The major objectives of orientation are to reduce the initial anxiety all new employees feel as they begin a new job; to familiarize new employees with the job, the work unit, and the organization as a whole; and to facilitate the outsider–insider transition. Job orientation expands on the information the employee obtained during the recruitment and selection stages. The new employee's specific duties and responsibilities are clarified as well as how his or her performance will be evaluated. This is also the time to rectify any unrealistic expectations new employees might hold about the job. Work unit orientation familiarizes the employee with the goals of the work unit, makes clear how his or her job contributes to the unit's goals, and provides an introduction to his or her co-workers. Organization orientation informs the new employee about the organization's objectives, history, philosophy, procedures, and rules. This information should include relevant personnel policies such as work hours, pay procedures, overtime requirements, and benefits. A tour of the organization's physical facilities is often part of the orientation.

Management has an obligation to make the integration of the new employee into the organization as smooth and as free of anxiety as possible. Successful orientation, whether formal or informal, results in an outsider–insider transition that makes the new member feel comfortable and fairly well-adjusted, lowers the likelihood of poor work performance, and reduces the probability of a surprise resignation by the new employee only a week or two into the job.[16]

WHAT IS EMPLOYEE TRAINING?

On the whole, planes don't cause airline accidents, people do. Most collisions, crashes, and other airline mishaps—nearly three-quarters of them—result from errors by the pilot or air traffic controller, or inadequate maintenance. Weather and structural failures typically account for the remaining accidents.[17] We cite these statistics to illustrate the importance of training in the airline industry. These maintenance and human errors could be prevented or significantly reduced by better employee training.

Employee training is a learning experience in that it seeks a relatively permanent change in employees such that their ability to perform on the job improves. Thus, training involves changing skills, knowledge, attitudes, or behavior.[18] This may mean changing what employees know, how they work; or their attitudes toward their jobs, co-workers, managers, and the organization. It has been estimated, for instance, that U.S. business firms alone spend billions each a year on formal courses and training programs to develop workers' skills.[19] Management, of course, is responsible for deciding when employees are in need of training and what form that training should take.

Determining training needs typically involves generating answers to several questions (see Exhibit 6–6). If some of these questions sound familiar, you have been paying close attention. It is precisely the type of analysis that took place when managers developed an organization structure to achieve their strategic goals—only now the focus is on the people.[20]

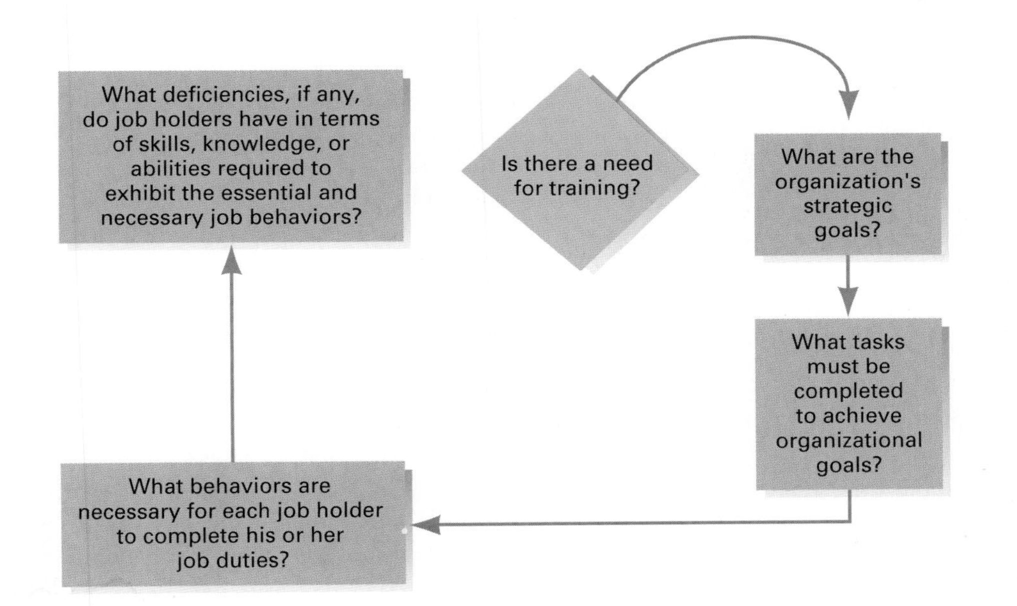

EXHIBIT 6–6
Determining if Training Is Needed

The leading questions in Exhibit 6–6 suggest the kinds of signals that can warn a manager when training may be necessary. The more obvious ones are related directly to productivity. There may be indications that job performance is declining, such as decreases in production numbers, lower quality, more accidents, and higher scrap or rejection rates. Any of these outcomes might suggest that worker skills need to be fine-tuned. Of course, we are assuming that the employee's performance decline is in no way related to lack of effort. Managers, too, must also recognize that training may be required because the workplace is constantly evolving. Changes imposed on employees as a result of job redesign or a technological breakthrough also require training.

How are employees trained? Most training takes place on the job. The prevalence of on-the-job training can be attributed to its simplicity and its usually lower cost. However, on-the-job training can disrupt the workplace and result in an increase in errors while learning takes place. Also, some skill training is too complex to learn on-the-job and should take place outside the work setting.

What are some of the typical methods used? Many different types of training methods are available. For the most part, however, we can classify them as on-the-job or off-the-job training. We have summarized the more popular training methods in Exhibit 6–7.

How can managers ensure that training is working? It is easy to generate a new training program, but if the training effort is not evaluated, any employee training efforts can be rationalized. It would be nice if all companies could boast the returns on investments in training that Neil Huffman Auto Group executives do; they claim they receive $230 in increased productivity for every dollar spent on training.[21] But such a claim cannot be made unless training is properly evaluated.

Can we determine how training programs are typically evaluated? The following approach is probably generalizable across organizations: Several managers, representatives from HRM, and a group of workers who have recently completed a training program are asked for their opinions. If the comments are generally positive, the program may get a favorable evaluation and the organization will continue it until someone decides, for whatever reason, that it should be eliminated or replaced.

EXHIBIT 6–7
Typical Training Methods

Sample On-the-Job Training Methods	
Job rotation	Lateral transfers allowing employees to work at different jobs. Provides good exposure to a variety of tasks.
Understudy assignments	Working with a seasoned veteran, coach, or mentor. Provides support and encouragement from an experienced worker. In the trades industry, this may also be an apprenticeship.
Sample Off-the-Job Training Methods	
Classroom lectures	Lectures designed to convey specific technical, interpersonal, or problem-solving skills.
Films and videos	Using the media to explicitly demonstrate technical skills that are not easily presented by other training methods.
Simulation exercises	Learning a job by actually performing the work (or its simulation). May include case analyses, experiential exercises, role playing, and group interaction.
Vestibule training	Learning tasks on the same equipment that one actually will use on the job but in a simulated work environment.

The reactions of participants or managers, while easy to acquire, are the least valid; their opinions are heavily influenced by factors that may have little to do with the training's effectiveness—difficulty, entertainment value, or the personality characteristics of the instructor. However, trainees' reactions to the training may, in fact, provide feedback on how worthwhile the participants viewed the training to be. Beyond general reactions, however, training must also be evaluated in terms of how much the participants learned; how well they are using their new skills on the job (did their behavior change?); and whether the training program achieved its desired results (reduced turnover, increased customer service, etc.).[22]

PERFORMANCE MANAGEMENT

It is important for managers to get their employees to reach performance levels that the organization considers desirable. How do managers ensure that employees are performing as well as they are supposed to? In organizations, the formal means of assessing the work of employees is through a systematic performance appraisal process.

WHAT IS A PERFORMANCE MANAGEMENT SYSTEM?

A **performance management system** is a process of establishing performance standards and evaluating performance in order to arrive at objective human resource decisions—such as pay increases and training needs—as well as to provide documentation to support any personnel actions. But how do you evaluate an employee's performance? That is, what are the specific techniques for appraisal? We have listed them in Exhibit 6–8.

performance management system
A process of establishing performance standards and evaluating performance in order to arrive at objective human resource decisions and to provide documentation to support personnel actions

The *written essay* requires no complex forms or extensive training to complete. However, a "good" or "bad" appraisal may be determined as much by the evaluator's writing skill as by the employee's actual level of performance. The use of *critical incidents* focuses the evaluator's attention on those critical or key behaviors that separate effective from ineffective job performance. The appraiser writes down anecdotes describing whatever the employee did that was especially effective or ineffective. The key here is that only specific behaviors are cited, not vaguely defined personality traits. One of the oldest and most popular methods of appraisal is by *adjective rating*

EXHIBIT 6–8
Performance Appraisal Methods

METHOD	ADVANTAGE	DISADVANTAGE
Written essay	Simple to use	More a measure of evaluator's writing ability than of employee's actual performance
Critical incidents	Rich examples behaviorally based	Time-consuming; lack quantification
Graphic rating scales	Provide quantitative data; less time-consuming than others	Do not provide depth of job behavior assessed
BARS	Focus on specific and measurable job behaviors	Time-consuming; difficult to develop measures
Multiperson	Compares employees with one another	Unwieldy with large number of employees
MBO	Focuses on end goals; results oriented	Time-consuming
360° Appraisal	More thorough	Time-consuming

Many global organizations—like Nokia—are using a performance appraisal process called 360-degree appraisal. Under this process, an employee is rated by a boss, peers, team members, customers, and suppliers.

360-degree appraisal
An appraisal device that seeks feedback from a variety of sources for the person being rated

scales. This method lists a set of performance factors such as quantity and quality of work, job knowledge, cooperation, loyalty, attendance, honesty, and initiative. The evaluator then goes down the list and rates each factor on an incremental scale. An approach that has received renewed attention involves *behaviorally anchored rating scales (BARS)*.[23] These scales combine major elements from the critical incident and graphic rating scale approaches. The appraiser rates an employee according to items along a numerical scale, but the items are examples of actual behavior on a given job rather than general descriptions or traits.[24]

Finally, an appraisal device that seeks performance feedback from such sources as the person being rated, bosses, peers, team members, customers, and suppliers has become very popular in organizations. It's called the **360-degree appraisal.**[25] It's being used in approximately 90 percent of the *Fortune* 1000 firms, which include such companies as Otis Elevator, DuPont, Nabisco, Pfizer, ExxonMobil, Cook Children Health Care System, General Electric, UPS, and Nokia.[26]

In today's dynamic organizations, traditional performance evaluation systems may be archaic.[27] Downsizing has given supervisors greater responsibility and more employees who report directly to them. Accordingly, in some instances, it is almost impossible for supervisors to have extensive job knowledge of each of their employees. Furthermore, the growth of project teams and employee involvement in today's companies places the responsibility of evaluation at points at which people are better able to make accurate assessments.[28]

The 360-degree feedback process also has some positive benefits for development concerns.[29] Many managers simply do not know how their employees view them and the work they have done. Research studies into the effectiveness of 360-degree performance appraisals are reporting positive results from more accurate feedback, empowering employees, reducing the subjective factors in the evaluation process, and developing leadership in an organization.[30]

Should we compare people with one another or against a set of standards?

The methods identified above have one thing in common. They require us to evaluate employees on the basis of how well their performance matches established or absolute criteria. Multiperson comparisons, on the other hand, compare one person's performance with that of one or more individuals. Thus, they are relative, not absolute, measuring devices. The three most popular forms of this method are group-order ranking, individual ranking, and paired comparison.

The *group-order ranking* requires the evaluator to place employees into a particular classification such as "top fifth" or "second fifth." If a rater has 20 employees, only 4 can be in the top fifth, and, of course, 4 must be relegated to the bottom fifth. The *individual ranking* approach requires the evaluator merely to list the employees in order from highest to lowest. Only one can be "best." In an appraisal of 30 employees, the difference between the first and second employee is assumed to be the same as that between the twenty-first and twenty-second. Even though some employees may be closely grouped, there can be no ties. In the *paired comparison* approach, each employee is compared with every other employee in the comparison group and rated as either the superior or weaker member of the pair. After all paired comparisons are made, each employee is assigned a summary ranking based on the number of superior scores he or she achieved. Although this approach ensures that each employee is compared against every other one, it can become unwieldy when large numbers of employees are being assessed.

Isn't MBO an appraisal approach too? We introduced management by objectives during our discussion of planning in Chapter 3. MBO, however, is also a mechanism for appraising performance.

Employees are evaluated by how well they accomplish a specific set of objectives that have been determined to be critical in the successful completion of their jobs. As you'll recall from our discussion in Chapter 3, these objectives need to be tangible, verifiable, and measurable. MBO's popularity among managerial personnel is probably due to its focus on end goals. Managers tend to emphasize such results-oriented outcomes as profit, sales, and costs. This emphasis meshes with MBO's concern with quantitative measures of performance. Because MBO emphasizes ends rather than means, this appraisal method allows managers to choose the best path for achieving their goals.

WHAT HAPPENS WHEN PERFORMANCE FALLS SHORT?

So far this discussion has focused on the performance management system. But what if an employee is not performing in a satisfactory manner? What can you do?

If, for some reason, an employee is not meeting his or her performance goals, a manager needs to find out why. If it is because the employee is mismatched for the job (a hiring error) or because he or she does not have adequate training, something relatively simple can be done; the manager can either reassign the individual to a job that better matches his or her skills or train the employee to do the job more effectively. If the problem is associated not with the employee's abilities but with his or her desire to do the job, it becomes a **discipline** problem. In that case, a manager can try counseling and, if necessary, can take disciplinary action such as verbal and written warnings, suspensions, and even terminations (see Exhibit 6–9).

discipline
Actions taken by a manager to enforce an organization's standards and regulations

Employee counseling is a process designed to help employees overcome performance-related problems. Rather than viewing the performance problem from a punitive standpoint (discipline), employee counseling attempts to uncover why employees have lost their desire or ability to work productively. More important, it is designed to find ways to fix the problem. In many cases, employees don't go from being productive one day to being unproductive the next. Rather, the change happens gradually and may be a function of what is occurring in their personal lives. Employee counseling attempts to assist employees in getting help to resolve whatever is bothering them.

employee counseling
A process designed to help employees overcome performance-related problems

The premise behind employee counseling is fairly simple: It is beneficial to both the organization and the employee. Just as it is costly to have a worker quit shortly after being hired, it is costly to fire someone. The time spent recruiting and selecting, orienting, training, and developing employees translates into money. If, however, an organization can help employees overcome personal problems and get them back on the job quickly, it can avoid these costs. But make no mistake about it, employee counseling is not intended to lessen the effect of an employee's poor performance, nor is it intended to reduce his or her responsibility to change inappropriate work behavior. If the employee can't or won't accept help, then disciplinary actions must be taken.

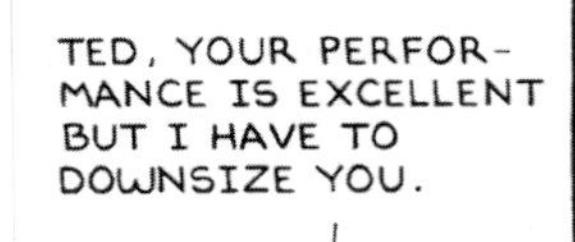

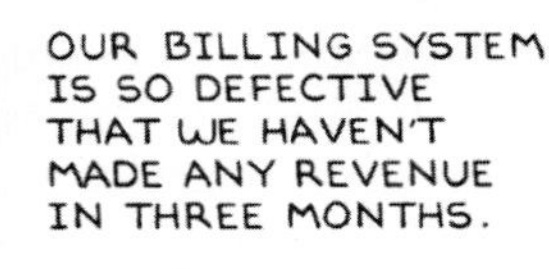

EXHIBIT 6–9
Performance Matters
Source: Dilbert reprinted by permission of United Features Syndicate, Inc.

COMPENSATION AND BENEFITS

You open the newspaper and the following job advertisement grabs your attention: "Wanted: Hardworking individual who is willing to work 60 hours a week in a less-than-ideal environment." The job pays no money but gives you the opportunity to say "I've done that." Sound intriguing to you? Probably not. Although there are exceptions, most of us work for money. What our jobs pay and what benefits we get fall under the heading of compensation and benefits. Determining what these will be is by no means easy.

HOW ARE PAY LEVELS DETERMINED?

compensation administration
The process of determining a cost-effective pay structure that will attract and retain competent employees, provide an incentive for them to work hard, and ensure that pay levels will be perceived as fair

How does management decide who gets paid $15.85 an hour and who receives $325,000 a year? The answer lies in **compensation administration**. The goals of compensation administration are to design a cost-effective pay structure that will attract and retain competent employees and to provide an incentive for these individuals to exert high energy levels at work. Compensation administration also attempts to ensure that pay levels, once determined, will be perceived as fair by all employees. Fairness means that the established pay levels are adequate and consistent for the demands and requirements of the job. Therefore, the primary determination of pay is the kind of job an employee performs. Different jobs require different kinds and levels of skills, knowledge, and abilities, and these vary in their value to the organization. So, too, do the responsibility and authority of various positions. In short, the higher the skills, knowledge, and abilities—and the greater the authority and responsibility—the higher the pay.

Although skills, abilities, and the like directly affect pay levels, other factors may come into play. Pay levels may be influenced by the kind of business, the environment surrounding the job, geographic location, and employee performance levels and seniority.[31] For example, private sector jobs typically provide higher rates of pay than comparable positions in public and not-for-profit jobs. Employees who work under hazardous conditions (say, bridge builders operating 200 feet in the air), work unusual hours (e.g., the midnight shift), or work in geographic areas where the cost of living is higher (e.g., New York City rather than Tucson, Arizona) are typically more highly compensated. Employees who have been with an organization for a long time may have had a salary increase each year.

Irrespective of the factors mentioned above, there is one other most critical factor—management's compensation philosophy. Some organizations, for instance, don't pay employees any more than they have to. In the absence of a union contract that stipulates wage levels, those organizations only have to pay minimum wage for most of their jobs. On the other hand, some organizations are committed to a compensation philosophy of paying their employees at or above area wage levels in order to emphasize that they want to attract and keep the best pool of talent.

WHY DO ORGANIZATIONS OFFER EMPLOYEE BENEFITS?

employee benefits
Nonfinancial rewards designed to enrich employees' lives

When an organization designs its overall compensation package, it has to look further than just an hourly wage or annual salary. It has to take into account another element, employee benefits. **Employee benefits** are nonfinancial rewards designed to enrich employees' lives. They have grown in importance and variety over the past several decades. Once viewed as "fringes," today's benefit packages reflect a considered effort to provide something that each employee values.

The benefits offered by an organization will vary widely in scope. Most organizations are legally required to provide Social Security and workers' and unemployment compensations, but organizations also provide an array of benefits such as paid time off from work, life and disability insurance, retirement programs, and health insurance.[32] The costs of some of these, such as retirement and health insurance benefits, are frequently paid by both the employer and the employee.

CURRENT ISSUES IN HUMAN RESOURCE MANAGEMENT

We'll conclude this chapter by looking at several human resource issues facing today's managers—workforce diversity, sexual harassment, labor–management cooperation, employee violence, and layoff-survivor sickness.

HOW CAN WORKFORCE DIVERSITY BE MANAGED?

We have discussed the changing makeup of the workforce in several places in this book. Let's now consider how workforce diversity will affect such basic HRM concerns as recruitment, selection, and orientation.[33]

Improving workforce diversity requires managers to widen their recruiting net. For example, the popular practice of relying on current employee referrals as a source of new job applicants tends to produce candidates who have similar characteristics to those of present employees. So managers have to look for applicants in places where they haven't typically looked before. To increase diversity, managers are increasingly turning to nontraditional recruitment sources such as women's job networks, over-50 clubs, urban job banks, disabled people's training centers, ethnic newspapers, and gay rights organizations. This type of outreach should enable an organization to broaden its pool of applicants.

Once a diverse set of applicants exists, efforts must be made to ensure that the selection process does not discriminate. Moreover, applicants need to be made comfortable with the organization's culture and be made aware of management's desire to accommodate their needs. For instance, at TGI Friday's, company management works diligently to accommodate differences and create workplace choices for a diverse workforce; so, too, do companies like Fresh Mex, Ben & Jerry's, and Lucent Technologies.[34]

Finally, orientation is often difficult for women and minorities. Many organizations today, such as Lotus and Hewlett-Packard, provide special workshops to raise diversity consciousness among current employees as well as programs for new employees that focus on diversity issues. The thrust of these efforts is to increase individual understanding of the differences each of us brings to the workplace. A number of companies also have special mentoring programs to deal with the reality that lower-level female and minority managers have few role models with whom to identify.[35]

Come inside and you'll notice a rich environment. No, not one with lavish furnishings. Rather, you see one in which company management works hard to accommodate differences and promote workplace choices for a diverse workforce.

WHAT IS SEXUAL HARASSMENT?

Sexual harassment is a serious issue in both public and private sector organizations. More than 15,000 complaints are filed with the EEOC each year,[36] and it's estimated that more than 20 percent of the women and 7 percent of the men working in today's organizations have reported being sexually harassed.[37] Settlements in some of these cases incurred a substantial cost to the companies in terms of litigation. It is estimated that it is the single largest financial risk facing companies today—and result in upwards of a 30 percent decrease in a company's stock price.[38] At Mitsubishi, for example, the company paid out more than $34 million to 300 women for the rampant sexual harassment to which they were exposed.[39] But it's more than just jury awards. Sexual harassment results in millions lost in absenteeism, low productivity, and turnover.[40] Sexual harassment, furthermore, is not just a U.S. phenomenon. It's a global issue. For instance, sexual harassment charges have been filed against employers in such countries as Japan, Australia, Netherlands, Belgium, New Zealand, Sweden, Ireland, and Mexico.[41] While discussions of sexual harassment cases oftentimes focus on the large awards granted by a court, there are other concerns for employers. Sexual harassment creates an unpleasant work environment for organization members and undermines their ability to perform their jobs. But just what is sexual harassment?

sexual harassment
Sexually suggestive remarks, unwanted touching and sexual advances, requests for sexual favors, or other verbal and physical conduct of a sexual nature

Any unwanted activity of a sexual nature that affects an individual's employment can be regarded as **sexual harassment**. It can occur between members of the opposite or the same sex—between employees of the organization or between employee and nonemployee.[42] Although such an activity has been generally protected under Title VII (sex discrimination) in the United States., in recent years this problem has gained more recognition. By most accounts, prior to the mid-1980s, occurrences were generally viewed as isolated incidents, with the individual committing the act being solely responsible (if at all) for his or her actions.[43] By the beginning of the new millennium, however, charges of sexual harassment have continued to appear in the headlines on an almost regular basis.

Much of the problem associated with sexual harassment is determining what constitutes this illegal behavior.[44] In 1993, the EEOC cited three situations in which sexual harassment can occur. These are instances where verbal or physical conduct toward an individual:

1. Creates an intimidating, offensive, or hostile environment;
2. Unreasonably interferes with an individual's work; or
3. Adversely affects an employee's employment opportunities.

For many organizations, it's the offensive or hostile environment issue that is problematic.[45] Just what constitutes such an environment? Challenging hostile environment situations gained much support from the Supreme Court case of *Meritor Savings Bank v. Vinson*.[46] This case stemmed from a situation in which Ms. Vinson initially refused the sexual advances of her boss. However, out of fear of reprisal, she ultimately conceded. But according to court records, it did not stop there. Vinson's boss continued to hassle Vinson, subjecting her to severe hostility which affected her job.[47] In addition to supporting hostile environment claims, the Meritor case also identified employer liability: That is, in sexual harassment cases, an organization can be held liable for sexual harassment actions by its managers, employees, and even customers![48]

Although the Meritor case has implications for organizations, how do organizational members determine if something is offensive? For instance, does sexually explicit language in the office create a hostile environment? How about off-color jokes? Pictures of women totally undressed? The answer is: It could! It depends on the people in the organization and the environment in which they work. What does this tell us? The point here is that we all must be attuned to what makes fellow employees uncomfortable—and if we don't know, then we should find out! Organizational success entering the new millennium will, in part, reflect how sensitive each employee is toward another in the company. At DuPont, for example, the corporate culture and diversity programs are designed to eliminate sexual harassment through awareness and respect for all individuals.[49] This means understanding one another and, most importantly, respecting others' rights. Similar programs exist at FedEx, General Mills, and Levi Strauss.

Is the action of this supervisor sexual harassment? The answer is, it depends. If the employee feels that such action is interfering with her work, and she has asked for the offensive behavior to stop and it hasn't, then she may be experiencing sexual harassment. Actions such as this may be part of the reason why more than 20 percent of all working women have reported instances of sexual harassment at work.

If sexual harassment carries with it potential costs to the organization, what can a company do to protect itself?[50] The courts want to know two things—did the organization know about, or should it have known about, the alleged behavior? And what did management do to stop it?[51] With the number and dollar amounts of the awards against organizations today, there is even a greater need for management to educate all employees on sexual harassment matters and to have mechanisms available to monitor employees. Furthermore, "victims" no longer have to prove that their psychological well-being is seriously affected. The U.S. Supreme Court ruled in 1993, in the case of *Harris v. Forklift Systems, Inc.*, that victims do not have to suffer substantial mental distress to receive a jury award. Furthermore, in June 1998, the Supreme Court ruled that sexual harassment may have occurred even if the employee had not experienced any "negative" job repercussions. In this case, Kimberly Ellerth, a marketing assistant at Burlington Industries, filed harassment charges against her boss because he "touched her, suggested she wear shorter skirts, and told her during a business trip that he could make her job 'very hard or very easy'." When Ellerth refused, the harasser never "punished" her; in fact, Kimberly even received a promotion during the time the harassment was ongoing. What the Supreme Court's decision in this case indicates is that "harassment is defined by the ugly behavior of the manager, not by what happened to the worker subsequently."[52]

Finally, whenever one is involved in a sexual harassment matter, managers must remember that the harasser may have rights, too.[53] This means that no action should be taken against someone until a thorough investigation has been conducted. Furthermore, the results of the investigation should be reviewed by an independent and objective individual before any action against the alleged harasser is taken. Even then, the harasser should be given an opportunity to respond to the allegation, and have a disciplinary hearing if desired. Additionally, an avenue for appeal should also exist for the alleged harasser—an appeal heard by someone in a higher level of management who is not associated with the case.

CAN UNIONS AND MANAGEMENT COOPERATE?

Historically, the relationship between a labor union and management has been based on conflict. The interests of labor and management have been basically at odds—each treating the other as the opposition. But times have changed somewhat. Management has become increasingly aware that successful efforts to increase productivity, improve quality, and lower costs require employee involvement and commitment. Similarly, some labor unions have come to recognize that they can help their members more by cooperating with management than fighting it.[54]

Unfortunately, current U.S. labor laws, passed in an era of mistrust and antagonism between labor and management, may be a barrier to both parties becoming cooperative partners. As a case in point, the National Labor Relations Act was passed to encourage collective bargaining and to balance workers' power against that of management. That legislation also sought to eliminate the then widespread practice of firms setting up company unions for the sole purpose of undermining the efforts of outside unions to organize their employees. So the law prohibits employers from creating or supporting a "labor organization." Ironically, labor laws—like the National Labor Relations Act—may have also presented a minor roadblock to management and labor cooperation in setting up employee committees.

Labor relations issues cross all national boundaries. These Polish mineworkers have combined their "forces" in an effort to deal effectively with management and address issues that directly affect them.

Although this issue has been the subject of congressional debate, the current legal environment doesn't prohibit employee-involvement programs in the United States. Rather, to comply with the law, management is required to give its employee-involvement programs independence. When such programs become dominated by management, they're likely to be interpreted as performing some functions of labor unions but being really controlled by management. What kinds of actions would indicate that an employee involvement program is not dominated by management? Some examples might include choosing program members through secret ballot elections, giving program members wide latitude in deciding what issues to deal with, permitting members to meet apart from management, and specifying that program members are not susceptible to dissolution by management whim. The key theme that labor

Scenes like this have become way too familiar in the United States. Workplace violence accounts for more than 1,000 people being murdered each year, and more than 1.5 million employees are assaulted on the job each year. It's an issue that management simply can't ignore.

laws appear to be conveying is that where employee involvement programs are introduced, members must have the power to make decisions and act independently of management.

CAN MANAGERS PREVENT WORKPLACE VIOLENCE?

Inasmuch as there is growing concern for the job safety for our workers, today a much greater emphasis is being placed on the increasing violence that has erupted on the job. No organization is immune from such happenstance, and the problem appears to be getting worse.[55] Shootings at a local post office by a recently disciplined employee; an upset purchasing manager stabs his boss because they disagreed over how some paperwork was to be completed; a disgruntled significant other enters the workplace and shoots his mate; an employee upset over having his wages garnished—incidents like these have become all too prevalent. Consider the following statistics. More than 1,000 employees are murdered, and more than 1.5 million employees are assaulted on the job each year. Homicide has become the number-two cause of work-related death in the United States.[56]

Two factors have contributed greatly to this trend—domestic violence and disgruntled employees.[57] The issue for companies, then, is to find a way to prevent the violence from occurring on the job—and to reduce their liability should an unfortunate event occur.[58] Because the circumstances of each incident are different, a specific plan of action for companies to follow is difficult to detail. However, several suggestions can be made. First, the organization must develop a plan to deal with the issue. This may mean reviewing all corporate policies to ensure that they are not adversely affecting employees. In fact, in many cases where the violent individuals caused mayhem in an office setting, and didn't commit suicide, one common factor arose. That is, these employees were not treated with respect or dignity. They were laid off without any warning, or they perceived themselves as being treated too harshly in the discipline process. Sound HRM practices can help to ensure that respect and dignity exist for employees, even in the most difficult of issues like terminations.

Organizations must also train their supervisory personnel to identify troubled employees before the problem results in violence. Employee assistance programs (EAPs) can be designed specifically to help these individuals. Rarely does an individual go from being happy to committing some act of violence overnight! Furthermore, if supervisors are better able to spot the types of demonstrated behaviors that may lead to violence, then those who cannot be helped through the EAP can be removed from the organization before others are harmed. Organizations should also implement stronger security mechanisms. For example, many women who are killed at work, following a domestic dispute, die at the hands of someone who didn't belong on company premises. These individuals, as well as violence paraphernalia—guns, knives, and so on—must be prevented from entering the facilities altogether.

Sadly, no matter how careful the organization is, and no matter how much it attempts to prevent workplace violence, some will occur. In those cases, the organization must be prepared to deal with the situation and to offer whatever assistance it can to deal with the aftermath.[59]

HOW DO "SURVIVORS" RESPOND TO LAYOFFS?

As we discussed in Chapter 2, one of the significant trends we witnessed was organizational downsizing. Because downsizing typically involves shrinking the organization's workforce, it is an issue in HRM that needs to be addressed.

Many organizations have done a fairly good job of helping layoff victims by offering a variety of job-help services, psychological counseling, support groups, severance pay, extended health insurance benefits, and detailed communications. Although some individuals react very negatively to being laid off (the worst cases involve returning to the former organization and committing a violent act), the assistance offered reveals that the organization does care about its former employees. Unfortunately, little is done for those who retain their jobs and have the task of keeping the organization going or even of revitalizing it.

It may surprise you to learn that both victims and survivors experience feelings of frustration, anxiety, and loss.[60] But layoff victims get to start over with a clean slate and a clear conscience. Survivors don't. A new syndrome seems to be popping up in more and more organizations: **layoff-survivor sickness**, a set of attitudes, perceptions, and behaviors of employees who survive involuntary staff reductions.[61] Symptoms include job insecurity, perceptions of unfairness, guilt, depression, stress from increased workload, fear of change, loss of loyalty and commitment, reduced effort, and an unwillingness to do anything beyond the required minimum.

layoff-survivor sickness
A set of attitudes, perceptions, and behaviors of employees who remain after involuntary employee reductions; include insecurity, guilt, depression, stress, fear, loss of loyalty, and reduced effort

To address this survivor syndrome, managers may want to provide opportunities for employees to talk to counselors about their guilt, anger, and anxiety.[62] Group discussions can also provide an opportunity for the survivors to vent their feelings. Some organizations have used downsizing as the spark to implement increased employee participation programs such as empowerment and self-managed work teams. In short, to keep morale and productivity high, every attempt should be made to ensure that those individuals who are still working in the organization know that they are valuable and much-needed resources.

Review, Comprehension, Application

CHAPTER SUMMARY

How will you know if you fulfilled the Learning Outcomes on page 168? You will have fulfilled the Learning Outcomes if you are able to:

1. **Describe the human resources management process.** The human resource management process seeks to staff the organization and to sustain high employee performance through strategic human resource planning, recruitment or downsizing, selection, orientation, training, performance appraisal, compensation and benefits, safety and health, and by dealing with contemporary issues in HRM.
2. **Identify the influence of government regulations on human resource decisions.** Since the mid-1960s, the U.S. government has greatly expanded its influence over HRM decisions by enacting new laws and regulations. Because of the government's effort to provide equal employment opportunities, management must ensure that key HRM decisions—recruitment, selection, training, promotions, and terminations—are made without regard to race, sex, religion, age, color, national origin, or disability. Financial penalties can be imposed on organizations that fail to follow these laws and regulations.
3. **Differentiate between job descriptions and job specifications.** A job description is a written statement of what a job holder does, how it is done, and why it is done. A job specification states the minimum acceptable qualifications that a potential employee must possess to successfully perform a given job.
4. **Contrast recruitment and downsizing options.** Recruitment seeks to develop a pool of potential job candidates. Typical sources include an internal search, advertisements, employee referrals, employment agencies, school placement centers, and temporary services. Downsizing typically reduces the labor supply within an organization through options such as firing, layoffs, attrition, transfers, reduced workweeks, early retirements, and job sharing.
5. **Explain the importance of validity and reliability in selection.** All HRM decisions must be based on factors or criteria that are both reliable and valid. If a selection device is not reliable, then it cannot be assumed to measure consistently. If a device is not valid, then no proven relationship exists between the criterion and successful job performance.

6. **Describe the selection devices that work best with various kinds of jobs.** Selection devices must match the job in question. Work sampling works best with low-level jobs; assessment centers work best for managerial positions. The validity of the interview as a selection device increases at progressively higher levels of management.
7. **Identify various training methods.** Employee training can be on-the-job or off-the-job. Popular on-the-job methods include job rotation, understudying, and apprenticeships. The more popular off-the-job methods are lectures, films, and simulation exercises.
8. **Explain the various techniques managers can use in evaluating employee performance.** Managers can use several techniques in evaluating employee performance, such as comparing employee performance against some set performance standard, comparing employees with one another, or measuring performance on the basis of preset objectives. One of the newer performance evaluation methods used in contemporary organizations is the 360-degree evaluation, whereby an employee is evaluated by bosses, peers, direct reports, if any, and possibly customers.
9. **Describe the goals of compensation administration and factors that affect wage structures.** Compensation administration attempts to ensure that pay levels will be perceived as fair by all employees. Fairness means that the established levels of pay are adequate and consistent for the demands and requirements of the job. Therefore, the primary determination of pay is the kind of job an employee performs.
10. **Explain what is meant by the terms *sexual harassment, labor–management cooperation, workplace violence,* and *layoff-survivor sickness.*** Sexual harassment encompasses sexually suggestive remarks, unwanted touching and sexual advances, requests for sexual favors, or other verbal and physical conduct of a sexual nature. Labor–management cooperation involves mutual efforts on the part of a labor union and the management of an organization. Workplace violence refers to the increase in violent crimes being committed at the work site. The layoff-survivor sickness is the set of attitudes, perceptions, and behaviors of employees who remain after involuntary staff reductions.

COMPANION WEBSITE

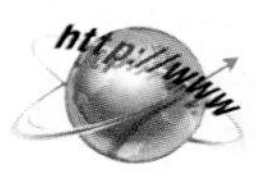

We invite you to visit the Robbins/DeCenzo companion Website at **www.prenhall.com/robbins** for this chapter's Internet resources, including an online study guide, Internet exercises, and "In the News" with full text articles provided by XanEdu.

READING FOR COMPREHENSION

1. How does HRM affect all managers?
2. Contrast reject errors and accept errors. Which are most likely to open an employer to charges of discrimination? Why?
3. What are the major problems of the interview as a selection device?
4. What is the relationship between selection, recruitment, and job analysis?
5. How are orientation and employee training alike? How are they different?
6. What can managers do to help prevent workplace violence?

LINKING CONCEPTS TO PRACTICE

1. Should an employer have the right to choose employees without government interference in the hiring process? Explain your position.
2. Do you think there are moral limits on how far a prospective employer should delve into an applicant's life by means of interviews, tests, and background investigations? Explain your position.
3. What in your view constitutes sexual harassment? Describe how companies can minimize sexual harassment in the workplace.
4. Why should managers be concerned with diversity in the workplace? What special HRM issues does diversity raise?
5. Victims of downsizing are not those employees who were let go. Rather, the victims are the ones who have kept their jobs. Do you agree or disagree with this statement? Defend your position.
6. Workplace violence is indicative of the violence that exists in our society. Accordingly, no amount of prevention can eliminate all workplace violence occurrences. Do you agree or disagree with the statement? Explain.

Management Workshop

Team Skill-Building Exercise

Laying Off Workers

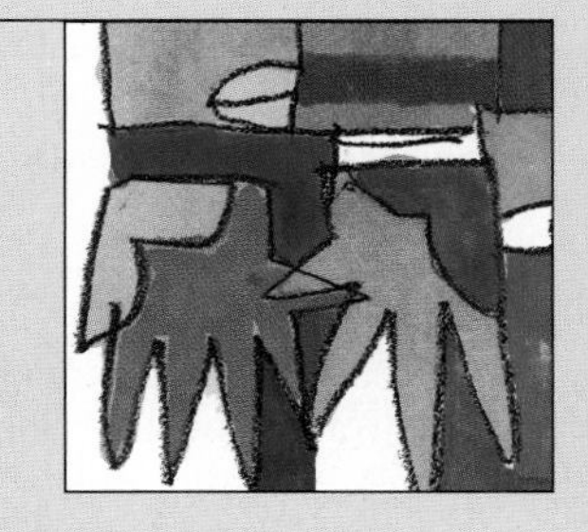

Every manager, at some point in his or her career, is likely to be faced with the difficult task of laying off employees. Assume that you are the manager in the internal auditing department of a 4,500-member corporation. You have been notified by top management that you must permanently reduce your staff by two individuals. Below are some data about your five employees.

Emma Connor: African-American female, age 32. Emma has been employed with your company for five years in the accounting department. Her evaluations over the past three years have been outstanding, above average, and outstanding. Emma has an MBA from a top-25 business school. She has been on short-term disability for the past few weeks because of the birth of her second child and is expected to return to work in 20 weeks.

Ron Johnson: White male, age 49. Ron has been with you for four months and has 11 years of experience in the company in payroll. He has an associate's degree in business administration and bachelor's and master's degrees in accounting. He's also a CPA. Ron's evaluations over the past three years in payroll have been average, but he did save the company $150,000 on a suggestion he made regarding using electronic time sheets.

Jose Hernandez: Hispanic male, age 31. Jose has been with the company almost four years. His evaluations over the past three years in your department have been outstanding. He is committed to getting the job done and devoting whatever it takes. He has also shown initiative by taking job assignments that no one else wanted, and he has recovered a number of overdue and uncollected accounts that you had simply thought should be written off as a loss.

Julie Sapp: White female, age 35. Julie has been with your company seven years. Four years ago, Julie was in an automobile accident while traveling on business to a customer's location. As a result of the accident, she was disabled and is wheelchair-bound. Rumors have it that she is about to receive several million dollars from the insurance company of the driver that hit her. Her performance during the past two years has been above average. She has a bachelor's degree in accounting and specializes in computer information systems.

Bobby Hayden: African-American male, age 43. Bobby just completed his double master's degree in taxation and law and recently passed the bar exam. He has been with your department for four years. His evaluations have been good to above average. Five years ago, Bobby won a lawsuit against your company for discriminating against him in a promotion to a supervisory position. Rumors have it that now, with his new degree, Bobby is actively pursuing another job outside the company.

Given these five brief descriptions, which two employees should be laid off? Discuss any other options that can be used to meet the requirement of downsizing by two employees without resorting to layoffs. Discuss what you will do to assist the two individuals who have been let go and to assist the remaining three employees. Then, in a group of three to five students, seek consensus on the questions posed above. Be prepared to defend your actions.

Understanding Yourself

Before you can develop other people, you must understand your present strengths. To assist in this learning process, we encourage you to complete the following self-assessments from the Prentice Hall Self-Assessment Library 2.0:

- What's the Right Organizational Culture for Me? (#42)
- Am I Experiencing Work–Family Conflict? (#44)

After you complete these assessments, we suggest that you print out the results and store them as part of your "portfolio of learning."

Developing Your Interviewing Skill

Interviewing Job Applicants

About the Skill

Every manager needs to develop his or her interviewing skills. The following discussion highlights the key behaviors associated with this skill.

Steps in Practicing the Skill

1. **Review the job description and job specification.** Reviewing pertinent information about the job provides valuable information about what you will assess the candidate on. Furthermore, relevant job requirements help to eliminate interview bias.
2. **Prepare a structured set of questions to ask all applicants for the job.** By having a set of prepared questions, you ensure that the information you wish to elicit is attainable. Furthermore, if you ask them all similar questions, you are able to better compare all candidates' answers against a common base.
3. **Before meeting a candidate, review his or her application form and resume.** Doing so helps you to create a complete picture of the candidate in terms of what is represented on the resume or application and what the job requires. You will also begin to identify areas to explore in the interview. That is, areas that are not clearly defined on the resume or application but that are essential for the job will become a focal point of your discussion with the candidate.
4. **Open the interview by putting the applicant at ease and by providing a brief preview of the topics to be discussed.** Interviews are stressful for job candidates. By opening with small talk (e.g., the weather) you give the candidate time to adjust to the interview setting. By providing a preview of topics to come, you are giving the candidate an agenda that helps the candidate to begin framing what he or she will say in response to your questions.
5. **Ask your questions and listen carefully to the applicant's answers.** Select follow-up questions that naturally flow from the answers given. Focus on the responses as they relate to information you need to ensure that the candidate meets your job requirements. Any uncertainty you may still have requires a follow-up question to probe further for the information.
6. **Close the interview by telling the applicant what is going to happen next.** Applicants are anxious about the status of your hiring decision. Be honest with the candidate regarding others who will be interviewed and the remaining steps in the hiring process. If you plan to make a decision in two weeks or so, let the candidate know what you intend to do. In addition, tell the applicant how you will let him or her know about your decision.
7. **Write your evaluation of the applicant while the interview is still fresh in your mind.** Don't wait until the end of your day, after interviewing several candidates, to write your analysis of a candidate. Memory can fail you. The sooner you complete your write-up after an interview, the better chance you have of accurately recording what occurred in the interview.

Practicing the Skill

Review and update your resume. Then have several friends critique it who are employed in management-level positions or in management training programs. Ask them to explain their comments, and make any changes to your resume that they think will improve it.

Now inventory your interpersonal and technical skills and any practical experiences that do not show up in your resume. Draft a set of leading questions you would like to be asked in an interview that would give you a chance to discuss the unique qualities and attributes you could bring to the job.

Developing Your Diagnostic and Analytical Skills

Creative Recruiting

After an organization has established its strategic direction and developed a corresponding employment plan, it must turn its attention to getting the right people. That's the fundamental basis of employment planning. The jobs that have been identified and their associated skills point to very specific types of employees that are required. But these employees don't just magically appear—nor do they frequently come knocking on the organization's door. Instead, the company must embark on an employment process of finding and hiring qualified people.

That process starts when the organization notifies the "public" that openings exist. The organization wants to get its information out in such a way that a large number of potentially qualified applicants will respond. Then, after several interactions with the most promising of these candidates, hopefully, employees are hired. These candidates will best demonstrate the skills, knowledge, and abilities to successfully perform the job. The key word in this interaction is hopefully!

There is a labor shortage for some jobs in the United States. Many types of jobs—from high-tech to service jobs—are getting more difficult to fill. For example, in the Information Technology (IT) arena, consider the following. There is an estimated need to fill more than 1.6 million IT jobs by 2005 alone.[63] If every person who has any IT skill and experience were hired, there would still be more than 800,000 jobs unfilled. That's a nightmare for organizations. But more importantly, what about the 800,000 that are hired. Competition for them is unbelievable. Compounding this is the realization that in areas where high-tech work flourishes, unemployment in those areas is well below 2 percent—about half the national average. Being such, how do you locate these potential applicants and entice them to join your organization? Let's look at what some companies have done.[64]

- A number of companies in the Silicon Valley area flash job opening advertisements on movie screens just before the main attraction film starts;
- Microsoft, in an effort to attract and retain its IT workers, significantly raised the salaries of their positions;
- OnLink Technology hires an airplane to fly above rush hour traffic in southern California carrying banners advertising jobs;
- Some organization recruiters show up at people's homes, offering them the corporate jet for a weekend to fly somewhere to think about joining the company;
- New start-up companies advertise at college career fairs advocating that joining the company now gets the new hire in pre-IPO;
- Cisco has gone into the high schools, replacing shop class with a "new economy" course on inputting computer codes. Some of these high school students may end up with jobs approaching $70,000 annually after graduating. Cisco is also doing the same with individuals in homeless shelters.

The use of creativity for searching for job candidates appears to be gaining momentum. Whenever labor shortages exist, recruiting efforts take on new proportions. It's also safe to say that a competitive advantage can be gained by targeting good talent and encouraging them to apply. Quite possibly that's what the CEO of Acteva, Inc., thought when she hired the driver of the automobile who just rear-ended her car. Impressed with how the driver reacted to this stressful event, the CEO talked about a job opening she had, and offered the job on the spot; it was accepted. Impressed with the company, the driver's significant other also joined the company two weeks later. In this case, the recruiting effort was no accident!

Questions

1. Describe the process by which organizations identify "open" positions, and the types of employees needed. What two primary documents serve as the basis for recording this information?
2. Creativity in recruiting is necessary, but what do you believe the potential pitfalls may be? Using the examples presented above, describe how the organizations may not meet their recruiting goals even though they are creatively recruiting.
3. Hiring someone like the CEO of Acteva hired can "fill" vacant positions. What are the employment law legal ramifications of such an action? Cite specific examples.

Enhancing Your Communication Skills

1. Visit your campus career center and make an appointment with a career counselor. During your meeting, ask the counselor for advice about how to succeed in interviews. Focus specifically on the kinds of things campus recruiters are looking for today, how you should prepare for the interview, and what kinds of questions you can expect to get in the interview. Once your appointment is completed, provide a three- to five- page summary of the interview, highlighting how the information can be useful for you in a future job search.
2. College faculty are frequently evaluated by their peers, their department chair, their students, and oftentimes other academic administrators. Do you believe this process is reflective of a 360-degree appraisal? Discuss and support your position. Are there other constituents that you believe should be part of a faculty member's evaluation? Explain.

3. Go to the EEOC's Web site <www.eeoc.gov>. Research the procedure one must follow to file an EEOC charge. Also review the sexual harassment data and summary statistics the EEOC collects. Ascertain the number of cases filed during the past three years for which data have been kept, how many cases were settled, and the amounts of the monetary benefits awarded.

C A R E E R   M O D U L E

Building Your Career

INTRODUCTION

Although career development has been an important topic in management-related courses for the past three decades, there have been some drastic changes in recent years. Thirty years ago, career development programs were designed to assist employees in advancing their work lives and to provide the information and assessment needed to help realize career goals. Career development was a way for an organization to attract and retain highly talented personnel. But those concerns are all but disappearing in today's organizations. Downsizing, restructuring, work process engineering, and the like have reshaped the organization's role in career development. Today, the individual—not the organization—is responsible for an employee's career.[1] Unfortunately, millions of employees have learned this the hard way over the past few years. This module has been created to better prepare you to take responsibility for managing your career.

MAKING A CAREER DECISION

career
The sequence of positions occupied by a person during the course of a lifetime

The best **career** is whatever offers the best match between what you want out of life and what you need. Good career choices should result in a series of positions that give you an opportunity to be a good performer, make you want to maintain your commitment to your career, lead to highly satisfying work, and give you the proper balance between work and personal life. A good career match, then, is one in which you are able to develop a positive self-concept, to do work that you think is important, and to lead the kind of life you desire. Creating that balance is referred to as career planning.

Career planning is designed to assist you in becoming more knowledgeable about your needs, values, and personal goals. This knowledge can be achieved through a three-step, self-assessment process.[2]

- ***Identify and organize your skills, interests, work-related needs, and values.*** The best place to begin is by drawing up a profile of your educational record. List each school attended from high school on. What courses do you remember liking most and least? In what courses did you score highest and lowest? In what extracurricular activities did you participate? Are there any specific skills that you acquired? Are there other skills in which you have gained proficiency? Next, begin to assess your occupational experience. List each job you have held, the organization you worked for, your overall level of satisfaction, what you liked most and least about the job, and why you left. It's important to be honest in covering each of these points.
- ***Convert this information into general career fields and specific job goals.*** Step 1 should have provided some insights into your interests and abilities. Now you need to look at how they can be converted into the kind of organizational setting or field of endeavor with which you will be a good match. Then you can become specific and identify distinct job goals.

What fields are available? In business? In government? In nonprofit organizations? Your answer can be broken down further into areas such as education, financial, manufacturing, social services, or health services. Identifying areas of interest is usually far easier than pinpointing specific occupations. When you are able to identify a limited set of occupations that interest you, you can start to align them with your abilities and skills. Will certain jobs require you to move? If so, would the location be compatible with your geographic preferences? Do you have the educational requirements necessary for the job? If not, what additional schooling will be needed? Does the job offer the status and earning potential to which you aspire? What is the long-term outlook for jobs in this field? Does the field suffer from cyclical employment? Because no job is without its drawbacks, have you seriously considered all the negative aspects? When you have fully answered questions such as these, you should have a relatively short list of specific job goals.

- ***Test your career possibilities against the realities of the organization or the job market by talking with knowledgeable people in the fields, organizations, or jobs you desire.*** These informational interviews should provide reliable feedback as to the accuracy of your self-assessment and the opportunities available in the fields and jobs that interest you.

GETTING INTO THE ORGANIZATION

In Chapter 6 we've briefly introduced you to the recruiting process in organizations. When recruiters make a decision to hire employees, information is often sent out announcing the job in some format. Seeing that announcement, and feeling like there's a potential match between what you can offer and what the organization wants, you need to throw your hat into the "hiring ring."

One of the more stressful situations you will face happens when you apply for a job. This occurs because generally there are no specific guidelines to follow to guarantee you success. However, several tips may increase your chances of finding employment. Even though getting a job interview should be one of your major goals in the hiring process, being offered an interview opportunity requires hard work. You should view getting a job as your job of the moment.

WHERE CAN I FIND JOBS ADVERTISED ON THE INTERNET?

Newspaper advertisements and employment agencies may be on their way to extinction as primary sources for conveying information about job openings and finding job candidates—the reason: Internet recruiting. Nearly four out of five companies currently use the Internet to recruit new employees by adding a recruitment section to their Web site.[3] Large organizations or those planning to do a lot of Internet recruiting often develop dedicated sites specifically designed for recruitment. They have the typical information you might find in an employment advertisement—qualifications sought, experience required, benefits provided. But they also allow the organization to showcase its products, services, corporate philosophy, and mission statement. This information increases the quality of applicants, as those whose values don't mesh with the organization tend to self-select themselves out. The best designed of those Web sites include an online response form, so applicants don't need to send a separate resume by mail, e-mail, or fax. Applicants only need to fill in a resume page and hit the "submit" button. Cisco Systems, Inc., for example, receives more than 80 percent of its resumes electronically.[4]

Facilitating the growth of Internet recruitment are commercial job-posting services that provide essentially electronic classified ads.[5] We've listed the Web site for the 100 most popular of these, by category, in Exhibit CM–1.

EXHIBIT CM–1 Internet Job-Posting Services/Top 100 Electronic Recruiters (www.interbiznet.com)

JOB HUNTER'S SITE MAP

Recruiting Tools

- ■ Net-Temps
- ❑ Contract Employment
- ❑ DICE
- ❑ Entertainment Recruit
- ❑ Recruiters OnLine

Print Publishers

- ■ TechCareers(CMP)
- ❑ Boston.com
- ❑ Career Finder
- ❑ Career Path
- ❑ Career Post
- ❑ Comm Career Fair
- ❑ Jobsmart.com
- ❑ Talent Scout
- ❑ Virtual Job Fair

Educational Institutions

- ■ RPI Career Rsrcs
- ❑ Job-Hunt
- ❑ JobTrak
- ❑ JobWeb
- ❑ Purdue University

International Recruiters

- ■ JobServe
- ❑ Asia-Net
- ❑ CareerChina
- ❑ Computing Japan
- ❑ Recruit Media

Recruiters, Non-Technical

- ■ Cool Works
- ❑ Adecco (was Adia)
- ❑ Christian & Timbers
- ❑ Interim.com
- ❑ Kelly Services
- ❑ Manpower
- ❑ Robert Half

Best Job Seekers Tools

- ■ Job Smart

Master Sites

- ■ Monster Board
- ❑ Best Jobs USA Today
- ❑ Career Magazine
- ❑ CareerCity
- ❑ CareerMosaic
- ❑ Careers OnLine
- ❑ Career WEB
- ❑ E-SPAN
- ❑ 4 Work
- ❑ ICE
- ❑ Intellimatch
- ❑ JobBank USA
- ❑ Nation Job Network
- ❑ Online Career Center
- ❑ TOPjobs(tm) USA

New Generation Recruiters

- ■ Tripod: Work & $
- ❑ About Work
- ❑ Bay Area Jobs
- ❑ Chivas Toolbox
- ❑ Dream Jobs
- ❑ Extreme Resume Drop
- ❑ GETAJOB!
- ❑ KRON
- ❑ OfficeNET
- ❑ Student Center
- ❑ Yahoo Classifieds

Recruiters, Technical

- ■ MindSource
- ❑ Contractors Direct
- ❑ Hot Jobs
- ❑ Pencom Career Ctr
- ❑ Technology Locator

Resume Databases

- ■ SkillSearch
- ❑ InPursuit's Network
- ❑ Technology Registry

Niche Markets

- ■ MedSearch America
- ❑ Aleph
- ❑ Dave-Net Webmasters
- ❑ Direct Marketing World
- ❑ Editor & Publisher
- ❑ IEEE Employment
- ❑ Job Digger
- ❑ MMWire Classifieds
- ❑ Online Sports - Careers
- ❑ Survival Systems
- ❑ Water Online

Corporations, Technical

- ■ Cisco Systems, Inc.
- ❑ HP Employment
- ❑ Macromedia
- ❑ Microsoft Employment
- ❑ National Semiconductor
- ❑ Texas Instruments

Manufacturing and Services

- ■ Arthur Andersen
- ❑ AT&T
- ❑ IDG Careers
- ❑ J.P. Morgan & Co.
- ❑ KPMG
- ❑ Monsanto Careers

Industry Suppliers

- ■ HR Live
- ❑ Austin Knight
- ❑ Enterprise
- ❑ Fidelity
- ❑ HR Online
- ❑ Personnel Journal
- ❑ Relocation Journal
- ❑ Restrac
- ❑ Resumix
- ❑ SHRM
- ❑ Staffing Industry

Pioneer's Award

- ■ Riley Guide

Source: www.interbiznet.com. Used with permission.

HOW DO YOU PREPARE YOUR RESUME?

All job applicants need to circulate information that reflects positively on their strengths. That information needs to be sent to prospective employers in a format that is understandable and consistent with the organization's hiring practices. In most instances, this is done through the resume.

No matter who you are or where you are in your career, you should have a current resume. Your resume is typically the primary information source that a recruiter will use in determining whether to grant you an interview. Therefore, your resume must be a sales tool; it must give key information that supports your candidacy, highlights your strengths, and differentiates you from other job applicants. Anything positive that distinguishes you from other applicants should be included. For example, things like volunteer or community service show that you are well-rounded, committed to your community, and willing to "help" others.

It's important to pinpoint a few key themes regarding resumes that may seem like common sense but are frequently ignored. First, if you are making a "paper" copy of your resume, it must be printed on a quality printer. The style of font should be easy to read (e.g., Courier or Times New Roman type fonts). Avoid any style that may be hard on the eyes, such as a script or italics font. A recruiter who must review 100 or more resumes a day is not going to look favorably at difficult-to-read resumes, so using an easy-to-read font will make the recruiter's job easier.

It is also important to note that many companies today are relying on computer software for making the first pass through resumes. Each resume is scanned for specific information like key job elements, experience, work history, education, or technical expertise. This has created two important aspects for resume writing that you need to be aware of. The computer matches key words in a job description. Thus, in creating a resume, standard job description phraseology should be used. Second (and this goes back to the issue of font type), the font used should be easily read by the scanner, and if it isn't, your resume may be put in the rejection file. Your resume should be copied on good-quality white or off-white paper (no off-the-wall colors). There are certain types of jobs—like a creative artist position—where this suggestion may be inappropriate. But these are the exceptions. You can't go wrong using a 20-weight bend paper that has some cotton content (about 20 percent). By all means, don't send standard duplicating paper—it may look as if you are mass-mailing resumes (even if you are).

Much of what we stated in the last few paragraphs also holds true if you are producing an electronic resume. Whether or not the electronic resume is required will often be designated in the advertisement you've read, or provided as direction in the Internet recruiting site where you saw the job opening. Many aggressive job candidates are setting up their own Web pages to "sell" their job candidacy—they're called Websumes. When they learn of a possible job opening, they encourage potential employers to "check me out at my Web site." There, applicants have standard resume information, supporting documentation, and sometimes a video where they introduce themselves to potential employers.

Finally, regardless of whether your resume is electronic or on paper, make sure it is carefully proofread. Because the resume is the only representation of you the recruiter has, a sloppy resume can be deadly. If it contains misspelled words or is grammatically incorrect, your chances for an interview will be significantly reduced. Proofread your resume several times, and if possible, let others proofread it.

ARE THERE WAYS TO EXCEL AT AN INTERVIEW?

Interviews play a critical role in determining whether you will get the job. Up to now, all the recruiter has seen is your well-polished cover letter and resume. Remember, however, that very few people, if any, get a job without an interview. No matter how qualified you are for a position, if you perform poorly in the interview, you're not likely to be hired!

The reason interviews are so popular is that they help the recruiter determine if you are a "good fit" for the organization, in terms of your level of motivation and interpersonal skills.[6] The following suggestions can help you make your interview experience successful.

First, do some homework. Do a search for the company on the Internet (or visit your library) and get as much information as possible on the organization. Develop a solid grounding in the company, its history, markets, financial situation—and the industry in which it competes.

The night before the interview, get a good night's rest. As you prepare for the interview, keep in mind that your appearance is going to be the first impression you make. Dress appropriately. Incorrect attire can result in a negative impression. In getting to the interview location, arrive about 15 minutes ahead of your scheduled interview. It's better for you to wait than to have to contend with something unexpected, like a traffic jam, that could make you late. Arriving early also gives you an opportunity to survey the office environment and gather clues about the organization. Pay attention to the layout of the waiting room, the formality of the receptionist, and anything else that can give you insights into what the organization may be like.[7]

When you meet the recruiter, give him or her a firm handshake. Make good eye contact and maintain it throughout the interview. Remember, your body language may be giving away secrets about you that you don't want an interviewer to pick up. Sit erect and maintain good posture. While you're undoubtedly nervous, try your best to relax. Recruiters know that you'll be anxious, and a good one will try to put you at ease. Being prepared for an interview can also help build your confidence and reduce the nervousness. You can start building that confidence by reviewing a set of questions most frequently asked by interviewers. You can usually get a copy of these from the career center at your college. Develop rough responses to these questions beforehand. This will lessen the likelihood that you'll be asked a question that catches you off guard. But, our best advice is to be yourself. Don't go into an interview with a prepared text and recite it from memory. Have an idea of what you would like to say, but don't rely on rehearsed responses. Experienced interviewers will see through this "overpreparedness" and are likely to downgrade their evaluation of you.

If possible, you should also try to go through several "practice" interviews.[8] Universities often have career days on campus, when recruiters from companies are on-site to interview students. Take advantage of them. Even if a job doesn't fit what you want, the practice will help you become more skilled at dealing with interviews. You can also practice with family, friends, career counselors, student groups, or your faculty advisor.

When the interview ends, thank the interviewer for his or her time, and for giving you this opportunity to talk about your qualifications. But don't think that "selling" yourself has stopped there. As soon as you get home, send a thank you letter to the recruiter for taking the time to interview you and giving you the opportunity to discuss your job candidacy. This little act of courtesy has a positive effect—use it to your advantage.

WHAT ARE SOME SUGGESTIONS FOR DEVELOPING A SUCCESSFUL MANAGEMENT CAREER?

Today, managing your career carries with it responsibility by both you and the organization. Let's look at these responsibilities.

WHAT ARE AN ORGANIZATION'S RESPONSIBILITIES FOR CAREER DEVELOPMENT?

What, if any, responsibility does the organization have for career development under the "new rules" in today's contemporary organization? Basically the organization's responsibility is to build employee self-reliance and to help employees maintain their marketability through continual learning. The essence of a contemporary career development program is built on providing support so employees can continually add to their skills, abilities, and knowledge. This support includes:

- ***Communicating clearly the organization's goals and future strategies.*** When people know where the organization is headed, they're better able to develop a personal plan to share in that future.
- ***Creating growth opportunities.*** Employees should have the opportunity to get new, interesting, and professionally challenging work experiences.
- ***Offering financial assistance.*** The organization should offer tuition reimbursement to help employees keep current.
- ***Providing the time for employees to learn.*** Organizations should be generous in providing paid time off from work for off-the-job training. Additionally, workloads should not be so demanding that they preclude employees from having the time to develop new skills, abilities, and knowledge.

HOW CAN YOU ENHANCE YOUR CAREER?

You should consider managing your career like entrepreneurs manage a small business. You should think of yourself as self-employed, even if employed in a large organization. In a world of "free agency," the successful career will be built on maintaining flexibility and keeping skills and knowledge up-to-date. The following suggestions are consistent with the view that you, and only you, hold primary responsibility for your career.

- ***Know yourself.*** Know your strengths and weaknesses. What talents can you bring to an employer? Personal career planning begins by being honest with yourself.
- ***Manage your reputation.*** Without appearing as a braggart, let others both inside and outside your current organization know about your achievements. Make yourself and your accomplishments visible.
- ***Build and maintain network contacts.*** In a world of high mobility, you need to develop contacts. Join national and local professional associations, attend conferences, and network at social gatherings.
- ***Keep current.*** Develop those specific skills and abilities that are in high demand. Avoid learning organization-specific skills that can't be transferred quickly to other employers.
- ***Balance your specialist and generalist competencies.*** You need to stay current within your technical specialty. But you also need to develop general competencies that give you the versatility to react to an ever-changing work environment. Overemphasis in a single functional area or even in a narrow industry can limit your mobility.
- ***Document your achievements.*** Employers are increasingly looking to what you've accomplished rather than the titles you've held. Seek jobs and assignments that will provide increasing challenges and that will also offer objective evidence of your competencies.
- ***Keep your options open.*** Always have contingency plans prepared that you can call on when needed. You never know when your group will be eliminated, your department downsized, your project canceled, or your company acquired in a takeover. "Hope for the best but be prepared for the worst" may be a cliché, but it's still not bad advice.

CHAPTER 7

Managing Change, Stress, and Innovation

LEARNING OUTCOMES

After reading this chapter, I will be able to:

1. Describe what change variables are within a manager's control.
2. Identify external and internal forces for change.
3. Explain how managers can serve as change agents.
4. Contrast the "calm waters" and "white-water rapids" metaphors for change.
5. Explain why people are likely to resist change.
6. Describe techniques for reducing resistance to change.
7. Identify what is meant by the term *organization development* (OD) and specify four popular OD techniques.
8. Explain the causes and symptoms of stress.
9. Differentiate between creativity and innovation.
10. Explain how organizations can stimulate innovation.

In a geographic region where currency crises, political upheavals, and natural disasters are an unavoidable fact of life, Panamerican Beverages, Inc., has learned how to not only survive, but actually thrive in a chaotic and unpredictable environment. Founded in 1941, Panamco is Latin America's largest Coca-Cola bottler and distributor. Its sales account for about 5 percent of Coke's worldwide unit case volume of soft-drink sales. In Latin America, Panamco sells approximately one-fourth of all soft drinks sold in the region![1]

William C. Cooling, chairman and CEO, is well aware of his company's strategic importance both to Coca-Cola and to numerous Latin American economies. He recognizes that one of the company's most important managerial responsibilities is keeping its employees focused on successful performance in a sea of change. This requires organizational members to adapt to an ever-changing marketplace. In fact, adaptability has become one of the company's core survival skills and the secret to its ever-expanding business. Other organizational factors important to its success include its democratic and decentralized management philosophy, logistical expertise, innovative merchandising strategies, and excellent financial stewardship.

Cooling has always encouraged managers at Panamco to focus on flexibility, good communication, and quick reaction. Local Latin American managers are given a lot of autonomy to make decisions and respond independently to market forces in their territories. They have the authority to implement their own programs and initiatives. Although Panamco's managers appreciate and support the need for continual adaptation to marketplace demands, many of its nonmanagerial employees often fail to understand why the company must be adaptive and responsive to change. This makes it imperative that Panamco's managers educate its employees about the importance and necessity of change.

THE PROBLEMS FACED BY PANAMCO'S ORGANIZATIONAL MEMBERS are not unique. Large companies, small businesses, entrepreneurial start-ups, universities, state and city governments, hospitals, and even the military are being forced to significantly change the way they do things. Although change has always been a part of the manager's job, it has become more so in recent years. In this chapter we discuss the reasons for this and the ways managers can deal with the stress that exists in the organization, stimulate innovation, and increase their organizations' adaptability.

WHAT IS CHANGE?

change
An alteration of an organization's environment, structure, technology, or people

Change is an alteration of an organization's environment, structure, technology, or people. If it weren't for change, the manager's job would be easy. Planning would be simplified because tomorrow would be no different from today. The issue of organization design would be solved because the environment would be free from uncertainty and there would be no need to adapt. Similarly, decision making would be dramatically simplified because the outcome of each alternative could be predicted with near pinpoint accuracy. It would, indeed, simplify the manager's job if, for example, competitors did not introduce new products or services, if customers didn't make new demands, if government regulations were never modified, if technology never advanced, or if employees' needs always remained the same.

However, change is an organizational reality. Handling change is an integral part of every manager's job. But what can a manager change? The options essentially fall into one of three categories: altering structure, technology, or people (see Exhibit 7–1). We'll look at these three areas of change later in this chapter.

EXHIBIT 7–1
Three Categories of Change

Structure		Technology		People
Authority relationships Coordinating mechanisms Job redesign Spans of control	+	Work processes Work methods Equipment	+	Attitudes Expectations Perceptions Behavior

FORCES FOR CHANGE

In Chapter 2 we pointed out that there are both external and internal forces that constrain managers. These same forces also bring about the need for change. Let's briefly review these factors.

WHAT EXTERNAL FORCES CREATE A NEED FOR CHANGE?

The external forces that create the need for change come from various sources. In recent years, the marketplace has affected firms such as Verizon and Home Depot by introducing new competition. Verizon, for example, is experiencing competition from cable companies to provide local phone service. Home Depot, too, must now contend with a host of aggressive competitors such as Lowe's and Menard's. Government laws and regulations are also an impetus for change. Just a dozen years ago, the passage of the Americans with Disabilities Act required thousands of businesses to widen doorways, reconfigure restrooms, and add ramps. Organizations continue to deal with the requirements of improving accessibility for the disabled.

Technology also creates the need for change. In the new millennium, the Internet and e-commerce have changed the way we get information and how products are sold. As we discussed in Chapter 3, recent developments in sophisticated equipment have created significant economies of scale for many organizations. For instance, new technology and competition from discount brokerage houses forced Merrill Lynch (the brokerage firm) to offer its clients the opportunity to make trades over the Internet without a broker. The assembly line in many industries is also undergoing dramatic change as employers continue to replace human labor with technologically advanced mechanical robots, and the fluctuation in labor markets is

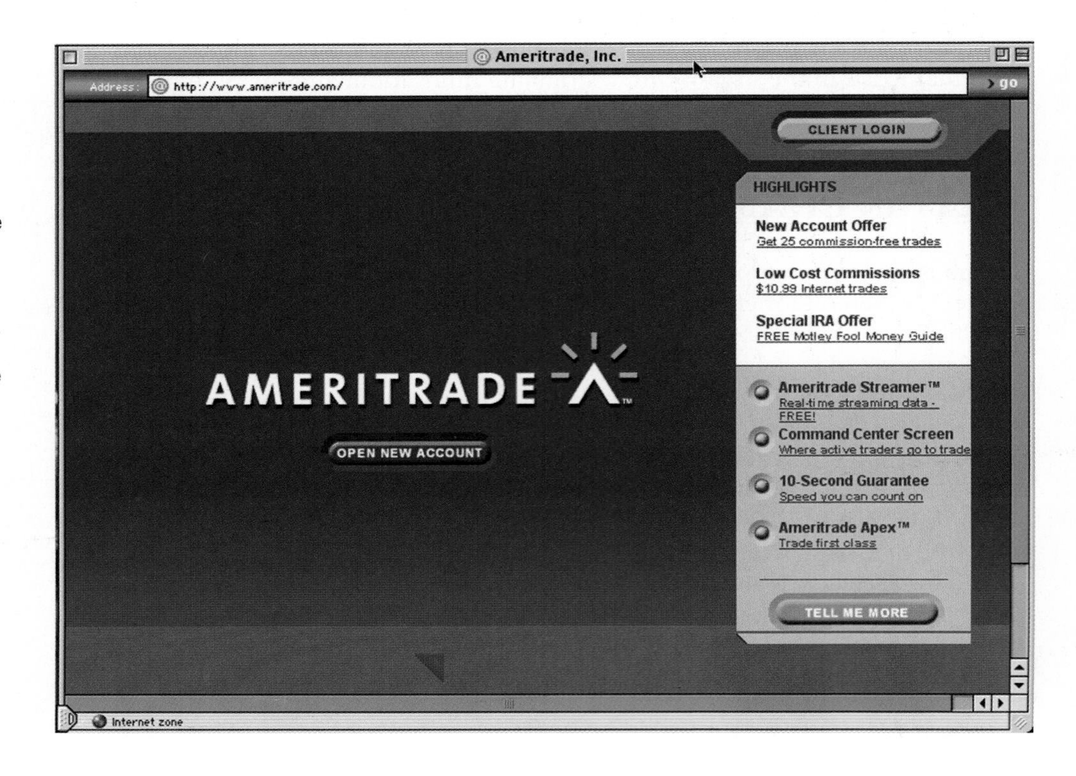

An organization like Merrill Lynch has made some dramatic changes in response to competition from companies such as Ameritrade. Merrill Lynch now offers its customers an opportunity to make trades over the Internet without the assistance of a stockbroker.

Source: The Ameritrade screen shot is the property of Ameritrade IP Company, Inc., is being displayed with the permission of Ameritrade IP Company, Inc., all rigts in the copyrightable content and trademarks are owned and reserved by Ameritrade IP Company, Inc., and that Ameritrade (R) is a registered trademark of Ameritrade IP Company, Inc.

forcing managers to initiate changes. For example, the shortage of registered nurses in the United States has led many hospital administrators to redesign jobs and to alter their rewards and benefits packages.

Economic changes, of course, affect almost all organizations. The dramatic decreases in interest rates in recent years fostered significant growth in the housing market. This meant more jobs, more employees hired, and significant increases in sales of other businesses that support the building industry. And changes occurring since September 11, 2001 have brought new and unprecedented life patterns to "life in America." As a case in point, the events of September 11th significantly reduced air travel. New security measures and lower traffic volumes have forced airlines to cut staff, redesign routes, and rethink almost every aspect of their business.

WHAT INTERNAL FORCES CREATE A NEED FOR CHANGE?

In addition to the external forces noted previously, internal forces can also stimulate the need for change. These internal forces tend to originate primarily from the internal operations of the organization or from the impact of external changes. [It is also important to recognize that these changes are a normal part of the organizational life cycle.[2]]

When management redefines or modifies its strategy, it often introduces a host of changes. For example, when Herman Miller Inc., developed a new strategy of competing more aggressively in the office furniture market, organizational members had to change how they performed their jobs—marketing efforts shifted dramatically, and manufacturing processes were revamped.[3] The introduction of new equipment represents another internal force for change. Employees may have their jobs redesigned, may need to undergo training to operate the new equipment, or be required to establish new interaction patterns within their work groups. An organization's workforce is rarely static. Its composition changes in terms of age, education, gender, nationality, and so forth. In a stable organization in which managers have been in their positions for years, there might be a need to restructure jobs in order to retain more ambitious employees by affording them some upward mobility. The compensation and benefits systems might also need to be reworked to reflect the needs of a diverse workforce and market forces in which certain skills are in short supply. Employee attitudes, such as increased job dissatisfaction, may lead to increased absenteeism, resignations, and even strikes. Such events will, in turn, often lead to changes in management policies and practices.

change agent
A person who initiates and assumes the responsibility for managing a change in an organization

HOW CAN A MANAGER SERVE AS A CHANGE AGENT?

Changes within an organization need a catalyst. People who act as catalysts and assume the responsibility for managing the change process are called **change agents**.[4]

Any manager can be a change agent. As we review the topic of change, we assume that it is initiated and carried out by a manager within the organization. However, the change agent can be a nonmanager—for example, an internal staff specialist or an outside consultant whose expertise is in change implementation. For major systemwide changes, internal management will often hire outside consultants to provide advice and assistance. Because these consultants are from the outside, they can offer an objective perspective that insiders usually lack. However, outside consultants may have an inadequate understanding of the organization's history, culture, operating procedures, and personnel. They are also prone to initiating more drastic changes than insiders—which can be either a benefit or a disadvantage—because they do not have to live with the repercussions after the change is implemented. In contrast, internal managers who act as change agents may be more thoughtful (and possibly more cautious) because they must live with the consequences of their actions.

No organization can sit idly and still compete effectively. At Herman Miller, the furniture manufacturer in Holland, Michigan, organizational members recognize this. CEO Michael Volkman wouldn't let success lure him into a false sense of security. Rather, he knew that to be a market leader, he had to change—and for Herman Miller, that meant significant infusions of technology into its manufacturing process.

TWO VIEWS OF THE CHANGE PROCESS

"calm waters" metaphor
A description of traditional practices in and theories about organizations that likens the organization to a large ship making a predictable trip across a calm sea and experiencing an occasional storm

"white-water rapids" metaphor
A description of the organization as a small raft navigating a raging river

We often use two metaphors to clarify the change process.[5] The **"calm waters" metaphor** envisions the organization as a large ship crossing a calm sea. The ship's captain and crew know exactly where they are going because they have made the trip many times before. Change surfaces as the occasional storm, a brief distraction in an otherwise calm and predictable trip. In the **"white-water rapids" metaphor**, the organization is seen as a small raft navigating a raging river with uninterrupted white-water rapids. Aboard the raft are half a dozen people who have never worked together before, who are totally unfamiliar with the river, who are unsure of their eventual destination, and who, as if things weren't bad enough, are traveling in a pitch-dark night. In the white-water rapids metaphor, change is a natural state and managing change is a continual process.

These two metaphors present very different approaches to understanding and responding to change. Let's take a closer look at each one.

WHAT IS THE "CALM WATERS" METAPHOR?

Until very recently, the "calm waters" metaphor dominated the thinking of practicing managers and academics. The prevailing model for handling change in calm waters is best illustrated in Kurt Lewin's three-step description of the change process[6] (see Exhibit 7–2).

According to Lewin, successful change requires unfreezing the status quo, changing to a new state, and freezing the new change to make it permanent. The status quo can be considered an equilibrium state. Unfreezing is necessary to move from this equilibrium. It can be achieved in one of three ways:

- The driving forces, which direct behavior away from the status quo, can be increased.
- The restraining forces, which hinder movement from the existing equilibrium, can be decreased.
- The two approaches can be combined.

Once unfreezing has been accomplished, the change itself can be implemented. However, the mere introduction of change does not ensure that it will take hold. The new situation, therefore, needs to be refrozen so that it can be sustained over time. Unless this last step is attended to, there is a strong chance that the change will be short-lived and employees will revert to the previous equilibrium state. The objective of refreezing the entire equilibrium state, then, is to stabilize the new situation by balancing the driving and restraining forces.

Note how Lewin's three-step process treats change as a break in the organization's equilibrium state. The status quo has been disturbed, and change is necessary to establish a new equilibrium state.[7] This view might have been appropriate to the relatively calm environment that most organizations faced in the 1950s, 1960s, and early 1970s, but the calm waters metaphor is increasingly obsolete as a description of the kinds of seas that current managers have to navigate.

EXHIBIT 7–2
The Change Process

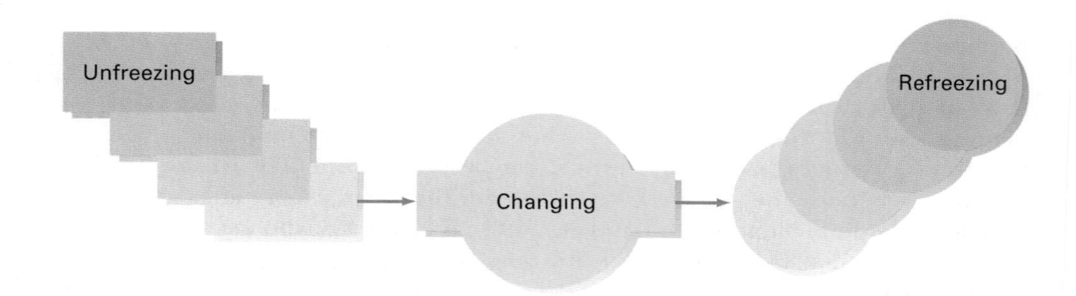

HOW DOES THE "WHITE-WATER RAPIDS" METAPHOR OF CHANGE FUNCTION?

This metaphor takes into consideration the fact that environments are both uncertain and dynamic. To get a feeling for what managing change might be like when you have to continually maneuver in uninterrupted rapids, imagine attending a college in which courses vary in length, so when you sign up, you don't know whether a course will last for two weeks or 30 weeks. Furthermore, the instructor can end a course any time he or she wants, with no prior warning. If that isn't bad enough, the length of the class session changes each time—sometimes it lasts 20 minutes, other times it runs for 3 hours—and the time of the next class meeting is set by the instructor during the previous class. Oh yes, there's one more thing. The exams are all unannounced, so you have to be ready for a test at any time. To succeed in this college, you would have to be incredibly flexible and be able to respond quickly to every changing condition. Students who are too structured or slow on their feet would not survive.

A growing number of managers are coming to accept that their job is much like what a student would face in such a college. The stability and predictability of the calm waters do not exist. Disruptions in the status quo are not occasional and temporary, to be followed by a return to calm waters. Many of today's managers never get out of the rapids. They face constant change, bordering on chaos. These managers are being forced to play a game they have never played before, which is governed by rules created as the game progresses.[8]

Is the white-water rapids metaphor merely an overstatement? No! Take the case of General Motors.[9] In the intensely competitive automotive manufacturing business, a company has to be prepared for any possibility. Cars are being surpassed by sport utility vehicles. Gasoline engines are still the fury of environmentalists who desire a more environment-friendly source of power for vehicles. Government regulators demand ever-increasing gasoline mileage. Customers want new and unique styles more frequently. And competition in the industry is fierce. While GM has focused on "big" competitors, new entrants into the marketplace—like Hyundai and Kia—pick away at market share. For GM to succeed, it must change, and continuously improve and revamp everything that it does! As one of GM's Advanced Portfolio Exploration Group (APEX) members stated, "change takes guts. It takes imagination. It takes commitment." These are all necessary ingredients for dealing with the chaotic world of business!

Change in a dynamic environment is typically filled with uncertainty. Just as white-water rafters have to deal with continuously changing environments, managers facing rapid and uncertain change must quickly and properly react to unexpected events.

DOES EVERY MANAGER FACE A WORLD OF CONSTANT AND CHAOTIC CHANGE?

Not every manager faces a world of constant and chaotic change, but the number of managers who don't is dwindling rapidly.[10] Managers in such businesses as women's apparel and computer software have long confronted a world of white-water rapids. They used to envy their counterparts in industries such as auto manufacturing, oil exploration, banking, publishing, telecommunications, and air transportation, who historically faced a stable and predictable environment. That might have been true in the 1960s, but not today.

Few organizations can treat change as the occasional disturbance in an otherwise peaceful world, and those few do so at great risk. Too much is changing too fast for any organization or its managers to be complacent. Most competitive advantages last less than 18 months. A firm such as People Express—a no-frills airline—was described in business periodicals as the model new-look firm; it went bankrupt a short time later. Southwest Airlines, however, uses this no-frills model extensively and is quite successful. The rules are being rewritten. What works for one organization may not work for another—and vice versa.

HOW DO ENTREPRENEURS HANDLE CHANGE?

We know from previous discussions that the context facing entrepreneurs is one of dynamic change. Both external and internal forces may bring about the need for making changes in the entrepreneurial venture. Entrepreneurs need to be alert to problems and opportunities that may create the need to change. In fact, of the many hats an entrepreneur wears, that of change agent may be one of the most important. If changes are needed in the entrepreneurial venture, often it is the entrepreneur who first recognizes the need for change and acts as the catalyst, coach and cheerleader, and chief change consultant. Change isn't easy in any organization, but it can be particularly challenging for entrepreneurial ventures. Even if a person is comfortable with taking risks, as entrepreneurs usually are, change can be hard. That's why it's important for an entrepreneur to recognize the critical roles he or she plays in stimulating and implementing change.

Since organizational change of any type can be disruptive and scary, the entrepreneur must assume the role of explaining the change and encouraging change efforts by supporting, explaining, getting employees excited about the change, building employees up, and motivating employees to put forth their best efforts; in other words, doing those things that coaches and cheerleaders do for a team.

Finally, the entrepreneur may have to guide the actual change process as changes in strategy, technology, products, structure, or people are being implemented. In this role, the entrepreneur answers questions, makes suggestions, gets needed resources, facilitates conflict, and does whatever else is necessary to get the change(s) implemented.

ORGANIZATIONAL CHANGE AND MEMBER RESISTANCE

Managers should be motivated to initiate change because they are concerned with improving their organization's effectiveness. However, change can be a threat to managers and nonmanagerial personnel as well. Organizations, and people within them, can build up inertia that propels them to resist any change, even if that change might be beneficial (see Details on a Management Classic). In this section, we review why people in organizations resist change and what can be done to lessen that resistance.

WHY DO PEOPLE RESIST CHANGE?

It's been said that most people hate any change that doesn't jingle in their pockets. This resistance to change is well documented.[11] But why do people resist change? An individual is likely to resist change for three reasons: uncertainty, concern over personal loss, and the belief that the change is not in the organization's best interest[12] (see Exhibit 7–3).

Changes substitute ambiguity and uncertainty for the known. No matter how much students may dislike some of the work associated with attending college, at least they know the ropes. They understand what is expected of them. When they leave college and venture out into the world of full-time employment, regardless of how eager they are to get out of college, they will have to trade the known for the unknown. Employees in organizations often hold the same dislike for uncertainty. For example, the introduction in manufacturing plants of six sigma processes means that employees will have to learn these new methods. Some employees who are accustomed to their work routines or who have inadequate math and statistics backgrounds may fear that they will be unable to meet the six sigma demands. They may, therefore, develop a negative attitude toward this methodology or behave dysfunctionally if required to use the process.

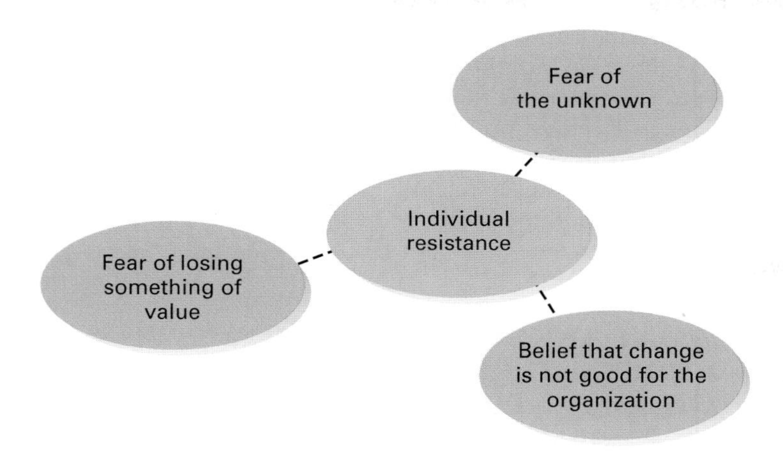

EXHIBIT 7-3
Why People Resist Change

The second cause of resistance is the fear of losing what one already possesses. Change threatens the investment in the status quo. The more people have invested in the current system, the more they resist change. Why? They fear the loss of their position, money, authority, friendships, personal convenience, or other benefits that they value. That is why senior employees resist change more than do relatively new employees. Senior employees generally have invested more in the current system and, therefore, have more to lose by adapting to a change.

Details on a Management Classic

Coch and French: Resistance to Change

One of the most famous studies on organizational change took place in the late 1940s at a Harwood Manufacturing Company plant, where pajamas were made.[13] The plant employed about 500 people and had a long history of disruptions every time changes were made in the way work progressed. Although the changes were typically minor—for example, workers who had formerly folded the tops that went with the pre-folded bottoms would be required to fold the bottoms as well—the employees resisted. They would complain bitterly and refuse to make the changes. Production decreased and grievances, absenteeism, and job turnover increased.

Harwood's management usually made these changes autocratically. Management would make the decision and then announce the changes to employees at a group meeting. The changes would be implemented immediately. Then, as mentioned, the employees would rebel. So Harwood's executives brought in a consultant as a change agent to help with their problem. As an experiment, the consultant arranged for the next change to be conducted in three groups, using three different methods. In the control group, the change was initiated in the usual manner—autocratically. The second group involved employee participation through selected representatives. These representatives, with management, worked out the details of the change, then tried the new methods and trained others in the new procedures. In the third group, all employees shared in the designing of the new methods with management.

The change agent gathered data over a 40-day period. What he found strongly supported the value of participation. In the control group, resistance occurred as before. Seventeen percent of the employees quit during the 40-day period, and grievances and absenteeism increased. However, in the representative and full-participation groups, there were no resignations, only one grievance, and no absenteeism. Moreover, participation was positively related to productivity. In the control group, output actually dropped from an average of 60 units per hour to 48 during the experimental period. The participation group generated 68 units per hour, and the total-participation group averaged 73 units per hour.

The Coch and French study still holds a major key for today's organizational change. That is, for permanent change to occur without extensive resistance, employees must be involved. Without employee involvement in matters that directly affect their work, companies run the risk of negating any possible gain a change can bring about, or worse, making the problem more serious than it was originally.

Research tells us that one way of reducing the resistance to change is to offer education and communication opportunities—like this employee session. By helping employees understand why the change is needed, and what effect it will have on them, resistance can be lessened.

A final cause of resistance is a person's belief that the change is incompatible with the goals and best interests of the organization. If an employee believes that a new job procedure proposed by a change agent will reduce productivity or product quality, that employee can be expected to resist the change. If the employee expresses his or her resistance positively (clearly expressing it to the change agent, along with substantiation), this form of resistance can be beneficial to the organization.

WHAT ARE SOME TECHNIQUES FOR REDUCING RESISTANCE TO ORGANIZATIONAL CHANGE?

When management sees resistance to change as dysfunctional, what actions can it take? Several strategies have been suggested for use by managers or other change agents in dealing with resistance to change.[14] These include education and communication, participation, facilitation and support, negotiation, manipulation and co-optation, and coercion. These tactics are summarized here and described in Exhibit 7–4.

Education and communication can help reduce resistance to change by helping employees see the logic of the change effort. This technique, of course, assumes that much of the resistance lies in misinformation or poor communication. *Participation* involves bringing those individuals directly affected by the proposed change into the decision-making process. Their participation allows these individuals to express their feelings, increase the quality of the process, and increase employee commitment to the final decision. *Facilitation and support* involve helping employees deal with the fear and anxiety associated with the change effort. This help may include employee counseling, therapy, new skills training, or a short paid leave of absence. *Negotiation* involves a bargain: exchanging something of value for an agreement to lessen the resistance to the change effort. This resistance technique may be quite useful when the resistance comes from a powerful source. *Manipulation and co-optation* refers to covert attempts to influence others about the change. It may involve twisting or distorting facts to make the change appear more attractive. Finally, *coercion* can be used to deal with resistance to change. Coercion involves the use of direct threats or force against the resisters.

MAKING CHANGES IN THE ORGANIZATION

What can a manager change? The manager's options, as we mentioned at the beginning of this chapter, fall into one of three categories: structure, technology, or people. Let's look more closely at each of these three areas.

Changing *structure* includes any alteration in authority relationships, coordination mechanisms, degree of centralization, job design, or similar organization structure variables. For instance, in our previous discussions we mentioned that work process engineering, restructuring, and empowering result in decentralization, wider spans of control, reduced work specialization, and work teams. These structural components give employees the authority and means to implement process improvements. For instance, the creation of work teams that cut across departmental lines allows those people who understand a problem best to solve that problem. In addition, cross-functional work teams encourage cooperative problem solving rather than "us versus them" situations.

Changing *technology* encompasses modification in the way work is processed or the methods and equipment used. The primary focus on technological change in continuous improvement initiatives is directed at developing flexible processes to

EXHIBIT 7–4 **Techniques for Reducing Resistance to Change**

TECHNIQUE	WHEN USED	ADVANTAGE	DISADVANTAGE
Education and communication	When resistance is due to misinformation	Clear up misunderstandings	May not work where mutual trust and credibility are lacking
Participation	When resisters have the expertise to make a contribution	Increases involvement and acceptance	Time-consuming, has potential for a poor solution
Facilitation and support	When resisters are fearful and anxiety-ridden	Can facilitate needed adjustments	Expensive; no guarantee of success
Negotiation	Necessary when resistance comes from a powerful group	Can "buy" commitment	Potentially high cost; opens door for others to apply pressure too
Manipulation and co-optation	When a powerful group's endorsement is needed	Inexpensive, easy way to gain support	Can backfire, causing change agent to lose credibility
Coercion	When a powerful group's endorsement is needed	Inexpensive, easy way to gain support	May be illegal; may undermine change agent's credibility

support better-quality operations. Employees committed to continuous improvements are constantly looking for things to fix. Thus, work processes must be adaptable to continual change and fine-tuning. This adaptability requires an extensive commitment to educating and training workers. The organization must provide employees with skills training in problem solving, decision making, negotiation, statistical analysis, and team-building, and they must be able to analyze and act on data.[15] For example, the infusion of technology and employee training has been the primary basis that has propelled Herman Miller to its market-leading position.[16]

Changes in *people* refers to changes in employee attitudes, expectations, perceptions, or behaviors. The human dimension of change requires a workforce committed to the organization's objectives of quality and continuous improvement. Again, this dimension necessitates proper education and training. It also demands a performance evaluation and reward system that supports and encourages continuous improvements. For example, successful programs put quality objectives into bonus plans for executives and incentives for operating employees.

HOW DO ORGANIZATIONS IMPLEMENT PLANNED CHANGES?

We know that most changes that employees experience in an organization do not happen by chance. Often, management makes a concerted effort to alter some aspect of the organization. Whatever happens—in terms of structure or technology—however, ultimately affects organizational members. The effort to assist organizational members with a planned change is referred to as organization development.

WHAT IS ORGANIZATION DEVELOPMENT?

Organization development (OD) facilitates long-term, organization-wide changes. Its focus is to constructively change the attitudes and values of organization members so that they can more readily adapt to and be more effective in achieving the new directions of the organization.[17] When OD efforts are planned, organization leaders are, in essence, attempting to change the organization's culture.[18] However, one of the

organization development (OD) An activity designed to facilitate planned, long-term organization-wide change that focuses on the attitudes and values of organizational members; essentially an effort to change an organization's culture

Ethical Dilemma in Management

The OD Intervention

OD interventions often produce positive change results. Interventions that rely on the participation of organization members can create openness and trust among co-workers and respect for others. Interventions can also help employees understand that the organization wants to promote risk taking and empowerment. "Living" these characteristics can lead to better organizational performance.

However, a change agent involved in an OD effort imposes his or her value system on those involved in the intervention, especially when the cause for that intervention is co-worker mistrust. To deal with this problem, the change agent may bring all affected parties together to openly discuss their perceptions of the dilemma.

Although many change agents are well versed in OD practices, sometimes they walk a fine line between success and failure. For personal problems to be resolved in the workplace, participants must disclose private, and often sensitive information. Even though an individual can refuse to divulge such information, doing so may carry negative ramifications. For example, it could lead to lower performance appraisals, fewer pay increases, or the perception that the employee is not a team player.

On the other hand, active participation can cause employees to speak their minds, but that, too, carries some risks. For instance, imagine in such a setting that an employee questions a manager's competence. This employee fully believes that the manager's behavior is detrimental to the work unit, but his or her reward for being open and honest could be retaliation from the boss. Although, at the time, the manager might appear to be receptive to the feedback, he or she may retaliate later. In either case—participation or not—employees could be hurt. Even though the intent is to help overcome worker mistrust, the result may be more backstabbing, more hurt feelings, and more mistrust (see Exhibit 7–5).

Do you think that co-workers can be too open and honest under this type of OD intervention? What do you think a change agent can do to ensure that employees' rights will be protected?

fundamental issues of OD is its reliance on employee participation to foster an environment in which open communication and trust exist.[19] Persons involved in OD efforts acknowledge that change can create stress for employees. Therefore, OD attempts to involve organizational members in changes that will affect their jobs and seeks their input about how the innovation is affecting them.

ARE THERE TYPICAL OD TECHNIQUES?

Any organizational activity that assists with implementing planned change can be viewed as an OD technique (see Ethical Dilemma in Management). However, the more popular OD efforts in organizations rely heavily on group interactions and cooperation. These include survey feedback, process consultation, team-building, and intergroup development.

survey feedback
A method of assessing employees' attitudes toward and perceptions of a change they are encountering by asking specific questions

Survey feedback efforts are designed to assess employee attitudes about and perceptions of the change they are encountering. Employees are generally asked to respond to a set of specific questions regarding how they view such organizational

EXHIBIT 7–5
Change, Dilbert Style
Source: DILBERT reprinted by permission of United Feature Syndicate, Inc.

aspects as decision making, leadership, communication effectiveness; and satisfaction with their jobs, co-workers, and management.[20] The data the change agent obtains are used to clarify problems that employees may be facing. As a result of this information, the change agent can take some action to remedy the problems.

"One of the fundamental issues behind OD is to foster an environment of communication and trust."

In **process consultation**, outside consultants help managers to perceive, understand, and act upon process events with which they must deal.[21] These might include, for example, workflow, informal relationships among unit members, and formal communications channels. Consultants give managers insight into what is going on. It is important to recognize that consultants are not there to solve these problems. Rather, they act as coaches to help managers diagnose the interpersonal processes that need improvement. If managers, with consultants' help, cannot solve the problem, consultants will often help managers locate experts who do have the requisite knowledge.

process consultation
The use of consultants from outside an organization to help change agents within the organization assess process events such as workflow, informal intraunit relationships, and formal communications channels

Organizations are made up of individuals working together to achieve some goals. Because organizational members are frequently required to interact with peers, a primary function of OD is to help them become a team. **Team-building** is generally an activity that helps work groups set goals, develop positive interpersonal relationships, and clarify the roles and responsibilities of each team member. There may be no need to address each area because the group may be in agreement and understand what is expected of it. The primary focus of team-building is to increase members' trust and openness toward one another.[22]

team-building
An activity that helps work groups set goals, develop positive interpersonal relationships, and clarify the roles and responsibilities of each team member

Whereas team-building focuses on helping a work group to become more cohesive, **intergroup development** attempts to achieve the same results among different work groups. That is, intergroup development attempts to change attitudes, stereotypes, and perceptions that one group may have toward another group. In doing so, better coordination among the various groups can be achieved.

intergroup development
An activity that attempts to make several work groups become more cohesive

STRESS: THE AFTERMATH OF ORGANIZATIONAL CHANGE

For many employees, change creates stress. A dynamic and uncertain environment characterized by restructurings, downsizings, empowerment, and personal-life matters has caused large numbers of employees to feel overworked and "stressed out." In this section, we will review specifically what is meant by the term *stress*, what causes stress, how to identify it, and what managers can do to reduce anxiety.

Not every stressor in our lives is negative. Happy moments, like getting married, having a child, or getting a promotion, can all create stress. We need to understand what causes us stress, and learn to manage what the cards of life "deal" us.

WHAT IS STRESS?

Stress is a dynamic condition in which an individual is confronted with an opportunity, constraint, or demand related to what he or she desires, and for which the outcome is perceived to be both uncertain and important. Stress is a complex issue, so let us look at it more closely. Stress can manifest itself in both a positive and a negative way. Stress is said to be positive when the situation offers an opportunity for one to gain something; for example, the "psyching-up" that an athlete goes through can be stressful, but this can lead to maximum performance. It is when constraints or demands are placed on us that stress can become negative.[23] Let us explore these two features—constraints and demands.

Constraints are barriers that keep us from doing what we desire. Purchasing a sport utility vehicle (SUV) may be your desire,

Having a stressful day? This employee is. After significant staffing cutbacks in the organization, this individual now does the work that was once handled by three people.

but if you cannot afford the $38,000 price, you are constrained from purchasing it. Accordingly, constraints inhibit you in ways that take the control of a situation out of your hands. If you cannot afford the SUV, you cannot get it. Demands, on the other hand, may cause you to give up something you desire. If you wish to go to a movie with friends on Tuesday night but have a major examination Wednesday, the examination may take precedence. Thus, demands preoccupy your time and force you to shift priorities.

Constraints and demands can lead to potential stress. When they are coupled with uncertainty about the outcome and the importance of the outcome, potential stress becomes actual stress. Regardless of the situation, if you remove the uncertainty or the importance, you remove stress. For instance, you may have been constrained from purchasing the SUV because of your budget, but if you just won one in a radio-sponsored contest, the uncertainty element is significantly reduced. Furthermore, if you are auditing a class for no grade, the importance of the major examination is essentially nil. However, when constraints or demands have an effect on an important event and the outcome is unknown, pressure is added—pressure resulting in stress.

While we are not attempting to minimize stress in people's lives, it is important to recognize that both good and bad personal factors may cause stress. Of course, when you consider the changes, like restructuring, that are occurring in U.S. companies, it is little wonder that stress is so rampant. Just how rampant? Stress-related problems amount to costs of nearly $300 billion annually for U.S. corporations in terms of "lost productivity, increased worker compensation claims, turnover, and health care costs."[24] And stress on the job knows no boundaries.

In Japan, there is a concept called **karoshi**, which means death from overworking—employees who die after working more than 3,000 hours in a year—18-plus hours each day with nearly every minute scheduled out in specific detail. Upwards of 10,000 individuals die each year from heart attack or stroke—having karoshi listed as the cause of death.[25] Many Japanese employees literally work themselves to death—with one in six working more than 3,100 hours annually. Employees in Australia, Germany, and Britain, too, have suffered the ill effects of stress—costing their organizations billions of dollars.[26]

"In Japan, upwards of 10,000 individuals die annually from being overworked!"

stress
A force or influence a person feels when he or she faces opportunities, constraints, or demands that he or she perceives to be both uncertain and important

karoshi
A Japanese term that refers to a sudden death caused by overworking

stressor
A factor that causes stress

ARE THERE COMMON CAUSES OF STRESS?

Stress can be caused by a number of factors called **stressors**. Factors that create stress can be grouped into two major categories—organizational and personal (see Exhibit 7–6).[27] Both directly affect employees and, ultimately, their jobs.

There is no shortage of factors within the organization that can cause stress. Pressures to avoid errors or complete tasks in a limited time period, a demanding supervisor, and unpleasant co-workers are a few examples. The discussion that follows organizes stress factors into five categories: task, role, and interpersonal demands; organization structure; and organizational leadership.

Task demands are factors related to an employee's job. They include the design of the person's job (autonomy, task variety, degree of automation), working conditions, and the physical work layout. Work quotas can put pressure on employees when their "outcomes" are perceived as excessive.[28] The more interdependence between an employee's tasks and the tasks of others, the more potential stress there is. *Autonomy*, on the other hand, tends to lessen stress. Jobs where temperatures, noise, or other working conditions are dangerous or undesirable can increase anxiety. So, too, can working in an overcrowded room or in a visible location where interruptions are constant.

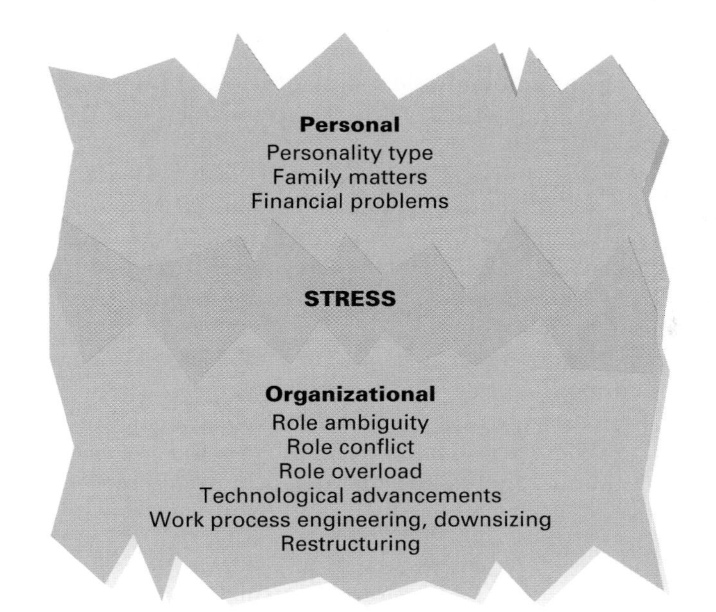

EXHIBIT 7-6
Major Stressors

Role demands relate to pressures placed on an employee as a function of the particular role he or she plays in the organization. **Role conflicts** create expectations that may be hard to reconcile or satisfy. **Role overload** is experienced when the employee is expected to do more than time permits. **Role ambiguity** is created when role expectations are not clearly understood and the employee is not sure what he or she is to do.

role conflicts
Work expectations that are hard to satisfy

role overload
Having more work to accomplish than time permits

role ambiguity
When role expectations are not clearly understood

Interpersonal demands are pressures created by other employees. Lack of social support from colleagues and poor interpersonal relationships can cause considerable stress, especially among employees with a high social need.

Organization structure can increase stress. Excessive rules and an employee's lack of opportunity to participate in decisions that affect him or her are examples of structural variables that might be potential sources of stress.

Organizational leadership represents the supervisory style of the organization's company officials. Some managers create a culture characterized by tension, fear, and anxiety. They establish unrealistic pressures to perform in the short run, impose excessively tight controls, and routinely fire employees who don't measure up. This style of leadership flows down through the organization to affect all employees.

Personal factors that can create stress include family issues, personal economic problems, and inherent personality characteristics. Because employees bring their personal problems to work with them, a full understanding of employee stress requires a manager to be understanding of these personal factors. There is also evidence that employees' personalities have an effect on how susceptible they are to stress. The most commonly used labels for these personality traits are Type A and Type B.

Type A personality is characterized by chronic feelings of a sense of time urgency, an excessive competitive drive, and difficulty accepting and enjoying leisure time. The opposite of Type A is **Type B personality**. Type Bs never suffer from time urgency or impatience. Until quite recently, it was believed that Type As were more likely to experience stress on and off the job. A closer analysis of the evidence, however, has produced new conclusions. It has been found that only the hostility and anger associated with Type A behavior is actually associated with the negative effects of stress. And Type Bs are just as susceptible to the same anxiety-producing elements. For managers, what is important is to recognize that Type A employees are more likely to show symptoms of stress, even if organizational and personal stressors are low.

type A personality
People who have a chronic sense of urgency and an excessive competitive drive

type B personality
People who are relaxed and easygoing and accept change easily

WHAT ARE THE SYMPTOMS OF STRESS?

What signs indicate that an employee's stress level might be too high? There are three general ways that stress reveals itself. These include physiological, psychological, and behavioral symptoms.

Most of the early discussions of stress focused heavily on health-related, or *physiological concerns.* This was attributed to the fact that high stress levels result in changes in metabolism, increased heart and breathing rates, increased blood pressure, headaches, and increased risk of heart attacks. Because detecting many of these requires the skills of trained medical personnel, their immediate and direct relevance to managers is negligible.

Of greater importance to managers are psychological and behavioral symptoms of stress. It's these things that can be witnessed in the person. The *psychological symptoms* can be seen as increased tension and anxiety, boredom, and procrastination—all of which can lead to productivity decreases. So too, can the *behavior-related symptoms*—changes in eating habits, increased smoking or substance consumption, rapid speech, or sleep disorders.

HOW CAN STRESS BE REDUCED?

employee assistance programs (EAPs)
Programs offered by organizations to help their employees overcome personal and health-related problems

wellness programs
Program offered by organizations to help their employees prevent health problems

Reducing stress is one thing that presents a dilemma for managers.[29] Some stress in organizations is absolutely necessary. Without it, people have no energy. Accordingly, whenever one considers stress reduction, what is at issue is reducing its dysfunctional aspects.

One of the first means of reducing stress is to make sure that employees are properly matched to their jobs, and that they understand the extent of their "authority." Furthermore, by letting employees know precisely what is expected of them, role conflict and ambiguity can be reduced. Redesigning jobs can also help ease work overload-related stressors. Employees should also have some input in those things that affect them. Their involvement and participation have been found to help lessen stress.

You must recognize that no matter what you do to eliminate organizational stressors, some employees will still be "stressed-out." You simply have little or no control over the personal factors. You also face an ethical issue when personal factors are causing stress. That is, just how far can you intrude in an employee's personal life? To help deal with this issue, many companies have started employee assistance and wellness programs. These employer-sponsored programs are designed to assist employees in areas like financial planning, legal matters, health, fitness, stress, and the like—where they are having difficulties.

How can managers tell if one of their employees is "stressed-out?" In many cases it's difficult to do. However, some cues regarding behavioral changes—like increased smoking or substance consumption—can be telltale signs.

Contemporary **employee assistance programs (EAPs)** are extensions of programs that had their start in U.S. companies in the 1940s.[30] Companies such as DuPont, Standard Oil, and Kodak recognized that a number of their employees were experiencing problems with alcohol. Formal programs were implemented on the company's site to educate these workers about the dangers of alcohol and to help them overcome their addiction. The rationale for these programs, which still holds today, is getting a productive employee back on the job as swiftly as possible. And there can be a benefit to the organization in terms of a return on investment. It is estimated that U.S. companies spend almost $1 billion each year on EAP programs. For most, studies suggest that these companies save up to $5.00 to $16 for every EAP dollar spent.[31] That, for most of us, is a significant return on investment!

In addition to EAP, many organizations are implementing wellness programs. A **wellness program** is designed to keep employees healthy.[32] These are varied and may focus on such things as smoking cessation, weight control, stress management, physical fitness, nutrition education, high-blood-pressure control, violence protection, work team problem intervention, and so on.[33] Wellness programs are designed to help cut employer health costs, and to lower absenteeism and turnover by preventing health-related problems.[34]

Employees at Gould Evans Goodman architectural firm in Kansas City, Missouri, relieve some of their stress while at work. Concerned about employees' well-being, company officials have installed sleep tents, gymnasiums, and art rooms. This employee gets some needed rest while at work, which can help to make him refreshed, and more productive.

STIMULATING INNOVATION

Innovate or die! These harsh words are increasingly becoming the rallying cry of today's managers.[35] In the dynamic world of global competition, organizations must create new products and services and adopt state-of-the-art technology if they are to compete successfully.[36] The standard of innovation toward which many organizations strive is that achieved by such companies as 3-M, DuPont, Motorola, and Whirlpool.[37] Their innovations have helped them become brand names known and products used in nearly every household.[38] But, these companies also know that today's innovation is short-lived. For instance, management at Black & Decker learned a valuable lesson about innovation when it brought its "SnakeLight" light to market in the mid-1990s. Projecting first-year sales of 200,000 units, the SnakeLight sold more than 600,000—backlogging orders for nearly 28 months. And the company's failure to "inject useful, useable and desirable changes into the product" led to Black & Decker's losing its market share to a competing product.[39]

What's the secret to success for innovative companies? What, if anything, can other managers do to make their organizations more innovative? In the following pages, we will try to answer those questions as we discuss the factors behind innovation.

HOW ARE CREATIVITY AND INNOVATION RELATED?

In general usage, **creativity** means the ability to combine ideas in a unique way or to make unusual associations between ideas. For example, when Felix Hoffman discovered a "pure and stable" form of acetylsalicylic acid, he pioneered the invention of the pharmaceutical industry's medicine for pain management.[40] And at Mattel, company officials have introduced "Project Platypus." This special division brings people from all disciplines—like engineering, marketing, design, and sales—to get employees to "think outside the box" in order to "understand the sociology and psychology behind children's play patterns." To help make this happen, team members embark on such activities as imagination exercises, group crying, and stuffed-bunny throwing.[41] The first Project Platypus product, Ello, hit the market in 2002 after two years in development.

creativity
The ability to combine ideas in a unique way or to make unusual connections

Innovation is the process of taking a creative idea and turning it into a useful product, service, or method of operation.[42] The innovative organization is characterized by the ability to channel its creative juices into useful outcomes. When managers talk about changing an organization to make it more creative, they usually mean that they want to stimulate innovation. The 3-M Company is aptly described as innovative because it has taken novel ideas and turned them into profitable products such as cellophane tape, Scotch Guard protective coatings, Post-It™ notepads, and diapers with elastic waistbands. Also innovative is the highly successful microchip manufacturer Intel. It leads all chip manufacturers in miniaturization, and the success of its Pentium IV chip gives the company a 75 percent share of the microprocessor market for IBM-compatible PCs. With $26 billion a year in sales, Intel's commitment to

innovation
The process of taking a creative idea and turning it into a useful product, service, or method of operation

staying ahead of the competition by introducing a stream of new and more powerful products is supported by annual expenditures exceeding $7 billion for its plant and equipment and nearly $4 billion for research and development.[43]

WHAT IS INVOLVED IN INNOVATION?

Some people believe that creativity is inborn; others believe that with training, anyone can be creative. The latter group views creativity as a fourfold process consisting of perception, incubation, inspiration, and innovation.[44]

Perception involves the way you see things. Being creative means seeing things from a unique perspective. One person may see solutions to a problem that others cannot or will not see at all. The movement from perception to reality, however, doesn't occur instantaneously. Instead, ideas go though a process of incubation. Sometimes, employees need to sit on their ideas. This doesn't mean sitting and doing nothing. Rather, during this incubation period, employees should collect massive amounts of data that are stored, retrieved, studied, reshaped, and finally molded into something new. During this period, it is common for years to pass. Think for a moment about a time you struggled for an answer on a test. Although you tried hard to jog your memory, nothing worked. Then suddenly, like a flash of light, the answer popped into your head. You found it! *Inspiration* in the creative process is similar. Inspiration is the moment when all your efforts successfully come together.

Although inspiration leads to euphoria, the creative work is not complete. It requires an innovative effort. Innovation involves taking that inspiration and turning it into a useful product, service, or way of doing things. Thomas Edison is often credited with saying that "Creativity is 1 percent inspiration and 99 percent perspiration." That 99 percent, or the innovation, involves testing, evaluating, and retesting what the inspiration found. It is usually at this stage that an individual involves others more in what he or she has been working on. That involvement is critical because even the greatest invention may be delayed, or lost, if an individual cannot effectively deal with others in communicating and achieving what the creative idea is supposed to do.

HOW CAN A MANAGER FOSTER INNOVATION?

Three sets of variables have been found to stimulate innovation. They pertain to the organization's structure, culture, and human resources practices.

How do structural variables affect innovation? On the basis of extensive research, we can make three statements regarding the effect of structural variables on innovation.[45] First, organic structures positively influence innovation because they have less work specialization and fewer rules and are more decentralized than mechanistic structures. They facilitate the flexibility, adaptation, and cross-fertilization that make the adoption of innovations easier.[46] Second, easy availability of plentiful resources is a key building block for innovation. An abundance of resources allows management to purchase innovations, bear the cost of instituting innovations, and absorb failures. Finally, frequent interunit communication helps to break down possible barriers to innovation by facilitating interaction across departmental lines.

How does an organization's culture affect innovation? Innovative organizations tend to have similar cultures.[47] They encourage experimentation. They reward both successes and failures. They celebrate mistakes.[48] For example, at the General Motors APEX unit, employees are encouraged to experiment and rewarded for experimenting with new products in the marketplace.[49] An innovative culture is likely to have the following seven characteristics:[50]

- ***Acceptance of ambiguity.*** Too much emphasis on objectivity and specificity constrains creativity.
- ***Tolerance of the impractical.*** Individuals who offer impractical, even foolish, answers to what-if questions are not stifled. What seems impractical at first might lead to innovative solutions.
- ***Low external controls.*** Rules, regulations, policies, and similar controls are kept to a minimum.
- ***Tolerance of risk.*** Employees are encouraged to experiment without fear of consequences should they fail. Mistakes are treated as learning opportunities.
- ***Tolerance of conflict.*** Diversity of opinions is encouraged. Harmony and agreement between individuals or units are not assumed to be evidence of high performance.
- ***Focus on ends rather than on means.*** Goals are made clear, and individuals are encouraged to consider alternative routes toward their attainment. Focusing on ends suggests that there might be several right answers to any given problem.
- ***Open systems focus.*** The organization closely monitors the environment and responds rapidly to changes as they occur.

What human resources variables affect innovation? Within the human resources category, we find that innovative organizations actively promote the training and development of their members so that their knowledge remains current. They offer their employees high job security to reduce the fear of getting fired for making mistakes, and encourage individuals to become champions of change.[51] Once a new idea is developed, champions of change actively and enthusiastically promote the idea, build support, overcome resistance, and ensure that the innovation is implemented. Research finds that champions have common personality characteristics: extremely high self-confidence, persistence, energy, and a tendency to take risks. Champions also display characteristics associated with dynamic leadership.[52] They inspire and energize others with their vision of the potential of an innovation and through their strong personal conviction about their mission. They are also good at gaining the commitment of others to support their mission. In addition, champions have jobs that provide considerable decision-making discretion. This autonomy helps them introduce and implement innovations.[53]

How important is innovation in an organization? If you ask Ronald DeFeo, he'll tell you it's one of the most important responsibilities he has to support. And to encourage innovation, DeFeo believes the organization's culture must be supportive, and there must be clear communication among organization members. That, to him, is imperative.

WHY DO ENTREPRENEURS VALUE INNOVATION?

In today's dynamic world of global competition, organizations must continually innovate new products and services if they want to compete successfully. We know that innovation is a key characteristic of entrepreneurial ventures. In fact, you might say that innovation is what makes the entrepreneurial venture "entrepreneurial."

What must an entrepreneur do to encourage innovation in the venture? Having an innovation-supportive culture is crucial. What does such a culture look like?[54] It's one in which employees perceive that supervisory support and organizational reward systems are consistent with a commitment to innovation. It's also in this type of culture that employees not perceive that their workload pressures are excessive or unreasonable. And research has shown that firms with cultures supportive of innovation tend to be smaller; they have fewer formalized human resources practices and less abundant resources.[55]

Although having an innovation-supportive culture is important, employees also need to be able to do something with those innovations. For instance, at Monarch Marking Systems, Inc., in Miamisburg, Ohio, employees know how to turn ideas into action. To improve the productivity levels in one particular area, an employee team pondered several potential remedies, tested theories, and ultimately implemented five solutions. The team's innovative solutions reduced the amount of time it took to change over the production line from 60 minutes to four minutes. In addition, the innovative solutions made the employees' jobs easier.[56]

Review, Comprehension, Application

CHAPTER SUMMARY

How will you know if you fulfilled the Learning Outcomes on page 202? You will have fulfilled the Learning Outcomes if you are able to:

1. **Describe what change variables are within a manager's control.** Managers can change the organization's structure by altering work specialization, rules and regulations, or centralization variables or by redesigning jobs; they can change the organization's technology by altering work processes, methods, and equipment, or they can change people by altering attitudes, expectations, perceptions, or behavior.
2. **Identify external and internal forces for change.** External forces for change include the marketplace, government laws and regulations, technology, labor markets, and economic changes. Internal forces of change include organizational strategy, equipment, the workforce, and employee attitudes.
3. **Explain how managers can serve as change agents.** Managers can serve as change agents by becoming the catalysts for change in their units and by managing the change process.
4. **Contrast the "calm waters" and "white-water rapids" metaphors for change.** The calm waters metaphor views change as a break in the organization's equilibrium state. Organizations are seen as stable and predictable, disturbed by only an occasional crisis. The white-water rapids metaphor views change as continual and unpredictable. Managers must deal with ongoing and almost chaotic change.
5. **Explain why people are likely to resist change.** People resist change because of the uncertainty it creates, fear of personal loss, and conviction that it might not be in the organization's best interest.
6. **Describe techniques for reducing resistance to change.** Six strategies have been proposed for reducing the resistance to change. They are education and communication, participation, facilitation and support, negotiation, manipulation and co-optation, and coercion.
7. **Identify what is meant by the term *organization development* and specify four popular OD techniques.** Organization development is an organizational activity designed to facilitate long-term organization-wide changes. Its focus is to constructively change the attitudes and values of organization members so that they can more readily adapt to and be more effective in achieving the new directions of the organization. The more popular OD efforts in organizations rely heavily on group interactions and cooperation and include survey feedback, process consultation, team-building, and intergroup development.
8. **Explain the causes and symptoms of stress.** Stress is the tension that individuals feel when they face opportunities, constraints, or demands that they perceive to be both uncertain and important. It can be caused by organizational factors, such as work overload, role conflict, and role ambiguity. Personal factors can also contribute to stress—a serious illness, death of a family member, divorce, financial difficulties, or personality type.
9. **Differentiate between creativity and innovation.** Creativity is the ability to combine ideas in a unique way or to make unusual associations between ideas. Innovation is the process of taking creative ideas and turning them into a useful product, service, or method of operation.
10. **Explain how organizations can stimulate innovation.** Organizations that stimulate innovation will have flexible structures, easy access to resources, and fluid communication; a culture that is relaxed, supportive of new ideas, and encourages monitoring of the environment; and creative people who are well trained, current in their fields, and secure in their jobs.

COMPANION WEBSITE

We invite you to visit the Robbins/DeCenzo companion Website at **www.prenhall.com/robbins** for this chapter's Internet resources, including an online study guide, Internet exercises, and "In the News" with full text articles provided by XanEdu.

READING FOR COMPREHENSION

1. Why is handling change an integral part of every manager's job?
2. Describe Lewin's three-step change process. How is it different from the change process needed in the white-water rapids metaphor of change?
3. How do work overload, role conflict, and role ambiguity contribute to employee stress?
4. How do creativity and innovation differ? Give an example of each.
5. How does an innovative culture make an organization more effective? Do you think an innovative culture could ever make an organization less effective? Why or why not?

LINKING CONCEPTS TO PRACTICE

1. Who are change agents? Do you think that a low-level employee could act as a change agent? Explain.
2. Why is organization development planned change? Explain how planned change is important for organizations in today's dynamic environment.
3. Which organization—DaimlerChrysler or Apple—do you believe would have more difficulty changing its culture? Explain your position.
4. "Managers have a responsibility to their employees who are suffering serious ill effects of work-related stress." Do you agree or disagree with the statement? Support your position.
5. Do you think changes can occur in an organization without a champion to foster new and innovative ways of doing things? Explain.

Management Workshop

Team Skill-Building Exercise

The Celestial Aerospace Company

Objectives

1. To illustrate how forces for change and stability must be managed in organizations.
2. To illustrate the effects of alternative change techniques on the relative strength of forces for change and forces for stability.

The Situation

The marketing division of the Celestial Aerospace Company (CAP) has gone through two major reorganizations in the past seven years. Initially, the structure changed from a functional to a matrix form, which did not satisfy some functional managers nor did it lead to organizational improvements. The managers complained that the structure confused the authority and responsibility relationships. In reaction to these complaints, senior management returned to the functional form, which maintained market and project teams that were managed by project managers with a few general staff personnel. No functional specialists were assigned to these groups. After the change, some problems began to surface. Project managers complained that they could not obtain the necessary assistance from functional staffs. It not only took more time to obtain necessary assistance but also created problems in establishing stable relationships with functional staff members. Because these problems affected customer services, project managers demanded a change in the organizational structure.

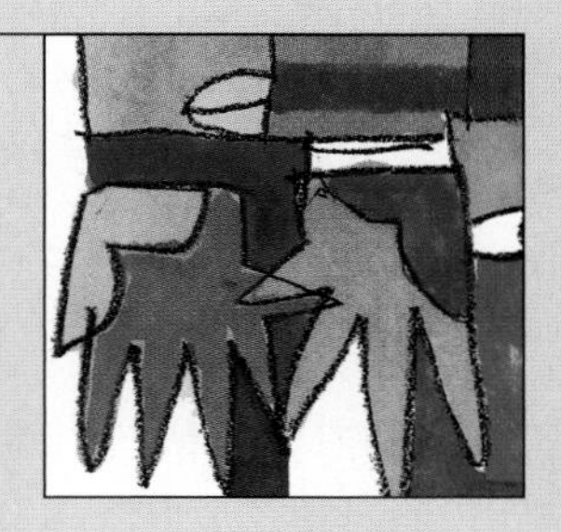

Faced with these complaints and demands from project managers, senior management is pondering yet another reorganization for the division. They have requested an outside consultant (you) to help them in their reorganization plan—one that will provide some stability in the structure, address their issues, and help the organization achieve its strategic goals.

Procedure

1. Divide into groups of five to seven and take the role of consultants.
2. Each group should identify the forces necessitating the change and the resistance to that change in the company.
3. Each group should develop a set of strategies for dealing with the resistance to change and for implementing those strategies.
4. Reassemble the class and hear each group's recommendations and explanations.
5. After each group has presented, the other consulting groups should pose probing questions about the presenting group's recommendations.

Understanding Yourself

Before you can develop other people you must understand your present strengths. To assist in this learning process, we encourage you to complete the following self-assessments from the Prentice Hall Self-Assessment Library 2.0:

- Am I a Type A? (#6)
- How Creative Am I? (8)
- How Well Do I Respond to Turbulent Change? (#47)
- How Stressful Is My Life? (#48)

After you complete these assessments, we suggest that you print out the results and store them as part of your "portfolio of learning."

Developing Your Change Management Skill

About the Skill

Managers play an important role in organizational change. That is, they often serve as a catalyst for the change—a change agent. However, managers may find that change is resisted by employees. After all, change represents ambiguity and uncertainty, or it threatens the status quo. How can this resistance to change be effectively managed? Here are some suggestions.[57]

Steps in Practicing the Skill

1. **Assess the climate for change.** One major factor in why some changes succeed while others fail is the readiness for change. Assessing the climate for change involves asking several questions. The more affirmative answers you get, the more likely it is that change efforts will succeed. Here are some guiding questions:
   - **a.** Is the sponsor of the change high enough in the organization to have power to effectively deal with resistance?
   - **b.** Is senior management supportive of the change and committed to it?
   - **c.** Is there a strong sense of urgency from senior managers about the need for change and is this feeling shared by others in the organization?
   - **d.** Do managers have a clear vision of how the future will look after the change?
   - **e.** Are there objective measures in place to evaluate the change effort and have reward systems been explicitly designed to reinforce them?
   - **f.** Is the specific change effort consistent with other changes going on in the organization?
   - **g.** Are managers willing to sacrifice their personal self-interests for the good of the organization as a whole?
   - **h.** Do managers pride themselves on closely monitoring changes and actions by competitors?
   - **i.** Are managers and employees rewarded for taking risks, being innovative, and looking for new and better solutions?
   - **j.** Is the organizational structure flexible?
   - **k.** Does communication flow both down and up in the organization?
   - **l.** Has the organization successfully implemented changes in the past?
   - **m.** Are employees satisfied with, and do they trust management?
   - **n.** Is there a high degree of interaction and cooperation between organizational work units?
   - **o.** Are decisions made quickly and do they take into account a wide variety of suggestions?

2. **Choose an appropriate approach for managing the resistance to change.** In this chapter, six strategies have been suggested for dealing with resistance to change—education and communication, participation, facilitation and support, negotiation, manipulation and co-optation, and coercion. Review Exhibit 7–4 (p. 211) for the advantages and disadvantages, and when it is best to use them.
3. **During the time the change is being implemented and after the change is completed, communicate with employees regarding what support you may be able to provide.** Your employees need to know that you are there to support them during change efforts. Be prepared to offer the assistance that may be necessary to help them enact the change.

Practicing the Skill

Read through the following scenario. Write down some notes about how you would handle the situation described. Be sure to refer to the three suggestions for managing resistance to change.

You're the nursing supervisor at a community hospital employing both emergency room and floor nurses. Each of these teams of nurses tends to work almost exclusively with others doing the same job. In your professional reading, you've come across the concept of cross-training nursing teams and giving them more varied responsibilities, which in turn has been shown to improve patient care while lowering costs. You call the two team leaders, Sue and Scott, into your office to discuss your plan to have the nursing teams move to this approach. To your surprise, they're both opposed to the idea. Sue says she and the other emergency room nurses feel they're needed in the ER, where they fill the most vital role in the hospital. They work special hours when needed, do whatever tasks are required, and often work in difficult and stressful circumstances. They think the floor nurses have relatively easy jobs for the pay they receive. Scott, leader of the floor nurse team, tells you that his group believes the ER nurses lack the special training and extra experience that the floor nurses bring to the hospital. The floor nurses claim they have the heaviest responsibilities and do the most exacting work. Because they have ongoing contact with the patients and their families, they believe they shouldn't be pulled away from vital floor duties to help ER nurses complete their tasks.

Developing Your Diagnostic and Analytical Skills

On the Open Seas

When you think of cruise ships, you may imagine gleaming white hulls, luxurious interiors, and sparkling blue-green seas. But the ships of the Royal Caribbean line have been busy polluting those seas for years.[58]

An aggressive five-year investigation by the U.S. government revealed a pollution scandal that included deliberate violations and cover-ups, and an uncaring and even defiant corporate culture. In the early 1990s, the firm now acknowledges, engine rooms on five ships were rigged to pour oily bilge directly overboard, illegally bypassing expensive onboard pollution-treatment devices that should have been used. Thousands of gallons of dry-cleaning fluid and photo-developing chemicals were unlawfully dumped into the Caribbean, Alaska's Inside Passage, New York Harbor, and even the port of Miami, where the firm has its own headquarters. One cruise ship was filmed trailing oil slicks across the water; ship's officers were caught by Coast Guard officials in the very act of polluting; and engine-room employees admitted to federal investigators that dumping was done at night to avoid detection.

Despite all the evidence, the cruise line hoped to avoid punishment and hired a team of lawyers to plead not that the firm was innocent, but rather that the U.S. government had no jurisdiction over it because it is a Liberian corporation whose ships are registered abroad. However, a federal judge in Miami was unmoved. Royal Caribbean finally pleaded guilty, receiving a $9 million fine and five years' corporate probation, and expressed deep regret over its role in polluting the very environment that made its business possible and profitable. By the time the investigation was over, the Justice Department had handed down another 21 charges to which the firm pled guilty. This time the fine was $18 million (making the total fine higher than that imposed on Exxon for the damage done by the *Valdez*), and several high-level managers were fired. A new vice president was brought in, a senior vice president of safety and environment was appointed, and new environmental standards approved by the government were imposed.

The company now intends to be a model of safe environmental practices. Employees wear tags that say "Save the Waves," passengers are reminded not to throw trash overboard, and on one ship's recent maiden voyage, patrons had to wait in line at a popular onboard restaurant because no one was allowed to sit in the outdoor booths. The reason? The ship's officers were worried that stiffer-than-usual winds might blow waxed-paper food wrappers overboard into the sea.

Questions

1. Describe the internal and external factors compelling change in Royal Caribbean's practices.
2. Why do you believe Royal Caribbean's management hired a senior vice president for safety and environment? What implications do you believe this hiring will have in making changes in the organization?
3. Do you believe employees on these ships should have been empowered with the responsibility to make changes that would have eliminated the pollution problem? Support your position.

Enhancing Your Communication Skills

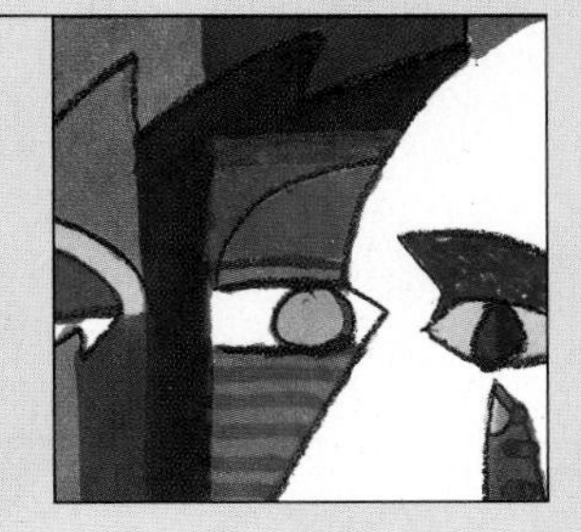

1. Describe a significant change event you experienced (like going from high school to college, changing jobs, etc.). How did you prepare for the change? What fears did you encounter and how did you overcome those fears? Knowing what you know now about the change, what would you do differently today that you didn't do then? How can you apply these should-haves to changes you'll face in the future?
2. Go to the employee assistance program provider Interlock's Web site www.interlock.com. Research the following information: (1) What are the components of an EAP and how does Interlock evaluate an EAP program's success? And (2) Identify how Interlock recommends implementing an EAP in an organization.
3. Business programs have traditionally focused on developing rationality, not creativity. That may be a mistake. Describe how you would promote student creativity in your business curriculum. Specify the kinds of courses or activities that you think should be included in business school classes that would foster creativity and innovation.

PART 4

Leading

CHAPTER 8

Foundations of Individual and Group Behavior

LEARNING OUTCOMES

After reading this chapter, I will be able to:

1. Define the focus and goals of organizational behavior.
2. Identify and describe the three components of attitudes.
3. Explain cognitive dissonance.
4. Describe the Myers-Briggs personality type framework and its use in organizations.
5. Define perception and describe the factors that can shape or distort perception.
6. Explain how managers can shape employee behavior.
7. Contrast formal and informal groups.
8. Explain why people join groups.
9. State how roles and norms influence employees' behavior.
10. Describe how group size affects group behavior.

MEET A REAL MANAGER!

"One Manager's Reflection" page 237

Brendan McGinity, Vice President of Development and Operations, NovaNET Learning, Inc.

What makes a person change his or her attitude toward a chosen career? Is it the conflict between the ideals and goals and the difficulty of achieving them? Is it a matter of chance? Or can it be strong personality traits that take an individual in other directions? For Anne Beiler, (see photo) founder of Auntie Anne's, (maker of hand-rolled soft pretzels), it's probably a combination of all three.

Anne Beiler grew up in Gap, Pennsylvania, a quiet Amish town with a population of 2,000. Her childhood was rooted in Mennonite traditions. Family values were the centerpiece of her early life—including working hard on the family farm, marrying young, and raising a family of her own. And for the first 38 years of her life, she followed that traditional path. In 1987, however, Beiler—somewhat restless after raising two children, and in need of some extra cash—decided to take an outside job. She became a manager of a food stand some two hours away from her home. While there, she noticed that hand-rolled pretzels were the best-selling item. Selling for 55 cents each, while costing less than 7 cents to make, they were quite profitable for the food-stand owner. Although she had never had a formal business course, Anne realized that selling pretzels could be very lucrative. Nearly a year later—tiring of the two-hour commute—She opened her own pretzel stand in the farmer's market in the heart of Gap.[1]

Anne's goal was to make her pretzel business successful enough to allow her and her family to work together. As in any new business start-up, Anne expected the early times to be difficult. But those "early times" didn't last long! Several weeks into the operation, business proved to be so good that Anne opened a second stall across town. Several months later, her brother paid Anne $2,500 for her pretzel recipe and the right to use the Auntie Anne's name to start a pretzel shop in the next town. Weeks later, she sold an additional 10 franchises to family and friends, generating almost $50,000 in revenues. By 1992, she had sold more than 100 franchises to individuals who paid several thousand dollars for the right to use Anne's pretzel recipe.

To gain more control of her life, Anne Beiler took a chance that paid off. Today, Auntie Anne's franchises sell for about $300,000 each—and she gets hundreds of requests for franchises each month. There are now 700 store locations in 43 states and 11 locations outside the United States. The company has also expanded its offerings to include cookies and frozen custard. It's rated as one of the top 500 woman-owned businesses in the United States, and it has achieved honors for being one of the best places to work.

Yet, even with this much success, Anne's traditions and values haven't changed much. She is still family oriented, donates thousands of dollars annually to charities, raises funds for the children's Miracle Network, and underwrites a Family Information Center, a not-for-profit counseling facility in Lancaster, Pennsylvania.

AN UNDERSTANDING OF ANNE BEILER'S PERSONALITY CAN HELP people who work with her to better understand and predict her behavior. And because personality is potent in shaping behavior, you can improve your ability to work with others by gaining insights into their personalities. In this chapter, we look at four psychological aspects—attitudes, personality, perception, and learning—and demonstrate how these things can help managers understand the behavior of those people with whom they have to work.

TOWARD EXPLAINING AND PREDICTING BEHAVIOR

The material in this and the following four chapters draws heavily on the field of study known as organizational behavior. Although it is concerned with the general area of behavior—that is, the actions of people—**organizational behavior (OB)** is concerned specifically with the actions of people at work.

organizational behavior (OB)
The study of the actions of people at work

One of the challenges of understanding organizational behavior is that it addresses some issues that are not obvious. Like an iceberg, a lot of organizational behavior is not visible to the naked eye (see Exhibit 8–1). What we tend to see when

EXHIBIT 8–1

The Organization As an Iceberg Metaphor

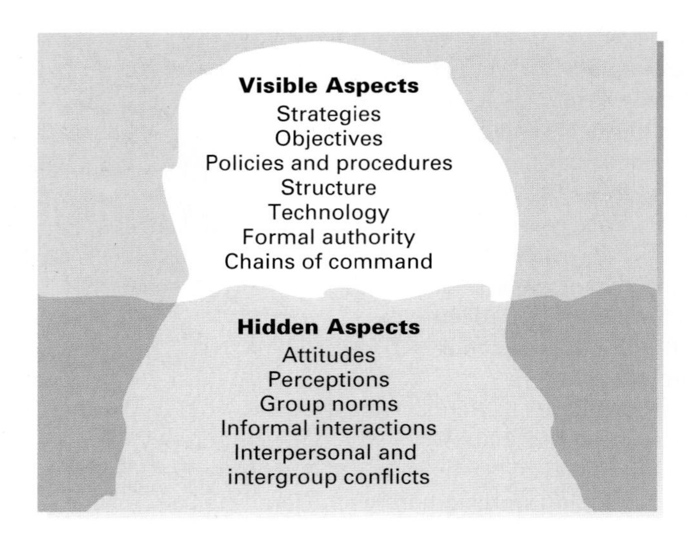

we look at organizations are their formal aspects—strategies, objectives, policies and procedures, structure, technology, formal authority, and chains of command. But, just under the surface lie informal elements that managers need to understand. OB provides managers with considerable insight into these important but hidden aspects of the organization.

WHAT IS THE FOCUS OF ORGANIZATIONAL BEHAVIOR?

Organizational behavior focuses primarily on two major areas. First, OB looks at individual behavior. Based predominantly on contributions from psychologists, this area includes such things as personality, perception, learning, and motivation. Second, OB is concerned with group behavior, which includes norms, roles, team-building, and conflict. Our knowledge about groups comes basically from the work of sociologists and social psychologists. Unfortunately, the behavior of a group of employees cannot be understood by merely summing up the actions of the individuals, because individuals in groups behave differently than individuals acting alone. You see this difference when individuals engage in some risk-taking behavior, like bungee jumping. The individuals might never engage in such behavior if they were to act alone. Put them together, add peer pressure, and they act differently. Therefore, because employees in an organization are both individuals and members of groups, we need to study them at two levels. This chapter provides the foundation for understanding individual and group behavior. In the next chapter, we will introduce basic concepts related to special cases of group behavior—when individuals come together as a work team.

WHAT ARE THE GOALS OF ORGANIZATIONAL BEHAVIOR?

The goals of OB are to explain and to predict behavior. Why do managers need this skill? Simply, in order to manage their employees' behavior. We know that a manager's success depends on getting things done through other people. The manager needs to be able to explain why employees engage in some behaviors rather than others and to predict how employees will respond to various actions the manager might take.

The employee behaviors we are specifically concerned about are employee *productivity*, *absenteeism*, and *turnover*.[2] The importance of productivity is obvious. Managers are concerned with the quantity and quality of output of each employee. But absence and turnover, especially in high rates—can adversely affect this output.

That's because when an employee isn't at work, he or she can't be productive. Furthermore, high turnover rates increase costs and often lead to less-experienced individuals performing the tasks.

There's a fourth type of behavior that is becoming important in determining employee performance. It's called *organizational citizenship*.[3] **Organizational citizenship** is behavior that is not directly part of an employee's formal job description. Rather, it's those behaviors that promote the effective functioning of the organization. For example, positive employee citizenship might include helping others on one's work team, volunteering for extra job activities, avoiding unnecessary conflicts, or making constructive statements about one work group and the overall organization.

How do you feel about employees having to go outside of the office to smoke? Is it appropriate? Or should employees be allowed to smoke at their desk? Your reaction to these questions reflects your attitude.

In addition to these behaviors, we will look at job satisfaction. Although job satisfaction is not a behavior—it's an attitude—it is an outcome with which many managers are concerned. That's because an employee's attitude may be linked to his or her productivity, absenteeism, and turnover. In the following pages, we address how an understanding of employee personality, perception, and learning can help us to predict and explain employee productivity, absence and turnover rates, and job satisfaction.

Attitudes are valuative statements, either favorable or unfavorable, concerning objects, people, or events. They reflect how an individual feels about something. When a person says, "I like my job," he or she is expressing an attitude about work.

To better understand this, we should look at an attitude as being made up of three components: cognition, affect, and behavior.[4] The **cognitive component of an attitude** is made up of the beliefs, opinions, knowledge, and information held by a person. For example, shortly after the 9/11 attacks, Congress spent weeks debating whether airport baggage screeners should be federal employees. Some claimed the current private airport screeners were adequately doing their jobs, even though evidence presented during the debate showed that knives, pepper spray, and a loaded gun were missed by airport screeners.[5] This belief held by some congressional leaders that private screeners were effective is an example of cognition. The **affective component of an attitude** is the emotional, or feeling, segment of an attitude. This component would be reflected in the statement, "I don't like Erica because she smokes." Cognition and affect can lead to behavioral outcomes. The **behavioral component of an attitude** refers to an intention to behave in a certain way toward someone or something. So, to continue our example, I might choose to avoid Erica because of my feelings about her. Looking at attitudes as being made up of three components—cognition, affect, and behavior—helps to illustrate the complexity of attitudes. For the sake of clarity, keep in mind that the term usually refers only to the affective component.

organizational citizenship
Behavior that is not directly part of an employee's formal job description

attitudes
Valuative statements concerning objects, people, or events

cognitive component of an attitude
The beliefs, opinions, knowledge, and information held by a person

affective component of an attitude
The emotional, or feeling, segment of an attitude

behavioral component of an attitude
An intention to behave in a certain way toward someone or something

Naturally, managers are not interested in every attitude an employee might hold. Rather, they are specifically interested in job-related attitudes, and the three most important and most studied are job satisfaction, job involvement, and organizational commitment.[6] *Job satisfaction* is an employee's general attitude toward his or her job. When people speak of employee attitudes, more often than not they mean job satisfaction. *Job involvement* is the degree to which an employee identifies with his or her job, actively participates in it, and considers his or her job performance important for self-worth. Finally, *organizational commitment* represents an employee's orientation toward the organization in terms of his or her loyalty to, identification with, and involvement in the organization.

DO AN INDIVIDUAL'S ATTITUDE AND BEHAVIOR NEED TO BE CONSISTENT?

Did you ever notice how people change what they say so that it doesn't contradict what they do? Perhaps a friend of yours had consistently argued that American-manufactured cars were poorly built and that he'd never own anything but a foreign import. Then his parents gave him a late model American-made car, and suddenly they weren't so bad. Or, when going through sorority rush, a new freshman believes that sororities are good and that pledging a sorority is important. If she fails to make a sorority, however, she may say, "I recognized that sorority life isn't all it's cracked up to be, anyway."

Research has generally concluded that people seek consistency among their attitudes and between their attitudes and their behavior. Individuals try to reconcile differing attitudes and align their attitudes and behavior so that they appear rational and consistent (see Ethical Dilemma in Management). They can correct it by altering either the attitudes or the behavior or by developing a rationalization for the discrepancy.

Ethical Dilemma in Management

Must Attitudes and Behaviors Align?

You work for a large international organization that manufacturers and sells computer drives. In your position as a recruiter, you have the primary responsibility to hire individuals to fill entry-level positions in the company. Your organization focuses on recent college graduates for these entry-level manufacturing and marketing positions. In doing so, the company has an opportunity to hire individuals who have the latest knowledge in their fields at a discounted price.

Your job requires you to travel extensively. In fact, over the past several years, you have made visits to 35 college campuses on three different continents during a semester. Your performance evaluation rests primarily on one factor—how many people you have hired.

Over the past several months, you have noticed a surge in pen positions. These are not new positions but replacements for employees who have quit. A little investigation on your part finds that, after about three years with the firm, entry-level employees quit. There is no upward mobility with the firm, and these employees burn out after working up to 12 hours a day, 6 days a week. Furthermore, you know that the benefits for entry-level employees—especially sick and vacation leave—aren't competitive with those offered by similar firms in the industry. So you think you know why these employees quit.

On the other hand, almost everyone who has quit has gone on to a bigger, better-paying job with more responsibility. To get the most productivity out of these employees, your firm invests heavily in their training. Almost all workers in these positions receive over 40 hours of specialized training each year and have jobs that offer excellent learning opportunities but little advancement. Top management believes it is better to hire new people than to pay the higher salaries that seniority and experience demand. Although you don't totally agree with management's treatment of these employees, you recognize that the company is giving many of them a great career start.

Should you disclose to college recruits during interviews that the jobs they are being considered for are dead-end positions in the organization? Why or why not? Would your response change if you were evaluated not only on how many people you hired, but also on how long they stay with the organization? Defend your position.

This college recruiter is attempting to hire college graduates for jobs that, in the past, people have quit after a couple of years. The recruiter knows that there is little upward mobility for these new hires. But the recruiter is evaluated on how many individuals are successfully brought into the organization. Should the recruiter tell the "entire story?"

WHAT IS COGNITIVE DISSONANCE THEORY?

Can we assume from this consistency principle that an individual's behavior can always be predicted if we know his or her opinion on a subject? The answer, unfortunately, cannot simply be a yes or a no.

Leon Festinger, in the late 1950s, proposed the theory of **cognitive dissonance** to explain the relationship between attitude and behavior.[7] Dissonance in this case means inconsistency. Cognitive dissonance refers to any incompatibility that an individual might perceive between two or more of his or her attitudes or between his or her behavior and attitude. Festinger argued that any form of inconsistency is uncomfortable and that individuals will attempt to reduce the dissonance and, hence, the discomfort. Therefore, individuals will seek a stable state with a minimum of dissonance.

cognitive dissonance
Any incompatibility between two or more attitudes or between behavior and attitudes

Of course, no individual can completely avoid dissonance. You know that cheating on your income tax is wrong, but you may fudge the numbers a bit every year and hope you won't be audited. Or you tell your children to brush after every meal even though you might not. So how do people cope? Festinger proposed that the desire to reduce dissonance is determined by the importance of the elements creating the dissonance, the degree of influence the individual believes he or she has over the elements, and the rewards that may be involved. Let's look at some examples of cognitive dissonance.

Suppose that the factors creating the dissonance are relatively unimportant. In this case, the pressure to correct the imbalance would be low. However, say that a corporate manager, Julia Bradley, believes strongly that no company should lay off employees. Unfortunately, Julia is placed in the position of having to make decisions that would trade off her company's strategic direction against her convictions on layoffs. She knows that, because of restructuring in the company, some jobs may no longer be needed, and the layoffs are in the best economic interest of her firm. What will she do? Undoubtedly, Julia is experiencing a high degree of cognitive dissonance. Because of the importance of the issues in this example, we cannot expect her to ignore the inconsistency. There are several paths that she can follow to deal with her dilemma. She can change her behavior (lay off employees). Or she can reduce dissonance by concluding that the dissonant behavior is not so important after all ("I've got to make a living, and in my role as a decision maker, I often have to place the good of my company above that of individual organizational members"). A third alternative would be for Julia to change her attitude ("There is nothing wrong in laying off employees"). Still another choice would be to seek out more consonant elements to outweigh the dissonant ones ("The long-term benefits to the surviving employees from our restructuring more than offset the costs associated with the retrenchment effort").

The degree of influence that individuals like Julia Bradley believe they have over the elements also will have an impact on how they react to the dissonance. If they perceive the dissonance to be uncontrollable—something about which they have no choice—they are less likely to feel a need for an attitude change. If, for example, the dissonance-producing behavior were required by the boss's directive, the pressure to reduce dissonance would be less than if the behavior were performed voluntarily. Dissonance would exist but it could be rationalized and justified. This is why it is so critical in today's organizations for their leaders to establish the ethical culture. Without their influence and support, reducing dissonance toward ethical behaviors is lessened.[8] Rewards also influence the degree to which individuals are motivated to reduce dissonance. High dissonance, when accompanied by high rewards, tends to reduce the tension inherent in the dissonance. The reward reduces dissonance by adding to the consistency side of the individual's balance sheet.

These moderating factors suggest that although individuals experience dissonance, they will not necessarily move directly toward consistency, that is, toward reduction of the dissonance. If the issues underlying the dissonance are of minimal importance, if an individual perceives that the dissonance is externally imposed and is substantially uncontrollable, or if rewards are significant enough to offset the dissonance, the individual will not be under great tension to reduce the dissonance.[9]

Why are these employees out having fun? It's all part of their management's belief that satisfied employees are happy employees. By offering their employees a "fun day," management is helping to create a culture that has a caring environment. One hoped for outcome of this culture is that it will lead to greater productivity and job satisfaction.

HOW CAN AN UNDERSTANDING OF ATTITUDES HELP MANAGERS BE MORE EFFECTIVE?

We know that employees can be expected to try to reduce dissonance. Therefore, not surprisingly, there is relatively strong evidence that committed and satisfied employees have low rates of turnover and absenteeism.[10] Because most managers want to minimize the number of resignations and absences—especially among their more productive employees—they should do those things that will generate positive job attitudes. Dissonance can be managed. If employees are required to engage in activities that appear inconsistent to them or that are at odds with their attitudes, managers should remember that pressure to reduce the dissonance is lessened when the dissonance is perceived as externally imposed and uncontrollable. The pressure is also lessened if rewards are significant enough to offset the dissonance.

But let's not confuse satisfied workers with productive workers. We need to be aware of a debate that has lasted almost eight decades: Are happy workers more productive? Several research studies of the past have important implications for managers.[11] They suggested that making employees satisfied would lead to high productivity. That suggestion, in part, explains why, in the 1930s, 1940s, and 1950s management spent considerable time doing things that would create a caring environment. For instance, company bowling teams, picnics, and credit unions all gave something to employees and made them happy, but the effect on productivity was questioned.[12] As a result, most researchers perceived that managers would get better results by directing their attention primarily to what would help employees become more productive.[13] Successful job performance should then lead to feelings of accomplishment, increased verbal recognition, increased pay and promotions opportunities,[14] and other rewards—all desirable outcomes—which then lead to satisfaction with the job.

PERSONALITY

Some people are quiet and passive. Some, like radio shock jocks Howard Stern and Don Geronimo, are loud and aggressive. When we describe people in terms such as quiet, passive, loud, aggressive, ambitious, extroverted, loyal, tense, or sociable, we are categorizing them in terms of personality traits. An individual's personality is the combination of the psychological traits that characterize that person.

CAN PERSONALITY PREDICT BEHAVIOR?

Literally dozens of traits are attributed to an individual's behavior. Through the years, researchers attempted to focus specifically on which traits would identify sources of one's personality. Two of these efforts have been widely recognized—the Myers-Briggs Type Indicator and the Big Five-model of personality.

Myers-Briggs Type Indicator (MBTI)
A method of identifying personality types

What is the Myers-Briggs Type Indicator? One of the more widely used methods of identifying personalities is the **Myers-Briggs Type Indicator (MBTI®)**. The MBTI uses four dimensions of personality to identify 16 different personality types based on the responses to an approximately 100-item questionnaire (see Exhibit 8–2). More than two million individuals take the MBTI each year in the United States alone. And it's used in such companies as Apple Computer, Honda, AT&T, Exxon, 3M, as well as many hospitals, educational institutions, and the U.S. Armed Forces.

The 16 personality types are based on the four dimensions noted in Exhibit 8–2. That is, the MBTI dimensions include extroversion versus introversion (EI), sensing versus intuitive (SN), thinking versus feeling (TF), and judging versus perceiving (JP). The EI dimension measures an individual's orientation toward the inner world of ideas (I) or the external world of the environment (E). The sensing-intuitive dimension indicates an individual's reliance on information gathered from the external world (S) or from the world of ideas (N). Thinking-feeling reflects one's preference for evaluating information in an analytical manner (T) or on the basis of values and beliefs (F). The judging-perceiving index reflects an attitude toward the external world that is either task completion oriented (J) or information seeking (P).[15]

How could the MBTI help managers? Proponents of the instrument believe that it's important to know these personality types because they influence the way people interact and solve problems. For example, if your boss is an intuitor and you are a sensor, you will gather information in different ways. An intuitor prefers gut reactions, whereas a sensor prefers facts. To work well with your boss, you have to present more than just facts about a situation and discuss how you feel. MBTI has also been found to be useful in focusing on growth orientations for entrepreneurial types as well as profiles supporting emotional intelligence (we'll look at emotional intelligence shortly).[16]

EXHIBIT 8–2 **Characteristics Frequently Associated with Myers-Briggs Types**

		SENSING TYPES S		INTUITIVE TYPES N	
		THINKING T	FEELING F	FEELING F	THINKING T
INTROVERTS I	JUDGING J	**ISTJ** Quiet, serious, dependable, practical, matter-of-fact. Value traditions and loyalty.	**ISFJ** Quiet, friendly, responsible, thorough, considerate. Strive to create order and harmony.	**INFJ** Seek meaning and connection in ideas. Committed to firm values. Organized and decisive in implementing vision.	**INTJ** Have original minds and great drive for their ideas. Skeptical and independent. Have high standards of competence for self and others.
	PERCEIVING P	**ISTP** Tolerant and flexible. Interested in cause and effect. Value efficiency.	**ISFP** Quiet, friendly, sensitive. Like own space. Dislike disagreements and conflicts.	**INFP** Idealistic, loyal to their values. Seek to understand people and help them fulfill their potential.	**INTP** Seek logical explanations. Theoretical and abstract over social interactions. Skeptical, sometimes critical. Analytical.
EXTROVERTS E	PERCEIVING P	**ESTP** Flexible and tolerant. Focus on here and now. Enjoy material comforts. Learn best by doing.	**ESFP** Outgoing, friendly. Enjoy working with others. Spontaneous. Learn best by trying a new skill with other people.	**ENFP** Enthusiastic, imaginative. Want a lot of affirmation. Rely on verbal fluency and ability to improvise.	**ENTP** Quick, ingenious, stimulating. Adept at generating conceptual possibilities and analyzing them strategically. Bored by routine.
	JUDGING J	**ESTJ** Practical, realistic, matter-of-fact, decisive. Focus on getting efficient results. Forceful in implementing plans.	**ESFJ** Warmhearted, cooperative. Want to be appreciated for who they are and for what they contribute.	**ENFJ** Warm, responsive, responsible. Attuned to needs of others. Sociable, facilitate others, provide inspirational leadership.	**ENTJ** Frank, decisive, assume leadership. Enjoy long-term planning and goal setting. Forceful in presenting ideas.

Source: Modified and reproduced by special permission of the publisher, Consulting Psychologists Press, Inc., Palo Alto, CA 94303, from *Introduction to Type*, 6th ed., by Isabel Myers-Briggs, and Katherine C. Briggs. Copyright 1998 by Consulting Psychologists Press, Inc. All rights reserved. Further reproduction is prohibited without publisher's written consent. *Introduction to Type* is a trademark of Consulting Psychologists Press, Inc. (The Myers-Briggs Type Indicator and MBTI are registered trademarks of Consulting Psychologists Press, Inc.)

Big Five model
Five-factor model of personality that includes extroversion, agreeableness, conscientiousness, emotional stability, and openness to experience

What is the Big Five model of personality? Another way of viewing personality is through five-factor model of personality—more typically called **the Big Five model.**[17] The Big Five factors are:

1. **Extroversion** A personality dimension that describes the degree to which someone is sociable, talkative, and assertive.
2. **Agreeableness** A personality dimension that describes the degree to which someone is good-natured, cooperative, and trusting.
3. **Conscientiousness** A personality dimension that describes the degree to which someone is responsible, dependable, persistent, and achievement oriented.
4. **Emotional stability** A personality dimension that describes the degree to which someone is calm, enthusiastic, and secure (positive) or tense, nervous, depressed, and insecure (negative).
5. **Openness to experience** A personality dimension that describes the degree to which someone is imaginative, artistically sensitive, and intellectual.

The Big Five model provides more than just a personality framework. Research has shown that important relationships exist between these personality dimensions and job performance.[18] For example, one study reviewed five categories of occupations: professionals (e.g., engineers, architects, attorneys), police, managers, sales, and semiskilled and skilled employees.[19] Job performance was defined in terms of employee performance ratings, training competency, and personnel data such as salary level. The results of the study showed that conscientiousness predicted job performance for all five occupational groups.[20] Predictions for the other personality dimensions depended on the situation and the occupational group. For example, extroversion predicted performance in managerial and sales positions, in which high social interaction is necessary.[21] Openness to experience was found to be important in predicting training competency. Ironically, emotional security was not positively related to job performance. Although it would appear logical that calm and secure workers would be better performers, that wasn't the case. Perhaps that result is a function of the likelihood that emotionally stable workers often keep their jobs and emotionally unstable people may not. Given that all those participating in the study were employed, the variance on that dimension was probably small.

emotional intelligence (EI)
An assortment of noncognitive skills, capabilities, and competencies that influence a person's ability to cope with environmental demands and pressures

The Big Five model tells us that this police officer will be more successful on the job because she possesses conscientiousness. This means the officer is responsible, dependable, persistent, and achievement oriented.

What is emotional intelligence? People who understand their own emotions and are good at reading others' emotions may be more effective in their jobs. That, in essence, is the theme of the underlying research on emotional intelligence.[22]

Emotional intelligence (EI) refers to an assortment of noncognitive skills, capabilities, and competencies that influence a person's ability to cope with environmental demands and pressures. It's composed of five dimensions:

- ***Self-awareness*** Being aware of what you're feeling.
- ***Self-management*** The ability to manage your own emotions and impulses.
- ***Self-motivation*** The ability to persist in the face of setbacks and failures.
- ***Empathy*** The ability to sense how others are feeling.
- ***Social skills*** The ability to handle the emotions of others.

Several studies suggest EI may play an important role in job performance.[23] For instance, one study looked at the characteristics of the Bell Lab engineers who were rated as stars by their peers. The scientists concluded that these stars were better at relating to others. That is, it was EI, not academic IQ that characterized high performers. A second study of Air Force recruiters generated similar findings: Top performing recruiters exhibited high levels of EI. Using these findings, the Air Force revamped its selection criteria. A follow-up investigation found that future hires who had high EI scores were 2.6 times more successful than those with low scores. Organizations like American Express have found that implementing emotional intelligence programs has helped them increase their effectiveness; with other organizations finding similar results that emotional intelligence has contributed to team effectiveness.[24] For instance, at Cooperative Printing in Minneapolis, a study of its 45 employees concluded that EI skills were twice as important in "contributing to excellence as intellect and expertise alone."[25] A poll of human resources managers asked this question: How important is it for your workers to demonstrate EI to move up the corporate ladder? Forty percent of the managers replied "very important." Another 16 percent said moderately important. Other studies have also indicated that emotional intelligence can be beneficial to quality improvements in contemporary organizations.[26]

The implications from the initial EI evidence is that employers should consider emotional intelligence as a criterion in their selection process—especially for those jobs that demand a high degree of social interaction.

locus of control
A personality attribute that measures the degree to which people believe that they are masters of their own fate

Machiavellianism ("Mach")
A measure of the degree to which people are pragmatic, maintain emotional distance, and believe that ends can justify means

CAN PERSONALITY TRAITS PREDICT PRACTICAL WORK-RELATED BEHAVIORS?

Five specific personality traits have proven most powerful in explaining individual behavior in organizations. These are locus of control, Machiavellianism, self-esteem, self-monitoring, and risk propensity.

Who has control over an individual's behavior? Some people believe that they control their own fate. Others see themselves as pawns of fate, believing that what happens to them in their lives is due to luck or chance. The **locus of control** in the first case is internal. In the second case, it is external; these people believe that their lives are controlled by outside forces.[27] A manager might also expect to find that externals blame a poor performance evaluation on their boss's prejudice, their co-workers, or other events outside their control, whereas "internals" explain the same evaluation in terms of their own actions.

The second characteristic is called **Machiavellianism ("Mach")** after Niccolo Machiavelli, who provided instruction in the sixteenth century on how to gain and manipulate power. An individual who is high in Machiavellianism is pragmatic, maintains emotional distance, believes that ends can justify means,[28] and is found to have beliefs that are less ethical.[29] "The philosophy, "if it works, use it," is consistent with a high Mach perspective. Do high Machs make good employees? That answer depends on the type of job and whether you consider ethical implications in evaluating performance. In jobs that require bargaining skills (a labor negotiator) or that have substantial rewards for winning (a commissioned salesperson), high Machs are productive. In jobs in which ends do not justify the means or that lack absolute standards of performance, it is difficult to predict the performance of high Machs.

Evidence has shown that employees in jobs that require a high degree of social interaction benefit greatly by having a high EI. Men's Warehouse seeks employees who demonstrate the five dimensions of emotional intelligence—self-awareness, self-management, self-motivation, empathy, and social skills.

self-esteem (SE)
An individual's degree of like or dislike for himself or herself

People differ in the degree to which they like or dislike themselves. This trait is called **self-esteem (SE)**.[30] The research on SE offers some interesting insights into organizational behavior. For example, SE is directly related to expectations for success. High SEs believe that they possess the ability to succeed at work. Individuals with high SE will take more risks in job selection and are more likely to choose unconventional jobs than are people with low SE.[31] The most common finding on self-esteem is that low SEs are more susceptible to external influence than are high SEs. Low SEs are dependent on positive evaluations from others. As a result, they are more likely to seek approval from others and more prone to conform to the beliefs and behaviors of those they respect than are high SEs. In managerial positions, low SEs will tend to be concerned with pleasing others and, therefore, will be less likely to take unpopular stands than will high SEs. Not surprisingly, self-esteem has also been found to be related to job satisfaction. A number of studies confirm that high SEs are more satisfied with their jobs than are low SEs.

self-monitoring
A measure of an individual's ability to adjust his or her behavior to external, situational factors

Another personality trait that has recently received increased attention is called **self-monitoring**.[32] It refers to an individual's ability to adjust his or her behavior to external, situational factors. Individuals high in self-monitoring can show considerable adaptability in adjusting their behavior to external, situational factors.[33] They are highly sensitive to external cues and can behave differently in different situations. High self-monitors are capable of presenting striking contradictions between their public persona and their private selves. Low self-monitors can't alter their behavior. They tend to display their true dispositions and attitudes in every situation; hence, there is high behavioral consistency between who they are and what they do. Evidence suggests that high self-monitors tend to pay closer attention to the behavior of others and are more capable of conforming than are low self-monitors.[34] We might also hypothesize that high self-monitors will be more successful in managerial positions that require individuals to play multiple, and even contradicting, roles.

The final personality trait influencing worker behavior reflects the willingness to take chances—the propensity for *risk taking*. A preference to assume or avoid risk has been shown to have an impact on how long it takes individuals to make a decision and how much information they require before making their choice. For instance, in one classic study, 79 managers worked on a simulated human resources management exercise that required them to make hiring decisions.[35] High risk-taking managers made more rapid decisions and used less information in making their choices than did the low risk-taking managers. Interestingly, the decision accuracy was the same for both groups.

Although it is generally correct to conclude that managers in organizations are risk-aversive, especially in large companies and government bureaus,[36] there are still individual differences on this dimension.[37] As a result, it makes sense to recognize these differences and even to consider aligning risk-taking propensity with specific job demands. For instance, a high risk-taking propensity may lead to effective performance for a stock trader in a brokerage firm. This type of job demands rapid decision making. The same holds true for the entrepreneur.[38] On the other hand, this personality characteristic might prove a major obstacle to accountants performing auditing activities, which might be better done by someone with a low risk-taking propensity.

HOW DO WE MATCH PERSONALITIES AND JOBS?

Obviously, individual personalities differ. So, too, do jobs. Following this logic, efforts have been made to match the proper personalities with the proper jobs. The best-documented personality job fit theory has been developed by psychologist John Holland.[39] His theory states that an employee's satisfaction with his or her job as well as his or her propensity to leave that job depends on the degree to which the individual's personality matches his or her occupational environment.

Learning from Experience: One Manager's Reflection

Brendan McGinty Vice President of Development and Operations, NovaNET Learning, Inc.

MATCHING PERSONALITIES AND JOBS

Describe the situation you faced. Back in 1993, we experienced a unique situation regarding the foundations of individual and group behavior, matching personalities and jobs, and the relative importance of these matters within the organization, when we privatized the NovaNET computer-based education system from the University of Illinois. It was a huge undertaking, essentially eliminating a research and development laboratory from a university environment and replacing it with a streamlined private company.

The university had been losing money on NovaNET and had decided to close down the research lab responsible for running the system. A private company, called University Communications, spun off from the university, had marketing rights to the system but no design or development control. In 1993, NovaNET consisted of approximately 6,000 separate programs teaching basic skills and other topics via computer to adult and young adult learners throughout the United States.

What action(s) did you take? I led the technology side of the privatization, and was responsible for figuring out how to run this wide area network while reducing the cost of operations. The university had 85 people running and supporting the system, and the privatizing company wanted to do the same with less than 20 full-time staff. However, I wanted to add the right kind of people in the right spots in the new organization, so I looked at the talent within the university's existing staff that had been running the system, and selected those that I felt would transition well from a university-based research lab to a more competitive environment.

On top of the sheer numbers and the task of finding those with the right makeup, there were many technical areas, from system programming to custom site installation to telecommunications, that needed to be covered in order to support the existing client base. Thus, matching personalities with jobs included not only the ability to do the job, but the ability to work on a part or parts of a large system and a large and growing team.

But not all of the team members had good communication skills. Some were introverted, some were arrogant, some had confidence problems, and yet all shared a common view: They were passionate about NovaNET and the good that it was doing for students around the country.

I needed to find a way to maximize the immense talent within the group and help them to see the big picture, the team picture, without suffocating their individuality or even their quirkiness.

What results occurred? For our early NovaNET team, the goal was to take superstar talent, individuals with eccentricities and immense knowledge, and put them in an environment where their individual talents could be showcased but they would work toward a common goal: improving the way education was delivered to students needing help across the country and beyond. We did so by providing structure and goals while allowing individuals to be individuals, and the results were dramatic. NovaNET grew exponentially, thanks to the University of Illinois greatest technology transfer triumphs.

Holland has identified six basic employee personality types. Exhibit 8–3 describes each of the six types, their personality characteristics, and examples of congruent occupations.

Holland's research strongly supports the hexagonal diagram in Exhibit 8–4.[40] This exhibit shows that the closer two fields or orientations are in the hexagon, the more compatible they are. For instance, Realistic and Social are opposite each other in the diagram. A person with a Realistic preference wants to work with objects, not people. A person with a Social preference wants to work with people,

EXHIBIT 8-3 **Holland's Typology of Personality and Sample Occupations**

TYPE	CHARACTERISTICS	PERSONALITY SAMPLE OCCUPATIONS
Realistic Prefers physical activities that require skill, strength, and coordination	Shy, genuine, persistent, stable, conforming, practical	Mechanic, drill-press operator, assembly-line worker, farmer
Investigative Prefers activities involving thinking, organizing, and understanding	Analytical, original, curious independent	Biologist, economist, mathematician, reporter
Social Prefers activities that involve helping and developing others	Sociable, friendly, cooperative, understanding	Social worker, teacher, counselor, clinical psychologist
Conventional Prefers rule-regulated, orderly, and unambiguous activities	Conforming, efficient, practical, unimaginative, inflexible	Accountant, corporate manager, bank teller, file clerk
Enterprising Prefers verbal activities where there are opportunities to influence others and attain power	Self-confident, ambitious, energetic domineering	Lawyer, real estate agent, public relations specialist, small business manager
Artistic Prefers ambiguous and unsystematic activities that allow creative expression	Imaginative, disorderly, idealistic, emotional, impractical	Painter, musician, writer, interior decorator

Source: Reproduced by special permission of the publisher, Psychological Assessment Resources, Inc., *Making Vocational Choices,* 3rd ed., copyright 1973, 1985, 1992, 1997 by Psychological Assessment Resources, Inc. All rights reserved.

no matter what else they do. Therefore, they have opposing preferences about working alone or with others. Investigative and Enterprising are opposing themes as are Artistic and Conventional preferences. An example of mutually reinforcing themes is the Social-Enterprising-Conventional (SEC) vocational preference structure. Stephanie, for example, likes working with people, being successful, and following established rules. That combination is perfect for someone who's going to succeed in a bureaucracy. But let's look at another employee, Rob. He's Realistic-Investigative-Artistic, preferring solitary work to large groups, asking questions to answering them, and making his own rules instead of following someone else's. How would Rob fit into Stephanie's bureaucracy? Probably not very well. In fact,

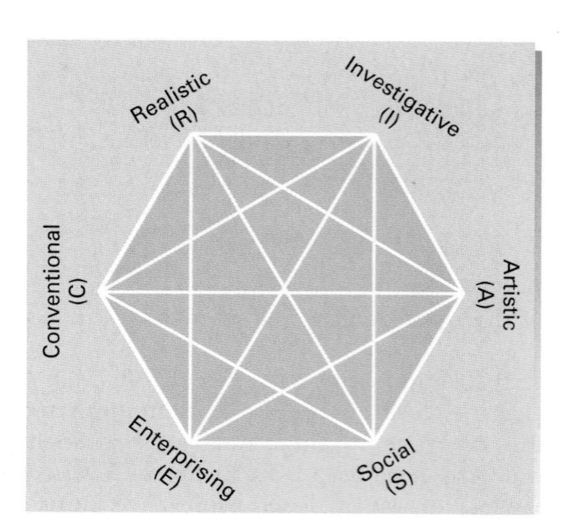

EXHIBIT 8-4

Relationship among Occupational Personality Types

Source: Reproduced by special permission of the publisher, Psychological Assessment Resources, Inc., *Making Vocational* Choices, 3rd ed., copyright 1973, 1985, 1992, 1997 by Psychological Assessment Resources, Inc. All rights reserved.

his preferred actions could be viewed as trouble making. Where then would Rob make a better fit? Possibly in a research lab? Both the preference of the scientist and the environment of the research lab are characterized by a lack of human interruptions and a concentration on factual material. That's consistent with the Realistic Investigative-Artistic profile.

What does all this mean? The theory argues that satisfaction is highest and turnover lowest when personality and occupation are in agreement.[41] Social individuals should be in social jobs, conventional people in conventional jobs, and so forth. A realistic person in a realistic job is in a more congruent situation than is a realistic person in an investigative job. A realistic person in a social job is in the most incongruent situation possible. The key points of this model are:

1. There do appear to be intrinsic differences in personality among individuals;
2. There are different types of jobs; and
3. People in job environments congruent with their personality types should be more satisfied and less likely to resign voluntarily than people in incongruent jobs.

HOW CAN AN UNDERSTANDING OF PERSONALITY HELP MANAGERS BE MORE EFFECTIVE?

The major value of a manager's understanding personality differences probably lies in employee selection.[42] Managers are likely to have higher performing and more satisfied employees if personality types are matched to compatible jobs. In addition, there may be other benefits. By recognizing that people approach problem solving, decision making, and job interactions differently, a manager can better understand why, for instance, an employee is uncomfortable with making quick decisions or why an employee insists on gathering as much information as possible before addressing a problem. Or, for instance, managers can expect that individuals with an external locus of control may be less satisfied with their jobs than those with an internal locus, and also that they may be less willing to accept responsibility for their actions.

DO PERSONALITY ATTRIBUTES DIFFER ACROSS NATIONAL CULTURES?

There certainly are no dominant personality types within a given country. You can, for instance, find high risk takers and low risk takers in almost any culture, yet a country's culture should influence the dominant personality characteristics of its population. We can see this influence by looking at the locus of control.

In Chapter 2, we introduced you to the issues of national cultures. One point of that discussion was that national cultures differ in terms of the degree to which people believe they control their environment. North Americans, for example, believe that they can dominate their environment, whereas other societies, such as Middle Eastern countries, believe that life is essentially preordained. Notice the close parallel to internal and external locus of control. We should expect a larger proportion of employees who have internal loci in the United States and Canadian workforces than in the workforces of Saudi Arabia or Iran.

As we have described throughout this section, personality traits influence employees' behavior. For global managers, understanding how personality traits differ takes on added significance when we adopt the perspective of national culture.

DO ENTREPRENEURS SHARE PERSONALITY CHARACTERISTICS?

Think of someone you know who is an entrepreneur. Maybe it's someone you know personally or maybe it's someone you've read about like Bill Gates of Microsoft, Oprah Winfrey of Harpo Productions, or Larry Ellison of Oracle. How would you describe this person's personality? One of the more researched areas of entrepreneurship has been

Can we describe some of the personality traits of Larry Ellison, the entrepreneurial CEO of Oracle? Research tells us that people such as Ellison have a high level of motivation, an abundance of self-confidence, and high energy levels. Such individuals are also moderate risk takers and have the ability to set and achieve goals.

the search to determine what, if any, psychological characteristics entrepreneurs have in common; what types of personality traits entrepreneurs have that might distinguish them from nonentrepreneurs; and what traits entrepreneurs have that might predict who will be successful.

Is there a classic "entrepreneurial personality?" Although trying to pinpoint specific personality characteristics that all entrepreneurs share is difficult, this hasn't stopped entrepreneurship researchers from looking for common traits.[43] For instance, one list of personality characteristics included the following: high level of motivation, abundance of self-confidence, ability to be involved for the long term, high energy level, persistent problem solver, high degree of initiative, ability to set goals, and moderate risk taker. Another list of characteristics of "successful" entrepreneurs included high energy level, great persistence, resourcefulness, the desire and ability to be self-directed, and relatively high need for autonomy.[44] A recent development in defining the entrepreneurial personality characteristics was the proposed use of a proactive personality scale to predict an individual's likelihood of pursuing entrepreneurial ventures—called proactive personality. **Proactive personality** describes those individuals who are more prone to take actions to influence their environment.[45] Obviously, an entrepreneur is likely to exhibit proactivity as he or she searches for opportunities and acts to take advantage of those opportunities. Various items on the proactive personality scale were found to be good indicators of a person's likelihood of becoming an entrepreneur. These included, for example, education and having an entrepreneurial parent.

proactive personality
Describes those individuals who are more prone to take actions to influence their environment

perception
The process of organizing and interpreting sensory impressions in order to give meaning to the environment

PERCEPTION

Perception is a process by which individuals organize and interpret their sensory impressions in order to give meaning to their environment. Research on perception consistently demonstrates that several individuals may look at the same thing, yet perceive it differently. One manager, for instance, can interpret the fact that her assistant regularly takes several days to make important decisions as evidence that the assistant is slow, disorganized, and afraid to make decisions. Another manager, with the same assistant, might interpret the approach as evidence that the assistant is thoughtful, thorough, and deliberate. The first manager would probably evaluate her assistant negatively, and the second manager would probably evaluate the person positively. The point is that none of us actually sees reality. We interpret what we see and call it reality. And, of course, as the preceding example illustrates, we act according to our perceptions.

WHAT INFLUENCES PERCEPTION?

How do we explain the fact that Cathy, a marketing supervisor for a large commercial petroleum products organization, age 45, noticed Bill's nose ring during his employment interview, and Sean, a human resources recruiter, age 22, didn't? A number of factors operate to shape and sometimes distort perception. These factors can reside in the perceiver, in the object or target being perceived, or in the context of the situation in which the perception is made.

When an individual looks at a target and attempts to interpret what he or she sees, that individual's personal characteristics will heavily influence the interpretation. These personal characteristics include attitudes, personality, motives, interests, past experiences, and expectations. The characteristics of the target being observed can also affect what is perceived. Loud people are more likely than quiet people to be

Old woman or young woman? Two faces or an urn? A knight on a horse?

EXHIBIT 8–5

Perceptual Challenges: What Do You See?

noticed in a group. So, too, are extremely attractive or unattractive individuals. Because targets are not looked at in isolation, the relationship of a target to its background also influences perception (see Exhibit 8–5 for an example), as does our tendency to group close things and similar things together.

The context in which we see objects or events is also important. The time at which an object or event is seen can influence attention, as can location, lighting, temperature, and any number of other situational factors.

HOW DO MANAGERS JUDGE EMPLOYEES?

Much of the research on perception is directed at inanimate objects. Managers, though, are more concerned with human beings. Our perceptions of people differ from our perceptions of such inanimate objects as computers, robots, or buildings because we make inferences about the actions of people that we don't, of course, make about inanimate objects. When we observe people, we attempt to develop explanations of why they behave in certain ways. Our perception and judgment of a person's actions, therefore, will be significantly influenced by the assumptions we make about the person's internal state. Many of these assumptions have led researchers to develop attribution theory.

What is attribution theory? Attribution theory has been proposed to develop explanations of how we judge people differently depending on what meaning we attribute to a given behavior.[46] Basically, the theory suggests that when we observe an

attribution theory
A theory based on the premise that we judge people differently depending on the meaning we attribute to a given behavior

Which of these two would you consider hiring as a consultant in your organization to assist with a computer problem you're having? If you chose the "man in the suit," maybe you ought to reconsider. The other gentleman is Jaron Lanier, the individual who's credited with developing the software that has made virtual reality commonplace in our society. Companies like Xerox, Kodak, American Express, and the U.S. Defense Department have used his services. Making a decision based on an initial perception may not always be the best approach.

individual's behavior, we attempt to determine whether it was internally or externally caused. Internally caused behavior is believed to be under the control of the individual. Externally caused behavior results from outside causes; that is, the person is seen as having been forced into the behavior by the situation. That determination, however, depends on three factors: distinctiveness, consensus, and consistency.

Distinctiveness refers to whether an individual displays a behavior in many situations or whether it is particular to one situation. Is the employee who arrived late to work today also the person co-workers see as a goof-off? What we want to know is whether this behavior is unusual. If it is, the observer is likely to give the behavior an external attribution. If this action is not unique, it will probably be judged as internal.

If everyone who is faced with a similar situation responds in the same way, we can say the behavior shows consensus. Our tardy employee's behavior would meet this criterion if all employees who took the same route to work today were also late. If consensus is high, you would be expected to give an external attribution to the employee's tardiness, whereas if other employees who took the same route made it to work on time, you would conclude the reason to be internal.

Finally, a manager looks for consistency in an employee's actions. Does the individual engage in the behaviors regularly and consistently? Does the employee respond the same way over time? Coming in 10 minutes late for work is not perceived in the same way if, for one employee, it represents an unusual case (she hasn't been late for several months), but for another it is part of a routine pattern (he is late two or three times a week). The more consistent the behavior, the more the observer is inclined to attribute it to internal causes.

Exhibit 8–6 summarizes the key elements in attribution theory. It would tell us, for instance, that if an employee, Mr. Flynn, generally performs at about the same level on other related tasks as he does on his current task (low distinctiveness), if other employees frequently perform differently—better or worse—than Mr. Flynn does on that current task (low consensus), and if Mr. Flynn's performance on this current task is consistent over time (high consistency), his manager or anyone else who is judging Mr. Flynn's work is likely to hold him primarily responsible for his task performance (internal attribution).

fundamental attribution error The tendency to underestimate the influence of external factors and overestimate the influence of internal or personal factors when making judgments about the behavior of others

Can attributions be distorted? One of the more interesting findings drawn from attribution theory is that errors or biases distort attributions. For instance, there is substantial evidence to support the hypothesis that when we make judgments about the behavior of other people, we have a tendency to underestimate the influence of external factors and overestimate the influence of internal or personal factors.[47] This is the **fundamental attribution error**, which can explain why a sales manager may be prone to attribute the poor performance of her sales agents to laziness rather than to

EXHIBIT 8–6

The Process of Attribution Theory

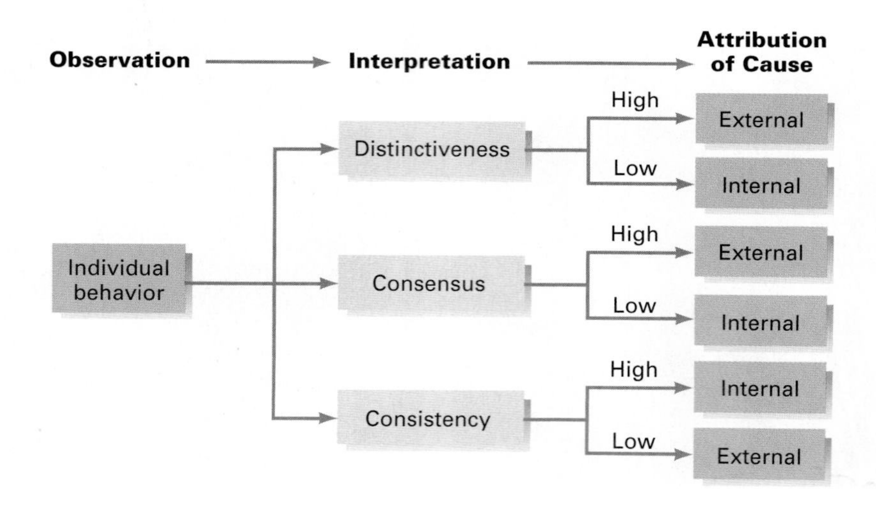

the innovative product line introduced by a competitor. Individuals also tend to attribute their own successes to internal factors such as ability or effort while putting the blame for failure on external factors such as luck. This is called the **self-serving bias** and suggests that feedback provided to employees in performance reviews will be predictably distorted by them, whether it is positive or negative.

self-serving bias
The tendency for individuals to attribute their own successes to internal factors while putting the blame for failures on external factors

WHAT SHORTCUTS DO MANAGERS USE IN JUDGING OTHERS?

Managers use a number of shortcuts to judge others. Perceiving and interpreting what others do are burdensome processes. As a result, individuals develop techniques for making the task more manageable. These techniques are frequently valuable; they allow us to make accurate perceptions rapidly and provide valid data for making predictions. However, they are not foolproof. They can and do get us into trouble. An understanding of these shortcuts can help us determine when they can result in significant distortions (see Exhibit 8–7).

Individuals cannot assimilate all they observe, so they are *selective.* They absorb bits and pieces. These bits and pieces are not chosen randomly; rather, they are selectively chosen depending on the interests, background, experience, and attitudes of the observer. Selective perception allows us to "speed read" others but not without the risk of drawing an inaccurate picture.

It is easy to judge others if we assume that they are similar to us. In *assumed similarity,* or the "like me" effect, the observer's perception of others is influenced more by the observer's own characteristics than by those of the person observed. For example, if you want challenge and responsibility in your job, you will assume that others want the same. People who assume that others are like them can, of course, be proven right, but most of the time they're wrong.

When we judge someone on the basis of our perception of a group to which he or she belongs, we are using the shortcut of *stereotyping.* "Most women won't relocate for a promotion," and "Older workers are less productive" are examples of stereotyping. If someone holds such stereotypes, that is what he or she will perceive—whether or not it's accurate. When stereotypes have no foundation, they distort judgments.

EXHIBIT 8–7 Distortions in Shortcut Methods in Judging Others

SHORTCUT	WHAT IT IS	DISTORTION
Selectivity	People assimilate certain bits and pieces of what they observe depending on their interests, background, experience, and attitudes	"Speed reading" others may result in an inaccurate picture of them
Assumed similarity	People assume that others are like them	May fail to take into account individual differences, resulting in incorrect similarities
Stereotyping	People judge others on the basis of their perception of a group to which the others belong	May result in distorted judgments because many stereotypes have no factual foundation
Halo effect	People form an impression of others on the basis of a single trait	Fails to take into account the total picture of what an individual has done
Self-fulfilling prophecy	People perceive others in a certain way, and, in turn, those others behave in ways that are consistent with the perception	May result in getting the behavior expected, not the true behavior of individuals

Was this fire predicted? If you recognize how escalation of commitment affects decision making, and how as time went on the more tense it was for both David Koresch, leader of the Branch Davidians, and the FBI, something dramatic was inevitable. Add to that the self-fulfilling prophecy by both groups to make their point—and disaster resulted in the 51-day siege. All told, 4 federal officers and 80 Branch Davidian members died.

When we form a general impression about an individual on the basis of a single characteristic such as intelligence, sociability, or appearance, we are being influenced by the *halo effect*. This effect frequently occurs, for instance, when students evaluate their classroom instructors. Students may isolate a single trait such as enthusiasm and allow their entire evaluation to be tainted by their perception of this one trait. An instructor might be assured, knowledgeable, and highly qualified, but if he or she lacks zeal, he or she may be rated lower on a number of other characteristics. Some companies, like Johnson & Johnson, use the halo effect as a competitive advantage. As Johnson & Johnson's chairman, Ralph Larsen, says, "consumers, even doctors, trust J & J more because it sells baby oil—it gives us a wonderful image that most companies would kill for."[48]

A final shortcut in judging others involves a manager's expectations of employees. It is the *self-fulfilling prophecy* (or the Pygmalion effect).[49] The self-fulfilling prophecy involves how a manager perceives others and how they, in turn, behave in ways that are consistent with the manager's expectations. For example, if a manager expects outstanding performance from his employees, they are not likely to disappoint him. They will work (or be perceived to work) up to the manager's expectations. On the other hand, if this same manager believes that he is supervising a group of underachievers, his employees will respond accordingly. As a result, the manager's expectations will become a reality as the employees work in such a way as to meet his low expectations. We've also seen evidence of how escalation of commitment (see Chapter 4) and self-fulfilling prophecy can interact with one another to create disaster, as was the case with the stand-off between the FBI and the Branch Davidian cult in Waco, Texas.[50]

HOW CAN AN UNDERSTANDING OF PERCEPTIONS HELP MANAGERS BE MORE EFFECTIVE?

Managers need to recognize that their employees react to perceptions, not to reality. Whether a manager's appraisal of an employee is actually objective and unbiased or whether the organization's wage levels are actually among the highest in the industry is less relevant than what employees perceive. If employees perceive appraisals to be biased or wage levels as low, they will behave as if those conditions actually existed. Employees organize and interpret what they see, creating the potential for perceptual distortion.

The message to managers should be clear. Pay close attention to how employees perceive both their jobs and management practices. Remember, the valuable employee who quits because of an inaccurate perception is just as great a loss to an organization as the valuable employee who quits for a valid reason.

LEARNING

The last individual behavior we introduce in this chapter is learning. It is included for the obvious reason that almost all complex behavior is learned. If we want to explain and predict behavior, we need to understand how people learn. What is learning? A psychologist's definition is considerably broader than the layperson's view that it's what we did when we went to school. In actuality, each of us is continually going to school. Learning occurs all the time. We constantly learn from our experiences. A workable definition here of **learning** is, therefore, any relatively permanent change in behavior that occurs as a result of experience. How do we learn? Two popular theories explain the process by which we acquire patterns of behavior: operant conditioning and social learning theory.

learning
Any relatively permanent change in behavior that occurs as a result of experience

WHAT IS OPERANT CONDITIONING?

operant conditioning
A behavioral theory that argues that voluntary, or learned, behavior is a function of its consequences

Operant conditioning argues that behavior is a function of its consequences. People learn to behave so as to get something they want or to avoid something they don't want. Operant behavior is voluntary or learned rather than reflexive or unlearned behavior. The tendency to repeat such behavior is influenced by the reinforcement or lack of reinforcement brought about by the consequences of the behavior. Reinforcement, therefore, strengthens a behavior and increases the likelihood that it will be repeated.

Building on earlier work in the field, the late Harvard psychologist B. F. Skinner extensively expanded our knowledge of operant conditioning.[51] Even his staunchest critics, who represent a sizable group, admit that his operant concepts work.

Behavior is assumed to be determined from without (learned) rather than from within (reflexive, or unlearned). Skinner argued that causing pleasing consequences to follow a specific form of behavior will increase the frequency of that behavior. People are most likely to engage in desired behaviors if they are positively reinforced for doing so. Rewards, for example, are most effective if they immediately follow the desired response. In addition, behavior that is not rewarded or is punished is less likely to be repeated.

You see illustrations of operant conditioning everywhere. For example, any situation in which it is either explicitly stated or implicitly suggested that reinforcements are contingent on some action on your part involves operant learning. Your instructor asserts that if you want a high grade in the course, you must supply correct answers on the test. A real estate agent finds that high income is contingent on generating many home listings and sales in his or her territory. Of course, the linkage can also teach the individual to engage in behaviors that work against the best interests of the organization. Assume that your boss tells you that if you will work overtime during the next three-week-long busy season, you will be compensated for it at the next performance appraisal. However, when performance appraisal time comes, you are given no positive reinforcement for your overtime work. The next time your boss asks you to work overtime, what will you do? You may decline. Your behavior can be explained by operant conditioning: If a behavior fails to be positively reinforced, the probability that the behavior will be repeated declines.

WHAT IS SOCIAL LEARNING THEORY?

Individuals can also learn by observing what happens to other people and by being told about something as well as by direct experience. For example, much of what we have learned comes from watching models—parents, teachers, peers, television and movie performers, bosses, and so forth. This view that we can learn through both observation and direct experience has been called **social learning theory**.[52]

social learning theory
The theory that people can learn through observation and direct experience

Social learning theory is an extension of operant conditioning—that is, it assumes that behavior is a function of consequences—but it also acknowledges the existence of observational learning and the importance of perception in learning. People respond to the way that they perceive and define consequences, not to the objective consequences themselves.

The influence of models is central to the social learning viewpoint. Four processes determine the influence that a model will have on an individual:

1. **Attentional processes** People learn from a model only when they recognize and pay attention to its critical features. We tend to be most influenced by repeatedly available models, which we think are attractive, important, or similar to us.

2. **Retention processes** — A model's influence will depend on how well the individual remembers the model's action, even after the model is no longer readily available.
3. **Motor reproduction processes** — After a person has seen a new behavior by observing the model, watching must be converted to doing. This process demonstrates that the individual can perform the modeled activities.
4. **Reinforcement processes** — Individuals will be motivated to exhibit the modeled behavior if positive incentives or rewards are provided. Behaviors that are reinforced will be given more attention, and will be learned better and performed more often than will behaviors that are not reinforced.

HOW CAN MANAGERS SHAPE BEHAVIOR?

shaping behavior
Systematically reinforcing each successive step that moves an individual closer to a desired behavior

Managers should be concerned with how they can teach employees to behave in ways that most benefit the organization. Thus, managers will often attempt to mold individuals by guiding their learning in graduated steps. This process is called **shaping behavior** (see Developing Your Skill at Shaping Behavior on page 254).

Consider the situation in which an employee's behavior is significantly different from that desired by management. If management reinforced the individual only when he or she showed desirable responses, there might be very little reinforcement.

We shape behavior by systematically reinforcing each successive step that moves the individual closer to the desired response. If an employee who has continually been 30 minutes late for work arrives only 20 minutes late, we can reinforce this improvement. Reinforcement would increase as responses more closely approximate the desired behavior.

There are four ways in which to shape behavior: positive reinforcement, negative reinforcement, punishment, or extinction. When a response is followed with something pleasant, such as when a manager praises an employee for a job well done, it is called *positive reinforcement.* Rewarding a response with the termination or withdrawal of something pleasant is called *negative reinforcement.* Managers who habitually criticize their employees for taking extended coffee breaks are using negative reinforcement. The only way these employees can stop the criticism is to shorten their breaks. *Punishment* penalizes undesirable behavior. Suspending an employee for two days without pay for showing up drunk is an example of punishment. Eliminating any reinforcement that is maintaining a behavior is called *extinction.* When a behavior isn't reinforced, it gradually disappears. Managers who wish to discourage employees from continually asking distracting or irrelevant questions in meetings can eliminate that behavior by ignoring those employees when they raise their hands to speak. Soon, the behavior will be diminished.

Both positive and negative reinforcement result in learning. They strengthen a desired response and increase the probability of repetition. Both punishment and extinction also result in learning; however, they weaken behavior and tend to decrease its subsequent frequency.

HOW CAN AN UNDERSTANDING OF LEARNING HELP MANAGERS BE MORE EFFECTIVE?

Managers can undoubtedly benefit from understanding the learning process. Because employees must continually learn on the job, the only issue is whether managers are going to let employee learning occur randomly or whether they are going to manage learning through the rewards they allocate and the examples they set. If marginal employees are rewarded with pay raises and promotions, they will have little reason to change their behavior. If managers want a certain type of behavior but reward a different type of behavior, it shouldn't surprise them to find that employees are learning to engage in the latter. Similarly, managers should expect that employees will look to them as models. Managers who are constantly late for work, take two hours for lunch, or help themselves to company office supplies for personal use should expect employees to read the message they are sending and model their behavior accordingly.

Why have these employees joined the company softball team? Research tells us they did so out of their need for security, status, self-esteem, affiliation, power, or goal achievement.

FOUNDATIONS OF GROUP BEHAVIOR

The behavior of individuals in groups is not the same as the sum total of all the individuals' behavior. Individuals act differently in groups than they do when they are alone. Therefore, if we want to understand organizational behavior more fully, we need to study groups.

WHAT IS A GROUP?

A **group** is two or more interacting and interdependent individuals who come together to achieve particular objectives. Groups can be either formal or informal. Formal groups are work groups established by the organization that have been given designated assignments and established tasks. Behaviors are stipulated by and directed toward organizational goals. In contrast, informal groups are of a social nature. These groups are natural formations that appear in the work environment in response to the need for social contact. Informal groups tend to form around friendships and common interests.

Why do people join groups? There is no single reason why individuals join groups. Because most people belong to a number of groups, it's obvious that different groups provide different benefits to their members. Most people join a group out of needs for security, status, self-esteem, affiliation, power, or goal achievement. We've listed these and described their perceived benefit in Exhibit 8–8.

group
Two or more interacting and interdependent individuals who come together to achieve particular objectives

WHAT ARE THE BASIC CONCEPTS OF GROUP BEHAVIOR?

The basic foundation for understanding group behavior includes roles, norms and conformity, status systems, and group cohesiveness. Let's take a closer look at each of those aspects.

EXHIBIT 8–8
Reasons Why People Join Groups

REASON	PERCEIVED BENEFIT
Security	Gaining strength in numbers; reducing the insecurity of standing alone
Status	Achieving some level of prestige from belonging to a particular group
Self-esteem	Enhancing one's feeling of self-worth—especially membership in a highly valued group
Affiliation	Satisfying one's social needs through social interaction
Power	Achieving something through a group action not possible individually; protecting group members from unreasonable demands of others
Goal achievement	Providing an opportunity to accomplish a particular task when it takes more than one person's talents, knowledge, or power to complete the job

What are roles? We introduced the concept of roles in Chapter 1 when we discussed what managers do. Of course, managers are not the only individuals in an organization who have roles. The concept of roles applies to all employees in organizations and to their lives outside the organization as well.

role
A set of expected behavior patterns attributed to someone who occupies a given position in a social unit

A **role** refers to a set of expected behavior patterns attributed to someone who occupies a given position in a social unit. Individuals play multiple roles, adjusting their roles to the group to which they belong at the time. In an organization, employees attempt to determine what behaviors are expected of them. They read their job descriptions, get suggestions from their bosses, and watch what their co-workers do. An individual who is confronted by divergent role expectations experiences role conflict. Employees in organizations often face such role conflicts. The credit manager expects her credit analysts to process a minimum of 30 applications a week, but the work group pressures members to restrict output to 20 applications a week so that everyone has work to do and no one gets laid off. A newly hired college instructor's colleagues want him to give out very few high grades in order to maintain the department's reputation for high standards, whereas students want him to give out lots of high grades to enhance their grade point averages. To the degree that the instructor sincerely seeks to satisfy the expectations of both his colleagues and his students, he faces role conflict.

How do norms and conformity affect group behavior? All groups have established **norms**, acceptable standards that are shared by the group's members. Norms dictate output levels, absenteeism rates, promptness or tardiness, the amount of socializing allowed on the job, and so on. Norms, for example, dictate the dress code of customer service representatives at one credit card processing company. Most workers who have little direct customer contact come to work dressed very casually. However, on occasion, a newly hired employee will come to work dressed in a suit. Those who do are often teased and pressured until their dress conforms to the group's standard.

norms
Acceptable standards shared by the members of a group

Although each group will have its own unique set of norms, common classes of norms appear in most organizations. These focus on effort and performance, dress, and loyalty. Probably the most widespread norms are related to levels of effort and performance. Work groups typically provide their members with very explicit cues on how hard to work, what level of output to have, when to look busy, when it's acceptable to goof off, and the like. These norms are extremely powerful in affecting an individual employee's performance. They are so powerful that performance predictions that are based solely on an employee's ability and level of personal motivation often prove wrong.

Some organizations have formal dress codes—even describing what is considered acceptable for corporate casual dress. However, even in the absence of codes, norms frequently develop to dictate the kind of clothing that should be worn to work. College seniors, when interviewing for their first postgraduate job, pick up this norm quickly. Every spring, on college campuses throughout the country, the students who are interviewing for jobs can be spotted; they are the ones walking around in the dark gray or blue pinstriped suits. They are enacting the dress norms that they have learned are expected in professional positions. Of course, acceptable dress in one organization may be very different from the norms of another.

Few managers appreciate employees who ridicule the organization. Similarly, professional employees and those in the executive ranks recognize that most employers view persons who actively look for another job unfavorably. People who are unhappy know that they should keep their job searches secret. These examples demonstrate that loyalty norms are widespread in organizations. This concern for demonstrating loyalty, by the way, often explains why ambitious aspirants to top management positions willingly take work home at night, come in on weekends, and accept transfers to cities in which they would otherwise prefer not to live. Because individuals desire acceptance by the groups to which they belong, they are suscepti-

Details on a Management Classic

Solomon Asch and Group Conformity

Does the desire to be accepted as a part of a group leave one susceptible to conforming to the group's norms? Will the group exert pressure that is strong enough to change a member's attitude and behavior? According to the research by Solomon Asch, the answer appears to be yes.

Asch's study involved groups of seven or eight people who sat in a classroom and were asked to compare two cards held by an investigator.[53] One card had one line; the other had three lines of varying length. As shown in Exhibit 8–9, one of the lines on the three-line card was identical to the line on the one-line card. The difference in line length was quite obvious; under ordinary conditions, subjects made errors of less than 1 percent. The object was to announce aloud which of the three lines matched the single line. But what happens if all the members of the group begin to give incorrect answers? Will the pressure to conform cause the unsuspecting subject (USS) to alter his or her answers to align with those of the others? That was what Asch wanted to know. He arranged the group so that the USS was unaware that the experiment was fixed. The seating was prearranged so that the USS was the last to announce his or her decision.

The experiment began with two sets of matching exercises. All the subjects gave the right answers. On the third set, however, the first subject gave an obviously wrong answer—for example, saying C in Exhibit 8–9. The next subject gave the same wrong answer, and so did the others, until it was the unsuspecting subject's turn. He knew that "B" was the same as "X" but everyone else said "C." The decision confronting the USS was this: Do you publicly state a perception that differs from the preannounced position of the others? Or do you give an answer that you strongly believe to be incorrect in order to have your response agree with the other group members? Asch's subjects conformed in about 35 percent of many experiments and many trials. That is, the subjects gave answers that they knew were wrong but were consistent with the replies of other group members.

For managers, the Asch study provides considerable insight into group behaviors. The tendency, as Asch showed, is for individual members to go along with the pack. To diminish the negative aspects of conformity, managers should create a climate of openness in which employees are free to discuss problems without fear of retaliation.

EXHIBIT 8–9
Examples of Cards Used in Asch Study

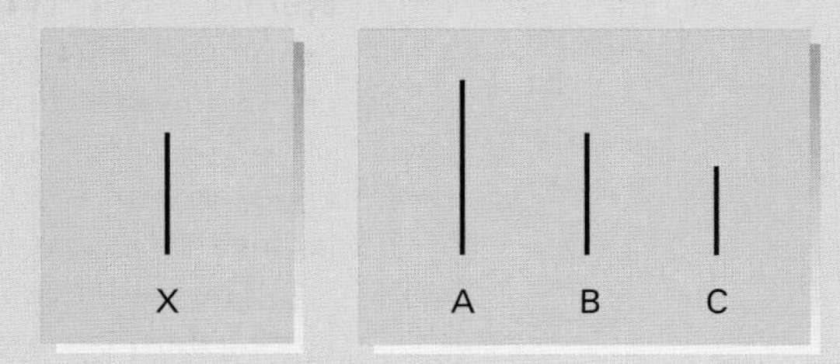

ble to conformity pressures. The impact of group pressures for conformity on an individual member's judgment and attitudes was demonstrated in the classic studies by Solomon Asch [54] (see Details on a Management Classic). Asch's results suggest that group norms press us toward conformity. We desire to be one of the group and to avoid being visibly different. We can generalize this finding to say that when an individual's opinion of objective data differs significantly from that of others in the group, he or she feels extensive pressure to align his or her opinion to conform with those of the others (see also groupthink, p. 120).

What is status and why is it important? **Status** is a prestige grading, position, or rank within a group. As far back as scientists have been able to trace human groupings, they have found status hierarchies: tribal chiefs and their followers, nobles and peasants, the haves and the have nots. Status systems are important factors in understanding behavior. Status is a significant motivator that has behavioral consequences when individuals see a disparity between what they perceive their status to be and what others perceive it to be.

status
A prestige grading, position, or rank within a group

Status may be informally conferred by characteristics such as education, age, skill, or experience. Anything can have status value if others in the group admire it. Of course, just because status is informal does not mean that it is unimportant or that there is disagreement on who has it or who does not. Members of groups have no problem placing people into status categories, and they usually agree about who is high, low, and in the middle.

It is important for employees to believe that the organization's formal status system is congruent. That is, there should be equity between the perceived ranking of an individual and the status symbols he or she is given by the organization. For instance, incongruence may occur when a supervisor earns less than his or her employees or when a desirable office is occupied by a lower-ranking individual. Employees may view such cases as a disruption to the general pattern of order and consistency in the organization.

Does group size affect group behavior? The size of a group affects the group's behavior. However, that effect depends on what criteria you are looking at.[55]

The evidence indicates, for instance, that small groups complete tasks faster than larger ones. However, if the group is engaged in problem solving, large groups consistently get better marks than their smaller counterparts. Translating these results into specific numbers is a bit more hazardous, but we can offer some parameters. Large groups—with a dozen or more members—are good for gaining diverse input. Thus, if the goal of the group is to find facts, larger groups should be more effective. On the other hand, smaller groups are better at doing something productive with those facts. Groups of approximately five to seven members tend to act more effectively.

One of the more disturbing findings is that, as groups get incrementally larger, the contribution of individual members often tends to lessen. That is, although the total productivity of a group of four is generally greater than that of a group of three, the individual productivity of each group member declines as the group expands. Thus, a group of four will tend to produce at a level of less than four times the average individual performance. The best explanation for this reduction of effort is that dispersion of responsibility encourages individuals to slack off; this behavior is referred to as **social loafing**.[56] When the results of the group cannot be attributed to any single person, the relationship between an individual's input and the group's output is clouded. In such situations, individuals may be tempted to become "free riders" and coast on the group's efforts. In other words, there will be a reduction in efficiency when individuals think that their contributions cannot be measured. The obvious conclusion from this finding is that managers who use work teams should also provide a means by which individual efforts can be identified.

social loafing
The tendency of an individual in a group to decrease his or her effort because responsibility and individual achievement cannot be measured

Are cohesive groups more effective? Intuitively, it makes sense that groups in which there is a lot of internal disagreement and lack of cooperation are less effective than are groups in which individuals generally agree, cooperate, and like each other. Research on this position has focused on **group cohesiveness**, the degree to which members are attracted to one another and share the group's goals. The more the members are attracted to one another and the more the group's goals align with their individual goals, the greater the group's cohesiveness.

group cohesiveness
The degree to which members of a group are attracted to each other and share goals

Previous research has generally shown that very cohesive groups are more effective than are those with less cohesiveness, but the relationship between cohesiveness and effectiveness is more complex.[57] A key moderating variable is the degree to which the group's attitude aligns with its formal goals or those of the larger organization. The more cohesive a group is, the more its members will follow its goals. If these goals are favorable (for instance, high output, quality work, cooperation with individuals outside the group), a cohesive group is more productive than a less cohesive group. But if cohesiveness is high and attitudes are unfavorable, productivity decreases. If cohesiveness is low and goals are supported, productivity increases, but not as much as when both cohesiveness and support are high. When cohesiveness is low and goals are not supported, cohesiveness has no significant effect upon productivity. These conclusions are summarized in Exhibit 8–10.

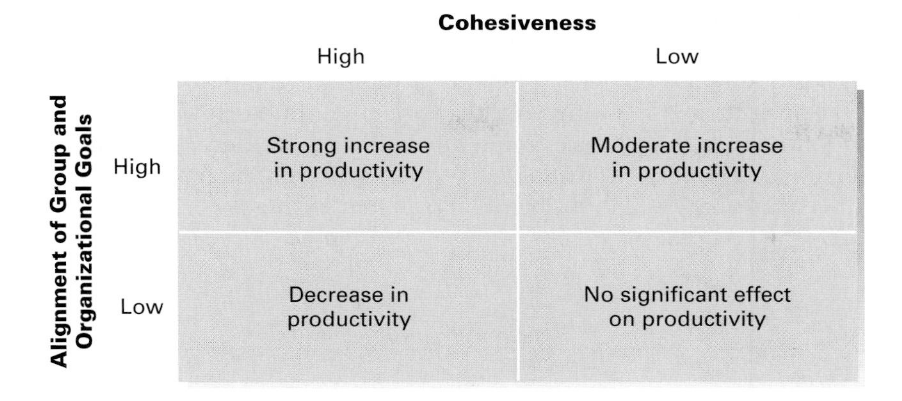

EXHIBIT 8–10

The Relationship Between Group Cohesiveness and Productivity

Review, Comprehension, Application

CHAPTER SUMMARY

How will you know if you fulfilled the Learning Outcomes on page 226? You will have fulfilled the Learning Outcomes if you are able to:

1. **Define the focus and goals of organizational behavior.** The field of organizational behavior is concerned with the actions of people—managers and operatives alike—in organizations. By focusing on individual and group-level characteristics, OB seeks to explain and predict behavior. Because they get things done through other people, managers will be more effective leaders if they have an understanding of behavior.
2. **Identify and describe the three components of attitudes.** Attitudes are made up of three components. The cognitive component involves the beliefs, opinions, knowledge, or information held by the person. The affective component is the emotional or feeling side of the individual, and the behavioral component of an attitude is one's intention to behave in a certain manner toward someone or something.
3. **Explain cognitive dissonance.** Cognitive dissonance refers to the relationship of attitudes and behavior. Cognitive dissonance is any incompatibility that an individual might perceive between two or more attitudes or between behavior and attitudes. Cognitive dissonance means that any form of inconsistency is uncomfortable and an individual will attempt to reduce the dissonance and the associated discomfort.
4. **Describe the Myers-Briggs personality type framework and its use in organizations.** The Myers-Briggs Type Indicator (MBTI) is a personality assessment test that asks individuals how they usually act or feel in different situations. The way the individual responds to the questions reveals one of 16 different personality types. The MBTI can help managers understand and predict employees' behaviors.
5. **Define perception and describe the factors that can shape or distort perception.** Perception is the process of organizing and interpreting sensory impressions in order to give meaning to the environment. Several factors operate to shape and sometimes distort perceptions. These factors can reside in the perceiver, in the target being perceived, or in the context of the situation in which the perception is being made.
6. **Explain how managers can shape employee behavior.** Managers can shape or mold employee behavior by systematically reinforcing each successive step that moves the employee closer to the desired response. Employee behavior can be shaped through positive reinforcement (providing a reward the employee desires), negative reinforcement (terminating or withdrawing something that an employee finds pleasant), punishment (penalizing undesirable behavior), or extinction (eliminating any reinforcement).
7. **Contrast formal and informal groups.** Formal groups are defined by the organization's structure, with designated work assignments establishing tasks. Informal groups are social alliances that are neither structured nor organizationally determined.
8. **Explain why people join groups.** People join groups because of their need for security (strength in numbers), status (a prestige that comes from belonging to a specific group), self-esteem (feelings of self-worth), affiliation (fulfilling one's social needs), power (achieving goals through a group), and goal achievement (if it takes more than one person's time and talents to accomplish some task).

9. **State how roles and norms influence employees' behavior.** A role refers to a set of behavior patterns expected of someone occupying a given position in a social unit. At any given time, employees adjust their role behaviors to the group of which they are a part. Norms are standards shared by group members. They informally convey to employees which behaviors are acceptable and which are unacceptable.

10. **Describe how group size affects group behavior.** Group size affects group behavior in a number of ways. Smaller groups are generally faster at completing tasks than are larger ones. However, larger groups are frequently better at fact finding because of their diversified input. As a result, larger groups are generally better at problem solving.

COMPANION WEBSITE

We invite you to visit the Robbins/DeCenzo companion Website at **www.prenhall.com/robbins** for this chapter's Internet resources, including an online study guide, Internet exercises, and "In the News" with full text articles provided by XanEdu.

READING FOR COMPREHENSION

1. How is an organization like an iceberg? Use the iceberg metaphor to describe the field of organizational behavior.
2. What role does role consistency play in one's attitude?
3. Clarify how individuals reconcile inconsistencies between attitudes and behaviors.
4. Describe what is meant by the term *emotional intelligence*. Provide an example of how it's used in contemporary organizations.
5. Name five different shortcuts used in judging others. What effect does each have on perception?
6. What is the most effective size for a group?

LINKING CONCEPTS TO PRACTICE

1. What behavioral predictions might you make if you knew that an employee had (1) an external locus of control, (2) a low Mach score, (3) low self-esteem, (4) high self-monitoring tendencies?
2. How might a manager use personality traits to improve employee selection in his department? Emotional intelligence? Discuss.
3. Describe the implications of social learning theory for managing people at work.
4. "Informal groups in an organization can be detrimental to management." Do you agree or disagree with that statement? Explain your position.
5. Discuss the organizational implications drawn from Asch's conformity studies.

VIDEO CASE APPLICATION

Praendex Incorporated: Matching the Right Personality to the Right Job

"What we do is help our clients to understand the special value of each one of the people who work with them so that they can create an environment that affords every single employee the opportunity to do the work that they can do best," says Dinah Daniels, president and chairman, Praendex Incorporated.

The Predictive Index (PI), a personality survey developed by Praendex, based in Wellesley-Hills, Massachusetts, is an assessment tool that is used to reveal the aptitudes and abilities of employees and job candidates. Based on psychological and sociological studies, the survey was created in 1955 by Ms. Daniel's father. [58] Not only does the survey give hiring managers insight into potential new employees, but it also allows them to better understand current employees to see whether they are in the right jobs for their personality traits.

The survey takes just minutes to complete and minutes to score, but the accuracy of its predictions has been astounding people around the world for nearly 50 years. The PI survey consists of a two-sided work sheet with lists of 86 adjectives on each side. On the first side people are asked to check off any words they feel describe how others expect them to act. On the second side, they are asked to select adjectives they believe pertain to them.

Once a company has made the commitment to use Praendex's program, a complete assessment of the positions in the organization is made, with particular attention given to the survey results of top performers in each job category. Managers are offered a three-day training course so that they can interpret the answers to the survey themselves.[59] Parendex software then produces charts of the responses that will give managers insights into an employee's motivational drive.

The results uncover "things like how intensely independent an individual is, what their pace of activity is, how they are going to relate to and interact with other people, and what their attention to detail is," says Senior Vice President Dennis LaRosee.

In this tight market, executives like Tom Loper, vice president of subscriber services, Lifeline Systems, Inc. need to understand how to hire and retain the best human resources possible. Lifeline Systems, Inc. is America's leading provider of emergency response systems for the elderly and disabled. Using the PI to hire people who are diligent and who will derive personal satisfaction from this demanding work, Tom Loper was able to improve the company's bottom line by best utilizing the capabilities of his employees. He is not alone.

Entrepreneur Larry Aramoff of Tatuck Booksellers used the Predictive Index to help members of his management team understand their own leadership styles in order to work more effectively with each other and the staff. In the process, he found someone to replace himself, freeing him to run other parts of the business for which he was better suited.[60]

Kathy Till, director of training for La-Z-Boy Furniture Galleries in Phoneix, Arizona, used the Predictive Index as an interview tool. She found that she was able to establish a sales force with a mix of personality styles to better accommodate different customer styles. She was able to identify and hire employees who could establish a rapport with their customers, ensuring repeat business and greater job satisfaction.[61]

Satisfied clients span 77 countries and vary from small businesses to large conglomerates. Here is a posting on the PI Web site from Kees Halken, managing director, Te Strake BV, The Netherlands: "PI training has proved to be invaluable to help develop our managers to their full potential. I would unhesitatingly recommend PI to all business—it's a beautiful tool!"[62]

These accolades attest to Dinah Daniel's recognition that today's executives are *very* aware of the value of people in their organizations. The answer to building a successful business does not lie foremost in our ability to grasp technological advances, but in our ability to understand each other and ourselves.

Questions

1. In the video Michael Roberts, senior lecturer Harvard Business School/Praendex board of directors, states that the Predictive Index gives managers and employees "a comfortable means of discussing the sensitive issue of personality in a neutral way rather than in a critical way." Do you agree with this statement? Explain.
2. Praendex Incorporated is advertising opportunities for talented consultants. The position requires a strong self-starter. The job description includes the following: "As a Predictive Index consultant you would sell and deliver the PI management techniques and methods to business executives and managers in your area. The freedom is there to set your own schedules and to have a great deal of control over the growth of your client base. You would have a chance to greatly impact the effectiveness and culture of a company.[63] Using John Holland's "Typology of Personality and Sample Occupations" (Exhibit 8–3), assess whether you would be a good candidate for this job.
3. In your opinion, would the Predictive Index be a good indicator of a person's emotional intelligence? Explain.
4. You are interested in applying for a position that is about to open up in your department. Your supervisor is aware of your aspirations, and you have been working extra hard to make a good impression. The company has just invested in Praendex's Predictive Index and will begin the program before the job is officially posted. Now you will be required to fill out the survey, along with everyone else who is eligible for this internal opening. How does this make you feel? Discuss the possibilities and the conflicts this presents.

Management Workshop

Team Skill-Building Exercise

The Salary Request

Objectives

a. To illustrate how perceptions can influence decisions.

b. To illustrate the effects of shortcuts used in evaluating others.

The Situation

a. Your instructor will give you a scenario involving an employee's salary increase request. You are to read it and make a recommendation (either favorable or unfavorable) about the raise.

Procedure

a. Divide into groups of five to seven and take the role of a manager making the decision.

b. Each group should identify its perceptions about the employee's work habits and other factors in support of its decision.

c. Reassemble the class and hear each group's recommendations and explanations.

Understanding Yourself

Before you can develop other people, you must understand your present strengths. To assist in this learning process, we encourage you to complete the following self-assessments from the Prentice Hall Self-Assessment Library 2.0:

- What's My Basic Personality? (#1)
- What's My MBTI Personality Type?(#2)
- What's My Locus of Control? (#3)
- How Does My Self-Esteem Rate? (#4)

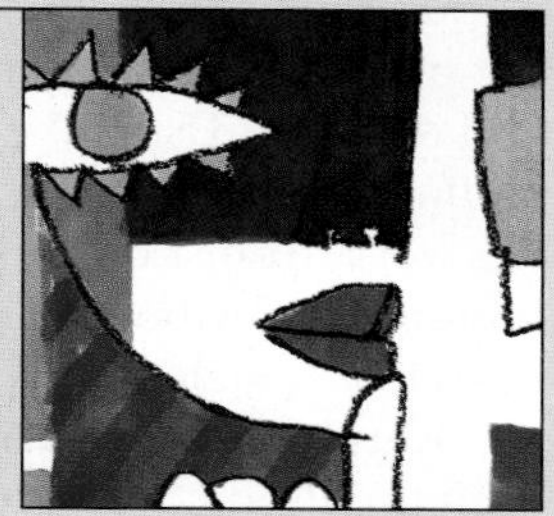

After you complete these assessments, we suggest that you print out the results and store them as part of your "portfolio of learning."

Developing Your Skill at Shaping Behavior

About the Skill

In today's dynamic work environments, learning is continual. But this learning shouldn't be done in isolation or without any guidance. Most employees need to be shown what is expected of them on the job. As a manager, you must teach your employees the behaviors that are most critical to their, and the organization's, success.

Steps in Practicing the Skill

1. **Identify the critical behaviors that have a significant impact on an employee's performance.** Not everything employees do on the job is equally important in terms of performance outcomes. A few critical behaviors may, in fact, account for the majority of one's results. These high impact behaviors need to be identified.
2. **Establish a baseline of performance.** This is obtained by determining the number of times the identified behaviors occur under the employee's present job conditions.
3. **Analyze the contributing factors to performance and their consequences.** A number of factors, such as the norms of a group, may be contributing to the baseline performance. Identify these factors and their effect on performance.
4. **Develop a shaping strategy.** The change that may occur will entail changing some element of performance—structure, processes, technology, groups, or the task. The purpose of the strategy is to strengthen the desirable behaviors and weaken the undesirable ones.

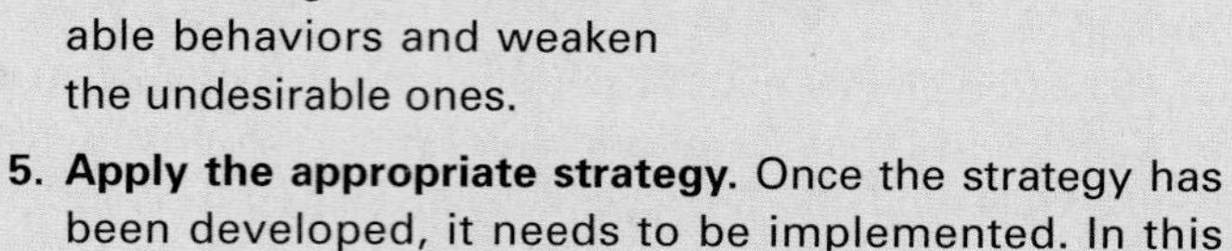

5. **Apply the appropriate strategy.** Once the strategy has been developed, it needs to be implemented. In this step, the intervention occurs.
6. **Measure the change that has occurred.** The intervention should produce the desired results in performance behaviors. Evaluate the number of times the identified behaviors now occur. Compare these with the baseline evaluation in step 2.
7. **Reinforce desired behaviors.** If the intervention has been successful and the new behaviors are producing the desired results, maintain these behaviors through reinforcement mechanisms.

Practicing the Skill

a. Imagine that your assistant is ideal in all respects but one—he or she is hopeless at taking phone messages for you when you are not in the office. Since you are often in training sessions and the calls are sales leads you are anxious to follow up, you have identified taking accurate messages as a high impact behavior for your assistant.

b. Focus on steps 3 and 4, and devise a way to shape your assistant's behavior. Identify some factors that might contribute to his or her failure to take messages—these could range from a heavy workload to a poor understanding of the task's importance (you can rule out insubordination). Then develop a shaping strategy by determining what you can change—the available technology, the task itself, the structure of the job, or some other element of performance.

c. Now plan your intervention, a brief meeting with your assistant in which you explain the change you expect. Recruit a friend to help you role play your intervention. Do you think you would succeed in a real situation?

Developing Your Diagnostic and Analytical Skills

Plumtree Living

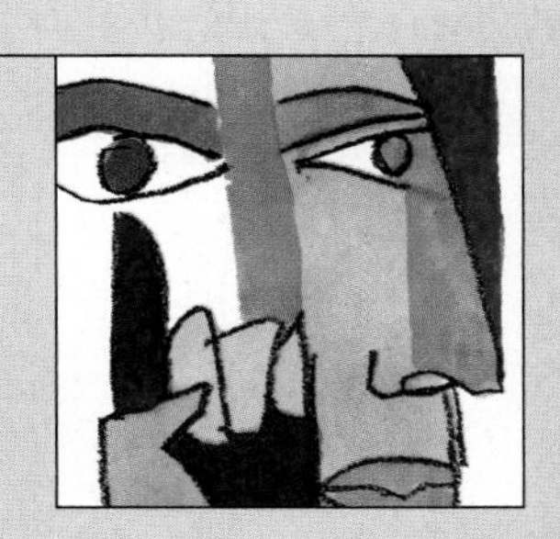

Imagine how it would feel if you were a new employee and your boss asked you to do something you had no idea how to do. Most people would feel inadequate or incompetent. Now imagine how strange and uncomfortable it would be if, after experiencing such an incident, you went home with the boss because the two of you are roommates—and have been friends since the fourth grade. This, in fact, is a situation faced by John Kim, an employee at Plumtree Software, Inc., the San Francisco–based portal manufacturer, and his boss, Glenn Kelman. Kelman is a cofounder and vice president of product management and marketing for Plumtree.[64] A third roommate, Conan Reidy, also works at the company. The three roommates are finding that mixing work and friendship can be tricky.

At home, the roommates are equals. They share a single bathroom, and the housework. However, at work, equality is nonexistent. For instance, a problem with office assignments erupted when Plumtree moved into its new headquarters. As part of the four-person management team, Kelman has a corner office with windows—and the amenities that a cofounder might expect. Reidy, who works in a cubicle, was annoyed at Kelman for not standing up for him when offices were assigned. However, Reidy didn't complain because he didn't want to get an office only because of this relationship with Kelman. Another problem brewing is that the roommates compete to outlast one another working late. Reidy's boss worries that he's going to burn out. Other awkward situations arise whenever the company's performance is being discussed. Kelman often wants to complain about work but has to stop himself. Whenever the company's president calls, Kelman goes into his bedroom and shuts the door. And, now that the company has decided to sell stock to the public, Kelman's financial wealth is expected to increase dramatically—which just may create some interesting emotional issues for the roommates. Although it might appear easy to say to the roommates "move out," it's too expensive to do so. Besides, these guys are best friends.

Questions

1. How could Kelman use information about emotions and attitudes to handle work matters with his roommates?
2. How might perception be affecting the work performance of Kim and Reidy? Do you perceive any difference now that the company has issued its IPO and Glenn Kelman stands to benefit financially? Explain your views.
3. Based on the information in the case, describe Glenn Kelman and Conan Reidy in terms of the Big Five model characteristics.

Enhancing Your Communication Skills

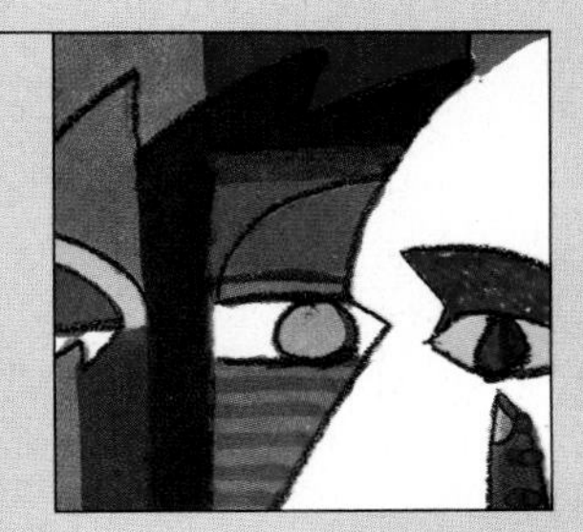

1. There has been a lengthy debate about the following two viewpoints in management: "Happy employees are productive employees" versus "Productive employees are happy employees." Which one of the two statements do you support? Explain and defend your position. Use examples to support your viewpoint.
2. Using the Self-Assessment Library, take the Myers-Briggs Type Indicator (Self-Assessment #2). Identify and describe your profile. What are the implications of this profile for your career choices?
3. Each semester, students are typically asked to evaluate their professors. In completing the evaluations, they use shortcuts in judging the effectiveness of their instructors. Using the information contained in Exhibit 8–7 (page 243), describe how each of these shortcuts may be applicable to a student evaluation of a professor. Then describe how specific distortions may exist.

CHAPTER 9

Understanding Work Teams

LEARNING OUTCOMES

After reading this chapter, I will be able to:

1. Explain the growing popularity of work teams in organizations.
2. Describe the five stages of team development.
3. Contrast work groups with work teams.
4. Identify four common types of work teams.
5. Explain what types of teams entrepreneurial organizations use.
6. List the characteristics of high-performing work teams.
7. Discuss how organizations can create team players.
8. Explain how managers can keep teams from becoming stagnant.
9. Describe the role of teams in continuous process improvement programs.

MEET A REAL MANAGER!

"One Manager's Reflection" page 266

Steve Peters, President/Owner, Cool Pictures & MultiMedia Presentations

"Revolutionize the international advertising world to create and control the buzz about brands across borders." That's the bold mission for StrawberryFrog, a small advertising agency with 40 people headquartered in Amsterdam. Yet for Karin Drakenberg (see photo), the Swedish chief executive of StrawberryFrog, the goal is not only ambitious, but, she and her employees feel, very achievable.[1] All employees of the organization are absolutely committed to making the mission statement a reality.

StrawberryFrog has never had a traditional, hierarchical organizational structure. Instead, it uses a "multicultural, open-room concept." Since its founding on Valentine's Day in 1999, the company depends on a network of about 200 people around the globe who can pitch in when they're needed to work on various projects. For example, the agency's graphic design work is done in Amsterdam, Brussels, San Francisco, and Sydney. With no cumbersome administrative bureaucracy to slow it down, the agency has landed some large ad campaigns—for such companies as Mitsubishi Europe, Sprint, Pharmacia and Upjohn, Sony Ericsson, Credit Suisse, Ikea, and *Elle*. The team at Strawberry Frog feels that good global campaigns are found in big ideas, not in big bureaucracies. The use of sophisticated technologies allow StrawberryFrog the same "Knowledge control as any of the big agencies—coupled with its speed, flexibility, and the quality of the work." The 20 or 30 languages spoken by StrawberryFrog employees together enables the company to effectively communicate with anyone in the world.

The key to strawberry Frog's approach is its model of virtual work teams. By relying on a web of freelancers around the globe, the agency enjoys a network of talent without all the unnecessary overhead and complexity of rigid work arrangements. The inspiration for this approach came from the film and construction industries. If you look at the film industry, workers are essentially "free agents" who move from project to project applying their skills—directing, talent search, costuming, makeup, acting, set design—as needed. And the construction industry has mastered the art of managing multiskilled teams all working together on one shared vision. Those are the hallmarks of what Drakenberg is attempting to do. It allows StrawberryFrog to win the attention of big advertisers seeking a twenty-first century image for their twentieth-century products. Given its success in just a few years in existence, it appears that its model of virtual teams is working.

LIKE KAREN DRAKENBERG, MANAGERS TODAY BELIEVE THAT THE use of teams will allow their organizations to increase sales or produce better products faster and at lower costs. Although the effort to create teams isn't always successful, well-planned teams can reinvigorate productivity and better position an organization to deal with a rapidly changing environment.

THE POPULARITY OF TEAMS

In the early 1970s, when companies such as Toyota, General Foods, and Volvo introduced teams, it made news because no one else was doing it. Today, it's just the opposite: It's the organization that doesn't use some form of team that is noteworthy. Pick up almost any business publication, and you will read how teams have become an essential part of work in companies such as Honeywell, General Electric, Saab, John Deere, Imperial Oil, Australian Airlines, Honda, Florida Power and Light, Shiseido, and FedEx. In fact, about 80 percent of all *Fortune* 500 companies are using teams in some part of their organization.[2]

How do we explain the current popularity of teams? The evidence suggests that teams typically outperform individuals when tasks require multiple skills, judgment, and experience.[3] As organizations restructure themselves to compete more effectively and efficiently, they are turning to teams as a better way to utilize employee talents.[4]

The majority of *Fortune* 500 companies are using teams in their organizations. At Deere & Company, for example, teams of employees have been found to outperform individuals when jobs require multiple skills, judgment, and experience.

Management has found that teams are more flexible and responsive to a changing environment than traditional departments or other forms of permanent work groupings.[5] Teams also can be quickly assembled, deployed, refocused, and disbanded.

Finally, teams may offer more that just increased efficiency and enhanced performance for the organization: They can serve as a source of job satisfaction.[6] Because team members are frequently empowered to handle many of the things that directly affect their work, teams serve as an effective means for management to enhance employee involvement, increase employee morale, and promote workforce diversity.

WHAT ARE THE STAGES OF TEAM DEVELOPMENT?

Team development is a dynamic process. Most teams find themselves in a continual state of change. But even though teams probably never reach stability, there's a general pattern to most teams' evolution. The five stages of team development, shown in Exhibit 9–1, are forming, storming, norming, performing, and adjourning.[7]

The first stage, **forming**, is characterized by a great deal of uncertainty about the group's purpose, structure, and leadership. Members are testing the waters to determine what types of behaviors are acceptable. This stage is complete when members have begun to think of themselves as part of a team.

The **storming** stage is one of intragroup conflict. Members accept the existence of the team but resist the control that the group imposes on individuality. Further, there is conflict over who will control the team. When stage II is complete, there will be relatively clear leadership within the team.

The third stage is one in which close relationships develop and members begin to demonstrate cohesiveness. There is now a stronger sense of team identity and camaraderie. This **norming** stage is complete when the team structure solidifies and members have assimilated a common set of expectations of appropriate work behav-

forming
The first stage of work team development, characterized by uncertainty about development, purpose, structure, and leadership

storming
The second stage of work team development, characterized by intragroup conflict

EXHIBIT 9–1
Stages of Team Development

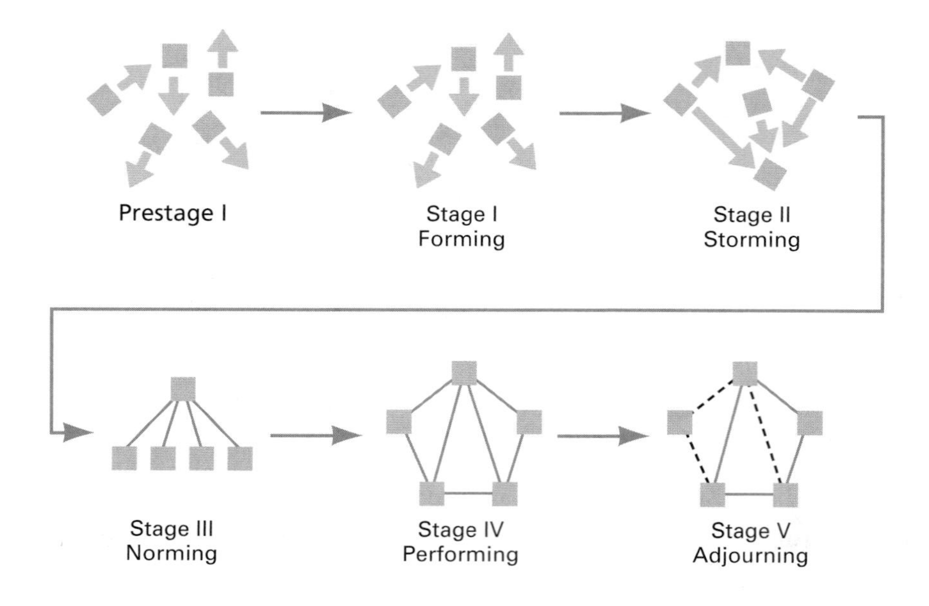

ior. The fourth stage is **performing**. The structure is fully functional and accepted by team members. Their energy is diverted from getting to know and understand each other to performing the necessary tasks. For permanent teams, performing is the last stage of their development. For temporary teams—those that have a limited task to perform—there is an **adjourning** stage. In this stage, the team prepares for its disbandment. A high level of task performance is no longer the members' top priority. Instead, their attention is directed toward wrapping up activities.

Recognizing that teams progress through these stages, one can pose an obvious question: Do they become more effective as they progress through each stage? Some researchers argue that the effectiveness of work units does increase at advanced stages, but it's not that simple.[8] Although that assumption may be generally true, what makes a team effective is complex. Under some conditions, high levels of conflict are conducive to high levels of group performance.[9] We might expect, then, to fine situations in which teams in Stage II outperform those in Stage III or IV. Similarly, teams do not always proceed clearly from one stage to the next. Sometimes, in fact, several stages are going on simultaneously—as when teams are storming and performing at the same time. Therefore, one should not always assume that all teams precisely follow this developmental process or that stage IV is always most preferable. Instead, it is better to think of these stages as a general framework, which should remind you that teams are dynamic entities, and can help you better understand the issues that may surface in a team's life.

norming
The third stage of work team development, in which close relationships develop and members begin to demonstrate cohesiveness

performing
The fourth stage of work team development, in which the structure is fully functional and accepted by team members

adjourning
The fifth and final stage of the development of temporary work teams, in which the team prepares for its disbandment

AREN'T WORK GROUPS AND WORK TEAMS THE SAME?

At this point, you may be asking yourself where this discussion is going. Aren't teams and groups the same thing? No. In this section, we define and clarify the difference between a work group and a work team.[10]

In the last chapter, we defined a group as two or more individuals who have come together to achieve certain objectives. A **work group** interacts primarily to share information and to make decisions that will help each group member perform within his or her area of responsibility. Work groups have no need or opportunity to engage in collective work that requires joint effort. Consequently, their performance is merely the summation of all the group members' individual contributions. There is no positive synergy that would create an overall level of performance greater than the sum of the inputs.

A **work team**, on the other hand, generates positive synergy through a coordinated effort. Their individual efforts result in a level of performance that is greater than the sum of those individual inputs.[11] Exhibit 9–2 highlights the main differences between work groups and work teams.

These descriptions should help to clarify why so many organizations have restructured work processes around teams. Management is looking for that positive synergy that will allow the organization to increase performance.[12] The extensive use

work group
A group that interacts primarily to share information and to make decisions that will help each member perform within his or her area of responsibility

work team
A group that engages in collective work that requires joint effort and generates a positive synergy

Work Teams		Work Groups
Collective performance	← Goal →	Share information
Positive	← Synergy →	Neutral (sometimes negative)
Individual and mutual	← Accountability →	Individual
Complementary	← Skills →	Random and varied

EXHIBIT 9–2
Comparing Work Teams and Work Groups

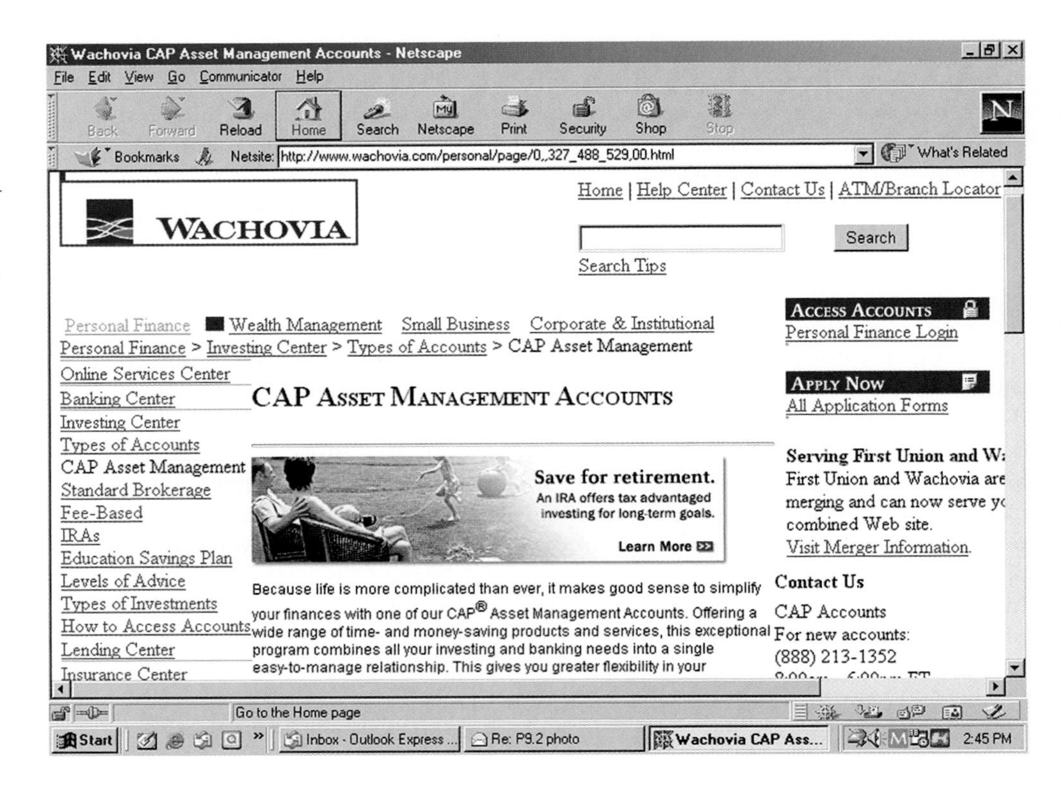

Are teams better performers than individual employees? In many cases, yes. At Wachovia Capital Management Group, investment fund teams have helped the organization improve its Morningstar rating from the 76th to the 31st percentile—meaning that people's investments are gaining value under the team arrangement.

of teams creates the potential for an organization to generate greater outputs with no increase in (or even fewer) inputs. For example, at Wachovia Asset Management Division of Wachovia Bank, mutual funds investment teams have significantly improved investment performance since its team structure was implemented in the late 1990s. As a result, Wachovia's teams have helped the bank improve its Morningstar financial rating—placing it in the 31st percentile; this is up from its place in the 76th percentile three years earlier.[13]

Recognize, however, that such increases are simply "potential." Nothing inherently magical in the creation of work teams guarantees that this positive synergy and its accompanying productivity will occur. Accordingly, merely calling a group a team doesn't automatically increase its performance.[14] As we show later in this chapter, successful or high-performing work teams have certain common characteristics. If management hopes to gain increases in organizational performance—like those as Wachovia—it will need to ensure that its teams possess those characteristics.

TYPES OF WORK TEAMS

Work teams can be classified on the basis of their objectives. The four most common forms of teams in an organization are functional teams, problem-solving teams, self-managed teams, and cross-functional teams (see Exhibit 9–3). A technology-based model for the twenty-first century, the virtual team, will also be discussed.

WHAT IS A FUNCTIONAL TEAM?

functional teams
A work team composed of a manager and the employees in his or her unit and involved in efforts to improve work activities or to solve specific problems within the particular functional unit

Functional teams are composed of a manager and the employees in his or her unit. Within this functional team, issues such as authority, decision making, leadership, and interactions are relatively simple and clear. Functional teams are often involved in efforts to improve work activities or to solve specific problems within a particular functions unit. For example, at the Marque, Inc., headquarters in Goshen, Indiana (manufacturers of emergency squad trucks), employees in all departments in the organization participate on teams, making decisions to "make their products faster, cheaper, and better."[15]

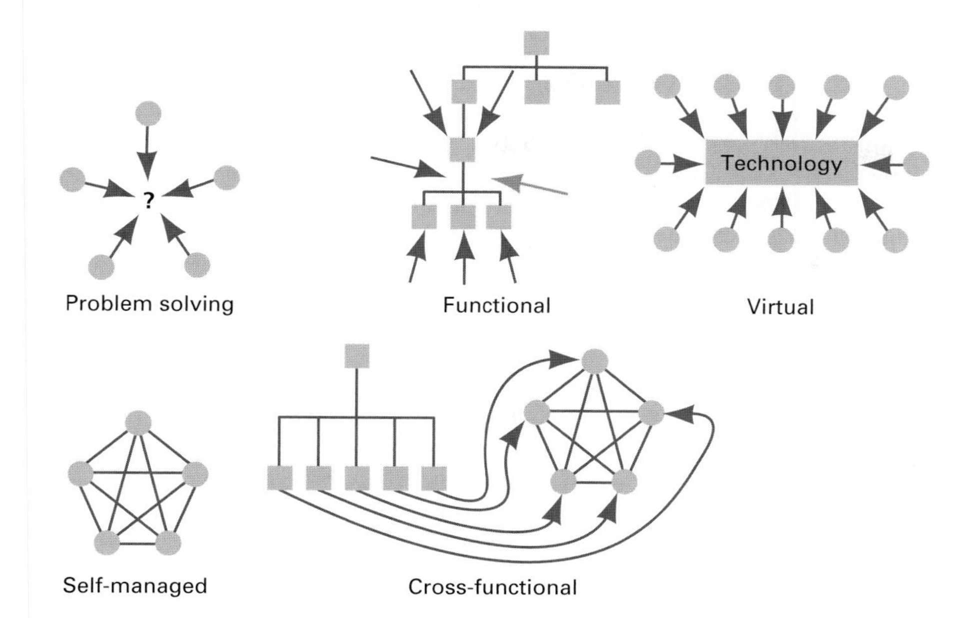

EXHIBIT 9-3
Types of Work Teams

HOW DOES A PROBLEM-SOLVING TEAM OPERATE?

Almost 25 years ago, teams were just beginning to grow in popularity, and the form they took was strikingly similar. These teams typically were composed of 5 to 12 hourly employees from the same department who met for a few hours each week to discuss ways of improving quality, efficiency, and the work environment. We call these **problem-solving teams**. In problem-solving teams, members share ideas or offer suggestions on how work processes and methods can be improved.[16] Some of the most widely practiced applications of problem-solving teams witnessed during the 1980s were **quality circles**, which are work teams of 8 to 10 employees and supervisors who share an area of responsibility. They meet regularly to discuss their quality problems, investigate causes of the problems, recommend solutions, and take corrective actions. They assume responsibility for solving quality problems, and they generate and evaluate their own feedback. Rarely, however, are these teams given the authority to unilaterally implement any of their suggestions. Instead, they make a recommendation to management, which usually makes the decision about the implementation of recommended solutions. Jo Egbert, general manager of Kimball Manufacturing in Boise, Idaho—makers of cables and electronic and electomechanical assemblies—recognized that her company needed to improve production operations and reduce "work-in-process inventory."[17] After several months of implementing and supporting problem-solving teams, Kimball Manufacturing employees reduced production time by 50 percent, and reduced work-in-process inventory from 14 to 3.5 days.

problem-solving teams
Work teams typically composed of 5 to 12 hourly employees from the same department who meet each week to discuss ways of improving quality, efficiency, and the work environment

quality circles
Work teams composed of 8 to 10 employees and supervisors who share an area of responsibility and who meet regularly to discuss quality problems, investigate the causes of the problem, recommend solutions, and take corrective actions but who have no authority

WHAT IS A SELF-MANAGED WORK TEAM?

Another type of team commonly being used in organizations is the self-directed or self-managed team. A **self-managed work team** is a formal group of employees that operates without a manager and is responsible for a complete work process or segment that delivers a product or service to an external or internal customer.[18] Nearly 70 percent of the *Fortune* 1000 organizations have implemented self-managed work teams.[19] Typically, this kind of team has control over its work pace, determines work assignments and when breaks are taken, and inspects its own work. Fully self-managed work teams even select their own members and have the members evaluate each other's performance.[20] As a result, supervisory positions take on decreased importance and may even be eliminated.[21]

self-managed work teams
A formal group of employees that operates without a manager and is responsible for a complete work process or segment that delivers a product or service to an external or internal customer

HOW DO CROSS-FUNCTIONAL TEAMS OPERATE?

cross-functional work team
A team composed of employees from about the same hierarchical level but from different work areas in an organization who are brought together to accomplish a particular task

The next type of team we will identify is the **cross-functional work team**, which consists of employees from about the same hierarchical level but from different work areas in the organization. Workers are brought together to accomplish a particular task.[22]

Many organizations have used cross-functional teams for years. For example, in the1960s, IBM created a large team made up of employees from across departments in the company to develop the highly successful System 360. However, the popularity of cross-functional work teams exploded in the late 1980s. All the major automobile manufacturers—including Toyota, DaimlerChrysler, Nissan, General Motors, Ford, Honda, and BMW have turned to this form of team in order to coordinate complex projects. For example, Hewlett-Packard's Medical Products Group has used cross-functional teams to decrease product development times and optimize their organizational resources.[23]

Cross-functional teams are also an effective way to allow employees from diverse areas within an organization to exchange information, develop new ideas, solve problems, and coordinate complex tasks.[24] But cross-functional teams can be difficult to manage.[25] The early stages of development (e.g., storming) are very often time-consuming as members learn to work with diversity and complexity. This difficulty with diversity, however, can be turned into an advantage. For example, remember our discussion of group decision making in Chapter 4. One of the tenets of that process was that groups provided more complete information and were more creative than individuals. The diversity of a work team can help identify creative or unique solutions. Furthermore, the lack of a common perspective caused by diversity usually means that team members will spend more time discussing relevant issues, which decreases the likelihood that a weak solution will be selected. However, keep in mind that the contribution that diversity makes to teams probably will decline over time.[26] As team members become more familiar with one another, they form a more cohesive group, but the positive aspect of this decline in diversity is that a team bond is built. It takes time to build trust and teamwork. Later in this chapter we present ways managers can help facilitate and build trust among team members.

virtual team
A team that meets electronically; allows groups to meet without concern for space or time

ARE VIRTUAL TEAMS A REALITY IN THE NEW MILLENNIUM?

A **virtual team** is an extension of the electronic meetings we discussed in Chapter 4. A virtual team allows groups to meet without concern for space or time and enables organizations to link workers together in a way that would have been impossible in the past.[27] Team members use computer technology to link physically dispersed members in order to achieve a common goal—using technological advances like conference calls, video conferencing, or e-mail to solve problems even though they may be geographically dispersed or several time zones away.[28] The advertising project teams at StrawberryFrog would be an example of a virtual team. So, too, are some of the team structures at Heineken, manufacturers of Heineken Beer.[29] Heineken uses virtual teams in many aspects of its advertising activities. For example, in an effort to increase Heineken sales, the company brought together people from "local and international companies with expertise in retailing, music, Web design, and advertising." By taking the best talent from each component, Heineken officials were better able to produce an advertising campaign that would lead to the company's goals—increasing the brand awareness, and sales of Heineken Beer.

Teams don't just pop out of thin air in an organization. Rather, they're the result of major changes that occur regarding how work gets done. This team of workers at the Toyota Camry plant in Erlanger, Kentucky, recognized that it takes a lot of care and a supportive organizational culture to give teams the opportunity to be successful. But through their efforts, team members have been able to enhance productivity and coordinate complex projects.

WHY DO ENTREPRENEURS USE TEAMS?

Employee work teams tend to be extremely popular in entrepreneurial ventures, and three types of teams appear to be common.[30] These include empowered functional teams (teams that have authority to plan and implement process improvements); self-directed teams (teams that are nearly autonomous and responsible for many activities that were once the jurisdiction of managers); and cross-functional teams (teams that include a hybrid grouping of individuals who are experts in various specialties and who work together on various tasks).

Entrepreneurial firms use teams because they facilitate the technology and market demands the organization is facing. Teams, entrepreneurs find, help the organization to make products faster, cheaper, and better. Additionally, teams permit entrepreneurs to tap into the collective wisdom of the venture's employees. Entrepreneurs have found that empowering employees to make decisions is one of the best ways for them to adapt to change.[31] Additionally, the team culture can improve the overall workplace environment and worker morale.

For team efforts to work, however, entrepreneurs must shift from the traditional command-and-collaboration style (we'll look at leadership styles in Chapter 11). Entrepreneurs must recognize that individual employees can understand the business and can innovate just as effectively as they can. For example, at marque, Inc., CEO Scott Jessup recognized that he wasn't the smartest person in the company when it came to production problems.[32] But he was smart enough to recognize that if his company wanted to expand its market share in manufacturing its medical emergency-squad vehicles, new levels of productivity needed to be reached. While the organization had enjoyed success with its functional teams, he decided to form a cross-functional team—bringing together people from production, quality assurance, and fabrication—who could spot production bottlenecks and other problems. More importantly, he gave the team the authority to resolve the constraints.

CHARACTERISTICS OF HIGH-PERFORMANCE WORK TEAMS

Teams are not automatic productivity enhancers. We know that they can also be disappointments for management. What common characteristics, then, do effective teams have? Research provides some insight into the primary characteristics associated with high-performance work teams.[33] Let's take a look at these characteristics as summarized in Exhibit 9–4.

What characteristics does a high-performing work team from Saturn possess? Research tells us they have an understanding of goals, trust one another, and have excellent communications. These teams also have an effective leader, and operate in a supportive organizational climate.

High-performance work teams have both a *clear understanding* of the goal and a belief that the goal embodies a worthwhile or important result. Moreover, the importance of these goals encourages individuals to redirect energy away from personal concerns and toward team goals. In high-performing work teams, members are committed to the team's goals; they know what they are expected to accomplish and understand how they will work together to achieve those goals. Effective teams are composed of competent individuals. They have the relevant technical skills and abilities to achieve the desired goals and the personal characteristics required to achieve excellence while working well with others. These same individuals are also capable of readjusting their work skills—called

EXHIBIT 9–4
Characteristics of High-performing Work Teams

job morphing—to fit the needs of the team. It's important not to overlook the personal characteristics. Not everyone who is technically competent has the skills to work well as a team member. High-performing team members possess both technical and interpersonal skills.

Effective teams are characterized by *high mutual trust* among members. That is, members believe in the integrity, character, and ability of one another.[34] But, as you probably know from your own personal relationships, trust is fragile. We'll look at the issue of trust in more detail in Chapter 11. Members of an effective team exhibit intense loyalty and dedication to the team. They are willing to do anything that has to be done to help their team succeed. We call this loyalty and dedication *unified commitment.* Studies of successful teams have found that members identify with their teams.[35] Members redefine themselves to include membership in the team as an important aspect of the self. Unified commitment, then, is characterized by dedication to the team's goal and a willingness to expend extraordinary amounts of energy to achieve them.

Not surprisingly, effective teams are characterized by *good communication.* Members are able to convey messages in a form that is readily and clearly understood. This includes nonverbal as well as spoken messages. Good communication is characterized by a healthy dose of feedback from team members and management. This helps to guide team members and to correct misunderstandings. Like two individuals who have been together for many years, members of high-performing teams are able to quickly and effectively share ideas and feelings.

When jobs are designed around individuals, job descriptions, rules and procedures, and other types of formalized documentation clarify employee roles.[36] Effective teams, on the other hand, tend to be flexible and continually make adjustments, so team members must possess adequate negotiating skills.[37] Because problems and relationships are regularly changing in teams, the members have to be able to confront and reconcile differences.

Effective leaders can motivate a team to follow them through the most difficult situations. How? Leaders help clarify goals. They demonstrate that change is possible by overcoming inertia. And they increase the self-confidence of team members, helping them to realize their potential more fully. The best leaders are not necessarily directive or controlling. Increasingly, effective team leaders are taking the roles of coach and facilitator (see Developing Your Coaching Skill, p. 276). They help guide and support the team, but they don't control it. This description obviously applies to self-managed teams, but it also increasingly applies to problem-solving and cross-functional teams in which members themselves are empowered. For some traditional managers, changing their role from boss to facilitator—from giving orders to working for the team—is a difficult transition. Although most managers relish the newfound shared authority, or come to understand its advantages through leadership training, some hard-nosed, dictatorial managers are just ill suited to the team concept and must be transferred or replaced.

The final condition for an effective team is a *supportive climate.* Internally, the team should be provided with a sound infrastructure. This includes proper training, an understandable measurement system with which team members can evaluate their overall performance, an incentive program that recognizes and rewards team activities, and a supportive human resources system. The infrastructure should support members and reinforce behaviors that lead to high levels of performance. Externally, management should provide the team with the resources needed to get the job done.

TURNING INDIVIDUALS INTO TEAM PLAYERS

So far, we have made a strong case for the value and growing popularity of work teams, but not every worker is inherently a team player. Some people prefer to be recognized for their individual achievements. In some organizations, too, work environments are such that only the strong survive. Creating teams in such an environment may meet some resistance. Finally, as we mentioned in Chapter 2, countries differ in terms of how conducive they are to individualism and collectivism. Teams fit well in countries that score high on collectivism. But what if an organization wants to introduce teams into an individualistic society (like that of the United States)? As one writer stated, regarding teams in the United States, Americans don't grow up learning how to function in teams. In school they don't get a team report card, or learn the names of the team of sailors who traveled with Columbus to America.[38] This limitation apparently would apply to Canadians, British, Australians, and others from individualistic societies.

WHAT ARE THE MANAGEMENT CHALLENGES OF CREATING TEAM PLAYERS?

The points raised are meant to dramatize that one substantial barrier to work teams is the individual resistance that may exist. Employees' success, when they are part of teams, is no longer defined in terms of individual performance. Instead, success is a function of how well the team as a whole performs. To perform well as team members, individuals must be able to communicate openly and honestly with one another, to confront differences and resolve conflicts, and to place lower priority on personal goals for the good of the team. For many employees, these are difficult, and sometimes impossible assignments.

The challenge of creating team players will be greatest where the national culture is highly individualistic and the teams are being introduced into an established organization that has historically valued individual achievement.[39] This describes, for instance, the environment that faced managers at AT&T, Ford, Motorola, and other large U.S Companies. These firms prospered by hiring and rewarding corporate stars, and they bred a competitive work climate that encouraged individual achievement and recognition. Employees in these types of organizations can experience culture shock caused by a sudden shift in the focus to teamwork.[40]

In contrast, the challenge for management is less demanding when teams are introduced in places in which employees have strong collectivist values—such as

Learning from Experience: One Manager's Reflection

Steve Peters President/Owner, Cool Pictures & MultiMedia Presentations

TURNING INDIVIDUALS INTO TEAM PLAYERS

Describe the situation you faced. As a new company formed to provide technology-based information for the classroom it was important that we develop a solid team. Our goal was not only to provide multimedia services but to differentiate our firm from others who were doing the same thing. It was decided that we would approach this differentiation opportunity in two ways: Never miss any deadlines; on the contrary, submit work early and continually work to be creative and to provide a quality product; and give the clients more than they pay for.

The difficulty of this task was reflected in the size of the firm. Unlike many who start a businesses, our goal was to remain somewhat small. This has the potential to create a vacuum when we are seeking creative talent as well as attempting to keep that talent.

What action(s) did you take? Our initial mistake was not developing a team attitude. The part-time employees rarely saw each other and had no idea what the other people's contributions were. Proper training was not provided, and in general the importance of everyone's contribution was not stressed.

What results occurred? While the tasks were always completed on time, the quality was often questionable. The team rarely took creative chances. Finally, the need to monitor more closely became a concern.

What did/should you have done differently? The selection of the team was based on known past performance so selection was not a problem. Training and communications were the problems. Initially, all those who were hired should have been brought together and provided with training. A weekly communications tool should have been implemented and input sought from everyone. Finally, a "Project of Quality" celebration signaling the end of a project should have been instituted for the team.

If you took a corrective action, what were the results? Now, everyone who is hired will be introduced to the team members. We stress the fact that it takes a collective effort if we are going to be successful in the long term. We also believe in investing in the employees. While the two full-time employees will be going to seminars and workshops this year, it is planned that in the future the part-time staff will also receive the same benefit. The president or graphics president will provide the personal touch by communicating in person with all employees two or three times a week during project development. Management must sit down and communicate with the individual. The goal is to remove any obstacles hampering the completion of the assigned tasks. Finally, there are social activities that include the team members and families celebrating a "Project of Quality" completion.

Today the need for close monitoring is past. In fact, just the opposite is true. Assign a project, communicate, remove obstacles, and provide support when requested and a quality end result will occur.

Japan or Mexico. The challenge of forming teams will also be less in new organizations that use teams as their initial form of structuring work. Saturn Corporation, for instance, is an American Organization. Although owned by General Motors, the company was designed around teams from its start. Everyone at Saturn was hired on the understanding that they would be working in teams, and the ability to be a good team player was a hiring prerequisite.

WHAT ROLES DO TEAM MEMBERS PLAY?

High-performing work teams carefully match people to various roles. One stream of research has identified nine potential roles that work team members often can play: creator-innovator, explorer-promoter, assessor-developer, thrust-organizer, concluder-producer, controller-inspector, upholder-maintainer, reporter-adviser, and linker[41] (see Exhibit 9–5). Let's briefly review each team role.

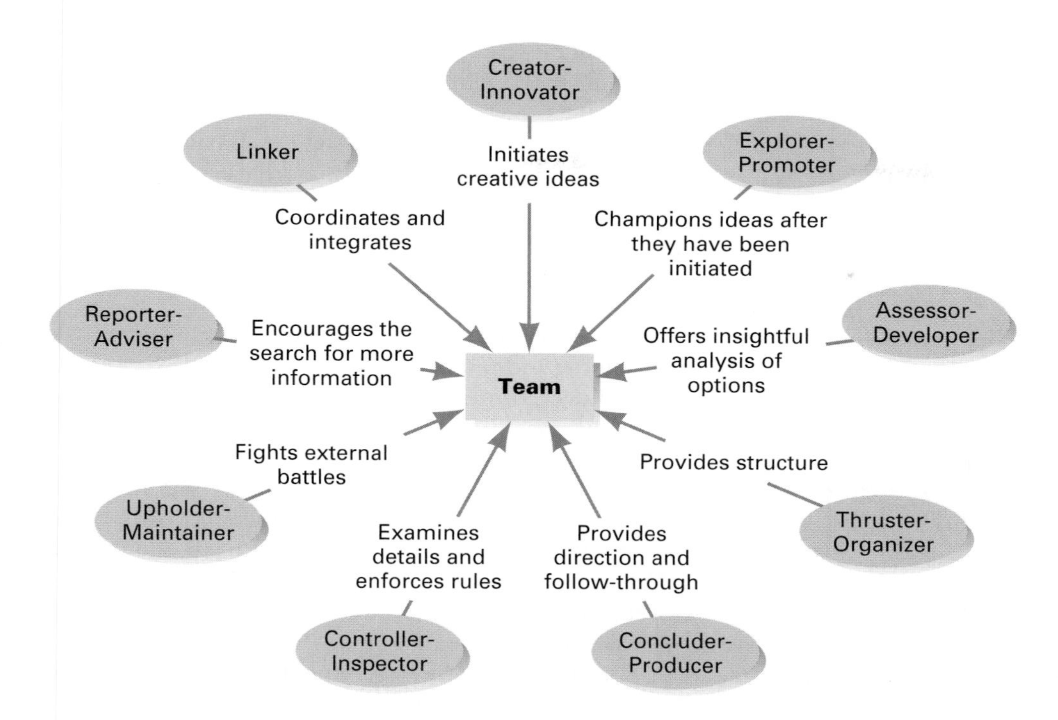

EXHIBIT 9-5

Team Member Roles

Source: Based on C. Margerison and D. McCann, *Team Management: Practical New Approaches* (London: Mercury Books, 1990).

Creator-innovators are usually imaginative and good at initiating ideas or concepts. They are typically very independent and prefer to work at their own pace on their own—and very often on their own time. *Explorer-promoters* like to take new ideas and champion their cause. These individuals are good at picking up ideas from the creator-innovators and finding the resources to promote those ideas. However, they often lack the patience and control skills to ensure that the ideas are followed through in detail. *Assessor-developers* have strong analytical skills. They're at their best given several different options to evaluate and analyze before a decision is made. *Thruster-organizers* like to set up procedures to turn ideas into reality and get things done. They set goals, establish plans, organize people, and establish systems to ensure that deadlines are met. And, somewhat like thruster-organizers, *concluder-producers* are concerned with result. Only their role focuses on keeping to deadlines and ensuring that all commitments are followed through. Concluder-producers take pride in producing a regular output to a standard.

Controller-inspectors have a high concern for establishing and enforcing rules and policies. They are good at examining details and making sure that inaccuracies are avoided. They want to check all the facts and figures to make sure they're complete. *Upholder-maintainers* hold strong convictions about the way things should be done. They will defend the team and fight its battles with outsiders while, at the same time, strongly supporting fellow team members. Accordingly, these individuals provide team stability. *Reporter-advisers* are good listeners and tend not to press their point of view on others. They tend to favor getting more information before making decisions. As such, they perform an important role in encouraging the team to seek additional information before making decisions and discouraging the team from making hasty decisions.

The last role—the *linkers*—overlaps the others. This role can be assumed by any actors of the previous eight roles. Linkers try to understand all views. They are coordinators and integrators. They dislike extremism and try to build cooperation among all team members. They also recognize the various contributions that other team members make and try to integrate people and activities despite differences that might exist.

If forced to, most individuals can perform any of these roles. However, most have two or three they strongly prefer. Managers need to understand the strengths that each individual can bring to a team; they need to select team members on the basis of an appropriate mix of individual strengths and allocate work assignments that fit each member's preferred style. By matching individual preferences with team role demand, managers increase the likelihood that the team members will work well together. Unsuccessful teams may have an unbalanced portfolio of individual talents, with too much energy being expended in one area and not enough in other areas.

HOW CAN A MANAGER SHAPE TEAM BEHAVIOR?

There are several options available for managers who are trying to turn individuals into team players (see Ethical Dilemma in Management). The three most popular ways include proper selection, employee training, and rewarding the appropriate team behaviors. Let's look at each of these.

What role does selection play? Some individuals already possess the interpersonal skills to be effective team players. When hiring team members, in addition to checking on the technical skills required to successfully perform the job, the organizations should ensure that applicants can fulfill team roles.

As we have mentioned before, some applicants have been socialized around individual contributions and, consequently, lack team skills, as might some current employees who are restructuring into teams. When faced with such candidates, a manager can do several things. First, and most obvious, if team skills are woefully lacking, don't hire that candidate. If successful performance requires interaction, rejecting such a candidate is appropriate. On the other hand, a candidate who has only some basic skills can be hired on a probationary basis and required to undergo training to shape him or her into a team player. If the skills aren't learned or practiced, the individual may have to be separated from the company for failing to achieve the skills necessary for performing successfully on the job.

Ethical Dilemma in Management

Does Everyone Have To Be a Team Player?

You're a production manager at the Saturn plant. One of your newest employees is Barbara Petersen, who has a bachelor's degree in engineering and a master's in business. You recently hired Barbara out of college for a position in supply chain management.

You've recently been chosen to head up a cross-functional team to look at ways to reduce inventory costs. This team would essentially be a permanent task force. You've decided to have team members come from supplier relations, cost accounting, transportations, and production systems. You've also decided to include Barbara on the team. While she has only been at Saturn for four months, you've been impressed with her energy, smarts, and industriousness. You think this would be an excellent assignment for her to increase her visibility in the company and expand her understanding of the company's inventory system.

When you called Barbara into your office to give her the good news, you were quite surprised by her response. "I'm not a team player," she said, "I didn't join clubs in high school. I was on the track team and I did well, but track is an individual sport. We were a team only in the sense that we rode together in the same bus to away meets. In college, I avoided the whole sorority thing. Some people may call me a loner. I don't think that's true. I can work well with others, but I hate meetings and committees. To me, they waste so much time. And anything you're working on with a group, you've got all these different personalities that you have to adjust for. I'm an independent operator. Give me a job and I'll get it done. I work harder than anyone I know—and I give my employer 150 percent. But I don't want my performance to be dependent on the other people in my group. They may not work as hard as I will. Someone is sure to shirk some of their responsibilities. I just don't want to be a team player."

What do you do? Should you give Barbara the option of joining the inventory cost reduction team? Is it unethical for you to require someone like Barbara to do his or her job as part of a team?

Can we train individuals to be team players? Performing well in a team involves a set of behaviors. As we discussed in the preceding chapter, new behaviors can be learned. Even a large portion of people who were raised on the importance of individual accomplishment can be trained to become team players. Training specialists can conduct exercises that allow employees to experience the satisfaction that teamwork can provide. The workshops usually cover such topics as team problem solving, communications, negotiations, conflict resolution, and coaching skills. It's not unusual, too, for these individuals to be exposed to the five stages of team development that we discussed earlier.[42] At Bell Atlantic, for example, trainers focus on how a team goes through various stages before it gels. And employees are reminded of the importance of patience, because teams take longer to do some things—such as make decisions —than do employees acting alone.[43]

What role do rewards play in shaping team players? The organization's reward system needs to encourage cooperative efforts rather than competitive ones. For instance, Lockheed Martin's Aeronautics company has organized its 20,000-plus employees into teams. Rewards are structured to return a percentage increase in the bottom line to the team members on the basis of achievements of the team's performance goals.

Promotions, pay raises, and other forms of recognition should be given to employees who are effective collaborative team members. This doesn't mean that individual contribution is ignored, but rather that it is balanced with selfless contributions to the team. Examples of behaviors that should be rewarded include training new colleagues, sharing information with teammates, helping resolve team conflicts, and mastering new skills in which the team is deficient.[44] Finally, managers cannot forget the inherent rewards that employees can receive from teamwork. Work teams provide camaraderie. It's exciting and satisfying to be an integral part of a successful team. The opportunity to engage in personal development and to help teammates grow can be a very satisfying and rewarding experience for employees.[45]

HOW CAN A MANAGER REINVIGORATE A MATURE TEAM?

The fact that a team is performing well at any given point in time is no assurance that it will continue to do so. Effective teams can become stagnant. Initial enthusiasm can give way to apathy. Time can diminish the positive value from diverse perspectives as cohesiveness increases. In terms of the five-stage development model, teams don't automatically stay at the performing stage. Familiarity and team success can lead to contentment and complacency. And, as that happens, the team may become less open to novel ideas and innovative solutions. Mature teams, also, are particularly prone to suffer from groupthink(see Chapter 4), as team members begin to believe they can read everyone's mind and assume that they know what the others are thinking. Consequently, team members become reluctant to express their thoughts and are less likely to challenge one another.

Another source of problems for mature teams is that their early successes are often due to having taken on easy tasks. It's normal for new teams to begin by taking on those issues and problems they can most easily handle. But as time passes, the easy problems are solved, and the team has to begin to tackle the more difficult issues. At this point, the team has frequently

Can rewards shape team members' behavior? That depends on the rewards offered. At Tape Resources, Inc., located in Virginia Beach, Virginia, rewards played a major role in team member behavior. Initially, incentives offered to just the sales team did not achieve the desired results. But when organizational members took it upon themselves to work together to benefit all employees, the team concept flourished, as did the company, with annual sales growth in the 24 percent range.

EXHIBIT 9–6

How to Reinvigorate Mature Teams

1. Prepare members to deal with the problems of maturity.
2. Offer refresher training.
3. Offer advanced training.
4. Encourage teams to treat their development as a constant learning experience.

established its processes and routines, and team members are often reluctant to change the workable system they have developed. When that happens, problems arise. Internal team processes no longer work smoothly. Communication bogs down, and conflict increases because problems are less likely to have obvious solutions. All in all, team performance may dramatically drop.

What can a manager do to reinvigorate mature teams—especially ones that are encountering the problems described above? We offer the following suggestions (see Exhibit 9–6). Prepare team members to deal with the problems of team maturity. Remind them that they are not unique. All successful teams eventually have to address maturity issues: Members shouldn't feel let down or lose their confidence in the team concept when the initial excitement subsides and conflicts begin to surface. When teams get into ruts, it may help to provide them with refresher training in communication, conflict resolution, team processes, and similar skills. This training can help team members regain their confidence and trust in each other. Offer advanced training. The skills that worked well with easy problems may be insufficient for some of the more difficult problems the team is addressing. Mature teams can often benefit from advanced training to help members develop stronger problem-solving, interpersonal, and technical skills. Encourage teams to treat their development as a constant learning experience. Just as organizations use continuous improvement programs, teams should approach their own development as part of a search for continuous improvement. Teams should look for ways to improve, to confront member and frustrations, and to use conflict as a learning opportunity.

CONTEMPORARY TEAM ISSUES

As we close this chapter, we will address two issues related to managing teams—continuous process improvement programs and diversity in teams.

WHY ARE TEAMS CENTRAL TO CONTINUOUS PROCESS IMPROVEMENT PROGRAMS?

One of the central characteristics of continuous process improvement programs is the use of teams. Why teams? Teams provide the natural vehicle for employees to share ideas and implement improvements. The essence of continuous improvement is process improvement, and employee participation is the linchpin of process improvement. In other words, continuous improvement requires management to encourage employees to share ideas and to act on what the employees suggest. As one author put it, "None of the various processes and techniques will catch on and be applied except in work teams. All such techniques and processes require high levels of communication and contact, response, adaptation, and coordination and sequencing. They require, in short, the environment that can be supplied only by superior work teams."[46]

HOW DOES WORKFORCE DIVERSITY AFFECT TEAMS?

Teams at Boeing have earned the respect of their peers by being recognized as one of America's best plant operations. How have they worked to achieve that honor? Part of their success is that each team sets its goals, which are critically linked to the organization's strategic plan. This includes a heavy emphasis on continuous improvements.

Managing diversity on teams is a balancing act. Diversity typically provides fresh perspectives on issues, but it makes it more difficult to unify the team and reach agreements. The strongest case for diversity on work teams arises when these teams are engaged in problem-solving and decision-making tasks.[47] Heterogeneous teams bring multiple perspectives to the discussion, thus increasing the likelihood that the team will identify creative or unique solutions.[48] Additionally, the lack of a common perspective usually means diverse teams spend more time discussing issues, which decreases the chances that a weak alternative will be chosen. However, keep in mind that the positive contribution that diversity makes to decision-making teams undoubtedly declines over time. As we pointed out in the previous chapter, diverse groups have more difficultly working together and solving problems, but this problem dissipates with time. Expect the value-added component of diverse teams to increase as members become more familiar with each other and the team becomes more cohesive.[49]

Studies tell us that members of cohesive teams have greater satisfaction, lower absenteeism, and lower attrition from the group.[50] Yet cohesiveness is likely to be lower on diverse teams. So here is a potential negative of diversity: It can be detrimental to group cohesiveness.[51] But again, referring to the previous chapter, the relationship between cohesiveness and group productivity is moderated by performance-related norms. We suggest that if the norms of the team are supportive of diversity, a team can maximize the value of heterogeneity while achieving the benefits of high cohesiveness. This makes a strong case for having team members participate in diversity training.[52]

Review, Comprehension, Application

CHAPTER SUMMARY

How will you know if you fulfilled the Learning Outcomes on page 256? You will have fulfilled the Learning Outcomes if you are able to:

1. **Explain the growing popularity of work teams in organizations.** Teams have become increasingly popular in organizations because they typically outperform individuals when the tasks require multiple skills, judgment, and experience. Teams are also more flexible and responsive to a changing environment. Teams may serve an effective means for management to enhance employee involvement, increase employee morale, and promote workforce diversity.
2. **Describe the five stages of team development.** The five stages of team development are forming, storming, norming, performing, and adjourning. In forming, people join the team and define the team's purpose, structure, and leadership. Storming is a stage of intragroup conflict over control issues. During the norming stage, close relationships develop and the team demonstrates cohesiveness. Performing is the stage at which the team is doing the task at hand. Finally, adjourning is the stage when teams with a limited task to perform prepare to be disbanded.
3. **Contrast work groups with work teams.** A work group interacts primarily to share information and to make decisions to help each member perform within his or her area of responsibility. Work groups have neither need nor opportunity to engage in collective work

that requires joint effort. Consequently, their performance is merely the summation of all the group members' individual contributions. There is no positive synergy that would create an overall level of performance greater than the sum of the inputs. A work team, on the other hand, generates positive synergy through a coordinated effort. Individual efforts result in a level of performance that is greater than the sum of those individual inputs.

4. **Identify four common types of work teams.** The four most popular types of teams are functional teams (a manager and the employees in his or her unit); problem-solving teams (typically 5 to 12 hourly employees from the same department who meet for a few hours each week to discuss ways of improving quality, efficiency, and the work environment); self-managed teams (a formal group of employees that operates without a manager and is responsible for a complete work process or segment that delivers a product or service to an external or internal customer); and cross-functional teams (employees from about the same hierarchical level but from different work areas in the organization, brought together to accomplish a particular task).
5. **Explain what types of teams entrepreneurial organizations use.** Entrepreneurial firms use teams because they are necessary to meet the technology and market demands the organization is facing. These include empowered functional teams (teams that have authority to plan and implement process improvements); self-directed teams (teams that are nearly autonomous and responsible for many activities that were once the jurisdiction of managers); and cross-functional teams (teams that include a hybrid grouping of individuals who are experts in various specialities and who work together on various tasks).
6. **List the characteristics of high-performing work teams.** High-performing work teams are characterized by clear goals, unified commitment, good communications, mutual trust, effective leadership, external support, internal support, negotiating skills, and relevant skills.
7. **Discuss how organizations can create team players.** Organizations can create team players by selecting individuals with the interpersonal skills to be effective team players, providing training to develop teamwork skills, and rewarding individuals for cooperative efforts.
8. **Explain how managers can keep teams from becoming stagnant.** As teams mature, they can become complacent. Managers need to support mature teams with appropriate advice, provide guidance where needed, and provide training to team members if these teams are to continue to improve.
9. **Describe the role of teams in continuous process improvement programs.** Continuous process improvement programs provide a natural vehicle for employees to share ideas and to implement improvements as part of the process. Teams are particularly effective for resolving complex problems.

COMPANION WEBSITE

We invite you to visit the Robbins/DeCenzo companion Website at **www.prehall.com/robbins** for this chapter's Internet resources, including an online study guide, Internet exercises, and "In the News" with full text articles provided by XanEdu.

READING FOR COMPREHENSION

1. Contrast (1) self-managed and cross-functional teams and (2) virtual and face-to-face teams.
2. What problems might surface in teams during each of the five stages of team development?
3. How do virtual teams enhance productivity?
4. In what ways can management invigorate stagnant teams?
5. Why do you believe mutual respect is important to developing high-performing work teams?

LINKING CONCEPTS TO PRACTICE

1. How do you explain the rapidly increasing popularity of work teams in countries such as the United States and Canada, whose national cultures place a high value on individualism?
2. "All work teams are work groups, but not all work groups are work teams." Do you agree or disagree with the statement? Discuss.
3. Would you prefer to work alone or as part of a team? Why? Support your response with data from your self-assessments.
4. Describe a situation in which individuals, acting independently, outperform teams in an organization.
5. Contrast the pros and cons of diverse teams.

VIDEO CASE APPLICATION

Engenia Software, Inc: Keeping Work Teams Productive 24/7

In 1999, as a result of his own frustration while working at IBM, CEO Jeffrey Crigler launched Engenia Software, Inc., based in Reston, VA. He was fascinated by the potential for network applications that would enable people to swap ideas, but was impatient with the slow pace of development at a large company like IBM.[53] With the introduction of Unity, Engenia has created a desktop that allows people inside and outside a corporation to collaborate across space and time. Jeffrey Crigler likens it to "having a very sophisticated beeper system" that allows users to keep track of every detail of a team project from a very high level. "It lets you concentrate on the underlying issues rather than running around and gathering up status," he says.

Joseph Rhyne is senior vice president of technology at Thompson Corporation, one of the world's largest online publishing companies. Regardless of where his travels take him, Rhyne uses Unity's digital "dashboard" to check on the exact status of the projects his teams are running without so much as an e-mail. "I can see if things are falling behind or need help," he says. Everything related to a project including documents, activities, and people shows up on the same customized, secured Web page. Any team member working anywhere in the world, at any time of day or night can be synchronized from his or her desktop to view the same page in real time.

Team members no longer have to worry about finding documents or about whose computer the files are on. "Even if the information is distributed all over the place," says Jeff Kay, chief technology officer, Engenia Software, Inc., Unity will bring it together. A user can access a workspace for a corporate project, get the latest changes made by co-workers and continue working online or off-line.

However, not even a sophisticated knowledge management tool like Unity can turn human beings into team players automatically. In our individualistic American culture, many ambitious people have long assumed that protecting knowledge is the path to power in the workplace. According to Ben Gottesman, executive editor, *PC Magazine*, "the Internet has made it very apparent that it is by exposing knowledge" within the context of teamwork that will give today's companies a competitive advantage. "But," says Gottesman, "it is taking time for individuals to realize that success lies in collaboration."

"Teams that we depend on to get our work done in most businesses are more and more becoming teams between companies," according to Jeffrey Crigley. "Businesses need to work with suppliers, outside contractors, consultants, and even people that might be competitors." Engenia's Unity uses intelligent "software agents" to help both virtual and brick-and-mortar companies coordinate the planning, execution, and reporting functions of complex projects.

Engenia Software, Inc.'s corporate literature describes Unity software as an innovative package that never sleeps, and is never distracted by meetings, travel, or other responsibilities. It is a software solution that does exactly what you would do if you had nothing else to do in life but spend 24 hours a day monitoring every step in your IT project.[54] The software reacts to obstacles in real-time and takes actions you want it to take as soon as the action is needed.

The header on Engenia's home page reads: "Always Current. Always Aware." Depending on your perspective, this could conjure up the quintessential butler who anticipates your every need or Big Brother watching your every move. As high-performing work teams become key to sustaining competitive advantage, businesses in all sectors will demand access to 'round the clock control. For as long as we still need to sleep, we will need software programs like Unity.

Questions

1. Briefly compare and contrast the advantages of Unity software to the manager of a virtual team like StrawberryFrog, with its benefits to the manager of a cross-functional team within a large corporation like General Electric.
2. Do you think that Unity's digital dashboard can help executives like Joseph Rhyne, senior vice president of technology, Thompson Corporation, to be more effective leaders? Explain.
3. According to Ben Gottesman, executive editor, *PC Magazine*, it is taking time for individuals to realize that success lies in collaboration or teamwork. What are some of the methods managers can use to ensure that their employees will perform well as members of a team?
4. If you are a fan of *PC Week*, you might have read a profile of Patrick Savage, a graduate of Virginia Polytechnic Institute and State University with a computer science degree. After six months of searching, he found his dream job as a software engineer at Engenia Software, Inc. He wanted a small innovative company where he could learn quickly, have access to new technologies, and a chance to make a difference. The article includes a picture of Patrick Savage riding a mountain bike against a beautiful sky and the following quote: "Engenia has a lot going for it. But I could also see myself moving on in a few years—there are just so many opportunities out there."[55] In your opinion will Patrick Savage make a good team player? Explain.

Management Workshop

Team Skill-Building Exercise

Building Effective Work Teams

Objective

This exercise is designed to allow class members to (1) experience working together as a team on a specific task and (2) analyze this experience.

Time

Teams will have 90 minutes to engage in steps 2 and 3. Another 45 to 60 minutes of class time will be used to critique and evaluate the exercise.

Procedure

1. Class members are assigned to teams of about six people.
2. Each team is required to:
   - **a.** Determine a team name
   - **b.** Compose a team song
3. Each team is to try to find the following items on its scavenger hunt:
   - **a.** A picture of a team
   - **b.** A newspaper article about a group or team
   - **c.** A piece of apparel with the college name or logo
   - **d.** A drinking straw
   - **e.** A ball of cotton
   - **f.** A piece of stationery from a college department
   - **g.** A Post-It™ pad
   - **h.** A 3.5" floppy disk
   - **i.** A beverage cup from McDonald's
   - **j.** A pet leash
   - **k.** A book by Ernest Hemingway
   - **l.** An ad brochure for a Ford product
   - **m.** A test tube
   - **n.** A pack of gum
   - **o.** A college catalog

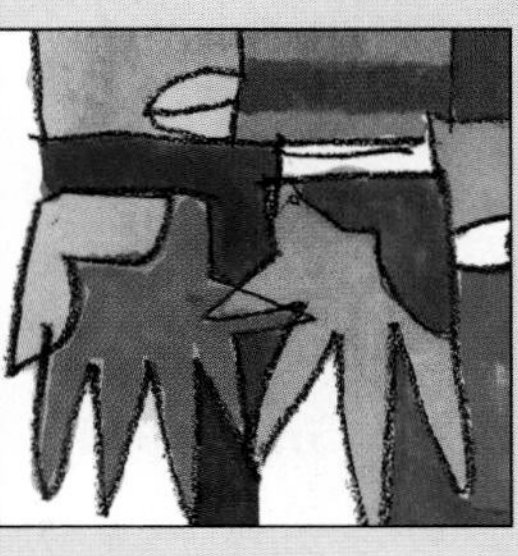

4. After 90 minutes, all teams are to be back in the classroom. (A penalty, determined by the instructor, will be imposed on late teams.) The team with the most items on the list will be declared the winner. The class and instructor will determine whether the items meet the requirements of the exercise.
5. Debriefing of the exercise will begin by having each team engage in self-evaluation. Specifically, each should answer the following:
   - **a.** What was the team's strategy?
   - **b.** What roles did individual members perform?
   - **c.** How effective was the team?
   - **d.** What could the team have done to be more effective?
6. Full class discussion will focus on issues such as:
   - **a.** What differentiated the more effective teams from the less effective teams?
   - **b.** What did you learn from this experience that is relevant to the design of effective teams?

Source: Adapted from M. R. Manning and P. J. Schmidt, "Building Effective Work Teams: A quick Exercise Based on a Scavenger Hunt," *Journal of Management Education* (August 1995): 392–98. © 1995. Reprinted by permission of Sage Publications, Inc.

Understanding Yourself

Before you can develop other people, you must understand your present strengths. To assist in this learning process, we encourage you to complete the following self-assessment from the Prentice Hall Self-Assessment Library 2.0:

- How Good Am I at Building and Leading a Team? (#30)

After you complete this assessment, we suggest that you print out the results and store them as part of your "portfolio of learning."

Developing Your Coaching Skill

Coaching Others

About the Skill

Effective managers are increasingly being described as coaches rather than bosses. Just like coaches, they're expected to provide instruction, guidance, advice, and encouragement to help team members improve their job performance.

Steps in Practicing the Skill

1. **Analyze ways to improve the team's performance and capabilities.** A coach looks for opportunities for team members to expand their capabilities and improve performance. How? You can use the following behaviors. Observe your team members' behaviors on a day-to-day basis. Ask questions of them: Why do you do a task this way? Can it be improved? What other approaches might be used? Show genuine interest in team members as individuals, not merely as employees. Respect them individually. Listen to each employee.
2. **Create a supportive climate.** It's the coach's responsibility to reduce barriers to development and to facilitate a climate that encourages personal performance improvement. How? You can use the following behaviors. Create a climate that contributes to a free and open exchange of ideas. Offer help and assistance. Give guidance and advice when asked. Encourage your team. Be positive and upbeat. Don't use threats. Ask, "What did we learn from this that can help us in the future?" Reduce obstacles. Assure team members that you value their contribution to the team's goals. Take personal responsibility for the outcome, but don't rob team members of their full responsibility. Validate the team members' efforts when they succeed. Point to what was missing when they fail. Never blame team members for poor results.
3. **Influence team members to change their behavior.** The ultimate test of coaching effectiveness is whether an employee's performance improves. You must encourage ongoing growth and development. How can you do this? Try the following behaviors. Recognize and reward small improvements and treat coaching as a way of helping employees to continually work toward improvement. Use a collaborative style by allowing team members to participate in identifying and choosing among improvement ideas. Break difficult tasks down into simpler ones. Model the qualities that you expect from your team. If you want openness, dedication, commitment, and responsibility from your team members, you must demonstrate these qualities yourself.

Practicing the Skill

Collaborative efforts are more successful when every member of the group or team contributes a specific role or task toward the completion of the goal. To improve your skill at nurturing team effort, choose two of the following activities and break each one into at least six to eight separate tasks or steps. Be sure to indicate which steps are sequential, and which can be done simultaneously with others. What do you think is the ideal team size for each activity you choose?

- **a.** Making an omelet
- **b.** Washing the car
- **c.** Creating a computerized mailing list
- **d.** Designing an advertising poster
- **e.** Planning a ski trip
- **f.** Restocking a supermarket's produce department

Developing Your Diagnostic and Analytical Skills

Tape Resources

Tape Resources is what many individuals would consider a classic small company. Headquartered in Virginia Beach, Virginia, Tape Resources sells blank videotapes and audiotapes to businesses like television stations and production companies. Some of its most popular tapes—from manufacturers such as Sony, Fuji, Maxell, and Panasonic—carry price tags ranging from $10 to $25. The company doesn't try to compete on price. Rather, its strategy is to offer superior customer service, or as company officials call it, "Legendary Customer Service." For many of its customers, this means that Tape Resources provides a guaranteed in-stock program and speedy delivery.[56]

The company has about 15 employees and annual sales approaching the $20 million mark. Its early sales grew more than 700 percent in just six short years. The company's owner, Seph Barnard, wanted that trend to continue. So he implemented a plan that he thought would excite his sales staff and promote teamwork among them. Salespeople at Tape Resources fill orders from repeat customers as well as from new ones who contact the company as a result of advertising campaigns. Once the sale is completed, it goes to the shipping department for packaging and delivery. Barnard added a commission incentive on top of the sales staff's salaries, but the new program was met with almost immediate resistance. Tension among staff became rampant. That's because the salespeople worked in the same offices as everyone else, but now they had an opportunity to make significantly more money than other employees. Employees who had been excluded from the incentive program—like those in shipping—became resentful.

Somewhat surprisingly, even the salespeople who would benefit from the added income started to have difficulties. Whereas once the salespeople cooperated and covered for one another, they now became reluctant to spend time away from the phones or to help others on specific tasks. They also didn't like it when another salesperson served a customer they had helped earlier—thereby taking away their commission. As a result of Barnard's "great incentive program," nearly all of the company's employees had become territorial and began looking out for "number one." Within six months, Barnard realized that he had made a mistake. All he wanted to do was to increase sales. Instead, his incentive plan increased resentment among team members.

While Barnard has since given up much of the control of his company to his chief operating officer, and takes frequent sabbaticals from work, his efforts have not been a waste of time. Employees took it upon themselves to recognize the importance of a team concept where all employees can benefit as the company benefits. For example, many of the employees formed a special team to win a sales contest sponsored by a tape manufacturer, which earned them an all-expenses-paid trip to Cancun, Mexico. It appears that when they, as a group, saw the benefit for all employees and not a select few, the team camaraderie and company good that Barnard had hoped for came to fruition—with annual sales increases in the 24 percent range.

Questions

1. Why do you believe the sales team incentive system failed? Cite specific examples to support your position.
2. While the initial "team concept" failed, employees later used many of the team concepts that ultimately worked for them—and made the organization grow. Why do you believe the "employee-formed" team was successful?
3. Using the nine characteristics of a high-performing work team (refer to Exhibit 9–4), describe each of the nine elements as they relate to this case. Use examples where appropriate. If a characteristic was not specifically cited in the case, describe how it may have been witnessed in this situation.

Enhancing Your Communication Skills

1. Teams create conflict among their members, and conflict can lead to lower productivity. Management, then, should not support the concept of teams. Build one argument to support this statement and another to show why the statement is false. Then, take a position on one side of the controversy and support your opinion.
2. Describe why work teams are more acceptable in Japan than in the United States or Canada. Explain how Japanese firms in the United States can still use teams even though the cultural dimensions are different.
3. Develop a presentation explaining whether you would prefer to work alone or as part of a team. What does your response indicate in terms of organizational cultures in which you might work? Explain.

CHAPTER 10

Motivating and Rewarding Employees

LEARNING OUTCOMES

After reading this chapter, I will be able to:

1. Describe the motivation process.
2. Define needs.
3. Explain the hierarchy of needs theory.
4. Differentiate Theory X from Theory Y.
5. Explain the motivational implications of the motivation-hygiene theory.
6. Describe the motivational implications of equity theory.
7. Explain the key relationships in expectancy theory.
8. Describe how managers can design individual jobs to maximize employee performance.
9. Explain the effect of workforce diversity on motivational practices.
10. Describe how entrepreneurs motivate their employees.

MEET A REAL MANAGER!

"One Manager's Reflection" Page 296

Mark Boice, Vice President, Warner Bodies

Angel Lorenzo (see photo) is a shift supervisor at Grupo M, the largest private employer in the Dominican Republic.[1] The company's 13,000 employees make clothes for Abercrombie & Fitch, Hugo Boss, and Tommy Hilfiger in 26 factories. Lorenzo began working at Grupo M as a sewing machine operator and then was promoted to quality control inspector. Now, Lorenzo manages 14 teams of machine operators.

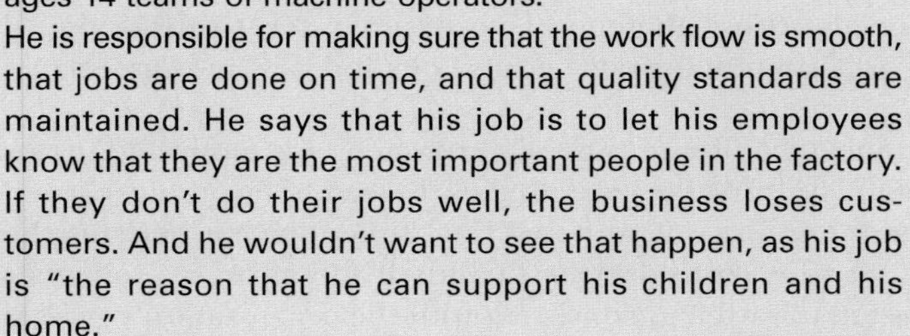

He is responsible for making sure that the work flow is smooth, that jobs are done on time, and that quality standards are maintained. He says that his job is to let his employees know that they are the most important people in the factory. If they don't do their jobs well, the business loses customers. And he wouldn't want to see that happen, as his job is "the reason that he can support his children and his home."

Grupo M defies the stereotypical image of garment manufacturers found in many third world countries. The company is not a sweatshop nor does it employ child labor. Its factories are clean, brightly lit, and nice places to work. And in a land of expansive poverty, Grupo M employees receive excellent pay and benefits. Their pay rates are nearly double the country's minimum wage levels. The company also lends money to employees to buy cars. If the vehicles they purchase are in need of service, they take them to the company garage where they are serviced at no cost to the employee. Employees also enjoy medical treatment at a company facility—again at no cost to them. And many of the employees bring their children to work with them and place them in the company's day care facility.

Fernando Capellan, the company's founder, envisioned an exemplary business that would be an innovator in the garment industry. Grupo M has earned a reputation as a remarkably progressive employer with cutting-edge labor practices. For instance, the company recently earned a corporate conscience award (from the U.S.-based Council on Economic Priorities) for "empowering employees," putting it on par with organizations like IBM and Pfizer. Capellan says, "We have proven that you don't have to run a factory like a sweatshop in order to be profitable and to grow. In fact, we believe that we have been able to innovate, to expand, and to do what we have done because of the way that we treat our people. Everything that we give to our workers gets returned to us in terms of efficiency, quality, loyalty, and innovation. It's just smart business."

And smart business it has become, as Grupo M is now the largest employer in the Dominican Republic. Through the efforts of its employees, the company is growing nearly 20 percent each year. Employee turnover is nearly nonexistent. Fernando Capellan understands that treating employees well can pay off in terms of employee motivation and company productivity.

IN THIS CHAPTER, WE PROVIDE INSIGHT INTO HOW MANAGERS can utilize motivation techniques to maximize employee behavior. We begin by defining motivation.

MOTIVATION AND INDIVIDUAL NEEDS

To understand what motivation is, let us begin by pointing out what motivation isn't. Why? Because some individuals incorrectly view motivation as a personal trait—that is, they think that some have it and others don't. In practice, this attitude would characterize the manager who labels a certain employee as unmotivated. Our knowledge of motivation, though, tells us that people can't be labeled in this way. We know that motivation is the result of the interaction between the individual and the situation which he or she faces. Certainly, individuals differ in motivational drive, but an individual's motivation varies from situation to situation. As we analyze the concept of motivation, keep in mind that level of motivation varies both among individuals and within individuals at different times.

We define **motivation** as the willingness to exert high levels of effort to reach organizational goals, conditioned by the effort's ability to satisfy some individual need. In less academic terms, motivation is a function of three key elements—effort,

motivation
The willingness to exert high levels of effort to reach organizational goals, conditioned by the effort's ability to satisfy some individual need

EXHIBIT 10–1 The Motivation Process

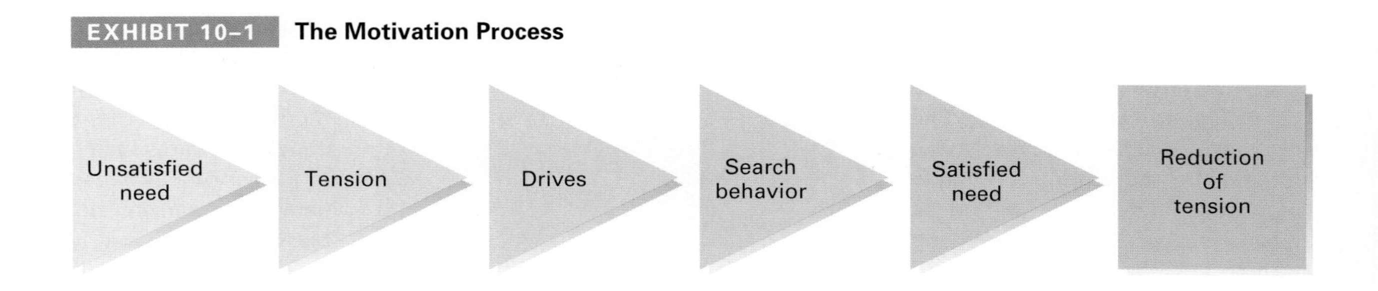

organizational goals, and needs. Although general motivation refers to effort toward any goal, here it refers to organizational goals because our focus is on work-related behavior.

The *effort* element is a measure of intensity. When someone is motivated, he or she tries hard. However, high levels of effort are unlikely to lead to favorable job performance outcomes unless the effort is channeled in a direction that benefits the organization.[2] Therefore, we must consider the quality of the effort as well as its intensity. Effort that is directed toward and consistent with the organization's goals is the kind of effort that we should be seeking. Finally, we treat motivation as a need-satisfying process. This is depicted in Exhibit 10–1.

need
An internal state that makes certain outcomes appear attractive

A **need**, in our definition, is some internal state that makes certain outcomes appear attractive. An unsatisfied need creates tension that stimulates drives within an individual. These drives generate a search behavior to find particular goals that, if attained, will satisfy the need and reduce the tension.

We can say that motivated employees are in a state of tension. To relieve this tension, they exert effort. The greater the tension, the higher the effort level. If this effort successfully leads to the satisfaction of the need, it reduces tension. Because we are interested in work behavior, this tension-reduction effort must also be directed toward organizational goals. Therefore, inherent in our definition of motivation is the requirement that the individual's needs be compatible and consistent with the organization's goals. When they aren't, individuals may exert high levels of effort that run counter to the interests of the organization. Incidentally, this situation is not so unusual. You may find that some employees spend a lot of time talking with friends at work, surfing their favorite Web sites, or playing computer games in order to satisfy their social needs. There is a high level of effort, but from an organizational perspective, it's being unproductively directed.

EARLY THEORIES OF MOTIVATION

The 1950s were a fruitful time for the development of motivation concepts. Three specific theories were formulated during this period that, although heavily attacked and now considered questionable, are probably still the best known explanations of employee motivation. These are the hierarchy of needs theory, Theories X and Y, and the motivation-hygiene theory. Although more valid explanations of motivation have been developed, you should know these early theories for at least two reasons. First, they represent the foundation from which contemporary theories grew. Second, practicing managers regularly use these theories and their terminology in explaining employee motivation. Let's take a look at them.

heirarchy of needs theory
Maslow's theory that there is a hierarchy of five human needs: physiological, safety, social, esteem, and self-actualization; as each need becomes satisfied, the next need becomes dominant

WHAT IS MASLOW'S HIERARCHY OF NEEDS THEORY?

Probably the best known theory of motivation is psychologist Abraham Maslow's **hierarchy of needs theory**.[3] He stated that within every human being exists a hierarchy of five types of needs. These include:

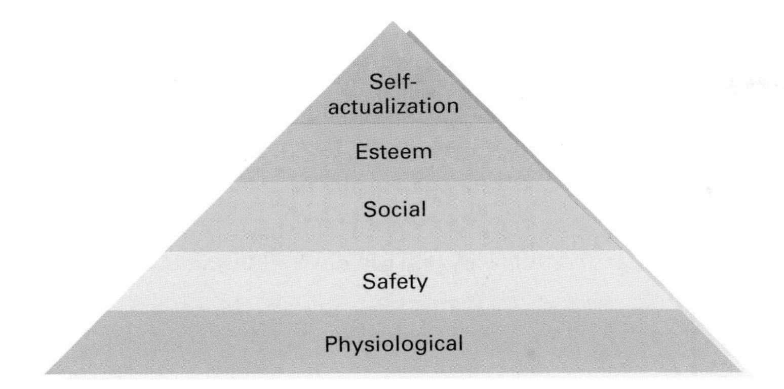

EXHIBIT 10–2
Maslow's Hierarchy of Needs
Source: *Motivation and Personality*, 2nd ed., by A. H. Maslow, 1970. Reprinted by permission of Prentice Hall, Inc., Upper Saddle River, New Jersey.

- ***Physiological needs*** Food, drink, shelter, sexual satisfaction, and other bodily requirements
- ***Safety needs*** Security and protection from physical and emotional harm
- ***Social needs*** Affection, belongingness, acceptance, and friendship
- ***Esteem needs*** Internal esteem factors such as self-respect, autonomy, and achievement and external esteem factors such as status, recognition, and attention
- ***Self-actualization needs*** Growth, achieving one's potential, and self-fulfillment; the drive to become what one is capable of becoming

As each level of need is substantially satisfied, the next need becomes dominant. As shown in Exhibit 10–2, the individual moves up the hierarchy. From a motivation viewpoint, the theory says that, although no need is ever fully gratified, a substantially satisfied need no longer motivates. If you want to motivate someone, according to Maslow, you need to understand where that person is in the hierarchy and focus on satisfying needs at or above that level.

Maslow's need theory has received wide recognition, particularly among practicing managers.[4] Its popularity can be attributed to the theory's intuitive logic and ease of understanding.[5] Unfortunately, however, research does not generally validate the theory. Maslow provided no empirical substantiation for his theory, and several studies that sought to validate it found no support.[6]

WHAT IS MCGREGOR'S THEORY X AND THEORY Y?

Douglas McGregor proposed two distinct views of the nature of human beings: a basically negative view, labeled **Theory X**, and a basically positive view, labeled **Theory Y**.[7] After viewing the way managers dealt with employees, McGregor concluded that a manager's view of human nature is based on a group of assumptions, either positive or negative (see Exhibit 10–3), and that the manager molds his or her behavior toward employees according to these suppositions.

Theory X
McGregor's term for the assumption that employees dislike work, are lazy, seek to avoid responsibility, and must be coerced to perform

Theory Y
McGregor's term for the assumption that employees are creative, seek responsibility, and can exercise self-direction

What does McGregor's analysis imply about motivation? The answer is best expressed in the framework presented by Maslow. Theory X assumes that physiological and safety needs dominate the individual. Theory Y assumes that social and esteem needs are dominant. McGregor himself held to the belief that the assumptions of Theory Y were more valid than those of Theory X. Therefore, he proposed that participation in decision making, responsible and challenging jobs, and good group relations would maximize work effort.

Unfortunately, there is no evidence to confirm that either set of assumptions is valid or that accepting Theory Y assumptions and altering one's actions accordingly will make one's employees more motivated. In the real world, effective managers do make Theory X assumptions. For instance, when Bob McCurry was vice president of Toyota's U.S.

EXHIBIT 10–3 Theory X and Theory Y Premises

THEORY X: A MANAGER WHO VIEWS EMPLOYEES FROM A THEORY X (NEGATIVE) PERSPECTIVE BELIEVES:
1 Employees inherently dislike work and, whenever possible, will attempt to avoid it.
2 Because employees dislike work, they must be coerced, controlled, or threatened with punishment to achieve desired goals.
3 Employees will shirk responsibilities and seek formal direction whenever possible.
4 Most workers place security above all other factors associated with work and will display little ambition.

THEORY Y: A MANAGER WHO VIEWS EMPLOYEES FROM A THEORY Y (POSITIVE) PERSPECTIVE BELIEVES:
1 Employees can view work as being as natural as rest or play.
2 Men and women will exercise self-direction and self-control if they are committed to the objectives.
3 The average person can learn to accept, even seek, responsibility.
4 The ability to make good decisions is widely dispersed throughout the population and is not necessarily the sole province of managers.

marketing operations, he essentially followed Theory X. He drove his staff hard and used a "crack the whip" style, yet he was been extremely successful at increasing Toyota's market share in a highly competitive environment. Moreover, former Warnco and Authentic Fitness CEO Linda Wachner was also Theory X oriented—oftentimes characterized as a combative, ruthless taskmaster, who took a $3 million investment and built a $1 billion company—before the company went bankrupt in 2002.[8]

Is there support for Maslow's Hierarchy of Needs theory of motivation in business today? That depends on whom you talk to. Although rigorous empirical research in academe has been unable to support the theory, people like Scott Litman, CEO of the Minneapolis-based e-commerce services firm, Imaginet, believes in it. As Litman puts it, "It's nice after a long week to get together to relax." Under Maslow's theory, we can conclude that Litman is expressing fulfillment of a social need.

WHAT IS HERZBERG'S MOTIVATION-HYGIENE THEORY?

The **motivation-hygiene theory** was proposed by psychologist Frederick Herzberg.[9] Believing that an individual's attitude toward his or her work can very well determine success or failure, Herzberg investigated the question of what people want from their jobs. He asked people to describe, in detail, situations in which they felt exceptionally good or bad about their jobs. Their responses were then tabulated and categorized. Exhibit 10–4 represents Herzberg's findings.

After analyzing the responses, Herzberg concluded that the replies of people who felt good about their jobs were significantly different from the replies they gave when they disliked their jobs. As seen in Exhibit 10–4, certain characteristics were consistently related to job satisfaction (on the left side of the figure) and others to job dissatisfaction (on the right side of the figure). *Intrinsic factors* such as achievement, recognition, and responsibility were related to job satisfaction.[10] When the people questioned felt good about their work, they tended to attribute these characteristics to themselves. On the other hand, when they were dissatisfied, they tended to cite extrinsic factors such as company policy and administration, supervision, interpersonal relationships, and working conditions.

The data suggest, said Herzberg, that the opposite of satisfaction is not dissatisfaction, as was traditionally believed. Removing dissatisfying characteristics from a job does not necessarily make the job satisfying. As illustrated in Exhibit 10–5, Herzberg proposed that his findings indicate that the opposite of "satisfaction" is "no satisfaction" and the opposite of "dissatisfaction" is "no dissatisfaction."

According to Herzberg, the factors that lead to job satisfaction are separate and distinct from those that lead to job dissatisfaction.

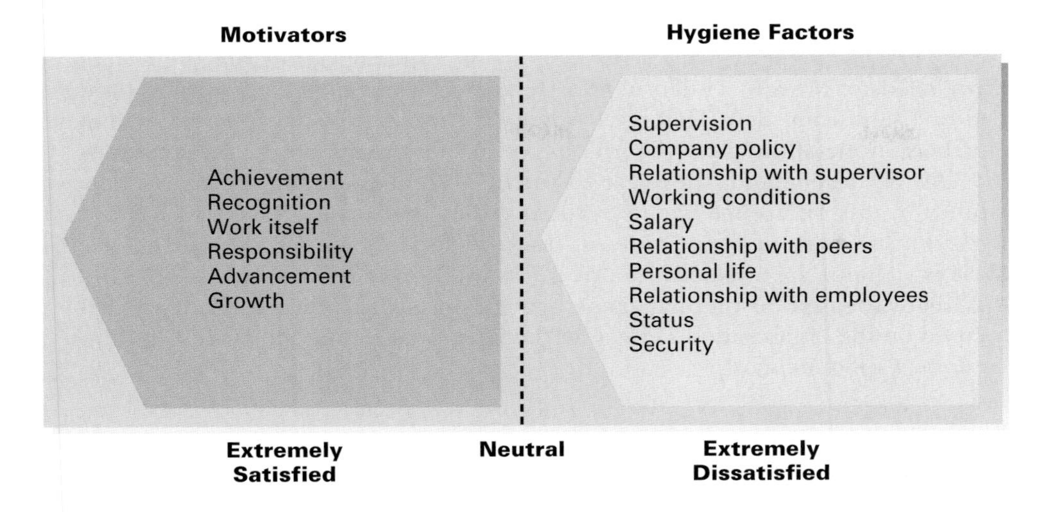

EXHIBIT 10-4
Herzberg's Motivation-Hygiene Theory

Therefore, managers who seek to eliminate factors that create job dissatisfaction can bring about peace but not necessarily motivation: They are placating their workforce rather than motivating it. Because they don't motivate employees, the factors that eliminate job dissatisfaction were characterized by Herzberg as **hygiene factors**. When these factors are adequate, people will not be dissatisfied, but neither will they be satisfied. To motivate people on their jobs, Herzberg suggested emphasizing **motivators**, those factors that increase job satisfaction.

The motivation-hygiene theory is not without its detractors, who criticize, for example, the methodology Herzberg used to collect data and his failure to account for situational variables.[11] Regardless of any criticism, Herzberg's theory has been widely popularized, and few managers are unfamiliar with his recommendations. Much of the enthusiasm for enriching jobs—that is, making them more challenging and giving more autonomy to work—can be attributed to Herzberg's findings and recommendations.

motivation-hygiene theory
Herzberg's theory that intrinsic factors are related to job satisfaction and extrinsic factors are related to job dissatisfaction

hygiene factors
Herzberg's term for factors, such as working conditions and salary, that, when adequate, may eliminate job dissatisfaction but do not necessarily increase job satisfaction

motivators
Herzberg's term for factors, such as recognition and growth, that increase job satisfaction

WHAT ARE THE SIMILARITIES AND DIFFERENCES AMONG THE EARLY THEORIES OF MOTIVATION?

Two critical questions posed about the early theories of motivation are: "How are they alike?" and "How are they different?". With close examination of the three theories, we can suggest the following.

Each of the three theories, as we mentioned earlier, is popular in the literature and practicing managers' minds. They make sense because they are intuitively logical. Each theory includes some lower-order and some higher-order needs. For

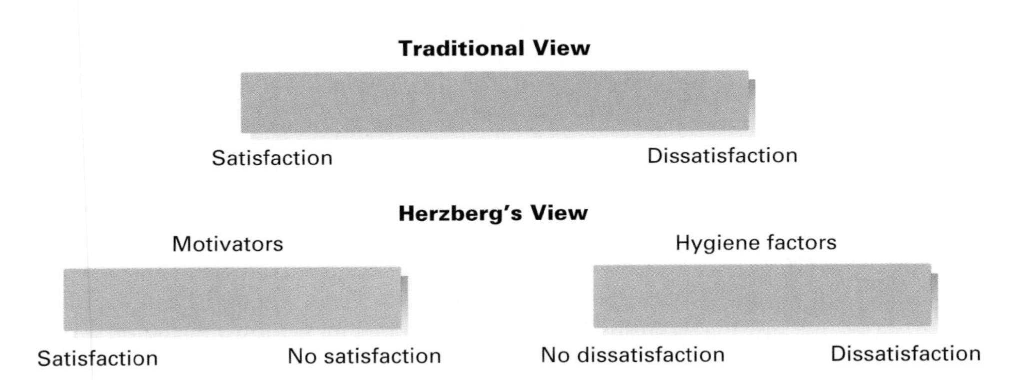

EXHIBIT 10-5
Contrasting Views of Satisfaction-Dissatisfaction

instance, Maslow's physiological and safety needs, McGregor's Theory X, and Herzberg's Hygiene factors are very similar in context. So, too, are the remaining three needs of Maslow, Theory Y, and Herzberg's Motivators. Each of the three has had one significant flaw. That is, as originally proposed by Maslow, McGregor, and Herzberg, none of the three theories has been substantiated by further research.

On the other hand, there are distinct differences among the three theories. Ironically, this difference is one of focus rather than context. That is, while each looked at motivation of individuals, they did so from a different perspective. In Maslow's Hierarchy of Needs theory, he focused on individual needs—or the self. McGregor focused on the manager's perception of the individual, while Herzberg focused on the organization's effect on the individual. Three similar results differentiated by a unique focus!

CONTEMPORARY THEORIES OF MOTIVATION

Although the three previous theories are well known, they unfortunately have not held up well under close examination. However, all is not lost. There are contemporary theories that all have reasonable degrees of valid supporting documentation. The following theories represent the contemporary views of employee motivation.

WHAT IS MCCLELLAND'S THREE-NEEDS THEORY?

three-needs theory
McClelland's theory that the needs for achievement, power, and affiliation are major motives in work

David McClelland and others have proposed the **three-needs theory**, which maintains that there are three major relevant motives or needs in work situations:

- ***Need for achievement (nAch)*** The drive to excel, to achieve in relation to a set of standards, to strive to succeed
- ***Need for power (nPow)*** The need to make others behave in a way that they would not have behaved otherwise
- ***Need for affiliation (nAff)*** The desire for friendly and close interpersonal relationships[12]

need for achievement
The drive to excel, to achieve in relation to a set of standards, and to strive to succeed

Some people have a compelling drive to succeed, but they are striving for personal achievement rather than for the rewards of success per se (nAch). They have a desire to do something better or more efficiently than it has been done before. This drive is the **need for achievement**. From his research on the achievement need, McClelland concluded that high achievers differentiate themselves by their desire to do things better.[13] They seek situations (1) in which they can assume personal responsibility for finding solutions to problems; (2) in which they can receive rapid and unambiguous feedback on their performance in order to tell whether they are improving; and (3) in which they can set moderately challenging goals (see Details on a Management Classic). High achievers are not gamblers; they dislike succeeding by chance. They prefer the challenge of working at a problem and accepting the personal responsibility for success or failure rather than leaving the outcome to chance or the actions of others. An important point is that they avoid what they perceive to be very easy or very difficult tasks.

need for power
The need to make others behave in a way that they would not have behaved otherwise

need for affiliation
The desire for friendly and close interpersonal relationships

The **need for power** (*nPow*) is the desire to have impact and to be influential. Individuals high in nPow enjoy being in charge, strive for influence over others, and prefer to be in competitive and status-oriented situations. The third need isolated by McClelland is the **need for affiliation** (*nAff*), which is the desire to be liked and accepted by others. This need has received the least attention from researchers. Individuals with high nAff strive for friendships, prefer cooperative situations rather than competitive ones, and desire relationships involving a high degree of mutual understanding.

Details on a Management Classic

David McClelland and the Three-Needs Theory

David McClelland helped us to understand motivation in an organizational setting by focusing on aspects of personality characteristics. Much of his research centered on achievement, power, and affiliation orientations. McClelland found that some people have a compelling drive to succeed for personal achievement rather than for rewards of success per se. The questions then are: How do you find out if someone is, for instance, a high achiever? What effect can that person's need for achievement have on an organization?[14]

In his research, McClelland used a projective test in which subjects responded to a set of pictures. Each picture was briefly shown to a subject, who then wrote a story based on the picture. The responses were then classified by McClelland as focusing on a need for achievement, power, or affiliation. Subjects who had a high need for achievement, however, shared some similarities.

High achievers perform best when they perceive their probability of success as being about 50 percent—that is, when they estimate they have a 50-50 chance of success. They dislike gambling when the odds are high because they get no satisfaction from happenstance success. Similarly, they dislike low odds (high probability of success) because then there is no challenge to their skills. They like to set goals that require stretching themselves a little. When there is an approximately equal chance of success or failure, there is optimum opportunity to feel successful and satisfied.

On the basis of extensive research, some reasonably well supported predictions can be made about the relationship of the achievement need and job performance. Although less research has been done on power and affiliation needs when compared to achievement needs, there are consistent findings in those areas, too. First, individuals with a high need for achievement prefer job situations with personal responsibility, feedback, and an intermediate degree of risk. When these characteristics are prevalent, high achievers are strongly motivated. The evidence consistently demonstrates, for instance, that high achievers are successful in entrepreneurial activities such as running their own businesses, managing self-contained units within a large organization, and in many sales positions. Second, a high need to achieve does not necessarily indicate that someone is a good manager—especially in large organizations. A high nAch salesperson at Hitachi, Ltd., does not necessarily make a good sales manager, and good sales managers in large organizations like General Electric or Unilever do not necessarily have a high need to achieve. Third, needs for affiliation and power are closely related to managerial success. The best managers are high in the need for power and low in the need for affiliation. Last, employees can be trained to stimulate their achievement need. If a job calls for a high achiever, management can select a person with a high nAch or develop its own candidate through achievement training.

HOW DO INPUTS AND OUTCOMES INFLUENCE MOTIVATION?

Employees don't work in a vacuum. They make comparisons. If someone offered you $60,000 a year on your first job upon graduation from college, you would probably grab the offer and report to work enthusiastic and certainly satisfied with your pay. But how would you react if you found out a month or so into the job that a co-worker—another recent graduate, your age, with comparable grades from a comparable college—was getting $65,000 a year? You probably would be upset. Even though, in absolute terms, $60,000 is a lot of money for a new graduate to make (and you know it!), that suddenly would not be the issue. The issue would now center on relative rewards and what you believe is fair. There is considerable evidence that employees make comparisons of their job inputs and outcomes relative to others and that inequities influence the degree of effort that employees exert.[15]

Developed by J. Stacey Adams, **equity theory** says that employees perceive what they get from a job situation (*outcomes*) in relation to what they put into it (*inputs*) and then compare their input-outcome ratio with the input-outcome ratios of relevant others. This relationship is shown in Exhibit 10–6. If workers perceive their ratio to be equal to those of the relevant others with whom they compare themselves, a state of equity exists. They perceive that their situation is fair—that justice prevails. If the ratios are unequal, inequity exists; that is, workers view themselves as underrewarded or overrewarded. When inequities occur, employees attempt to correct them.

equity theory
Adams's theory that employees perceive what they get from a job situation (outcomes) in relation to what they put into it (inputs) and then compare their input-outcome ratio with the input-outcome ratios of relevant others

EXHIBIT 10–6
Equity Theory Relationships

PERCEIVED RATIO COMPARISON*	EMPLOYEE'S ASSESSMENT
$\frac{\text{Outcomes A}}{\text{Inputs A}} < \frac{\text{Outcomes B}}{\text{Inputs B}}$	Inequity (underrewarded)
$\frac{\text{Outcomes A}}{\text{Inputs A}} = \frac{\text{Outcomes B}}{\text{Inputs B}}$	Equity
$\frac{\text{Outcomes A}}{\text{Inputs A}} > \frac{\text{Outcomes B}}{\text{Inputs B}}$	Inequity (overrewarded)

* Person A is the employee, and Person B is a relevant other or referent.

referent
In equity theory, the other persons, the systems, or the personal experiences against which individuals compare themselves to assess equity

The **referent** with whom employees choose to compare themselves is an important variable in equity theory.[16] The three referent categories have been classified as "other," "system," and "self." The *other* category includes individuals with similar jobs in the same organization and friends, neighbors, or professional associates. On the basis of information through word of mouth, newspapers, and magazine articles on issues such as executive salaries or a recent union contract, employees compare their pay with that of others.

The *system* category considers organizational pay policies and procedures and the administration of that system. It considers organization-wide pay policies, both implied and explicit. Patterns by the organization in terms of allocation of pay are major determinants in this category.

The *self* category refers to input-outcome ratios that are unique to the individual. It reflects personal experiences and contacts. This category is influenced by criteria such as previous jobs or family commitments.

The choice of a particular set of referents is related to the information available about referents as well as to the perceived relevance. On the basis of equity theory, when employees perceive an inequity, they might (1) distort either their own or others' inputs or outcomes, (2) behave so as to induce others to change their inputs or outcomes, (3) behave so as to change their own inputs or outcomes, (4) choose a different comparison referent, and/or (5) quit their job.

Equity theory recognizes that individuals are concerned not only with the absolute rewards they receive for their efforts, but also with the relationship of those rewards to what others receive.[17] They make judgments concerning the relationship between their inputs and outcomes and the inputs and outcomes of others. On the basis of one's inputs, such as effort, experience, education, and competence, one compares outcomes such as salary levels, raises, recognition, and other factors. When people perceive an imbalance in their input-outcome ratio relative to those of others, they experience tension. This tension provides the basis for motivation as people strive for what they perceive to be equity and fairness.

The theory establishes four propositions relating to inequitable pay, listed in Exhibit 10–7, that have generally been proven to be correct.[18] Research consistently confirms the equity thesis: Employee motivation is influenced significantly by relative rewards as well as by absolute rewards. Whenever employees perceive inequity, they will act to correct the situation.[19] The result might be lower or higher productivity, improved or reduced quality of output, increased absenteeism, or voluntary resignation.

However, from the preceding discussion, we should not conclude that equity theory is without problems. The theory leaves some key issues still unclear.[20] For instance, how do employees define inputs and outcomes? How do they combine and weigh their inputs and outcomes to arrive at totals? When and how do the factors change over time? Regardless of these problems, equity theory has an impressive amount of research support and offers us some important insights into employee motivation.

EXHIBIT 10–7
Equity Theory Propositions

1 **If paid according to time, overrewarded employees will produce more than equitably paid employees.** Hourly and salaried employees will generate a high quantity or quality of production in order to increase the input side of the ratio and bring about equity.

2 **If paid according to quantity of production, overrewarded employees will produce fewer but higher-quality units than equitably paid employees.** Individuals paid on a piece-rate basis will increase their effort to achieve equity, which can result in greater quality or quantity. However, increases in quantity will only increase inequity, because every unit produced results in further overpayment. Therefore, effort is directed toward increasing quality rather than quantity.

3 **If paid according to time, underrewarded employees will produce less or poorer-quality output.** Effort will be decreased, which will bring about lower productivity or poorer-quality output than equitably paid subjects produce.

4 **If paid according to quantity of production, underrewarded employees will produce a large number of low-quality units in comparison with equitably paid employees.** Employees on piece-rate pay plans can bring about equity because trading off quality of output for quantity will increase rewards with little or no increase in contributions.

DOES JOB DESIGN INFLUENCE MOTIVATION?

What differentiates one job from another? We know that a traveling salesperson's job is different from that of an emergency room nurse. And we know that both of those jobs have little in common with the job of an editor in a newsroom or that of a component assembler on a production line. But what is it that allows us to draw these distinctions? We can answer these questions through the **job characteristics model (JCM)** developed by J. Richard Hackman and Greg R. Oldham.[21]

According to Hackman and Oldham, any job can be described in terms of the following five core job dimensions:

1. **Skill variety** The degree to which the job requires a variety of activities so the worker can use a number of different skills and talents
2. **Task identity** The degree to which the job requires completion of a whole and identifiable piece of work
3. **Task significance** The degree to which the job affects the lives or work of other people
4. **Autonomy** The degree to which the job provides freedom, independence, and discretion to the individual in scheduling the work and in determining the procedures to be used in carrying it out
5. **Feedback** The degree to which carrying out the work activities required by the job results in the individual's obtaining direct and clear information about the effectiveness of his or her performance

Exhibit 10–8 presents the model. Notice how the first three dimensions—skill variety, task identity, and task significance—combine to create meaningful work. What we mean is that if these three characteristics exist in a job, we can predict that the person will view his job as being important, valuable, and worthwhile. Notice, too, that jobs that possess autonomy give the job incumbent a feeling of personal responsibility for the results and that, if a job provides feedback, the employee will know how effectively he or she is performing.

From a motivational point of view, the JCM suggests that internal rewards are obtained when an employee *learns* (knowledge of results

What is it that will make Shakibria Anderson's job as a consultant with the Los Angeles-based consulting firm Monitor meaningful? Is it her starting salary in excess of $50,000? According to the JCM, three dimensions—skill variety, task identity, and task significance—combine to provide the main elements of motivation. In addition, Shakibria's ability to work autonomously and receive proper feedback will assist in creating that meaningful and productive job.

EXHIBIT 10–8

The Job Characteristics Model

Source: J. R. Hackman, "Work Design," in J. R. Hackman and J. L. Suttle, eds., *Improving Life at Work* (Glenview, IL: Scott, Foresman, 1977), p. 129.

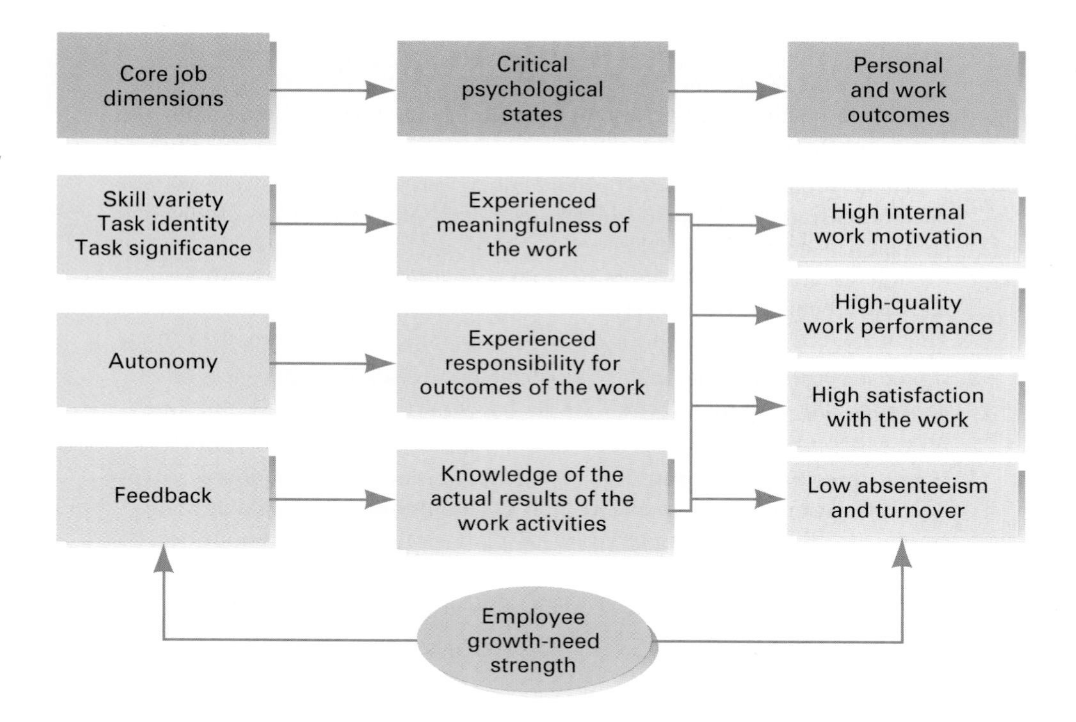

job characteristics model (JCM) Hackman and Oldham's job description model: The five core job dimensions are skill variety, task identity, task significance, autonomy, and feedback

job enrichment Vertically expanding a job by adding planning and evaluation responsibilities.

through feedback) that he or she *personally* (experienced responsibility through autonomy of work) has performed well on a task that he or she *cares* about (experienced meaningfulness through skill variety, task identity, and/or task significance). The more these three conditions characterize a job, the greater the employee's motivation, performance, and satisfaction and the lower his or her absenteeism and the likelihood of resigning. As the model shows, the links between the job dimensions and the outcomes are moderated by the strength of the individuals's growth need (the person's desire for self-esteem and self-actualization). This means that individuals are more likely to experience the critical psychological states and respond positively when their jobs include the core dimensions than are individuals with a low growth need. This may explain the mixed results with **job enrichment** (vertical expansion of a job by adding planning and evaluation responsibilities): Individuals with low growth need don't tend to achieve high performance or satisfaction by having their jobs enriched.

The JCM provides significant guidance to managers for job design for both individuals and teams (see Exhibit 10–9).[22] The suggestions in Exhibit 10–9, which are based on the JCM, specify the types of changes in jobs that are most likely to improve in each of the five core job dimensions.

EXHIBIT 10–9

Guidelines for Job Redesign

Source: J. R. Hackman and J. L. Suttle eds., *Improving Life at Work* (Glenview. IL: Scott. Foresman. 1977). With permission of the authors.

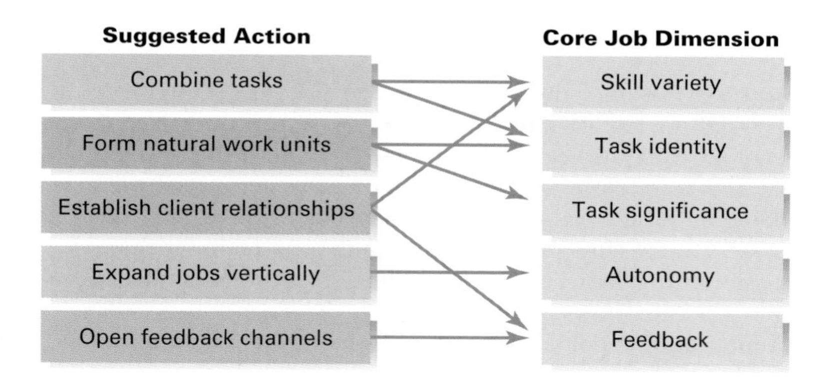

WHY IS EXPECTANCY THEORY CONSIDERED A COMPREHENSIVE THEORY OF MOTIVATION?

The most comprehensive and widely accepted explanation of motivation to date is Victor Vroom's expectancy theory.[23] Although the theory has its critics,[24] most of the research evidence supports it.[25]

Expectancy theory states that an individual tends to act in a certain way on the basis of the expectation that the act will be followed by a given outcome and the attractiveness of that outcome to the individual. It includes three variables or relationships:

expectancy theory
Vroom's theory that an individual tends to act in a certain way, in the expectation that the act will be followed by given outcome, and according to the attractiveness of that outcome

1. **Effort–performance linkage** The probability perceived by the individual that exerting a given amount of effort will lead to performance
2. **Performance–reward linkage** The degree to which the individual believes that performing at a particular level will lead to the attainment of a desired outcome
3. **Attractiveness** The importance that the individual places on the potential outcome or reward that can be achieved on the job. This variable considers the goals and needs of the individual[26]

Although this might sound complex, it really is not that difficult to visualize. The theory can be summed up in the following questions: (1) How hard do I have to work to achieve a certain level of performance?, and (2) Can I actually achieve that level? What reward will performing at that level get me? How attractive is this reward to me, and does it help achieve my goals? Whether one has the desire to produce at any given time depends on one's particular goals and one's perception of the relative worth of performance as a path to the attainment of those goals.

How does expectancy theory work? Exhibit 10–10 illustrates a very simple version of expectancy theory that expresses its major contentions. The strength of a person's motivation to perform (*effort*) depends on how strongly that individual believes that he or she can achieve what is being attempted. If this goal is achieved (*performance*), will he or she be adequately rewarded by the organization? If so, will the reward satisfy his or her individual goals (*attractiveness*)? Let us consider the four steps inherent in the theory and then attempt to apply it.

First, what perceived outcomes does the job offer the employee? Outcomes may be positive: pay, security, companionship, trust, employee benefits, a chance to use talent or skills, or congenial relationships. On the other hand, an employee may view the outcomes as negative: fatigue, boredom, frustration, anxiety, harsh supervision, or threat of dismissal. Reality is not relevant here: The critical issue is what the employee perceives the outcome to be, regardless of whether his or her perceptions are accurate.

Second, how attractive does an employee consider these outcomes to be? Are they valued positively, negatively, or neutrally? This obviously is an internal issue and takes into account the individual's personal attitudes, personality, and needs. The individual who finds a particular outcome attractive—that is, values it positively—would rather attain it than not attain it. Others may find it negative and, therefore, prefer not attaining it to attaining it. Still others may be neutral.

EXHIBIT 10–10 Simplified Expectancy Theory

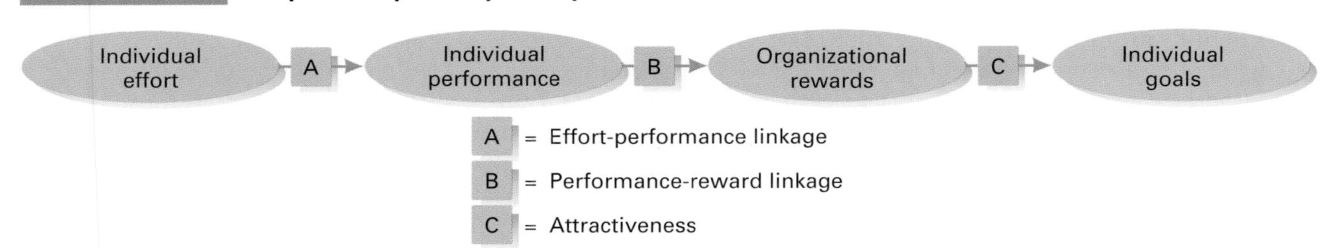

Third, what kind of behavior must the employee exhibit to achieve these outcomes? The outcomes are not likely to have any effect on an employee's performance unless the employee knows, clearly and unambiguously, what he or she must do to achieve them[27] (see Ethical Dilemma in Management). For example, what does "doing well" mean in terms of performance appraisal? What criteria will be used to judge the employee's performance?

Fourth and last, how does the employee view his or her chances of doing what is asked? After the employee has considered his or her own competencies and ability to control those variables that will determine success, what probability does he or she assign to successful attainment?[28]

How can expectancy theory be applied? Let's use a classroom analogy as an illustration of how one can use expectancy theory to explain motivation.

Most students prefer an instructor to tell them what is expected in the course. They want to know what the assignments and examinations will be like, when they are due or have to be taken, and how much weight each carries in the final term grade. They also like to think that the amount of effort they exert in attending classes, taking notes, and studying will be reasonably related to the grade they will earn in the course. Let's assume that you, as a student, feel this way. Consider that five weeks into a class you are really enjoying (we'll call it MNGT 301), an examination is returned to you. You studied hard for this examination, and you have consistently made As and Bs on examinations in other courses in which you have expended similar effort. The reason you work so hard is to make top grades, which you believe are important for getting a good job upon graduation. Also, although you are not sure,

Ethical Dilemma in Management

Rewarding Appropriate Behavior

You have just been hired as a supervisor at the Charlotte, North Carolina–based Quality Travel Agency. Customers call you to arrange travel plans. You look up airline flights, times, and fares on your computer and help customers make travel reservations that work best for them. You also provide customers assistance in reserving rental cars, finding suitable hotel accommodations, and booking tours and cruises.

Many car rental agencies and hotels frequently run contests for the sales representative who reserves the most cars for a particular firm or books the most clients for a specific hotel chain. The rewards for doing so are very attractive, too. One car rental firm offers to place employees' names in a monthly drawing to win $2,500 if they book just 20 reservations. If they book 100 in the same amount of time, they're eligible for a $10,000 prize. If they book 200 clients, they receive an all-expenses-paid, four-day Caribbean vacation for two. These incentives are attractive enough for you to "steer" customers toward those companies, even though it might not be the best or the cheapest for them. Your supervisor doesn't discourage participation in these programs. In fact, you view it as a bonus for your hard work.

Do you believe that there is anything wrong with your doing business with these car rental and hotel firms that offer kickbacks? What ethical issues do you see in this case for (1) you and (2) your customers? How could your organization design a performance reward system that would encourage you to high levels of bookings, while at the same time not compromise ethical practices and good customer service?

Your incentives reward you for steering customers toward certain companies. Even though it may be a bit more expensive for your customers, they find it acceptable. But, it has a significant benefit for you. Do you suggest this for your customers even though it is more advantageous for you? Or do you put the customers' interests in front of yours?

you might want to go on to graduate school, and you think grades are important if you are going to get into a good graduate school.

Well, the results of that first examination are in. The class average was 76. Ten percent of the class scored an 88 or higher and got an A. Your grade was 54; the minimum passing mark was 60. You're upset. You're frustrated. Even more, you're perplexed. How could you possibly have done so poorly on the examination when you usually score in the top range in other classes by preparing as you did for this one?

Several interesting things are immediately evident in your behavior. Suddenly, you may no longer be driven to attend MNGT 301 classes regularly. You may find several reasons why you don't want to study for the course, either. When you do attend classes, you may find yourself daydreaming—the result is an empty notebook instead of several pages of notes. One would probably be correct in saying that you lack motivation in MNGT 301. Why did your motivation level change? You know and we know, but let's explain it in expectancy terms.

If we use Exhibit 10–10 (page 289) to understand this situation, we might say the following: Studying for MNGT 301 (*effort*) is conditioned by the correct answers on the examination (*performance*), which will produce a high grade (*reward*), which will lead, in turn, to the security, prestige, and other benefits that accrue from obtaining a good job (*individual goal*).

The attractiveness of the outcome, a good grade, is high. But what about the performance–reward linkage? Do you feel that the grade you received truly reflects your knowledge of the material? In other words, did the test fairly measure what you know? If it did, then this linkage is strong. If you think it didn't, then at least part of the reason for your reduced motivational level is your belief that the test was not a fair measure of your performance. If the test was an essay type, maybe you believe that the instructor's grading method was poor. Was too much weight placed on a question that you thought was trivial? Maybe the instructor does not like you and was biased in grading your paper. These are examples of perceptions that influence the performance–reward linkage and your level of motivation.

Another possible demotivating force may be the effort–performance relationship. If, after you took the examination, you believe that you could not have passed it regardless of the amount of preparation you had done, then your desire to study may drop. Possibly, the instructor assumed that you had a considerably broader background in the subject matter. Maybe the course had several prerequisites that you did not know about, or possibly you had the prerequisites but took those courses several years ago. The result is the same: You place a low value on your effort leading to answering the examination questions correctly; hence, your motivational level decreases, and you reduce your effort.

Can we relate this classroom analogy to a work setting? What does expectancy theory say that can help us motivate our employees? Let's summarize some of the issues surrounding the theory. First, expectancy theory emphasizes payoffs or rewards. As a result, managers have to believe that the rewards they offer will align with what the employee wants. As such, it is a theory based on self-interest, wherein each individual seeks to maximize his or her expected satisfaction. Second, expectancy theory stresses that managers understand why employees view certain outcomes as attractive or unattractive. They will want to reward individuals with those things they value positively. Third, the expectancy theory emphasizes expected behaviors. Do individuals know what is expected of them and how they will be appraised? Unless employees see this connection between performance and rewards, organizational goals may not be met. Finally, the theory is concerned with perceptions. The facts are irrelevant. An individual's own perceptions of performance, reward, and goal satisfaction will determine his or her level of effort, not the objective outcomes themselves. Accordingly, there must be continuous feedback to align perceptions with reality.

"Expectancy theory is filled with perceptions—relevant or not. The individual's perception of the outcome will determine the effort expended."

HOW CAN WE INTEGRATE THE CONTEMPORARY THEORIES OF MOTIVATION?

There is a tendency to view the motivation theories in this chapter independently. Doing so is a mistake. Many of the ideas underlying the theories are complementary and your understanding of how to motivate people is maximized when you see how the theories fit together.[29]

Exhibit 10–11 visually integrates much of what we know about motivation. Its basic foundation is the simplified expectancy model in Exhibit 10–10. Let's work through Exhibit 10–11, beginning at the left.

The individual effort box has an arrow leading into it. This arrow flows out of the individual's goals. This goals–effort loop reminds us that goals direct behavior. Expectancy theory predicts that an employee will exert a high level of effort if he or she perceives a strong relationship between effort and performance, performance and rewards, and rewards and satisfaction of personal goals. Each of these relationships, in turn, is influenced by certain factors. If effort is to lead to good performance, the individual must have the requisite ability to perform, and the performance evaluation system that measures the individual's performance must be perceived as fair and objective. The performance–reward relationship will be strong if the individual perceives that performance (rather than seniority, personal favorites, or other criteria) is rewarded. Thus, if management has designed a reward system that is seen by employees as paying off for good performance, the rewards will reinforce and encourage continued good performance. The final link in expectancy theory is the rewards–goals relationship. Need theories come into play at this point. Motivation is high to the degree that the rewards an individual received for his or her high performance satisfy the dominant needs consistent with his or her individual goals.

A closer look at Exhibit 10–11 will also reveal that the model considers the need for achievement, equity, and the JCM theories. The high achiever is not motivated by the organization's assessment of his or her performance or organizational rewards, hence the jump from effort to individual goals for those with a high nAch. Remember

EXHIBIT 10–11 Integrating Theories of Motivation

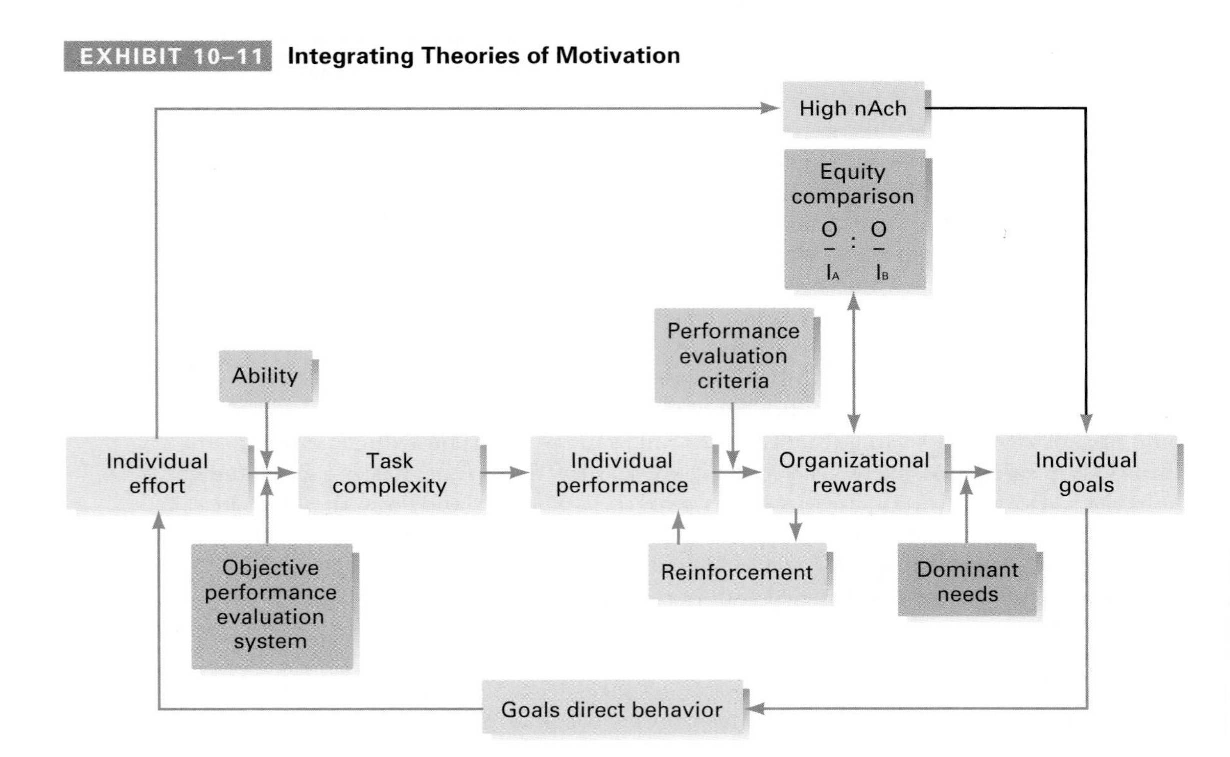

that high achievers are internally driven as long as the jobs they are doing provide them with personal responsibility, feedback, and moderate risks. They are not concerned with the effort–performance, performance–rewards, or rewards–goal linkages. Rewards also play the key part in equity theory. Individuals will compare the rewards (outcomes) they receive from the inputs they make with the input-outcome ratio of relevant others, and inequities may influence the effort expended.

Finally, we can see the JCM in this exhibit. Task characteristics (job design) influence job motivation at two places. First, jobs that score high in motivating potential are likely to lead to higher actual job performance because the employee's motivation is stimulated by the job itself. So jobs that are high in complexity (that is, have motivating potential) increase the linkage between effort and performance. Second, jobs that score high in motivating potential also increase an employee's control over key elements in his or her work. Therefore, jobs that offer autonomy, feedback, and similar complex task characteristics help to satisfy the individual goals of those employees who desire greater control over their work.

If you were a manager concerned with motivating your employees, what specific recommendations could you draw from this integration? Although there is no simple, all encompassing set of guidelines, we offer the following suggestions, which draw on the essence of what these theories have taught us about motivating employees (see Developing Your Skill at Motivating Employees on page 305).

CONTEMPORARY ISSUES IN MOTIVATION

In this final section, we address some contemporary motivation issues facing today's managers. These include motivating a diversified workforce, pay-for-performance programs, motivating minimum wage employees, motivating professional and technical employees, and flexible work schedule options. We'll also look at what entrepreneurs do to motivate their employees.

WHAT IS THE KEY TO MOTIVATING A DIVERSE WORKFORCE?

To maximize motivation in today's diversified workforce, management needs to think in terms of *flexibility*.[30] For instance, studies tell us that men place considerably more importance on autonomy in their jobs than do women. In contrast, the opportunity to learn, convenient work hours, and good interpersonal relations are more important to women than to men.[31] Managers need to recognize that the motivation of a single mother with two dependent children, who is working full time to support her family, may be very different from the needs of a young, single, part-time worker or the needs of the older employee who is working to supplement his or her pension income. Employees have different personal needs and goals that they're hoping to satisfy through their jobs. A diverse array of rewards is needed to motivate employees with such varied needs.

Motivating a diverse workforce also means that managers must be flexible enough to accommodate cultural differences. The theories of motivation we have been studying were developed largely by U.S. psychologists and were validated in studies of American workers. Therefore, these theories need to be modified for different cultures.[32] Take, for instance, Maslow's Hierarchy of Needs. The hierarchy aligns well with the American culture. The self-interest concept is consistent with capitalism, as is the extremely high value placed on individualism. But in countries where collectivism and uncertainty avoidance characteristics are strong—such as Japan, Greece, and Mexico—security needs would be on top of the needs hierarchy, not self-actualization. Because almost all the motivation theories presented in this chapter are based on the self-interest motive, they should be applicable to employees in countries such as Great Britain and Australia, where capitalism and individualism are highly valued. In countries with high scores on the quality of life dimension, such as Denmark, Sweden, Norway, the Netherlands, and Finland, social needs would be at the top of the needs hierarchy.

The need for achievement concept is another aspect of a motivation theory with a U.S. bias. The view that a high need for achievement acts as an internal motivator presupposes the existence of two cultural characteristics: a willingness to accept a moderate degree of risk and a concern with performance. These characteristics would exclude countries with high uncertainty avoidance scores and high quality of life ratings. The remaining countries are, predictably, such countries as New Zealand, South Africa, Ireland, the United States, and Canada that have large populations influenced by British and U.S. cultural norms.

Although equity theory has a strong following in the United States, evidence suggests that in collectivist cultures—especially in the former socialist countries of Central and Eastern Europe—employees expect rewards to reflect their individual needs as well as their performance.[33] Moreover, consistent with the legacy of communism and centrally planned economies, employees exhibit an entitlement attitude—that is, they expect outcomes to be greater than their inputs.[34]

Don't assume, however, from the comments in the past few paragraphs that there aren't any cross-cultural consistencies with respect to motivation. Several studies among employees in other countries indicate that some aspects of motivation theory are, in fact, transferable.[35] For instance, the motivational techniques presented earlier in this chapter were shown to be effective in changing performance-related behaviors of Russian textile mill workers. However, we should not assume that motivation concepts are universally applicable. Managers must recognize that to motivate employees in any environment, they must adjust their motivational techniques to fit the culture.

pay-for-performance programs Compensation plans such as piece-rate plans, profit sharing, and the like that pay employees on the basis of some performance measure

SHOULD EMPLOYEES BE PAID FOR PERFORMANCE OR TIME ON THE JOB?

What's in it for me? That's a question every person consciously or unconsciously asks before engaging in any form of behavior. Our knowledge of motivation tells us that people act in order to satisfy some need. Before they do anything, therefore, they look for a payoff or reward. Although many different rewards may be offered by organizations, most of us are concerned with earning an amount of money that allows us to satisfy our needs and wants. Because pay is an important variable in motivation, we need to look at how we can use pay to motivate high levels of employee performance. This concern explains the logic behind pay-for-performance programs.

How do we pay for performance? This Sheetrock hanger receives compensation for each piece of Sheetrock hung. Accordingly, the individual's total compensation is directly related to the work performed and directly attributable to the person's effort.

Pay-for-performance programs pay employees on the basis of some performance measure.[36] Piece-rate plans, gainsharing, wage-incentive plans, profit sharing, and lump-sum bonuses are examples of pay-for-performance programs. What differentiates these forms of pay from the more traditional compensation plans is that instead of paying an employee for time on the job, his or her pay is adjusted to reflect some performance measures.[37] These performance measures might include such things as individual productivity, team or work group productivity, departmental productivity, or the overall organization's profits for a given period.[38] For example, at British Telecom, a pay-for-performance program was "designed to improve productivity and work-life balance."[39] By focusing on work performance, and not simply attendance at work, productivity increased by more than 5 percent, and quality of service by more than 8 percent. And employees, too, say their salaries rise by a comparable amount!

Performance-based compensation is probably most compatible with expectancy theory. That is, employees should perceive a strong relationship between their performance and the rewards they receive if motivation is to be maximized. If rewards are allocated solely on nonperformance factors—such as seniority, job title, or across-the-board cost-of-living raises—then employees may be likely to reduce their efforts.

Pay-for-performance programs are gaining in popularity in organizations. One study found that approximately 80 percent of firms surveyed were providing some form of pay for performance for salaried employees.[40] The growing popularity can be explained in terms of both motivation and cost control. From a motivation perspective, making some or all of a worker's pay conditional on performance measures focuses his or her attention and effort on that measure, then reinforces the continuation of that effort with rewards. However, if the employee, team, or the organization's performance declines, so, too, does the reward. Thus, there is an incentive to keep efforts, productivity, and motivation strong.[41]

A recent extension of the pay-for-performance concept is called **competency-based compensation**.[42] A competency-based compensation program pays and rewards employees on the basis of the skills, knowledge, or behaviors employees possess. These competencies may include such behaviors and skills as leadership, problem solving, decision making, or strategic planning. Pre-set pay levels, called **broad-banding**, are established on the basis of the degree to which these competencies exist. Pay increases in a competency-based system are typically awarded for growth in personal competencies as well as for the contributions one makes to the overall organization. Accordingly, an employee's rewards are tied directly to how capable he or she is of contributing to the achievement of the organization's goals and objectives.

competency-based compensation
A program that pays and rewards employees on the basis of skills, knowledge, or behaviors they possess

broad-banding
Pre-set pay level, based on the degree competencies exist

stock options
A program that allows employees to purchase company stock at a fixed price

A variation of pay-for-performance programs in organizations today is the offering of stock options. **Stock options** have been a common incentive offered to executives. They generally allow certain individuals to purchase, at some time in the future, a specific amount of the company's stock at a fixed price. Under the assumption that good management will increase the company's profitability and, therefore, the price of the stock, stock options are viewed as performance-based incentives.[43] The clear intent of these programs is to reward those individuals who are fulfilling the "strategic and political contingencies" of the organization, as well as stakeholder interests.[44] It should be pointed out, however, that the use of stock options is heavily influenced by the current status of the tax laws.[45]

While stock option programs are designed to "reward performance," a more fundamental question today is: Do stock options encourage managers to engage in unethical accounting practices and/or manipulation of performance data?[46] Newspapers and the popular press recently have been flooded with reports of "indiscretions" in the accounting practices of some U. S. firms like Enron and Adelphia. Stories cite top management decisions to engage in questionable accounting practices to inflate stock prices and bolster their stock options.[47] What is even more sinister, some of these corporate leaders have been accused of withholding accurate financial data long enough to sell off their stocks at significant profits. When the "truth" becomes known, many shareholders (many of whom are company employees) watch their stock values plummet.[48] Ironically, in Chapter 2 we discussed the point that one way for companies to be socially responsible was for to them to properly police themselves. When that fails to happen, actions of managers at some companies have led to new legislation to reform the corporate governance and accounting practices of public companies.[49]

The failure of corporate leaders to act responsibly has led to growing concerns for corporate financial reforms. Accounting irregularities and billions of dollars of losses now being uncovered have angered investors, and have caused an economic downturn in the United States. Because of these conditions, President Bush passed federal legislation to "police" the financial activities of publicly held corporations. What effect this will have on companies is unknown—but clearly, had corporate leaders acted responsibly in the first place, this legislation would not have been needed.

HOW CAN MANAGERS MOTIVATE MINIMUM-WAGE EMPLOYEES?

Imagine for a moment that your first managerial job after graduating from college involves overseeing a group of minimum-wage employees. Offering more pay to these employees for high levels of performance is out of the question. Your company just can't afford it.[50] What are your motivational options at this point? One of the toughest motivational challenges facing many managers today is how to achieve high performance levels among minimum-wage workers.

One trap many managers fall into is thinking that employees are motivated only by money. Although money is important as a motivator, it's not the only reward that people seek and that managers can use. What are some other types of rewards? Many companies use employee recognition programs such as employee of the month, quarterly employee performance award ceremonies, or other celebrations of employee accomplishment. For instance, at many fast-food restaurants such as McDonald's and Wendy's, you'll often see plaques hanging in prominent places that feature the "Crew Member of the Month." These types of programs highlight employees whose performance has been of the type and level the organization wants to encourage. Many managers also recognize the power of praise, but you need to be sure that these "pats on the back" are sincere and done for the right reasons; otherwise, employees can interpret such actions as manipulative.

Learning from Experience: One Manager's Reflection

Mark Boice Vice President, Warner Bodies

MOTIVATING MINIMUM-WAGE EMPLOYEES

Describe the situation you faced. Warner hired me out of college in 1977. The company was experiencing extremely high turnover. Although management was willing to do anything to retain employees, most would rarely stay more than two weeks. Many employees would spend three to four hours taking the necessary tests to be hired at Warner, but would then spend only a couple of hours on the job before quitting.

What action(s) did you take? We decided to increase the benefit packages and create a 401(k) plan for the employees. And, an exit interview was designed to determine people's reasons for leaving the company.

What results occurred? Employee turnover was not reduced. They would simply walk out without informing management or participating in the new exit interview.

What did/should you have done differently? I wanted to find why the employees were leaving. Since the exit interview was worthless, I decided to work in the shop for one month to learn what it was that they disliked.

I learned that employees were comparing their hourly rates to those other places around the community, without taking benefits into consideration. They were leaving Warner for another company if they could make $.25 an hour more somewhere else.

If you took action, what were the results? We started to change our approach to motivating employees. Instead of trying to just find out what our employees wanted, we started educating them on what to look for. We held meetings explaining the benefits packages that we were giving. By comparing them to other companies' packages, we were able to show people why they should stay at Warner. We dropped the 401(k) plan and started a profit-sharing program that paid dividends to retiring employees regardless of their investments.

By working in the shop, I also received more respect from the entire workforce. I was able to motivate them better. They believed in me and looked at me as a fellow employee instead of management. Warner now has less than a five percent turnover.

I learned that I need to educate my employees. Now, instead of taking for granted that they compare our benefits to others, I teach them how to compare. We have gone on to open our accounting books to our employees and we have taught them how to read all of the financials.

I also learned to work with all of the employees on all decisions. I now involve them in everything from human relations to product development. They have knowledge that I do not have in certain areas, and they have much better communication channels with other employees. Remember, your best engineer may be the employee welding on the line.

We know from the motivation theories presented earlier that rewards are only part of the motivation equation. We need to look at other elements such as empowerment and career development assistance. We can look to job design and expectancy theories for these insights. In service industries such as travel and hospitality, retail sales, child care, and maintenance, where pay for front-line employees generally doesn't get much above the minimum-wage level, successful companies are empowering these front-line employees with more authority to address customers' problems. If we use the JCM to examine this change, we can see that this type of job redesign provides enhanced motivating potential because employees now experience increased skill variety, task identity, task significance, autonomy, and feedback. Also, employees, facing this situation often want to better themselves professionally. They need guidance, assistance in self-assessment, and training. By providing these to minimum-wage employees, you're preparing them for the future—one that hopefully promises better pay. For many, this is a strong motivator![51]

How does management motivate this professional employee? It's suggested that work itself provides the motivation. The individual wants to feel important, wants autonomy, and expects to have access to educational opportunities. The individual also seeks recognition for a job well done.

WHAT'S DIFFERENT IN MOTIVATING PROFESSIONAL AND TECHNICAL EMPLOYEES?

What do a graphic artist at the TBWA Chiat/Day advertising agency, a programmer at Microsoft, and a lawyer at a major New York law firm have in common? They're professional and technical employees, and they have a strong and long-term commitment to their field of expertise. Their loyalty, however, is more often to their profession than to their employer. To keep current in their field, they need to regularly update their knowledge, and their commitment to their profession or technical field means they rarely define their workweek in terms of nine-to-five or five days a week.[52]

So what motivates these types of employees? Money and promotions into management typically are low on their priority list. Why? They tend to be well paid, and they enjoy what they do. In contrast, job challenge tends to be ranked high. They like to tackle problems and find solutions. Their chief reward is the work itself. Professional and technical employees generally also value support. They want others to think that what they are working on is important.[53] The above points imply that managers should provide professional and technical employees with new assignments and challenging projects. Give them autonomy to follow their interests and allow them to structure their work in ways they find productive. Reward them with educational opportunities—training, workshops, conferences—that allow them to keep current in their field and to network with their peers. Also reward them with recognition. Managers should ask questions and engage in other actions that demonstrate to their professional and technical employees that they're sincerely interested in what they're doing.

WHAT CAN MANAGEMENT DO TO IMPROVE WORK-LIFE BALANCE?

Wayne Chandler is the classic "morning person." He rises each day at 5:00 A.M. sharp, full of energy. On the other hand, as he puts it, "I'm usually ready for bed right after the 7:00 P.M. news." Wayne's work schedule as a claims processor at Chubb Insurance is flexible. It allows him some degree of freedom as to when he comes to work and when he leaves. His office opens at 6:00 A.M. and closes at 7:00 P.M. It's up to him how he schedules his eight-hour day within this thirteen-hour period. He's at the job when he's most alert and can be home to take care of his son when he gets out of school.

Many employees continue to work an eight-hour day, five days a week. They are full-time employees who report to a fixed organizational location and start and leave at a fixed time. But, consistent with managers' attempts to increase their organizations' flexibility and support work-family balances, a number of scheduling options have been introduced to give management and employees more flexibility.[54] In addition to an increased use of temporary and contingent workers, contemporary companies are looking at other options: flextime, job sharing, and telecommuting.

flextime
A scheduling option that allows employees to select what their work hours will be within some specified parameters

How does flextime work? **Flextime** is a scheduling option that allows employees, within specific parameters, to decide when to go to work. Wayne Chandler's work schedule at Chubb Insurance is an example of flextime. But what specifically is it?

Flextime is short for flexible work hours. Employees have to work a specific number of hours a week, but they are free to vary the hours of work within certain limits. Each day consists of a common core, usually six hours, with a flexibility band surrounding the core. For example, exclusive of a one-hour lunch break, the core may be 9:00 A.M. to 3:00 P.M., with the office actually opening at 6:00 A.M. and closing at 6:00 P.M. All employees are required to be at their jobs during the common core period, but they are allowed to schedule their other two hours before or after the core time. Some flextime programs allow extra hours to be accumulated and turned into a free day off each month. Flextime has become a popular scheduling option—especially important for professional employees and Gen-Xers.[55] For instance, a recent study of firms' practices to enhance work/life benefits found that about 60 percent offered employees some form of flextime.[56]

"Some benefits of flextime are improved motivation and morale; reduced absenteeism; higher-quality, more diverse workforce."

The potential benefits of flextime are numerous—for both the employee and the employer. They include improved employee motivation and morale, reduced absenteeism as a result of enabling employees to better balance work and family responsibilities, increased wages due to productivity gains, and the ability of the organization to recruit higher-quality and more diverse employees.[57]

Flextime's major drawback, however, is that it is not applicable to every job. It works well with job tasks for which an employee's interaction with people outside his or her department is limited. It is not a viable option when key people must be available during standard hours, when workflow requires tightly determined scheduling, or when specialists are called upon to maintain coverage of all functions in a unit.

job sharing
A type of part-time work that allows two or more workers to split a traditional 40-hour-a-week job

Can employees share jobs? **Job sharing** is a special type of part-time work. It allows two or more individuals to split a traditional 40-hour-a-week job. So, for example, one person might perform the job from 8:00 A.M. to noon while another performs the same job from 1:00 P.M. to 5:00 P.M., or both could work full, but alternate, days.

Job sharing is growing in popularity, with 57 percent of large organizations offering it.[58] Job sharing allows the organization to draw upon the talents of more than one individual for a given job. It provides the opportunity to acquire skilled workers—for instance, single parents with young children and retirees—who might not be available on a full-time basis.[59] Furthermore, it is an option for managers to use to minimize layoffs.[60] The major drawback, from management's perspective, is finding compatible pairs of employees who can successfully coordinate the intricacies of one job.

telecommuting
A system of working at home on a computer that is linked to the office

What is telecommuting? **Telecommuting** capabilities that exist today have made it possible for employees to be located anywhere on the globe and still do their jobs. With this potential, companies no longer have to consider locating near their workforce. For example, if Progressive Auto Insurance in Nebraska finds that it is having problems attracting qualified local applicants for its claims-processing jobs, and a pool of qualified workers is available in Berlin, Maryland, Progressive doesn't need to establish a facility in Maryland. Rather, by providing these employees with computer equipment and appropriate ancillaries, the work can be done hundreds of miles away and then be transmitted to the "home" office.

Telecommuting also offers an opportunity for a business in a high-labor-cost area to have its work done in an area where lower wages prevail. Take the publisher in New York City who finds manuscript editing costs have skyrocketed. By having that work done by a qualified editor in Pawleys Island, South Carolina, the publisher could reduce labor costs. Likewise, not having to provide office space to this editor in the city, given the cost per square foot of real estate in the area, adds to the cost savings. Telecommuting employees do their work at home on a computer that is linked to an organization's facility.[61] Currently, more than 16 million people work at home in the United States—and the number is expected to double by 2005.[62] It's used at such companies as AT&T, Merrill Lynch, Hewlett-Packard, and IBM. Telecommuting is also found in other countries—for example, nearly 8 percent of all European workers telecommute.[63]

What do you do when you really love your job, but love raising your children more? For Kristen Durrett and Nancy Oliphant, account executives at Emmis Communications Corporation in Indianapolis, Indiana, both pregnant with their second child, the decision was easy—just convince management to permit them to share one full-time job—which happened! Durrett works on Mondays and Tuesdays, Oliphant on Thursdays and Fridays—with both at the job on Wednesday. Sharing one full-time salary and commissions evenly, and the benefits package associated with the position, Durrett and Oliphant have worked this shared arrangement for more than two years. As their boss states, "They work off each other's strengths."

Much of the challenge for employers in telecommuting revolves around training managers in how to establish and ensure appropriate work quality and on-time completion. Traditional "face-time" is removed in such work arrangements, and managers' need to "control" the work will have to change. Instead, there will have to be more employee involvement, allowing workers the discretion to make those decisions that affect them. For instance, although a due date is established for the work assigned to employees, managers must recognize that home workers will work at their own pace. That may mean that, instead of an individual focusing work efforts over an eight-hour period, he or she may work two hours here, three hours at another time, and another three late at night. The emphasis, then, will be on the final product, not the means by which it is accomplished.

Work at home may also require managers to rethink their compensation policy. Will it pay workers by the hour, on a salary basis, or by the job performed? More than likely, because certain jobs, like claims processing, can be easily quantified and standards set, pay plans will be in the form of pay for actual work done. Beyond the compensation issue, managers must also anticipate potential legal problems that may arise from telecommuting.[64] For example, what if the employee works more than 40 hours during the work week? Will that employee be entitled to overtime pay? The answer is yes! As such, alternative work-site activities will have to be monitored by managers to ensure that employees are not abusing overtime privileges, and that those workers who rightfully should be paid overtime are compensated.

Because telecommuting employees are often full-time employees of an organization, as opposed to contingent or temporary workers, it will be the organization's responsibility to ensure the health and safety of the off-premise work site. Equipment provided by the company, for example, that leads to an employee injury or illness is the responsibility of the organization. Although management cannot constantly monitor workers in their homes, it must ensure that these workers understand the proper techniques for using the equipment. Additionally, if accidents or injuries occur, employees must understand the regulations for reporting them. Generally, that means, for instance, reporting them within 48 hours, at which time management must investigate immediately.

For employees, the two big advantages of telecommuting are the decrease in time and stress of commuting in congested areas and the increase in flexibility in coping with family demands.[65] But it may have some potential drawbacks. For instance, will telecommuting employees miss the social contact that a formal office provides? Will they be less likely to be considered for salary increases and promotions? Is being out of sight equivalent to being out of mind? Will nonwork-related distractions such as children, neighbors, and the proximity of the refrigerator significantly reduce productivity for those without superior willpower and discipline? Answers to these questions are central in determining whether telecommuting will continue to expand in the future.

WHAT DO ENTREPRENEURS DO TO MOTIVATE EMPLOYEES?

At Sapient Corporation, which creates Internet and software systems for e-commerce and for automating back-office tasks such as billing and inventory, cofounders Jerry Greenberg and J. Stuart Moore recognized that employee motivation was critically important to their company's ultimate success. They designed their organization so that individual employees are part of an industry-specific team that works on an entire project rather than on one small piece of it. Their rationale was that people often feel frustrated when they're doing a small part of a job and never get to see the whole job from start to finish. They figured people would be more productive if they got the opportunity to participate in all phases of a project. Their approach seems to be working: *Fortune* named Sapient one of the 100 Fastest Growing Companies in the new millennium.[66]

When you're motivated to do something, don't you find yourself energized and willing to work hard at doing whatever it is you're excited about? Wouldn't it be great if all of a venture's employees were energized, excited, and willing to work hard at their jobs? Having motivated employees is an important goal for any entrepreneur, and employee empowerment is an important motivational tool entrepreneurs can use. Employee empowerment—giving employees the power to make decisions and take actions on their own—is an important motivational approach. Why? Because successful entrepreneurial ventures must be quick and nimble, ready to pursue opportunities and go off in new directions. Empowered employees can provide that flexibility and speed. When employees are empowered, they often display stronger work motivation, better work quality, higher job satisfaction, and lower turnover. For example, the employees at Butler International, Inc., a technology consulting services firm based in Montvale, New Jersey, work at client locations. Ed Kopko, president and CEO, recognized that employees had to be empowered to do their jobs if they were going to be successful. The company's commitment to and success with employee empowerment led to its being awarded the Arthur Andersen Global Best Practices Award for Motivating and Retaining Employees.[67]

How does entrepreneur Ed Kopko motivate his employees at Butler International, Inc., the technology consulting firm? He empowers his employees to do their jobs the best they can. The have the power to make decisions and take actions on their own.

Another entrepreneurial venture that has found employee empowerment to be a strong motivational approach is Stryker Instruments in Kalamazoo, Michigan. Each of the company's 40 production units (consisting of about 40 employees each) has responsibility for its operating budget, cost-reduction goals, customer-service levels, inventory management, training, production planning and forecasting, purchasing, human resources management, safety, and problem solving. In addition, unit members work closely with marketing, sales, and R&D during new-product introductions and continuous improvement projects. Says one team supervisor, "Stryker lets me do what I do best and rewards me for that privilege."[68]

Empowerment is a philosophical concept that entrepreneurs have to "buy into." This doesn't come easily. In fact, it's hard for many entrepreneurs to do. Their lives are tied up in their businesses. They've built them from the ground up. But continuing to grow the entrepreneurial venture is eventually going to require handing over more responsibilities to employees. How can entrepreneurs empower employees? For many entrepreneurs, it's a gradual process. They can begin by using participative decision making in which employees provide input into decisions. Although getting employees to participate in decisions isn't quite taking the full plunge into employee empowerment, it, at least, is a way to begin tapping into the collective array of employees' talents, skills, knowledge, and abilities.

Another way to empower employees is through delegation—the process of assigning certain decisions or specific job duties to employees. By delegating decisions and duties, the entrepreneur is turning over the responsibility for carrying them out.

When an entrepreneur is finally comfortable with the idea of employee empowerment, fully empowering employees means redesigning their jobs so they have discretion over the way they do their work. It's allowing employees to do their work effectively and efficiently by using their creativity, imagination, knowledge, and skills. If an entrepreneur implements employee empowerment properly—that is, with complete and total commitment to the program and with appropriate employee training—results can be impressive for the entrepreneurial venture and for the empowered employees. The business can enjoy significant productivity gains, quality improvements, more satisfied customers, increased employee motivation, and improved morale. Employees can enjoy the opportunities to do a greater variety of work that is more interesting and challenging. In addition, employees are encouraged to take the initiative in identifying and solving problems and doing their work. For example, at Mine Safety Appliances in Murrysville, Pennsylvania, employees are empowered to change their work processes in order to meet the organization's challenging quality improvement goals. Getting to this point took an initial 40 hours of classroom instruction per employee in areas such as engineering drawing, statistical process control, quality certifications, and specific work instruction. However, the company's commitment to an empowered workforce has resulted in profitability increasing 91 percent over the last five years, 95 percent of the company's employees achieving multiskill certifications, and the company being named Home Depot's Supplier of the Year in 1999 in its first year of supplying the company.[69]

Review, Comprehension, Application

CHAPTER SUMMARY

How will you know if you fulfilled the Learning Outcomes on page 278? You will have fulfilled the Learning Outcomes if you are able to:

1. **Describe the motivation process.** Motivation is the willingness to exert high levels of effort toward organizational goals, conditioned by the efforts' ability to satisfy some individual need. The motivation process begins with an unsatisfied need, which creates tension and drives an individual to search for goals that, if attained, will satisfy the need and reduce the tension.
2. **Define needs.** Needs are internal states that make certain outcomes appear attractive. Because needs may be unfulfilled, people attempt to do something. That "something" is behavior designed to satisfy an unfulfilled need.
3. **Explain the hierarchy of needs theory.** The hierarchy of needs theory states that there are five needs—physiological (food, water, shelter); safety (freedom from emotional and physical harm); social (affection, belongingness, friendship); esteem (self-respect, autonomy, achievement); and self-actualization (achieving one's potential)—that individuals attempt to satisfy in a step-like progression. A substantially satisfied need no longer motivates.
4. **Differentiate Theory X from Theory Y.** Theory X is basically a negative view of human nature, assuming that employees dislike work, are lazy, seek to avoid responsibility, and must be coerced to perform. A Theory X employee is motivated by fear of losing job security. Theory Y is basically positive, assuming that employees are creative, seek responsibility, and can exercise self-direction. A Theory Y employee is motivated by challenging work and empowerment.
5. **Explain the motivational implications of the motivation-hygiene theory.** The motivations-hygiene theory states that not all job factors can motivate employees. The presence or absence of certain job characteristics or hygiene factors can only placate employees but do not lead to satisfaction or motivation. Factors that people find intrinsically rewarding such as achievement, recognition, responsibility, and growth act as motivators and produce job satisfaction.
6. **Describe the motivational implications of equity theory.** In equity theory, individuals compare their job's input-outcome ratio with those of relevant others. If they perceive that they are underrewarded, their motivation declines. They may adjust the quantity and quality of their work, leave the organization, or simply compare themselves to another relevant other. When individuals perceive that they are overrewarded, they often are motivated to work harder in order to justify their pay. Oftentimes both quality and quantity of work will increase.

7. **Explain the key relationships in expectancy theory.** The expectancy theory states that an individual tends to act in a certain way based on the expectation that the act will be followed by a given outcome and on the attractiveness of that outcome to the individual. The theory's prime components are the relationships between effort and performance, performance and rewards, and rewards and individual goals.
8. **Describe how managers can design individual jobs to maximize employee performance.** Managers can design individual jobs to maximize employee performance by combining tasks, creating natural work units, establishing client relationships, expanding jobs vertically, and opening feedback channels.
9. **Explain the effect of workforce diversity on motivational practices.** Maximizing motivation in contemporary organizations requires that managers be flexible in their practices. They must recognize that employees have different personal needs and goals that they are attempting to satisfy through work. Managers must also recognize that cultural differences may play a role, too. Various types of rewards must be developed to meet and motivate these diverse needs, as well as training opportunities and career development assistance.
10. **Describe how entrepreneurs motivate their employees.** Employee empowerment is an important motivational tool that entrepreneurs use. Entrepreneurs use participative decision making and delegation. They allow employees to do their work effectively and efficiently by using their creativity, imagination, knowledge, and skills. As a result, the business will be more flexible and is likely to achieve productivity gains, quality improvements, more satisfied customers, increased employee motivation, and improved morale.

COMPANION WEBSITE

We invite you to visit the Robbins/DeCenzo companion Website at **www.prenhall.com/robbins** for this chapter's Internet resources, including an online study guide, Internet exercises, and "In the News" with full text articles provided by XanEdu.

READING FOR COMPREHENSION

1. How do needs affect motivation?
2. Contrast lower-order and higher-order needs in Maslow's needs hierarchy.
3. Describe the three needs in the three-needs theory.
4. What are some of the possible consequences of employees perceiving an inequity between their inputs and outcomes and those of others?
5. What are some advantages of using pay-for-performance to motivate employee performance? Are there drawbacks? Explain.

LINKING CONCEPTS TO PRACTICE

1. What role would money play in (1) the hierarchy of needs theory, (2) motivation-hygiene theory, (3) equity theory, (4) expectancy theory, and (5) motivating employees with a high nAch?
2. If you accept Theory Y assumptions, how would you be likely to motivate employees?
3. Would an individual with a high nAch be a good candidate for a management position? Explain.
4. What difficulties do you think workforce diversity causes for managers who are trying to use equity theory?
5. Describe several means that you might use to motivate (1) a minimum-wage employee or (2) professional and technical employees. Which of your suggestions do you think is best? Support your position.

VIDEO CASE APPLICATION

Novasoft Information Technology: Turning Employee Perks into Company Profits

The list of Novasoft Values is impressive: respect for clients and employees; achievement through teamwork; conduct business with integrity; reward entrepreneurship; just do it; simple form, lean staff; and deliver what is promised. These values come straight from CEO Neil Bhaskar, and he lives by them, staying up all night or working all weekend to deliver a report to a client on time. He believes in doing whatever it takes to earn a new account or satisfy a loyal customer.

In 1993, Neil Bhaskar started his business, based in Lawrenceville, New Jersey, with one employee. Today the software consulting company has 400 people working in London, Singapore, and India; boasting a revenue growth of 300 percent a year. By 1998, he was steadily building the company by recruiting highly qualified engineers and computer programmers from India. When the U.S. government began turning away foreign visas and placed economic sanctions on India, he quickly began tapping local colleges for talent. "You don't stop production because the cost of your raw material increases," says Bhaskar. Quick thinking in the face of adversity allowed him to propel his entrepreneurial venture forward.

The competition to keep skilled workers is fierce among New Jersey's technology companies. "I want to be the employer of choice and create a company with a difference," says Bhaskar. "Part of my mission is to have fun while you do things." He uses a balance scorecard to track client and employee acquisition, retention, and satisfaction. "My style is not like the industrial age command-and-control management style; mine is a teamwork style that offers freedom to do things. But with freedom comes responsibility. The responsibility includes a predetermined set of goals for each employee, regardless of job type."

According to Neil Bhaskar, "Christmas comes four times a year." Each quarter at the company is a Nova Year, and each Nova Year brings a quarterly review and a quarterly bonus of up to a week's pay.[70] Incentives come in enticing packages at Novasoft, where star performers can earn an overseas vacation for two, a Mercedes Benz or a Rolex for meeting their objectives. "My board of directors bashes me up every time I give a car away, but it has been a great help in creating self-esteem," claims Bhaskar.[71] Administrative staffers including receptionists and secretaries will soon get leases on new Volkswagen Beetles.

Clients like Fuller Bulk Handling reap the efforts of Novasoft's motivated staff. When the Bethlehem, Pennsylvania, company turned to Novasoft to implement a software package that would integrate their three separate computer systems, CEO Jack Hilbert was more than pleased. Not only did Novasoft experts finish the installation a previous consulting company had failed to complete, but they also introduced him to new Internet possibilities for the company to use in the future.

Novasoft appeared on *Working Woman* magazine's list of 100 Best Companies for Working Mothers in 2001. The company has been named twice to *Inc.* magazine's list of the country's 500 fastest growing privately held companies. For CEO Neil Bhaskar, however, the "ultimate kick is to see how many people in my company become millionaires."

In case you were wondering, Bhaskar drives a black Mercedes.[72]

Questions

1. Based on McClelland's three needs theory, would a high achiever make a good candidate for a sales force position at Novasoft? Explain. You may refer to Exhibit 10–11 in your text to support your answer.
2. Do you think that the organization-wide pay policy at Novasoft is perceived by the company's employees to be fair and equitable? Explain.
3. Based on the video you have just seen, define the three variables of Expectancy Theory as they would apply to a member of Novasoft's sales force.
4. Using your text and your knowledge of Novasoft values, what are some of the motivational factors the company provides for its technical experts? Consider how the needs of the sales force may differ from the needs of the software professionals.

Management Workshop

Team Skill-Building Exercise

How Can You Motivate Others?

This exercise is designed to help increase your awareness of how and why you motivate others and to help focus on the needs of those you are attempting to motivate.

Step 1

Break into groups of five to seven people. Each group member is to individually respond to the following:

Situation 1: You are the owner and president of a 50-employee organization. Your goal is to motivate all 50 employees to their highest effort level.

Task 1: On a separate piece of paper, list the factors you would use to motivate your employees. Avoid general statements such as "give them a raise." Rather, be as specific as possible.

Task 2: Rank (from highest to lowest) all the factors listed in Task 1 above.

Situation 2: Consider now that you are one of the 50 employees who have been given insight as to what motivates you.

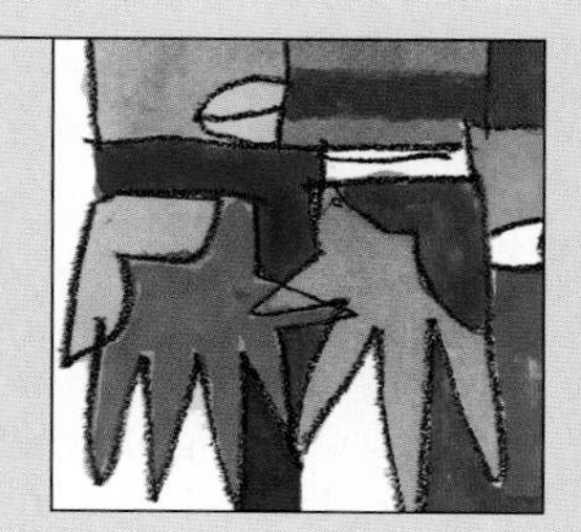

Task 3: As an employee, list those factors that would most effectively motivate you. Again, be as specific as possible.

Task 4: Rank (from highest to lowest) all the factors listed in Task 3.

Step 2

Each member should share his or her prioritized lists (the lists from Tasks 2 and 4) with the other members of the group.

Step 3

After each member has presented his or her lists, the group should respond to the following questions:

1. Are each individual's lists (Task 2 and Task 4) similar or dissimilar? What do the differences or similarities suggest to you?
2. What have you learned about how and why to motivate others, and how can you apply these data?

Understanding Yourself

Before you can develop other people, you must understand your present strengths. To assist in this learning process, we encourage you to complete the following self-assessments from the Prentice Hall Self-Assessment Library 2.0:

- What Do I Value? (#9)
- What Rewards Do I Value Most? (#14)
- What's My View on the Nature of People? (#15)

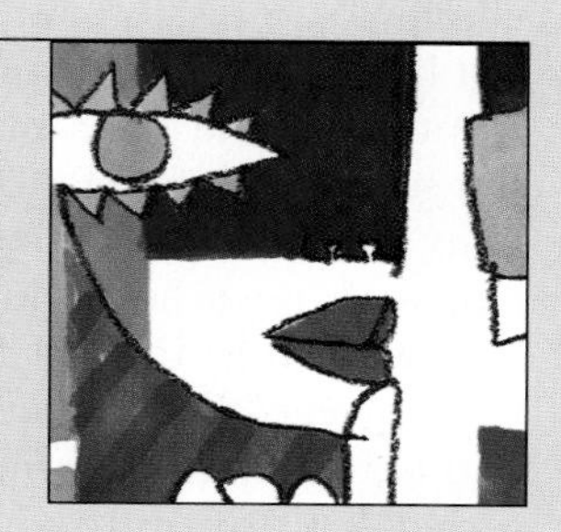

After you complete these assessments, we suggest that you print out the results and store them as part of your "portfolio of learning."

Developing Your Skill at Motivating Employees

Maximizing Employee Effort

About the Skill

There is no simple, all-encompassing set of motivational guidelines, but the following suggestions draw on the essence of what we know about motivating employees.

Steps Practicing the Skill

1. **Recognize individual differences.** Almost every contemporary motivation theory recognizes that employees are not homogeneous. They have different needs. They also differ in terms of attitudes, personality, and other important individual variables.
2. **Match people to jobs.** There is a great deal of evidence showing the motivational benefits of carefully matching people to jobs. People who lack the necessary skills to perform successfully will be disadvantaged.
3. **Use goals.** You should ensure that employees have hard, specific goals and feedback on how well they are doing in pursuit of those goals. In many cases, these goals should be participatively set.
4. **Ensure that goals are perceived as attainable.** Regardless of whether goals are actually attainable, employees who see goals as unattainable will reduce their effort. Be sure, therefore, that employees feel confident that increased efforts can lead to achieving performance goals.
5. **Individualize rewards.** Because employees have different needs, what acts as a reinforcer for one may not do so for another. Use your knowledge of employee differences to individualize the rewards over which you have control. Some of the more obvious rewards that you can allocate include pay, promotions, autonomy, and the opportunity to participate in goal setting and decision making.
6. **Link rewards to performance.** You need to make rewards contingent on performance. Rewarding factors other than performance will only reinforce the importance of those other factors. Key rewards such as pay increases and promotions should be given for the attainment of employees' specific goals.
7. **Check the system for equity.** Employees should perceive that rewards or outcomes are equal to the inputs given. On a simplistic level, experience, ability, effort, and other obvious inputs should explain differences in pay, responsibility, and other obvious outcomes.
8. **Don't ignore money.** It's easy to get so caught up in setting goals, creating interesting jobs, and providing opportunities for participation that you forget that money is a major reason why most people work. Thus, the allocation of performance-based wage increases, piece-work bonuses, employee stock ownership plans, and other pay incentives are important in determining employee motivation.

Practicing the Skill

Employees at Zero Knowledge Systems in Montreal can get their laundry washed, dried, and folded for them at work. At Gymboree Corp's California headquarters the benefits include free cookies and milk and daily breaks for "recess." Arcnet, a New Jersey architectural firm, gives the use of a BMW to employees who stay more than a year. The firm believes the car makes a more lasting impression on employees than cash.

All of the following traditional and offbeat benefits are currently offered at various U.S. firms. Rank-order them for yourself, putting those that are most likely to motivate you at the top of your list. Now look at your top five choices. How do you think you will rank them in 10 years? Why?

Flextime
Telecommuting
Dental insurance
Tuition refund
Matching gift plan
Vision insurance
Health club
Life insurance
On-site day care
Employee assistance program
Laundry/dry cleaning service
Company car
Subsidized cafeteria
Paid vacation
Profit sharing
Stock purchase plan
Ability to keep frequent flier miles
Pets at work
Management program
Daily naptime
Free snacks/candy
Year-end bonus
Clothing allowance
Flexible spending plan
Free lunch
Retirement plan
Paid sick days
Children's college tuition
Annual birthday gift
Nonwork-related courses
Company-sponsored sports team
Free uniform
Transportation voucher
Family picnics and parties
Child and elder care referral services
Benefits for unmarried domestic partners

Sources: Kim Clark, "Perking Up the Office," *U.S. News & World Report* (November 22, 1999), p. 73; Lynn Brenner, "Perks that Work," *BusinessWeek Frontier* (October 11, 1999), pp. F22–40.

Developing Your Diagnostic and Analytical Skills

Kindergarten and Corporate America

Maybe Robert Fulghum, author of *All I Really Need to Know I Learned in Kindergarten* (Ballantine Publishing Group, 1993), has taught individuals in corporate America a thing or two. For Sean McLaughlin, CEO of Eze Castle Software, there's no doubt how kindergarten principles improved his company.[73]

Eze Castle, headquartered in Boston, Massachusetts, develops software that is used for security trading. This six-year-old company has grown to more than 90 employees, with annual revenues exceeding $13 million. During its first few years, this start-up venture prospered, in part due to the attention paid to every detail in managing the company. But success appeared to come at a price. Workers became complacent. Some decisions were made without any regard to "the bottom line," such as paying more than $100 a month to a contractor to water the few plants in the office. Furthermore, employees began to spend their time on activities not related to work. In one case, the company's T1 Internet connection service fee soared because of excessive traffic brought about by most employees downloading MP3 files so they'd have music at their desks. As McLaughlin put it, his company culture had taken on bureaucratic tendencies—"acting with large company sloppiness rather than start-up frugality." But two major events changed this.

First, within a two-week time period, two key administrative assistants quit. No one knew what to do. Supplies were no longer available, as stock items were not replenished. Mail was not delivered—it simply stayed bagged in the mail room. Even when a few tried to handle the mail situation, they couldn't. They didn't know who was who in the organization. Second, while getting away from it all for a day, McLaughlin attended his daughter's kindergarten class. There he witnessed how chores were divided among the classmates, and how serving refreshments was intended for all students to socialize.

Thinking about what he had seen, and what was happening at Eze, McLaughlin identified eight separate tasks that would make work more enjoyable for employees. These included stocking the kitchen, cleaning and organizing dishes, maintaining the supply closet, sorting and distributing mail, cleaning the kitchen, overseeing the reception area, arranging snack breaks, and acting as an ombudsman (the one who would oversee and coordinate the seven previous activities). These activities would be done by employees on a rotating basis—each person typically having one assignment to a task every three months. By doing so, McLaughlin also would not have to replace the administrative assistants. Instead, he could take the money saved from their salaries and benefits and share it with employees. Once presented with the idea, Eze employees at first began their tasks reluctantly. While some questioned the need for such activities, especially cleaning up, they participated.

With cookies-and-milk breaks every afternoon at 2:30, employees from all parts of the company enjoyed the socializing. They began to get to know one another, and understand what was happening in the organization. Meanwhile, managers used some of the saved administrative assistant salary monies to support both internal and external service activities that were important to them. For example, one committee has recommended that a company gym be built; while another has been supporting Boston area homeless shelters by conducting food drives.

Since McLaughlin's changes, he's noticed something remarkable. Employee morale has increased. Teams have formed in the organization that are once again focusing on the "good of the organization." One team, for instance, has recommended that they all turn off their lights and computers each evening before leaving the building. This suggestion alone is saving Eze more than $3,000 per month, reducing its electric bill by more than 75 percent.

McLaughlin learned something else at that kindergarten class: that sharing can be good, and when people share, they can be happier. At Eze Software, productivity is up, costs are down, and the employees would not think of missing their afternoon milk and cookies!

Questions

1. What is your reaction to this "employee plan" implemented by Sean McLaughlin? Do you believe it is too simplistic? Defend your position.
2. Do you believe such programs as described in this case can be successfully used at other companies? Why or why not?
3. Do special conditions have to exist for such a system to work? Explain. How do these conditions relate to the motivation process?
4. Relate McLaughlin's new program to suggestions made in this chapter regarding motivation in entrepreneurial firms.

Enhancing Your Communication Skills

1. Develop a two- to three-page response to the following questions. What motivates me? What rewards can an employer provide that will make me give the extra effort? How realistic is it that I will find such an organization? (*Note*: You may want to use information from the Self-Assessments in this exercise.)
2. Randomly contact 25 fellow students on your campus. Ask them to identify the top three rewards they want from an employer. Keep a log of these responses. Provide a two- to three-page report about your findings. What did the sample respondents indicate they wanted most? Given the responses, which of the motivation theories discussed in this chapter appear to be best supported? Explain your reasoning.

3. Go to <www.chartcourse.com> and visit the Web site Free Articles. Review two articles, specifically: Gregory P. Smith, "Managing Negative Employees and Other Energy Suckers," and Gregory P. Smith, "Recognize, Reinforce and Reward the Right Behavior." Discuss the implications of the articles' content to the motivation process discussed in this chapter.

C H A P T E R 1 1

Leadership and Trust

LEARNING OUTCOMES

After reading this chapter, I will be able to:

1 Define leader and explain the difference between managers and leaders.

2 Summarize the conclusions of trait theories of leadership.

3 Describe the Fiedler contingency model.

4 Summarize the path-goal model of leadership.

5 Explain situational leadership.

6 Identify the qualities that characterize charismatic leaders.

7 Describe the skills that visionary leaders exhibit.

8 Explain the four specific roles of effective team leaders.

9 Identify the five dimensions of trust.

MEET A REAL MANAGER!

"One Manager's Reflection" page 327

Adele Sacarelli, President, TeamworkWins LTD

Are leaders born, or do they rise out of adversity? That question has been part of an age-old debate on leadership. While proponents of both sides of the argument cite specific cases to support their positions, Rudolph Giuliani (see photo), the former mayor of New York City, provides a strong case for the power of adversity.[1]

For most of his career, Giuliani was often regarded as a hard-nosed, nothing-but-business individual. He built his career tackling tough issues such as cleaning up the streets of New York City by reducing crime, and vagrancy, and clamping down on businesses that catered to the seedier side of life. Giuliani's no-nonsense approach to fighting crime first earned him accolades as a prosecuting attorney when he tackled the stronghold of organized crime in the New York area. His strength and conviction in these cases made him a local hero to many, ultimately catapulting him into the job of mayor.

As mayor, he continued his autocratic ways. He ordered city employees to do certain things—and expected them to be done correctly. He was regarded as an individual who had no heart, no compassion. Giuliani carried on his mayoral duties in a decisive manner—to some people's dismay. His crime-fighting tactics, for instance, drew severe criticism from minority groups. Several well-publicized police shootings, which drew national attention, were defended by Giuliani in an "ends-justify-the-means" approach. Many of these same individuals were thrilled that his eight years in office were quickly drawing to a close in early 2001. The so-called "tyrant of New York City" was about to leave!

In the spring of 2001, Giuliani's personal life changed dramatically. He was diagnosed with prostate cancer, and became embattled with his wife of two decades over their legal separation. Both of these events were national news. But Giuliani persevered. He continued to display his hard-nosed approach to managing the City. While he opted not to run for a New York State Senate seat opposing Hillary Rodham Clinton, he was not about to let his personal life interfere with who he was.

At 8:46 on the morning of September 11, 2001, Rudy Giuliani's life (as well as the world's) changed. Here he was, the iron-fisted mayor, faced with the worst terrorist attack this country had ever seen. What would he do? How would he react? Everyone's attention turned to the mayor of New York. That moment in history exposed a side of this man that had never before been seen. He began leading the people of New York through some of the darkest days in U. S. history.

Giuliani quickly took control, first ensuring the safety of the city. He closed bridges and called for military air support. But he also gave aid and comfort to those at ground zero. He inspired and encouraged people by his words, and displayed emotions that few thought he possessed. He was visible—in fact, as some say, he was everywhere. He was seen with the firefighters as they searched for their comrades. He was even seen "running for his life" as the second World Trade tower collapsed. He was on television keeping the world informed about what was happening. Giuliani was quickly hailed by almost everyone as a compassionate leader who would not let the tragedy destroy his city, nor his nation.

Did world events bring out the best in Rudy Giuliani? You bet it did! He rose to the occasion. He guided all of his people—supporters and critics alike—through one of the most difficult periods in recent times. For his efforts, countless people were thankful. In fact, *Time* magazine selected Giuliani as its 2001 "Person of the Year."

RUDY GIULIANI'S STORY TELLS US SOMETHING ABOUT LEADERSHIP. On one hand, it's the leaders in organizations who make things happen. However, the ways that they do this may differ widely.

MANAGERS VERSUS LEADERS

Let's begin by clarifying the distinction between managers and leaders. Writers frequently use the two terms synonymously. However, they aren't necessarily the same. Managers are appointed; they have legitimate power that allows them to reward and punish. Their ability to influence is based on the formal authority inherent in their positions. In contrast, leaders may either be appointed or may emerge from within a group. Leaders can influence others to perform beyond the actions dictated by formal authority.

"Not all leaders are managers, nor are all managers leaders."

Should all managers be leaders? Conversely, should all leaders be managers? Because no one yet has been able to demonstrate through research or logical argument that leadership ability is a handicap to a manager, we can state that all managers should ideally be leaders. However, not all leaders necessarily have capabilities in other managerial functions, and thus not all should hold managerial positions. The fact that an individual can influence others does not mean that he or she can also plan, organize, and control. Given (if only ideally) that all managers should be leaders, we can pursue the subject from a managerial perspective. Therefore, by **leaders** we mean those who are able to influence others and who possess managerial authority.

leaders
People who are able to influence others and who possess managerial authority

TRAIT THEORIES OF LEADERSHIP

Ask the average person on the street what comes to mind when he or she thinks of leadership. You're likely to get a list of qualities such as intelligence, charisma, decisiveness, enthusiasm, strength, bravery, integrity, and self-confidence.[2] These responses represent, in essence, **trait theories of leadership**. The search for traits or characteristics that differentiate leaders from nonleaders, though done in a more sophisticated manner than our on-the-street survey, dominated the early research efforts in the study of leadership.

trait theories of leadership
Theories that isolate characteristics that differentiate leaders from nonleaders

Is it possible to isolate one or more traits in individuals who are generally acknowledged to be leaders—for instance, U.S. national security advisor Condoleezza Rice, Larry Ellison of Oracle, British Prime Minister Tony Blair, Chairman Kazuo Inamori of Kyocera, or Meg Whitman of eBay—that nonleaders do not possess? We may agree that these individuals meet our definition of a leader, but they have utterly different characteristics. If the concept of traits were to prove valid, all leaders would have to possess specific characteristics.

Research efforts at isolating these traits resulted in a number of dead ends. Attempts to identify a set of traits that would always differentiate leaders from followers and effective leaders from ineffective leaders failed. Perhaps it was a bit optimistic to believe that a set of consistent and unique personality traits could apply across the board to all effective leaders, whether they were in charge of the Washington Wizards basketball team, Nextel, Cedars Sinai Hospital, Volvo, Merck, United Way, or Outback Steakhouse.

However, attempts to identify traits consistently associated with leadership have been more successful. Six traits on which leaders are seen to differ from nonleaders include drive, the desire to lead, honesty and integrity, self-confidence, intelligence, and job-relevant knowledge.[3] These traits are briefly described in Exhibit 11–1.

Yet traits alone do not sufficiently explain leadership. Explanations based solely on traits ignore situational factors. Possessing the appropriate traits only makes it more likely that an individual will be an effective leader. He or she still has to take the right actions. And what is right in one situation is not necessarily right for another situation. So, although there has been some resurgent interest in traits during the past two decades, a major movement away from trait theories began as early as the 1940s. Leadership research from the late 1940s through the mid-1960s emphasized the preferred behavioral styles that leaders demonstrated.

What traits characterize leaders like Meg Whitman, president and CEO of eBay? Research has identified six: drive, the desire to lead, honesty and integrity, self-confidence, intelligence, and job-relevant knowledge. Using these traits to the best of her ability, Whitman has made eBay the leading online marketplace for selling goods and services.

EXHIBIT 11–1

Six Traits That Differentiate Leaders from Nonleaders

1. **Drive** Leaders exhibit a high effort level. They have a relatively high desire for achievement, they're ambitious, they have a lot of energy, they're tirelessly persistent in their activities, and they show initiative.
2. **Desire to lead** Leaders have a strong desire to influence and lead others. They demonstrate the willingness to take responsibility.
3. **Honesty and integrity** Leaders build trusting relationships between themselves and followers by being truthful or nondeceitful and by showing high consistency between word and deed.
4. **Self-confidence** Followers look to leaders for an absence of self-doubt. Leaders, therefore, need to show self-confidence in order to convince followers of the rightness of goals and decisions.
5. **Intelligence** Leaders need to be intelligent enough to gather, synthesize, and interpret large amounts of information and to be able to create visions, solve problems, and make correct decisions.
6. **Job-relevant knowledge** Effective leaders have a high degree of knowledge about the company, industry, and technical matters. In-depth knowledge allows leaders to make well-informed decisions and to understand the implications of those decisions.

Source: Reprinted from "Leadership: Do Traits Really Matter?" by S. A. Kirkpatrick and E. A. Locke by permission of *Academy of Management Executive*, May 1991, pp. 48–60. © 1991 by Academy of Management Executive.

BEHAVIORAL THEORIES OF LEADERSHIP

The inability to explain leadership solely by traits led researchers to look at the behavior of specific leaders. Researchers wondered whether there was something unique in the behavior of effective leaders. For example, do leaders tend to be more democratic than autocratic?

It was hoped that the **behavioral theories of leadership approach** would not only provide more definitive answers about the nature of leadership, but, if successful, it would also have practical implications quite different from those of the trait approach. If trait research had been successful, it would have provided a basis for selecting the right people to assume formal positions in organizations requiring leadership. In contrast, if behavioral studies were to turn up critical behavioral determinants of leadership, we could train people to be leaders. That's precisely the premise behind the management development programs at, for example, most of the *Fortune* 1000 companies.[4]

behavioral theories of leadership
Theories that isolate behaviors that differentiate effective leaders from ineffective leaders

A number of studies looked at behavioral styles. We shall briefly review three of the most popular studies: Kurt Lewin's studies at the University of Iowa, the Ohio State group, and the University of Michigan studies. Then we shall see how the concepts that those studies developed could be used to create a grid for appraising leadership styles.

ARE THERE IDENTIFIABLE LEADERSHIP BEHAVIORS?

One of the first studies of leadership behavior was done by Kurt Lewin and his associates at the University of Iowa.[5] In their studies, the researchers explored three leadership behaviors or styles: autocratic, democratic, and laissez faire. An **autocratic style** is that of a leader who typically tends to centralize authority, dictate work methods, make unilateral decisions, and limit employee participation. A leader with a **democratic style** tends to involve employees in decision making, delegates authority, encourages participation in deciding work methods and goals, and uses feedback as an opportunity to coach employees. The democratic style can be further classified in

autocratic style of leadership
The term used to describe a leader who centralizes authority, dictates work methods, makes unilateral decisions, and limits employee participation

democratic style of leadership
The term used to describe a leader who involves employees in decision making, delegates authority, encourages participation in deciding work methods and goals, and uses feedback to coach employees

laissez-faire style of leadership The term used to describe a leader who gives employees complete freedom to make decisions and to decide on work methods

two ways: consultative and participative. A *democratic-consultative leader* seeks input and hears the concerns and issues of employees but makes the final decision him or herself. In this capacity, the democratic-consultative leader is using the input as an information-seeking exercise. A *democratic-participative leader* often allows employees to have a say in what's decided. Here, decisions are made by the group, with the leader providing one input to that group. Finally, the **laissez-faire** leader generally gives his or her employees complete freedom to make decisions and to complete their work in whatever way they see fit. A laissez-faire leader might simply provide necessary materials and answer questions.

Lewin and his associates wondered which one of the three leadership styles was most effective. On the basis of their studies of leaders from boys' clubs, they concluded that the laissez-faire style was ineffective on every performance criterion when compared with both democratic and autocratic styles. Quantity of work done was equal in groups with democratic and autocratic leaders, but work quality and group satisfaction were higher in democratic groups. The results suggest that a democratic leadership style could contribute to both good quantity and high quality of work.

Later studies of autocratic and democratic styles of leadership showed mixed results. For example, democratic leadership styles sometimes produced higher performance levels than autocratic styles, but at other times they produced group performance that was lower than or equal to that of autocratic styles. Nonetheless, more consistent results were generated when a measure of employee satisfaction was used.

Group members' satisfaction levels were generally higher under a democratic leader than under an autocratic one.[6] Did this mean that managers should always exhibit a democratic style of leadership? Two researchers, Robert Tannenbaum and Warren Schmidt, attempted to provide that answer.[7]

Tannenbaum and Schmidt developed a continuum of leader behaviors (see Exhibit 11–2). The continuum illustrates that a range of leadership behaviors, all the

EXHIBIT 11–2 Continuum of Leader Behavior

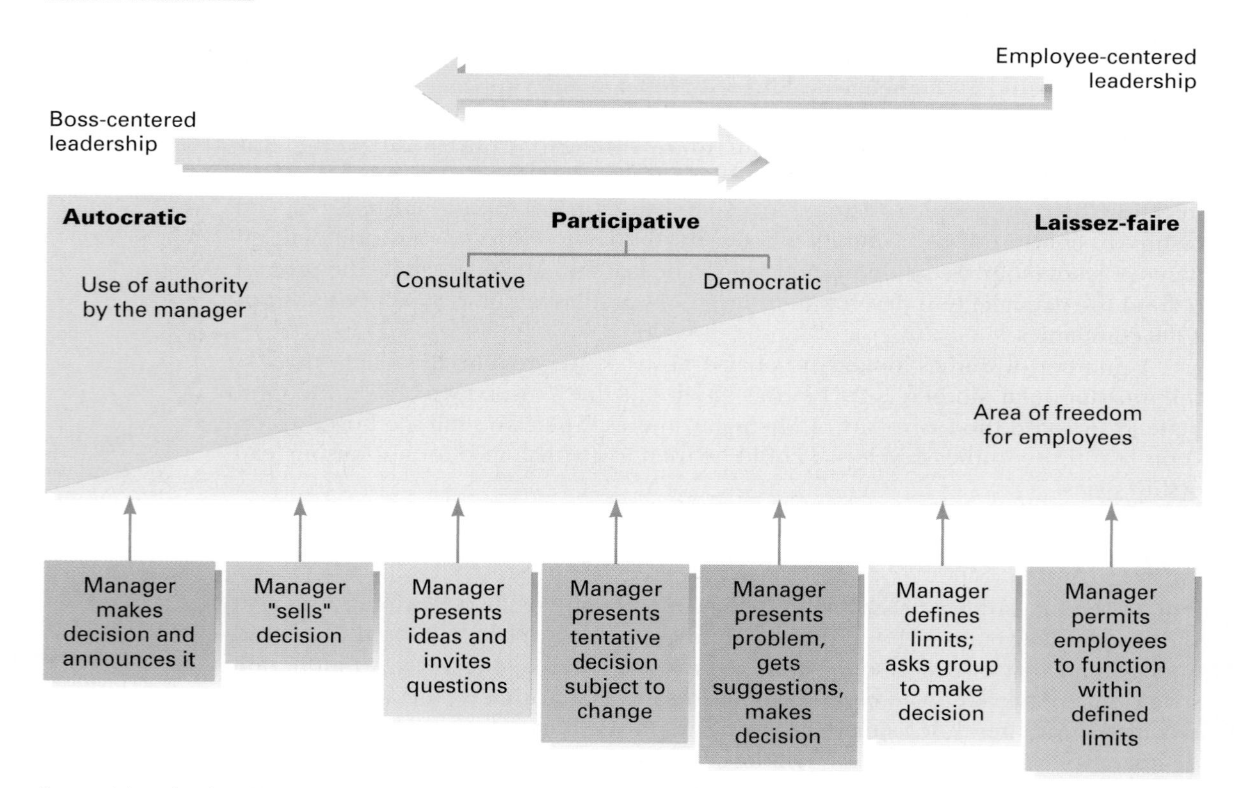

Source: Adapted and reprinted by permission of the *Harvard Business Review*. An exhibit from "How to Choose a Leadership Pattern" by R. Tannenbaum and W. Schmidt, May–June 1973. Copyright © 1973 by the President and Fellows of Harvard College; all rights reserved.

way from boss-centered (autocratic) on the left side of the model to employee-centered (laissez-faire) on the right side of the model, is possible. In deciding which leader behavior from the continuum to use, Tannenbaum and Schmidt proposed that managers look at forces within themselves (such as comfort level with the chosen leadership style), forces within the employees (such as readiness to assume responsibility), and forces within the situation (such as time pressures). They suggested that managers should move toward more employee-centered styles in the long run because such behavior would increase employees' motivation, decision quality, teamwork, morale, and development.

This dual nature of leader behaviors—that is, focusing on the work to be done and focusing on the employees—is also a key characteristic of the Ohio State and University of Michigan studies.

WHY WERE THE OHIO STATE STUDIES IMPORTANT?

The most comprehensive and replicated of the behavioral theories resulted from research that began at Ohio State University in the late 1940s.[8] These studies sought to identify independent dimensions of leader behavior. Beginning with over 1,000 dimensions, the researchers eventually narrowed the list down to two categories that accounted for most of the leadership behavior described by employees. They called these two dimensions initiating structure and consideration.

Initiating structure refers to the extent to which a leader is likely to define and structure his or her role and those of employees in the search for goal attainment. It includes behavior that attempts to organize work, work relationships, and goals. For example, the leader who is characterized as high in initiating structure assigns group members to particular tasks, expects workers to maintain definite standards of performance, and emphasizes the meeting of deadlines.

initiating structure
The extent to which a leader defines and structures his or her role and the roles of employees to attain goals

Consideration is defined as the extent to which a leader has job relationships characterized by mutual trust and respect for employees' ideas and feelings. A leader who is high in consideration helps employees with personal problems, is friendly and approachable, and treats all employees as equals. He or she shows concern for his or her followers' comfort, well-being, status, and satisfaction.

consideration
The extent to which a leader has job relationships characterized by mutual trust, respect for employees' ideas, and regard for their feelings

Extensive research based on these definitions found that a leader who is high in initiating structure and consideration (a high-high leader) achieved high employee performance and satisfaction more frequently than one who rated low on either consideration, initiating structure, or both. However, the high-high style did not always yield positive results. For example, leader behavior characterized as high on initiating structure led to greater rates of grievances, absenteeism, and turnover, and lower levels of job satisfaction for workers performing routine tasks. Other studies found that high consideration was negatively related to performance ratings of the leader by his or her manager. In conclusion, the Ohio State studies suggested that the high-high style generally produced positive outcomes, but enough exceptions were found to indicate that situational factors needed to be integrated into the theory.

WHAT WERE THE LEADERSHIP DIMENSIONS OF THE UNIVERSITY OF MICHIGAN STUDIES?

Leadership studies undertaken at the University of Michigan's Survey Research Center, at about the same time as those being done at Ohio State, had similar research objectives: to locate the behavioral characteristics of leaders that were related to performance effectiveness. The Michigan group also came up with two dimensions of leadership behavior, which they labeled employee oriented and production oriented.[9] Leaders who were **employee oriented** emphasized interpersonal relations; they took a personal interest in the needs of their employees and accepted individual differences among members. The **production-oriented** leaders, in contrast, tended to emphasize the technical or task aspects of the job, were concerned mainly with accomplishing their group's tasks, and regarded group members as a means to that end.

employee oriented
The term used to describe a leader who emphasizes interpersonal relations, takes a personal interest in the needs of employees, and accepts individual differences

production oriented
The term used to describe a leader who emphasizes the technical or task aspects of a job, is concerned mainly with accomplishing tasks, and regards group members as a means to accomplishing goals

The conclusions of the Michigan researchers strongly favored leaders who were employee oriented. Employee-oriented leaders were associated with higher group productivity and higher job satisfaction. Production-oriented leaders were associated with lower group productivity and lower worker satisfaction.

WHAT IS THE MANAGERIAL GRID?

managerial grid
A two-dimensional view of leadership style that is based on concern for people versus concern for production

The **managerial grid** is a two-dimensional view of leadership style developed by Robert Blake and Jane Mouton.[10] They proposed a managerial grid based on the styles of "concern for people" and "concern for production," which essentially represent the Ohio State dimensions of consideration and initiating structure and the Michigan dimensions of employee orientation and production orientation.

The grid, depicted in Exhibit 11–3 has nine possible positions along each axis, creating 81 different positions into which a leader's style may fall. The grid does not show the results but rather the dominating factors in a leader's thinking in regard to getting the results. That is, although there are 81 positions on the grid, the five key positions identified by Blake and Mouton focus on the four corners of the grid and a middle-ground area.

Blake and Mouton concluded that managers perform best using a 9,9 style. Unfortunately, the grid offers no answers to the question of what makes an effective leader, but only a framework for conceptualizing leadership style. In fact, there is little substantive evidence to support the conclusion that a 9,9 style is most effective in all situations.[11]

WHAT DID THE BEHAVIORAL THEORIES TEACH US ABOUT LEADERSHIP?

We have described the most popular and important attempts to explain leadership in terms of behavior. There have been other efforts,[12] but they faced the same problem that confronted the early behavioral researchers: They had very little success in iden-

EXHIBIT 11–3

The Managerial Grid

Source: Adapted and reprinted by permission of the *Harvard Business Review*. An Exhibition from "Breakthrough in Organization Development" by R. R. Blake, J. A. Mouton, L. B. Barnes, and L. E. Greine November–December 1964, p. 136. Copyright © 1964 by the President and Fellows of Harvard College; all rights reserved.

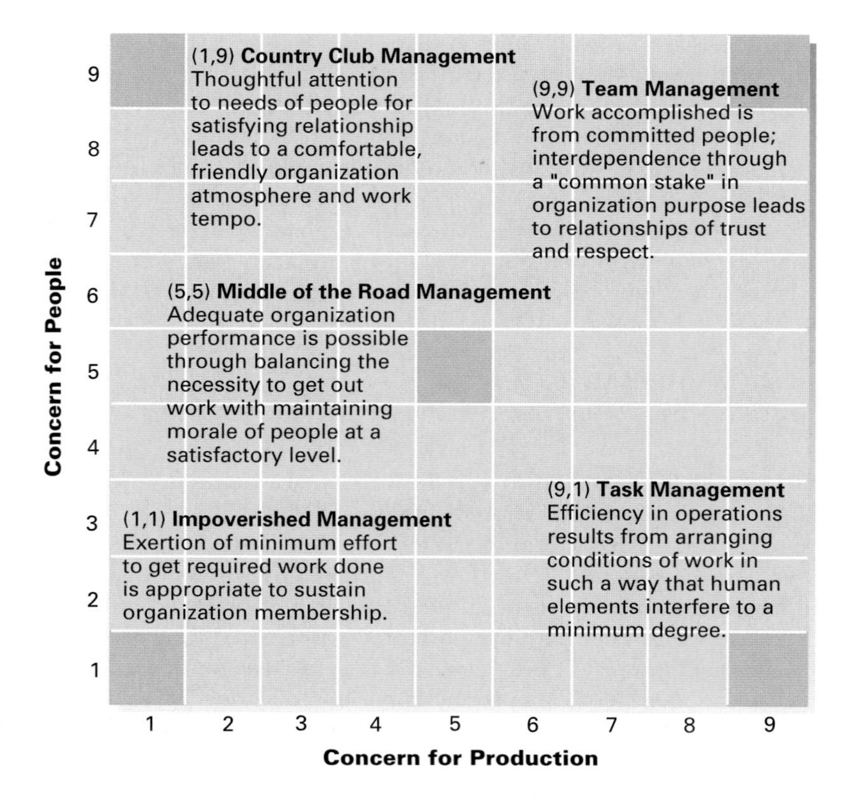

tifying consistent relationships between patterns of leadership behavior and successful performance. General statements could not be made because results would vary over different ranges of circumstances. What was missing was a consideration of the situational factors that influence success or failure. For example, would Mother Teresa have been a great leader of the poor at the turn of the century? Would Ralph Nader have risen to lead a consumer activist group had he been born in 1834 rather than in 1934 or in Costa Rica rather than in Connecticut? It seems quite unlikely, yet the behavioral approaches we have described could not clarify such situational factors. These uncertainties—the application of certain leadership styles in all situations—led researchers to try to better understand the effect of the situation on effective leadership styles.

Are the Army's elite, the 101st Airborne Rangers, born leaders? Probably not. Rather, members of this elite group become leaders in their field by learning what to do and how to do it. Behavioral leadership theorists would say, then, that they are trained in knowing when to focus on results and when to take into account a people orientation.

CONTINGENCY THEORIES OF LEADERSHIP

It became increasingly clear to students of the leadership phenomenon that predicting leadership success was more complex than isolating a few traits or preferable behaviors. The failure to obtain consistent results led to a new focus on situational influences. The relationship between leadership style and effectiveness suggested that under condition a, style X would be appropriate, whereas style Y would be more suitable for condition b, and style Z for condition c. But what were the conditions a, b, c, and so forth? It was one thing to say that leadership effectiveness depended on the situation and another to be able to isolate situational conditions.

Several approaches to isolating key situational variables have proved more successful than others and, as a result, have gained wider recognition. We shall consider four: the Fiedler model, path-goal theory, the leader-participation model, and Hersey and Blanchard's situational leadership theory.

WHAT IS THE FIEDLER MODEL?

The first comprehensive contingency model for leadership was developed by Fred Fiedler.[13] His model proposes that effective group performance depends on the proper match between the leader's style of interacting with his or her subordinates and the degree to which the situation gives control and influence to the leader.

Fiedler developed an instrument, which he called the **least-preferred co-worker (LPC) questionnaire**, that purports to measure the leader's behavioral orientation—either task oriented or relationship oriented. Then, he isolated three situational criteria—leader member relations, task structure, and position power—that could be manipulated so as to create the proper match with the behavioral orientation of the leader. In a sense, the **Fiedler contingency model** is an outgrowth of trait theory, because the LPC questionnaire is a simple psychological test. Fiedler, however, went significantly beyond trait and behavioral approaches in attempting to isolate situations, relating his personality measure to his situational classification and then predicting leadership effectiveness as a function of the two. This description of the Fiedler model is somewhat abstract (see Details on a Management Classic).

least-preferred co-worker (LPC) questionnaire
A questionnaire that measures whether a person is task or relationship oriented

Fiedler contingency leadership model
The theory that effective group performance depends on the proper match between the leader's style of interacting with employees and the degree to which the situation gives control and influence to the leader

The Fiedler contingency model of leadership proposes matching an individual's least-preferred co-worker score and an assessment of three contingency variables to achieve maximum leadership. In his studies of over 1,200 groups, in which he compared relationship-versus task-oriented leadership styles in each of eight situational categories, Fiedler concluded that task-oriented leaders tend to perform best in situations that are either very favorable or very unfavorable to

Details on a Management Classic

The Fielder Contingency Model of Leadership

Fred Fiedler believed that an individual's basic leadership style is a key factor in leadership success, so he began by trying to find out the leader's basic style using the LPC questionnaire, which contains 16 contrasting adjectives (such as pleasant-unpleasant, efficient-inefficient, open-guarded, supportive-hostile). The questionnaire asks the respondent to think of all the co-workers he or she has ever had and to describe the one person he or she *least enjoyed* working with by rating that person on a scale of 1 to 8 for each of the 16 sets of contrasting adjectives. Fiedler believed that, on the basis of the answers to this LPC questionnaire, he could determine a respondent's basic leadership style. His premise was that what you say about others tells more about you than it tells about the person you're describing. If the least-preferred co-worker was described in relatively positive terms (a high LPC score), then the respondent was primarily interested in good personal relations with co-workers. That is, if you essentially described the person you are least able to work with in favorable terms, Fiedler would label you relationship oriented. In contrast, if the least-preferred co-worker is seen in relatively unfavorable terms (a low LPC score), the respondent is primarily interested in productivity and thus would be labeled task oriented. Notice that Fiedler assumed that an individual's leadership style is fixed, that is, either relationship oriented or task oriented. This assumption is important because it means that if a situation requires a task-oriented leader and the person in that leadership position is relationship oriented, either the situation has to be modified or the leader replaced for optimum effectiveness. Fiedler argued that leadership style is innate to a person—you can't change your style to fit changing situations.

After an individual's basic leadership style has been assessed through the LPC, it is necessary to match the leader with the situation. The three situational factors or contingency dimensions identified by Fiedler are defined as follows:

- ***Leader–member relations*** The degree of confidence, trust, and respect employees have in their leader
- ***Task structure*** The degree to which the job assignments of employees are structured or unstructured
- ***Position power*** The degree of influence a leader has over power variables such as hiring, firing, discipline, promotions, and salary increases

So, the next step in the Fiedler model is to evaluate the situation in terms of these three contingency variables. Leader–member relations are either good or poor, task structure either high or low, and position power either strong or weak. Fiedler stated that the better the leader–member relations, the more highly structured the job, and the stronger the position power, the more control or influence the leader has. For example, a very favorable situation (in which the leader has a great deal of control) might involve a payroll manager who is well respected and whose subordinates have confidence in him or her (good leader–member relations); where the activities to be done—such as wage computation, check writing, report filing—are specific and clear (high task structure); and where the job provides considerable freedom to reward and punish subordinates (strong position power). On the other hand, an unfavorable situation might be that of the disliked chairman of a voluntary United Way fund-raising team. In this job, the leader has very little control. All together, by mixing the three contingency variables, there are potentially eight different situations or categories in which a leader could find himself or herself. Fiedler concluded that task-oriented leaders perform best in situations that are very favorable or very unfavorable to them. A moderately favorable situation, however, is best handled through relationship-oriented leadership.

them (see Exhibit 11–4). Fiedler predicted that, when faced with a category I, II, III, VII, or VIII situation, task-oriented leaders would perform well. Relationship-oriented leaders, however, perform best in moderately favorable situations—categories IV through VI.

Remember that according to Fiedler, an individual's leadership style is fixed. Therefore, there are really only two ways in which to improve leader effectiveness. First, you can change the leader to fit the situation. For example, if a group situation rates as highly unfavorable to the leader but is currently led by a relationship-oriented manager, the group's performance could be improved by

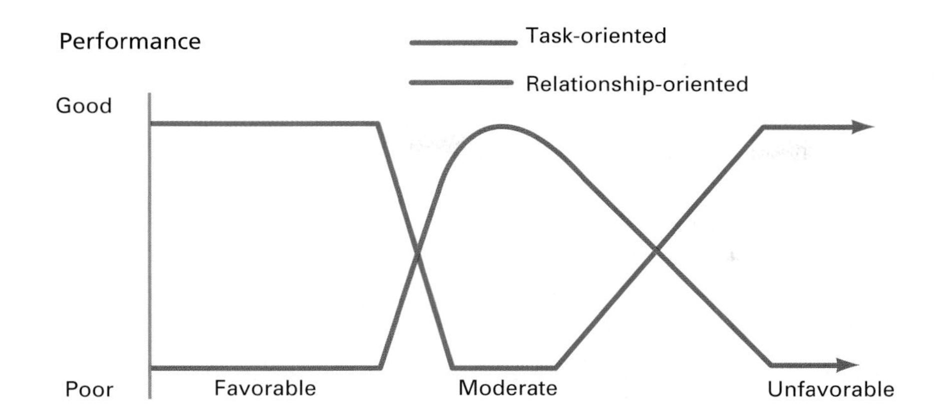

Category	I	II	III	IV	V	VI	VII	VIII
Leader–member relations	Good	Good	Good	Good	Poor	Poor	Poor	Poor
Task structure	High	High	Low	Low	High	High	Low	Low
Position power	Strong	Weak	Strong	Weak	Strong	Weak	Strong	Weak

EXHIBIT 11-4

The Findings of the Fiedler Model

replacing that manager with one who is task oriented. The second alternative would be to change the situation to fit the leader by restructuring the tasks or by increasing or decreasing the power that the leader has to control such factors as salary increases, promotions, and disciplinary actions.

As a whole, the major studies undertaken that tested the overall validity of the Fiedler model lead to a generally positive conclusion. That is, there is considerable evidence to support at least substantial parts of the model.[14] Even though Fielder may not have identified all the situational variables that affect leadership, the ones he did identify do appear to contribute substantially to our understanding of situational factors.[15] But there are problems with the LPC and the practical use of the model that need to be addressed. For instance, the logic underlying the LPC is not well understood, and studies have shown that respondents' LPC scores are not stable. Also, the contingency variables are complex and difficult for practitioners to assess. It's often difficult in practice to determine how good the leader–member relations are, how structured the task is, and how much position power the leader has.

HOW DOES PATH-GOAL THEORY OPERATE?

One of the most respected approaches to leadership is **path-goal theory**. Developed by Robert House, path-goal theory is a contingency model of leadership that extracts key elements from the Ohio State leadership research and the expectancy theory of motivation (see Chapter 10).[16]

path-goal theory
The theory that it is a leader's job to assist followers in attaining their goals and to provide the necessary direction and support

The essence of the theory is that it is the leader's job to assist his or her followers in attaining their goals and to provide the necessary direction and support to ensure that their goals are compatible with the overall objectives of the group or organization. The term path-goal is derived from the belief that effective leaders clarify the path to help their followers get from where they are to the achievement of their work goals and make the journey along the path easier by reducing roadblocks and pitfalls.

"According to path-goal theory, a leader's job is to assist his or her followers in attaining their goals."

According to path-goal theory, a leader's behavior is acceptable to the degree that employees view it as an

According to path-goal theory, this platoon leader's job is to assist his platoon members in attaining their goals and provide them direction and support in achieving those goals for the benefit of the military operation.

immediate source of satisfaction or as a means of future satisfaction. A leader's behavior is motivational to the degree that it (1) makes employee need satisfaction contingent on effective performance and (2) provides the coaching, guidance, support, and rewards that are necessary for effective performance. To test these statements, House identified four leadership behaviors. The *directive leader* lets employees know what is expected of them, schedules work to be done, and gives specific guidance as to how to accomplish tasks. This type of leadership closely parallels the Ohio State dimension of initiating structure. The *supportive leader* is friendly and shows concern for the needs of employees. This type of leadership is essentially synonymous with the Ohio State dimension of consideration. The *participative leader* (a la Lewin's democratic consultative style) consults with employees and uses their suggestions before making a decision. The *achievement-oriented* leader sets challenging goals and expects employees to perform at their highest levels. In contrast to Fiedler's view of a leader's behavior, House assumes that leaders are flexible. Path-goal theory implies that the same leader can display any or all of these leadership styles, depending on the situation.[17]

As Exhibit 11–5 illustrates, path-goal theory proposes two classes of situational or contingency variables that moderate the leadership behavior–outcome relationship—environmental variables that are outside the control of the employee (task structure, the formal authority system, and the work group) and variables that are part of the personal characteristics of the employee (locus of control, experience, and perceived ability). Environmental factors determine the type of leader behavior required if employee outcomes are to be maximized, and personal characteristics of the employee determine how the environment and leader behavior are interpreted. The theory proposes that leader behavior will be ineffective when it is redundant to

EXHIBIT 11–5
Path-Goal Theory

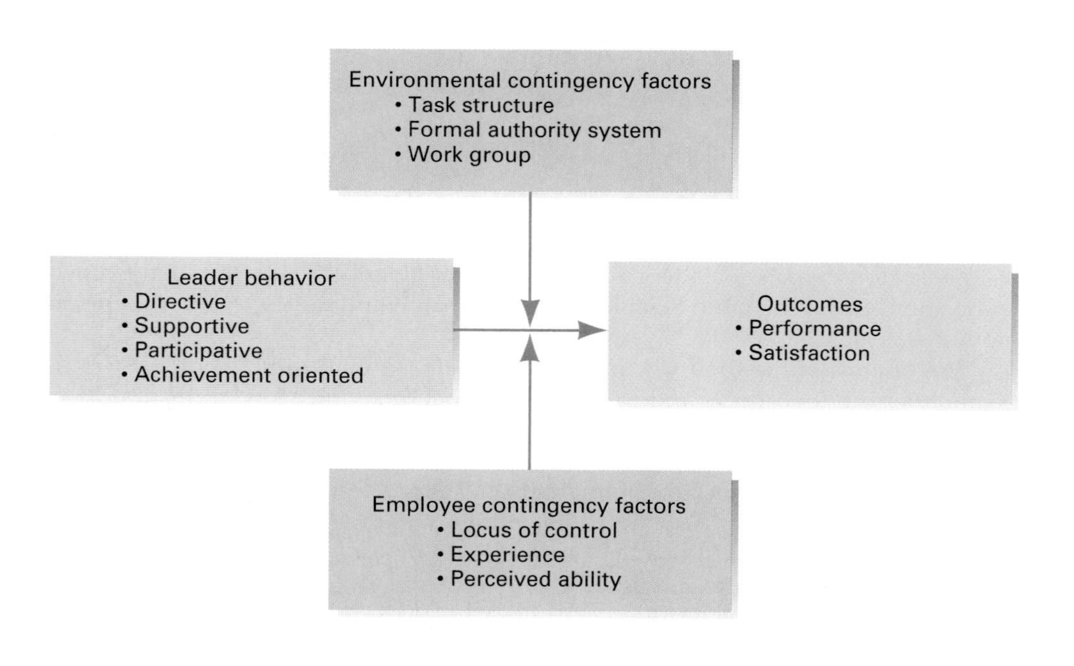

sources of environmental structure or incongruent with subordinate characteristics.

Research to validate path-goal predictions has been generally encouraging, although not every study found positive support.[18] However, the majority of the evidence supports the logic underlying the theory. That is, employee performance and satisfaction are likely to be positively influenced when the leader compensates for shortcomings with the employee or the work setting. But if the leader spends time explaining tasks when those tasks are already understood or the employee has the ability and experience to handle them without interference, the employee is likely to see such directive behavior as redundant or even insulting.

Ken Chenault, CEO of American Express, confirms the path-goal theory of leadership in that a person's leadership style is to assist followers in attaining their goals. As a directive leader, Chenault lets his staff know precisely what is expected of them, works with his employees in understanding how to do their jobs, and gives them specific guidance as to how to accomplish their goal of being one of America's most admired companies.

WHAT IS THE LEADER-PARTICIPATION MODEL?

Back in 1973, Victor Vroom and Phillip Yetton developed a **leader-participation model** that related leadership behavior and participation to decision making.[19] Recognizing that task structures have varying demands for routine and nonroutine activities, these researchers argued that leader behavior must adjust to reflect the task structure. Vroom and Yetton's model was normative. That is, it provided a sequential set of rules to be followed in determining the form and amount of participation in decision making in different types of situations. The model was a decision tree incorporating seven contingencies (whose relevance could be identified by making yes or no choices) and five alternative leadership styles.

More recent work by Vroom and Arthur Jago has revised that model.[20] The new model retains the same five alternative leadership styles but expands the contingency variables to twelve—from the leader's making the decision completely by himself or herself to sharing the problem with the group and developing a consensus decision. These variables are listed in Exhibit 11–6.

Research testing the original leader-participation model was very encouraging.[21] But, unfortunately, the model is far too complex for the typical manager to use regularly. In fact, Vroom and Jago have developed a computer program to guide managers through all the decision branches in the revised model. Although we obviously cannot do justice to this model's sophistication in this discussion, it has provided us with some solid, empirically supported insights into key contingency variables related to leadership effectiveness. Moreover, the leader-participation model confirms that leadership research should be directed at the situation rather than at the person. That is, it probably makes more sense to talk about autocratic and participative situations than autocratic and participative leaders. As House did in his path-goal theory, Vroom, Yetton, and Jago argue against the notion that leader behavior is inflexible. The leader-participation model assumes that the leader can adapt his or her style to different situations.[22]

Leader-participation model
A leadership theory that provides a sequential set of rules for determining the form and amount of participation a leader should exercise in decision making according to different types of situations

HOW DOES SITUATIONAL LEADERSHIP OPERATE?

Paul Hersey and Kenneth Blanchard's leadership model has gained a strong following among management development specialists. Called **Situational Leadership (SL)**, it shows how a leader should adjust his or her leadership style to reflect what followers need.[23] This model has been incorporated into leadership training programs at many of the *Fortune* 500 companies, and over 10 million managers a year from a wide variety of organizations are learning its basic elements.[24]

situational leadership (SL) theory
A model of leadership behavior that reflects how a leader should adjust his or her leadership style in accordance with the readiness of followers.

Situational Leadership is a contingency theory that focuses on the followers. Successful leadership is achieved by selecting the right leadership style, which Hersey and Blanchard argue is contingent on the follower's level of readiness. Before we

EXHIBIT 11–6

Contigency Variables in the Revised Leader-Participation Model

QR: Quality Requirement	How important is the technical quality of this decision?
CR: Commitment Requirement	How important is employee commitment to the decision?
LI: Leader Information	Do you have sufficient information to make a high-quality decision?
ST: Problem Structure	Is the problem well structured?
CP: Commitment Probability	If you were to make this decision by yourself, is it reasonably certain that your employees would be committed to the decision?
GC: Goal Congruence	Do employees share the organizational goal to be attained in solving this problem?
CO: Employee Conflict	Is conflict among employees over preferred solutions likely?
SI: Employee Information	Do employees have sufficient information to make a high-quality decision?
TC: Time Constraint	Does a critically severe time constraint limit your ability to involve employees?
GD: Geographical Dispersion	Are the costs involved in bringing together geographically dispersed employees prohibitive?
MT: Motivation Time	How important is it to you to minimize the time it takes to make the decision?
MD: Motivation-Development	How important is it to you to maximize the opportunities for employee development?

Source: V. H. Vroom and A. G. Jago, *The New Leadership: Managing Participation in Organizations* (Upper Saddle River, NJ: Prentice Hall, 1988), pp. 111–12. Reprinted by permission of Prentice Hall, Inc., Upper Saddle River, New Jersey.

proceed, let's clarify two points: Why focus on the followers? And what is meant by the term *readiness*?[25]

The emphasis on the followers in leadership effectiveness reflects the reality that it is the followers who accept or reject the leader. Regardless of what the leader does, effectiveness depends on the actions of his or her followers. This important dimension has often been overlooked or underemphasized in most leadership theories. **Readiness**, as defined by Hersey and Blanchard, refers to the extent that people have the ability and the willingness to accomplish a specific task.

readiness
The situational leadership model term for a follower's ability and willingness to perform

Hersey and Blanchard identify four specific behaviors—from highly directive to highly laissez-faire (see Exhibit 11–7). The most effective behavior depends on a follower's ability and motivations.[26] So, SL says if a follower is unable and unwilling, the leader needs to display high task orientation to compensate for the follower's lack of ability and high relationship orientation to get the follower to buy into the leader's desires. At the other end of the readiness spectrum, if followers are able and willing, the leader doesn't need to do much.

SL has an intuitive appeal. It acknowledges the importance of followers and builds on the idea that leaders can compensate for the lack of ability and motivation of their followers. Yet research efforts to test and support the theory have generally been mixed.[27] Why? Possible explanations include internal ambiguities and inconsistencies of the model itself as well as problems with research methodology in tests of the theory. So, in spite of its intuitive appeal and wide popularity, at least at this point in time, any endorsement of SL has to be guarded.

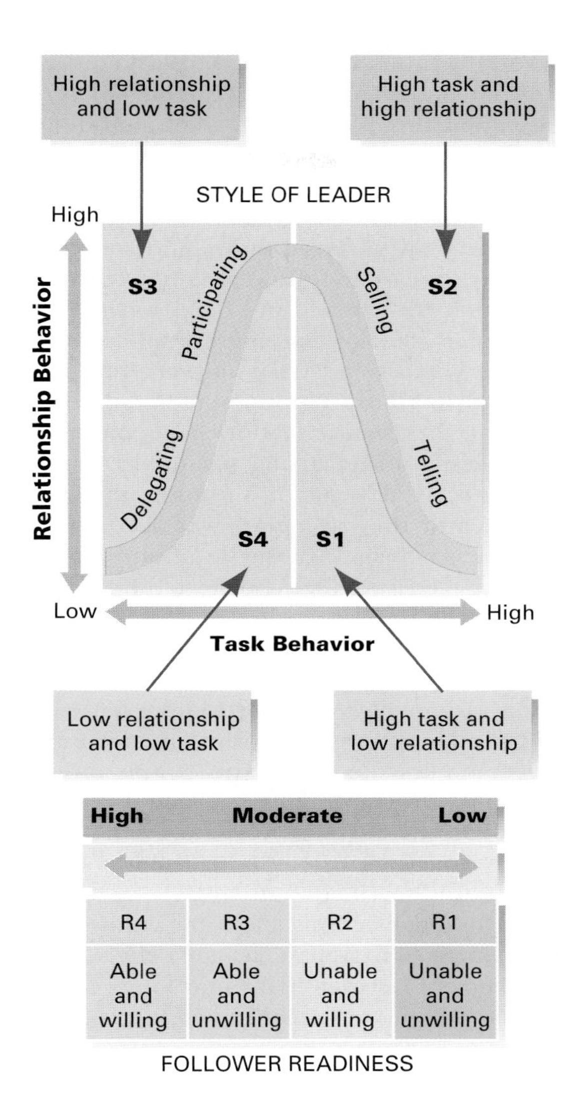

EXHIBIT 11-7

Hersey and Blanchard's Situational Leadership Model

Source: Reprinted with permission from the Center for Leadership Studies. Situational Leadership® is a registered trademark of the Center for Leadership Studies, Escondido, California. All rights reserved.

EMERGING APPROACHES TO LEADERSHIP

We'll conclude our review of leadership theories by presenting three emerging approaches to the subject: charismatic leadership, visionary leadership, and transactional versus transformational leadership. If there is one theme that underlies these approaches, it is that they take a more practical view of leadership than previous theories have (with the exception of trait theories, of course). That is, these approaches look at leadership the way the average person on the street does.

WHAT IS CHARISMATIC LEADERSHIP THEORY?

In Chapter 8, we discussed attribution theory in relation to perception. **Charismatic leadership theory** is an extension of that theory. It says that followers make attributions of heroic or extraordinary leadership abilities when they observe certain behaviors.[28] Studies on charismatic leadership have, for the most part, attempted to identify those behaviors that differentiate charismatic leaders from their noncharismatic counterparts.[29] Some examples of individuals frequently cited as being charismatic include John F. Kennedy, Martin Luther King Jr., Mary Kay Ash (founder of Mary Kay Cosmetics), and Herb Kelleher (former CEO of Southwest Airlines).

charismatic leadership theory
The theory that followers make attributions of heroic or extraordinary leadership abilities when they observe certain behaviors

What leadership traits does Tom Coughlin, executive vice president and vice chairman, Wal-Mart Stores, Inc. (USA), Durain and Tom's Club USA, possess that helped him become a leader for this "giant" of a company. Researchers would say that Coughlin's traits include his compelling vision, the consistency of his actions, his ability to communicate his vision to others, and the ability to capitalize on his personal strengths.

Several authors have attempted to identify personal characteristics of the charismatic leader. Robert House (of path-goal fame) has identified three: extremely high confidence, dominance, and strong convictions.[30] Warren Bennis, after studying 90 of the most effective and successful leaders in the United States, found that they had four common competencies: They had a compelling vision or sense of purpose; they could communicate that vision in clear terms that their followers could readily identify with; they demonstrated consistency and focus in the pursuit of their vision; and they knew their own strengths and capitalized on them.[31] The most comprehensive analysis, however, has been completed by Jay Conger and Rabindra Kanungo at McGill University.[32] They concluded that charismatic leaders have an idealized goal that they want to achieve and a strong personal commitment to that goal; they are perceived as unconventional, they are assertive and self-confident, and they are perceived as agents of radical change rather than as managers of the status quo. Exhibit 11–8 summarizes the key characteristics that appear to differentiate charismatic leaders from noncharismatic ones.

How do charismatic leaders influence followers? The evidence suggests a four-step process.[33] It begins with the leader stating an appealing vision. This vision provides a sense of community for followers by linking the present with a better future for the organization. The leader then communicates high expectations and expresses confidence that followers can attain them. This enhances follower self-esteem and self-confidence. Next, the leader conveys, through words and actions, a new set of values,[34] and by his or her behavior sets an example for followers to imitate. Finally, the charismatic leader makes self-sacrifices and engages in unconventional behavior to demonstrate courage and convictions about the vision.

What can we say about the charismatic leader's effect on his or her followers? There is an increasing body of research that shows impressive correlations between charismatic leadership and high performance and satisfaction among followers.[35]

EXHIBIT 11–8

Key Characteristics of Charismatic Leaders

1. **Self-confidence** Charismatic leaders have complete confidence in their judgment and ability.
2. **Vision** They have an idealized goal that proposes a future better than the status quo. The greater the disparity between this idealized goal and the status quo, the more likely that followers will attribute extraordinary vision to the leader.
3. **Ability to articulate the vision** They are able to clarify and state the vision in terms that are understandable to others. This articulation demonstrates an understanding of the followers' needs and, hence, acts as a motivating force.
4. **Strong convictions about the vision** Charismatic leaders are perceived as being strongly committed and willing to take on high personal risk, incur high costs, and engage in self-sacrifice to achieve their vision.
5. **Behavior that is out of the ordinary** They engage in behavior that is perceived as being novel, unconventional, and counter to norms. When successful, these behaviors evoke surprise and admiration in followers.
6. **Appearance as a change agent** Charismatic leaders are perceived as agents of radical change rather than as caretakers of the status quo.
7. **Environmental sensitivity** They are able to make realistic assessments of the environmental constraints and resources needed to bring about change.

Source: Based on J. A. Conger and R. N. Kanungo, "Behavioral Dimensions of Charismatic Leadership," in J. A. Conger and R. N. Kanungo, *Charismatic Leadership* (San Francisco; Jossey-Bass, 1988), p. 91.

People working for charismatic leaders are motivated to exert extra work effort and, because they like and respect their leaders, express greater satisfaction.

If charisma is desirable, can people learn to be charismatic leaders? Or are charismatic leaders born with their qualities? While a small minority still think charisma cannot be learned, most experts believe that individuals can be trained to exhibit charismatic behaviors, and can thus enjoy the benefits that accrue to being labeled "a charismatic leader."[36] But it's important to note that charismatic leadership may not always be needed to achieve high levels of employee performance. Charisma appears to be most appropriate when the followers' task has a ideological component or when the environment involves a high degree of stress and uncertainty.[37] This may explain why, when charismatic leaders surface, it's more likely to be in politics, religion, wartime, or when a business firm is in its infancy or facing a life-threatening crisis.

The late Mary Kay Ash of Mary Kay® cosmetics had a visionary leadership style. Her ability to create the vision of women as entrepreneurs selling products that improved their self-image provided the inspiration for the cosmetic company to grow throughout the decades.

WHAT IS VISIONARY LEADERSHIP?

The term *vision* appeared in our previous discussion of charismatic leadership, but visionary leadership goes beyond charisma. In this section, we review recent revelations about the importance of visionary leadership.

Visionary leadership is the ability to create and articulate a realistic, credible, attractive vision of the future for an organization or organizational unit that grows out of and improves upon the present.[38] This vision, if properly selected and implemented, is so energizing that it in effect jump starts the future by calling forth the skills, talents, and resources to make it happen.[39]

visionary leadership
The ability to create and articulate a realistic, credible, attractive vision of the future that grows out of and improves upon the present

A review of various definitions finds that a vision differs from other forms of direction setting in several ways: A vision has clear and compelling imagery that offers an innovative way to improve, which recognizes and draws on traditions, and connects to actions that people can take to realize change. Vision taps people's emotions and energy. Properly articulated, a vision creates the enthusiasm that people have for sporting events and other leisure-time activities, bringing this energy and commitment to the workplace.[40]

The key properties of a vision seem to be inspirational possibilities that are value centered, realizable, and have superior imagery and articulation.[41] Visions should be able to create possibilities that are inspirational, unique, and offer a new order that can produce organizational distinction. A vision is likely to fail if it doesn't offer a view of the future that is clearly and demonstrably better for the organization and its members. Desirable visions fit the times and circumstances and reflect the uniqueness of the organization. People in the organization must also believe that the vision is attainable. It should be perceived as challenging yet do-able. Visions that have clear articulation and powerful imagery are more easily grasped and accepted.

What are some examples of visions? Rupert Murdoch had a vision for the future for the communications industry that combined entertainment and media. Through his News Corporation, Murdoch has successfully integrated a broadcast network, TV stations, movie studio, publishing, and global satellite distribution. Mary Kay Ash's vision of women as entrepreneurs selling products that improved their self-image gave impetus to her cosmetics company. Michael Dell has created a vision of a business that allows Dell Computer to sell and deliver a finished PC directly to a customer in fewer than eight days.

"A vision should create enthusiasm, bringing energy and commitment to the organization."

What skills do visionary leaders exhibit? Once the vision is identified, these leaders appear to have three

What is it that makes Sandy Leitch, chief executive of Zurich Financial Services, UKISA/Asia Pacific, a charismatic leader? Research tells us that he pays attention to the concerns and development needs of his employees; helps his employees look at problems in new ways; and excites, arouses, and inspires them to put out extra effort to achieve organizational goals. Given the success of Allied Zurich in the past few years, Leitch's results illustrate the goals that can be achieved by a charismatic leader.

qualities that are related to effectiveness in their visionary roles.[42] First is the ability to explain the vision to others. The leader needs to make the vision clear in terms of required actions and aims through clear oral and written communication. Former President Ronald Reagan—the so-called great communicator—used his years of acting experience to help him articulate a simple vision for his presidency: a return to happier and more prosperous times through less government, lower taxes, and a strong military. Second is the ability to express the vision not just verbally but through the leader's behavior. This requires behaving in ways that continually convey and reinforce the vision. Herb Kelleher at Southwest Airlines lived and breathed his commitment to customer service. He was famous within the company for jumping in, when needed, to help check in passengers, load baggage, fill in for flight attendants, or do anything else to make the customer's experience more pleasant. The third skill is the ability to extend the vision to different leadership contexts. This is the ability to sequence activities so the vision can be applied in a variety of situations. For instance, the vision has to be as meaningful to the people in accounting as to those in marketing and to employees in Zurich as well as in Nashville.

ARE ENTREPRENEURS VISIONARY LEADERS?

The last topic we want to discuss in this section is the role of the entrepreneur as a leader. In this role, the entrepreneur has certain leadership responsibilities in the organization.

Today's successful entrepreneur must be like the leader of a jazz ensemble that excels in improvisation, innovation, and creativity. Max DePree, former head of Herman Miller, Inc., a leading office furniture manufacturer known for its innovative leadership, said it best in his book *Leadership Jazz*:

> Jazz band leaders must choose the music, find the right musicians, and perform—in public. But the effect of the performance depends on so many things—the environment, the volunteers playing the band, the need for everybody to perform as individuals and as a group, the absolute dependence of the leader on the members of the band, the need for the followers to play well. . . . The leader of the jazz band has the beautiful opportunity to draw the best out of the other musicians. We have much to learn from jazz band leaders, for jazz, like leadership, combines the unpredictability of the future with the gifts of individuals.[43]

The way an entrepreneur leads the venture should be much like the jazz leader—drawing out the best of other individuals even given the unpredictability of the situation. And one way that an entrepreneur does this is through the vision he or she creates for the organization. In fact, often the driving force through the early stages of the entrepreneurial venture is the visionary leadership of the entrepreneur. The entrepreneur's ability to articulate a coherent, inspiring, and attractive vision of the future is a key test of his or her leadership. If an entrepreneur can do this, the results can be worthwhile. A study contrasting visionary and nonvisionary companies showed that visionary companies outperformed the nonvisionary ones by six times on standard financial criteria, and their stocks outperformed the general market by 15 times.

HOW DO TRANSACTIONAL LEADERS DIFFER FROM TRANSFORMATIONAL LEADERS?

The third area we touch on is the continuing interest in differentiating transformational leaders from transactional leaders.[44] As you will see, because transformational leaders are also charismatic, there is some overlap between this topic and our discussion on charismatic leadership.

Most of the leadership theories presented in this chapter—for instance, the Ohio State studies, Fiedler's model, path-goal theory, the leader-participation model, and Hersey and Blanchard's situational leadership model—address the issue of **transactional leaders**. These leaders guide or motivate their followers in the direction of established goals by clarifying role and task requirements, but another type of leader (transformational) inspires followers to transcend their own self-interests for the good of the organization and is capable of having a profound and extraordinary effect on his or her followers. **Transformational leaders** include such individuals as Bill Gates of Microsoft and Jeff Bezos of Amazon.com.[45] They pay attention to the concerns and developmental needs of individual followers; they change followers' awareness of issues by helping those followers to look at old problems in new ways; and they are able to excite, arouse, and inspire followers to put out extra effort to achieve group goals.

transactional leaders
Leaders who guide or motivate their followers toward established goals by clarifying role and task requirements

transformational leaders
Leaders who inspire followers to transcend their own self-interests for the good of the organization and are capable of having a profound and extraordinary effect on followers

Transactional and transformational leadership should not be viewed as opposing approaches to getting things done.[46] Transformational leadership is built on transactional leadership. Transformational leadership produces levels of employee effort and performance that go beyond what would occur with a transactional approach alone.[47] Moreover, transformational leadership is more than charisma. "The purely charismatic [leader] may want followers to adopt the charismatic's world view and go no further; the transformational leader will attempt to instill in followers the ability to question not only established views but eventually those established by the leader."[48]

The evidence supporting the superiority of transformational leadership over the transactional variety is overwhelmingly impressive. For instance, a number of studies with U.S., Canadian, and German military officers found, at every level, that transformational leaders were evaluated as more effective than their transactional counterparts.[49] Managers at FedEx who were rated by their followers as transformational leaders were evaluated by their immediate supervisors as the highest performers and the most promotable.[50] Transformational leadership has also been found to be linked to building trust among organizational members.[51] In summary, the overall evidence indicates that transformational leadership, as compared with transactional leadership, is more strongly correlated with lower turnover rates, higher productivity, and higher employee satisfaction.[52]

CONTEMPORARY LEADERSHIP ISSUES

As you may have inferred from the preceding discussions of the various theories, models, and roles of leadership, the concept of effective leadership is continually being refined as researchers continue to study leadership in organizations (see Ethical Dilemma in Management). Let's take a closer look at some of the contemporary issues in leadership: team leadership, leadership and national culture, emotional intelligence and leadership, the relevance of leadership, and entrepreneurial leadership.

WHAT IS TEAM LEADERSHIP?

Leadership increasingly exists within a team context. As teams grow in popularity, the role of the team leader takes on heightened importance.[53] This role is different from the traditional leadership role performed by first-line supervisors. J. D. Bryant, a supervisor at Texas Instruments' Forest Lane plant in Dallas, found that out.[54] One day he was happily overseeing a staff of 15 circuit board assemblers. The next day he was informed that the company was moving to teams and that he was to become a facilitator. "I'm supposed to teach the teams everything I know and then let them make their own decisions," he said. Confused about his new role, he admitted there was no clear plan on what he was supposed to do. In this section, we consider the challenge of being a team leader, review the new roles that team leaders take on, and offer some tips on how to perform effectively in this position.

Many leaders are not equipped to handle the change to teams. As one prominent consultant noted, "even the most capable managers have trouble making the

Ethical Dilemma in Management

Do Men and Women Lead Differently?

Are there gender differences in leadership styles? Are men more effective leaders, or, does that honor belong to women? Even asking those questions is certain to evoke reactions on both sides of the debate.

The evidence indicates that the two sexes are more alike than different in the ways they lead.[55] Much of this similarity is based on the fact that leaders, regardless of gender, perform similar activities in influencing others. That's their job, and the two sexes do it equally well. The same holds true in other professions. For instance, although the stereotypical nurse is a woman, men are equally effective and successful in this career.

Saying the sexes are more alike than different still means the two are not exactly the same.[56] The most common difference lies in leadership styles. Women tend to use a more democratic style. They encourage participation of their followers and are willing to share their positional power with others. In addition, women tend to influence others best through their ability to be charmingly influential.[57] Men, on the other hand, tend to typically use a task-centered leadership style. This includes directing activities of others and relying on their positional power to control the organization's activities. But surprisingly, even this difference is blurred. All things considered, when a woman is a leader in a traditionally male-dominated job (such as that of a police officer), she tends to lead in a manner that is more task centered.

Further compounding this issue are the changing roles of leaders in today's organizations. With an increased emphasis on teams, employee involvement, and interpersonal skills, democratic leadership styles are more in demand. Leaders need to be more sensitive to their followers' needs and more open in their communications; they need to build more trusting relationships. And many of these factors are behaviors that women have typically grown up developing.

So what do you think? Is there a difference between the sexes in terms of leadership styles? Do men or women make better leaders? Would you prefer to work for a man or a woman? What's your opinion?

transition because all the command and control type things they were encouraged to do before are no longer appropriate. There's no reason to have any skill or sense of this."[58] This same consultant estimated that "probably 15 percent of managers are natural team leaders; another 15 percent could never lead a team because it runs counter to their personality. [They're unable to sublimate their dominating style for the good of the team.] Then there's that huge group in the middle: Team leadership doesn't come naturally to them, but they can learn it."[59]

The challenge for most managers, then, is in becoming an effective team leader.[60] They have to learn the patience to share information, the ability to trust others and to give up authority, and the understanding of when to intervene.[61] Effective leaders have mastered the difficult balancing act of knowing when to leave their teams alone and when to intercede. New team leaders may try to retain too much control at a time when team members need more autonomy, or they may abandon their teams at times when the teams need support and help.[62]

A study of 20 organizations that had reorganized themselves around teams found certain common responsibilities that all leaders had to assume. These included coaching, facilitating, handling disciplinary problems, reviewing team/individual performance, training, and communication.[63] Many of these responsibilities apply to managers in general. A more meaningful way to describe the team leader's job is to focus on two priorities: managing the team's external boundary and facilitating the team process.[64] We've broken these priorities down into four specific roles (see Exhibit 11–9).

First, team leaders are *liaisons with external constituencies.* These include upper management, other internal teams, customers, and suppliers. The leader represents the team to other constituencies, secures needed resources, clarifies others' expectations of the team, gathers information from the outside, and shares this information with team members.

Second, team leaders are *troubleshooters.* When the team has problems and asks for assistance, team leaders sit in on meetings and help to resolve the problems. This rarely relates to technical or operational issues because the team members typically know more about the tasks than does the team leader. The leader is most likely to contribute by asking penetrating questions, helping the team talk through problems,

EXHIBIT 11-9
Team Leader Roles

Coaches	Liaisons with external constituents
Effective Team Leadership Roles	
Conflict managers	Troubleshooters

and getting needed resources from external constituencies.[65] For instance, when a team in an aerospace firm found itself shorthanded, its team leader took responsibility for getting more staff. He presented the team's case to upper management and got approval through the company's human resources department.

Third, team leaders are *conflict managers*. When disagreements surface, they help process the conflict. What's the source of the conflict? Who is involved? What are the issues? What resolution options are available? What are the advantages and disadvantages of each? By getting team members to address questions such as these, the leader minimizes the disruptive aspects of intrateam conflicts.

Finally, team leaders are *coaches*. They clarify expectations and roles, teach, offer support, cheerlead, and whatever else is necessary to help team members improve their work performance.[66]

Learning from Experience: One Manager's Reflection

Adele Sacarelli President, TeamworkWins LTD

EFFECTIVE TEAM LEADERSHIP

Describe the situation you faced. One of the team members/employees who faced significant learning challenges was unable to complete a task because he didn't understand the task.

What action did you take? I became impatient, harsh, critical, judgmental, and I communicated poorly. I had asked him to do something and when I checked on the task, I felt it was not done to my satisfaction. I immediately made a judgment about the person and his performance. I then spoke to the employee in a manner that was less than understanding.

What results occurred? The employee took it personally, and difficulties then ensued. There were personality conflicts and disagreements about what was said and agreed upon. There were differences of opinion on what was said in the original conversation, causing the job to be delayed and thereby affecting customer relations.

What did/should you have done differently? I reacted out of my own frustration. I should have asked myself if I had communicated effectively to the employee. I should have taken the time to understand the employee and how he processed information, and spoken to him less harshly so as to not offend him.

If you took corrective action, what were the results? Ultimately, I changed my approach and communicated in a way the employee understood, without making any judgments or assumptions. He then completed the task to my satisfaction and the goal of pleasing the customer was achieved.

DOES NATIONAL CULTURE AFFECT LEADERSHIP?

We've learned in this chapter that leaders don't use any single style. They adjust their style to the situation. Although not mentioned explicitly in any of the theories we presented, certainly national culture is an important situational factor determining which leadership style will be most effective.[67] We propose that you consider it as another contingency variable. It can help explain, for instance, why executives at the highly successful Asia Department Store in central China blatantly bragged about practicing "heartless" management, requiring new employees to undergo two to four weeks of military training with units of the People's Liberation Army in order to increase their obedience, and conducted the store's in-house training sessions in a public place at which employees could openly suffer embarrassment from their mistakes.[68]

National culture affects leadership style because leaders cannot choose their styles at will: They are constrained by the cultural conditions that their followers have come to expect. Consider the following: Korean leaders are expected to be paternalistic toward employees.[69] Arab leaders who show kindness or generosity without being asked to do so are seen by other Arabs as weak.[70] Japanese leaders are expected to be humble and speak infrequently.[71] And Scandinavian and Dutch leaders who single out individuals for public praise are likely to embarrass those individuals rather than energize them.[72]

Remember that most leadership theories were developed in the United States, using U.S. subjects. Therefore, they have an American bias. They emphasize follower responsibilities rather than rights; assume hedonism rather than commitment to duty or altruistic motivation; assume centrality of work and democratic value orientation; and stress rationality rather than spirituality, religion, or superstition.[73]

Will national culture affect leadership? National culture does affect leadership in that leaders are often constrained by cultural conditions that their followers have come to expect. For example, Korean leaders are expected to be paternalistic toward employees. If they are not, they may not have the effect on leadership and motivation that they would like.

As a guide for adjusting your leadership style, you might consider the value dimensions of national culture presented in Chapter 2.[74] For example, a manipulative or autocratic style is compatible with high power distance, and we find high power distance scores in Arab, Far Eastern, and Latin countries. Power distance rankings should also be good indicators of employee willingness to accept participative leadership. Participation is likely to be most effective in such low power distance cultures such as Norway, Finland, Denmark, and Sweden. Not incidentally, this may explain (1) why a number of leadership theories (the more obvious being ones like the University of Michigan behavioral studies and the leader-participation model) implicitly favor the use of a participative or people-oriented style, (2) the emergence of development-oriented leader behavior found by Scandinavian researchers, and (3) the recent enthusiasm for empowerment in North America.

HOW DOES EMOTIONAL INTELLIGENCE AFFECT LEADERSHIP?

We introduced emotional intelligence (EI) in our discussion of emotions in Chapter 8. We revisit the topic here because of recent studies indicating that EI—more than I.Q., expertise, or any other single factor—is the best predictor of who will emerge as a leader.[75]

As our trait research demonstrated, leaders need basic intelligence and job-relevant knowledge. But I.Q. and technical skills are "threshold capabilities." They're necessary but not sufficient requirements for leadership. It's the possession of the five components of emotional intelligence—self-awareness, self-management, self-motivation, empathy, and social skills—that allows an individual to become a star performer. Without EI, a person can have outstanding training, a highly analytical mind, a long-term vision, and an endless supply of terrific ideas but still not make a great leader. This is especially true as individuals move up in an organization. The evidence indicates that the higher the rank of a person considered to be a star performer, the more that EI capabilities surface as the reason for his or her effectiveness. Specifically, when star performers were compared with average ones in senior management positions, nearly 90 percent of the difference in their effectiveness was attributable to EI factors rather than basic intelligence.

Interestingly, it's been pointed out that the maturing of Rudolph Giuliani's leadership effectiveness closely followed the development of his emotional intelligence. As indicated in the opening vignette, for the better part of the eight years he was mayor of New York, Giuliani ruled with an iron fist. He talked tough, picked fights, and demanded results. The result was a city that was cleaner, safer, and better governed—but also more polarized. Critics called Giuliani a tin-eared tyrant. In the eyes of many, something important was missing from his leadership. That something, his critics acknowledged, emerged as the World Trade Center collapsed. It was a newfound compassion to complement his command: a mix of resolve, empathy, and inspiration that brought comfort to millions.[76] It's likely that Giuliani's emotional capacities and compassion for others were stimulated by a series of personal hardships—including prostate cancer and the highly visible breakup of his marriage—both of which had taken place less than a year before the terrorist attacks on the World Trade Center![77]

EI has been shown to be positively related to job performance at all levels. But it appears to be especially relevant in jobs that demand a high degree of social interaction. And of course, that's what leadership is all about. Great leaders demonstrate their EI by exhibiting all five of its key components—self-awareness; self-management; self-motivation; empathy; and social skills (see pp. 233–235).

The recent evidence makes a strong case for concluding that EI is an essential element in leadership effectiveness. As such, it should probably be added to the list of traits associated with leadership that we described earlier in the chapter.

IS LEADERSHIP ALWAYS IMPORTANT?

In keeping with the contingency spirit, we conclude this section by offering this opinion: The belief that a particular leadership style will always be effective *regardless* of the situation may not be true. Leadership may not always be important. Data from numerous studies demonstrate that, in many situations, any behaviors a leader exhibits are irrelevant. Certain individual, job, and organizational variables can act as substitutes for leadership or neutralize the leader's ability to influence his or her followers.[78]

Neutralizers make it impossible for leader behavior to make any difference in follower outcomes. They negate the leader's influence. Substitutes, on the other hand, make a leader's influence not only impossible, but also unnecessary. They act as a replacement for the leader's influence. For instance, characteristics of employees such as experience, training, professional orientation, or indifference toward organizational regards can substitute for, or neutralize the effect of leadership. Experience and training, for instance, can replace the need for a leader's support or ability to create structure and reduce task ambiguity. Jobs that are inherently unambiguous and routine or that are intrinsically satisfying may place fewer demands on the leadership variable. Organizational characteristics such as explicit formalized goals, rigid rules and procedures, and cohesive work groups can substitute for leadership.

This realization that leaders don't always have an effect on followers should not be that alarming. After all, we have introduced a number of variables (for example, attitudes, personality, ability, and group norms) that have been documented as having an effect on employee performance and satisfaction. Yet supporters of the leadership concept have tended to place an undue burden on this variable for explaining and predicting behavior. It is too simplistic to consider employees as guided to goal accomplishment solely by the actions of a leader. It's important, therefore, to recognize that leadership is another variable in organizational effectiveness. In some situations, it may contribute a lot to explaining employee productivity, absence, turnover, citizenship, and satisfaction. But in other situations, it may contribute little toward that end.

BUILDING TRUST: THE ESSENCE OF LEADERSHIP

Trust, or lack of trust, is an increasingly important issue in today's organizations.[79] The actions by leaders at WorldCom, Adelphia, and Enron in 2001 and 2002 have led to a precipitous drop in the public's trust in corporate leaders. Many individuals simply see such leaders as greedy and opportunistic. Those are not characteristics that lead to developing trusting relationships!

We briefly introduced you to trust in Chapter 9 in our discussion of high-performing work teams. In this chapter, we want to further explore this issue of trust by defining what trust is and showing you how trust is a vital component of effective leadership.[80]

WHAT IS TRUST?

trust
The belief in the integrity, character, and ability of a leader

Trust is a positive expectation that another will not—through words, actions, or decisions—act opportunistically.[81] Most important, trust implies familiarity and risk. The phrase "positive expectation" in our definition assumes knowledge of and familiarity with the other party. Trust is a history-dependent process based on relevant but limited samples of experience.[82] It takes time to form, building incrementally and accumulating (see Developing Your Trust-Building Skill on page 336). Most of us find it hard, if not impossible, to trust someone immediately if we don't know anything about them. At the extreme, in the case of total ignorance, we can gamble but we can't trust.[83] But as we get to know someone and the relationship matures, we gain confidence in our ability to make a positive expectation.

The word *opportunistically* refers to the inherent risk and vulnerability in any trusting relationship. Trust involves making oneself vulnerable as when, for example, we disclose intimate information or rely on another's promises.[84] By its very nature, trust provides the opportunity to be disappointed or to be taken advantage of.[85] But trust is not taking risk per se; rather it is a willingness to take risk.[86] So when we trust someone, we expect that he or she will not take advantage of us. This willingness to take risks is common to all trust situations.[87]

What are the key dimensions that underlie the concept of trust? Research has identified five: integrity, competence, consistency, loyalty, and openness[88] (see Exhibit 11–10).

Integrity refers to honesty, conscientiousness, and truthfulness.[89] Of all five dimensions, this one seems to be most critical. "Without a perception of the other's 'moral character' and 'basic honesty,' other dimensions of trust [are] meaningless."[90]

Competence encompasses an individual's technical and interpersonal knowledge and skills. Does the person know what he or she is talking about? You're unlikely to listen to or depend upon someone whose abilities you don't respect. You need to believe that a person has the skills and abilities to carry out the things he or she promises.

Consistency relates to an individual's reliability, predictability, and good judgment in handling situations. Inconsistencies between words and actions decrease trust.[91] This dimension is particularly relevant for managers. "Nothing is noticed more quickly . . . than a discrepancy between what executives preach and what they expect their associates to practice."[92] *Loyalty* is the willingness to protect and save face for another person. Trust requires that you can depend on someone not to act oppor-

EXHIBIT 11–10
Five Dimensions of Trust

■ Integrity	Honesty and truthfulness
■ Competence	Technical and interpersonal knowledge and skills
■ Consistency	Reliability, predictability, and good judgment
■ Loyalty	Willingness to protect and save face for a person
■ Openness	Willingness to share ideas and information freely

Source: Adapted and reproduced with permission of publisher from: J. K. Butler Jr., and R. S. Cantrell, "A Behavioral Decision Theory Approach to Modeling Dyadic Trust in Superiors and Subordinates."

tunistically. The final dimension of trust is *openness*. Can you rely on the person to give you the full truth?

WHY IS TRUST CRITICAL TO LEADERSHIP?

Trust appears to be a primary attribute associated with leadership.[93] In fact, if you look back at our discussion of leadership traits, honesty and integrity were found to be among the six traits consistently associated with leadership.

As one author noted: "Part of the leader's task has been, and continues to be, working with people to find and solve problems, but whether leaders gain access to the knowledge and creative thinking they need to solve problems depends on how much people trust them. Trust and trustworthiness modulate the leader's access to knowledge and cooperation."[94] When followers trust a leader, they are willing to be vulnerable to the leader's actions—confident that their rights and interests will not be abused.[95] People are unlikely to look up to or follow someone who they perceive as dishonest or who is likely to take advantage of them. Honesty, for instance, consistently ranks at the top of most lists of characteristics admired in leaders. "Honesty is absolutely essential to leadership. If people are going to follow someone willingly, whether it be into battle or into the boardroom, they first want to assure themselves that the person is worthy of their trust."[96]

Now, more than ever, managerial and leadership effectiveness depends on the ability to gain the trust of followers.[97] For instance, work process engineering, downsizing, stock prices tumbling, and the increased use of temporary employees have undermined a lot of employees' trust in management. Moreover, contemporary management practices such as empowerment and the use of work teams require trust to be effective.[98] A survey of employees by a firm in Chicago found 40 percent agreed with the statement: I often don't believe what management says.[99] In times of change and instability, people turn to personal relationships for guidance, and the quality of these relationships is largely determined by level of trust. That's why Robert Eckert spent considerable hours in the cafeteria with his employees shortly after assuming the duties of leadership of the ailing Mattel Company.[100]

WHAT ARE THE THREE TYPES OF TRUST?

There are three types of trust in organizational relationships: deterrence based, knowledge based, and identification based.[101] Let's briefly look at each of these.

Deterrence-based trust The most fragile relationships are founded on **deterrence-based trust**. One violation or inconsistency can destroy the relationship. This form of trust is based on fear of reprisal if the trust is violated. Individuals who are in this type of relationship act because they fear the consequences of not following through on their obligations. Deterrence-based trust will work only to the degree that punishment is possible, consequences are clear, and the punishment is actually imposed if the trust is violated. To be sustained, the potential loss of future interaction with the other party must outweigh the profit

deterrence-based trust
Trust based on fear of reprisal if the trust is violated

One of the first things Robert Eckert, CEO of Mattel, did shortly after assuming his duties was to visit employees in the cafeteria. He did this to build relationships with the employees in an attempt to develop a bond of trust between them. He was hoping that these personal relationships would assist him and the company during its time of change and instability.

potential that comes from violating expectations. Moreover, the potentially harmed party must be willing to introduce harm (for example, I have no qualms about speaking badly of you if you betray my trust) to the person acting distrustingly.

Most new relationships begin on a base of deterrence. Take, as an illustration, a situation of selling your car to a friend of a friend. You don't know the buyer. You might be motivated to refrain from telling this buyer about all the problems that you know the car has. Such behavior would increase your chances of selling the car and securing the highest price. However, you don't withhold information; you openly share the car's flaws. Why? Probably because of fear of reprisal. If the buyer later thinks you deceived him, he is likely to share this with your mutual friend. If you knew that the buyer would never say anything to the mutual friend, you might be tempted to take advantage of the opportunity. If it's clear that the buyer would tell and that your mutual friend would think considerably less of you for taking advantage of this buyer friend, your honesty could be explained in deterrence terms.

Another example of deterrence-based trust is a new manager–employee relationship. As an employee, you typically trust a new boss even though there is little experience to base that trust on. The bond that creates this trust lies in the authority held by the boss and the punishment he or she can impose if you fail to fulfill your job-related obligations.

knowledge-based trust
Trust based on the behavioral predictability that comes from a history of interaction

Knowledge-based trust Most organizational relationships are rooted in **knowledge-based trust**. That is, trust is based on the behavioral predictability that comes from a history of interaction. It exists when you understand someone well enough to be able to accurately predict his or her behavior.

Knowledge-based trust relies on information rather than deterrence. Knowledge of the other party and predictability of his or her behavior replaces the contracts, penalties, and legal arrangements more typical of deterrence-based trust. This knowledge develops over time, largely as a function of experience that builds confidence of trustworthiness and predictability. The better you know someone, the more accurately you can predict what he or she will do. Predictability enhances trust even if the other person is predictably untrustworthy because the ways that the other will violate the trust can be predicted. The more communication and regular interaction you have with someone, the more this form of trust can be developed and depended upon.

Interestingly, at the knowledge-based level, trust is not necessarily broken by inconsistent behavior. If you believe you can adequately explain or understand another's apparent violation, you can accept it, forgive the person, and move on in the relationship. However, the same inconsistency at the deterrence level is likely to irrevocably break the trust.

In an organizational context, most manager–employee relationships are knowledge based. Both parties have enough experience working with each other to know what to expect. A long history of consistently open and honest interactions, for instance, is not likely to be permanently destroyed by a single violation.

identification-based trust
Trust based on an emotional connection between the parties

Identification-based trust The highest level of trust is achieved when there is an emotional connection between the parties. It allows one party to act as an agent for the other and substitute for that person in interpersonal transactions. This is called **identification-based trust**. Trust exists because the parties understand each other's intentions and appreciate the other's wants and desires. This mutual understanding is developed to the point that each can effectively act for the other. Controls are minimal at this level. You don't need to monitor the other party because unquestioned loyalty exists.

The best example of identification-based trust is a long-term, happy marriage. A spouse comes to learn what's important to his or her partner and anticipates those actions. The partner, in turn, takes this for granted. Increased identification enables each to think like the other, feel like the other, and respond like the other.

You see identification-based trust occasionally in organizations among people who have worked together for long periods of time and have a depth of experience that allows them to know each other inside and out. This is also the type of trust that managers ideally seek in teams. Team members are so comfortable and trusting of each other that they can anticipate each other and freely act in each others' absence. Realistically, in the current work world, most large corporations have broken the bonds of identification trust that they may have built with long-term employees. Broken promises have led to a breakdown in what was, at one time, a bond of unquestioned loyalty. It's likely to have been replaced with knowledge-based trust.

Review, Comprehension, Application

CHAPTER SUMMARY

How will you know if you fulfilled the Learning Outcomes on page 308? You will have fulfilled the Learning Outcomes if you are able to:

1. **Define leader and explain the difference between managers and leaders.** A leader is able to influence others. Managers are appointed. They have legitimate power that allows them to reward and punish, and their ability to influence is founded upon the formal authority inherent in their positions. Leaders may either be appointed or emerge from within a group. Leaders can influence others to perform beyond the actions dictated by formal authority.
2. **Summarize the conclusions of trait theories of leadership.** Six traits have been found in which leaders differ from nonleaders—drive (exerting high energy levels); the desire to lead (wanting to influence others and willingness to take responsibility); honesty and integrity (being truthful and nondeceitful; and being consistent in one's actions); self-confidence (an absence of self-doubt); intelligence (ability to gather, synthesize, and interpret large amounts of information); and job-relevant knowledge (knowledge about the company and the industry to assist in making well-informed decisions). Yet possession of these traits is no guarantee of leadership because one can't ignore situational factors.
3. **Describe the Fiedler contingency model.** Fiedler's contingency model of leadership focuses on the belief that an individual's basic leadership style is a key factor in leadership success. To determine one's basic style, Fiedler created the least-preferred co-worker questionnaire containing 16 contrasting adjectives. Fiedler's contingency model identifies three situational variables: leader–member relations, task structure, and position power. In situations that are highly favorable or highly unfavorable, task-oriented leaders tend to perform best. In moderately favorable or unfavorable situations, relations-oriented leaders are preferred.
4. **Summarize the path-goal model of leadership.** The path-goal model proposes two classes of contingency variables—those in the environment and those that are part of the personal characteristics of the subordinate. Leaders select a specific type of behavior—directive, supportive, participative, or achievement oriented—that is congruent with the demands of the environment and the characteristics of the subordinate.
5. **Explain situational leadership.** Situational leadership theory, developed by Hersey and Blanchard, proposes four leadership styles—telling, selling, participating, and delegating. Which style a leader chooses to use depends on the followers' readiness—their willingness and ability to do the job. As followers reach higher levels of readiness, the leader responds by reducing control over and involvement with the employee.
6. **Identify the qualities that characterize charismatic leaders.** Charismatic leaders are self-confident (assured of their actions); possess a vision of a better future (have an idealized goal for a better future); articulate the vision (clearly state the vision to others in understandable terms); have a strong belief in that vision (willing to take high personal risk to achieve the vision); engage in unconventional behaviors (focus on behaviors that are novel, unconventional, and counter to norms); are perceived as agents of radical change

(don't accept the status quo); and are sensitive to the environment around them (make realistic assessments of the constraints they'll face and the resources they'll need to achieve their vision).

7. **Describe the skills that visionary leaders exhibit.** Several skills are associated with visionary leaders. Although possessing these skills is not a guarantee that someone will be a visionary leader, visionary leaders typically exhibit them frequently. The skills include: (1) having the ability to explain, both orally and in writing, the vision to others in a way that is clear in terms of required actions; (2) having the ability to express the vision through one's behavior so it reinforces to organizational members the importance of the vision; and (3) being able to extend the vision to different leadership contexts, gaining commitment and understanding from organizational members regardless of their department affiliation or their location.
8. **Explain the four specific roles of effective team leaders.** Team leaders often have a variety of responsibilities. To be effective in their jobs, team leaders need to be involved in four specific roles. These are: liaisons with external constituencies (representing the team to other constituencies, both internal and external to the organization); troubleshooters (sitting in on meetings to assist in resolving problems that arise for team members); conflict managers (helping to process the disagreements that surface among team members); and coaches (clarifying expectations and roles, teaching, cheerleading, and offering support to team members).
9. **Identify the five dimensions of trust.** The five dimensions of trust include integrity, competence, consistency, loyalty, and openness. Integrity refers to one's honesty and truthfulness. Competence involves an individual's technical and interpersonal knowledge and skills. Consistency relates to an individual's reliability, predictability, and good judgment in handling situations. Loyalty is an individual's willingness to protect and save face for another person. Openness means that you can rely on the individual to give you the whole truth.

COMPANION WEBSITE

We invite you to visit the Robbins/DeCenzo companion Website at **www.prenhall.com/robbins** for this chapter's Internet resources, including an online study guide, Internet exercises, and "In the News" with full text articles provided by XanEdu.

READING FOR COMPREHENSION

1. Discuss the strengths and weaknesses of the trait theory of leadership.
2. What is the managerial grid? Contrast this approach to leadership with that developed by the Ohio State and Michigan groups.
3. How is a least-preferred co-worker determined? What is the importance of one's LPC for the Fiedler theory of leadership?
4. What are the contingencies of the path-goal theory of leadership?
5. What similarities, if any, can you find among Fiedler's model, path-goal theory, and Hersey and Blanchard's situational leadership?
6. How might leadership in Pacific Rim nations contrast with leadership in the United States or Canada?

LINKING CONCEPTS TO PRACTICE

1. "All managers should be leaders, but not all leaders should be managers." Do you agree or disagree with that statement? Support your position.
2. Do you think trust evolves out of an individual's personal characteristics or out of specific situations? Explain.
3. "Charismatic leadership is always appropriate in organizations." Do you agree or disagree? Support your position.
4. Contrast the three types of trust. Relate them to your experience in personal relationships.
5. When might leaders be irrelevant?

VIDEO CASE APPLICATION

enews.com: The Mercurial Champion of the Magazine Industry

The rapport is instantaneous. Seated in front of his eel-shaped phone, Brian Hecht, CEO and president of enews.com exudes enthusiasm. In 1992, Hecht graduated from Harvard University with a degree in journalism, never dreaming that he would one day be at the helm of a growing Internet business. The company started out as The Electronic Newsstand, originally conceived of as a circulation-boosting Web site for *The New Republic*, where Hecht had interned as a student. He became friendly with the magazine's owner who asked him to serve as editor-in-chief for the Electronic Newsstand in 1995. Two years later, Hecht had single-handedly piloted the site into an online Mecca of sales, marketing, and distribution for the entire magazine industry.

Brian Hecht envisioned the site as a consumer product, accountable to its users, not just to its magazine clients. He created three new venues for magazine lovers on the enews.com Web site. He added "off the rack," media commentary and interviews; "Monster Magazine List;" consisting of more than 2,000 links to online magazines, and "Magazine Monitor;" a daily summary of magazine features. His goal was to make enews.com the magazine equivalent of leading online bookseller Amazon.com.[102]

Today, Hecht has convinced magazine publishers who find they can no longer depend on sweepstakes to find new subscribers that the Internet is "a better way." Barnes & Noble was so impressed with the way enews.com ran its magazine site that they are now equity partners, as well as business partners with the dot-com.

Preparation and maintenance of the enews.com Web site is an ongoing process, vital to the firm's success. "What we're trying to do is make sure that browsers who log onto the site are able to find what they are looking for very quickly and buy it without too much hassle," says Lauren Ogle, vice president production. "It is basically about giving people a good search experience." For Brian Hecht the business is all about getting enews.com recognized as *the* source for magazines, "regardless of whether readers get it digitally downloaded to their handheld computer or the traditional way." The company has recently branched out to include a special page for newspaper subscriptions to some of the top papers in the country including *USA Today, The Wall Street Journal,* and *The New York Times.*

The excitement Hecht finds in the Internet has a lot to do with its accessibility. "The relationship between an idea and an action is closer on the Internet," he says. "Entrepreneurs are in a valuable place."[103] He is riveted by the possibilities offered by the World Wide Web, and his ebullience is not lost on his employees. They describe him as "incredibly energetic, excited about what he does." One enews.com staffer puts it like this: "He never stays satisfied. He always says 'OK, what can I do next?' He takes a split second of satisfaction and then he moves on." They seem unanimously appreciative of the noncorporate environment. The young employees relish the kind of "kookiness" their workplace both accommodates and inspires.

Brian Hecht is open about his intentions vis-à-vis his employees. "I've always grown this business to be a stable, long term, profitable business and that will benefit the entire company." Everyone at enews.com participates in a stock option plan and everyone, it seems, is happily sharing their CEO's ambitions for the future of the magazine industry. Even in this age of information overload, Brian Hecht is confident that the allure of magazines will never fade.

Questions

1. Discuss the path-goal theory as it might be applied to Brian Hecht and his employees at enews.com, taking into account leadership behavior, employee satisfaction, and work setting.
2. What skills does Brian Hecht exhibit that would characterize him as a visionary leader? Explain.
3. What role, if any, does emotional intelligence play in Brian Hecht's success? Explain.
4. Based on the comments of enews.com employees, who appeared in the video, has Brian Hecht succeeded in building trust? Explain. Consider why this is critical in today's dot-com environment.

Management Workshop

Team Skill-Building Exercise

The Pre-Post Leadership Assessment

Objective

To compare characteristics intuitively related to leadership with leadership characteristics found in leadership theory.

Procedure

Identify three people (e.g., friends, relatives, previous boss, public figures) whom you consider to be outstanding leaders. List why you feel each individual is a good leader. Compare your lists of the three individuals. Which traits, if any, are common to all three? Your instructor will lead the class in a discussion of leadership characteristics based on your lists. Students will call out what they identified, and your instructor will write the traits on the chalkboard. When all students have shared their lists, class discussion will focus on the following:

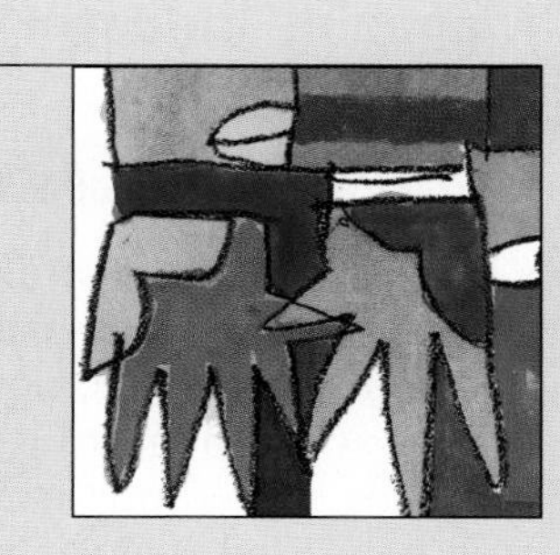

- What characteristics consistently appeared on students' lists?
- Were these characteristics more trait oriented or behavior oriented?
- Under what situations were these characteristics useful?
- What, if anything, does this exercise suggest about leadership attributes?

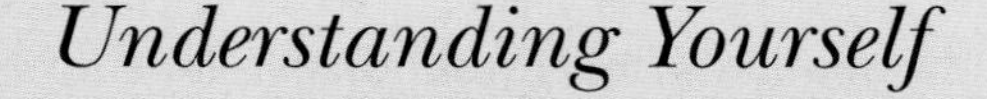

Understanding Yourself

Before you can develop other people, you must understand your present strengths. To assist in this learning process, we encourage you to complete the following self-assessments from the Prentice Hall Self-Assessment Library 2.0:

- How Flexible Am I? (#4)
- What Is My Leadership Style? (#27)
- How Willing Am I to Delegate? (#40)

After you complete these assessments, we suggest that you print out the results and store them as part of your "portfolio of learning."

Developing Your Trust-Building Skill

About the Skill

Given the importance trust plays in the leadership equation, today's leaders should actively seek to build trust with their followers. Here are some suggestions for achieving that goal.[104]

Steps in Practicing the Skill

1. **Practice openness.** Mistrust comes as much from what people don't know as from what they do know. Openness leads to confidence and trust. So keep people informed; make clear the criteria on how decisions are made; explain the rationale for your decisions; be candid about problems; and fully disclose relevant information.
2. **Be fair.** Before making decisions or taking actions, consider how others will perceive them in terms of objectivity and fairness. Give credit where credit is due; be objective and impartial in performance appraisals; and pay attention to equity perceptions in reward distributions.
3. **Speak your feelings.** Leaders who convey only hard facts come across as cold and distant. When you share your feelings, others will see you as real and human. They will know who you are and their respect for you will increase.
4. **Tell the truth.** If honesty is critical to credibility, you must be perceived as someone who tells the truth. Followers are more tolerant of being told something they "don't want to hear" than of finding out that their leader lied to them.

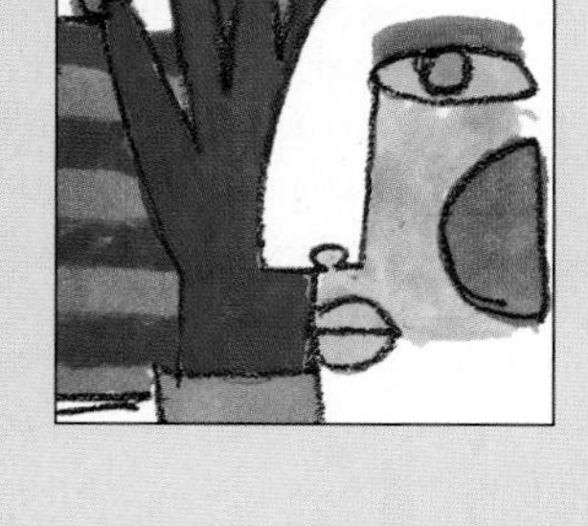

5. **Be consistent.** People want predictability. Mistrust comes from not knowing what to expect. Take the time to think about your values and beliefs. Then let them consistently guide your decisions. When you know your central purpose, your actions will follow accordingly, and you will project a consistency that earns trust.
6. **Fulfill your promises.** Trust requires that people believe that you are dependable. So you need to keep your word. Promises made must be promises kept.
7. **Maintain confidences.** You trust those whom you believe to be discrete and whom you can rely on. If people make themselves vulnerable by telling you something in confidence, they need to feel assured

that you won't discuss it with others or betray that confidence. If people perceive you as someone who leaks personal confidences or someone who can't be depended on, you won't be perceived as trustworthy.

8. **Demonstrate confidence.** Develop the admiration and respect of others by demonstrating technical and professional ability. Pay particular attention to developing and displaying your communication, negotiating, and other interpersonal skills.

Practicing the Skill

You are a new manager. Your predecessor, who was very popular and who is still with your firm, concealed from your team how far behind they are on their goals this quarter. As a result, your team members are looking forward to a promised day off that they are not entitled to and will not be getting.

It's your job to tell them the bad news. How will you do it?

Developing Your Diagnostic and Analytical Skills

The Sonic Boom

D. L. Rogers, based in Bedford, Texas, owns 65 franchises of Sonic Corporation, a chain of fast-food drive-in restaurants, in six states. Jack Hartnett, Rogers' president, leads by combining ingredients from the stone age and new age.[105]

Hartnett prides himself on knowing everything about his employees. If they've got marital problems or credit card debt, he wants to know. And he thinks nothing of using that information if he thinks it can help. For instance, how many executives counsel employees on their sex lives? Hartnett does. When the wife of one of his managers called Hartnett to say her husband was impotent and she didn't know what to do, Hartnett had the answer. He met the couple in a motel room where he prodded the fellow into confessing to an affair and begging for forgiveness.

Is Hartnett intrusive? Yes, but he doesn't consider it a problem. "There are no secrets here," he says. No subject is too delicate for his ears. And his defense? He's merely doing what any good friend might do. Also, he believes that the more he knows about his workers, the more he can help them stay focused at work and happy at home.

Hartnett plays golf with his managers, sends them personally signed birthday cards, and drops by their homes to take them to dinner. But if you think he's "Mr. Nice Guy," think again. He bad-mouths academic theories that propound that leaders need to persuade workers to "buy-in" to the leader's vision. Hartnett instructs his employees to "do it the way we tell you to do it." He's perfectly comfortable using the authority in his position to make rules and dish out punishments. One of Hartnett's basic rules is, "I will only tell you something once." Break one of his rules twice and you're fired!

The managers who work for Hartnett are well-compensated for meeting his demanding requirements. These individuals earn an average of $72,000 annually. This compares with industry averages of just over $40,000. Additionally, managers receive partnership opportunities giving them part ownership in their stores—resulting in several managers earning more than $150,000 annually.

Does Hartnett seem inconsistent? Maybe. He believes in openness, integrity, and honesty. But he expects as much as he gives. It's not an option. So he's "your best friend" and at the same tine, he's rigid and autocratic. He admits to purposefully keeping everybody slightly off balance "so they'll work harder."

Hartnett's approach to leadership seems to be effective. His per store revenues are nearly 18 percent higher than the chain's average, and profits are 25 percent above the norm. Moreover, people seem to like working for him. In an industry known for high turnover, Hartnett's managers stay about nine years compared with the industry average of less than two.

Questions

1. Is Jack Hartnett a transactional or transformational leader? Support you position.
2. How would you describe Jack Hartnett's leadership style? Cite specific examples where appropriate.
3. What situational variables do you think explain his success at Rogers?

Enhancing Your Communication Skills

1. Think about a person in your life (a parent, a supervisor, a teacher, etc.) who has influenced you so that you enthusiastically gave 110 percent. Describe the characteristics of this person. Pick one of the contemporary leadership theories in this chapter and explain how your leader demonstrated the attributes of your selected theory.
2. Develop a two- to three-page discussion when responding to the following question. What kind of activities could a full-time college student pursue that might lead to the perception that he or she is a charismatic leader?
3. Prepare a presentation that compares and contrasts male versus female leadership styles. Which style works best, and when?

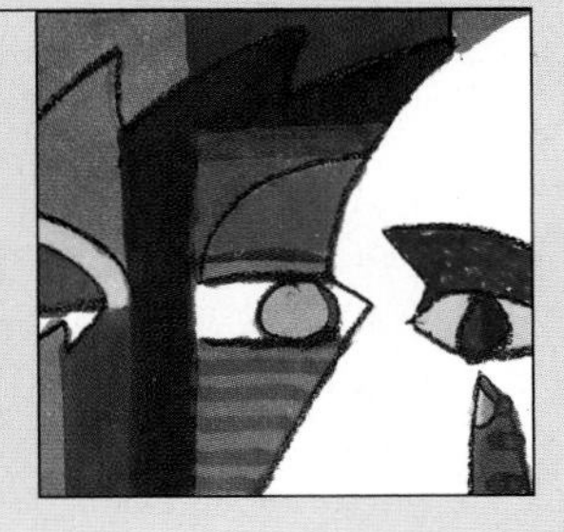

C H A P T E R 1 2

Communication and Interpersonal Skills

LEARNING OUTCOMES

After reading this chapter, I will be able to:

1. Define communication and explain why it is important to managers.
2. Describe the communication process.
3. List techniques for overcoming communication barriers.
4. Describe the wired and wireless technologies affecting organizational communications.
5. Identify behaviors related to effective active listening.
6. Explain what behaviors are necessary for providing effective feedback.
7. Describe the contingency factors influencing delegation.
8. Identify behaviors related to effective delegating.
9. Describe the steps in analyzing and resolving conflict.
10. Explain why a manager might stimulate conflict.
11. Contrast distributive and integrative bargaining.

MEET A REAL MANAGER

"One Manager's Reflection" page 355

Lori A. De Gasso, Studio Manager, Yoga Zone LLC

One of the fundamental requirements in labor–management relationships is that both sides come to the bargaining table and negotiate in good faith. This good-faith bargaining requires both sides to attempt to work toward a settlement. But good-faith bargaining provides no guarantee that an agreement will be reached. On the contrary, serious disagreements do arise at times, resulting in negotiations breaking off. We've witnessed this occurrence countless times over the decades—with truckers, newspaper personnel, airline pilots and flight attendants, communications workers, coal miners, and professional athletes. Recent efforts in Major League Baseball demonstrate that good-faith negotiations don't have to lead to walk-outs or strikes if the parties are determined to reach an agreement. Don Fehr, president of the Baseball Players' Union and players' representative, and Rob Manfred, Major League Baseball's executive vice president of labor relations and human resources and representative of the owners (pictured here), made it their goal to work through even the toughest of issues facing Major League Baseball in the summer of 2002.[1]

Since 1972, there have been eight work stoppages in Major League Baseball. Lasting anywhere from two to 232 days, nearly 2,000 baseball games have been cancelled. In 1994, for example, nearly 1,000 games were never played, including the World Series. This was the first time in modern history that the World Series had been cancelled.

One major factor influencing recent negotiations has been fan support. During the past three decades, baseball fans have grown less tolerant of the players' and owners' tactics. For example, to offset the costs of "playing the game," management has drastically raised ticket prices. Had it not been for the Cal Ripken "streak of consecutive games played," or Mark McGwire's and Sammy Sosa's chase of Roger Maris' season high home run record in the late 1990s, public sentiment toward professional baseball might have waned even more. By 2002, the game appeared to be winning back fan support. The big question was, would the players and the owners be able to come to a satisfactory agreement or would they initiate the ninth work stoppage in 30 years—and possibly administer a fatal blow to professional baseball?

Contract negotiations appeared doomed from the start. The owners were proposing eliminating two teams. The rich teams were getting richer and the highest players getting wealthier—creating increasing inequalities among teams and between players. Early in the negotiations, owners and players were miles apart on several key issues—like minimum salaries, drug testing, and revenue sharing. Neither side appeared willing to move toward consensus, and fans grew increasingly outspoken against both players and owners. Many threatened to never go to a ball game if there was a strike. Nevertheless, the players' union set a strike date. The task facing Fehr and Manfred was daunting—the sports world was watching their every move. In labor–management negotiations, deliberations often go to the "eleventh hour." This case was no different. But only hours before the strike deadline, in spite of a lot of rhetoric, a settlement was reached.

In the end, neither side got exactly what it wanted. Typically, neither does. But through the persistent negotiation efforts of Manfred and Fehr, a compromise was reached. And in doing so, they just may have saved America's favorite pastime!

IN THIS CHAPTER, WE PRESENT BASIC CONCEPTS IN INTERPERSONAL communication and explain the communication process, methods of communicating, barriers to effective communication, and ways to overcome those barriers. In addition, we review several communication-based interpersonal skills—active listening, providing feedback, delegating, managing conflict, and negotiating—that managers must be proficient in to be able to manage effectively in today's organizations.

UNDERSTANDING COMMUNICATION

The importance of effective communication for managers cannot be overemphasized for one specific reason: Everything a manager does involves communicating. Not *some* things but *everything*! A manager can't formulate strategy or make a decision without information. That information has to be communicated. Once a decision is made, communication must again take place. Otherwise, no one will know that a decision has been made. The best idea, the most creative suggestion, or the finest plan cannot take form without communication. Managers, therefore, need effective communication skills. We are not suggesting, of course, that good communication skills alone make a successful manager. We can say, however, that ineffective communication skills can lead to a continuous stream of problems for the manager.

HOW DOES THE COMMUNICATION PROCESS WORK?

Communication can be thought of as a process or flow. Communication problems occur when there are deviations or blockages in that flow. Before communication can take place, a purpose, expressed as a message to be conveyed, is needed. It passes between a source (the sender) and a receiver. The message is encoded (converted to symbolic form) and is passed by way of some medium (channel) to the receiver, who re-translates (decodes) the message initiated by the sender. The result is a transference of meaning from one person to another.[2]

communication process
The transferring and understanding of meaning

encoding
The conversion of a message into some symbolic form

Exhibit 12–1 depicts the **communication process**. This model is made up of seven parts: (1) the communication source, (2) encoding, (3) the message, (4) the channel, (5) decoding, (6) the receiver, and (7) feedback.

The source initiates a message by **encoding** a thought. Four conditions affect the encoded message: skill, attitudes, knowledge, and the social cultural system. Our message in our communication to you is dependent upon our writing skills; if the authors of textbooks are without the requisite writing skills, their messages will not reach students in the form desired. One's total communicative success includes speaking, reading, listening, and reasoning skills as well. As we discussed in Chapter 8, our attitudes influence our behavior. We hold predisposed ideas on numerous topics, and our communications are affected by these attitudes. Furthermore, we are restricted in our communicative activity by the extent of our knowledge of the particular topic. We cannot communicate what we don't know, and should our knowledge be too extensive, it's possible that our receiver will not understand our message. Clearly, the amount of knowledge the source holds about his or her subject will affect the message he or she seeks to transfer. And, finally, just as attitudes influence our behavior, so does our position in the social cultural system in which we exist. Your beliefs and values, all part of your culture, act to influence you as a communicative source.

message
A purpose to be conveyed

The **message** is the actual physical product from the source. When we speak, the speech is the message. When we write, the writing is the message. When we paint, the picture is the message. When we gesture, the movements of our arms, the expressions on our faces are the message.[3] Our message is affected by the code or group of symbols we use to transfer meaning, the content of the message itself, and the decisions that we make in selecting and arranging both codes and content.[4]

channel
The medium by which a message travels

The **channel** is the medium through which the message travels. It is selected by the source, who must determine which channel is formal and which one is informal.

EXHIBIT 12–1 The Communication Process

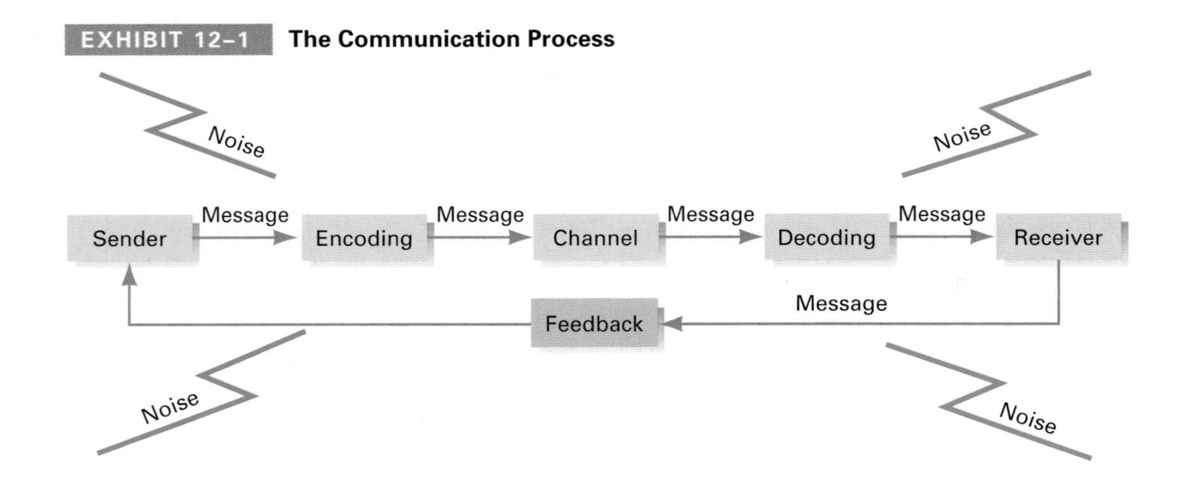

Formal channels are established by the organization and transmit messages that pertain to the job-related activities of members. They traditionally follow the authority network within the organization. Other forms of messages, such as personal or social, follow the informal channels in the organization.

The receiver is the person to whom the message is directed. However, before the message can be received, the symbols in it must be translated into a form that can be understood by the receiver. This is the **decoding** of the message. Just as the encoder was limited by his or her skills, attitudes, knowledge, and social cultural system, the receiver is equally restricted. Accordingly, the source must be skillful in writing or speaking; the receiver must be skillful in reading or listening, and both must be able to reason. One's knowledge, attitudes, and cultural background influence one's ability to receive, just as they do the ability to send.

The primary purpose of any communication is to get a message from the sender to the receiver in the way the message was intended. How that is accomplished may vary. For example, this international sign for "no smoking" clearly identifies the purpose of the message. It's clear and specific. Accordingly, symbols such as these transfer meaning and aid understanding.

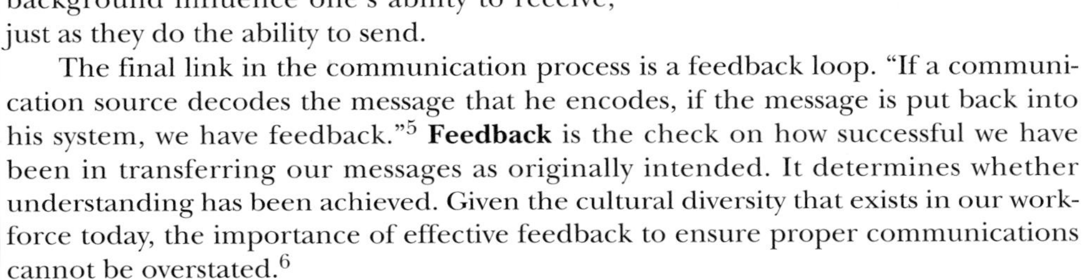

The final link in the communication process is a feedback loop. "If a communication source decodes the message that he encodes, if the message is put back into his system, we have feedback."[5] **Feedback** is the check on how successful we have been in transferring our messages as originally intended. It determines whether understanding has been achieved. Given the cultural diversity that exists in our workforce today, the importance of effective feedback to ensure proper communications cannot be overstated.[6]

ARE WRITTEN COMMUNICATIONS MORE EFFECTIVE THAN VERBAL ONES?

decoding
A receiver's translation of a sender's message

feedback
The degree to which carrying out the work activities required by a job results in the individual's obtaining direct and clear information about the effectiveness of his or her performance

Written communications include memos, letters, e-mail, organizational periodicals, bulletin boards, or any other device that transmits written words or symbols. Why would a sender choose to use written communications? Because they are tangible, verifiable, and more permanent than the oral variety. Typically, both sender and receiver have a record of the communication. The message can be stored for an indefinite period of time. If there are questions about the content of the message, it is physically available for later reference. This feature is particularly important for complex or lengthy communications. For example, the marketing plan for a new product is likely to contain a number of tasks spread out over several months. By putting it in writing, those who have to initiate the plan can readily refer to the document over the life of the plan. A final benefit of written communication comes from the process itself. Except in rare instances, such as when presenting a formal speech, more care is taken with the written word than with the spoken word. Having to put something in writing forces a person to think more carefully about what he or she wants to convey. Therefore, written communications are more likely to be well thought out, logical, and clear.

Of course, written messages have their drawbacks. Writing may be more precise, but it also consumes a great deal of time. You could convey far more information to your college instructor in a one-hour oral exam than in a one-hour written exam. In fact, you could probably say in 10 to 15 minutes what takes you an hour to write. The other major disadvantage is feedback or, rather, lack of it. Oral communications allow the receivers to respond rapidly to what they think they hear. However, written communications don't have a built-in feedback mechanism. Sending a memo is no assurance that it will be received; if it is received, there is no guarantee that the recipient will interpret it as the sender meant. The latter point is also relevant in oral communiques, but it's easier in such cases merely to ask the receiver to summarize what you have said. An accurate summary presents feedback evidence that the message has been received and understood.

IS THE GRAPEVINE AN EFFECTIVE WAY TO COMMUNICATE?

grapevine
An unofficial channel of communication

The **grapevine** is the unofficial way that communications take place in an organization. It is neither authorized nor supported by the organization. Rather, information is spread by word of mouth—and even through electronic means. Ironically, this is a two-way process—good information passes among us rapidly; bad information, even faster.[7] The grapevine gets information out to organizational members as quickly as possible.

The biggest question raised about grapevines, however, focuses on the accuracy of the rumors. Research on this topic has found somewhat mixed results. In an organization characterized by openness, the grapevine may be extremely accurate. In an authoritative culture, the rumor mill may not be accurate. But even then, although the information flowing is inaccurate, it still contains some element of truth. Rumors about major layoffs, plant closings, and the like may be filled with inaccurate information regarding who will be affected or when it may occur. Nonetheless, the reports that something is about to happen are probably on target.

"The grapevine motto: Good information passes among people fairly rapidly—bad information, even faster!"

HOW DO NONVERBAL CUES AFFECT COMMUNICATIONS?

body language
Nonverbal communication cues such as facial expressions, gestures, and other body movements

Some of the most meaningful communications are neither spoken nor written. These are nonverbal communications. A loud siren or a red light at an intersection tells you something without words. A college instructor doesn't need words to know that students are bored; their eyes get glassy or they begin to read the school newspaper during class. Similarly, when papers start to rustle and notebooks begin to close, the message is clear: Class time is about over. The size of a person's office and desk or the clothes he or she wears also convey messages to others. However, the best known areas of nonverbal communication are body language and verbal intonation.

Body language refers to gestures, facial configurations, and other movements of the body.[8] A snarl, for example, says something different from a smile. Hand motions, facial expressions, and other gestures can communicate emotions or temperaments such as aggression, fear, shyness, arrogance, joy, and anger.[9]

Nonverbal communication frequently signifies what's going on with a person. It's painfully obvious by looking at this individual that he is upset, and not happy about a given situation. One doesn't need expressed words to recognize that!

Verbal intonation refers to the emphasis someone gives to words or phrases. To illustrate how intonations can change the meaning of a message, consider the student who asks the instructor a question. The instructor replies, "What do you mean by that?" The student's reaction will vary, depending on the tone of the instructor's response. A soft, smooth tone creates a different meaning from one that is abrasive with a strong emphasis on the last word. Most of us would view the first intonation as coming from someone who sincerely sought clarification, whereas the second suggests that the person is aggressive or defensive. The adage, "it's not what you say but how you say it," is something managers should remember as they communicate.

The fact that every oral communication also has a nonverbal message cannot be overemphasized.[10] Why? Because the nonverbal component is likely to carry the greatest impact. Research indicates that from 65 to 90 percent of the message of every face-to-face conversation is interpreted through body language. Without complete agreement between the spoken words and the body language that accompanies it, receivers are more likely to react to body language as the "true meaning."[11]

WHAT BARRIERS EXIST TO EFFECTIVE COMMUNICATION?

A number of interpersonal and intrapersonal barriers help to explain why the message decoded by a receiver is often different from that which the sender intended. We summarize the more prominent barriers to effective communication in Exhibit 12–2 and briefly describe them here.

verbal intonation
An emphasis given to words or phrases that conveys meaning

Filtering **Filtering** refers to the way that a sender manipulates information so that it will be seen more favorably by the receiver. For example, when a manager tells his boss what he feels that boss wants to hear, he is filtering information (see Ethical Dilemma in Management). Does this happen much in organizations? Sure it does. As information is passed up to senior executives, it has to be condensed and synthesized by underlings so upper management doesn't become overloaded with information. The personal interests and perceptions of what is important to those doing the synthesizing are going to cause filtering. Those doing the condensing filter communications through their personal interests and perceptions of what is important.

filtering
The deliberate manipulation of information to make it appear more favorable to the receiver

The extent of filtering tends to be the function of the number of vertical levels in the organization and the organization culture. The more vertical levels there are in an organization, the more opportunities there are for filtering. As organizations become less dependent on strict hierarchical arrangements and instead use more collaborative, cooperative work arrangements, information filtering may become less of a problem. In addition, the ever-increasing use of e-mail to communicate in organizations reduces filtering because communication is more direct as intermediaries are bypassed. Finally, the organizational culture encourages or discourages filtering by the type of behavior it rewards. The more that organizational rewards emphasize style and appearance, the more managers will be motivated to filter communications in their favor.

Selective perception The second barrier is **selective perception**. We've mentioned selective perception before in this book. The term appears again here because the receivers in the communication process selectively see and hear based on their needs, motivations, experience, background, and other personal characteristics. Receivers also project their interests and expectations into communications as they decode them. The employment interviewer who expects a female job applicant to put her family ahead of

selective perception
Selective hearing communications based on one's needs, motivations, experience, or other personal characteristics

EXHIBIT 12–2
Barriers to Effective Communication

BARRIER	DESCRIPTION
Filtering	The deliberate manipulation of information to make it appear more favorable to the receiver.
Selective Perception	Receiving communications on the basis of what one selectively sees and hears depending on his or her needs, motivation, experience, background, and other personal characteristics.
Information Overload	When the amount of information one has to work with exceeds one's processing capacity.
Emotions	How the receiver feels when a message is received.
Language	Words have different meanings to different people. Receivers will use their definition of words communicated.
Gender	How males and females react to communication may be different; and they each have a different communication style.
National Culture	Communication differences arising from the different languages that individuals use to communicate and the national culture of which they are a part.

Technology and fast-paced communications have entered into every aspect of workers' lives. While such systems can be very beneficial, they can create problems. Employees are now available 24/7. They can be reached wherever they are—or at the very least, have messages sent to them that need addressing. As a result, the bombardment of information can sometimes overload individuals. When this happens, communications may break down, resulting in a communication barrier known as information overload.

her career is likely to see that tendency in female applicants, regardless of whether the applicants would do so or not. As we said in Chapter 8, we don't see reality; rather, we interpret what we see and call it reality.

Information overload Individuals have a finite capacity for processing data. For instance, consider the international sales representative who returns home to find that she has more than 600 e-mails waiting for her. It's not possible to fully read and respond to each one of those messages without facing **information overload**. Today's typical executive frequently complains of information overload.[12] The demands of keeping up with e-mail, phone calls, faxes, meetings, and professional reading create an onslaught of data that is nearly impossible to process and assimilate. What happens when individuals have more information than they can sort out and use? They tend to select out, ignore, pass over, or forget information. Or they may put off further processing until the overload situation is over. In any case, the result is lost information and less effective communication.

Emotions How a receiver feels when a message is received influences how he or she interprets it. You'll often interpret the same message differently, depending on whether you're happy or distressed. Extreme emotions are most likely to hinder effective communications. In such instances, we often disregard our rational and objective thinking processes and substitute emotional judgments. It's best to avoid reacting to a message when you're upset because you're not likely to be thinking clearly.

information overload
The result of information exceeding processing capacity

jargon
Technical language

Language Words mean different things to different people. "The meanings of words are not in the words; they are in us."[13] Age, education, and cultural background are three of the more obvious variables that influence the language a person uses and the definitions he or she applies to words. Columnist George F. Will and rap artist Nelly both speak English. But the language one uses is vastly different from how the other speaks.

In an organization, employees usually come from diverse backgrounds and, therefore, have different patterns of speech. Additionally, the grouping of employees into departments creates specialists who develop their own **jargon** or technical language.[14] In large organizations, members are also frequently widely dispersed geographically—even operating in different countries—and individuals in each locale will use terms and phrases that are unique to their area.[15] And the existence of vertical levels can also cause language problems. The language of senior executives, for instance, can be mystifying to operative employees not familiar with management jargon. Keep in mind that while we may speak the same language, our use of that language is far from uniform. Senders tend to assume that the words and phrases they use mean the same to the receiver as they do to them. This, of course, is incorrect and creates communication barriers. Knowing how each of us modifies the language would help minimize those barriers.

Gender Do men and women communicate in the same way? The answer is no. And the differences between men and women may lead to significant misunderstandings and misperceptions.[16]

Deborah Tannen's research on how men and women communicate has uncovered some interesting insights. She found that when men talk, they do so to emphasize status and independence; whereas women talk to create connections and intimacy. For instance, men frequently complain that women talk on and on about their problems. Women, however, criticize men for not listening. When a man hears a woman talking about a problem, he frequently asserts his desire for independence and control by providing solutions. Many women, in contrast, view conversing about a problem as a means of promoting closeness. The woman presents the problem to gain support and connection, not to get the man's advice.

Effective communication between the sexes is important in all organizations if they are to meet organizational goals. But how can we manage the various differences in communication styles? To keep gender differences from becoming persistent barriers to effective communication requires acceptance, understanding, and a commitment to communicate adaptively with each other. Both men and women need to acknowledge that there are differences in communication styles, that one style isn't better than the other, and that it takes real effort to talk with each other successfully.

National culture Finally, communication differences can also arise from the different languages that individuals use to communicate and the national culture of which they are a part.[17] For example, let's compare countries that place a high value on individualism (such as the United States) with countries where the emphasis is on collectivism (such as Japan).[18]

In the United States, communication patterns tend to be oriented to the individual and clearly spelled out. U.S. managers rely heavily on memoranda, announcements, position papers, and other formal forms of communication to state their positions on

Ethical Dilemma in Management

Distorting Information Purposely

The issue of withholding information is always a concern for supervisors. And because it's so closely intertwined with interpersonal communication, this might be a good time to think about ethical dilemmas that supervisors face relating to the intentional distortion of information. Read through the following incidents.[19]

- ***Incident 1:*** You're an accountant with a large accounting firm. One of your clients is the CFO of a large energy conglomerate. The CFO has just seen his company's losses from activities they are involved in. Rather than show the losses on the corporate income statement, the CFO would like for you to verify that these losses rightfully belong to a subsidiary company. In doing so, the company's stock prices will not be affected. What do you do?
- ***Incident 2:*** As a sales manager, you just received your department's sales report for last month. Sales are down considerably. Your boss, who works 2,000 miles away in another city, is unlikely to see last month's sales figures. You're optimistic that sales will pick up this month and next so that your overall quarterly numbers will be right on target. You also know that your boss is the type of person who hates to hear bad news. You're having a phone conversation today with your boss. He happens to ask in passing how last month's sales went. What do you tell him?
- ***Incident 3:*** You represent a high profile individual that is a friend of a CEO of a company. Your client has invested money in that company. One day you are advised to sell the stocks before news about the company that will drastically reduce the company's stock price becomes public. Your client says the timing was coincidental. You believe otherwise. What do you tell the Securities and Exchange Commission when they contact you about the incident?
- ***Incident 4:*** An employee asks you about a rumor she's heard that your department and all its employees will be transferred from New York to Pittsburgh. You know the rumor to be true, but you'd rather not let the information out just yet. You're fearful that it could hurt departmental morale and lead to premature resignations. What do you say to your employee?

These four incidents illustrate potential dilemmas that supervisors face relating to evading the truth, distorting facts, or lying to others. And here's something else that makes the situation even more problematic: It might not always be in the best interest of a supervisor or those in his or her department to provide full and complete information. Keeping communications fuzzy can cut down on questions, permit faster decision making, minimize objections, reduce opposition, make it easier to deny one's earlier statements, preserve the freedom to change one's mind, permit one to say "no" diplomatically, help to avoid confrontation and anxiety, and provide other benefits that work to the advantage of the manager.

Is it unethical to purposely distort communications to get a favorable outcome? What about "little white lies" that really don't hurt anybody? Are these ethical? What guidelines could you suggest for managers who want guidance in deciding whether distorting information is ethical or unethical?

issues. U.S. supervisors may hoard information in an attempt to make themselves look good (filtering) and as a way of persuading their employees to accept decisions and plans. And for their own protection, lower-level employees also engage in this practice.

In collectivist countries, such as Japan, there's more interaction for its own sake and a more informal manner of interpersonal contact. The Japanese manager, in contrast to the U.S. manager, engages in extensive verbal consultation with employees over an issue first and draws up a formal document later to outline the agreement that was made. The Japanese value decisions by consensus, and open communication is an inherent part of the work setting. Also, face-to-face communication is encouraged.[20]

Cultural differences can affect the way a manager chooses to communicate.[21] And these differences undoubtedly can be a barrier to effective communication if not recognized and taken into consideration.

HOW CAN MANAGERS OVERCOME COMMUNICATION BARRIERS?

Given these barriers to communication, what can managers do to overcome them? The following suggestions should help make communication more effective (see also Exhibit 12–3).

Why use feedback? Many communication problems can be directly attributed to misunderstandings and inaccuracies. These problems are less likely to occur if the manager uses the feedback loop in the communication process. This feedback can be verbal or nonverbal.

If a manager asks a receiver, "Did you understand what I said?" the response represents feedback. Feedback should include more than "yes" and "no" answers. The manager can ask a set of questions about a message in order to determine whether the message was received as intended. Better yet, the manager can ask the receiver to restate the message in his or her own words. If the manager then hears what was intended, understanding and accuracy should be enhanced. Feedback also includes subtler methods than direct questioning or the summarizing of messages. General comments can give a manager a sense of the receiver's reaction to a message. In addition, performance appraisals, salary reviews, and promotions represent important forms of feedback.

Of course, feedback does not have to be conveyed in words. Actions may speak louder than words. The sales manager who sends out a directive to his or her staff describing a new monthly sales report that all sales personnel will need to complete receives feedback if some of the salespeople fail to turn in the new report. This feedback suggests that the sales manager needs to clarify the initial directive. Similarly, when you give a speech to a group of people, you watch their eyes and look for other nonverbal clues to tell you whether they are getting your message.

EXHIBIT 12–3
Overcoming Barriers to Effective Communication

Use Feedback	Check the accuracy of what has been communicated—or what you think you heard.
Simplify Language	Use words that the intended audience understands.
Listen actively	Listen for the full meaning of the message without making premature judgment or interpretation—or thinking about what you are going to say in response.
Constrain Emotions	Recognize when your emotions are running high. When they are, don't communicate until you have calmed down.
Watch Nonverbal Cues	Be aware that your actions speak louder than your words. Keep the two consistent.

EXHIBIT 12–4

Using Simple Language?

Source: DILBERT, reprinted by permission of United Feature Syndicate, Inc.

Why should simplified language be used? Because language can be a barrier, managers should choose words and structure their messages in ways that will make those messages clear and understandable to the receiver (see Exhibit 12–4). The manager should consider the audience to whom the message is directed so that the language will be tailored to the receivers. Remember, communication is effective when a message is both received and understood. Understanding is improved by simplifying the language used to the intended audience. This means, for example, that a hospital administrator should always try to communicate in clear, easily understood terms and that the language used in messages to the surgical staff should be different from that used with office employees. Jargon can facilitate understanding when it is used within a group that knows what it means, but it can cause innumerable problems when used outside that group.

Why must we listen actively? When someone talks, we hear. But too often we don't listen. Listening is an active search for meaning, whereas hearing is passive. In listening, two people are thinking—the receiver and the sender.

Many of us are poor listeners. Why? Because listening is difficult, and it's usually more satisfying to be the talker. Listening, in fact, is often more tiring than talking. It demands intellectual effort. Unlike hearing, active listening demands total concentration. The average person speaks at a rate of about 150 words per minute, whereas we have the capacity to hear and process at the rate of nearly 1,000 words per minute.[22] The difference obviously leaves idle time for the brain and opportunities for the mind to wander.

active listening
Listening for full meaning without making premature judgment or interpretations

Active listening is enhanced by empathy with the sender—that is, by placing yourself in the sender's position. Because senders differ in attitudes, interests, needs, and expectations, empathy makes it easier to understand the actual content of a message. An empathic listener reserves judgment on the message's content and carefully listens to what is being said. The goal is to improve one's ability to receive the full meaning of a communication without having it distorted by premature judgments or interpretations. We'll return to active listening as an interpersonal skill shortly.

Why must we constrain emotions? It would be naive to assume that managers always communicate in a fully rational manner. We know that emotions can severely cloud and distort the transference of meaning. A manager who is emotionally upset over an issue is likely to misconstrue incoming messages and fail to express his or her outgoing messages clearly and accurately. What can the manager do? The simplest answer is to stop communicating until he or she has regained composure.

Why the emphasis on nonverbal cues? If actions speak louder than words, then it's important to watch your actions to make sure that they align with and reinforce the words that go along with them. We noted that nonverbal messages carry a great deal of weight. Given this fact, the effective communicator watches his or her nonverbal cues to ensure that they, too, convey the desired message.

COMMUNICATIONS AND INFORMATION TECHNOLOGY

Information technology has radically changed the way organizational members communicate. For example, it has significantly improved a manager's ability to monitor individual and team performance, it has allowed employees to have more complete information to make faster decisions, and it has provided employees more opportunities to collaborate and share information. In addition, information technology has made it possible for people in organizations to be fully accessible 24 hours a day, 7 days a week, regardless of where they are. Employees don't have to be at their desks with their computers turned on in order to communicate with others in the organization. Three developments in information technology appear to have the most significant effect on current managerial communication: networked computer systems, wireless capabilities, and knowledge management systems.

WHAT ARE THE NETWORKED COMMUNICATION CAPABILITIES?

In a networked computer system, an organization links its computers together through compatible hardware and software, creating an integrated organizational network. Organization members can then communicate with each other and tap into information whether they're down the hall, across town, or anywhere on the globe. Although the mechanics of how network systems work are beyond the scope of this book, we'll address some of its communication applications. These include e-mail, instant messaging, voice mail, fax, electronic data interchange, intranets and extranets, and the talking Internet.

E-mail is the instantaneous transmission of messages on computers that are linked together. Messages wait at a receiver's computer and are read at the receiver's convenience. E-mail is fast and cheap and can be used to send the same message to many people at the same time. It's a quick and convenient way for organization members to share information and communicate. E-mail messages may also contain attached files, which enables the receiver to obtain a hard copy of a document.

Some organization members who find e-mail slow and cumbersome are also using instant messaging (IM). This is interactive, real-time communication that takes place among computer users who are logged on to the computer network at the same time. IM first became popular among teens and preteens who wanted to communicate with their friends online. Now it's moving to the workplace. With IMs, there's no waiting around for a colleague to read e-mail. Whatever information needs to be communicated can be done so instantaneously. However, there are a couple of drawbacks to instant messaging. It requires groups of users to be logged on to the organization's computer network at the same time. This leaves the network open to security breaches.

A voice-mail system digitizes a spoken message, transmits it over the network, and stores the message on a disk for the receiver to retrieve later.[23] This capability allows information to be transmitted even though a receiver may not be physically present to take the information. Receivers can choose to save the message for future use, delete it, or route it to other parties.

Facsimile or fax machines allow the transmission of documents containing both text and graphics over ordinary telephone lines. A sending fax machine scans and digitizes the document, a receiving fax machine reads the scanned information and reproduces it in hard-copy form. Information that is best viewed in printed form can be easily and quickly shared by organization members.

Electronic data interchange (EDI) is a way for organizations to exchange business transaction documents such as invoices or purchase orders, using direct, computer-to-

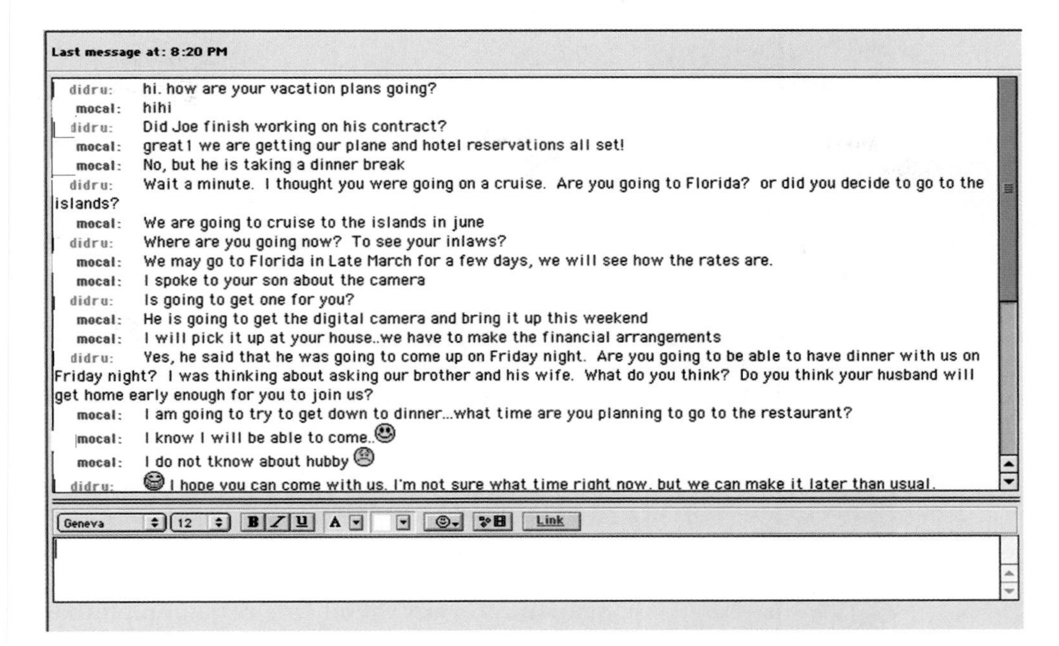

Technology has enhanced communications in a number of ways. Although e-mail enables communications to take place between two people, it is sometimes slow and cumbersome. Instant messaging allows real-time communication between two computer users logged on to the same network.

computer networks. Organizations often use EDI with vendors, suppliers, and customers because it saves time and money. How? Information on transactions is transmitted from one organization's computer system to another through an interorganizational telecommunications network. The printing and handling of paper documents at one organization are eliminated as is the inputting of data at the other organization.

Meetings—one-on-one, team, divisional, or organization-wide—have always been one way to share information. The limitations of technology used to dictate that meetings take place among people in the same physical location. But that's no longer the case. Teleconferencing allows a group of people to confer simultaneously using telephone or e-mail group communications software. If meeting participants can see each other over video screens, the simultaneous conference is called videoconferencing. Work groups, large and small, which might be in different locations, can use these communication network tools to collaborate and share information. Doing so is oftentimes much less expensive than incurring travel costs for bringing members together from several locations.

Networked computer systems have allowed the development of organizational intranets and extranets. An intranet is an organizational communication network that uses Internet technology but is accessible only to organizational employees. Many organizations are using intranets as ways for employees to share information and collaborate on documents and projects—as well as access company policy manuals and employee-specific materials, like employee benefits—from different locations.[24] An extranet is an organizational communication network that uses Internet technology and allows authorized users inside the organization to communicate with certain outsiders such as customers or vendors. Most of the large auto manufacturers, for example, have extranets that allow faster and more convenient communication with dealers.

Finally, the Internet is now being used for voice communication. Popular Web sites such as Yahoo! let users chat verbally with each other. America Online has introduced a Web browser that lets users click on a button to talk to others. Similarly, a number of companies are moving to Internet-based voice communications. For instance, in the New Jersey offices of Merrill Lynch, 6,500 Internet phones have been installed for employees to use in conference calls or for instant messaging communication.[25]

Just your typical day for Susan Sharin, an investment advisor in a company near Eastford, Connecticut. It's up early in the morning, do some Yoga, then turn on the computer and manage the $25 million under her control. All this from the privacy of her 14-acre homestead—eliminating the 42-mile commute to her former office.

HOW DO WIRELESS CAPABILITIES AFFECT COMMUNICATIONS?

While the communication possibilities for a manager in a networked world are exciting, the real potential is yet to come. Networked computer systems require organizations and organizational members to be connected by wires. Wireless communication relies on signals sent through air or space without any physical connection, using such devices as microwave signals, satellites, radio waves and radio antennas, or infrared light rays. Wireless smart phones, notebook computers, and other pocket communication devices have spawned a whole new way for managers to "keep in touch." Globally, millions of users have wireless technology that allows them to send and receive information from anywhere. One result: Employees no longer have to be at their desks with their computers plugged in and turned on in order to communicate with others in the organization. As technology continues to improve in this area, we'll see more and more organization members using wireless communication as a way to collaborate and share information.[26]

HOW DOES KNOWLEDGE MANAGEMENT AFFECT COMMUNICATIONS?

knowledge management
Includes cultivating a learning culture in which organizational members systematically gather knowledge and share it with others

Part of a manager's responsibility in fostering an environment conducive to learning and effective communications is to create learning capabilities throughout the organization. This must extend from the lowest to the highest levels in all areas. How can managers do this? An important step is understanding the value of knowledge as a major resource, just like cash, raw materials, or office equipment. To illustrate the value of knowledge, think about how you register for college classes. Do you talk to others who have had a certain professor? Do you listen to their experiences with this individual and make your decision based on what they have to say (their knowledge about the situation)? If you do, you're tapping into the value of knowledge. But in an organization, just recognizing the value of accumulated knowledge or wisdom isn't enough. Managers must deliberately manage that base of knowledge. **Knowledge management** involves cultivating a learning culture in which organizational members systematically gather knowledge and share it with others in the organization so as to achieve better performance.[27] For instance, accountants and consultants at Ernst and Young, one of the Big Five professional service firms, documents best practices that they have developed, unusual problems they have dealt with, and other work information. This "knowledge" is then shared with all employees through computer-based applications and through community of interest teams that meet regularly throughout the company. Many other organizations—General Electric, Toyota, Hewlett-Packard—have recognized the importance of knowledge management to being a learning organization (see Chapter 2, pp. 44–45). The technologies available in today's organizations are permitting knowledge management to improve and facilitate organizational communications and decision making.

DEVELOPING INTERPERSONAL SKILLS

Would it surprise you to know that more managers are probably fired because of poor interpersonal skills than for a lack of technical ability?[28] Moreover, a survey of top executives at *Fortune* 500 companies found that interpersonal skills were the most important consideration in hiring senior-level employees.[29] Because managers ultimately get things done through others, competencies in leadership, communication, and other interpersonal skills are prerequisites to managerial effectiveness.[30] Therefore, the rest of this chapter focuses on key interpersonal skills that every manager needs.[31]

WHY ARE ACTIVE LISTENING SKILLS IMPORTANT?

A few pages ago, we briefly mentioned that the ability to listen is too often taken for granted because we tend to confuse hearing with listening. Listening requires paying attention, interpreting, and remembering sound stimuli.

Effective listening is active rather than passive. In passive listening, you resemble a tape recorder. You absorb and remember the words spoken. If the speaker provides you with a clear message and makes his or her delivery interesting enough to keep your attention, you'll probably hear most of what the speaker is trying to communicate. Active listening requires you to get inside the speaker's mind to understand the communication from his or her point of view. As you will see, active listening is hard work.[32] You have to concentrate, and you have to want to fully understand what a speaker is saying.[33] Students who use active listening techniques for an entire 75-minute lecture are as tired as their instructor when the lecture is over because they have put as much energy into listening as the instructor put into speaking.

There are four essential requirements for active listening: (1) intensity, (2) empathy, (3) acceptance, and (4) a willingness to take responsibility for completeness.[34] As noted, the human brain is capable of handling a speaking rate that is about six times as fast as that of the average speaker. That leaves a lot of time for daydreaming. The active listener concentrates *intensely* on what the speaker is saying and tunes out the thousands of miscellaneous thoughts (about money, sex, vacation, parties, exams, and so on) that create distractions. What do active listeners do with their idle brain time? They summarize and integrate what has been said. They put each new bit of information into the context of what preceded it.

Empathy requires you to put yourself into the speaker's shoes. You try to understand what the speaker wants to communicate rather than what you want to hear. Notice that empathy demands both knowledge of the speaker and flexibility on your part. You need to suspend your own thoughts and feelings and adjust what you see and feel to your speaker's world. In that way, you increase the likelihood that you'll interpret the message in the way the speaker intended.

An active listener demonstrates *acceptance*. He or she listens objectively without judging content. This is no easy task. It's natural to be distracted by what a speaker says, especially when we disagree with it. When we hear something we disagree with, we have a tendency to begin formulating our mental arguments to counter what is being said. Of course, in doing so, we miss the rest of the message. The challenge for the active listener is to absorb what's being said and withhold judgment on content until the speaker is finished.

Active listening requires us to listen attentively to the speaker, and in many cases, develop empathy for what the speaker is saying. In this case, the listener is demonstrating empathy by "feeling" the speaker's words

The final ingredient of active listening is taking *responsibility for completeness*. That is, the listener does whatever is necessary to get the full intended meaning from the speaker's communication. Two widely used active listening techniques are listening for feeling as well as for content and asking questions to ensure understanding.

Just how, though, can you develop effective listening skills? The literature on active listening emphasizes eight specific behaviors (see Developing Your Active Listening Skill on page 369). As you review these behaviors, ask yourself whether they describe your listening practices. If you're not currently using these techniques, there's no better time than right now to begin developing them.

WHY ARE FEEDBACK SKILLS IMPORTANT?

Ask a manager about the feedback he or she gives to employees, and you're likely to get a qualified answer. If the feedback is positive, it's likely to be given promptly and enthusiastically. Negative feedback is often treated very differently.[35] Like most of us, managers don't particularly enjoy communicating bad news. They fear offending the receiver or having to deal with his or her emotions. The result is that negative feedback is often avoided, delayed, or substantially distorted. The purposes of this section are to show you the importance of providing both positive and negative feedback and to identify specific techniques to help make your feedback more effective.

What is the difference between positive and negative feedback? We know that managers treat positive and negative feedback differently. So, too, do receivers. You need to understand this fact and adjust your feedback style accordingly.

Positive feedback is more readily and accurately perceived than negative feedback. Furthermore, whereas positive feedback is almost always accepted, negative feedback often meets resistance.[36] Why? The logical answer appears to be that people want to hear good news and block out the rest. Positive feedback fits what most people wish to hear and already believe about themselves. Does this mean, then, that you should avoid giving negative feedback? No! What it means is that you need to be aware of potential resistance and learn to use negative feedback in situations in which it's most likely to be accepted.[37] What are those situations? Research indicates that negative feedback is most likely to be accepted when it comes from a credible source or if it's objective. Subjective impressions carry weight only when they come from a person with high status and credibility.[38] This suggests that negative feedback that is supported by hard data—numbers, specific examples, and the like—is more likely to be accepted. Negative feedback that is subjective can be a meaningful tool for experienced managers, particularly those in upper levels of the organization who have built the trust and earned the respect of their employees. From less experienced managers, those in the lower ranks of the organization, and those whose reputations have not yet been established, negative feedback that is subjective in nature is not likely to be well received.

How do you give effective feedback? There are six specific suggestions that we can make to help you become more effective in providing feedback.[39] We summarize them in Exhibit 12–5 and discuss them further on the next page.

EXHIBIT 12–5
Suggestions for Effective Feedback

- Focus on specific behavior
- Keep feedback impersonal
- Keep feedback goal oriented
- Make feedback well-timed
- Ensure understanding
- Direct negative feedback toward behavior that the receiver can control

- ***Focus on specific behaviors.*** Feedback should be specific rather than general. Avoid statements such as "You have a bad attitude" or "I'm really impressed with the good job you did." They are vague, and, although they provide information, they do not tell the receiver enough so that he or she can correct the "bad attitude," or on what basis you concluded that a good job has been done so the person knows what behaviors to repeat.
- ***Keep feedback impersonal.*** Feedback, particularly the negative kind, should be descriptive rather than judgmental or evaluative. No matter how upset you are, keep the feedback focused on job-related behaviors and never criticize someone personally because of an inappropriate action. Telling people they are incompetent, lazy, or the like is almost always counterproductive. It provokes such an emotional reaction that the performance deviation itself is apt to be overlooked. When you are criticizing, remember that you are censuring job-related behavior, not the person. You might be tempted to tell someone he or she is rude and insensitive (which might just be true); however, that is hardly impersonal. It's better to say something more specific, like, "You've interrupted me three times with questions that weren't urgent when you knew I was talking long distance to a customer in Brazil."
- ***Keep feedback goal oriented.*** Feedback should not be given primarily to "dump" or "unload" on another person. If you have to say something negative, make sure it is directed toward the receiver's goals. Ask yourself whom the feedback is supposed to help. If the answer is essentially you ("I've got something I just want to get off my chest"), bite your tongue and hold the comment. Such feedback undermines your credibility and lessens the meaning and influence of future feedback sessions.
- ***Make feedback well timed.*** Feedback is most meaningful to a receiver when there is a very short interval between his or her behavior and the receipt of feedback about that behavior. For example, a new employee who makes a mistake is more likely to respond to his or her manager's suggestions for improving right after the mistake or at the end of the work day rather than during a performance review session six months from now. If you have to spend time recreating a situation and refreshing someone's memory of it, the feedback you are providing is likely to be ineffective. Moreover, if you are particularly concerned with changing behavior, delays in providing timely feedback on the undesirable actions lessen the likelihood that the feedback will bring about the desired change. Of course, making feedback prompt merely for promptness sake can backfire if you have insufficient information or if you are upset. In such instances, well timed could mean somewhat delayed.
- ***Ensure understanding.*** Is your feedback concise and complete enough that the receiver clearly and fully understands your communication? Remember that every successful communication requires both transference and understanding of meaning. If feedback is to be effective, you need to ensure that the receiver understands it. As suggested in our discussion of listening techniques, ask the receiver to rephrase the message to find out whether he or she fully captured the meaning you intended.
- ***Direct negative feedback toward behavior that the receiver can control.*** There is little value in reminding a person of some shortcoming over which he or she has no control. Negative feedback should be directed toward behavior that the receiver can do something about. For instance, criticizing an employee who's late for work because she forgot to set her alarm clock is valid. Criticizing her for being late for work when the subway she takes to work every day had a power failure, stranding her for 90 minutes, is pointless. There is nothing she could have done to correct what happened—short of finding a different means of traveling to work, which may be unrealistic. In addition, when negative feedback is given concerning something that the receiver can control, it might be a good idea to indicate specifically what can be done to improve the situation. Such suggestions take some of the sting out of the criticism and offer guidance to receivers who understand the problem but don't know how to resolve it.

WHAT ARE EMPOWERMENT SKILLS?

As we've described in various places throughout this text, managers are leading more and more by empowering their employees. Millions of employees and teams of employees are making key operating decisions that directly affect their work. They're developing budgets, scheduling workloads, controlling inventories, solving quality problems, and engaging in activities that until recently were viewed exclusively as part of the manager's job.[40]

The increased use of empowerment is being driven by two forces. First is the need for quick decisions by those who are most knowledgeable about the issue. That requires moving decisions to lower levels. If organizations are to successfully compete in a dynamic global economy, they have to be able to make decisions and implement changes quickly. Second is the reality that the downsizing of organizations during the past two decades has left many managers with considerably larger spans of control than they had previously. In order to cope with the demands of an increased load, managers had to empower their employees. Two aspects of this empowering effect are understanding the value of delegating and knowing how to do it.

delegation
The assignment of authority to another person to carry out specific activities

Delegation is the assignment of authority to another person to carry out specific activities. It allows an employee to make decisions—that is, it is a shift of decision-making authority from one organizational level to another, lower one (see Exhibit 12–6). Delegation, however, should not be confused with participation. In participative decision making, there is a sharing of authority. With delegation, employees make decisions on their own. That's why delegation is such a vital component of worker empowerment!

Don't managers abdicate their responsibility when they delegate? When done properly, delegation is not abdication. The key word here is *properly*. If you, as a manager, dump tasks on an employee without clarifying the exact job to be done, the range of the employee's discretion, the expected level of performance, the time frame in which the tasks are to be completed, and similar concerns, you are abdicating responsibility and inviting trouble.[41] Don't fall into the trap, however, of assuming that, to avoid the appearance of abdicating, you should minimize delegation. Unfortunately, that is how many new and inexperienced managers interpret the situation. Lacking confidence in their employees or fearful that they will be criticized for their employees' mistakes, these managers try to do everything themselves.

EXHIBIT 12–6
Effective Delegation

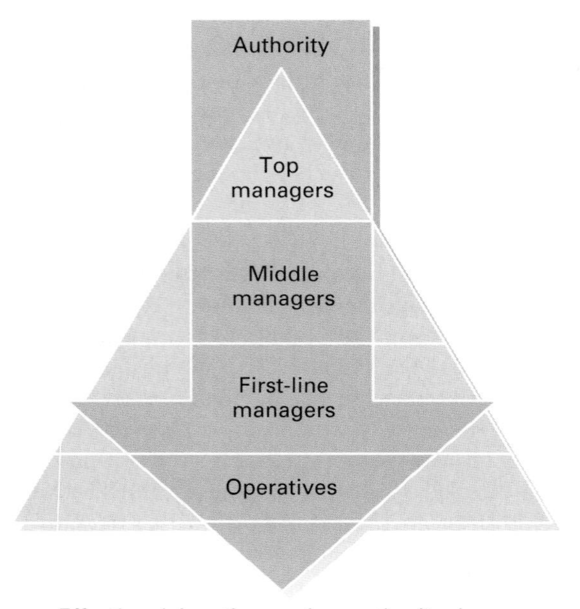

Effective delegation pushes authority down vertically through the ranks of an organization.

Learning from Experience: One Manager's Reflection

Lori A. De Gasso Studio Manager, Yoga Zone LLC

DELEGATING EFFECTIVELY

Describe the situation you faced. I have a lot of day-to-day responsibilities in my position as studio manager of our Old Brookville, New York, location. I have more than 30 employees that I oversee in different aspects of the company, which produces yoga-related products, videos and DVD's, and a television series shown daily on Wisdom television. There is a front-desk reception staff with whom I work closely, as well as yoga instructors, pilates instructors, and massage therapists. On any given day I interact and speak with at least 10 to 15 employees. Some of the responsibilities I have are ordering, receiving, inventory control, generating reports, payroll, dealing with customer issues, and hiring and firing. Although these responsibilities can take up most of the day, I also deal with unexpected issues that can and do arise. This is why I need to delegate some of my work to other employees in order to get it done in a reasonable amount of time.

One particular situation I faced with delegating was when I needed to take some personal time off for medical reasons and was forced to be away from my job for almost a month. I was not expecting to be away so long so I did not plan on having someone cover for me during that time. I was mainly concerned with the day-to-day work, which was taken care of.

What action(s) did you take? Because I was away for so long, most of my other work had piled up for weeks, since I had never thought to show someone exactly what to do. My hands were tied and it was hard for me to deal with because I am not the type of person to leave work undone.

What results occurred? The result was that it took me twice as long to catch up once I got back. In looking back now I realize how important it is to delegate because you never know what can happen. You may think that you're on top of it or that you are the only one who can handle it, but things happen and it's always better to be prepared.

What did/should you have done differently? I have not taken time off since this occurred, but I have been more diligent in delegating work to my employees. I learned that getting help is okay and doing this makes work enjoyable, which in turn creates a more productive and peaceful atmosphere.

It might very well be true that you are capable of doing tasks better, faster, or with fewer mistakes. The catch is that your time and energy are scarce resources. It is not possible for you to do everything yourself. As a manager, you'll need to delegate to be effective in your job. This fact suggests two important points. First, you should expect and accept some mistakes by your employees. Mistakes are part of delegation. They are often good learning experiences for employees as long as their costs are not excessive. Second, to ensure that the costs of mistakes don't exceed the value of the learning, you need to put adequate controls in place. As we will discuss shortly, delegation without feedback controls that let you know where there are potentially serious problems is a form of abdication.

How much authority should a manager delegate? Should he or she keep authority centralized, delegating only the minimal amount to complete the delegated duties? What contingency factors should be considered in determining the degree to which authority is delegated? Exhibit 12–7 presents the most widely cited contingency factors to provide some guidance in making those determinations.

How do you delegate effectively? Assuming that delegation is in order, how do you delegate? A number of methods have been suggested for differentiating the effective delegator from the ineffective one.[42]

EXHIBIT 12–7 **Contingency Factors in Delegation**

- **The size of the organization** The larger the organization, the greater the number of decisions that have to be made. Because top managers in an organization have only so much time and can obtain only so much information, in larger organizations they become increasingly dependent on the decision making of lower-level managers. Therefore, managers in large organizations resort to increased delegation.
- **The importance of the duty or decision** The more important a duty or decision (as expressed in terms of cost and impact on the future of an organization), the less likely it is be delegated. For instance, a department head may be delegated authority to make expenditures up to $7,500, and division heads and vice presidents up to $50,000 and $125,000, respectively.
- **Task complexity** The more complex the task, the more difficult it is for top management to possess current and sufficient technical information to make effective decisions. Complex tasks require greater expertise, and decisions about them should be delegated to the people who have the necessary technical knowledge.
- **Organizational culture** If management has confidence and trust in employees, the culture will support a greater degree of delegation. However, if top management does not have confidence in the abilities of lower-level managers, it will delegate authority only when absolutely necessary. In such instances, as little authority as possible is delegated.
- **Qualities of employees** A final contingency consideration is the qualities of employees. Delegation requires employees with the skills, abilities, and motivation to accept authority and act on it. If these are lacking, top management will be reluctant to relinquish authority.

- ***Clarify the assignment.*** First determine what is to be delegated and to whom. You need to identify the person who is most capable of doing the task and then determine whether he or she has the time and motivation to do the job. Assuming that you have a willing employee, it is your responsibility to provide clear information on what is being delegated, the results you expect, and any time or performance expectations you hold. Unless there is an overriding need to adhere to specific methods, you should ask an employee only to provide the desired results. That is, get agreement on what is to be done and the results expected, but let the employee decide by which means the work is to be completed. By focusing on goals and allowing the employee the freedom to use his or her own judgment as to how those goals are to be achieved, you increase trust between you and the employee, improve the employee's motivation, and enhance accountability for results.
- ***Specify employees' range of discretion.*** Every act of delegation comes with constraints. You are delegating authority to act but not unlimited authority. You are delegating the authority to act on certain issues within certain parameters. You need to specify what those parameters are so that employees know, in no uncertain terms, the range of their discretion. When those parameters have been successfully communicated, both you and employees will have the same idea of the limits to the latter's authority and how far they can go without further approval.
- ***Allow employees to participate.*** One of the best ways to decide how much authority will be necessary is to allow employees who will be held accountable for the tasks to participate in that decision. Be aware, however, that participation can present its own set of potential problems as a result of employees' self-interest and biases in evaluating their own abilities. Some employees might be personally motivated to expand their authority beyond what they need and beyond what they are capable of handling. Allowing such people too much participation in deciding what tasks they should take on and how much authority they must have to complete those tasks can undermine the effectiveness of the delegation process.
- ***Inform others that delegation has occurred.*** Delegation should not take place in a vacuum. Not only do you and your employees need to know specifically what has been delegated and how much authority has been granted; anyone else who is likely to be affected by the delegation act needs to be informed. This includes people outside the organization as well as inside it. Essentially, you need to convey what has been delegated (the task and amount of authority) and to whom.

Failure to inform others makes conflict likely and decreases the chances that your employees will be able to accomplish the delegated act efficiently.

- ***Establish feedback controls.*** To delegate without instituting feedback controls is inviting problems. There is always the possibility that employees will misuse the discretion they have been given. Controls to monitor employees' progress increase the likelihood that important problems will be identified early and that the task will be completed on time and to the desired specification. Ideally, these controls should be determined at the time of initial assignment. Agree on a specific time for completion of the task, and then set progress dates by which the employees will report on how well they are doing and on any major problems that have surfaced. These controls can be supplemented with periodic spot checks to ensure that authority guidelines are not being abused, organization policies are being followed, proper procedures are being met, and the like. Too much of a good thing can be dysfunctional. If the controls are too constraining, employees will be deprived of the opportunity to build self-confidence. As a result, much of the motivational aspect of delegation may be lost. A well-designed control system, which we will elaborate on in more detail in the next chapter, permits your employees to make small mistakes but quickly alerts you when big mistakes are imminent.

HOW DO YOU MANAGE CONFLICT?

The ability to manage conflict is undoubtedly one of the most important skills a manager needs to possess.[43] A study of middle- and top-level executives by the American Management Association revealed that the average manager spends approximately 20 percent of his or her time dealing with conflict.[44] The importance of conflict management is reinforced by a survey of the topics managers consider most important in management development programs; conflict management was rated as more important than decision making, leadership, or communication skills.[45]

What is conflict management? When we use the term **conflict**, we are referring to perceived differences resulting in some form of interference or opposition. Whether the differences are real is irrelevant. If people perceive differences, then a conflict state exists. In addition, our definition includes the extremes, from subtle, indirect, and highly controlled forms of interference to overt acts such as strikes, riots, and wars.

conflict
Perceived difference resulting in interference or opposition

Over the years, three differing views have evolved toward conflict in organizations[46] (see Exhibit 12–8). One argues that conflict must be avoided, that it indicates

EXHIBIT 12–8 Three Views of Conflict

Traditional view	The early approach assumed that conflict was bad and would always have a negative impact on an organization. Conflict became synonymous with violence, destruction, and irrationality. Because conflict was harmful, it was to be avoided. Management had a responsibility to rid the organization of conflict. This traditional view dominated management literature during the late nineteenth century and continued until the mid-1940s.
Human relations view	The human relations position argued that conflict was a natural and inevitable occurrence in all organizations. Because conflict was inevitable, the human relations approach advocated acceptance of conflict. This approach rationalized the existence of conflict; conflict cannot be eliminated, and there are times when it may even benefit the organization. The human relations view dominated conflict thinking from the late 1940s through the mid-1970s.
Interactionist view	The current theoretical perspective on conflict is the interactionist approach. Although the human relations approach accepts conflict, the interactionist approach encourages conflict on the grounds that a harmonious, peaceful, tranquil, and cooperative organization is prone to become static, apathetic, and nonresponsive to needs for change and innovation. The major contribution of the interactionist approach, therefore, is that it encourages managers to maintain ongoing minimum level of conflict—enough to keep units viable, self-critical, and creative.

traditional view of conflict
The view that all conflict is bad and must be avoided

human relations view of conflict
The view that conflict is natural and inevitable and has the potential to be a positive force

interactionist view of conflict
The view that some conflict is necessary for an organization to perform effectively

functional conflict
Conflict that supports an organization's goals

dysfunctional conflict
Conflict that prevents an organization from achieving its goals

a malfunctioning within the organization. We call this the **traditional view of conflict**. A second, the **human relations view of conflict**, argues that conflict is a natural and inevitable outcome in any organization and that it need not be evil but, rather, that it has the potential to be a positive force in contributing to an organization's performance. The third and most recent perspective proposes not only that conflict can be a positive force in an organization but also that some conflict is absolutely necessary for an organization or units within an organization to perform effectively. We label this third approach the **interactionist view of conflict**.

Can conflict be positive and negative? The interactionist view does not propose that all conflict is good. Rather, some conflicts support the goals of the organization; these are **functional conflicts** of a constructive form. Other conflicts prevent an organization from achieving its goals; these are **dysfunctional conflicts** of a destructive form.

Of course, it is one thing to argue that conflict can be valuable, but how does a manager tell whether a conflict is functional or dysfunctional? Unfortunately, the demarcation is neither clear nor precise. No one level of conflict can be adopted as acceptable or unacceptable under all conditions. The type and level of conflict that promote a healthy and positive involvement toward one department's goals may, in another department or in the same department at another time, be highly dysfunctional. Functionality or dysfunctionality, therefore, is a matter of judgment. Exhibit 12–9 illustrates the challenge facing managers. They want to create an environment within their organization or organizational unit in which conflict is healthy but not allowed to run to pathological extremes. Neither too little nor too much conflict is desirable. Managers should stimulate conflict to gain the full benefits of its

EXHIBIT 12–9

Conflict and Organizational Performance

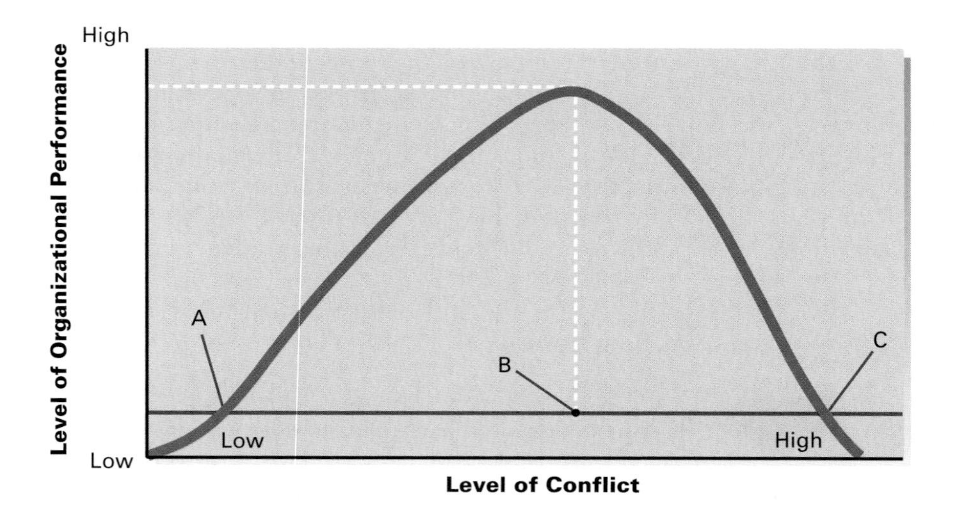

Situation	Level of Conflict	Type of Conflict	Organization's Internal Characteristics	Level of Organizational Performance
A	Low or none	Dysfunctional	Apathetic Stagnant Unresponsive to change Lack of new ideas	Low
B	Optimal	Functional	Viable Self-critical Innovative	High
C	High	Dysfunctional	Disruptive Chaotic Uncooperative	Low

functional properties yet reduce its level when it becomes a disruptive force. Because we have yet to devise a sophisticated measuring instrument for assessing whether a given conflict level is functional or dysfunctional, it remains for managers to make intelligent judgments concerning whether conflict levels in their units are optimal, too high, or too low.

If conflict is dysfunctional, what can a manager do? In the following sections, we review conflict resolution skills. Essentially, you need to know your basic conflict handling style as well as those of the conflicting parties to understand the situation that has created the conflict and to be aware of your options.

What appears to be the source of this conflict? There may be many, but on the face value of the situation, it appears that there is some communication difference between the two. For whatever reason, they have lost the ability to effectively discuss a matter between them, which is now causing a conflict.

What are the conflict-handling styles? Conflict in any organization is inevitable. Whenever you put people together and arrange them into some type of structure (formal or informal), there is a good probability that some individuals will perceive that others have negatively affected or are about to negatively affect something that they care about. How then do we deal with the conflict? The research of Kenneth W. Thomas has given us some insight.[47]

Thomas recognized that in these conflict-laden situations, one must first determine the intention of the other party. That is, one has to speculate about the other person's purpose for causing the conflict in order to respond to that behavior. Thomas concluded that one's response will depend on his or her cooperativeness or assertiveness. *Cooperativeness* is the degree to which an individual attempts to rectify the conflict by satisfying the other person's concerns.

Assertiveness is the degree to which an individual will attempt to rectify the conflict to satisfy his or her own concerns. Using these two dimensions, Thomas was able to identify four distinct conflict-handling techniques plus one middle-of-the-road combination. These were competing (assertive but uncooperative), collaborating (assertive and cooperative), avoiding (unassertive and uncooperative), accommodating (unassertive but cooperative), and compromising (midrange on both assertiveness and cooperativeness). Managers essentially can draw on any of these five conflict resolution options to reduce excessive conflict. Each has particular strengths and weaknesses, and no one option is ideal for every situation. Exhibit 12–10 describes when each is best used. You should consider each a tool in your conflict management tool chest. You might be better at using some tools than others, but the skilled manager knows what each tool can do and when each is likely to be most effective.[48]

Thomas recognized that one conflict resolution method is not appropriate in all situations. Rather, the situation itself must dictate the technique. For instance, *forcing* is most appropriate when a quick, decisive action is vital or against people who take advantage of noncompetitive behaviors. *Collaboration* is appropriate when one is attempting to merge insights from different people, and *avoidance* works well when the potential for disruption outweighs the benefits of resolving the conflict. *Accommodation* can assist in issues that are more important to others than to you or when harmony and stability are important to you. Finally, *compromise* works well in achieving temporary settlements to complex issues or reaching a solution when time constraints dictate and parties are about equal in power.

Which conflicts do you handle? Not every conflict justifies your attention. Some might not be worth the effort; others might be unmanageable. Not every conflict is worth your time and effort to resolve. Avoidance might appear to be a cop-out, but it can sometimes be the most appropriate response. You can improve your overall management effectiveness and your conflict management skills, in particular, by avoiding trivial conflicts. Choose your battles judiciously, saving your efforts for the ones that count.

Regardless of our desires, reality tells us that some conflicts are unmanageable.[49] When antagonisms are deeply rooted, when one or both parties wish to prolong a

EXHIBIT 12-10

Conflict Management: What Works Best and When

STRATEGY	BEST USED WHEN
Avoidance	Conflict is trivial, when emotions are running high and time is needed to cool them down, or when the potential disruption from an assertive action outweighs the benefits of resolution
Accommodation	The issue under dispute isn't that important to you or when you want to build up credits for later issues
Forcing	You need a quick resolution on important issues that require unpopular actions to be taken and when commitment by others to your solution is not critical
Compromise	Conflicting parties are about equal in power, when it is desirable to achieve a temporary solution to a complex issue, or when time pressures demand an expedient solution
Collaboration	Time pressures are minimal, when all parties seriously want a win-win solution, and when the issue is too important to be compromised

conflict, or when emotions run so high that constructive interaction is impossible, your efforts to manage the conflict are unlikely to meet with much success. Don't be lured into the naive belief that a good manager can resolve every conflict effectively. Some aren't worth the effort; some are outside your realm of influence. Still others may be functional and, as such, are best left alone.

Who are the conflict players? If you choose to manage a conflict situation, it is important that you take the time to get to know the players. Who is involved in the conflict? What interests does each party represent? What are each player's values, personality, feelings, and resources? Your chances of success in managing a conflict will be greatly enhanced if you can view the conflict situation through the eyes of the conflicting parties.

What are the sources of the conflict? Conflicts don't pop out of thin air. They have causes. Because your approach to resolving a conflict is likely to be determined largely by its causes, you need to determine the source of the conflict. Research indicates that, although conflicts have varying causes, they can generally be separated into three categories: communication differences, structural differences, and personal differences.[50]

Communication differences are disagreements arising from semantic difficulties, misunderstandings, and noise in the communication channels. People are often quick to assume that most conflicts are caused by lack of communication, but, as one author has noted, there is usually plenty of communication going on in most conflicts.[51] As we pointed out at the beginning of this chapter, many people equate good communication with having others agree with their views. What might at first look like an interpersonal conflict based on poor communication is usually found, upon closer analysis, to be a disagreement caused by different role requirements, unit goals,[52] personalities, value systems, or similar factors. As a source of conflict for managers, poor communication probably gets more attention than it deserves.

As we discussed in Chapter 5, organizations are horizontally and vertically differentiated. This *structural differentiation* creates problems of integration, which frequently cause conflicts. Individuals disagree over goals, decision alternatives, performance criteria, and resource allocations. These conflicts are not caused by poor communication or personal animosities. Rather, they are rooted in the structure of the organization itself.

The third conflict source is *personal differences*. Conflicts can evolve out of individual idiosyncrasies and personal value systems. The bad chemistry between some people makes it hard for them to work together. Factors such as background, education, experience, and training mold each individual into a unique personality with a particular set of values. Thus, people may be perceived as abrasive, untrustworthy, or strange. These personal differences can create conflict.

How does a manager stimulate conflict? What about the other side of conflict management—situations that require managers to stimulate conflict? The notion of stimulating conflict is often difficult to accept. For almost all of us the term conflict has a negative connotation, and the idea of purposely creating conflict seems to be the antithesis of good management. Few of us enjoy being in conflict situations, yet evidence demonstrates that there are situations in which an increase in conflict is constructive.[53] Although there is no clear demarcation between functional and dysfunctional conflict, and there is no definitive method for assessing the need for more conflict, an affirmative answer to one or more of the following questions may suggest a need for conflict stimulation.[54]

- Are you surrounded by "yes" people?
- Are employees afraid to admit ignorance and uncertainties to you?
- Is there so much concentration by decision makers on reaching a compromise that they lose sight of values, long-term objectives, or the organization's welfare?
- Do managers believe that it is in their best interest to maintain the impression of peace and cooperation in their unit, regardless of the price?
- Are decision makers excessively concerned about hurting the feelings of others?
- Do managers believe that popularity is more important for obtaining organizational rewards than competence and high performance?
- Do managers put undue emphasis on obtaining consensus for their decisions?
- Do employees show unusually high resistance to change?
- Is there a lack of new ideas?

We know a lot more about resolving conflict than about stimulating it. That's only natural, because human beings have been concerned with the subject of conflict reduction for hundreds, maybe thousands, of years. The dearth of ideas on conflict stimulation techniques reflects the very recent interest in the subject. The following are some preliminary suggestions that managers might want to use.[55]

The initial step in stimulating functional conflict is for managers to convey to employees the message, supported by actions, that conflict has its legitimate place. This step may require changing the culture of the organization. Individuals who challenge the status quo, suggest innovative ideas, offer divergent opinions, and demonstrate original thinking need to be rewarded visibly with promotions, salary, and other positive reinforcers.

As far as Franklin D. Roosevelt's administration, and probably before, the White House consistently has used communication to simulate conflict. Senior officials plant possible decisions with the media through the infamous "reliable source" route. For example, the name of a prominent judge is leaked as a possible Supreme Court appointment. If the candidate survives the public scrutiny, his or her appointment will be announced by the president. However, if the candidate is found lacking by the media and the public, the president's press secretary or other high-level official may make a formal statement such as, "At no time was this candidate under consideration." Regardless of party affiliation, occupants of the White House have regularly used the reliable source method as a conflict stimulation technique. It is all the more popular because of its handy escape mechanism. If the conflict level gets too high, the source can be denied and eliminated.

Ambiguous or threatening messages also encourage conflict. Information that a plant might close, that a department is likely to be eliminated, or that a layoff is imminent can reduce apathy, stimulate new ideas, and force reevaluation—all positive outcomes of increased conflict. Another widely used method for shaking up a stagnant unit or organization is to bring in outsiders either from outside or by internal transfer with backgrounds, values, attitudes, or managerial styles that differ from those of present members. Many large corporations have used this technique during the past decade to fill vacancies on their boards of directors. Women, minority group members, consumer activists, and others whose backgrounds and interests differ significantly from those of the rest of the board have been selected to add a fresh perspective.

We also know that structural variables are a source of conflict. It is, therefore, only logical that managers look to structure as a conflict stimulation device. Centralizing decisions, realigning work groups, increasing formalization, and increasing interdependencies between units are all structural devices that disrupt the status quo and increase conflict levels.

devil's advocate
A person who purposely presents arguments that run counter to those proposed by the majority or against current practices

Finally, one can appoint a **devil's advocate**, a person who purposely presents arguments that run counter to those proposed by the majority or against current practices. He or she plays the role of the critic, even to the point of arguing against positions with which he or she actually agrees. A devil's advocate acts as a check against groupthink and practices that have no better justification than "that's the way we've always done it around here." When thoughtfully listened to, the advocate can improve the quality of group decision making. On the other hand, others in the group often view advocates as time wasters, and their appointment is almost certain to delay any decision process.

WHAT ARE NEGOTIATION SKILLS?

We know that lawyers and auto salespeople spend a significant amount of time on their jobs negotiating. But so, too, do managers. They have to negotiate salaries for incoming employees, cut deals with their bosses, work out differences with their peers, and resolve conflicts with employees. Others, like Don Fehr and Rob Manfred in this chapter's opening vignette, have to negotiate labor contracts and other agreements with people outside their organizations. For our purposes, we will define **negotiation** as a process in which two or more parties who have different preferences must make a joint decision and come to an agreement. To achieve this goal, both parties typically use a bargaining strategy.

negotiation
A process in which two or more parties who have different preferences must make a joint decision and come to an agreement

How do bargaining strategies differ? There are two general approaches to negotiation—distributive bargaining and integrative bargaining.[56] Let's see what is involved in each.

You see a used car advertised for sale in the newspaper. It appears to be just what you've been looking for. You go out to see the car. It's great, and you want it. The owner tells you the asking price. You don't want to pay that much. The two of you then negotiate over the price. The negotiating process you are engaging in is called **distributive bargaining**. Its most identifying feature is that it operates under zero sum conditions.[57] That is, any gain you make is at the expense of the other person and vice versa. Every dollar you can get the seller to cut from the price of the used car is a dollar you save. Conversely, every dollar more he or she can get from you comes at your expense. Thus, the essence of distributive bargaining is negotiating over who gets what share of a fixed pie. Probably the most widely cited examples of distributive bargaining are traditional labor–management negotiations over wages and benefits. Typically, labor's representatives come to the bargaining table determined to get as much as they can from management. Because every cent more that labor negotiates increases management's costs, each party bargains aggressively and often treats the other as an opponent who must be defeated. In distributive bargaining, each party has a target point that defines what he or she would like to achieve. Each also has a resistance point that marks the lowest acceptable outcome (see Exhibit 12–11). The area between their resistance points is the set-

distributive bargaining
Negotiation under zero-sum conditions, in which any gain made by one party involves a loss to the other party

EXHIBIT 12-11 **Determining the Bargaining Zone**

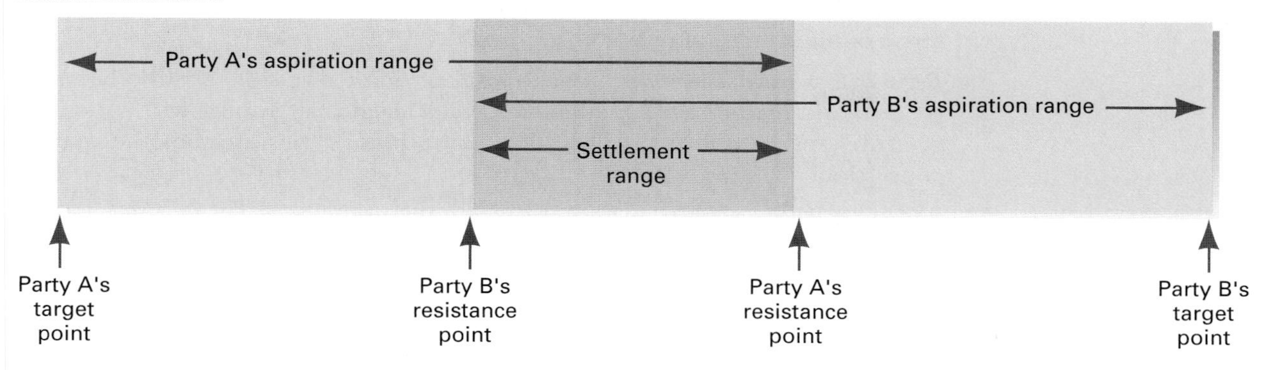

tlement range. As long as there is some overlap in their aspiration ranges, there exists a settlement area in which each one's aspirations can be met.

When engaged in distributive bargaining, you should try to get your opponent to agree to your specific target point or to get as close to it as possible. Examples of such tactics are persuading your opponent of the impossibility of getting to his or her target point and the advisability of accepting a settlement near yours; arguing that your target is fair, but your opponent's isn't; and attempting to get your opponent to feel emotionally generous toward you and thus accept an outcome close to your target point.

A sales representative for a women's sportswear manufacturer has just closed a $25,000 order from an independent clothing retailer. The sales rep calls in the order to her firm's credit department. She is told that the firm can't approve credit to this customer because of a past slow pay record. The next day, the sales rep and the firm's credit manager meet to discuss the problem. The sales rep doesn't want to lose the business. Neither does the credit manager, but he also doesn't want to get stuck with an uncollectible debt. The two openly review their options. After considerable discussion, they agree on a solution that meets both their needs. The credit manager will approve the sale, but the clothing store's owner will provide a bank guarantee that will assure payment if the bill isn't paid within 60 days.

The sales–credit negotiation is an example of **integrative bargaining**. In contrast to distributive bargaining, integrative problem solving operates under the assumption that there is at least one settlement that can create a win-win solution. In general, integrative bargaining is preferable to distributive bargaining. Why? Because the former builds long-term relationships and facilitates working together in the future. It bonds negotiators and allows each to leave the bargaining table feeling that he or she has achieved a victory. Distributive bargaining, on the other hand, leaves one party a loser. It tends to build animosities and deepen divisions between people who have to work together on an ongoing basis.

integrative bargaining
Negotiation in which there is at least one settlement that involves no loss to either party

Why, then, don't we see more integrative bargaining in organizations? The answer lies in the conditions necessary for this type of negotiation to succeed. These conditions include openness with information and frankness between parties, a sensitivity by each party to the other's needs, the ability to trust one another, and a willingness by both parties to maintain flexibility.[58] Because many organizational cultures and intraorganizational relationships are not characterized by openness, trust, and flexibility, it isn't surprising that negotiations often take on a win-at-any-cost dynamic. With that in mind, let's look at some suggestions for negotiating successfully.

How do you develop effective negotiation skills? The essence of effective negotiation can be summarized in the following seven recommendations.[59]

- ***Research the individual with whom you'll be negotiating.*** Acquire as much information as you can about the person with whom you'll be negotiating. What is that individual's interests and goals? What people must he or she appease? What is his or her strategy? This information will help you to better understand his or her behavior, to predict his or her responses to your offers, and to frame solutions in terms of his or her interests.

- ***Begin with a positive overture.*** Research shows that concessions tend to be reciprocated and lead to agreements. As a result, begin bargaining with a positive overture—perhaps a small concession—and then reciprocate the other party's concessions.
- ***Address problems, not personalities.*** Concentrate on the negotiation issues, not on the personal characteristics of the individual with whom you're negotiating. When negotiations get tough, avoid the tendency to attack the other party. Remember it's that person's ideas or position that you disagree with, not with him or her personally.
- ***Pay little attention to initial offers.*** Treat an initial offer as merely a point of departure. Everyone has to have an initial position, and initial positions tend to be extreme and idealistic. Treat them as such.
- ***Emphasize win-win solutions.*** If conditions are supportive, look for an integrative solution. Frame options in terms of the other party's interests and look for solutions that can allow this individual, as well as yourself, to declare a victory.
- ***Create an open and trusting climate.*** Skilled negotiators are better listeners, ask more questions, focus on their arguments more directly, are less defensive, and have learned to avoid words or phrases that can irritate the person with whom they're negotiating (such as a "generous offer," "fair price," or "reasonable arrangement"). In other words, they're better at creating an open and trusting climate that is necessary for reaching a win-win settlement.
- ***If needed, be open to accepting third-party assistance.*** When stalemates are reached, consider the use of a neutral third party—a mediator, an arbitrator, or a conciliator. Mediators can help parties come to an agreement, but they don't impose a settlement.[60] Arbitrators hear both sides of the dispute, then impose a solution. Conciliators are more informal and act as a communication conduit, passing information between the parties, interpreting messages, and clarifying misunderstandings.

Being chairman of Viacom's Motion Picture Group does not make giving presentations any easier for Sherry Lansing. Every time she takes the stage, she must deliver remarks that address the audience's needs. Her presentation preparations are designed to focus on the critical issues, making her points, and then answering questions. In doing so, Sherry is able to make more effective presentations for her organization.

WHAT IS AN EFFECTIVE PRESENTATION?

Most of us remember that first time in a class when we were required to give a five-minute presentation. It was typically a time of high anxiety—the realization that we'd have to get up in front of a group of people and talk. The nervousness, the excuses, the sweat rolling off the brow were all indicators that time was getting near. And then it was over, and some people hoped that they'd never have to get up and give a speech again.

The ability to deliver effective presentations is an important skill for career success. Unfortunately, it's only been within the past several years that organizations have started spending time helping employees, or students, in making presentations.[61] For example, you'll probably notice that upper-level business courses are frequently requiring students to make group presentations. The same is true for businesses. More and more companies are offering training to their employees about how to make effective presentations.

How do you make a presentation? Although podium fright is not unusual—even for the most skilled speaker—one cannot overlook the importance of presentation skills to your success in management. So what can you do to enhance your presentation skills? Let's look at some suggestions.[62]

- ***Prepare for the presentation.*** An actress and performer, Ethel Merman, was once asked, just before a major performance, if she was nervous. Her answer: "Why should I be nervous? I know what I'm going to do! The audience should be nervous. They don't know what's going to happen!" What the Merman quote tells us is that when preparing for a presentation, you must identify the key issues you want to express. In essence, why are you making the presentation? You also need to know who will be in your audience so you can anticipate their needs and speak their language. The better you prepare and anticipate questions that may be thrown at you, the more comfortable you will be in the presentation.
- ***Make your opening comments.*** The first few minutes of a presentation should be spent welcoming your audience, describing what you know about the issues your audience faces, citing your experience or credentials, and identifying your presentation's agenda. If you want your audience to do something at the end of your presentation—like approve your budget request, buy something, or so forth—tell them in your opening comments what you want them to do. By telling them ahead of time what you'd like at the end of your presentation, you frame the presentation and assist in having the audience actively listen to you.
- ***Make your points.*** This is the heart of your presentation. It's where you'll discuss the pertinent elements of presentation. Here you justify why you should get funding or why your particular product or service should be purchased. In the discussion, you need to describe why your ideas are important and how they will benefit your listeners. Any supporting data you have should be presented at this time.
- ***End the presentation.*** The end of a presentation includes nothing new. Rather, in the conclusion, you restate what you know about the issues facing your audience and what you recommended. If you had a request for action in the introductory part, you now come back to the action and seek closure on it. If the presentation is simply an information-sharing experience, there may not be an action requested of the audience.
- ***Answer questions.*** In many cases, questions will be posed at the end of your presentation. However, questions may come at any point in the presentation and may even be invited by you at the beginning. Regardless of where questions are asked, there are a few simple rules to follow. First, clarify the question. This requires you to actively listen to the question. If you are not sure what the question is, ask for clarification. Don't assume you know what the questioner is asking. When you understand the question, answer it. Then go back to the questioner and make sure your response answered the question. If it didn't, you'll probably get another question. Handle it the same way.

What about delivery issues? The importance of delivering an effective presentation is open to debate. One side of the debate focuses on having a polished presentation, flashy multimedia support, and speaking without the irritating mannerisms that distract from a presentation. There's no doubt that overindulgence in any of these can decrease the effectiveness of a presentation.

But don't make the assumption that your speech has to be perfect. The other side of the debate promotes being natural in your presentation but ensuring that you address what's important to the listener. If your audience is interested in what you have to say, they'll listen. They'll overlook a casual "um" or "ah" and disregard your hand gestures. So, put your effort into presenting the material and meeting the audience's needs. Any quirks in your mannerisms or your delivery will not matter greatly.

Review, Comprehension, Application

CHAPTER SUMMARY

How will you know if you fulfilled the Learning Outcomes on page 338? You will have fulfilled the Learning Outcomes if you are able to:

1. **Define communication and explain why it is important to managers.** Communication is the transference and understanding of meaning. It is important because everything a manager does—making decisions, planning, leading, and all other activities—requires that information be communicated.
2. **Describe the communication process.** The communication process begins with a communication sender (a source) who has a message to convey. The message is converted to symbolic form (encoding) and passed by way of a channel to the receiver, who decodes the message. To ensure accuracy, the receiver should provide the sender with feedback as a check on whether understanding has been achieved.
3. **List techniques for overcoming communication barriers.** Some techniques for overcoming communication barriers include using feedback (ensuring that the message was, in fact, received as intended), simplifying language (using language that is understood by your audience), listening actively (to capture the true meaning of the message being sent), constraining emotions (not allowing emotions to distort your ability to properly interpret the message), and watching nonverbal cues (aligning the nonverbal with the verbal).
4. **Describe the wired and wireless technologies affecting organizational communications.** Information technology has effectively aided communications in organizations through wired and wireless technologies. Wired technologies include: e-mail (instantaneous transmission of messages on computers that are linked together); instant messaging (interactive real-time communication that takes place among computer users who are logged on to the computer network at the same time); voice mail (digitizing a spoken massage, transmitting it over the network and storing the message on a disk for the receiver to retrieve later); fax (transmission of documents containing both text and graphics over ordinary telephone lines); electronic data interchange (a way for organizations to exchange business transaction documents such as invoices or purchase orders, using direct computer-to-computer networks); intranets (an organizational communication network that uses Internet technology but is accessible only by organizational employees), and extranets (an organizational communication network that uses Internet technology and allows authorized users inside the organization to communicate with certain outsiders such as customers or vendors); and the talking Internet (using the Internet for voice communication). The wireless side includes signals sent through air or space without any physical connection using such things as microwave signals, satellites, radio waves and radio antennas, or infrared light rays.
5. **Identify behaviors related to effective active listening.** Behaviors related to effective active listening are making eye contact, exhibiting affirmative nods and appropriate facial expressions, avoiding distracting actions or gestures, asking questions, paraphrasing, avoiding interruption of the speaker, not overtalking, and making smooth transitions between the roles of speaker and listener.
6. **Explain what behaviors are necessary for providing effective feedback.** In order to provide effective feedback, you must focus on specific behaviors; keep feedback impersonal, goal oriented, and well timed; ensure understanding; and direct negative feedback toward behavior that the recipient can control.
7. **Describe the contingency factors influencing delegation.** Contingency factors guide managers in determining the degree to which authority should be delegated. These factors include the size of the organization (larger organizations are associated with increased delegation); the importance of the duty or decision (the more important a duty or decision is, the less likely it is to be delegated); task complexity (the more complex the task is, the more likely it is that decisions about the task will be delegated); organizational culture (confidence and trust in subordinates are associated with delegation); and qualities of subordinates (delegation requires subordinates with the skills, abilities, and motivation to accept authority and act on it).
8. **Identify behaviors related to effective delegating.** Behaviors related to effective delegating are clarifying the assignment, specifying the employee's range of discretion, allowing the employee to participate, informing others that delegation has occurred, and establishing feedback controls.
9. **Describe the steps in analyzing and resolving conflict.** The steps to be followed in analyzing and resolving conflict situations begin by identifying your underly-

ing conflict-handling style. Second, select only conflicts that are worth the effort and that can be managed. Third, evaluate the conflict players. Fourth, assess the source of the conflict. Finally, choose the conflict resolution option that best reflects your style and the situation.

10. **Explain why a manager might stimulate conflict.** A manager might want to stimulate conflict if his or her unit suffers from apathy, stagnation, a lack of new ideas, or unresponsiveness to change. A manager can stimulate conflict by changing the organization's culture through the use of communications, by bringing in outsiders, by restructuring the organization, or by appointing a devil's advocate.
11. **Contrast distributive and integrative bargaining.** Distributive bargaining creates a win-lose situation because the object of negotiation is treated as fixed in amount. Integrative bargaining treats available resources as variable and hence creates the potential for win-win solutions.

COMPANION WEBSITE

We invite you to visit the Robbins/DeCenzo companion Website at **www.prenhall.com/robbins** for this chapter's Internet resources, including an online study guide, Internet exercises, and "In the News" with full text articles provided by XanEdu.

READING FOR COMPREHENSION

1. Which type of communication do you believe is most effective in a work setting? Why?
2. Why are effective interpersonal skills so important to a manager's success?
3. How has information technology enhanced a manager's communication effectiveness?
4. What is conflict? Should some conflict be encouraged?
5. Contrast the traditional, human relations, and interactionist views of conflict. Which of the three views do you think most managers have? Do you think this view is appropriate?
6. What are the five primary conflict resolution techniques?
7. What can a manager do if he or she wants to be a more effective negotiator?

LINKING CONCEPTS TO PRACTICE

1. Ineffective communication is the fault of the sender. Do you agree or disagree with this statement? Support your position.
2. Describe why effective communication isn't synonymous with agreement between the communicating parties.
3. "As technology improves, employees will be working more, be accessible to employers more, and be suffering from information overload." Do you agree or disagree with the statement? Defend your position.
4. How might a manager use the grapevine to his or her advantage? Support your response.
5. Using what you have learned about active listening in this chapter, would you describe yourself as a good listener? Are there any areas in which you are deficient? If so, how could you improve your listening skills?
6. Assume that you found an apartment that you wanted to rent and the ad had said: "$750/month, negotiable." What could you do to improve the likelihood that you would negotiate the lowest possible price?

VIDEO CASE APPLICATION

Linx Communication, Inc.: One-Number Connectivity for On-the-Go Professionals

Linx Communication, Inc.'s Web-enabled one-number follow-me service promises relief to anyone in any industry who is overrun by phone calls and electronic messages. Based in Newton, Massachusetts, the company was founded in 1996 by a unique team of telecommunication executives and entrepreneurs. Alice Hsin, president and CEO, is a nationally recognized expert in the telecommunications industry. She has worked with professionals in Japan, the United Kingdom, Korea, Taiwan, Singapore, and China. Linx customers include America Online, Apple Computer, and Compaq.

The appeal of Linx's unified communication solutions spans across industries and around the globe. "Our services are flexible and easy to use," says Alice Hsin. "Subscribers can control their communications without having their communications control them." Sales executives who are always on the road and need to stay in contact with company headquarters, clients, and family no longer have to check three different phones for voice mail, faxes, and office calls. Physicians who are burdened by pagers, cell phones, office voice mail, hospital phones, and faxes all in the course of a typical day, can now navigate their complicated routines more productively.[63]

All this convenience is "completely browser based so there is nothing to buy and nothing to install," according to Jeff Schlueter, vice president of marketing and product development. LinxConnect provides a single point of access to all calls, messages, and faxes through a single local or toll free phone number, or Internet connection. A visual representation of the message inventory appears automatically on the user's computer screen via the Linx Web site. Subscribers can easily see how long a message is, who it came from, and when it came in. "If a message is urgent," Schlueter explains, "I can listen immediately and call back by clicking on a button that places a call back out to the desktop, completing the call back to the other party."

Linx is setting the pace for the latest trend in hosted applications. "All you need to do is concentrate on what you are good at—conducting your business—and let us take care of all your communications solutions," says Alice Hsin. Her approach resonates in today's competitive environment, where outsourcing is becoming a popular way of cutting costs and increasing productivity. Linx services are being used to further connectivity worldwide by mobile individuals, small to medium businesses, and large organizations alike.

According to a news article from teledotcom's January 2000 newsletter (www.teledotcom.com), LinxConnect is now popular on America's college campuses. "We're finding that we can design very cost-effective programs for college students," says Jeff Schlueter. "The student market is geographically concentrated and therefore easy to reach," he explains. Gen Y students are quick to accept this new technological advance in communications, especially since it can simplify changing dorm phone numbers as often as the situation demands.

Linx's most useful feature may be its least advertised: The option of making yourself unavailable. With Linx you can choose to transfer calls to your voice mail or to a colleague and just take a break once in a while. Remember, it's your life and you're in control, so relax, even if it is only for a catnap.

Questions

1. Based on Jeff Schlueter's explanation of LinxConnect's on-screen representation of the message inventory, what impact does the service have on knowledge management? As a manager, consider how it might effect empowerment of employees.
2. In your view does Linx's unified messaging really simplify the lives of business professionals around the globe, or will it serve only to exacerbate information overload in the long run? Support your opinion using what you have learned from the text.
3. How important is using your active listening skills when viewing this video as a student of management? How important is using your active listening skills when viewing this video as an entrepreneur considering a subscription to Linx for his/her new venture? Explain.
4. Using this video as her forum, would you say that Alice Hsin has delivered an effective presentation of her company? Explain. Take into account the speaker's verbal and nonverbal cues, as well as any barriers you may have experienced as a listener.

Management Workshop

Team Skill-Building Exercise

Active Listening

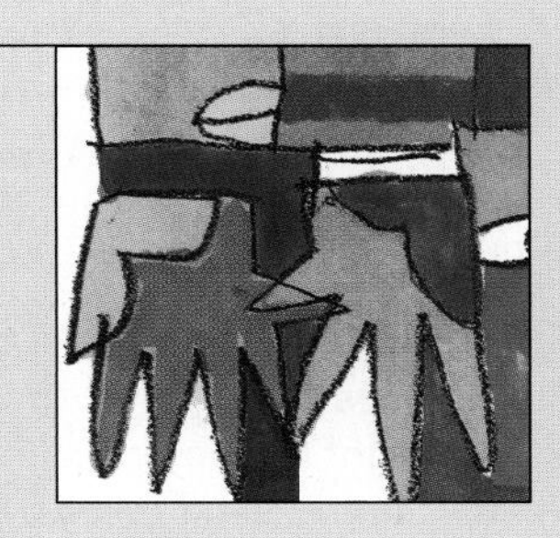

Purpose

To reinforce the idea that good listening skills are necessary for managers and that as communicators we can motivate listeners to actively listen.

Time Required

Approximately 30 minutes.

Procedure

Most of us, if we would admit it, are at times pretty poor listeners. This is probably because active listening is very demanding.[64] This exercise is specifically designed to dramatize how difficult it is to listen actively and to accurately interpret what is being said. It also points out how emotions can distort communication.

Your instructor will read you a story and ask you some follow-up questions. You will need a clean piece of paper and a pencil.

Understanding Yourself

Before you can develop other people, you must understand your present strengths. To assist in this learning process, we encourage you to complete the following self-assessments from the Prentice Hall Self-Assessment Library 2.0:

- How Good Are My Listening Skills? (#22)
- How Good Am I at Giving Feedback? (#23)

After you complete these assessments, we suggest that you print out the results and store them as part of your "portfolio of learning."

Developing Your Active Listening Skill

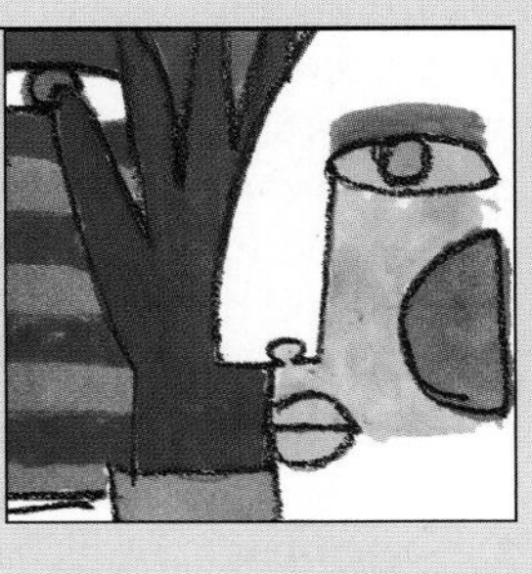

About the Skill

Active listening requires you to concentrate on what is being said. It's more than just hearing the words. It involves a concerted effort to understand and interpret the speaker's message.

Steps in Practicing the Skill

1. **Make eye contact.** How do you feel when somebody doesn't look at you when you're speaking? If you're like most people, you're likely to interpret this behavior as aloofness or disinterest. Making eye contact with the speaker focuses your attention, reduces the likelihood that you will become distracted, and encourages the speaker.
2. **Exhibit affirmative nods and appropriate facial expressions.** The effective listener shows interest in what is being said through nonverbal signals. Affirmative nods and appropriate facial expressions, when added to good eye contact, convey to the speaker that you're listening.
3. **Avoid distracting actions or gestures that suggest boredom.** In addition to showing interest, you must avoid actions that suggest that your mind is somewhere else. When listening, don't look at your watch, shuffle papers, play with your pencil, or engage in similar distractions. They make the speaker feel that you're bored or disinterested or indicate that you aren't fully attentive.

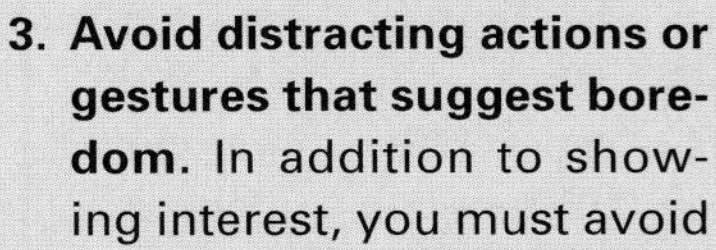

4. **Ask questions.** The critical listener analyzes what he or she hears and asks questions. This behavior provides clarification, ensures understanding, and assures the speaker that you're listening.

5. **Paraphrase using your own words.** The effective listener uses phrases such as: "What I hear you saying is . . . or Do you mean . . .?" Paraphrasing is an excellent control device to check on whether you're listening carefully and to verify that what you heard is accurate.
6. **Avoid interrupting the speaker.** Let the speaker complete his or her thought before you try to respond. Don't try to second-guess where the speaker's thoughts are going. When the speaker is finished, you'll know it.
7. **Don't overtalk.** Most of us would rather express our own ideas than listen to what someone else says. Talking might be more fun and silence might be uncomfortable, but you can't talk and listen at the same time. The good listener recognizes this fact and doesn't overtalk.
8. **Make smooth transitions between the roles of speaker and listener.** The effective listener makes transitions smoothly from speaker to listener and back to speaker. From a listening perspective, this means concentrating on what a speaker has to say and practicing not thinking about what you're going to say as soon as you get your chance.

Practicing the Skill

Ask a friend to tell you about his or her day and listen without interrupting. When your friend has finished speaking, ask two or three questions if needed to obtain more clarity and detail. Listen carefully to the answers. Now summarize your friend's day in no more than five sentences.

How well did you do? Let your friend rate the accuracy of your paraphrase (and try not to interrupt).

Developing Your Diagnostic and Analytical Skills

Rolling in Dough

Semifreddi's is an artisan-bread bakery (bakers of specialty breads and bread shaped in unusual and artistic ways), in Emeryville, California. CEO Tom Frainier has built a company whose annual revenues are over $7 million.[65] He describes himself as an "accessible, available, and communicative guy." However, language barriers are proving to be a challenge for Tom and his employees. That's because most of the employees are from Mexico, Laos, China, Peru, Cambodia, Yemen, and Vietnam. Even though his workers have limited English-language skills, Tom feels that he is communicating sufficiently well with his diverse workforce because no major problems have arisen—at least yet.

Consider the recent matter when customers began making comments about the lack of parking on one side of the bakery. Always when there were issues to be discussed, he called an employee meeting. He asked workers not to park in the spaces reserved for customers. Some employees misunderstood and thought he was telling them not to drive to work. Tom later said that his mistake was talking slowly and loudly and assuming that his employees would understand him. However, the miscommunication over the parking issue was minor in comparison to another of Tom's communication challenges.

Tom is a firm supporter of open-book management, a management approach that entails regularly "opening up the financial statements" to employees and sharing this information with them in order to make them more a part of the business. He recently gathered employees from different work shifts for a meeting, and rattled off a bunch of numbers. Then Tom asked them if they understood the information. All heads nodded in agreement. Tom later said, "I didn't realize that they were just being polite." His desire to involve employees by letting them see the financial results of their work, however, wasn't having the desired impact. Tom recognized that he needed to make some changes in his communications.

He promoted to management positions two Latino workers who helped Frainier convey messages to the Spanish-speaking employees. He holds meetings for smaller groups of employees now—grouping them according to their English proficiency. Furthermore, he now has a translator at every meeting. As a result of his actions, employees now raise a significant number of questions in their effort to understand. And Tom, he's happy, as he attributes increasing employee morale and an additional $400,000 in annual revenue to the changes he made in communications.

Questions

1. What communication difficulties does a diversified workforce present for managers like Tom Frainier?
2. What suggestions would you make to Tom (beyond what he has done) so he could further improve his communication effectiveness?
3. Do you believe there is a direct link between communications and employee morale and productivity? Explain your position.

Enhancing Your Communication Skills

1. Develop a report describing what you can do to improve the likelihood that your verbal communications will be received and understood as you intended them to be.
2. Do some research on male versus female communication styles. Provide a summary of what you've found. Do men and women communicate differently? If so, what are the implications of your findings for managers?
3. Search on the Internet for common communication shortcuts used by e-mail users. Identify 15 acronyms and describe what they mean. How should these acronyms be used? Describe any barriers these acronyms may cause a user; a receiver.

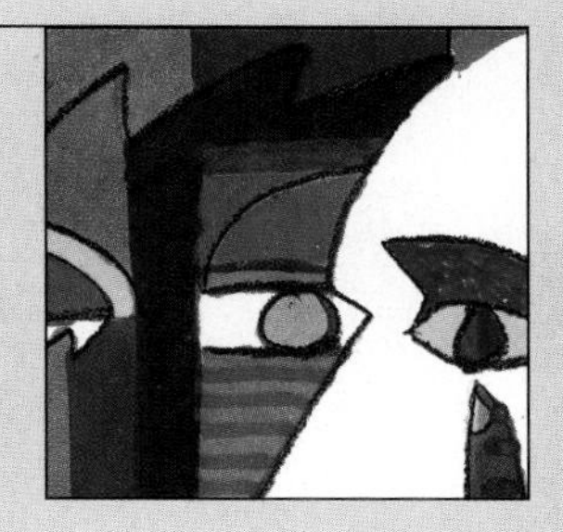

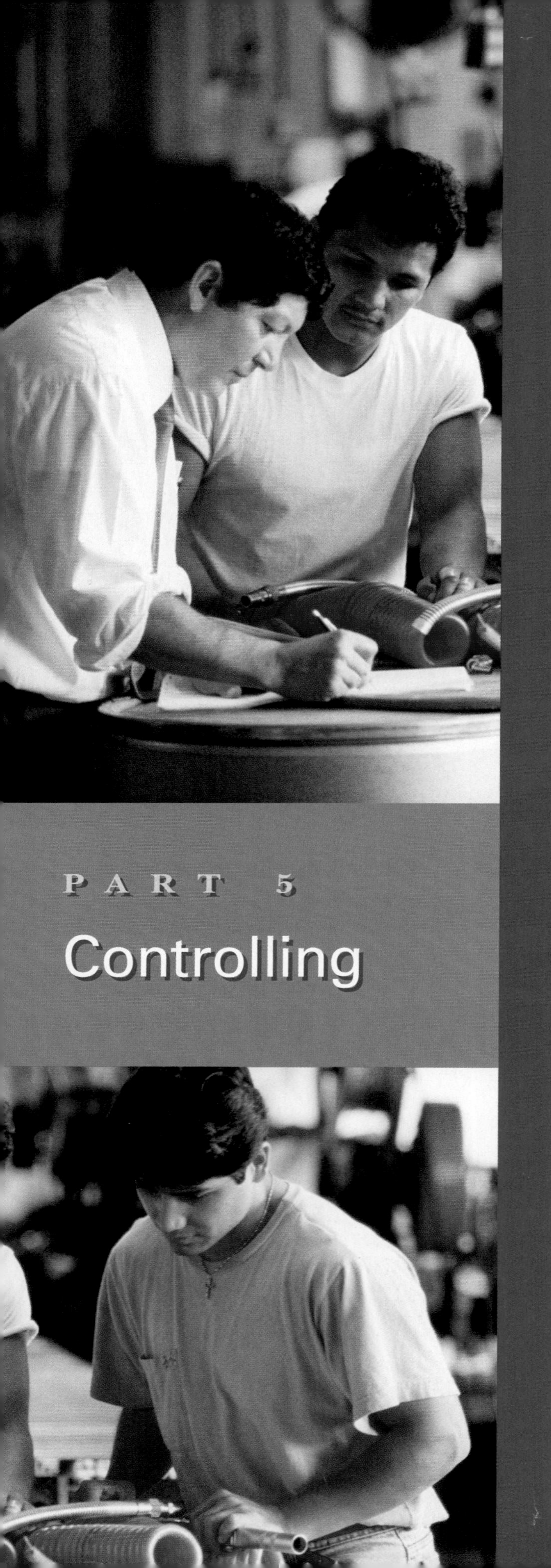

PART 5

Controlling

CHAPTER 13

Foundations of Control

LEARNING OUTCOMES

After reading this chapter, I will be able to:

1. Define control.
2. Describe three approaches to control.
3. Explain why control is important.
4. Describe the control process.
5. Distinguish among the three types of control.
6. Describe the qualities of an effective control system.
7. Identify the contingency factors in the control process.
8. Explain how controls can become dysfunctional.
9. Describe how national differences influence the control process.
10. Identify the ethical dilemmas in employee monitoring.
11. Describe how an entrepreneur controls for growth.

The management process is fairly straightforward. You plan to set your goals and you obtain and organize the necessary resources to make the plans a reality. You hire employees who possess the skills, knowledge, and abilities to successfully perform the often complex required tasks. Then you monitor the activities making sure you are on target. Where goals are not being met, you make the necessary changes. These are the fundamentals of management that serve as the foundation for operating an effective and efficient organization. In some organizations—like Enron, Adelphia, WorldCom, and Tyco International—these fundamentals have been ignored or abused. Executives in these organizations sadly have demonstrated that these fundamentals can be misused, especially when the controls that exist to protect the enterprise become dysfunctional. The fall of the Enron empire (see photo) is a clear example of this situation.[1]

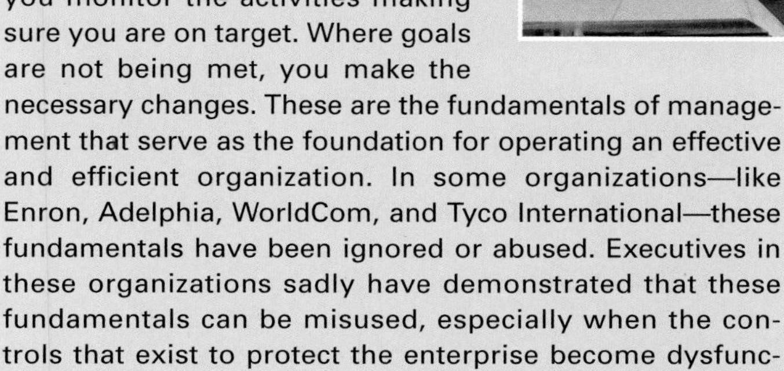

Enron executives distorted internal financial data and released misleading profit reports through the use of complex accounting transactions. For instance, through some clever accounting maneuvers, Enron simply kept hundreds of millions of dollars in debt off its balance sheets. And by the creative use of partnerships, Enron executives created financial obligations that never showed up on the books. Although such a practice was in accordance with generally accepted accounting principles, had Enron executives classified the partnerships as subsidiaries, they would have had to account for the losses incurred by a number of them.

Compounding these potential problematic partnerships, Enron executives also engaged in bartering activities. By swapping telecommunications network capabilities with other companies, Enron recorded the barter sales as revenues, even though no cash ever changed hands. Furthermore, through another creative accounting practice—called derivatives—Enron hid losses it incurred on its investments in financing unsuccessful businesses.

Should Enron executives have been able to get away with these financial shenanigans? Not if proper controls had been established. Part of those controls are independent audits. And Enron had one of the largest U.S. accounting firms, Arthur Andersen, vouching for its accounting practices. Unfortunately for Enron investors and Arthur Andersen (this fiasco eventually led to the demise of Arthur Andersen as a going concern and the loss of 70,000 jobs), Andersen either never knew about Enron's financial manipulations or chose to ignore them.

The controls that had been established to protect investors in publicly held organizations were not working properly at the least—or worse, stretched to their limits by greed. As investigations continue into the Enron debacle, with criminal charges being brought, and convictions achieved, one thing is certain—the control systems failed. This once giant energy company is gone, as well as the livelihoods and retirements of thousands of employees and investors. The fact that this string of events could reach such epic proportions is a lesson in controlling and ethics for all of us!

THE ENRON EXAMPLE ILLUSTRATES HOW DYSFUNCTIONAL control systems can be detrimental to an organization's performance. As we show in this chapter, effective management requires a well-designed control system—one that assists the organization in achieving its strategic goals.

WHAT IS CONTROL?

Control is the management function involving the process of monitoring activities to ensure that they are being accomplished as planned and correcting any significant deviations. Managers cannot really know whether their units are performing properly until they have evaluated what activities have been done and have compared the actual performance with the desired standard. An effective control system ensures that activities are completed in ways that lead to the attainment of the organization's goals. The effectiveness of a control system is determined by how well it facilitates goal achievement. The more it helps managers achieve their organization's goals, the better the control system.[2]

control
The process of monitoring activities to ensure that they are being accomplished as planned and of correcting any significant deviations

When we introduced organizations in Chapter 1, we stated that every organization attempts to effectively and efficiently reach its goals. Does that imply, however,

EXHIBIT 13–1

Characteristics of Three Approaches to Control Systems

TYPE OF CONTROL	CHARACTERISTICS
Market	Uses external market mechanisms, such as price competition and relative market share, to establish standards used in system. Typically used by organizations with clearly specified and distinct products or services and that face considerable marketplace competition.
Bureaucratic	Emphasizes organizational authority. Relies on administrative and hierarchical mechanisms, such as rules, regulations, procedures, policies, standardization of activities, well-defined job descriptions, and budgets to ensure that employees exhibit appropriate behaviors and meet performance standards.
Clan	Regulates employee behavior by the shared values, norms, traditions, rituals, beliefs, and other aspects of the organization's culture. Often used by organizations in which teams are common and technology is changing rapidly.

that the control systems organizations use are identical? In other words, would Nokia, Royal Dutch Shell, France Telecom, and Wal-Mart all have the same type of control system? Probably not. Although similarities may exist, there are generally three different approaches to designing control systems. These are market, bureaucratic, and clan controls[3] as summarized in Exhibit 13–1.

market control
An approach to control that emphasizes the use of external market mechanisms such as price competition and market share

Market control emphasizes the use of external market mechanisms. Controls are built around such criteria as price competition or market share. Organizations using a market control approach usually have clearly specified and distinct products and services and considerable competition. Under these conditions, the various divisions of the organization are typically turned into profit centers and evaluated by the percentage of total corporate profits each generates. For instance, at Matsushita, each of the various divisions—which produces such products as videos, home appliances, and industrial equipment—is evaluated according to its contribution to the company's total profits. Using these measures, managers make decisions about future resource allocations, strategic changes, and other work activities that may need attention.

bureaucratic control
An approach to control that emphasizes authority and relies on administrative rules, regulations, procedures, and policies

A second approach to control systems is **bureaucratic control**, a control approach that emphasizes authority and relies on administrative rules, regulations, procedures, and policies. This type of control depends on standardization of activities, well-defined job descriptions to direct employee work behavior, and other administrative mechanisms—such as budgets—to ensure that organizational members exhibit appropriate work behaviors and meet established performance standards. At BP Amoco, managers of various divisions are allowed considerable autonomy and freedom to run their units as they see fit. Yet they are expected to stick closely to their budgets and stay within corporate guidelines.

clan control
An approach to designing control systems in which employee behaviors are regulated by the shared values, norms, traditions, rituals, beliefs, and other aspects of the organization's culture

Clan control is an approach to designing control systems in which employee behaviors are regulated by the shared values, norms, traditions, rituals, beliefs, and other aspects of the organization's culture. In contrast to bureaucratic control, which is based on strict hierarchical mechanisms, clan control depends on the individual and the group (the clan) to identify appropriate and expected work-related behaviors and performance measures. Clan control is typically found in organizations in which teams are widely used and technologies change often. For instance, organizational members at SAS Institute (the Cary, NC–based software company), employees are well aware of the expectations regarding appropriate work behavior and performance standards. The organizational culture—through the shared values, norms, and stories about the company's founder, Jim Goodnight—conveys to individuals what's really important in the organization as well as what is not. Rather than relying on prescribed administrative controls, SAS employees are guided and controlled by the clan's culture.[4]

It is important to recognize that most organizations do not totally rely on just one of these three approaches to design an appropriate control system. Instead, an organization typically chooses to emphasize either bureaucratic or clan control and then add some market control measures. The key, however, in any of the approaches is to design an appropriate control system that helps the organization effectively and efficiently reach its goals.

What kind of control systems are SAS Institute managers using in their dealings with employees? At SAS, it's clan control. (Pictured is Jim Goodnight, president and CEO of SAS Institute.) Their approach is designed to control employee behaviors by regulating shared values, norms, traditions, beliefs, and other aspects of the organization's culture. At SAS Institute, such a system has had a profound effect—as the company has become the largest privately held software company in the world, with more than 3.5 million customers in more than 100 countries, and annual revenues exceeding the $1 billion mark.

THE IMPORTANCE OF CONTROL

Planning can be done; an organization structure can be created to efficiently facilitate the achievement of objectives, and employees can be directed and motivated. Still, as we saw with Enron, there is no assurance that activities are going as planned and that the goals are, in fact, being attained. Control is the final link in the functional chain of management. However, the value of the control function lies predominantly in its relation to planning and delegating activities.

In Chapter 3, we described objectives as the foundation of planning. Objectives give specific direction to managers. However, just stating objectives or having employees accept your objectives is no guarantee that the necessary actions have been accomplished. The effective manager needs to follow up to ensure that the actions others are supposed to take and the objectives they are supposed to achieve are, in fact, being taken and achieved.

THE CONTROL PROCESS

The control process consists of three separate and distinct steps: (1) measuring actual performance, (2) comparing actual performance against a standard, and (3) taking managerial action to correct deviations or inadequate standards (see Exhibit 13–2). Before we consider each step in detail, you should be aware that the control process assumes that standards of performance already exist, having been created in the planning function. If managers use some variation of mutual goal setting, then the objectives set are, by definition, tangible, verifiable, and measurable. In such instances, those objectives are the standards against which progress is measured and compared. If goal setting is not practiced, then standards are the specific performance indicators that management uses. Our point is that these standards are developed in the planning function; planning must precede control.

WHAT IS MEASURING?

To determine actual performance, a manager must acquire information about it. The first step in control, then, is measuring. Let's consider how we measure and what we measure.

How do managers measure? Four common sources of information frequently used to measure actual performance are personal observation, statistical reports, oral reports, and written reports. Each has particular strengths and weaknesses; however, use of a combination of them increases both the number of input sources and the probability of receiving reliable information.

EXHIBIT 13-2 **The Control Process**

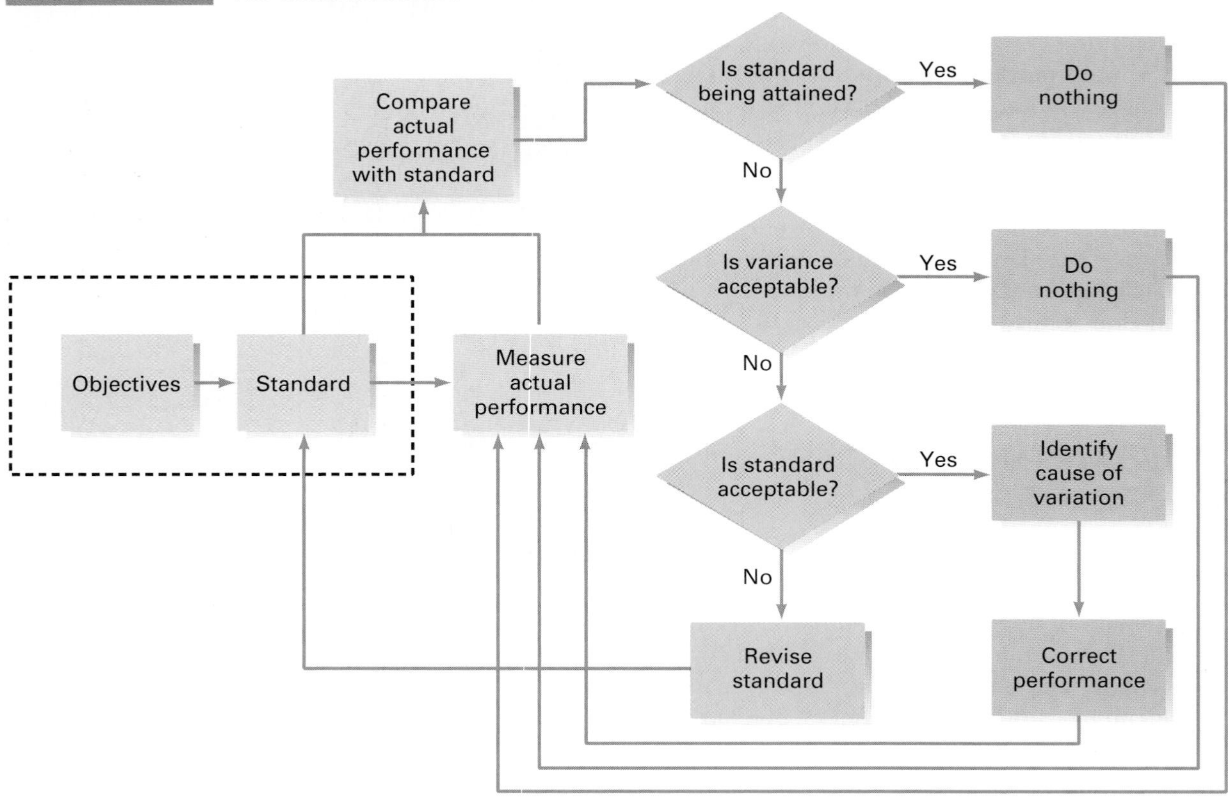

Management by walking around (MBWA)
A phrase used to describe when a manager is out in the work area interacting with employees

Personal observation provides first-hand, intimate knowledge of the actual activity—information that is not filtered through others. It permits intensive coverage because minor as well as major performance activities can be observed, and it provides opportunities for the manager to read between the lines. **Management by walking around (MBWA)** is a phrase that is used to describe when a manager is out in the work area, interacting directly with employees, and exchanging information about what's going on. MBWA can pick up factual omissions, facial expressions, and tones of voice that may be missed by other sources. Unfortunately, in a time when quantitative information suggests objectivity, personal observation is often considered an inferior information source. It is subject to perceptual biases; what one manager sees, another might not. Personal observation also consumes a good deal of time. Finally, this method suffers from obtrusiveness. Employees might interpret a manager's overt observation as a sign of a lack of confidence or of mistrust.

The widespread use of computers has led managers to rely increasingly on *statistical reports* for measuring actual performance. This measuring device, however, isn't limited to computer outputs. It also includes graphs, bar charts, and numerical displays of any form that managers can use for assessing performance. Although statistical information is easy to visualize and effective for showing relationships, it provides limited information about an activity. Statistics report on only a few key areas and may often ignore other important, often subjective, factors.

Information can also be acquired through *oral reports*—that is, through conferences, meetings, one-to-one conversations, or telephone calls. In organizations in which employees work in a cultural environment, this approach may be the best way to keep tabs on work performance. For instance, at the Ken Blanchard Companies in Escondido, California, managers are expected to hold one-on-one meetings with each of their employees at least once every two weeks.[5] The advantages and disadvantages of this method of measuring performance are similar to those of personal observation. Although the information is filtered, it is fast, allows for feedback, and permits expression and tone of voice as well as words themselves to convey meaning.

Historically, one of the major drawbacks of oral reports has been the problem of documenting information for later reference. However, our technological capabilities have progressed in the past couple of decades to the point where oral reports can be efficiently taped and become as permanent as if they were written.

Actual performance may also be measured by *written reports*. Like statistical reports, they are slower yet more formal than first- or second-hand oral measures. This formality also often gives them greater comprehensiveness and conciseness than is found in oral reports. In addition, written reports are usually easy to catalog and reference.

Given the varied advantages and disadvantages of each of these four measurement techniques, managers should use all four for comprehensive control efforts.

How can a manager measure the progress of work in an organization? One means is for the manager to get out into the work setting to personally observe what is happening.

What do managers measure? What managers measure is probably more critical to the control process than how they measure. Why? The selection of the wrong criteria can result in serious dysfunctional consequences. Besides, what we measure determines, to a great extent, what people in the organization will attempt to excel at.[6] For example, assume that your instructor has required a total of 10 writing assignments from the exercises at the end of each textbook chapter. But, in the grade computation section of the syllabus, you notice that these assignments are not scored. In fact, when you ask your professor about this, she replies that these writing assignments are for your own enlightenment and do not affect your grade for the course; grades are solely a function of how well you perform on the three exams. We predict that you would, not surprisingly, exert most, if not all, of your effort toward doing well on the three exams.

"What we measure is probably more critical to the control process than how we measure. The selection of the wrong criteria can result in a seriously dysfunctional consequence."

Some control criteria are applicable to any management situation. For instance, because all managers, by definition, direct the activities of others, criteria such as employee satisfaction or turnover and absenteeism rates can be measured. Most managers have budgets for their area of responsibility set in monetary units (dollars, pounds, francs, lire, and so on). Keeping costs within budget is, therefore, a fairly common control measure. However, any comprehensive control system needs to recognize the diversity of activities among managers. For example, a production manager in a paper tablet manufacturing plant might use measures of the quantity of tablets produced per day, tablets produced per labor hour, scrap tablet rate, or percentage of rejects returned by customers. On the other hand, the manager of an administrative unit in a government agency might use number of document pages produced per day, number of orders processed per hour, or average time required to process service calls. Marketing managers often use measures such as percent of market held, number of customer visits per salesperson, or number of customer impressions per advertising medium.

As you might imagine, some activities are more difficult to measure in quantifiable terms. It is more difficult, for instance, for a manager to measure the performance of a medical researcher or a middle school counselor than of a person who sells life insurance. But most activities can be broken down into objective segments that allow for measurement. The manager needs to determine what value a person, department, or unit contributes to the organization and then convert the contribution into standards.

CVS uses a variety of controls to ensure that its pharmacies are operating efficiently and that they are meeting customers' needs. These include ensuring adequate stock, providing proper pharmaceutical advice, assisting patients in ensuring proper coordination of medications, and helping customers lower their costs.

Most jobs and activities can be expressed in tangible and measurable terms. When a performance indicator cannot be stated in quantifiable terms, managers should look for and use subjective measures. Certainly, subjective measures have significant limitations. Still, they are better than having no standards at all and ignoring the control function. If an activity is important, the excuse that it is difficult to measure is inadequate. In such cases, managers should use subjective performance criteria. Of course, any analysis or decisions made on the basis of subjective criteria should recognize the limitations of the data.

How do managers compare actual performance to planned goals? The comparing step determines the degree of discrepancy between actual performance and the standard. Some variation in performance can be expected in all activities; it is therefore critical to determine the acceptable **range of variation** (see Exhibit 13–3). Deviations beyond this range become significant and should receive the manager's attention. In the comparison stage, managers are particularly concerned with the size and direction of the variation. An example should help make this clearer.

range of variation
The acceptable parameters of variance between actual performance and the standard

Pat Welsh is the sales manager for South Atlantic Distributors. The company distributes imported beers in several states in the South. Welsh prepares a report during the first week of each month that summarizes sales for the previous month, classified by brand name. Exhibit 13–4 displays both the standard and actual sales figures (in hundreds of cases) for the month of July.

Should Pat be concerned about the July performance? Sales were a bit higher than originally targeted, but does that mean there were no significant deviations? Even though overall performance was generally quite favorable, several brands might need to be examined more closely by Pat. However, the number of brands that deserve attention depends on what Pat believes to be *significant.* How much variation should Welsh allow before corrective action is taken?

The deviation on several brands is very small and undoubtedly not worthy of special attention. These include Molson, Moosehead, and Amstel Light. Are the shortages for Corona and Dos Equis brands significant? That's a judgment Pat must make. Heineken sales were 15 percent below the goal. This brand needs attention. Welsh

EXHIBIT 13–3
Defining an Acceptable Range of Variation

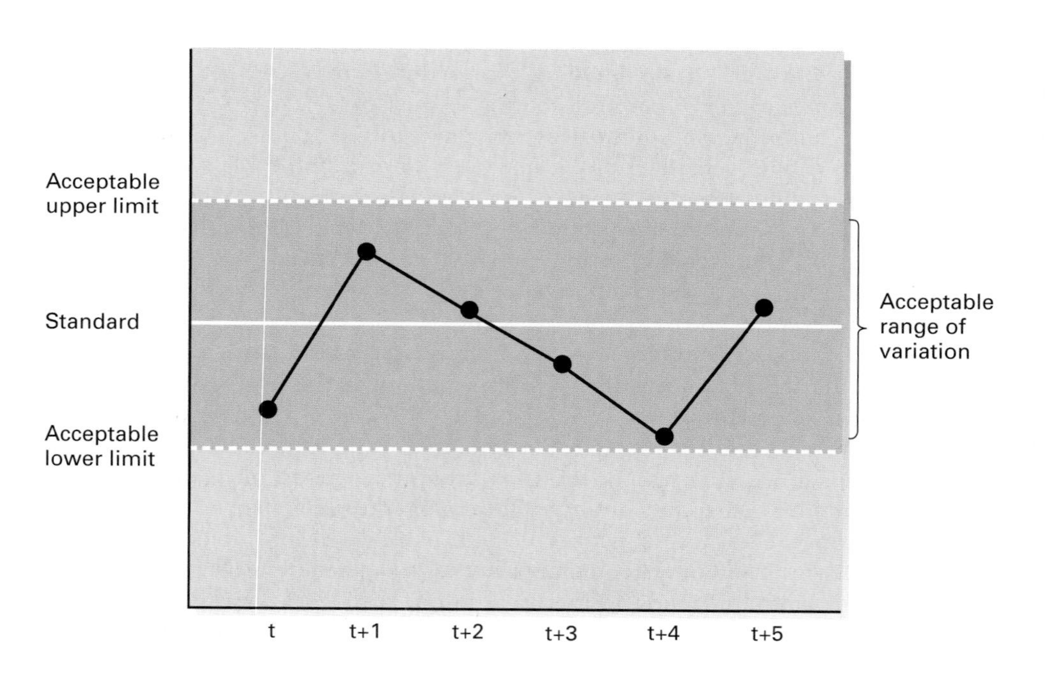

EXHIBIT 13–4

Mid-Western Distributors' Sales Performance for July (hundreds of cases)

BRAND	STANDARD	ACTUAL	OVER (UNDER)
Heineken	1,075	913	(162)
Molson	630	634	4
Beck's	800	912	112
Moosehead	620	622	2
Labatt's	540	672	132
Corona	160	140	(20)
Amstel Light	225	220	(5)
Dos Equis	80	65	(15)
Tecate	170	286	116
Total cases	4,300	4,464	164

should look for a cause. In this case, Pat attributes the loss to aggressive advertising and promotion programs by the big domestic producers, Anheuser-Busch and Miller. Because Heineken is the best-selling import, it is most vulnerable to the promotion clout of the big domestic producers. If the decline in Heineken is more than a temporary slump, Welsh will need to cut back on inventory stock.

An error in understating sales can be as troublesome as an overstatement. For instance, is the surprising popularity of Tecate (up 68 percent) a one-month aberration, or is this brand increasing its market share? Our South Atlantic example illustrates that both overvariance and undervariance require managerial attention.

WHAT MANAGERIAL ACTION CAN BE TAKEN?

The third and final step in the control process is managerial action. Managers can choose among three courses of action: They can do nothing, they can correct the actual performance, or they can revise the standard. Because doing nothing is fairly self-explanatory, let's look more closely at the latter two choices.

Correct actual performance If the source of the variation has been deficient performance, the manager will want to take corrective action.[7] Examples of such corrective action might include changes in strategy, structure, compensation practices, or training programs; the redesign of jobs; or the replacement of personnel.

A manager who decides to correct actual performance has to make another decision: Should he or she take immediate or basic corrective action? **Immediate corrective action** corrects problems at once and gets performance back on track. **Basic corrective action** asks how and why performance has deviated and then proceeds to correct the source of deviation. It is not unusual for managers to rationalize that they do not have the time to take basic corrective action and therefore must be content to perpetually put out fires with immediate corrective action. Effective managers, however, analyze deviations and, when the benefits justify it, take the time to permanently correct significant variances between standard and actual performance.

immediate corrective action
Correcting a problem at once to get performance back on track

basic corrective action
Determining how and why performance has deviated and then correcting the source of deviation

To return to our example of South Atlantic Distributors, Pat Welsh might take basic corrective action on the negative variance for Heineken. He might increase promotion efforts, increase the advertising budget for this brand, or reduce future orders with the manufacturer. The action Welsh takes will depend on the assessment of each brand's potential sales.

Revise the standard It is also possible that a variance was a result of an unrealistic standard—that is, the goal may have been too high or too low. In such cases the standard needs corrective attention, not the performance. In our example, the sales manager might need to raise the standard for Tecate to reflect its increasing popularity, much as, in sports, athletes adjust their performance goals upward during a season if they achieve their season goal early.

The more troublesome problem is the revising of a performance standard downward. If an employee or unit falls significantly short of its target, the natural response is for the employee or unit to blame the standard. For instance, students who make a low grade on a test often attack the grade cutoff points as too high. Rather than accept the fact that their performance was inadequate, the students argue that the standards were unreasonable. Similarly, salespeople who fail to meet their monthly quota may attribute the failure to an unrealistic quota. It may be true that standards are too high, resulting in a significant variance and demotivating those employees being assessed against it. However, keep in mind that if employees or managers don't meet the standard, the first thing they are likely to attack is the standard itself. If you believe that the standard is realistic, hold your ground. Explain your position, reaffirm to the employee or manager that you expect future performance to improve, and then take the necessary corrective action to turn that expectation into reality.

TYPES OF CONTROL

Management can implement controls before an activity commences, while the activity is going on, or after the activity has been completed. The first type is called feedforward control; the second is concurrent control, and the last is feedback control (see Exhibit 13–5).

WHAT IS FEEDFORWARD CONTROL?

feedforward control
Control that prevents anticipated problems

The most desirable type of control—**feedforward control**—prevents anticipated problems because it takes place in advance of the actual activity. It's future-directed.[8] For instance, when McDonald's opened its first restaurant in Moscow, it sent company quality control experts to help Russian farmers learn techniques for growing high-quality potatoes, and sent bakers to teach the processes for baking high-quality breads. Why? Because McDonald's strongly emphasizes product quality no matter what the geographical location. It wants a cheeseburger in Moscow to taste like one in Hartford, Connecticut. Another example of feedforward control is the scheduled aircraft maintenance programs done by the major airlines. These are designed to detect, and it's hoped, prevent structural damage that might lead to an airline disaster.

The key to feedforward control, therefore, is taking managerial action before a problem occurs. Feedforward controls allow management to prevent problems rather than having to cure them later. Unfortunately, these controls require timely and accurate information that is often difficult to develop. As a result, managers frequently have to use one of the other two types of control.

EXHIBIT 13–5
Types of Control

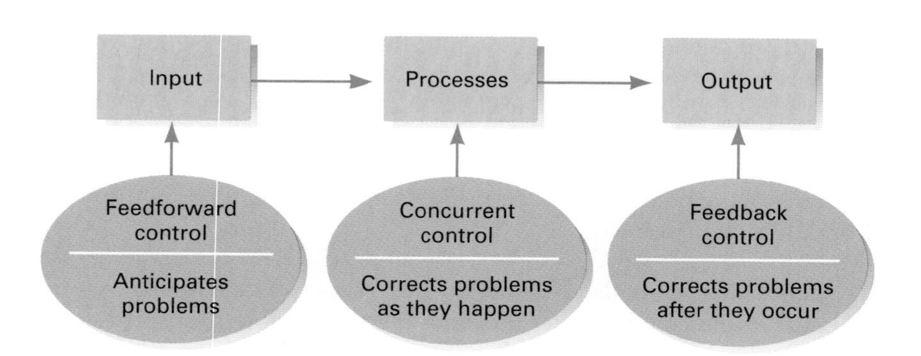

WHEN IS CONCURRENT CONTROL USED?

Concurrent control, as its name implies, takes place while an activity is in progress. When control is enacted while the work is being performed, management can correct problems before they become too costly.

The best known form of concurrent control is direct supervision. When a manager directly oversees the actions of an employee, the manager can concurrently monitor the employee's actions and correct problems as they occur. Although there is obviously some delay between the activity and the manager's corrective response, the delay is minimal. Technical equipment (such as computers and computerized machine controls) can be designed to include concurrent controls. For example, you may have experienced concurrent control when using a computer program such as word-processing that alerts you to a misspelled word or incorrect grammatical usage. In addition, many organizational quality programs rely on concurrent controls to inform workers of whether their work output is of sufficient quality to meet standards.

How important is feedforward control? In the airlines, it may be the difference between life and death. Questions were raised about the maintenance on the MD-83 aircraft that was used by the Alaska Air pilots for Flight 261 on January 31, 2000. Was poor feedforward control a contributing factor? While it's been debated, the fact remains, something mechanical went wrong with this plane—leading to the death of 88 individuals.

concurrent control
Control that takes place while an activity is in progress

feedback control
Control that takes place after an action

WHY IS FEEDBACK CONTROL SO POPULAR?

The most popular type of control relies on feedback. The control takes place after the action. The control report that Pat Welsh (from our South Atlantic Distributors example) used for assessing beer sales is an example of **feedback control**.

The major drawback of this type of control is that by the time the manager has the information the damage has already been done. It's analogous to locking the barn door after the horse has been stolen. But for many activities, feedback is the only viable type of control available. For example, financial statements are an example of feedback controls. If, for instance, the income statement shows that sales revenues are declining, the decline has already occurred. So at this point, the manager's only option is to try to determine why sales decreased and to correct the situation.

Feedback has two advantages over feedforward and concurrent control.[9] First, feedback provides managers with meaningful information on the effectiveness of their planning effort. Feedback that indicates little variance between standard and actual performance is evidence that planning was generally on target. If the deviation is great, a manager can use that information to make new plans more effective. Second, feedback control can enhance employee motivation. People want information on how well they have performed. Feedback control provides that information (see Developing Your Performance Feedback Skill on page 398).

CONTROL IMPLICATIONS FOR MANAGERS

A $165 million NASA Mars Polar Lander probe disappears without a trace. Marriott International implements its First Ten program, setting a standard for hassle-free guest check-in (based on the belief that guests ideally should be in their rooms within the first ten minutes of their arrival). Better financial controls implemented by CEO Pamela D. A. Reeve improve the financial results of

Could better controls have prevented the disappearance of the Mars Polar Lander? That debate continues. It's safe to say, however, that in most cases, without effective control systems in place, managers may have insufficient information to resolve problems, make decisions, or take appropriate actions. While their presence alone won't avert disasters, effective controls are an important function of managing properly.

Lightbridge, a Massachusetts-based company that helps telecommunications carriers acquire new clients and retain them.[10] As these examples illustrate, controlling plays an important role in results and is an important function of managing. Without controls, managers would have insufficient information to resolve problems, make decisions, or take appropriate actions. How can managers perform the control function effectively and efficiently? To answer this question, we're going to look a the qualities of an effective control system, the contingency factors that affect the design of control systems, and how controls need to be adjusted for national differences.

WHAT ARE THE QUALITIES OF AN EFFECTIVE CONTROL SYSTEM?

Effective control systems tend to have certain qualities in common.[11] The importance of these qualities varies with the situation, but we can generalize that the following characteristics should make a control system effective.

- ***Accuracy*** A control system that generates inaccurate information can result in management's failing to take action when it should or responding to a problem that doesn't exist. An accurate control system is reliable and produces valid data.
- ***Timeliness*** Controls should call management's attention to variations in time to prevent serious infringement on a unit's performance. The best information has little value if it is dated. Therefore, an effective control system must provide timely information.
- ***Economy*** A control system must be economically reasonable. Any system of control has to justify the benefits that it gives in relation to the costs it incurs. To minimize costs, management should try to impose the least amount of control necessary to produce the desired results.
- ***Flexibility*** Controls must be flexible enough to adjust to problems or to take advantage of new opportunities. Few organizations face environments so stable that there is no need for flexibility. Even highly mechanistic structures require controls that can be adjusted as times and conditions change.
- ***Understandability*** Controls that cannot be understood have no value. It is sometimes necessary, therefore, to substitute less complex controls for sophisticated devices. A control system that is difficult to understand can cause unnecessary mistakes, frustrate employees, and eventually be ignored.
- ***Reasonable criteria*** Control standards must be reasonable and attainable. If they are too high or unreasonable, they no longer motivate. Because most employees don't want to risk being labeled incompetent by accusing superiors of asking too much, employees may resort to unethical or illegal shortcuts. Controls should, therefore,

enforce standards that challenge and stretch people to reach higher performance levels without demotivating them or encouraging deception.

- ***Strategic placement*** Management can't control everything that goes on in an organization. Even if it could, the benefits couldn't justify the costs. As a result, managers should place controls on factors that are strategic to the organization's performance. Controls should cover the critical activities, operations, and events within the organization. That is, they should focus on places at which variations from standard are most likely to occur or at which a variation would do the greatest harm. If a department's labor costs are $100,000 a month and postage costs are $150 a month, a 5 percent overrun in the former is more critical than a 20 percent overrun in the latter. Hence, we should establish controls for labor and a critical dollar allocation, whereas postage expenses would not appear to be critical.
- ***Emphasis on the exception*** Because managers can't control all activities, they should place their strategic control devices where those devices can call attention only to the exceptions. An exception system ensures that a manager is not overwhelmed by information on variations from standard. For instance, if management policy gives supervisors the authority to give annual raises up to $500 a month, approve individual expenses up to $1,500, and make capital expenditures up to $10,000, then only deviations above those amounts require approval from higher levels of management. These checkpoints become controls that are part of the authority constraints and free higher levels of management from reviewing routine expenditures.
- ***Multiple criteria*** Managers and employees alike will try to look good on the criteria that are controlled. If management controls by using a single measure such as unit profit, effort will be focused only on looking good on that standard. Multiple measures of performance widen this narrow focus. Multiple criteria have a dual positive effect. Because they are more difficult to manipulate than a single measure, they can discourage employee efforts to merely look good. In addition, because performance can rarely be objectively evaluated from a single indicator, multiple criteria make possible more accurate assessments of performance.
- ***Corrective action*** An effective control system not only indicates when a significant deviation from standard occurs but also suggests what action should be taken to correct the deviation. That is, it ought to both point out the problem and specify the solution. This form of control is frequently accomplished by establishing if–then guidelines; for instance, if unit revenues drop more than 5 percent, then unit costs should be reduced by a similar amount.

WHAT FACTORS AFFECT CONTROL?

Although our generalizations about effective control systems provide guidelines, their validity is influenced by situational factors. What types of continency factors will affect the design of an organization's control system? These include size of the organization, one's position in the organization's hierarchy, degree of decentralization, organizational culture, and importance of an activity (see Exhibit 13–6).

Control systems should vary according to the size of the organization. A small business relies on informal and more personal control devices. Concurrent control through direct supervision is probably most cost-effective. As organizations increase in size, direct supervision is likely to be supported by an expanding formal system. Very large organizations will typically have highly formalized and impersonal feedforward and feedback controls.

The higher one moves in the organization's hierarchy, the greater the need for multiple sets of control criteria, tailored to the unit's goals. This reflects the increased ambiguity in measuring performance as a person moves up the hierarchy. Conversely, lower-level jobs have clearer definitions of performance, which allow for a narrower interpretation of job performance.

The greater the degree of decentralization, the more managers will need feedback on the performance of their employees' decisions. Because managers who delegate authority are ultimately responsible for the actions of those to whom it is delegated, they will want proper assurances that their employees' decisions are both effective and efficient.

The organizational culture may be one of trust, autonomy, and openness or one of fear and reprisal. In the former, we can expect to find informal self-control and, in the latter, externally imposed and formal control systems to ensure that performance is within standards. As with leadership styles, motivation techniques, organizational structuring, conflict management techniques, and the extent to which organiza-

EXHIBIT 13–6

Contingency Factors in the Design of Control Systems

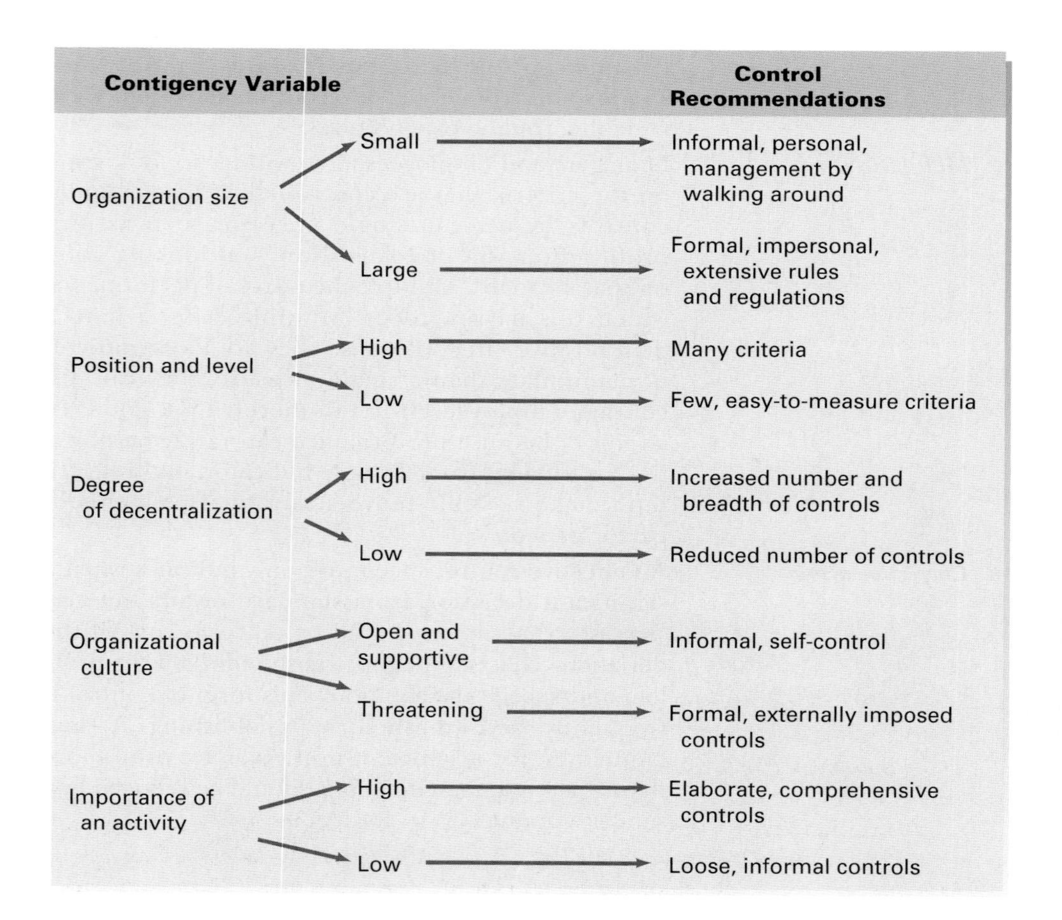

tional members participate in decision making, the type and extent of controls should be consistent with the organization's culture.

Finally, the importance of an activity influences whether, and how, it will be controlled. If control is costly and the repercussions from error small, the control system is not likely to be elaborate. However, if an error can be highly damaging to the organization, extensive controls are likely to be implemented—even if the cost is high.

DO CONTROLS NEED TO BE ADJUSTED FOR CULTURAL DIFFERENCES?

The concepts of control that we've discussed are appropriate for organizational units that aren't geographically distant or culturally distinct. But what about global organizations? Would control systems be different, and what should managers know about adjusting controls for national differences?

Methods of controlling employee behavior and operations can be quite different in different countries. In fact, the differences in organizational control systems of global organizations are primarily in the measurement and corrective action steps of the control process. In a global corporation, for instance, managers of foreign operations tend not to be closely controlled by the home office if for no other reason than that distance keeps managers from being able to observe work directly. Because distance creates a tendency for formalized controls, the home office of a global company often relies on extensive, formal reports for control. The global company may also use the power of information technology to control work activities. For instance, IYG Holding Company (a wholly owned subsidiary of Ito-Yokado Co., Ltd., and Seven-Eleven Japan Co., Ltd, that own the 7-Eleven convenience store chain) uses automated cash registers not only to record sales and monitor inventory, but also to schedule tasks for store managers and to track their use of the built-in analytical graphs and forecasts. If managers don't use them enough, they're told to increase their activities.[12]

Technology's impact on control is most evident in comparisons of technologically advanced nations with more primitive countries. Organizations in technologically advanced nations such as the United States, Japan, Canada, Great Britain, Germany, and Australia use indirect control devices—particularly computer-related reports and analyses—in addition to standardized rules and direct supervision to ensure that activities are going as planned. In less technologically advanced countries, direct supervision and highly centralized decision making are the basic means of control.

Also, constraints on what corrective action managers can take may affect managers in foreign countries because laws in some countries do not allow managers the option of closing facilities, laying off employees, or bringing in a new management team from outside the country. Finally, another challenge for global companies in collecting data is comparability. For instance, a company's manufacturing facility in Mexico might produce the same products as a facility in Scotland. However, the Mexican facility might be much more labor intensive than its Scottish counterparts (to take advantage of lower labor costs in Mexico). If the top-level executives were to control costs by, for example, calculating labor costs per unit or output per worker, the figures would not be comparable. Managers in global companies must address these types of global control challenges.

THE DYSFUNCTIONAL SIDE OF CONTROL

Have you ever noticed that some of the people who work in the college registrar's office don't seem to care much about students' problems? At times they appear to be so fixated on ensuring that every rule is followed that they lose sight of the fact that their job is to help students, not to hassle them.

At the Chronic Fatigue and Immune Dysfunction Syndrome Association of America, executives were spending thousands of dollars each year on research. As the association's CEO, Kim Keeney stated, "we're in this business to go out of business." That's why they

"Some employees may manipulate measures to give the appearance they are performing well."

kept funding research projects. They would raise money, and use the monies for research support—making available millions of dollars for research. While the association's executives were excited about the opportunity to raise awareness of the disease and pursue a cure, they recognized one thing: They had no idea where their money was being spent. Without controlling for research outcomes, they believe more than $12 million was misspent by one of the organizations to whom they had given money.[13]

This example illustrates what can happen when controls are lacking. Similar results occur when controls are inflexible or control standards are unreasonable, too. That's because people lose sight of the organization's overall goals. Instead of the organization running the controls, the controls can sometimes run the organization.

Because control systems don't monitor everything, problems can occur when individuals or organizational units attempt to look good exclusively on control measures. The result again is something that is dysfunctional. More often than not, this dysfunctionality is caused by incomplete measures of performance. If the control system evaluates only the quantity of output, people will ignore quality. Similarly, if the system measures activities rather than results, people will spend their time attempting to look good on the activity measures.

To avoid being reprimanded by managers, people may engage in behaviors that are designed solely to influence the information system's data output during a given control period. Rather than actually performing well, employees may manipulate measures to give the appearance that they are performing well. That's precisely one of the key factors in the Enron scandal. Evidence indicates that the manipulation of control data is not a random phenomenon. It depends on the importance of an activity. Organizationally important activities are likely to make a difference in a person's rewards; therefore, there is a great incentive to look good on those particular measures.[14] When rewards are at stake, individuals tend to manipulate data to appear in a favorable light by, for instance, distorting actual figures, emphasizing successes, and suppressing evidence of failures. On the other hand, only random errors have been found to occur when the distribution of rewards is unaffected.[15]

Our conclusion is that controls have both an upside and a downside. Failure to design flexibility into a control system can create problems more severe than those the controls were implemented to prevent.

CONTEMPORARY ISSUES IN CONTROL

There are issues that can arise as managers design efficient and effective control systems. Technological advances in computer hardware and software , for example, have made the process of controlling much easier. But these advances in technology brought with them difficult questions regarding what managers have the right to know about employees and how far they can go in controlling employee behavior (see Ethical Dilemma in Management). In this section, we're going to look at two contemporary issues in control—workplace privacy and employee theft.

IS MY WORK COMPUTER REALLY MINE?

If you work, do you think you have a right to privacy at your workplace? What can your employer find out about you and your work? You might be surprised by the answers. Employers can (and most often do), among other things, read your e-mail (even those marked personal or confidential), tap your phone, and monitor your computer work.[16] And these actions aren't all that uncommon. Today, nearly 80 percent of all businesses surveyed by the American Management Association indicate they monitor employees.[17]

Why do managers feel they must monitor what employees are doing? A big reason is that employees are hired to work, not to surf the Web checking stock prices, placing bets at online casinos, or shopping for presents for family or friends. Recreational on-the-job

Ethical Dilemma in Management

Invasion of Privacy?

Technological advances have made the process of managing an organization much easier. But technological advancements have also provided employers a means of sophisticated employee monitoring. Although most of this monitoring is designed to enhance worker productivity, it could, and has been, a source of concern over worker privacy. These advantages have also brought with them difficult questions regarding what managers have the right to know about employees and how far they can go in controlling employee behavior, both on and off the job.

What can your employer find out about you and your work? You might be surprised by the answers! Consider the following:

- The mayor of Colorado Springs, Colorado, reads the electronic mail messages that city council members send to each other from their homes. He defended his actions by saying he was making sure that e-mail to each other was not being used to circumvent his state's "open meeting" law that requires most council business to be conducted publicly.
- The U.S. Internal Revenue Service's internal audit group monitors a computer log that shows employee access to taxpayers' accounts. This monitoring activity allows management to check and see what employees are doing on their computers.
- American Express has an elaborate system for monitoring telephone calls. Daily reports are provided to supervisors that detail the frequency and length of calls made by employees, as well as how quickly incoming calls are answered.
- Managements in several organizations require employees to wear badges at all times while on company premises. These badges contain a variety of data that allow employees to enter certain locations in the organization. Smart badges, too, can transmit where the employee is at all times!

Just how much control should a company have over the private lives of its employees? Where should an employer's rules and controls end? Does the boss have the right to dictate what you do on your own free time and in your own home? Could, in essence, your boss keep you from engaging in riding a motorcycle, skydiving, smoking, drinking alcohol, or eating junk food? Again, the answers may surprise you. What's more, employer involvement in employees' off-work lives has been going on for decades. For instance, in the early 1900s, Ford Motor company would send social workers to employees' homes to determine whether their off-the-job habits and finances were deserving of year-end bonuses. Other firms made sure employees regularly attended church services. Today, many organizations, in their quest to control safety and health insurance costs, are once again delving into their employees' private lives.

Is "big brother" watching? Technology has made it possible for employers to watch nearly every movement of their employees. Should they be permitted to do this? They do it, but what effect does it have on employee motivation? That question is yet to be answered.

Although controlling employees' behaviors on and off the job may appear unjust or unfair, nothing in our legal system prevents employers from engaging in these practices. Rather, the law is based on the premise that "if employees don't like the rules, they have the option of quitting."

Managers, too, typically defend their actions in terms of ensuring quality, productivity, and proper employee behavior. For instance, an IRS audit of its southeastern regional offices found that 166 employees took unauthorized looks at the tax returns of friends, neighbors, and celebrities.

When does management's need for information about employee performance cross over the line and interfere with a worker's right to privacy?[18] Is any action by management acceptable as long as employees are notified ahead of time that they will be monitored? And what about the demarcation between monitoring work and nonwork behavior? When employees do work-related activities at home during evenings and weekends, does management's prerogative to monitor employees remain in force? What's your opinion?

Web surfing has been said to cost a billion dollars in wasted computer resources and billions of dollars in lost work productivity annually. That's a significant cost to businesses.

Another reason that managers monitor employee e-mail and computer usage is that they don't want to risk being sued for creating a hostile workplace environment because of an offensive message or inappropriate images displayed on a co-worker's. Establish what actually happened and can help managers react quickly.[19] Consider what happened at Chevron. They settled a sexual harassment lawsuit for $2.2 million because offensive e-mails—like "25 reasons why beer is better than women"—were readily circulated on the company's e-mail system. Organizations like Citigroup and Morgan Stanley Dean Witter have also been taken to court by employees for racist e-mail proliferating on their systems.[20] As one researcher pointed out, federal law views a company's e-mail no differently than if offensive materials were circulated on a company's letterhead.[21]

Finally, managers want to ensure that company secrets aren't being leaked. Although protecting intellectual property is important for all businesses, it's especially important in high-tech industries. Managers need to be certain that employees are not, even inadvertently, passing along information to others who could use that information to harm the company.

The consequences of inappropriate workplace computer usage also can be serious for employees and companies.[22] For instance, shortly before Christmas in 1999, 23 workers at a *New York Times* administrative center in Norfolk, Virginia, were fired, and a number of other employees were reprimanded for violating the company's policy that prohibits using the corporate e-mail system to "create, forward, or display any offensive or disruptive messages, including photographs, and audio material." A number of Xerox employees were dismissed for spending as much as eight hours a day browsing X-rated and e-shopping Web sites during work hours. Two executives at Salomon Smith Barney were fired after a routine check of corporate e-mail turned up pornographic material. And Lockheed Martin's e-mail system crashed for six hours after an employee sent 60,000 co-workers an e-mail (asking them to respond back using an attached e-receipt) about a national prayer day. Since Lockheed depended heavily on its internal e-mail communication system, this crash cost the company hundreds of thousands of dollars.

Even with all the workplace monitoring that managers can do, employees in the United States do have some protection from the Federal Electronic Communications Privacy Act of 1986 (EPCA).[23] The ECPA prohibits unauthorized interception of electronic communication. Although this law gives employees some privacy protection, it doesn't make workplace electronic monitoring illegal, as employers are allowed to monitor communications for business reasons or when employees have been notified of this practice. A similar law, the Data Protection Act of 1998, permits much of the same for companies in the United Kingdom.[24] Although employees may think that it's unfair for a company to monitor their work electronically and to fire them for what they feel are minor distractions, the courts have ruled that since the computer belongs to the company, it has a right to monitor anything on its system.[25] The point here is that there needs to be a balance between management's need to know and the effect employee monitoring may have on employee morale.[26]

One interesting facet to the employee monitoring debate centers around protecting the enterprise. Since September 11, 2001, many government agencies and private organizations have been increasing their computer surveillance in an effort to support "homeland security."[27] Because computer systems can and have been hacked, significant data can be lost. Moreover, a terrorist attack on U.S. computer systems could prove extremely damaging to the U.S. economy. As such, we can anticipate even more system monitoring and significantly more surveillance of many of the "normal" activities in our daily lives.

IS EMPLOYEE THEFT ON THE RISE?

Would it surprise you to find out that nearly 85 percent of all organizational theft and fraud is committed by employees—not outsiders?[28] And it's costly. It's estimated that U.S. companies lose about $29 billion annually from employee theft and fraud.[29]

Employee theft is defined as any unauthorized taking of company property by employees for their personal use.[30] It can range from embezzlement to fraudulent filing of expense reports to removing equipment, parts, software, and office supplies from company premises. Although retail businesses have long faced particularly serious potential losses from employee theft, loose financial controls at start-ups and small companies and the ready availability of information technology have made employee stealing an escalating problem in all kinds and sizes of organizations. In fact, a recent survey of U.S. businesses indicated that more than 35 percent of employees admitted to stealing from their employers.[31] That number is even higher when you include theft by employees who have been laid off.[32] It's a control issue that managers need to educate themselves about and with which they must be prepared to deal.[33]

employee theft
Any unauthorized taking of company property by employees for their personal use

Why do employees steal? The answer depends on whom you ask.[34] Experts in various fields—industrial security, criminology, clinical psychology—all have different perspectives. The industrial security people propose that people steal because the opportunity presents itself through lax controls and favorable circumstances. Criminologists say it's because people have financial-based pressures (such as personal financial problems) or vice-based pressures (such as gambling debts). And the clinical psychologists suggest that people steal because they can rationalize whatever they're doing as being correct and appropriate behavior ("everyone does it," "they had it coming," "this company makes enough money and they'll never miss anything this small," "I deserve this for all that I put up with," and so forth).[35] Although each of these approaches provides compelling insights into employee theft and has been instrumental in programs designed to deter it, unfortunately, employees continue to steal.

What can managers do? Under certain circumstances as part of a theft investigation in the organization, an employer could require an employee to submit to a polygraph (lie detector test).[36] There are also other means available. Let's look at some suggestions for managing employee theft. We can use the concepts of feedforward, concurrent, and feedback control to identify measures for deterring or reducing employee theft. We've presented this in Exhibit 13–7

EXHIBIT 13–7 Control Measures for Deterring or Reducing Employee Theft or Fraud

FEEDFORWARD	CONCURRENT	FEEDBACK
Careful prehiring screening.	Treat employees with respect and dignity.	Make sure employees know when theft or fraud has occurred—not naming names but letting people know this is not acceptable.
Establish specific policies defining theft and fraud and discipline procedures.	Openly communicate the costs of stealing.	Use the services of professional investigators.
Involve employees in writing policies.	Let employees know on a regular basis about their successes in preventing theft and fraud.	Redesign control measures.
Educate and train employees about the policies.	Use video surveillance equipment if conditions warrant.	Evaluate your organization's culture and the relationships of managers and employees.
Have professionals review your internal security controls.	Install "lock-out" options on computers, telephones, and e-mail. Use corporate hot lines for reporting incidences. Set a good example.	

Sources: Based on A.H. Bell and D.M. Smith, "Protecting the Company Against Theft and Fraud," *Workforce Online*, (www.workforce.com), December 3, 2000; J.D. Hansen, "To Catch a Thief," *Journal of Accountancy*, March 2000, pp. 43–46; and J. Greenberg, "The Cognitive Geometry of Employee Theft," in *Dysfunctional Behavior in Organizations: Nonviolent and Deviant Behavior* (Stamford, CT: JAI Press, 1998), pp. 147–93.

ENTREPRENEURS AND CONTROL

Entrepreneurs must look at controlling their ventures' operations in order to prosper in both the short and the long run. Those unique control issues that face entrepreneurs include managing growth, managing downturns, and exiting the venture.

HOW MUST THE ENTREPRENEUR CONTROL FOR GROWTH?

William Williams, cofounder of Glory Foods, has taken an unusual approach to managing growth—slow down the process. His company, based in Columbus, Ohio, sells "down-home-tasting" Southern specialities that are quick and easy to prepare. These items are an alternative to the traditional Southern cooking that takes hours of preparation. Glory Foods has successfully cornered a market niche by following a conservative path to growth. Williams' decision to move slowly was based mostly on the fact that he didn't want to dilute the founders' equity positions down to minority levels in order to acquire the increased financing needed to grow. Although the slow growth approach may have taken more time, Williams and his partners felt it was worth it because they still have total control over what happens in the company.[37]

Growth is a natural and desirable outcome for entrepreneurial ventures. In fact, it's part of our definition of entrepreneurship. Entrepreneurial ventures pursue growth.[38] However, growth doesn't have to be frantic and chaotic. Growing slowly can be just as successful, as William Williams discovered at Glory Foods.

Growth doesn't occur just randomly or by luck. Successfully pursuing growth typically requires an entrepreneur to manage all the challenges associated with growing. This entails planning, organizing, and controlling for growth.

Planning for growth As we said earlier in this chapter, controlling is tied closely to planning. And the best growth strategy is a well-planned one.[39] Ideally, the decision to grow doesn't come about spontaneously, but instead is part of the venture's overall business goals and plans. Rapid growth without planning can be disastrous. Entrepreneurs need to address growth strategies as part of their business planning but shouldn't be overly rigid in that planning. The plans should be flexible enough to exploit unexpected opportunities that arise. With plans in place, the successful entrepreneur must then organize for growth.

Organizing for growth The key challenges for an entrepreneur in organizing for growth include finding capital, finding people, and strengthening the organizational culture.

Having enough capital is a major challenge facing growing entrepreneurial ventures. The money issue never seems to go away. It does take capital to expand. The process of finding capital to fund growth is much like going through the initial financing of the venture. However, this time, hopefully, the venture has a successful track record to back up the request. If it doesn't, it may be extremely difficult to acquire the necessary capital. That's why we said earlier that the best growth strategy is a planned one. Part of that planning should be how growth will be financed. For example, the Boston beer company which produces Samuel Adams grew 30 percent to 60 percent a year for 12 years by focusing almost exclusively on increasing its top-selling product line. However, the company was so focused on increasing market share that it had few financial controls and an inadequate financial infrastructure. During periods of growth, cash flow difficulties would force company president and brew master Jim Koch to tap into a pool of unused venture capital funding. However, when a chief financial officer joined the company in the late 1980s, he developed a financial structure that enabled the company to manage its growth more efficiently and effectively by setting up a plan for funding growth.[40]

Another important issue that a growing entrepreneurial venture needs to address is finding people. Even if the venture is growing quickly, this challenge may be intensified because of the time constraints. It's important to plan, as much as possible, the number and types of employees needed to support the increasing workload as the venture

- Keep the lines of communication open—inform employees about major issues.
- Establish trust by being honest, open, and forthright about the challenges and rewards of being a growing organization.
- Be a good listener—find out what employees are thinking and facing.
- Be willing to delegate duties.
- Be flexible—be willing to change your plans if necessary.
- Provide consistent and regular feedback by letting employees know the outcomes—good and bad.
- Reinforce the contributions of each person by recognizing employees' efforts.
- Continually train employees to enhance their capabilities and skills.
- Maintain the focus on the venture's mission even as it grows.
- Establish and reinforce a "we" spirit since a successful growing venture takes the coordinated efforts of all the employees.

EXHIBIT 13-8

Suggestions for Achieving a Supportive Growth-Oriented Culture

grows. Also, it may be necessary to provide additional training and support to employees to help them handle the increased pressures associated with a growing organization.

Finally, when a venture is growing, it's important to create a positive, growth-oriented culture that enhances the opportunities to achieve success, both organizationally and individually. This sometimes can be difficult to do, particularly when changes are occurring rapidly. However, the values, attitudes, and beliefs that are established and reinforced during these times are critical to the entrepreneurial venture's continued and future success. Exhibit 13–8 lists some suggestions that entrepreneurs might use to ensure that their venture's culture is one that embraces and supports a climate in which organizational growth is viewed as desirable and important. Keeping employees focused and committed to what the venture is doing is critical to the ultimate success of its growth strategies. If employees don't buy into the direction in which the entrepreneurial venture is headed, it's unlikely the growth strategies will be successful.

Controlling for growth Maintaining good financial records and financial controls over cash flow, inventory, customer data, sales orders, receivables, payables, and costs should be a priority of every entrepreneur—whether pursuing growth or not. However, it's particularly important to reinforce these controls when the entrepreneurial venture is expanding. It's all too easy to let things "get away" or to put off doing them when there's an unrelenting urgency to get things done. Rapid growth, or even slow growth, does not excuse the need to have effective controls in place. In fact, it's particularly important to have established procedures, protocols, and processes and to use them. Even though mistakes and inefficiencies can never be entirely eliminated, at least an entrepreneur should ensure that every effort is being made to achieve high levels of productivity and organizational effectiveness. For example, at Green Gear Cycling, CEO Alan Scholz recognized the importance of controlling for growth. How? By following a "customer for life" strategy. By continually monitoring customer relationships and orienting organizational work decisions around their possible impacts on customers, Green Gear's employees hope to keep customers for life. That's significant because they figure that if they could keep a customer for life, the value would range from $10,000 to $25,000 per lifetime customer.[41]

HOW DOES THE ENTREPRENEUR MANAGE DOWNTURNS?

Although organizational growth is a desirable and important goal for entrepreneurial ventures, what happens when things turn sour—when the growth strategies don't result in the intended outcomes and, in fact, result in a decline in performance? Nobody likes to fail, especially entrepreneurs. However, when an entrepreneurial venture faces times of trouble, what can be done? The first step is recognizing that a crisis is brewing.

"The first step in managing a downturn is recognizing that a crisis is brewing."

How does Alan Scholz control the growth in Green Gear Cycling? By employing his "customer for life" strategy, he continually monitors customer relationships and orients work decisions around their possible effect on the customers. A customer for life at Green Gear would add an additional $10,000 to $25,000 per customer to the bottom line.

Recognizing crisis situations An entrepreneur should be alert to the warning signs of a business in trouble. Some signals of potential performance decline include inadequate cash flow, excess number of employees, unnecessary and cumbersome administrative procedures, fear of conflict and taking risks, tolerance of work incompetence, lack of a clear mission or goals, and ineffective or poor communication within the organization.[42]

Another perspective on recognizing performance declines revolves around what is known as the "**boiled frog phenomenon**."[43] The "boiled frog" is a classic psychological response experiment. In one case, a live frog that's dropped into a boiling pan of water reacts instantaneously and jumps out of the pan. But, in the second case, a living frog that's dropped into a pan of mild water that is gradually heated to the boiling point, fails to react and dies. A small firm may be particularly vulnerable to the boiled frog phenomenon because the entrepreneur may not recognize the "water heating up"—that is, the subtly declining situation. When changes in performance are gradual, a serious response may never be triggered or may come too late to do anything about the situation. So what dos this teach us? That entrepreneurs need to be alert to the signals that the venture's performance may be worsening. Entrepreneurs cannot wait until the water has reached the boiling point to react.[44]

"boiled frog phenomenon"
A classical psychological response experiment

When things turn for the worse Although an entrepreneur hopes never to have to deal with the organizational downturns, declines, or crises, there may come a time when he or she must do just that. After all, nobody likes to think about things going bad or taking a turn for the worse. But that's exactly what the entrepreneur needs to do—think about it before it happens, using feedforward control.[45] It's important to have an up-to-date plan for covering bad times. It's just like mapping out exit routes from your home in case of a fire. An entrepreneur wants to be prepared before an emergency hits. This plan should focus on providing specific details for controlling the most fundamental and critical aspects of running the business—things like revenues, costs, and debt. Beyond having a plan for controlling the venture's critical financial inflows and outflows, other actions would involve identifying specific strategies for cutting costs and restructuring the venture.

HOW DOES THE ENTREPRENEUR EXIT THE VENTURE?

Getting out of an entrepreneurial venture might seem a strange thing for an entrepreneur to do. However, there may come a point when the entrepreneur decides it's time to move on. That decision may be based on the fact that the entrepreneur hopes to cash out on the investment in the venture—called **harvesting**—or that the entrepreneur is facing serious organizational performance problems and wants to get out. It may even be the entrepreneur's desire to focus on other pursuits (either personal or business related). The issue involved with exiting the venture includes choosing a proper business valuation method and knowing what's involved in the process of selling a business.

harvesting
When an entrepreneur hopes to cash out on the investment he or she made in the business

Business evaluation method Valuation techniques generally fall into three categories: (1) asset valuations; (2) earnings valuations; and (3) cash flow valuations.[46] Setting a value on a business can be a little tricky. In many cases, the entrepreneur has sacrificed much for the business and sees it as his or her "baby." Calculating the value of the "baby" based on objective standards such as cash flow or some multiple of net profits can sometimes be a shock. That's why it's important for an entrepreneur who wishes to exit a venture to get a comprehensive business valuation prepared by professionals.

Other exiting considerations Although the hardest part of preparing to exit a venture is valuing it, other factors also should be considered.[47] This includes such matters as deciding who sells the business, determining the tax implications of the venture's sale, establishing how potential buyers are to be screened, and determining when to tell employees about the sale. The process of exiting the entrepreneurial venture should be approached as carefully as the process of launching it. If the entrepreneur is selling the venture on a positive note, he or she wants to realize the value built up in the business. If the venture is being exited because of declining performance, the entrepreneur wants to maximize the potential return.

Review, Comprehension, Application

CHAPTER SUMMARY

How will you know if you fulfilled the Learning Outcomes on page 372. You will have fulfilled the Learning Outcomes if you are able to:

1. **Define control.** Control is a management function that focuses on the process of monitoring activities to ensure that they are being accomplished as planned. Control also includes correcting any significant deviations that may exist between goals and actual results.
2. **Describe three approaches to control.** Three approaches to control are market control, bureaucratic control, and clan control. Market control emphasizes the use of external marketing mechanisms such as price competition and relative market share to establish standards used in the control system. Bureaucratic control emphasizes organizational authority and relies on administrative rules, regulations, procedures, and policies. Under clan control, employee behaviors are regulated by the shared values, norms, traditions, rituals, beliefs, and other aspects of organizational culture.
3. **Explain why control is important.** Control is important as a function of management because it involves determining whether objectives are being accomplished as planned. Furthermore, control is also useful for determining whether delegated authority is being abused.
4. **Describe the control process.** In the control process, management must first have standards of performance derived from the objectives it formed in the planning stage. Management must then measure actual performance and compare that performance against the standards. If a variance exists between standards and performance, management can adjust performance, adjust the standards, or do nothing, according to the situation.
5. **Distinguish among the three types of control.** There are three types of control: feedforward, concurrent, and feedback control. Feedforward control is future-directed and designed to prevent problems by anticipating them. Concurrent control takes place while an activity is in progress. Feedback control, the most frequently found in organizations, takes place after an activity or an event has occurred.
6. **Describe the qualities of an effective control system.** An effective control system is accurate, timely, economical, flexible, and understandable. It uses reasonable criteria, has strategic placement, emphasizes the exception, uses multiple criteria, and suggests corrective action.
7. **Identify the contingency factors in the control process.** A number of contingency factors in organizations affect the control process. The most frequent contingency factors in control systems include the size of the organization, the manager's level in the organization's hierarchy, the degree of decentralization, the organization's culture, and the importance of the activity.
8. **Explain how controls can become dysfunctional.** Controls can be dysfunctional when they redirect behavior away from an organization's goals. This dysfunction can occur as a result of inflexibility or unreasonable standards. In addition, when rewards are at stake, individuals are likely to manipulate data so that their performance will be perceived positively.
9. **Describe how national differences influence the control process.** Methods of controlling employee behavior and operations can be quite different according to the geographic location or cultural environment. As a result, control systems focus primarily on measurement and corrective action steps of the control process.
10. **Identify the ethical dilemmas in employee monitoring.** The ethical dilemmas in employee monitoring revolve around the rights of employees versus the rights of employers. Employees are concerned with protecting their workplace privacy and intrusion into their personal lives. Employers, in contrast, are primarily concerned with enhancing productivity and

controlling safety and health costs, and protecting their organization from claims of harassment.

11. **Describe how an entrepreneur controls for growth.** Entrepreneurs must maintain good financial records and financial controls over cash flow, inventory, customer data, sales orders, receivables, payables, and costs. These items need to be the priority of every entrepreneur—whether he or she is pursuing growth or not. It's particularly important, however, to reinforce these controls when the entrepreneurial venture is expanding.

COMPANION WEBSITE

We invite you to visit the Robbins/DeCenzo companion Website at **www.prenhall.com/robbins** for this chapter's Internet resources, including an online study guide, Internet exercises, and "In the News" with full text articles provided by XanEdu.

READING FOR COMPREHENSION

1. What is the role of control in management?
2. Name four methods managers can use to acquire information about actual organizational performance.
3. Contrast immediate and basic corrective action.
4. What are the advantages and disadvantages of feedforward control?
5. What can management do to reduce the dysfunctionality of controls?

LINKING CONCEPTS TO PRACTICE

1. How are planning and control linked? Is the control function linked to the organizing and leading functions of management? Explain.
2. In Chapter 7 we discussed the "white water rapids" view of change. Do you think it's possible to establish and maintain effective standards and controls in this type of atmosphere?
3. Why do you believe feedback control is the most popular type of control? Justify your response.
4. Why is what is measured probably more critical to the control process than how it is measured?
5. "Organizations have the right to monitor employees—both on and off the job." Build an argument supporting this statement and an argument disagreeing with the statement.

VIDEO CASE APPLICATION

YOUpowered: Safeguarding the Consumer's Online Privacy in the Name of Good Business

For lawyers and ethicists, privacy issues revolving around Internet use in the workplace and at home are just heating up. Consumers are increasingly wary of security problems in cyberspace and reluctant to have personal information fall into the wrong hands. YOUpowered gives both businesses and consumers an ethical solution to their needs through permission-based personalization, by detecting and blocking cookies.

These aren't the kind of cookies you enjoy with your milk. According to David Zimmerman, Ph.D., chief technology officer, YOUpowered, there are "good" cookies and "bad" cookies, cookies being the invisible software dropped on your hard drive by nearly every company with a Web site.

The "bad" cookies record and track your every move, and may be used by organizations to send you unwanted promotions and clutter your home computer screen with ads. Dr. Zimmerman believes that giving consumers control over their personal Internet profiles is the best response to the surreptitious, seemingly unstoppable, use of cookies by the e-business community. Using ORBY, individuals create their own digital profiles including name, password, address, job, and credit card numbers. They are notified on-screen about what information is being collected and can opt in or out of sharing their personal responses.

YOUpowered benefits the business community as well, by compiling online behavior information about surfer's Web activities and habits. YOUpowered's Orby software enables companies to build a strong customer base of people whose privacy preferences are compatible with the company's Web site. Orby's goal is to support a closer relationship between businesses and clients based on consumer confidence.

Two e-businesses that have integrated ORBY are MaxManager, a service that stores and organizes online shopping orders and receipts, and @once.com, an online marketer for companies like Nintendo, Egghead, and J.Crew. Both companies are committed to the idea that being open with Web site visitors will foster consumer trust *and* repeat business.

"A consumer should have access to their information," says Matthew Ellice, privacy officer, @once.com. "They should know exactly what their on-site experience will entail and what they can expect." Orby works together with an application called Consumer Trust to disclose what a firm would like to know, what they will use the data for, how long they plan to keep it, and whether they intend to do future "e-mailings."

Do you think that being observed silently by invisible bits of software while making online Christmas purchases in your own living room is an invasion of your privacy? No one seems to know the answer. The ethical and legal issues surrounding organizational monitoring of people at home and at work remain murky. Yet, the use of electronic surveillance monitoring devices have become commonplace in American businesses. In the face of soaring Internet crime, it is certainly defensible. Cyber thieves, among them many rank and file employees, are stealing millions if not billions of dollars a year from businesses in the United States and abroad. According to the *New York Times*, "thieves are not just diverting cash from company bank accounts, they are pilfering valuable information like business development strategies, new product specifications, or contract bidding plans and selling the data to competitors."[48]

Founded in 1997, New York City based YOUpowered is the leading provider of Web-wide Smart Personalization solutions for today's e-business community. Here in America, where defending one's right to privacy is endemic to the national character, YOUpowered's Orby is likely to be in demand.

Questions

1. How might the manager of a small virtual advertising business use ORBY to help him or her improve feedforward control, concurrent control, or feedback control? Explain.
2. When asked about MaxManager's decision to implement ORBY, Dan Berg, vice president of business development replied: "Those of us who have started these online and Internet companies are consumers and users of the Internet as well. I don't want my information disseminated in ways I don't know about." Analyze his answer from an entrepreneurial viewpoint, as well as a personal stance.
3. As an employee at @once, would you expect the organizational culture to dictate concern for employee privacy? Explain. Under these circumstances would you feel it was an invasion of your privacy for @once management to have accessed your personal health information upon filing your insurance claim after an unplanned hospital stay or would you reason that human resource personnel are accustomed to dealing with these issues and not take action? Explain. If you chose not to let the incident go, what form of action would you take?

Management Workshop

Team Skill-Building Exercise

The Paper Plane Corporation

Purposes

1. To integrate the management functions.
2. To apply planning and control concepts specifically to improve organizational performance.

Required Knowledge

Planning, organizing, and controlling concepts.

Time Required

Approximately one hour.

Procedure

Any number of groups of six participants each are used in this exercise. These groups may be directed simultaneously in the same room. Each person should have assembly instructions (Exhibit 13–9) and a summary sheet, plus ample stacks of paper (standard copying paper). The room should be large enough that each group of six can work without interference from other groups. A working space should be provided for each group. The participants are doing an exercise in production methodology. Each group must work independently of the other groups. Each group will choose a manager and an inspector, and the remaining participants will be employees. The objective is to make paper airplanes in the most profitable manner possible. The facilitator will give the signal to start. This is a 10-minute, timed event involving competition among the groups. After the first round, each group should report its production and profits to the entire group. Each group reports the manner in which it planned, organized, and controlled the production of the paper airplanes. This same procedure is followed for as many rounds as there is time.

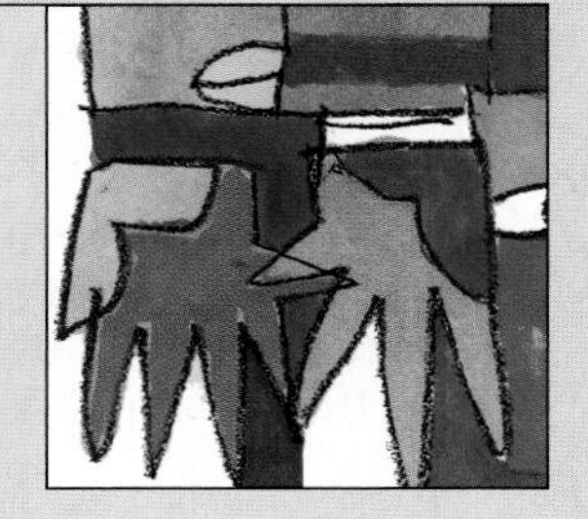

Your group is the complete workforce for Paper Plane Corporation. Established in 1943, Paper Plane has led the market in paper plane production. Currently under new management, the company is contracting to make aircraft for the U.S. Air Force. You must establish a plan and organization to produce these aircraft. You must fulfill your contract with the Air Force under the following conditions:

1. The Air Force will pay $20,000 per airplane.
2. The aircraft must pass a strict inspection.
3. A penalty of $25,000 per airplane will be subtracted for failure to meet the production requirements (bid planes not made or defective planes).
4. Labor and other overhead will be computed at $300,000.
5. Cost of materials will be $3,000 per bid plane. If you bid for ten but make only eight, you must pay the cost of materials for those you failed to make or that did not pass inspection.

Understanding Yourself

For the past 12 chapters, we have been suggesting that you complete a number of self-assessments in an effort to better understand your strengths and development areas. We've also suggested that you print the results of each assessment and store them as part of your "portfolio of learning." In the spirit of monitoring plans, it's now time to revisit your completed self-assessments and analyze your results. Here are some guiding questions for you to consider in your analysis.

1. What strengths and development areas have you uncovered about yourself?
2. Do you believe these assessments to be an accurate reflection of you? Why or why not?
3. How will knowledge of these strengths and development areas be useful in planning your career?
4. What will you do to focus on your development areas? How will you know if you're making progress on them?

EXHIBIT 13–9 Paper Plane Data Sheet

Instructions for Aircraft Assembly

Step 1: Take a sheet of paper and fold it in half, then open it back up.

Step 2: Fold upper corners toward the middle.

Step 3: Fold the corners to the middle again.

Step 4: Fold in half.

Step 5: Fold both wings down.

Step 6: Fold tail fins up.

Completed aircraft

Round 1		
Bid: [number of planes] x $20,000 per plane	=	
Result: [number of planes] x $20,000 per plane	=	
Less:		
overhead	=	$300,000
[number of bid planes] x $3,000 cost of raw materials	=	
[number of unmade or defective planes] x $25,000 penalty	=	
Profit [result – (overhead + raw materials + penalty)]:	=	
Round 2		
Bid: [number of planes] x $20,000 per plane	=	
Result: [number of planes] x $20,000 per plane	=	
Less:		
overhead	=	$300,000
[number of bid planes] x $3,000 cost of raw materials	=	
[number of unmade or defective planes] x $25,000 penalty	=	
Profit [result – (overhead + raw materials + penalty)]:	=	
Round 3		
Bid: [number of planes] x $20,000 per plane	=	
Result: [number of planes] x $20,000 per plane	=	
Less:		
overhead	=	$300,000
[number of bid planes] x $3,000 cost of raw materials	=	
[number of unmade or defective planes] x $25,000 penalty	=	
Profit [result – (overhead + raw materials + penalty)]:	=	

Source: Based on an exercise in J. H. Donnelly, Jr., J. L. Gibson, and J. M. Ivancevich, *Fundamentals of Management*, 8th ed. (Burr Ridge, IL: Irwin, 1992), pp. 285–89. With permission.

Developing Your Performance Feedback Skill

About the Skill

In this chapter, we introduced several suggestions for providing feedback. One of the more critical feedback sessions will occur when you, as a manager, are using feedback control to address performance issues.

Steps in Practicing the Skill

1. **Schedule the feedback session in advance and be prepared.** One of the biggest mistakes you can make is to treat feedback control lightly. Simply calling in an employee and giving feedback that is not well organized serves little purpose for you and your employee. For feedback to be effective, you must plan ahead. Identify the issues you wish to address and cite specific examples to reinforce what you are saying. Furthermore, set aside the time for the meeting with the employee. Make sure that what you do is done in private and can be completed without interruptions. That may mean closing your office door (if you have one), holding phone calls, and the like.
2. **Put the employee at ease.** Regardless of how you feel about the feedback, you must create a supportive climate for the employee. Recognize that giving and getting this feedback can be an emotional event even when the feedback is positive. By putting your employee at ease, you begin to establish a supportive environment in which understanding can take place.
3. **Make sure the employee knows the purpose of this feedback session.** What is the purpose of the meeting? That's something any employee will be wondering. Clarifying what you are going to do sets the appropriate stage for what is to come.
4. **Focus on specific rather than general work behaviors.** Feedback should be specific rather than general. General statements are vague and provide little useful information—especially if you are attempting to correct a problem.
5. **Keep comments impersonal and job related.** Feedback should be descriptive rather than judgmental or evaluative, especially when you are giving negative feedback. No matter how upset you are, keep the feedback job related and never criticize someone personally because of an inappropriate action. You are censuring job-related behavior, not the person.
6. **Support feedback with hard data.** Tell your employee how you came to your conclusion on his or her performance. Hard data help your employees to identify with specific behaviors. Identify the "things" that were done correctly and provide a detailed critique. And, if you need to criticize, state the basis of your conclusion that a good job was not completed.
7. **Direct the negative feedback toward work-related behavior that the employee controls.** Negative feedback should be directed toward work-related behavior that the employee can do something about. Indicate what he or she can do to improve the situation. This practice helps take the sting out of the criticism and offers guidance to an individual who understands the problem but doesn't know how to resolve it.

8. **Let the employee speak.** Get the employee's perceptions of what you are saying, especially if you are addressing a problem. Of course, you're not looking for excuses, but you need to be empathetic to the employee. Get his or her side. Maybe there's something that has contributed to the issue. Letting the employee speak involves your employee and just might provide information you were unaware of.
9. **Ensure that the employee has a clear and full understanding of the feedback.** Feedback must be concise and complete enough so that your employee clearly and fully understands what you have said. Consistent with active listening techniques, have your employee rephrase the content of your feedback to check whether it fully captures your meaning.
10. **Detail a future plan of action.** Performing doesn't stop simply because feedback occurred. Good performance must be reinforced, and new performance goals set. However, when there are performance deficiencies, time must be devoted to helping your employee develop a detailed, step-by-step plan to correct the situation. This plan includes what has to be done, when, and how you will monitor the activities. Offer whatever assistance you can to help the employee, but make it clear that it is the employee, not you, who has to make the corrections.

Practicing the Skill

Think of a skill you would like to acquire or improve, or a habit you would like to break. Perhaps you would like to learn a foreign language, start exercising, quit smoking, ski better, or spend less. For the purpose of this exercise, assume you have three months to make a start on your project and all the necessary funds. Draft a plan of action that outlines what you need to do, when you need to do it, and how you will know that you have successfully completed each step of your plan. Be realistic, but don't set your sights too low either.

Review your plan. What outside help or resources will you require? How will you get them? Add these to your plan.

Could someone else follow the steps you've outlined to achieve the goal you set? What modifications would you have to make, if any?

Developing Your Diagnostic and Analytical Skills

SiloCaf

At the Port of New Orleans, the largest coffee port in the United States, one company is handling an old-fashioned product in a new-fashioned way. Frederico Pacorini's SiloCaf, a fully computerized bulk-coffee storage, handling, and processing facility, is a place where tradition meets technology and where control is taking on a new perspective.[49]

SiloCaf was founded in 1933 as a freight-forwarding company that moved products from one location to another. Today, however, the company primarily moves coffee, and the way that it controls and monitors its entire processing operation is about as technologically advanced as possible. Why has SiloCaf invested in technology for such a seemingly simple product? The primary reason is that consumers want the same flavor each time they purchase a can of coffee. However, coffee is a natural product, and coffee beans may vary from crop to crop. Getting consistent flavor is difficult without some way to control the coffee blend. That's crucial to a big company like Folger's, that demands consistency in taste. Nearly one-third of all coffee processed in the United States comes through the New Orleans facility. Without the technology, the company simply could not meet customer demands. As a result, SiloCaf is addressing these challenges by using information systems and computer technology.

Mossimo Toma is SiloCaf's systems and resources manager. He is responsible for overseeing the coffee-blending process. Each week, several million pounds of coffee beans come into SiloCaf's warehouse from all over the world. More than 2 million pounds of coffee are processed in every 12-hour shift. Once the coffee has been processed, it's loaded into standard one-pound bags, larger bulk packages, or into 2,000-pound super-sacks, and shipped to a coffee-roasting company. At any one time, SiloCaf has from 35 to 40 million pounds of coffee in its facility for processing. If you consider the price of a pound of coffee, SiloCaf has an extremely valuable resource in its possession. Actually, SiloCaf never owns the coffee. Rather, it's owned by the roasting company or the dealer who delivers the coffee to the roasting company.

All the mechanical parts in SiloCaf's New Orleans facility have been brought from Italy, where the company first developed its technology. Frederico Pacorini, the son of the founder and manager of the New Orleans facility, says that technology in a business like theirs is important because it allows them to make all the blends they need for the coffee roasters and to optimize the process of making the various coffee blends. SiloCaf's employers receive continually updated statistical reports for each one of the scales used to blend coffee. The reports enable them to check the consistency of the scales' performance, which is important for achieving the consistency that the coffee drinker wants. In addition, the technology also helps employees to oversee the cleaning, sorting, and bagging of raw coffee beans before they are shipped to roasters.

You might think that this high-tech control would be expensive. It's not! SiloCaf's solution to the blend-consistency challenge is to use technology that is relatively simple and inexpensive. In fact, the company's investment was a mere 1 percent of all plant investment expenditures.

Enhancing Your Communication Skills

1. "Controls have to be sophisticated for them to be effective." Present both sides of the argument (for and against) this statement. Conclude your presentation with a persuasive statement of why you agree or disagree.
2. Describe how you can use the concepts of control in your own personal life. Be specific in your examples and think in terms of the feedforward, concurrent, and feedback controls that you use for different parts of your life.
3. Visit the Society of Human Resource Management's Web site for HR News, <www.shrm.org/hrnews>, and research the latest information on privacy issues and employee monitoring. Describe the pros and cons of having employees monitored and the latest technology that is used to enhance monitoring activities for the organization.

CHAPTER 14

Operations and Value Chain Management

LEARNING OUTCOMES

After reading this chapter, I will be able to:

1. Define operations management and the transformation process.
2. Describe three reasons operations management is important to all managers.
3. Differentiate between a service and a manufacturing organization.
4. Define value chain management.
5. Explain the organizational and managerial requirements for value chain management.
6. Identify the benefits and obstacles to value change management.
7. Discuss technology's role in operations management.
8. Explain what is meant by the term *just-in-time management.*
9. Describe what is meant by the term *quality control.*
10. Explain the concept of project management.

Have you ever given any thought to what goes into a successful surgical procedure on the ears, nose, or throat (ENT)? If you're like most readers, unless you've experienced a medical problem like chronic sinusitis or ear infections, you probably haven't. But if you ever have to have surgery on your ears, nose, or throat, you'll be happy that Medtronic Xomed is in business. This Jacksonville, Florida, company is a leader in medical devices that are used in ENT surgery. What makes them unique in their industry is how they identified what they call their "value stream mapping" process.[1]

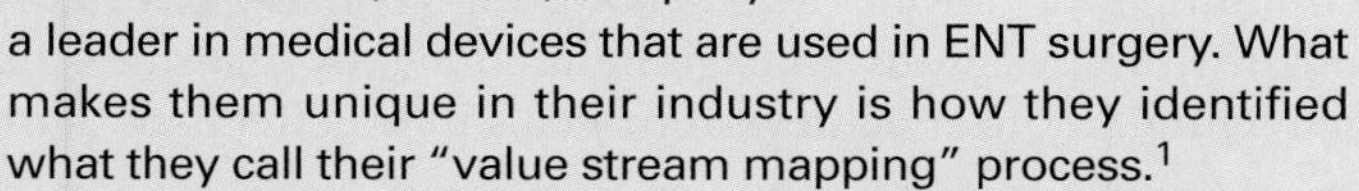

At Medtronic, value stream is defined as "the process of documenting the flow from supplier through production to delivery of products to doctors, hospitals, and surgery centers that are the plant's final customers." This process permits company officials, like Jon Swanson, the director of manufacturing (see photo), to understand in a systematic way what is happening in his firm's manufacturing process. Swanson is also able to determine which activities add value to the finished product, which ones don't and are wasteful, and how the entire process can be improved.

In the first three years since implementing their value stream process, Medtronic Xomed managers have seen significant improvements, For instance, production lead time for supplies has been cut from 253 to 129 days. Furthermore, the time between when an order is placed and when it's delivered to the customer has been reduced by more than 50 percent. Production costs have fallen by 38 percent, and employee productivity has increased by 40 percent. Additionally, the plant's operating efficiency is now approaching 99 percent—something unheard of just three short years ago. And all of these outcomes have come with 50 percent less plant space, brought about by a significant decrease in inventory.

How does Medtronic Xomed maintain these successes? According to Swanson, it's simple. You take care of the people who produce the products. Employees have become active participants in the value streaming process, and spend considerable time each year in training. With top management support and employees actively participating, value streaming has become ingrained in the Medtronic Xomed culture. And it helped the company's Jacksonville facility achieve the distinction of being chosen by *Industry Week* magazine as one of America's best plants, in 2002.

TECHNOLOGY HAS COMPLETELY CHANGED MEDTRONIC XOMED'S business, and it is having a similar impact on most organizations. In this chapter, we focus on the transformation process, productivity, and technology transfer. We want to look at the important role that value chain management and e-manufacturing are having on contemporary organizations. In doing so, we've entered the realm of operations management. We'll also take a look at one critical aspect of operations management with a discussion of project management.

THE IMPORTANCE OF OPERATIONS MANAGEMENT

The term **operation management** refers to the design, operation, and control of the transformation process that converts such resources as labor and raw materials into goods and services that are sold to customers.[2] Exhibit 14–1 portrays a simplified overview of the transformation process of creating value by converting inputs into outputs. The system takes inputs—people, technology, equipment, materials, and information—and transforms them through various processes, procedures, and work activities into finished goods and services. These processes flow throughout the organization. For example, department members in marketing, finance, research and development, human resources, and accounting convert inputs into outputs such as sales, increased market share, high rates of return on investments, new and innovative

operations management
The study and application of the transformation process

EXHIBIT 14–1
The Transformation Process

Inputs
- People
- Technology
- Capital
- Equipment
- Materials
- Information

Transformation Process

Outputs
- Goods
- Services

products, motivated and committed employees, and accounting reports. As a manager, you'll need to be familiar with operations management concepts, regardless of the area in which you're managing, in order achieve your goals more effectively and efficiently.

Why is operations management so important to organizations and managers? There are three reasons. First, it encompasses processes in all organizations—services as well as manufacturing.[3] Second, it's important in effectively and efficiently managing productivity. And third, it plays a strategic role in an organization's competitive success.

HOW DO SERVICE AND MANUFACTURING FIRMS DIFFER?

transformation process
The process through which an organization creates value by turning inputs (people, capital, equipment, materials) into outputs (goods or services)

manufacturing organization
Organization that produces physical goods

service organization
An organization that produces nonphysical outputs such as educational, medical, or transportation services

All organizations produce goods or services through the **transformation process**. Simply stated, every organization has an operations system that creates value by transforming inputs into finished goods and services outputs.

Every organization produces something. This is obvious with firms who manufacturer products like cars, cell phones, or food products. After all, **manufacturing organizations** produce physical goods. It's easy to see the operations management (transformation) process at work in these types of organizations because raw materials are turned into recognizable physical products. But that transformation process isn't as readily evident in **service organizations** because they produce nonphysical outputs in the form of services. For instance, hospitals provide medical and health care services that help people manage their personal health; taxi companies provide transportation services that move people from one location to another; cruise lines provide vacation and entertainment services; and residential plumbers and electricians ensure that we have electricity and running water where we live. All of these service organizations transform inputs into outputs. For example, look at your college. College administrators bring together inputs—instructors, books, academic journals, multimedia classrooms, and similar resources—to transform the "unenlightened" students into educated and skilled individuals.

The reason we're making this point is that the economies of developed countries have gone from being dominated by the creation and sales of manufactured goods to the creation and sales of services. In fact, most of the world's industrialized nations are predominantly service economies. In the United States, for example, nearly 80 percent of all private sector jobs are now in service industries.[4] Similar percentages can be found in the United Kingdom (73 percent), Australia (71 percent), Germany (68 percent), Mexico (68 percent), Canada (66 percent), and Japan (63 percent).[5]

HOW DO WE IMPROVE PRODUCTIVITY?

productivity
Outputs (labor + capital + materials)

Productivity is closely tied into the transformation process, and improving productivity has become a major goal in virtually every organization. By **productivity**, we mean the overall output of goods and services produced divided by the inputs needed to generate that output. For countries, high productivity can lead to economic growth and development. Employees can receive higher wages, and company profits can increase without causing inflation. For individual organizations, increased productivity lowers costs and allows firms to offer more competitive prices.

Increasing productivity is key to global competitiveness. For instance, a great deal of Japan's economic prosperity in the 1980s can be explained in terms of improved manufacturing productivity in business. As Japanese businesses became more competitive, U.S. businesses responded by making dramatic improvements to increase their efficiency.[6] For example, U.S. Technical Ceramics in Morgan Hill, California, invested in a diamond-coated cutting tool which resulted in a 300 percent increase in parts being produced. The cutting-tool investment also "prevented downtime," and significantly increased employee productivity.[7] Dispatch Industries in Minneapolis, Minnesota, designers and manufacturers of thermal processing equipment, has had similar outcomes, increasing productivity by 30 percent and enhancing product quality by increasing the efficiency of its workforce.[8]

What is a manufacturing organization? It is one in which physical goods are produced. At Ford's Volvo assembly plant, advanced robotics are spot-welding the frame of this soon-to-be Volvo automobile. When the assembly's complete, a physical good—in this case a vehicle—will be produced. The technology used in such plants has helped productivity to increase—but also has led to fewer employees. In the United States, for example, only about 20 percent of the jobs are in manufacturing organizations.

Organizations that hope to succeed globally are looking for ways to improve productivity. For example, McDonald's drastically reduced the amount of time it takes to cook its French fries—now only 65 seconds as compared to the 210 seconds it once took— saving time and other resources.[9] And Skoda Auto AS, the Czech car company owned by Germany's Volkswagen AS, improved its productivity through an intensive restructuring of its manufacturing process and now produces 500 cars per day, almost doubling the number it was capable of producing just a few years ago.[10]

Productivity is composite of people and operations variables. To improve productivity, managers must focus on both. W. Edwards Deming, a management consultant and quality expert (see Chapter 2), believed that managers, not workers, were the primary source of increased productivity. His 14 points for improving management's productivity reveals Deming's understanding of the interplay between people and operations. High productivity can't come solely from good "people management." The truly effective organization will maximize productivity by successfully integrating people into the overall operations system. For instance, Vicky Combs, vice president for Grove Madsen Industries in Las Vegas, a company that supplies electrical equipment to Las Vegas casinos, used to spend considerable time and energies discussing, both on the phone and in person, her designs with plant engineers from organizations who manufactured her products. Now, with the aid of her computer, she's able to "feed her design directly to the manufacturer's assembly line 2,050 miles away," and work begins on the assembly shortly after the request is received.[11]

WHAT STRATEGIC ROLE DOES OPERATIONS MANAGEMENT PLAY?

The era of modern manufacturing originated nearly a century ago in the United States, primarily in Detroit's automobile factories. Then the success that U.S. manufacturers experienced during World War II led manufacturing executives to naively believe that troublesome production problems had been conquered and required little managerial attention. So these executives focused on improving other functional areas such as finance and marketing. From the late 1940s through the mid-1970s, manufacturing activities in the United States were taken for granted, and to some extent, slighted. With an occasional exception (such as the defense and aerospace industries), corporate managers gave manufacturing little attention.

Meanwhile, as U.S. executives neglected the production side of their businesses, managers in Japan, Germany, and other countries took the opportunity to develop modern, computer-based, and technologically advanced facilities that fully integrated manufacturing into strategic planning decisions. The competitions' success realigned world manufacturing leadership. U.S. manufacturers discovered that foreign goods were being made not only less expensively but also with better quality. By the late 1970s, U.S. executives recognized that they were facing a true crisis, and responded. They heavily invested in improving manufacturing technology, increased the corporate authority and visibility of manufacturing executives, and began incorporating existing and future production requirements into the organization's overall strategic plan. Today, successful manufacturers recognize the crucial role that operations management plays as part of the overall organizational strategy to establish and maintain global leadership.

The strategic role that operations management plays in successful organizational performance can be seen clearly as more organizations move toward managing their operations from a value chain perspective.

VALUE CHAIN MANAGEMENT

It's 11:45 P.M. and you're listening to voice mail from your parents saying they want to buy you a computer for your birthday this year. They want you to order it so you have it to help you in your studies this semester. You go to the library and log on to Dell Computer's Web site and configure your dream machine that will serve even your most demanding computing needs for the remainder of your college years. You hit the order button and within three or four days, your computer is delivered to your dorm, built to your specifications, ready to set up and use immediately. Or consider Deere and Company's Horicon Works, which makes lawn and garden tractors. Managers set a goal of seven-day delivery for any tractor to any dealer in North America. Similarly, at Wainwright Industries in St. Peters, Missouri, employees produce stampings for a General Motors van assembly plant that's located six miles away. However, employees also operate a warehouse/just-in-time (JIT) sequencing facility dedicated to serving that GM customer. This warehouse handles some 1,500 parts made by 50 different suppliers, including Wainwright's products. Every seven minutes or so, a truck leaves the warehouse to make deliveries to the GM plant with the parts arranged in racks sequenced by color, size, and style as they will be needed on the van assembly line.[12]

How does value chain management affect the work at Wainwright Industries in St. Peters, Missouri? This plant, which produces stampings for a GM van assembly plant, also provides just-in-time parts warehousing for the GM facility. In doing so, Wainwright handles some 1,500 parts made by more than 50 different suppliers, making deliveries to GM about every 7 minutes—with parts arranged by color, size, and style as they are needed on the assembly line.

As these example show, closely integrated work activities among many different players are possible. They're being made possible through value chain management.[13] The concepts of value chain management are transforming operations management strategies and turning organizations around the world into the finely tuned models of efficiency and effectiveness, strategically positioned to exploit competitive opportunities as they arise.[14] In this section, we'll define value chain management, describe its goals, outline the requirements for successfully implementing it, explain its benefits, and briefly review the obstacles to its successful implementation.

WHAT IS VALUE CHAIN MANAGEMENT?

Years ago, John Deere and Company officials believed the most profitable way to do business was to build a significant number of lawn and garden tractors and ship them out to their dealers. While such processes helped Deere level out tractor production, it led to significant inventory and carrying costs. And not knowing what demand for their tractors they might face, delivery to dealers took nearly a month. By adopting a value chain management approach, Deere has decreased inventory by 50 percent, and increased delivery rates to dealers to 7 days or less.

Every organization needs customers if it's going to survive and prosper. Even not-for-profit organizations, like churches and government agencies, must have customers who use its services or purchase its products. Customers want some type of value from the goods and services they purchase, or use, and these end users determine what has value.[15] Organizations must provide that value to attract and keep customers. **Value** is the performance characteristics, features, and attributes, or any other aspects of goods and services for which customers are willing to give up resources (usually money). For example, when you purchase Britney Spears' new CD at Best Buy, a slice of pizza at a Sbarro's, or a haircut from your local hair salon, you're exchanging money in return for the value you desire from these products—providing music entertainment during your evening study time, alleviating your lunchtime hunger pangs, or looking professionally groomed for the job interview you have next week.

How is value provided to customers? Through the transformation of raw materials and other resources into some product or service that end users need or desire—in the form they want, when they want it. However, that seemingly simple act of turning a variety of resources into something that customers value and are willing to pay for involves a vast array of interrelated work activities performed by different participants. That is, this entire process involves the value chain. The **value chain** is the entire series of organizational work activities that add value at each step beginning with the processing of raw materials and ending with a finished product in the hands of end users. The value chain can encompass anything from the supplier's suppliers to the customer's customers.[16]

The concept of value chain was popularized by Michael Porter in his book *Competitive Advantage: Creating and Sustaining Superior Performance.*[17] He wanted managers to understand the sequence of organizational activities that created value for customers. Although he primarily focused on what was happening within a single organization, he did emphasize that managers must understand how their organization's value chain fits into the industry's overall creation of value. In some cases, that's difficult to do. For example, there are a number of things that organizations do that creates no value to the customer. It may please management or appease labor unions, but it doesn't do anything to make the customer happy. Consider, for instance, the movie industry. A lot of film producers spend significant amounts of money on things that do little to make a movie better. Money well spent in this case is that which is "up on the screen where customers can see it." The money spent, however, for catering, limo services, and private jets for stars doesn't add value because those things don't end up on the screen. As such, it doesn't create value. A similar claim could be made about management. As one noted management writer pointed out, "managers are not value-added. A customer never buys a product because of the caliber of management. Management is, by definition, indirect. So if possible, less is better. One of the goals of reengineering [work process engineering] is to minimize the necessary amount of management."[18]

value
The performance characteristics, features, and attributes, or any other aspects of goods and services for which customers are willing to give up resources

value chain
The entire series of organizational work activities that add value at each step beginning with the processing of raw materials and ending with a finished product in the hands of end users

Value chain management is the process of managing the entire sequence of integrated activities and information about product flows along the entire value chain. In contrast to **supply chain management**, which is internally oriented and focuses on the efficient flow of incoming materials to the organization, value chain management is externally oriented and focuses on both incoming materials and outgoing products and services. And although supply chain management is efficiency oriented (it's goal is to reduce costs and make the organization more productive), value chain management is effectiveness oriented and aims to create the highest value for customers.[19]

"The value chain is the entire series of organizational work activities that adds value to the customer."

value chain management
A method of improving the process of creating and transferring documents by automating the flow of information

supply chain management
Management of the facilities, functions, and activities involved in producing and delivering a product or service from suppliers to customers

WHAT ARE THE GOALS OF VALUE CHAIN MANAGEMENT?

Who has the power in the value chain? Is it the supplier providing needed resources and materials? After all, they have the ability to dictate prices and quality. Is it the manufacturer that assembles those resources into a valuable product or service? Their contribution in creating a product or service is quite obvious. Is it the distributor that makes sure the product or service is available where and when the customer needs it? Actually, it's none of these. In value chain management, ultimately customers are the ones with the power.[20] They're the ones who define what value is and how it's created and provided. Using value chain management, managers seek to find that unique combination in which customers are offered solutions that truly meet their needs and at a price that can't be matched by competitors.[21] For example, in an effort to better anticipate customer demand and replenish customer stocks, Shell Chemical Company developed a supplier inventory management order network. The software used in this network allows managers to track shipment status, calculate safety stock levels, and prepare resupply schedules.[22] This in turn allows Shell Chemical to provide its customers with the abilities to purchase goods when desired and to receive them immediately.

A good value chain is one in which a sequence of participants works together as a team, each adding some component of value such as faster assembly, more accurate information, or better customer response and service—the overall process.[23] The better the collaboration among the various chain participants, the better the customer solutions. When value is created for customers and their needs and desires are satisfied, everyone along the chain benefits. For example, at Iomega Corporation, a manufacturer of personal computer storage devices such as zip drives, managing the value chain started first with improved relationships with internal suppliers, then expanded out to external suppliers and customers. As the company's experience with value chain management intensified and improved, so did its connection to customers, which ultimately pays off for all its value chain partners.[24]

business model
A strategic design for how a company intends to profit from its broad array of strategies, processes, and activities

WHAT ARE THE VALUE CHAIN MANAGEMENT REQUIREMENTS?

The dynamic, competitive environment facing contemporary global organizations demands new solutions.[25] Understanding how and why value is determined by the marketplace has led some organizations to experiment with a new **business model**—that is, a strategic design for how a company intends to profit from its broad array of strategies, processes, and activities. For example, IKEA, the home furnishings manufacturer, transformed itself from a small, Swedish mail-order furniture operation into the world's largest retailer of home furnishings by reinventing the value chain in the home furnishings industry. The company offers customers well-designed products at substantially lower prices in return for the customers' willingness to take on certain key tasks traditionally done by manufacturers and retailers—such as getting the furniture home and assembling it.[26] The company's adoption of a new business model and willingness to abandon old methods and processes have worked well for IKEA.

So what does successful value chain management require? Exhibit 14–2 summarizes the six main requirements: coordination and collaboration, technology investment, organizational processes, leadership, employees/human

What was IKEA's new business model that helped it transform its home furnishings operations? IKEA management understood that customers wanted well-designed products at lower costs. To achieve this balance, IKEA managers recognized that the customer could do certain tasks typically done by the manufacturer—such things as transporting and assembling the furniture.

EXHIBIT 14–2

Six Requirements for Successful Value Chain Management

resources, and organizational culture and attitudes. Let's look at each of these elements more closely.

Coordination and collaboration For the value chain to achieve its goal of meeting and exceeding customers' needs and desires, comprehensive and seamless integration among all members of the chain is absolutely necessary. All partners in the value chain must identify things that they may not value but that customers do. And sharing information and being flexible as far as who in the value chain does what are important steps in building coordination and collaboration. This sharing of information and analysis requires open communication among the various value chain partners. For example, Furon company, a manufacturer of specialty polymer products, believes that better communication with customers and with suppliers has facilitated timely delivery of goods and services and opened up additional business opportunities for all its value chain partners.[27]

Technology investment Successful value chain management isn't possible without a significant investment in information technology. The payoff from this investment is that information technology can be used to restructure the value chain to better serve end users.[28] For example, Rollerblade, Inc., invested significant amounts of dollars in developing a Web site and used it to educate customers about its products. Although the company has chosen not to sell its products over the Web for fear of antagonizing its dealer network, managers remain flexible about the issue and would reconsider if they felt that value could be better delivered to customers by doing so.[29]

What types of technology are important? According to experts, the key tools include a supporting enterprise resource planning software (ERP) system that links all of an organization's activities, sophisticated work planning and scheduling software, customer relationship management systems, business intelligence capabilities, and e-business connections with trading network partners.[30] For instance, Dell Computer manages its supplier relationships almost exclusively online. The company has one Web site for customers and one for suppliers. The supplier Web site is the primary mode of communication between Dell and 33 of its largest suppliers. The company's investment in this type of information technology allows it to meet customers' needs in a way that competitors haven't been able to match.[31]

Organizational processes Value chain management radically changes **organizational processes**—that is, the way organizational work is done.[32] Managers must critically evaluate all organizational processes from beginning to end by looking at core competencies—the organization's unique skills, capabilities, and resources—to determine where value is being added. Non-value-adding activities should be eliminated. Questions

organizational processes
The way organizational work is done

such as "Where can internal knowledge be leveraged to improve flow of material and information,?" "How can we better configure our product to satisfy both customers and suppliers?" "How can the flow of material and information be improved?" and "How can we improve customer service?" should be asked for each process. For example when managers at Deere and Company implemented value chain management in its Worldwide Commercial and Consumer Equipment Division, a thorough process evaluation revealed that work activities needed to be better synchronized and interrelationships between multiple links in the value chain better managed. They changed numerous work processes division-wide in order to do this.[33]

We can identify three important conclusions about how organizational processes must change. First, better demand forecasting is necessary and possible because of closer ties with customers and suppliers. For example, in an effort to make sure that Listerine was on the store shelves when customers wanted it, Wal-Mart and Warner-Lambert's Consumer Group (now a division of Pfizer, Inc.) collaborated on improving product demand forecast information. Through their mutual efforts, the partners boosted Wal-Mart's sales of Listerine by $6.5 million. Customers also benefitted because they were able to purchase the product when and where they wanted it.

Second, selected functions may need to be done collaboratively with other partners in the value chain (see Ethical Dilemma in Management). This collaboration may even extend to sharing employees. For instance, Saint-Gobain Performance Plastics, headquartered in Northboro, Massachusetts, places its own employees in customer sites and brings employees of suppliers and customers to work on its premises. Saint-Gobain's CEO says this type of collaboration is essential if an organization wants to "go from being a mere component supplier to being a solutions provider."[34]

Finally, new measures are needed for evaluating the performance of various activities along the value chain. Because the goal in value chain management is meeting and exceeding customers' needs and desires, managers need a better picture of how well this value is being created and delivered to customers. For instance, when Nestlé USA implemented a value chain management approach, it redesigned its measurement system to focus on one consistent set of factors, including accuracy of demand forecasts and production plans, on-time delivery, and customer service levels. This allowed management to more quicky identify problems and take actions to resolve them.[35]

Ethical Dilemma in Management

The Bully Supplier

What happens when one partner in the value chain wields its power like a bully? That seems to be an apt description of what some large retailers are doing in the e-commerce arena.

Manufacturers are learning that big retailers—the companies they've always depended on to sell most of their products—can be e-commerce bullies. Instead of manufacturers using their Web sites to sell products and risking the wrath of their customers (that is, the retailers), most choose to refer potential online buyers to the "dealer nearest you." As a result, manufacturers are feeling the "squeeze" in letting retailers dictate some of their organizational practices. For example, Rubbermaid Home Products, a division of Newell Rubbermaid, Inc., up until mid-1999, sold a wide array of its products online. However, its Web site today has been stripped of its e-commerce capability because of a letter sent by Home Depot to most of its suppliers recommending that they not sell their products to consumers over the Web.[36]

Do you consider such "bully" behavior ethical? Why or why not? Would successful value chain management even be possible given bullying behavior by some organizations? Explain.

Leadership The importance of leadership of value to value chain management is plain and simple—successful value chain management isn't possible without strong and committed leadership.[37] From top organizational levels to lower levels, managers must support, facilitate, and promote the implementation and ongoing practice of value chain management. J. Michael Hagan, CEO of Furon Company, describes his role as follows: "Value is a mind-set that not only has to be driven from the top down, but also from the bottom up. Everyone has to be asking whether a given task adds value, and if it doesn't why do it."[38] Managers must make a serious commitment to identifying what value is, how that value can best be provided, and how successful those efforts have been. That type of organizational atmosphere or culture in which all efforts are focused on delivering superb customer value isn't possible without a serious commitment on the part of the organization's leaders.

Also, it's important that leaders outline expectations for what's involved in the organizations' pursuit of value chain management. Ideally, this should start with a vision or mission statement that expresses the organization's commitment to identifying, capturing, and providing the highest possible value to customers. For example, when American Standard Companies began its pursuit of value chain management, the CEO attended dozens of meetings across the country explaining the changing competitive environment and why the company needed to create better working relationships with its value chain partners.[39] Throughout the organization, then, managers should clarify expectations regarding each employee's role in the value chain. Being clear about expectations also extends to partners. For example, managers at American Standard identified clear requirements for suppliers and were prepared to drop any that couldn't meet them. The company was so serious about its expectations that it did cut hundreds of suppliers from air conditioning, bath and kitchen, and vehicle control systems businesses. The upside, though, was that those suppliers that met the expectations benefitted from more business and American Standard had partners who could deliver better value to customers.

Employees/human resources We know from our discussions of management theories and approaches throughout this textbook that employees are the organization's most important resource. So, not surprisingly, employees must play an important part in value chain management. Three main human resources requirements for value chain management are flexible approaches to job design, an effective hiring process, and ongoing training.

Flexibility is the key description of job design in a value chain management organization. Traditional functional job roles—such as marketing, sales, accounts payable, customer service representative, and so forth—are inadequate in a value chain management environment. Instead, jobs need to be designed around work processes that link all functions involved in creating and providing value to customers. This type of flexible job design supports the company's commitment to providing superb customer value.[40] In designing jobs for a value chain approach, the focus needs to be on how each activity performed by an employee can best contribute to the creation and delivery of customer value. That requires flexibility in what employees do and how they do it.

The fact that jobs in a value chain management organization must be flexible contributes to the second requirement: Flexible jobs require employees who are flexible. In a value chain organization, employees may be assigned to work teams that tackle a given process and are often asked to do different things on different days, depending on need. In an environment focusing on collaborative relationships that may change as customer needs change, employees' ability to be flexible is critical. Accordingly, the organization's hiring process must be designed to identify those employees who have the ability to quickly learn and adapt.

Finally, the need for flexibility also requires that there be a significant investment in continual and ongoing employee training. Whether the training involves learning how to use information technology software, how to improve the flow of materials throughout the chain, how to identify activities that add value, how to make better decisions faster, or how to improve any number of other potential work activities, managers must see to it that employees have the knowledge and tools they need to do their jobs. For example, at defense contractor Alenia Marconi Systems, based in Portsmouth, England, ongoing training is part of the company's commitment to efficiently and effectively meeting the needs of customers. Employees continually receive technical training as well as training in strategic issues including the importance of emphasizing people and customers, not just sales and profits.[41]

Organizational culture and attitudes The last requirement for value chain management is having a supportive organizational culture and attitudes. Those cultural attitudes include sharing, collaborating, openness, flexibility, mutual respect, and trust. And these attitutdes encompass not only the internal partners in the value chain but external partners as well. For instance, American Standard has chosen to practice these attitudes the old-fashioned way—with lots of face time and telephone calls. One of the company's suppliers, St. Louis–based White Rogers, described their relationship as follows: "Their goals are our goals, because both companies focus on growth. The keys to the relationship are mutual respect and open communications at all levels. No one has to go through a liaison. If our engineers need to talk to theirs, we just go right to the source."[42] However, as we mentioned earlier, Dell Computer has taken a completely different approach, as it works with its value chain partners almost exclusively through cyberspace.[43] Both approaches, however, reflect each company's commitment to developing long-lasting, mutually beneficial, and trusting relationships that best meet customers' needs.

WHAT ARE THE BENEFITS OF VALUE CHAIN MANAGEMENT?

Collaborating with external and internal partners takes significant investments in time, energy, and other resources, and a serious commitment by all chain partners. Yet, there are several significant benefits that organizations receive from value chain management. Exhibit 14–3 highlights the results of a survey of manufacturers that had embarked on value chain management initiatives and the benefits they perceived.[44] Let's take a look at what this exhibit is telling us.

EXHIBIT 14–3 Value Chain Benefits

Value chain survey respondents indicated the following are a "major benefit" from sharing information with partners:

	% OF COMPANIES IN EXCELLENT OR VERY GOOD CHAINS	% OF COMPANIES IN POOR CHAINS	% OF ALL COMPANIES
Increased sales	41%	14%	26%
Cost savings	62%	22%	40%
Increased market share	32%	12%	20%
Inventory reductions	51%	18%	35%
Improved quality	60%	28%	39%
Accelerated delivery times	54%	27%	40%
Improved logistics management	43%	15%	27%
Improved customer service	66%	22%	44%

Source: G. Taninecz, "Forging the Chain," *Industry Week*, May 15, 2000, p. 44.

Improved customer service was the major benefit that companies (44 percent) reported. Managing from a value chain perspective gives organizations a better handle on customer needs at all points along the chain. As value chain partners collaborate and optimize their processes to better meet customers' needs, customer service *should* improve.

The next two most cited benefits from value chain management reported by companies were cost savings and accelerated delivery times (40 percent). As inefficiencies and non-value-added activities are driven out of the value chain, companies will achieve cost savings in different work activities and areas. In addition, as value chain partners collaborate by sharing information and linking important activities, delivery times can be accelerated.

The next most important benefit cited by survey respondents was improved quality (39 percent). As work processes are evaluated for value-added potential, quality should be one of the measures used.

Inventory reductions were the next most important benefit identified by survey respondents (35 percent). Inventory storage—both raw materials and finished products—can represent a significant cost for organizations. Through close and careful collaboration among value chain partners, the flow of materials and information through the chain can be improved, leading to inventory reductions. For example, Straightline Source, a division of U.S. Steel, found that working with its customers to "manage the flow of steel into their operations to meet their production requirements on a just-in-time basis," helped its customers to reduce inventory levels as well as significantly decrease the potential for stock-outs.[45]

As Exhibit 14–3 shows, additional benefits of value chain mangement include improved logistics management, increased sales, and increased market share.

"The most cited benefits from value chain mangement were improved customer service, cost savings, and accelerated delivery times."

ARE THERE OBSTACLES TO VALUE CHAIN MANAGEMENT?

As desirable as the value chain management benefits can be, managers must deal with several obstacles in managing the value chain. The primary obstacles to having an efficient and effectively operating value chain management process include organizational barriers, cultural attitudes, required capabilities, and people (see Exhibit 14–4).

Organizational barriers Organizational barriers are among the most difficult obstacles managers handle. These barriers include refusal or reluctance to share information, unwillingness to accept change, and security issues. Without shared information, close coordination and collaboration are impossible. And the reluctance or refusal of employees to accept change can impede efforts

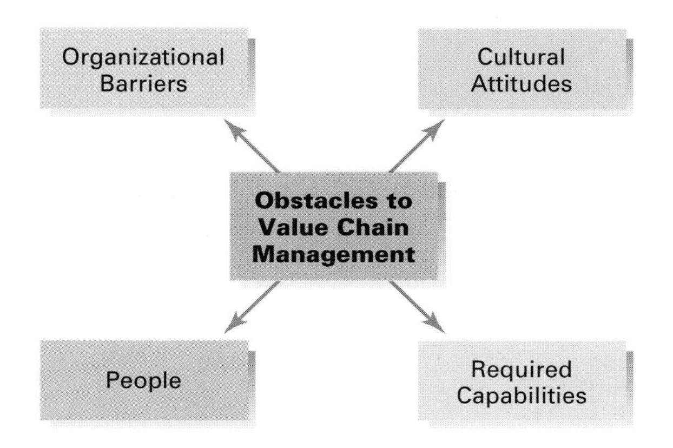

EXHIBIT 14–4
Obstacles to Successful Value Chain Management

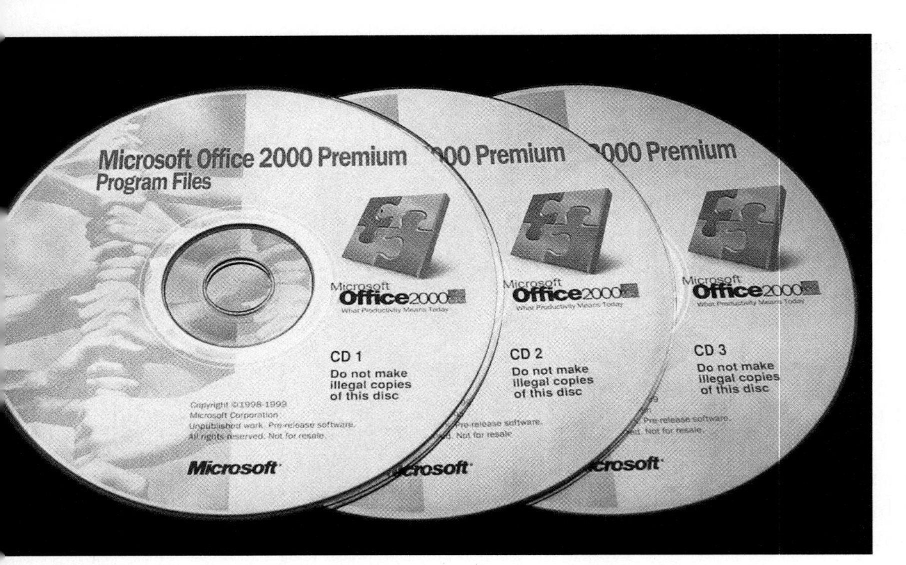

What is the value of Microsoft's Windows 2000 installation software CD? That depends on how you measure the value. Some might say that the value is the value placed on the CD itself—a few dollars. But the intellectual property contained on that CD is really where the value lies. And it's worth significantly more than "just the value of the CD."

toward successful implemenation of value chain management. Finally, because value chain management relies heavily on a substantial information technology infrastructure, system security and Internet security breaches are issues that need to be addressed. If an organization such as the Pentagon can have its Web site breached, then all organizations are vulnerable.[46]

Cultural attitudes An absence of cultural attitudes—especially trust and control—also can be an obstacle to value chain management. The trust issue is a critical one, from the perspective of both a lack of trust and too much trust. To be effective, partners in a value chain must trust each other. There must be mutual respect for, and honesty about, each partner's activities all along the chain. When that trust doesn't exist, the partners will be reluctant to share information, capabilities, and processes. But too much trust can also be a problem. For instance, many organizations are vulnerable to theft of **intellectual property**. This is proprietary information that's critical to a firms's efficient and effective operation. A study by the Amercian Society for Industrial Security found that those cultivating a trusting relationship with a company pose the most serious threat for intellectual property loss.[47] Although value chain partners need to trust each other, the potential for theft can be minimized by better understanding each other's operations and by being careful with proprietary intellectual property.

intellectual property
Proprietary information that is critical to a firm's efficient and effective operation

Another cultural attitude that can be an obstacle to successful value chain management is the belief that when an organization collaborates with external and internal partners, it no longer controls its own destiny. However, this needn't be the case. Even with the intense collaboration that must take place, organizations can still control critical decisions, including what customers value, how much they value what they desire, and what distribution channels are important.[48]

Required capabilities We know from our earlier discussions of requirements for successful implementation of value chain management that there are a number of capabilities that value chain partners must have—including extreme coordination and collaboration, the ability to configure products to satisfy customers and suppliers, and the ability to educate internal and external partners. These are essential to capturing and maximizing the value of the value chain, but often are difficult to achieve. Many of the companies we've described throughout this discussion—American Standard, Deere, and Dell—endured critical and often difficult self-evaluations of their capabilities and processes in order to become more effective and efficient at managing their value chains.

People The final obstacle to successful value chain management can be an organization's members. Without their unwavering commitment and willingness to make it work, value chain management isn't going to be successful. If employees refuse or are reluctant to be flexible, it will be difficult to make the necessary adjustments to changing situational demands. If they're not willing to be flexible in what work they do, and how and with whom they work, critical collaboration and cooperation throughout the value chain will be hard to achieve.

In addition, value chain management takes an incredible amount of time and energy on the part of an organization's employees. Managers must motivate those high levels of effort from employees.[49]

CONTEMPORARY ISSUES IN OPERATIONS MANAGEMENT

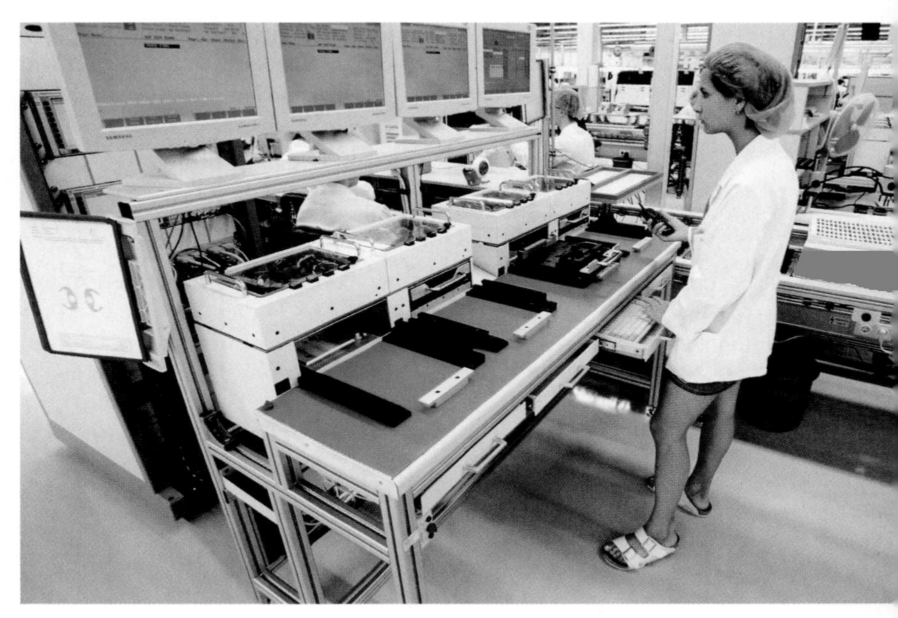

What does it take to make the value chain work properly? One of the more critical elements is the people. After all, it's the employees who do the work. But while significant energy is expended in hiring and training employees, one additional aspect is needed—employee motivation. This employee at Flextronics in Savar, Hungary, has all the up-to-date skills needed to do her job. But long work days, little time off, and excessive work loads created a motivation barrier. That was something that Flextronics managers didn't expect, but quickly addressed when the problem became known.

Capitalize on e-manufacturing technology. Make sure the parts arrive just in time. And make sure what is produced is of the highest quality. These issues are at the top of managers' list for improving operations management. While the previous discussion has focused on the external aspects, such as collaborating with supply chain partners, internal matters, too, must be addressed. Because managers consider them essential for making products and services competitive in global markets, we'll briefly look at each of these in this section.

Technology's role in e-manufacturing As we know from our previous discussion of value chain management, today's competitive marketplace has put a tremendous pressure on organizations to deliver products and services in a timely manner that customers value.[50] Smart companies are looking at ways to harness Web-based technology to improve operations management.[51] For example, Schneider Automation Inc. (a North Andover, Massachusetts–based division of the French multinational, Schneider Electric, SA) implemented its Transparent Factory Initiative. This is a framework for linking plant-floor automation with enterprise-wide business network systems. The company had millions of device sensors and actuators on its factory floors. But each of these ran on stand-alone software and did not connect to the factory's system network. Schneider managers saw a prime opportunity to capitalize on information technology solutions to manage its operations more effectively and efficiently by linking all of these components together.[52]

Although e-manufacturing is being driven by the recognition that the customer is king, managers still need to realize that the organization's production activities must be more responsive. For instance, operations managers need systems that can reveal available capacity, status of orders, and product quality while products are in the process of being manufactured—not just after the fact. To connect more closely with customers, operations across the enterprise, including manufacturing, must be synchronized. To avoid production and delivery bottlenecks, the manufacturing function must be a full partner in the entire e-business architecture.

What's making this type of extensive involvement and collaboration possible is **technology**. Technology is allowing manufacturing plants to control costs particularly in the areas of predictive maintenance, remote diagnostics, and utility cost savings. For instance, let's look at how e-manufacturing technology is affecting the equipment maintenance function. New generations of Internet-compatible equipment contain embedded Web servers that can communicate proactively. That is, if a piece of equipment breaks or reaches certain preset parameters that it's about to break, it can ask for help. This is similar to the "check engine" warning light on late-model cars. Such a warning tells you that something is amiss and needs attention. But technology can do more than sound an alarm or light up an indicator button. Some devices have the ability to initiate an e-mail or signal a pager at a supplier, the maintenance department, or contractor describing the specific problem and requesting parts and service. Such e-enabled maintenance control can prevent equipment breakdowns and subsequent production downtime.

technology
How an organization transforms its inputs into outputs

Just-in-time inventory practice Large companies such as Boeing, Toyota, and General Electric have billions of dollars tied up in inventories. It is not unusual for even small firms to have a million dollars or more tied up in inventories. So anything management can do to significantly reduce the size of its inventory will improve

just-in-time (JIT) inventory systems
Systems in which inventory items arrive when needed in the production process instead of being stored in stock

kanban
Japanese for card or signal; refers to a system of cards in shipping containers that uses the just-in-time concept (a card orders a shipment when a container is opened)

productivity. **Just-in-time (JIT)** inventory systems change the technology by which inventories are managed. Inventory items arrive when they are needed in the production process instead of being stored in stock. With JIT, the ultimate goal is to have only enough inventory on hand to complete the days's work—thereby reducing a company's lead time, inventory, and its associated costs.

In Japan, JIT systems are called **kanban**, a word that gets to the essence of the just-in-time concept.[53] Kanban is Japanese for card or signal. Japanese suppliers ship parts in containers. Each container has a card, or kanban, slipped into a side pocket. When a production worker at the manufacturing plant opens a container, he or she takes out the card and sends it back to the supplier. Receipt of the card initiates the shipping of a second container of parts that, ideally, reaches the production worker just as the last part in the first container is being used up. It was this simple "card" system that helped the Dana Corporation win the 2000 National Association of Manufacturers award for Workforce Excellence.[54] This system, coupled with a few other operations management projects is helping the company save nearly $300,000 annually. It's also credited with decreasing inventory costs by 20 percent and reducing parts-dispatching errors by more than 50 percent at Waterville TG, the Quebec-based manufacturer of sealing systems for automotive assembly lines.[55]

quality control
Ensuring that what is produced meets some preestablished standard

The ultimate goal of a JIT inventory system is to eliminate raw material inventories by coordinating production and supply deliveries precisely. When the system works as designed, it results in a number of positive benefits for a manufacturer: reduced inventories, reduced set-up time, better workflow, shorter manufacturing time, less space consumption, and even higher quality. Of course, suppliers who can be depended on to deliver quality materials on time must be found. Because there are no inventories, there is no slack in the system to compensate for defective materials or delays in shipments.

Continuous improvement and quality control We have discussed continuous improvement previously, describing it as a comprehensive, customer-focused program to continuously improve the quality of the organization's processes, products, and services. Quality improvement initiatives, however, aren't possible without having some way to monitor and evaluate their progress. Whether it involves standards for inventory control, defect rate raw materials procurement, or any other operations management area, controlling for quality is important. And it's the responsibility of every member of the organization.

How does quality control work? The premise behind quality control is to test a random selection of products for certain characteristics—for example, weight, strength, color, taste, finish, etc.—to ensure that it meets some preestablished standard.

Whereas continuous improvement programs emphasize actions to prevent mistakes, quality control emphasizes identifying mistakes that may have already occurred. What do we mean by **quality control**? It refers to monitoring quality—weight, strength, consistency, color, taste, reliability, finish, or any one of many characteristics—to ensure that it meets some preestablished standard. Quality control will probably be needed at one or more points, beginning with the receipt of inputs. It will continue with work in process and all steps up to the final product. Assessments at intermediate stages of the transformation process typically are part of quality control. Early detection of a defective part or process can save the cost of further work on the item.

Before implementing any quality control measures, managers need to ask whether they except to examine 100 percent of the items produced or only a sample. The inspection of every item makes sense if the cost of continuous evaluation is very low or if the consequences of a statistical error are very high (as in the manufacturing of a drug used in open-heart surgery). Statistical samples are usually less costly, and sometimes they're the only viable option, For example, if the quality test destroys the product as it does when testing flash bulbs, fireworks, or home pregnancy tests, then sampling has to be used.

MANAGING PROJECTS

project
One-time-only set of activities with a definite beginning and ending point in time

project management
Task of getting the activities done on time, within budget, and according to specifications

A **project** is a one-time-only set of activities with a definite beginning and ending point.[56] Projects vary in size and scope, from a NASA space shuttle launch to a wedding. **Project management** is the task of getting the activities done on time, within budget, and according to specifications.

Project management has actually been around for a long time in industries such as construction and movie making, but now it has expanded into almost every type of business, What explains the growing popularity of project management? It fits well with a dynamic environment and the need for flexibility and rapid response. Organizations are increasingly undertaking projects that are somewhat unusal or unique, have specific deadlines, contain complex interrelated tasks requiring specialized skills, and are temporary in nature. These types of projects don't lend themselves well to the standardized operating procedures that guide routine and continuous organizational activities.[57]

In the typical project, team members are temporarily assigned to and report to a project manager, who coordinates the project's activities with other departments ad reports directly to a senior executive. The project is temporary: It exists only long enough to complete its specific objectives. Then it's wound down and closed up; members move on to other projects, return to their permanent departments, or leave the organization.

WHAT ARE SOME POPULAR SCHEDULING TOOLS?

If you were to observe a group of supervisors or department managers for a few days, you would see them regularly detailing what activities have to be done, the order in which they are to be done, who is to do each, and when they are to be completed. The managers are doing what we call scheduling. The following discussion reviews some useful scheduling devices. How do you use a Gantt chart? The **Gantt chart** is a planning tool developed around the turn of the century by Henry Gantt (see History Module). The idea behind the Gantt chart is relatively simple. It is essentially a bar graph, with time on the horizontal axis and the activities to be scheduled on the vertical axis. The bars show output, both planned and actual, over a period of time. The Gantt chart visually shows when tasks are supposed to be done and compares the assigned date with the actual progress on each. This simple but important device allows managers to detail easily what has yet to be done to complete a job or project and to assess whether it is ahead of, behind, or on schedule.

Gantt chart
A planning tool that shows in bar graph form when tasks are supposed to be done and compares that with the actual progress on each

Exhibit 14–5 shows a Gantt chart that was developed for book production by a manager in a publishing firm. Time is expressed in months across the top of the

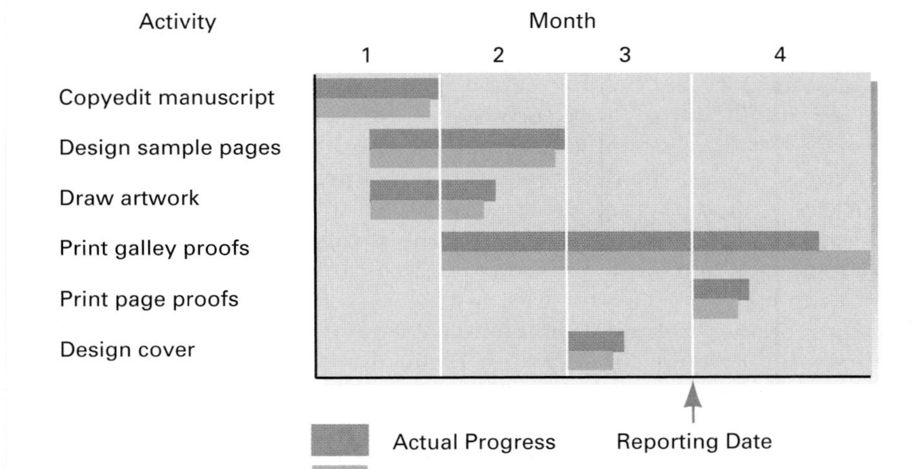

EXHIBIT 14–5
A Sample Gantt Chart

EXHIBIT 14–6
A Sample Load Chart

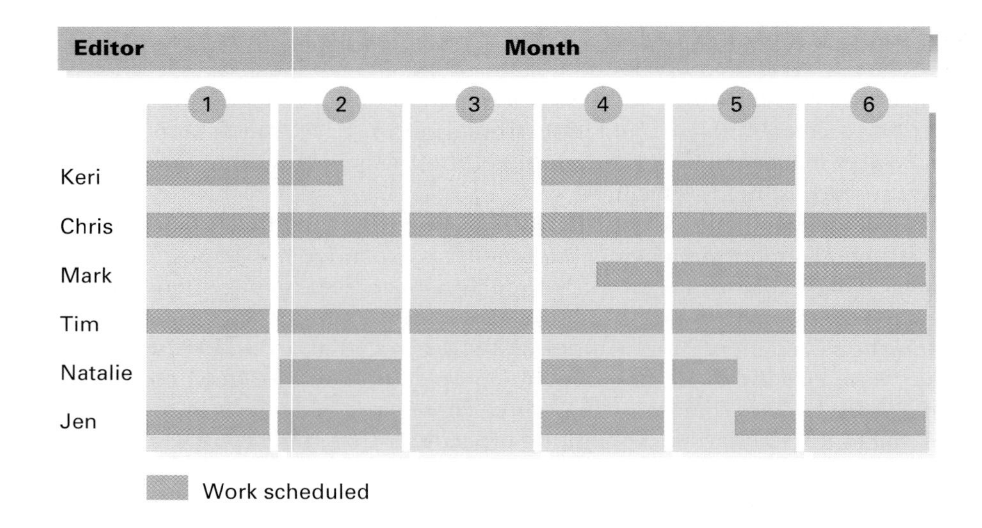

chart. Major activities are listed down the left side. The planning comes in deciding what activities need to be done to get the book finished, the order in which those activities need to be done, and the time that should be allocated to each activity. The gold shading represents actual progress made in completing each activity.

A Gantt chart, then, actually becomes a managerial control device as the manager looks for deviations from the plan. In this case, most activities were completed on time. However, if you look at the "print galley proofs" activity, you will notice that it actually took two weeks longer than planned to do this. Given this information, the manager might want to take some corrective action—either to make up the lost two weeks or to ensure that no further delays will occur. At this point, the manager can expect that the book will be published at least two weeks late if no corrective action is taken.

load chart
A modified version of a Gantt Chart, the load chart lists either whole departments or specific resources

A modified version of the Gantt chart is a **load chart**. Instead of listing activities on the vertical axis, load charts list either whole departments or specific resources. This information allows managers to plan and control for capacity utilization. In other words, load charts schedule capacity by work stations. For example, Exhibit 14–6 shows a load chart for six production editors at the same publishing firm. Each editor supervises the design and production of several books. By reviewing the load chart, the executive editor who supervises the six production editors can see who is free to take on a new book. If everyone is fully scheduled, the executive editor might decide not to accept any new projects, to accept some new projects and delay others, to ask the editors to work overtime, or to employ more production editors.

WHAT IS A PERT NETWORK ANALYSIS?

Gantt and load charts are helpful as long as the activities or projects being scheduled are few and independent of each other. But what if a manager had to plan a large project—such as a complex reorganization, the launching of a major cost-reduction campaign, or the development of a new product—that required coordinating inputs from marketing, production, and product design personnel? Such projects require coordinating hundreds or thousands of activities, some of which must be done simultaneously and some of which cannot begin until earlier activities have been completed. If you are constructing a shopping mall, you obviously cannot start erecting walls until the foundation has been laid. How, then, can you schedule such a complex project? You could use the program evaluation and review technique.

PERT network analysis
A flowchart-like diagram that depicts the sequence of activities needed to complete a project and the time or costs associated with each activity

The program evaluation and review technique—usually just called PERT, or the **PERT network analysis**—was originally developed in the late 1950s for coordinating the more than 3,000 contractors and agencies working on the Polaris submarine weapon system. This project was incredibly complicated, with hundreds of thousands of activities that had to be coordinated. PERT is reported to have cut two years off the completion date for the polaris project.

A PERT network is a flowchart-like diagram that depicts the sequence of activities needed to complete a project and the time or costs associated with each activity. With a PERT network, a project manager must think through what has to be done, determine which events depend on one another, and identify potential trouble spots (see Exhibit 14–7). PERT also makes it easy to compare the effects alternative actions will have on scheduling and costs. PERT allows managers to monitor a project's progress, identify possible bottlenecks, and shift resources as necessary to keep the project on schedule.

To understand how to construct a PERT network, you need to know three terms: events, activities, and critical path. Let us define these terms, outline the steps in the PERT process, and then develop an example. **Events** are end points that represent the completion of major activities. Sometimes called milestones, events indicate that something significant has happened (such as receipt of purchased items) or an important component is finished. In PERT, events represent a point in time. **Activities**, on the other hand, are the actions that take place. Each activity consumes time, as determined on the basis of the time or resources required to progress from one event to another. The **critical path** is the longest or most time-consuming sequence of events and activities required to complete the project in the shortest amount of time. Let's apply PERT to a construction manager's task of building a 6,500-square-foot custom home.

events
End points that represent the completion of major activities

activities
Actions that take place

critical path
The longest or most time-consuming sequence of events and activities required to complete a project in the shortest amount of time

As a construction manager, you recognize that time really is money in your business. Delays can turn a profitable job into a money loser. Accordingly, you must determine how long it will take to complete the house. You have carefully dissected the entire project into activities and events. Exhibit 14–8 outlines the major events in

EXHIBIT 14–7
Developing PERT Charts

Developing a PERT network requires the manager to identify all key activities needed to complete a project, rank them in order of dependence, and estimate each activity's completion time. This procedure can be translated into five specific steps:

1. Identify every significant activity that must be achieved for a project to be completed. The accomplishment of each activity results in a set of events or outcomes.
2. Ascertain the order in which these events must be completed.
3. Diagram the flow of activities from start to finish, identifying each activity and its relationship to all other activities. Use circles to indicate events and arrows to represent activities. The result is a flowchart diagram that we call the PERT network.
4. Compute a time estimate for completing each activity, using a weighted average that employs an optimistic time estimate (t_o) of how long the activity would take under ideal conditions, a most-likely estimate (t_m) of the time the activity normally should take, and a pessimistic estimate (t_p) that represents the time that an activity should take under the worst possible conditions. The formula for calculating the expected time (t_e) is then

$$t_e = \frac{t_o + 4t_m + t_p}{6}$$

5. Finally, using a network diagram that contains time estimates for each activity, the manager can determine a schedule for the start and finish dates of each activity and for the entire project. Any delays that occur along the critical path require the most attention because they delay the entire project. That is, the critical path has no slack in it; therefore, any delay along that path immediately translates into a delay in the final deadline for the completed project.

EXHIBIT 14–8

Major Activities in Building a Custom Home

EVENT	DESCRPTION	TIME (WEEKS)	PREDECESSOR ACTIVITY
A	Approve design and get permits	3	None
B	Perform excavation/lot clearing	1	A
C	Pour footers	1	B
D	Erect foundation walls	2	C
E	Frame house	4	D
F	Install windows	0.5	E
G	Shingle roof	0.5	E
H	Install brick front and siding	4	F,G
I	Install electrical, plumbing, and heating and A/C rough-ins	6	E
J	Install insulation	0.25	I
K	Install Sheetrock	2	J
L	Finish and sand Sheetrock	7	K
M	Install interior trim	2	L
N	Paint house (interior and exterior)	2	H, M
O	Install all cabinets	0.5	N
P	Install flooring	1	N
Q	Final touch-up and turn over house to homeowner	1	O, P

the construction project and your estimate of the expected time required to complete each activity. Exhibit 14–9 depicts the PERT network based on the data in Exhibit 14–8.

How Does PERT Operate? Your PERT network tells you that if everything goes as planned, it will take just over 32 weeks to build the house. This time is calculated by tracing the network's critical path: A B C D E F G H I J K L M N P Q. Any delay in completing the events along this path will delay the completion of the entire project. For example, if it took six weeks instead of four to frame the house (event E), the entire project would be delayed by two weeks (or the time beyond that expected). But a one-week delay for installing the brick (event H) would have little effect because that event is not on the critical path. By using PERT, the construction manager would know that no corrective action would be needed. Further delays in installing the brick, however, could present problems—for such delays may, in actuality, result in a new critical path. Now back to our original critical path dilemma.

Notice that the critical path passes through N, P, and Q. Our PERT chart (Exhibit 14–9) tells us that these three activities take four weeks. Wouldn't path N O Q be faster? Yes. The PERT network shows that it takes only 3.5 weeks to complete that path. So why isn't N O Q on the critical path? Because activity Q cannot begin until both activities O and P are completed. Although activity O takes half a week, activity P takes one full week. So, the earliest we can begin Q is after one week. What happens to the difference between the critical activity (activity P) time and the noncritical activity (activity O) time? The difference, in this case half a week, becomes slack time. **Slack time** is the time difference between the critical path and all other paths. What use is there for slack? If the project manager notices some slippage on a critical activity, perhaps slack time from a noncritical activity can be borrowed and temporarily assigned to work on the critical one.

slack time
The time difference between the critical path and all other paths

EXHIBIT 14–9 **A PERT Network for Building a Custom Home**

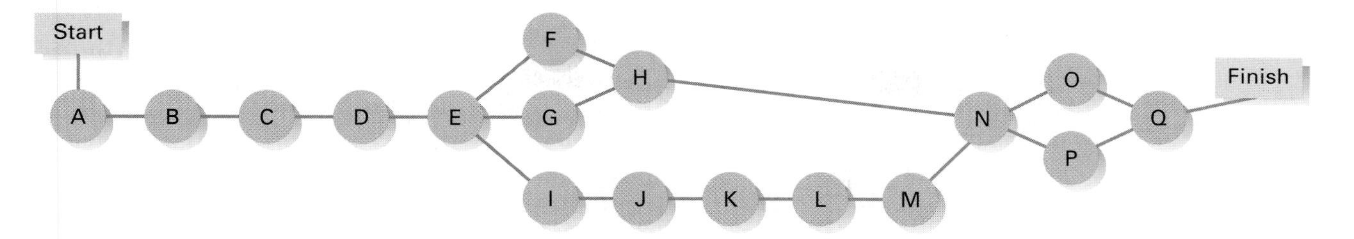

Isn't PERT both a planning and a control tool? Not only does PERT help us estimate the times associated with schelduling a project, it also give us clues about where our controls should be placed. Because any event on the critical path that is delayed will delay the overall project (making us not only late but probably also over budget), our attention needs to be focused on the critical activities at all times. For example, if activity F (installing windows) is delayed by a week because supplies have not arrived, that is not a major issue. It's not on the critical path. But if activity P (installing flooring) is delayed from one week to two weeks, the entire project will be delayed by one week. Consequently, anything that has the immediate potential for delaying a project (critical activities) must be monitored very closely.

Review, Comprehension, Application

CHAPTER SUMMARY

How will you know if you fulfilled the Learning Outcomes on page 400? You will have fulfilled the Learning Outcomes if you are able to:

1. **Define operations management and the transformation process.** Operations management refers to the design, operation, and control of the transformation process. The transformation process is the essence of operations management. Inputs (people, materials, etc.) are brought together and are transformed through the organization's work activities and processes into finished goods and services.
2. **Describe three important reasons operations management is important to all managers.** Operations management is important to organizations and its managers because it encompasses both services and manufacturing, it's important in effectively and efficiently managing productivity; and operations management plays a strategic role in an organization's competitive success.
3. **Differentiate between a service and a manufacturing organization.** A service organization is one that produces nonphysical outputs in the form of services. A manufacturing organization is one that produces a physical good. Other than the physical goods versus nonphysical goods elements, the operations management aspects of both organizations are similar.
4. **Define value chain management.** Value chain management is the process of managing the entire sequence of integrated activities and information about product flows along the entire value chain.
5. **Explain the organizational and managerial requirements for value chain management.** There are six main requirements for successful value chain management. These include: (1) coordination and collaboration among value chain partners, including sharing information and being flexible about who does what; (2) an investment in a technology infrastructure to support collaboration and sharing; (3) appropriate organizational processes (the ways organizational work is done), including better demand forecasting, collaborative work, and better metrics for evaluating the performance of various activities along the value chain; (4) strong and committed leadership; (5) appropriate employee approaches, including flexible job design, an effective hiring process, and ongoing training; and (6) supportive organizational culture and attitudes.

6. **Identify the benefits and obstacles to value change management.** Benefits from the value chain include improved customer service, cost savings, accelerated delivery times, improved quality, inventory reduction, improved logistics management, increased sales, and increased market share. Obstacles to successful implementation of value chain management include organizational barriers, cultural attitudes, required capabilities, and people.
7. **Discuss technology's role in operations management.** Organizations use technology to manage operations more effectively and efficiently by monitoring such information as available capacity, status of orders, and product quality; by connecting with customers and suppliers; and by controlling costs.
8. **Explain what is meant by the term just-in-time management.** Just-in-time inventory systems change the technology with which inventories are managed. Inventory items arrive when they are needed in the production process instead of being stored in stock.
9. **Describe what is meant by the term quality control.** Quality control refers to monitoring quality—weight, strength, consistency, color, taste, reliability, finish, or any one of myriad characteristics—to ensure that it meets some preestablished standard. Quality control continues throughout the production process such that early detection of a defective part or process can save the cost of further work on the item.
10. **Explain the concept of project management.** Project management involves getting a project's activities done on time, within budget, and accomplished to specifications. A project is a one-time only set of activities that has a definite beginning and ending point in time.

COMPANION WEBSITE

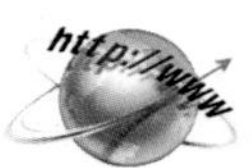

We invite you to visit the Robbins/DeCenzo companion Website at **www.prenhall.com/robbins** for this chapter's Internet resources, including an online study guide, Internet exercises, and "In the News" with full text articles provided by XanEdu.

READING FOR COMPREHENSION

1. What is operations management and how is it used in both manufacturing and service organizations?
2. What strategic role does operations management play?
3. What is the goal of value chain management?
4. How do leadership, employees, and organizational culture and attitudes contribute to value chain management?
5. What types of organizational benefits does value chain management provide?
6. List the essential steps in the project management process.

LINKING CONCEPTS TO PRACTICE

1. Explain why managing productivity is important in operations management.
2. Who has the power in the value chain? Explain your response.
3. How might operations management apply to other managerial functions besides control?
4. Which is more critical for success in organizations—continuous improvement or quality control? Support your position.
5. Describe how six sigma and ISO 9000 programs (see Chapter 3) are related to value chain management.

VIDEO CASE APPLICATION

Photon Dynamics, Inc.: High-Tech Quality Control for High-Tech Products

Manufacturers of printed circuit boards, automotive glass, and flat panel displays all turn to Photon Dynamics, Inc. to give them a competitive edge. When it comes to quality control, this company, based in San Jose, California, offers high-tech equipment that can test, repair, and inspect components right on the assembly line. Founded in 1986, the company has about 370 employees and sales officers and customer support services in Texas, China, The Netherlands, Taiwan, Canada, Korea, and Japan.[58]

"Our technology really replaces human inspection," says Vincent Solitto, president and CEO. The challenges of value chain management facing makers of cell phones, palm pilots, flat screen TV's, desktop monitors, and all the latest devices are often complex and always urgent. In response to their needs Photon Dynamics has incorporated artificial-intelligence techniques derived from military applications into its automated inspection systems. The technology can actually correct the production process in order to eliminate defects.

Originally this smart-vision technology was created to spot enemy planes and tanks. Photon Dynamics has commercialized it, helping clients like Sanmina to eliminate the need for highly skilled assembly line operations. This sophisticated machinery is capable of catching 100 percent of defects in printed circuit boards.[59] That equipment allowed us to automate the inspection process improving our yields, reducing our throughput, and improving our quality; which all put together resulted in a substantial reduction in our manufacturing cost for our customer base." says Randy Furr, president and CEO of Sanmina.

He is not the only client to realize the advantages of Photon Dynamics' technology. At Philips Electronics, managers are already planning for the next trend in flat panel display screens. Here is what Hafiz Haq, senior vice president, Philips Components, Philips Electronics, has to say: "We will need continuous addition of capacity of generation-five equipment, which is considered to be the largest glass available for the manufacturing of liquid-crystal displays (LCDs). Photo Dynamics makes equipment which will enable various sizes of displays to be tested very early in the life cycle."

Not only does the management team at Photon Dynamics understand their clients, it understands the pressures of the marketplace first hand. In 1997, when the notebook computer market took a dive, demand for Photon Dynamics' products fell and prices were cut in half. Just as the company's sales office opened in South Korea, the Asian economic crisis hit. By the spring of 1998, Photon Dynamics' stock had gone from nine dollars a share to two dollars a share. Solitto laid off seven of his one hundred employees and trimmed inventory. Three of his top executives quit. He found himself handling their jobs and overseeing manufacturing while still acting as CEO. Despite the departures, he motivated the remaining employees to work together to rebuild the business. Even though he delayed pay raises for everyone, he assured people he would protect their jobs. He held weekly meetings for everyone on the staff to answer questions and keep rumors from killing morale. He focused on three committed customers in Korea and Japan, fine-tuning products for them and establishing personal relationships with them. Solitto told himself, "If I ever get out of this, I will never be strapped for cash again."[60] To that end, he changed the business model of the company to encompass geographical diversification.

"I love the company. I love our technology. We're in a great position in several new markets," says Solitto today. Photon Dynamics has emerged, once again, as a high-tech leader. For more than a decade, the company has been developing cutting-edge systems to enable its clients around the world to sell a high-quality product back to their customers. After all, in value chain management, it is ultimately the customers who have the power.

Questions

1. What role does Photon Dynamics play in helping Sanmina to achieve quality control? Explain.
2. What role does Photon Dynamics play in value chain management at Philips Electronics? Discuss the importance of quality control.
3. Brett Hodess, senior semiconductor equipment analyst, Merrill Lynch, predicts that Photon Dynamics' orders will increase as more factory openings take place for the manufacture of flat panel displays. What effect, if any, might this have on the company's value chain management? Consider coordination, collaboration, technology investment, and organizational process requirements in your answer.
4. Explain how leadership, employees/human resources, and organizational culture and attitudes at Photon Dynamics might contribute to successful value chain management as the company prepares for the challenge of more orders to fill.

Management Workshop

Team Skill-Building Exercise

Designing Your University

Break into groups of four or five students. Your team's task is to assess how you believe technology will change the way your college disseminates information to students a decade from now. Specifically, what do you believe the typical college's teaching technologies will look like in the year 2010? To assist you in this activity, here are questions to consider:

1. Will there still be a need for a college campus spanning several hundred acres?
2. Do you believe every student will be required to have a laptop for classes?
3. Will there be computers in every classroom, coupled with hi-tech media technologies?
4. Do you believe students will be required to physically come to campus for their classes?
5. What role will distance learning and telecommuting have in classroom activities?

You have 30 minutes to discuss these issues and develop your responses. Appoint someone on your team to make a presentation to the class on your findings.

Developing Your Collaboration Skill

About the Skill

Collaboration is the teamwork, synergy, and cooperation used by individuals when they seek a common goal. Given that value chain management is contingent on all partners working together, collaboration is critically important to the process.

Steps in Practicing the Skill

1. **Look for common points of interest.** The best way to start working together in a collaborative fashion is to seek commonalities that exist among the parties. Common points of interest enable communications to be more effective.
2. **Listen to others.** Collaboration is a team effort. Everyone has valid points to offer, and each individual should have an opportunity to express his or her ideas.
3. **Check for understanding.** Make sure you understand what the other person is saying. Use feedback where necessary.
4. **Accept diversity.** Not everything in a collaborative effort will "go your way." Be willing to accept different ideas and different ways of doing things. Be open to these ideas, and the creativity that surrounds them.
5. **Seek additional information.** Ask individuals to provide additional information. Encourage others to talk and more fully explain suggestions. This brainstorming opportunity can assist in finding creative solutions.
6. **Don't become defensive.** Collaboration requires open communications. Discussions may focus on things you and others may not be doing, or need to do better. Don't take the constructive feedback as personal criticism. Focus on the topic being discussed, not on the person delivering the message. Recognize that you cannot always be right![61]

Practicing the Skill

Interview managers from three different organizations about how they collaborate with others. What specific tips have they discovered for effectively collaborating with others? What problems have they encountered when collaborating? How have they dealt with these problems?

Developing Your Diagnostic and Analytical Skills

Gummy Bears

Titus Lokananta represents an interesting global phenomenon. He's an Indonesian Cantonese with a German passport working for a Mexican company in the Czech Republic! As plant manager for the food company Grupo Industrial Bimbo SA, his plant, located in the Czech Republic, produces sweet, gooey gummy bears.[62]

Many Mexican multinationals are turning themselves into global powerhouses and fervently support globalization. Bimbo is a good example. In the late 1980s, a buyer for McDonald's stopped by the company's baked goods facilities in Mexico in search of a local supplier of buns. It only took a single bite for the buyer to reject Bimbo's product. That rejection inspired Bimbo's chairman to invest significant resources in baking a bun good enough for McDonald's. And it worked! Bimbo has progressed from being McDonald's preferred supplier to being its exclusive one. As McDonald's has moved into foreign markets, so has Bimbo. Today Bimbo's global workface of around 16,000 makes much of the sliced bread, snacks, and tortillas eaten by consumers in Latin America, as well as candy and cakes in over 16 countries. It's hoping that the gummy factory in the Czech Republic can become a strong contributor to the company's global business.

In 1995, Bimbo realized that its candy-making technology was obsolete. To improve it, it began to do contract work for Park Lane Confectionery of Germany. After learning all it could from the Germans, Bimbo bought Park Lane from its bankrupt owners. The company selected Lokananta, one of its liaisons at Park Lane, to run the Czech candy factory.

Lokananta hired back most of the factory's former workforce and went to work boosting productivity. One of his first managerial actions was persuading assembly line workers to take lunch breaks in shifts so production lines could run continuously. Now ready for the next challenge—boosting quality.

Questions

1. What do you believe Lokananta could do to implement a quality program in this plant?
2. Why do believe Lokananta wants everyone to take breaks at the same time? What effect do you believe this will have on employee productivity? Employee morale?
3. How could value chain management be used at Grupo Industrial Bimbo?

Enhancing Your Communication Skills

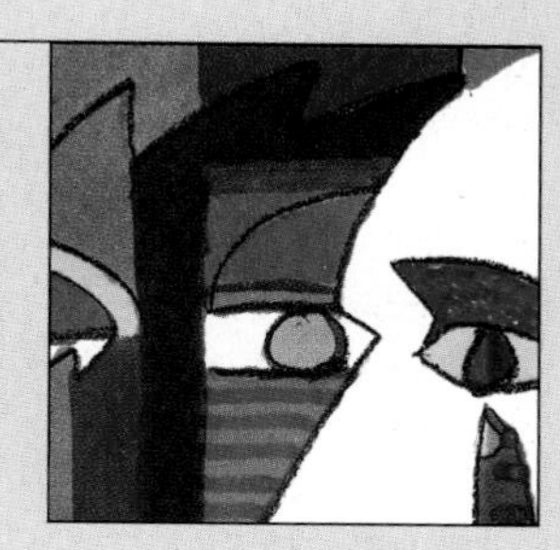

1. Discuss how you could use value chain management in your everyday life.
2. Choose a large organization you're interested in studying. Research this company to find out what types of operations management strategies it's using. Focus on describing what it's doing that's unusual or effective, or both.
3. Discuss the various types of enterprise resource planning software(ERP) commercially available to organizations. What do these software programs claim as their benefits? What is involved in implementing an ERP system in an organization?

Notes

Chapter 1

1. Opening vignette is based on C. Dawson, L. Armstrong, J. Muller, and K. Kerwin, "The Americanization of Toyota," *BusinessWeek* (April 15, 2002), pp. 52–54.
2. U. S. Census Bureau, *Statistical Abstract of the United States: 2001* (Washington, DC: Government Printing Office, 2001), p. 380.
3. Y. Hayashi, "Dodge and Cox Bets on International Fund," *Wall Street Journal* (December 31, 2001), p. C15.
4. S. DeCarlo, "Bragging Rights," *Forbes* (April 1, 2002), p. 40; and M. Veverka, "Plugged In: Capellas is the Key to Making H-P/Compaq Work," *Barron's* (March 25, 2002), p. T-3.
5. B. Leonard, "GM Drives HR to the Next Level," *HRMagazine* (March 2002), pp. 46–50.
6. H. Fayol, *Industrial and General Administration* (Paris: Dunod, 1916).
7. H. Koontz and C. O'Donnell, *Principles of Management: An Analysis of Managerial Functions* (New York: McGraw-Hill, 1955).
8. H. Mintzberg, *The Nature of Managerial Work* (New York: Harper & Row, 1973).
9. See, for example, T. Kellner, "One Man's Trash," *Forbes* (March 4, 2002), pp. 96–98.
10. Office of Advocacy, U.S. Small Business Administration, *Small Business Economic Indicators* (Washington, DC: Government Printing Office, 2001).
11. H. Etemad and Y. Lee, "Technological Capabilities and Industrial Concentrations in NICs and Industrialized Countries: Taiwanese SMEs versus South Korean Chaebols, *International Journal of Entrepreneurship and Innovation Management* (March 2001), p. 329.
12. J. Lee, "The Tao of Business," *Asian Business* (August 2001), pp. 48–49.
13. R. L. Katz, "Skills of an Effective Administrator," *Harvard Business Review*, September–October 1974, pp. 901–2.
14. See, for example, J. G. Harris, D. W. DeLong, and A. Donnellon, "Do You Have What It Takes to Be an E-manager?" *Strategy and Leadership* (August 2001), pp. 10–14; and C. Fletcher and C. Baldry, "A Study of Individual Differences and Self-Awareness in the Context of Multi-source Feedback," *Journal of Occupational and Organizational Psychology* (September 2000), pp. 303–19.
15. See, for example, R. D. Pathak, V. S. Dhar, D. M. Pestonjee, and N. Reddy, "Effect of Personal and Situational Variables on Managerial Effectiveness: An Empirical Study," *International Journal of Management* (March 2002), pp. 27–37; and "An Interview: Horace Deets of AARP," *Nonprofit Management and Leadership* (Fall 2001), pp. 87–94.
16. S. Agut and R. Grau, "Managerial Competency Needs and Training Requests: The Case of the Spanish Tourist Industry," *Human Resource Development Quarterly* (Spring 2002), pp. 31–51; and H. W. Goldstein, K. P. Yusko, and V. Nicolopoulos, "Exploring Black-White Subgroup Differences of Managerial Competencies," *Personnel Psychology* (Winter 2001), pp. 783–807.
17. "The High Performance Managerial Competencies," www.brefigroup.co.uk (April 15, 2002), pp. 1–2.
18. L. Lavelle, F. F. Jespersen, and M. Arndt, "Executive Pay," *BusinessWeek* (April 15, 2002), pp. 87–100.
19. Ibid., p. 81.
20. See, for example, S. Bates, "Piecing Together Executive Compensation," *HR Magazine* (May 2002), pp. 60–68.
21. For a discussion on one of these companies, see D. Brady, "The Education of Jeff Immelt," *BusinessWeek* (April 29, 2002), pp. 80–87.
22. See, for example, G. Colvin, "The Great CEO Pay Heist," *Fortune* (June 25, 2001), pp. 64–70; L. Lavelle, "The Artificial Sweetener in CEO Pay," *BusinessWeek* (March 26, 2001), p. 104; and L. Lavelle, "CEO Pay: The More Things Change...," *BusinessWeek* (October 16, 2000), p. 108.
23. L. Lavelle, "CEO Pay: Nothing Succeeds Like Failure," *BusinessWeek* (September 11, 2000), p. 48.
24. A. Tobias, "Are They Worth It?" *Parade Magazine* (March 3, 2002), p. 9.
25. www.masshightech.com, accessed December 21, 2002.
26. www. deploysolutions.com.
27. Case application is based on "Macronix 2001 Fourth Quarter Report," www.macronix.com (February 2, 2002), p. 1; C. Karmin, "Emerging Markets, Off to Strong Start This Year, May Enjoy Another Boost if Fed Cuts U.S. Rates," *Wall Street Journal* (January 31, 2001), p. C14; F. Hung, "Macronix Signs Five-year IC Deal with Tower—Flash Maker Will Receive Wafers While Tower Gains Asian Access," *Electronic Buyers' News* (August 21, 2001), p. 10; and W. Royal, "Made in Taiwan," *Industry Week* (February 15, 1999), pp. 68–70.

History Module

1 See, for example, R. Brillinger, "Management History's Broad Sweep and Putting People in Project Management," *Canadian HR Reporter* (August 14, 2000), p. 8.
2 A. Smith, *An Inquiry into the Nature and Causes of Wealth of Nations* (New York: Modern Library, 1937). Originally published in 1776.
3 F. W. Taylor, *The Principles of Scientific Management* (New York: Harper, 1911).
4 C. D. Wredge and R. M. Hodgetts, "Frederick W. Taylor's 1899 Pig Iron Observations: Examining Fact, Fiction, and Lessons for the New Millennium," *Academy of Management Journal* (December 2000), 1283–91; W. D. Eggers, "The Rise of eGov," *Wall Street Journal* (August 30, 2001), p. A-12; D. Organ, "The Great Restructuring of 1787–1789," *Business Horizons* (March/April 2001), pp. 1-2; J. R. Hough and M. A. White, "Using Stories to Create Change: The Object Lesson of Frederick Taylor's 'Pig-Tale'," *Journal of Management* (January 2001), pp. 585–600; and "PBS Film Examines the Life and Works of Frederick Taylor," *IIE Solutions* (April 2000), p. 13.
5 F. B. Gilbreth, *Motion Study* (New York: D. Van Nostrand, 1911); and F. B. Gilbreth and L. M. Gilbreth, *Fatigue Study* (New York: Sturgis and Walton, 1916).
6 Gilbreth, *Motion Study.*
7 H. Fayol, *Industrial and General Administration* (Paris: Dunod, 1916).
8 M. Weber, *The Theory of Social and Economic Organizations*, ed. T. Parsons, trans. A. M. Henderson and T. Parsons (New York: Free Press, 1947).
9 H. B. Jones, "Magic, Meaning and Leadership: Weber's Model and the Empirical Literature," *Human Relations* (June 2001), pp. 753–71.
10 R. A. Owen, *A New View of Society* (New York: E. Bliss and White, 1825).
11 H. Munsterberg, *Psychology and Industrial Efficiency* (Boston: Houghton Mifflin, 1913).
12 M. P. Follett, *The New State: Group Organization the Solution of Popular Government* (London: Longmans, Green, 1918).
13 C. I. Barnard, *The Functions of the Executive* (Cambridge, MA: Harvard University Press, 1938).
14 E. Mayo, *The Human Problems of an Industrial Civilization* (New York: Macmillan, 1933); and F. J. Roethlisberger and W. J. Dickson, *Management and the Worker* (Cambridge, MA: Harvard University Press, 1939).
15 Mayo, *The Human Problems of an Industrial Civilization.*

16 J. M. Bartunek and M. G. Seo, "Qualitative Research Can Add New Meanings to Quantitative Research," *Journal of Organizational Behavior* (March 2002), pp. 237–42.

17 D. Carnegie, *How to Win Friends and Influence People* (New York: Simon & Schuster, 1936).

18 A. Maslow, "*A Theory of Human Motivation," Psychological Review* (July 1943), pp. 370–96. See also Maslow, *Motivation and Personality* (New York: Harper & Row, 1954).

19 D. McGregor, *The Human Side of Enterprise* (New York: McGraw-Hill, 1960).

20 D. A. Wren, *The Evolution of Management Thought* (New York: John Wiley & Sons, 1993), p. 127.

21 C. C. Holt, "Learning How To Plan Production, Inventories, and Work Force," *Operations Research* (January/February 2002), pp. 96–99.

22 Ibid., p. 51.

23 R. Shirali, "Grasping the Guru," *Asian Business* (June 2000), p. 56.

24 See also, P. R. Carson, P. A. Lanier, and K. D. Carson, "A Historical Examination of Early 'Believers' in the Quality Management Movement: The Shaker Example," *TQM Magazine* (January 2000), p. 37.

25 H. Koontz, "The Management Theory Jungle," *Journal of the Academy of Management* (December 1961), pp. 174–88.

26 H. Koontz, ed., *Toward a Unified Theory of Management* (New York: McGraw-Hill, 1964).

27 R. L. Priem and J. Rosenstein, "Is Organization Theory Obvious to Practitioners? A Test of One Established Theory," *Organization Science* (September/October 2000), pp. 509–24.

28 See, for example, A. J. Shenhar, "One Size Does Not Fit All Projects: Exploring Classical Contingency Domains," *Management Science* (March 2001), pp. 394–414.

Chapter 2

1. L. Grant, "Container Store's Workers Huddle Up to Help You Out," *USA Today* (April 30, 2002), pp. B1–2.
2. Material in this section is adapted from S. D. Trujillo, "The Third Wave," *Executive Excellence* (January 2002), p. 19; R. W. Rice, "The World of Work in 2010," *CMA Management* (December 2001/January 2002), pp. 38–41; "The Third Wave of Revolution," *Monthly Labor Review* (February 2001), p. 59; and A. Toffler, *The Third Wave* (New York: Bantam Books, 1981).
3. B. Goldberg, "Contrarian Thoughts About Older Workers," *Financial Executive* (January/February 2002), p. 28; A. L. Liput, "Workforce 2000: Legal Issues in a Diverse Workforce," *The Human Resource Professional* (May/June 2000), pp. 19–21; J. Laabs, "Strategic HR Won't come Easily," *Workforce* (January 2000), pp. 52–56; and S. J. Wells, "A Female Executive Is Hard to Find," *HR Magazine* (June 2001), pp. 40–49.
4. M. Conlin, M. Mandel, M. Arndt, and W. Zellner, "Suddenly It's the Big Freeze," *BusinessWeek* (April 16, 2001), pp. 38–39; B. Blackstone and R. Christie, "Top Economic Index Declines as Growth Continues, Though at More Modest Pace," *Wall Street Journal* (March 23, 2001), p. A2; "Strategic Value Configuration Logics and the 'New' Economy; A Service Economy Revolution," *International Journal of Service Industry Management* (January 2001), p. 70; and "Time for Change," *Business Asia* (March 6, 2001), pp. 1–3.
5. B. B. Hughes, "Global Social Transformation: The Sweet Spot, the Steady Slog, and the Systemic Shift," *Economic Development and Cultural Change* (January 2001), pp. 423–58; C. R. Greer, "E-Voice: How Information Technology Is Shaping Life within Unions," *Journal of Labor Research* (Spring 2002), pp. 215–35; R. A. Miller, "The Four Horsemen of Downsizing and the Tower of Babel," *Journal of Business Ethics* (January 2001), pp. 147–51; and R. L. Schott, "The Origins of Bureaucracy: An Anthropological Perspective," *International Journal of Public Administration* (January 2000), pp. 53–78.
6. R. D. Hof and S. Hamm, "How E-Biz Rose, Fell, and Will Rise Again," *BusinessWeek* (May 13, 2002), pp. 64–72.
7. See, for example, "The Forbes 500s" *Forbes* (March 26, 2002), pp. 48–55.
8. C. Y. Chen, "The World's Most Admired Companies 2002," *Fortune* (March 4, 2002), pp. 91–93; N. Stein, "Global Most Admired: The World's Most Admired Companies," *Fortune* (October 2, 2000), p. 182; "Global Most Admired: And the Winners Are..." *Fortune* (October 2, 2000), pp. 191–94; and K. Capell, H. Dawley, W. Zellner, and K. N. Anhalt, "Wal-Mart's Not-So-Secret British Weapon," *BusinessWeek* (January 14, 2000), p. 132.
9. See Stephen P. Robbins and Mary Coulter, *Management*, 7th ed. (Upper Saddle River, NJ: Prentice Hall, 2001), p. 95.
10. P. Kenis and D. Knoke, "How Organizational Field Networks Shape Interorganizational Tie-formation Rates," *Academy of Management Review* (April 2002), pp. 275–93; K. Maddox, "IBM, Genesys Enter Alliance," *B to B* (April 8, 2002), p. 18; and S. Branch, "Brown-Forman, Bacardi Unit Form Strategic Alliance," *Wall Street Journal* (April 4, 2002), p. B2.
11. See, for instance, Whirlpool Corporation Worldwide, <www.whirlpool.com/whr/worldwide/index.htm>.
12. "Global Business: Getting the Frameworks Right," *Organization for Economic Cooperation and Development* (April 2000), p. 20.
13. R. D. Pathak, V. S. Chauhan, U. Dhar, D. M. Pestonjee, and N. Reddy, "Effect of Personal and Situational Variables on Managerial Effectiveness," *International Journal of Management* (March 2002), pp. 27–37; C. W. Holsapple and K. D. Joshi, "Organizational Knowledge Resources," *Decision Support Systems* (May 2001), pp. 39; and P. Lillrank and H. Kostama, "Product/Process Culture and Change Management in Complex Organizations," *International Journal of Technology Management* (January–March 2001), pp. 73–82.
14. G. Hofstede, *Cultures Consequences: International Differences in Work Related Values* (Beverly Hills, CA: Sage Publications, 1980), pp. 25–26; and Hofstede, "The Cultural Relativity of Organizational Practices and Theories," *Journal of International Business Studies* (Fall 1983), pp. 75–89.
15. For an interesting discussion of collectivism and teams, see C. Gomez, B. L Kirkman, and D. Shapiro, "The Impact of Collectivism and In-Group Membership on the Evaluation Generosity of Team Members," *Academy of Management Journal* (December 2000), pp. 1097–1106.
16. Hofstede called this dimension "masculinity versus femininity," but we've changed his terms because of their strong sexist connotation.
17. R. Bourke, "Configuring No Two Alike," *Computer-Aided Design* (November/December 2001), p. 38.
18. R. M. Kesner, "Running Information Services as a Business: Managing IS Commitments within the Enterprise," *Information Strategy* (Summer 2002), pp. 15–35.
19. T. George and E. Colkin, "Spring Cleaning for University Tech Offerings," *Information Week* (April 22, 2002), pp. 88–90.
20. H. F. Gale, Jr., T. R. Wojan, and J. C. Olmsted, "Skills, Flexible Manufacturing Technology, and Work Organization," *Industrial Relations* (January 2002), pp. 48–79.
21. E. Strout, "Launching an E-Business: A Survival Guide," *Sales & Marketing Management* (July 2000), pp. 90–92.
22. Cited in "World E-Commerce Growth," *Forrester* <www.forrester.com/ER/Press/ForrFind/0,1768,0,00.htm>; "ActivMedia Report: Real Numbers Behind 'Net Profits 2000," <www.activmediaresearch.com/real_numbers_2000.htm>.
23. R. D. Hof and S. Hamm, "How E-Biz Rose, Fell, and Will Rise Anew," *BusinessWeek* (May 13, 2002), pp. 64–72.
24. Ibid., p. 67.
25. "Telecommuting: Managing Off-Site Staff for Small Business," *The Canadian Manager* (Spring 2002), p. 27.
26. See, for example, Wayne F. Casio, "Managing a Virtual Workplace," *Academy of Management Executive* 14, no. 3 (March 2000), pp. 81–89.
27. J. Friedland and R. Wartzman, "A Look at Enron Figures Set to Testify Before Congress Today," *Wall Street Journal* (February 7,

2002), pp. A18; R. Karlgaard, "Enron End Notes," *Forbes* (March 4, 2002), p. 37; and R. Karlgaard, "My Ken Lay," *Forbes* (April 1, 2002), p. 35.
28. S. C. Awe, "Good Work: When Excellence and Ethics Meet," *Library Journal* (March 15, 2002), p. 42.
29. J. Useem, "Fortune 5 Hundred: No 2-Exxon's African Adventure," *Fortune* (April 15, 2002), pp. 102–14; and J. Rossant, J. Ewing, and B. Brenner, "The Corporate Cleanup Goes Global," *BusinessWeek* (May 6, 2002), pp. 80–82.
30. D. Dearlove and S. Crainer, "Enterprise Goes Social," *Chief Executive* (March 2002), p. 18; and "Bronze Winner: Ben & Jerry's Citizen Cool," *Brandweek* (March 18, 2002), p. R-24.
31. B. W. Husted, "A Contingency Theory of Corporate Social Performance," *Business and Society* (March 2000), pp. 24–48.
32. See, for instance, N. A. Ibrahim, J. P. Angelidis, and D. P. Howell, "The Corporate Social Responsiveness Orientation of Hospital Directors: Does Occupational Background Make a Difference?" *Health Care Management Review* (Spring 2000), pp. 85–92.
33. W. Acar, K. E. Aupprele, and R. M. Lowy, "An Empirical Exploration of Measures of Social Responsibility Across the Spectrum of Organizational Types," *International Journal of Organizational Analysis* (January 2001), pp. 26–57.
34. See P. Paul, "Corporate Responsibility," *American Demographics* (May 2002), p. 24.
35. Also see, J. A. Byrne, L. Lavelle, N. Byrnes, and M. Vickers, "How to Fix Corporate Governance," *BusinessWeek* (May 6, 2002), pp. 69–78.
36. S. A. DiPiazza, "Ethics in Action," *Executive Excellence* (January 2002), pp. 15–16.
37. "Coming Clean," *Money* (May 2002), p. 33.
38. J. Liedtka, "Ethics and the New Economy," *Business and Society Review* (Spring 2002), p. 1.
39. "Only in America: Starwood Hotels Survey," *Readers Digest* (September 2002), p. 19.
40. B. R. Gaumnitz and J. C. Lere, "Contents of Codes of Ethics of Professional Business Organizations in the United States," *Journal of Business Ethics* (January 2002), pp. 35–49.
41. M. K. Zachary, "Protection for the Ethical Employee–Part 1, Common Law Wrongful Discharge Claims," *Supervision* (May 2002), pp. 23–26; and C. Hymowitz, "In the Lead: Managers Must Respond to Employee Concerns About Honest Business," *Wall Street Journal* (February 19, 2002), p. B1.
42. S. P. Sethi, "Standards for Corporate Conduct in the International Arena: Challenges and Opportunities for Multinational Corporations," *Business and Society Review* (Spring 2002), pp. 20–40; N. Asgary and M. C. Mitschow, "Toward a Model for International Business Ethics," *Journal of Business Ethics* (March 2002), pp. 239–46; R. Berenbeim, "Global Ethics," *Executive Excellence* (May 2000), p. 7; and W. Royal, "Ethical Dilemmas," *Industry Week* (May 1, 2000), p. 8.
43. T. F. Shea, "Employees' Report Car on Supervisors' Ethics: No Improvement," *HR Magazine* (April 2002), p. 29.
44. See also, A. G. Peace, J. Weber, K. S. Hartzel, and J. Nightingale, "Ethical Issues in eBusiness: A Proposal for Creating the eBusiness Principles," *Business and Society Review* (Spring 2002), pp. 41–60.
45. This section is adapted from Stephen P. Robbins and Mary Coulter, *Management*, 7th ed. (Upper Saddle River, NJ: Prentice Hall, 2001), pp. 144–45.
46. M. Robinson, "The Ten Commandments of Intrapreneurs," *New Zealand Management* (December 2001), pp. 95–98.
47. J. Fox, "America's Most Admired: What's So Great About GE?" *Fortune* (March 4, 2002), pp. 64–67.
48. J. S. Hornsby, D. F. Kuratko, and S. A. Zahara, "Middle Managers' Perception of the Internal Environment for Corporate Entrepreneurship: Assessing a Measurement Scale," *Journal of Business Venturing* (May 2002), pp. 253–73; and F. Batten, "Out of the Blue and into the Black," *Harvard Business Review*, April 2002, pp. 112–19.
49. P. E. Drucker, *Innovation and Entrepreneurship* (New York: Harper & Row, 1985).
50. O. C. Richard, "Racial Diversity, Business Strategy, and Firm Performance: A Resource-Based View," *Academy of Management Journal* (April 2000), pp. 164–77.
51. A. S. Wellner, "Taping a Silver Mine," *HR Magazine* (March 2002), pp. 26–32; and Neal Thompson, "American Work Force Is Seeing More Gray," *Baltimore Sun* (October 8, 2000), pp. A1, A13.
52. B. Leonard, "Not All Training Programs Have Felt the Full Squeeze of Corporate Belt-Tightening," *HR Magazine* (April 2002), p. 25; and R. Koonce, "Redefining Diversity," *Training and Development* (December 2001), pp. 22–33.
53. B. Benham, "Get Your Share," *Working Woman* (April 2001), pp. 54–58.
54. See also, L. Grensing-Pophal, "A Balancing Act on Diversity Audits," *HR Magazine* (November 2001), pp. 87–95; and T. Minton-Eversole, "Coke Also Reviews Benefits Program During Its Diversity Analysis," *HR News* (December 2001), p. 4.
55. L. Grensing-Pophal, "Reaching for Diversity," *HR Magazine* (May 2002), pp. 53–56.
56. See, for instance, "Friends of the Family: 100 Best Companies for Working Mothers—16th Annual Survey," *Working Mother* (October 2001), pp. 60–148; and S. D. Brown, "Head of the Class," *Black Enterprise* (May 2002), pp. 39–44.
57. See, for instance, P. Cappelli, J. Constantine, and C. Chadwick, "It Pays to Value Family: Work and Family Trade-Offs Reconsidered," *Industrial Relations* (April 2000), pp. 175–98; M. A. Verespej, "Balancing Act," *Industry Week* (May 15, 2000), pp. 81–85; and R. C. Barnett and D. T. Hall, "How to Use Reduced Hours to Win the War for Talent," *Organizational Dynamics* (March 2001), p. 42.
58. M. Conlin, "The New Debate over Working Moms," *BusinessWeek* (November 18, 2000), pp. 102–3.
59. "The New World of Work: Flexibility Is the Watchword," *BusinessWeek* (January 10, 2000), p. 36.
60. See, for example, "U. S. Employers Polish Image to Woo a Demanding New Generation," *Manpower Argus* (February 2000), p. 2.
61. L. L. Martins, K. B. Eddleston, and J. F. Veiga, "Moderators of the Relationship Between Work-Family Conflict and Career Satisfaction," *Academy of Management Journal* (May 2002), pp. 399–409.
62. N. Grossman, "Shrinking the Work Force in an Economic Slowdown," *Compensation and Benefits Management* (Spring 2002), pp. 12–23.
63. E. Florian, "Layoff Count," *Fortune* (March 18, 2002), p. 32; and M. Murphy, "Ciena Cuts 22% of Its Work Force in an Effort to Realign the Company," *Wall Street Journal* (March 27, 2002), p. B3.
64. "Human Resources," *Business Asia* (March 11, 2002), pp. 6–8; D. Michaels, "British Airways to Cut More Jobs and Routes to Address Losses," *Wall Street Journal* (February 14, 2002), p. A15; and T. Waddel, "Contracting Out–Is In," *New Zealand Management* (November 2000), p. 92.
65. L. M. Gossett, "The Long-Term Impact of Short-Term Workers," *Management Communication Quarterly* (August 2001), pp. 115–20.
66. C. Serant, "Solectron Opts to Lease Lucent Plant in Three-year, $2B Outsourcing Deal," *EBN* (April 1, 2002), p. 10.
67. See K. J. Bannan, "Breakaway (A Special Report)—Getting Help—Together: By Bundling Job-Recruiting Efforts, Small Firms Seek Attention—and Leverage," *Wall Street Journal* (April 23, 2001), p. A12.
68. U. S. Bureau of Labor Statistics, "Contingent and Alternative Employment Arrangements" (Washington, DC: Government Printing Office, 2001), p. 1.
69. D. Eisenberg, "The Coming Job Boom," *Time* (May 6, 2002), pp. 40–44.
70. Ibid., p. 41.
71. D. Eisenberg, "Firms Brace for Worker Shortage," *Time* (May 6, 2002), p. 44.
72. A. J. Rucci, S. P. Kirn, and R .T. Quinn, "The Employee Customer Profit Chain at Sears," *Harvard Business Review* January–February 1998, pp. 83–97.

73. S. Daley, "A Spy's Advice to French Retailers: Politeness Pays," *New York Times*, (December 26, 2000), p. A4.
74. See, for instance, B. Schneider, D. E. Bowen, M. G. Ehrhart, and K. M. Holcombe, "The Climate for Service: Evolution of a Construct," in N. M. Ashkanasy, C. P. M. Wilderom, and M. F. Peterson (eds.), *Handbook of Organizational Culture and Climate* (Thousand Oaks, CA: Sage, 2000), pp. 21–36; M. D. Hartline, J. G. Maxham III, and D. O. McKee, "Corridors of Influence in the Dissemination of Customer-Oriented Strategy to Customer Contact Service Employees," *Journal of Marketing* (April 2000), pp. 35–50; and L. A. Bettencourt, K. P. Gwinner, and M. L. Meuter, "A Comparison of Attitude 'Personality' and Knowledge Predictors of Service-Oriented Organizational Citizenship Behaviors," *Journal of Applied Psychology* (February 2001), pp. 29–41.
75. A. Gabor, "He Made America Think About Quality," *Fortune* (October 30, 2000), pp. 292–93.
76. See, for example, J. McElroy, "Six Lessons for Ford," *Ward's Auto World* (December 2001), p. 17.
77. "Continuous Improvement: Ten Essential Criteria," *Measuring Business Excellence* (January 2002), p. 49.
78. "Winning with Kaizen," *IIE Solutions* (April 2002), p. 10.
79. S. Freeman, "Chrysler to Alter Jeep Suspension after Reviewers Question Safety," *Wall Street Journal* (April 17, 2002), p. D8.
80. J. A. M. Coyle-Shapiro, "Changing Employee Attitudes: The Independent Effects of TQM and Profit Sharing on Continuous Improvement Orientation," *Journal of Applied Behavioral Science* (March 2002), pp. 57–77.
81. M. Budman, "Jim Champy Puts His 'X' on Reengineering," *Across the Board* (March/April 2002), pp. 15–16.
82. See, for example, R. McAdam, "Large Scale Innovation—Reengineering Methodology in SMEs: Positivistic and Phenomenological Approaches," *International Small Business Journal* (February 2002), pp. 33–52; and T. Kontzer, "A Better Way to Manage Rules," *Information Week* (April 29, 2002), p. 48.
83. www.beyondcomponents.com.
84. "Petopia.com Withdraws Its Plans to Go Public, Sells Its Assets to Petco," *Wall Street Journal* (February 5, 2001), p. B2; and L. G. Crovits, "How to Think About Dot-Coms Coming Down," *Wall Street Journal* (December 21, 2000), p. A16.

Chapter 3

1. Opening vignette based on D. Fenn, "A Bigger Wheel," *Inc.* (November 2000), pp. 78–88.
2. Material in this section is based on C. Gilbert and J. L. Bower, "Disruptive Change: When Trying Harder Is Part of the Problem," *Harvard Business Review*, May 2002, pp. 94–101; R. J. Herbold, "Inside Microsoft: Balancing Creativity and Discipline," *Harvard Business Review*, January 2002, pp. 72–79; B. Von Oetinger, "The Renaissance Strategist," *The Journal of Business Strategy* (November/December 2001), pp. 38–42; T. K. Das and B. S. Teng, "Inabilities of Strategic Alliances: An Internal Tensions Perspective," *Organizational Science* (January/February 2000), pp. 77–101; P. D. Cameron, "Life After Planning," *CMA Management* (June 2001), pp. 14–17; H. Mintzberg, *The Rise and Fall of Strategic Planning* (New York: Free Press, 1994); and D. Miller, "The Architecture of Simplicity," *Academy of Management Review* (January 1993), pp. 116–38.
3. See, for example, J. A. Pearce II, K. K. Robbins, and R. B. Robinson Jr., "The Impact of Grand Strategy and Planning Formality on Financial Performance," *Strategic Management Journal* (March/April 1987), pp. 125–34; L. C. Rhyne, "Contrasting Planning Systems in High, Medium, and Low Performance Companies," *Journal of Management Studies* (July 1987), pp. 363–85; J. A. Pearce II, E. B. Freeman, and R. B. Robinson Jr., "The Tenuous Link Between Formal Strategic Planning and Financial Performance," *Academy of Management Review* (October 1987), pp. 658–75; D. K. Sinha, "The Contribution of Formal Planning to Decisions," *Strategic Management Journal* (October 1990), pp. 479–92; and C. C. Miller and L. B. Cardinal, "Strategic Planning and Firm Performance: A Synthesis of More Than Two Decades of Research," *Academy of Management Journal* (March 1994), pp. 1649–85.
4. M. M. Buechner, "Recharging Sears," *Time* (May 27, 2002), pp. 50–52; and L. Grant and J. Swartz, "A Really Good Fit," *USA Today* (May 14, 2002), p. B1.
5. E. A. Locke, "Toward a Theory of Task Motivation and Incentives," *Organizational Behavior and Human Performance* (May 1968), pp. 157–89.
6. The concept of management by objectives is generally attributed to Peter F. Drucker, *The Practice of Management* (New York: Harper & Row, 1954). See also J. F. Castellano and H. A. Roehm, "The Problem with Managing by Objectives and Results," *Quality Progress* (March 2001), pp. 39–46; J. Loehr and T. Schwartz, "The Making of a Corporate Athlete," *Harvard Business Review* January 2001, pp. 120–28; and A. J. Vogl, "Drucker, of Course," *Across the Board"* (November/December 2000), p. 1.
7. M. Green, J. Garrity, and B. Lyons, "Pitney Bowes Calls for New Metrics," *Strategic Finance* (May 2002), pp. 30–35.
8. See, for example, E. A. Locke, "Toward a Theory of Task Motivation and Incentives," *Organizational Behavior and Human Performance,* (May 1968), pp. 157–89; E. A. Locke, K. N. Shaw, L. M. Saari, and G. P. Latham, Goal Setting and Task Performance: 1969–1980, *Psychological Bulletin* (July 1981), pp. 12–52; E. A. Locke and G. P. Latham, *A Theory of Goal Setting and Task Performance* (Upper Saddle River, NJ: Prentice Hall, 1990); P. Ward and M. Carnes, "Effects of Posting Self-Set Goals on Collegiate Football Players' Skill Execution During Practice and Games," *Journal of Applied Behavioral Analysis* (Spring 2002), pp. 1–12; D. W. Ray, "Productivity and Profitability," *Executive Excellence* (October 2001), p. 14; and D. Archer, "Evaluating Your Managed System," *CMA Management* (January 2000), pp. 12–14.
9. T. D. Ludwig and E. S. Geller, "Intervening to Improve the Safety of Delivery Drivers: A Systematic Behavioral Approach," *Journal of Organizational Behavior Management* (April 4, 2000), pp. 11–24; P. Latham and L. M. Saari, "The Effects of Holding Goal Difficulty Constant on Assigned and Participatively Set Goals," *Academy of Management Journal* (March 1979), pp. 163–68; M. Erez, P. C. Earley, and C. L. Hulin, "The Impact of Participation on Goal Acceptance and Performance: A Two Step Model," *Academy of Management Journal* (March 1985), pp. 50–66; and G. P. Latham, M. Erez, and E. A. Locke, "Resolving Scientific Disputes by the Joint Design of Crucial Experiments by the Antagonists: Application to the Erez Latham Dispute Regarding Participation in Goal Setting," *Journal of Applied Psychology* (November 1988), pp. 753–72.
10. See, for instance, J. R. Crow, "Crashing with the Nose Up: Building a Cooperative Work Environment," *Journal for Quality and Participation* (Spring 2002), pp. 45–50; and E. C. Hollensbe and J. P. Guthrie, "Group Pay-for-Performance Plans: The Role of Spontaneous Goal Setting," *Academy of Management Review* (October 2000), pp. 864–72.
11. J. F. Castellano and H. A. Roehm, "The Problems with Managing by Objectives and Results," *Quality Progress* (March 2001), pp. 39–46.
12. See, for instance, P. P. Carson and K. D. Carson, "Deming versus Traditional Management Theorists on Goal Setting: Can Both Be Right?" *Business Horizons* (September/October 1994), pp. 145–58.
13. R. E. Silverman, "GE Goes Back to Future—Immelt's Familiar Troubles," *Wall Street Journal* (May 7, 2002), p. B1.
14. M. L. Frigo, "Strategy, Business Execution, and Performance Measures," *Strategic Finance* (May 2002), pp. 6–8.
15. P. D. Brewer, V. L. Brewer, and M. Hawksley, "Strategic Planning for Continuous Improvement in a College of Business," *The Mid-Atlantic Journal of Business* (June/September 2000), pp. 123–32.
16. G. Sutton, "Manager's Journal—Faddish Business: Cubicles Do Not a Utopia Make," *Wall Street Journal* (January 7, 2002), p. A24.
17. "A Restatement of Purpose," *Fast Company* (October 2001), p. 2.
18. J. Tan, "Impact of Ownership Type on Environment-Strategy and Performance: Evidence from a Transitional Company," *Journal of*

Management Studies (May 2002), pp. 333–54; and H. Li, "How Does New Venture Strategy Matter in the Environment-Performance Relationship," *Journal of High Technology Management Research* (Autumn 2001), pp. 183–204.
19. S. Chip, "For Tyco Electronics, Life Is Extreme Sport," *EBN* (May 20, 2002), p. 1.
20. A. H. Peterson, "E-Scan Analyzes Service Trends and Opportunities," *Credit Union Magazine* (June 2000), pp. 45–46.
21. See, for instance, "R. M. Beal, "Competing Effectively: Environmental Scanning, Competitive Strategy, and Organizational Performance in Small Manufacturing Firms," *Journal of Small Business Management* (January 2000), pp. 27–47.
22. E. Abels, "Hot Topics: Environmental Scanning," *American Society for Information Science* (February/March 2002), pp. 16–17.
23. B. Subramanian, "Business Intelligence Using Smart Technologies: Environmental Scanning Using Data Mining and Competitor Analysis Using Scenarios and Manual Simulation," *Competitiveness Review* (January 2002), p. 115.
24. See, for example, L. Lavelle, "The Case of the Corporate Spy," *BusinessWeek* (November 26, 2001), pp. 56–58; C. Britton, "Deconstructing Advertising: What Your Competitor's Advertising Can Tell You About Their Strategy," *Competitive Intelligence* (January/February 2002), pp. 15–19; and L. Smith, "Business Intelligence Progress in Jeopardy," *Information Week* (March 4, 2002), p. 74.
25. S. Greenbard, "New Heights in Business Intelligence," *Business Finance* (March 2002), pp. 41–46; K. A. Zimmermann, "The Democratization of Business Intelligence," *KN World* (May 2002), pp. 20–21; and C. Britton, "Deconstructing Advertising: What Your Competitor's Advertising Can Tell You About Their Strategy," *Competitive Intelligence* (January/February 2002), pp. 15–19.
26. L. Weathersby, "Take This Job and ***** It," *Fortune* (January 7, 2002), p. 122.
27. B. Aker, "Sometimes the Giants Do Fall," *Competitive Intelligence* (March/April 2002), pp. 45–46.
28. E. K. Valentin, "SWOT Analysis from a Resource-Based View," *Journal of Marketing Theory and Practice* (Spring 2001), pp. 54–69.
29. M. F. Turner, "How Does Your Company Measure Up?" *Black Enterprise* (November 2001), p. 52.
30. W. M. Bulkeley, "IBM's New CEO Sees Cost-cutting, Earnings Growth," *Wall Street Journal* (May 16, 2002), p. B6; and S. E. Ante and I. Sager, "IBM's New Boss," *BusinessWeek* (February 11, 2002), p. 86.
31. "UAL Gets Tax Refund Totaling $450 Million, Plans Charge for Avolar," *Wall Street Journal* (May 27, 2002), p. B2.
32. See, for example, J. B. Barney, "Organizational Culture: Can It Be a Source of Sustained Competitive Advantage?"*Academy of Management Review* (July 1986), pp. 656–65; C. Scholz, "Corporate Culture and Strategy: The Problem of Strategic Fit," *Long Range Planning* (August 1987), pp. 78–87; T. Kono, "Corporate Culture and Long Range Planning," *Long Range Planning* (August 1990), pp. 91–99; and C. M. Fiol, "Managing Culture as a Competitive Resource: An Identity Based View of Sustainable Competitive Advantage," *Journal of Management* (March 1991), pp. 191–211.
33. "Can Stolid Old Saab Become Sexy New Saab?" *BusinessWeek* (May 13, 2002), p. 102; and A. Taylor, "Finally GM Is Looking Good," *Fortune* (April 1, 2002), pp. 69–74.
34. R. Smith and S. Solomon, "Ebber's Exit Hurts WorldCom's Biggest Fan," *Wall Street Journal* (May 3, 2002), p. C1.
35. L. Grant, "Wal-Mart Bagging Success As a Grocer," *USA Today* (June 6, 2002), p. 3B
36. R. Berner and S. Anderson, "Wal-Mart Is Eating Everybody's Lunch," *BusinessWeek* (April 15, 2002), p. 43.
37. N. Byrnes and J. Foster, "A Touch of Indigestion," *BusinessWeek* (March 4, 2002), pp. 66–68; and R. Frank and S. Hensley, "Pfizer to Buy Pharmacia for $60 Billion," *Wall Street Journal* (July 15, 2002), p. A1.
38. J. D. Ward, "Responding to Fiscal Stress: A State-Wide Survey of Local Governments in Louisiana. A Research Note," *International Journal of Public Administration* (June 2001), pp. 565–71.
39. B. Orwall, D. Solomon, and S. Beatty, "The Bigger Picture: Why the Possible Sale of AT&T Broadband Spooks 'Content' Firms—Disney and Others Are Facing Prospect of Losing Power to Fewer, Larger Systems—The Zeros Are a Lot More," *Wall Street Journal* (August 27, 2001), p. A1; and B. Schlender, "Steve Jobs' Apple," *Fortune* (January 24, 2000), pp. 65–76.
40. "Jif, Crisco Find a New Home with Smucker," *USA Today* (June 3, 2002), p. 7B.
41. See, for example, M. E. Porter, *Competitive Strategy: Techniques for Analyzing Industries and Competitors* (New York: Free Press, 1980); Porter, *Competitive Advantage: Creating and Sustaining Superior Performance* (New York: Free Press, 1985).
42. N. Argyres and A. M. McGahan, "Introduction: Michael Porter's Competitive Strategy," *Academy of Management Executive* (May 2002), pp. 41–42; and N. Argyres and A. M. McGahan, "An Interview with Michael Porter," *Academy of Management Executive* (May 2002), pp. 43–52.
43. F. K. Wang and W. Lee, "Learning Curve Analysis in Total Productive Maintenance," *Omega* (December 2001), pp. 491–99.
44. F. Jossi, "Take a Peek Inside," *HR Magazine* (June 2002), pp. 46–52; and R. A. Martins, "Continuous Improvement Strategies and Production Competitive Criteria: Some Findings in Brazilian Industries," *Total Quality Management* (May 2001), pp. 281–91.
45. "New Range Rover Debuts at North American International Auto Show," www.ford.com (January 7, 2002), p. 1.
46. See, for example, "ISO 9000 and ISO 14000," *International Organization for Standardization* www.iso.ch/iso/en/iso9000-14000/index.htm (2001).
47. T. B. Schoenrock, "ISO 9000: 2000 Gives Competitive Edge," *Quality Progress* (May 2002), p. 107.
48. See, for instance, L. P. Dodd, Jr., "The Team Approach to ISO 9000: 2000 at Standard Aero Alliance," *Journal for Quality and Participation* (Spring 2002), pp. 41–44; and S. Smith, "The Cutting Edge of Environmental Management," *Occupational Hazards* (February 2002), pp. 33–37.
49. "Member Bodies," *International Organization for Standardization* www.iso.ch/iso/en/memberlist.membersummary (2002); and "Survey Shows Continued Growth of ISO 9000 and 14000," *Quality Progress* (October 2001), p. 20.
50. M. Henricks, "ISO A Go-Go," *Entrepreneur* (December 2001), p. 85.
51. A. A. King and M. J. Lenox, "Lean and Green? An Empirical Examination of the Relationship Between Lean Production and Environmental Performance," *Production and Operations Management* (Fall 2001), pp. 244–56.
52. C. Mitman, "Get ISO Certified on Time and Within Budget," *Quality* (November 2001), pp. 46–48.
53. M. Henricks, "ISO A Go-Go," *Entrepreneur* (December 2001), p. 85.
54. "Green Belt Training Starts February 4; Other Courses On-Line," *Quality Progress* (February 2002), p. 13; J. M. Lucas, "The Essential Six Sigma," *Quality Progress* (January 2002), pp. 27–31, and D. Treichler, R. Carmichael, A. Kusmanoff, J. Lewis, and G. Berthiez, "Design for Six Sigma: 15 Lessons Learned," *Quality Progress* (January 2002), p. 33.
55. T. Aeppel, "Career Journal: Nicknamed 'Nag,' She's Just Doing Her Job," *Wall Street Journal* (May 14, 2002), p. B1.
56. G. Eckes, "Making Six Sigma Last (and Work)," *Ivey Business Journal* (January/February 2002), pp. 77–81.
57. "Six Sigma Gets Its Day," *Quality* (January 2002), p. 48.
58. "Is 99.9% Good Enough?" *Training* (March 1991), p. 38. See also, J. Petty, "When Near Enough Is Not Good Enough," *Australian CPA* (May 2000), pp. 34–35.
59. M. Arndt, "Quality Isn't Just for Widgets," *BusinessWeek* (July 22, 2002), pp. 72–74.
60. N. F Krueger, Jr, "The Cognitive Infrastructure of Opportunity Emergence," *Entrepreneurship Theory and Practice* (Spring 2000), p. 6.

61. P. Drucker, *Innovation and Entrepreneurship* (New York: Harper & Row, 1985).
62. B. McClean, "This Entrepreneur Is Changing Underwear," *Fortune* (September 18, 2000), p. 60.
63. A. Cohen, "eBay's Bid to Conquer All," *Time* (February 5, 2001), pp. 48–51.
64. S. McFarland, "Cambodia's Internet Service Is in Kids' Hands," *Wall Street Journal* (May 15, 2000), p. A–9.
65. Information on Whole Foods Market from Hoovers Online www.hoovers.com, May 27, 2002.
66. A. Eisenberg, "What's Next? New Fabrics Can Keep Wearers Healthy and Smelling Good," *New York Times* (February 3, 2000), p. D1.
67. Material for developing a business plan can be found at Small Business Administration, *The Business Plan Workbook* (Washington, DC, May 17, 2001); and C. Etkin and B. Coutts, "SBA: Small Business Administration Home Page," *Library Journal* (April 15, 2002), p. 46. Readers may also find useful such software as Business Plan Pro Software, smallbizmanager.com.
68. Adapted from "TeamFuel Raises $5.5 Million to Challenge Fuel Procurement Supply Chain," www.teamfuel.com/corporate/index.html (January 23, 2001), p. 1; and "The Top 500 Women-Owned Businesses," *Working Woman* (June 1999), pp. 52–54.

Chapter 4

1. E. Brown, "Analyze This," *Forbes* (April 2002), pp. 96–98.
2. See, for example, A. Nagurney, J. Dong, and P. L. Mokhtarian, "Multicriteria Network Equilibrium Modeling with Variable Weights for Decision-Making in the Information Age with Applications to the Telecommuting and Teleshopping," *Journal of Economic Dynamics and Control* (August 2002), pp. 1629–50.
3. J. Sawyer, "Problem-Solving Success Tips," *Business and Economic Review* (April–June, 2002), pp. 23–24.
4. See J. Figueira and B. Ray, "Determining the Weights of Criteria in the Electre Type of Methods with a Revised Simos' Procedure," *European Journal of Operational Research* (June 1, 2002), pp. 317–26.
5. For instance, see M. Elliott, "Breakthrough Thinking," *IIE Solution* (October 2001), pp. 22–25; and B. Fazlollahi and R. Vahidov, "A Method for Generation of Alternatives by Decision Support Systems," *Journal of Management Information Systems* (Fall 2001), pp. 229–50.
6. D. Miller, Q. Hope, R. Eisenstat, N. Foote, and J. Galbraith, "The Problem of Solutions: Balancing Clients and Capabilities," *Business Horizons* (March/April 2002), pp. 3–12.
7. R. DeYoung, "Practical-Theoretical Approach in the Application of Theory Models of Organizational Behavior," *Journal of American Academy of Business* (March 2002), pp. 361–64.
8. This section is based on S. P. Robbins, *Essentials of Organizational Behavior*, 7th ed. (Upper Saddle River, NJ: Prentice Hall, Inc., 2003); C. W. Wang and R. Y. Horng, "The Effects of Creative Problem Solving Training on Creativity, Cognitive Type, and R & D Performance," *R & D Management* (January 2002), pp. 35–46; S. Caudron, "Creativity 101," *Workforce* (March 2002), pp 20, 24; and T. M. Amabile, "Motivating Creativity in Organizations," *California Management Review* (Fall 1997), pp. 42–52.
9. See A. Kuhberger, D. Komunska, and J. Perner, "The Disjunction Effect: Does It Exist for Two-Step Gambles?" *Organizational Behavior and Human Decision Processes* (July 2001), pp. 250–64; H. Mintzberg and F. Westley, "Decision Making: It's Not What You Think," *MIT Sloan Management Review* (Spring 2001), pp. 89–93; and P. M. Buhler, "Decision-Making: A Key to Successful Management," *Supervision* (February 2001), pp. 13–15.
10. M. Augier, "Subline Simon: The Consistent Vision of Economic Psychology's Nobel Laureate," *Journal of Economic Psychology* (June 2001), pp. 307–34; and H. K. Hvide, "Pragmatic Beliefs and Overconfidence," *Journal of Economic Behavior and Organization* (May 2002), pp. 15–28.
11. D. Dequech, "Bounded Rationality, Institutions, and Uncertainty," *Journal of Economic Issues* (December 2001), pp. 911–29.
12. H. A. Simon, *Administrative Behavior*, 3rd ed. (New York: Free Press, 1976); D. E. Agosto, "Bounded Rationality and Satisficing in Young People's Web-Based Decision Making," *Journal of the American Society for Information Science and Technology* (January 2002), pp. 16–27; and J. Forest and C. Mehier, "John R. Commons and Herbert A. Simon on the Concept of Rationality," *Journal of Economic Issues* (September 2001), pp. 591–605.
13. See, for example, P. Bromiley, "Debating Rationality: Nonrational Aspects of Organizational Decision Making/Rational Choice Theory and Organizational Theory: A Critique," *Academy of Management Review* (January 1999), pp. 157–59. See also, L. Anderlini and D. Canning, "Structural Stability Implies Robustness to Bounded Rationality," *Journal of Economic Theory* (December 2001), pp. 395–422.
14. See N. McK. Agnew and J. L. Brown, "Bounded Rationality: Fallible Decisions in Unbounded Decision Space," *Behavioral Science* (July 1986), pp. 148–61; D. R. A. Skidd, "Revisiting Bounded Rationality," *Journal of Management Inquiry* (December 1992), pp. 343–47; C. G. Lundberg and B. M. Nagle, "Post-Decision Inference Editing of Supportive and Counter Indicative Signals Among External Auditors in a Going Concern Judgement," *European Journal of Operational Research* (January 16, 2002), pp. 264–81; and P. D. Windschitl and M. E. Yong, "The Influence of Alternative Outcomes on Gut-Level Perceptions of Certainty," *Organizational Behavior and Human Decision Processes* (May 2001), pp. 109–34.
15. G. McNamara, H. Moon, and P. Bromiley, "Banking on Commitment: Intended and Unintended Consequences of an Organization's Attempt to Attenuate Escalation of Commitment," *Academy of Management Journal* (April 2002), pp. 443–52; H. Moon, "Looking Forward and Looking Back: Integrating Completion and Sunk-Cost Effects within an Escalation-of-Commitment Progress Decision," *Journal of Applied Psychology* (February 2001), pp. 104–13; H. Moon, "The Two Faces of Conscientiousness: Duty and Achievement Striving in Escalation of Commitment Dilemmas," *Journal of Applied Psychology* (June 2001), pp. 533–40.
16. "Rusnak Pleads Innocent in Allfirst Case," *Baltimore Sun* (June 12, 2002), p. B1.
17. A. Regalado, "Experiments in Controversy—Ethicists, Bodyguards Monitor Scientists' Effort to Create Copy of Human Embryo," *Wall Street Journal* (July 13, 2001), p. B1; and Stem-Cell Research is Forging Ahead in Europe," *Wall Street Journal* (July 13, 2001), p. B6.
18. R. D. Hof and H. Green, "How Amazon Cleared that Hurdle," *BusinessWeek* (February 4, 2002), p. 59.
19. B. L. Killingsworth, M. B. Hayden, and R. Schellenberger, "A Network Expert System Management System of Multiple Domains," *Journal of Information Science* (March–April 2001), p. 81.
20. See, for example, D. Mitchell and R. Pavur, "Using Modular Neural Networks for Business Decisions," *Management Decision* (January–February 2002), pp. 58–64.
21. S. Balakrishnan, N. Popplewell, and M. Thomlinson, "Intelligent Robotic Assemble," *Computers & Industrial Engineering* (December 2000), p. 467.
22. F. Harvey, "A Key Role in Detecting Fraud Patterns: Neural Networks," *Financial Times* (January 23, 2002), p. 3.
23. See, for example, G. A. Williams and R. B. Miller, "Change the Way You Persuade," *Harvard Business Review*, May 2002, pp. 65–73; J. A. Andersen, "Intuition in Managers: Are Intuitive Managers More Effective?" *Journal of Managerial Psychology* (January 2000), pp. 46–63; and G. Walsh, T. Henning-Thurau, V. Wayne-Mitchell, and K. P. Wiedmann, "Consumers' Decision-Making Styles as a Basis for Market Segmentation," *Journal of Targeting, Measurement and Analysis for Marketing* (December 2001), pp. 117–31.
24. See, for instance, C. K. W. DeDreu and M. A. West, "Minority Dissent and Team Innovation: The Importance of Participation in Decision Making," *Journal of Applied Psychology* (December 2001), pp. 1191–1201.

25. S. Mohammed, "Toward an Understanding of Cognitive Consensus in a Group Decision-Making Context," *Journal of Applied Behavioral Science* (December 2001), p. 408.
26. S. Mohammed, "Cognitive Diversity and Consensus in Group Decision Making: The Role of Inputs, Processes, and Outcomes," *Organizational Behavior and Human Decision Processes* (July 2001), pp. 310–35.
27. R. A. Meyers, D. E. Brashers, and J. Hanner, "Majority-Minority Influence: Identifying Argumentative Patterns and Predicting Argument-Outcome Links," *Journal of Communication* (Autumn 2000), pp. 3–30.
28. I. L. Janis, *Groupthink* (Boston: Houghton Mifflin, 1982). See also, C. R. Leana, "A Partial Test of Janis' Groupthink Model: Effects of Group Cohesiveness and Leader Behavior on Defective Decision Making," *Journal of Management* (Spring 1985), p. 517; G. Morehead and J. R. Montanari, "An Empirical Investigation of the Groupthink Phenomenon," *Human Relations* (May 1986), pp. 399–410; W. Auer-Rizzi and M. Berry, "Business vs. Cultural Frames of Reference in Group Decision Making: Interactions Among Austrian, Finnish, and Swedish Business Students," *Journal of Business Communications* (July 2000), pp. 264–92; and P. Smith, "Groupthink or Nuke Think," *New Zealand Management* (March 2001), pp. 48–49.
29. See, for instance, T. Horton, "Groupthink in the Boardroom," *Directors and Boards* (Winter 2002), p. 9.
30. See, for example, T. W. Costello and S. S. Zalkind, eds., *Psychology in Administration: A Research Orientation* (Upper Saddle River, NJ: Prentice Hall, 1963), pp. 429–30; R. A. Cooke and J. A. Kernaghan, "Estimating the Difference between Group versus Individual Performance on Problem Solving Tasks," *Group and Organization Studies* (September 1987), pp. 319–42; and L. K. Michaelsen, W. E. Watson, and R. H. Black, "A Realistic Test of Individual versus Group Consensus Decision Making," *Journal of Applied Psychology* (October 1989), pp. 834–39. See also, J. Hollenbeck, D. R. Ilgen, J. A. Colquitt, and A. Ellis, "Gender Composition, Situational Strength, and Team Decision-Making Accuracy: A Criterion Decomposition Approach," *Organizational Behavior and Human Decision Processes* (May 2002), pp. 445–75.
31. See, for example, L. K. Michaelsen, W. E. Watson, and R. H. Black, "A Realistic Test of Individual vs. Group Consensus Decision Making," *Journal of Applied Psychology* (October 1989), pp. 834–39; and P. W. Pease, M. Beiser, and M. E. Tubbs, "Framing Effects and Choice Shifts in Group Decision Making," *Organizational Behavior and Human Decision Processes* (October 1993), pp. 149–65.
32. J. Wagstaff, "Brainstorming Requires Drinks," *Far Eastern Economic Review* (May 2, 2002), p. 34.
33. T. Kelley, "Six Ways to Kill a Brainstormer," *Across the Board* (March/April 2002), p. 12.
34. K. L. Dowling and R. D. St. Louis, "Asynchronous Implementation of the Nominal Group Technique: Is It Effective," *Decision Support Systems* (October 2000), pp. 229–48.
35. See also, B. Andersen and T. Fagerhaug, "The Nominal Group Technique," *Quality Progress* (February 2000), p. 144.
36. J. Burdett, "Changing Channels: Using the Electronic Meeting System to Increase Equity in Decision Making," *Information Technology, Learning, and Performance Journal* (Fall 2000), pp. 3–12.
37. "Fear of Flying," *Business Europe* (October 3, 2001), p. 2.
38. "VC at Nestlé," *Business Europe* (October 3, 2001), p. 3.
39. M. Roberti, "Meet Me on the Web," *Fortune: Tech Supplement* (Winter 2002), p. 10.
40. See also, J. A. Hoxmeier and K. A. Kozar, "Electronic Meetings and Subsequent Meeting Behavior: Systems as Agents of Change," *Journal of Applied Management Studies* (December 2000), pp. 177–95.
41. See, for instance, P. Berthon, L. F. Pitt, and M. T. Ewing, "Corollaries of the Collective: The Influence of Organizational Culture and Memory Development on Perceived Decision-Making Context," *Academy of Market Science Journal* (Spring 2001), pp. 135–50.
42. J. de Haan, M. Yamamoto, and G. Lovink, "Production Planning in Japan: Rediscovering Lost Experiences or New Insights," *International Journal of Production Economics* (May 6, 2001), pp. 101–9.
43. www.mindbox.com.
44. R. Julavits, "MindBox attacks Fear of Internet," American Banker (October 2000), p. 9.
45. L. Normant, "Cathy Hughes: Ms. Radio," *Ebony* (May 2000), pp. 23–24.

Quantitative Module

1. Readers are encouraged to see R. S. Russell and B. W. Taylor III, *Quantitative Analysis for Management*, 8th ed. (Upper Saddle River, NJ: Prentice Hall, 2003); and L. P. Ritzman and L. J. Krajewski, *Foundations of Operations Management* (Upper Saddle River, NJ: Prentice Hall, 2003).
2. J. Schmid, "Getting to Breakeven," *Catalog Age* (November 2001), pp. 89–90.
3. We want to acknowledge and thank Professor Jeff Storm of Virginia Western Community College for his assistance in this example.

Chapter 5

1. Based on "Trufresh Wins American Tasting Award for Their Protein Perfect Salmon Servings and Farm Raised Atlantic Salmon Portions," www.trufresh.com, January 2000; "Salmon Is Designed for Health Care," *Restaurant & Institutions* (July 2, 2000), p. 1; "Self-Heating Meals Give Guard More Choices," *Government Food Service* (July 2001), p. 1; and "Fish with All the Trimmings," *Newsday* (July 2, 2001), p. 23.
2. For the historical purists, Adam Smith referred to work specialization as division of labor.
3. See, for instance, A. Takeishi, "Knowledge Partitioning in the Interfirm Division of Labor: The Case of Automotive Product Development," *Organizational Science* (May/June 2002), pp. 321–28; S. Prasso and D. Fairlamb, "One Currency, Many Pink slips," *Business Week* (January 28, 2002), p. 10; and J. Z. Muller, "Great Minds, Imperfect Markets," *Wall Street Journal* (June 21, 2001), p. A16.
4. R. Preston, "Inside Out," *Management Today* (September 2001), p. 37; and R. D. Clarke, "Over Their Heads," *Black Enterprise* (December 2000), p. 79.
5. L. Urwick, *The Elements of Administration* (New York: Harper & Row, 1944), pp. 52–53. See also, J. H. Gittel, "Supervisory Span, Relational Coordination, and Flight Departure Performance: A Reassessment of Post-Bureaucracy Theory," *Organizational Science* (July/August 2001), pp. 468–83.
6. "Span of Control vs. Span of Support," *The Journal for Quality and Participation* (Fall 2000), p. 15.
7. P. C. Light, "From Pentagon to Pyramids: Whacking at Bloat," *Government Executive* (July 2001), p. 100.
8. See, for instance, D. Van Fleet, "Span of Management Research and Issues," *Academy of Management Journal* (September 1983), pp. 546–52; and S. H. Cady and P. M. Fandt, "Managing Impressions with Information: A Field Study of Organizational Realities," *Journal of Applied Behavioral Science* (June 2001), pp. 180–204.
9. Stanley Milgram, *Obedience to Authority* (New York: Harper & Row, 1974).
10. R. S. Benchley, "Following Orders," *Chief Executive* (March 2002), p. 6.
11. B. S. Moskal, "A Shadow between Values and Reality," *Industry Week* (May 16, 1994), pp. 23–26. See also J. Contreras, "Looking for Bad Guys," *Newsweek* (April 16, 2001), p. 41; and K. Kranhold, "Southby's Former Chief Portrays Herself as Deputy Following Orders to Collude," *Wall Street Journal* (November 21, 2001), p. B6.
12. See J. R. P. French and B. Raven, "The Bases of Social Power," in D. Cartwright and A. F. Zander, eds., *Group Dynamics: Research and Theory* (New York: Harper & Row, 1960), pp. 607–23.

13. Henri Fayol, *General and Industrial Management*, trans. C. Storrs (London: Pitman Publishing, 1949), pp. 19–42.
14. J. Zabojnik, "Centralized and Decentralized Decision Making in Organizations," *Journal of labor Economics* (January 2002), pp. 1–22.
15. See P. Kenis and D. Knoke, "How Organizational Field Networks Shape InterOrganizational Tie-Formation Rates," *Academy of Management Review* (April 2002), pp. 275–93.
16. E. Kelly, "Keys to Effective Virtual Global Teams," *The Academy of Management Executive* (May 2001), pp. 132–33; and D. Ancona, H. Bresman, and K. Kaeufer, "The Comparative Advantage of X-Team," *MIT Sloan Management Review* (Spring 2002), pp. 33–39.
17. T. Burns and G. M. Stalker, *The Management of Innovation* (London: Tavistock, 1961).
18. D. Dougherty, "Re-imagining the Differentiation and Integration of Work for Sustained Product Innovation," *Organization Science* (September/October 2001), pp. 612–31.
19. A. D. Chandler Jr., *Strategy and Structure: Chapters in the History of the Industrial Enterprise* (Cambridge, MA: MIT Press, 1962).
20. I. Scales, "Thinking Local; Acting Local," *America's Network* (May 1, 2002), p. 10; and A. Burton-Jones, "Daunting Paradox," *Across the Board* (May/June 2002), pp. 60–63.
21. R. Dhawan, "Firm Size and Productivity Differential: Theory and Evidence from a Panel of US Firms," *Journal of Economic Behavior & Organization* (March 2001), pp. 269–93; and E. Pentecost, "The Determinants of Technology Diffusion: Evidence from the UK Financial Sector," *The Manchester School* (March 2002), pp. 185–203.
22. C. C. Miller, W. H. Glick, Y. D. Wang, and G. Huber, "Understanding Technology Structure Relationships: Theory Development and Meta Analytic Theory Testing," *Academy of Management Journal* (June 1991), pp. 370–99. See also, M. J. Lopez-Eguilaz, "The Impact of Technological Innovation: Situation in Spain, the Case of Navarra," *International Journal of Entrepreneurship and Innovation Management* (February 2001), pp. 276–94; and J. Teresko, "Strategic Design: Building the World's Next Plants," *Industry Week* (May 2002), pp. 22–27.
23. J. Woodward, *Industrial Organization: Theory and Practice* (London: Oxford University Press, 1965); and C. Perrow, *Organizational Analysis: A Sociological Perspective* (Belmont, CA: Wadsworth, 1970).
24. See, for instance, P. M. Blau and R. A. Schoenherr, *The Structure of Organizations* (New York: Basic Books, 1971).
25. See, for example, H. M. O'Neill, "Restructuring, Reengineering and Rightsizing: Do the Metaphors Make Sense?" *Academy of Management Executive* 8, no. 4 (1994), pp. 9–30; R. K. Reger, J. V. Mullane, L. T. Gustafson, and S. M. DeMarie, "Creating Earthquakes to Change Organizational Mindsets," *Academy of Management Executive* 8, no. 4 (1994), pp. 31–41; and J. Tan, "Impact of Ownership Type on Environment-Strategy Linkage and Performance: Evidence from a Transitional Company," *The Journal of Management Studies* (May 2002), pp. 333–54.
26. J. C. Linder and S. Cantrell, "It's All in the Mind(set)," *Across the Board* (May/June 2002), pp. 38–42; and B. Holland, "Management's Sweet Spot," *New Zealand Management* (March 2002), pp. 60–61.
27. M. Song, "Samsung Electronics Net Rises 54%," *Wall Street Journal* (April 22, 2002), p. B4.
28. H. Mintzberg, *Structure in Fives: Designing Effective Organizations* (Upper Saddle River, NJ: Prentice Hall, 1983), p. 157. See also, D. Pal and J. Sarkar, "Spatial Competition Among Multi-Store Firms," *International Journal of Industrial Organization* (February 2002), pp. 163–90; and R. Metters and V. Vargas, "Organizing Work in Service Firms," *Business Horizons* (July/August 2000), pp. 23–32.
29. See, for instance, J. Galbraith, "Matrix Organization Designs: How to Combine Functional and Project Forms," *Business Horizons* (February 1971), pp. 29–40; L. R. Burns, "Matrix Management in Hospitals: Testing Theories of Structure and Development," *Administrative Science Quarterly* (September 1989), pp. 349–68; and J. Wolf and W. G. Egelhoff, "A Reexamination and Extension of International Strategy-Structure Theory," *Strategic Management Journal* (February 2002), pp. 181–89.
30. See, for example, Z. Laslor and A. I. Goldberg, "Matrix Structures and Performance: The Search for Optimal Adjustment to Organizational Objectives," *IEEE Transactions on Engineering Management* (May 2001), pp. 144–156.
31. M. Dufficy, "Training for Success in a New Industrial World," *Industrial and Commercial Training* (February 2001), pp. 48–54.
32. R. L. Cross, A. Yan, and M. R. Louis, "Boundary Activities in 'Boundaryless' Organizations: A Case Study of a Transformation to a Team-Based Structure," *Human Relations* (June 2000), pp. 841–68.
33. D. Drickhamer, "Europe's Best Plants: Mission Critical," *Industry Week* (March 2002), pp. 44–46.
34. C. Garvey, "Steer Teams with the Right Pay," *HR Magazine* (May 2002), pp. 70–78.
35. J. Bozarth, "The Boundaryless Organization," *Training* (May 2002), p. 60.
36. K. R. T. Larsen and C. R. McInerney, "Preparing to Work in the Virtual Organization," *Information and Management* (May 2002), pp. 445–56; P. R. Sparrow, "New Employee Behaviors, Work Designs and Forms of Work Organization: What Is in Store for the Future of Work?" *Journal of Managerial Psychology* (March 2000), pp. 202–18; and P. Auditore, "Enabling Knowledge Management in Today's Knowledge Economy," *KM World* (January 2002), pp. S8–S9.
37. E. Schonfeld, "eBay's Secret Ingredient," *Business 2.0* (March 2002), p. 3.
38. See T. C. Lawton and K. P. Michaels, "Advancing to the Virtual Value Chain: Learning from the Dell Model," *Irish Journal of Management* (December 2001), pp. 91–112.
39. M. Biggs, "Tomorrow's Workforce," *InfoWorld* (September 18, 2000), pp. S59–S61.
40. See also, W. M. Fitzpatrick and D. R. Burke, "Form, Functions, and Financial Performance Realities for the Virtual Organization," *SAM Advanced Management Journal* (Summer 2000), pp. 13–20; and E. Kelley, "Keys to Effective Virtual Global Teams," *The Academy of Management Executive* (May 2001), pp. 132–33.
41. Initial work on the Learning Organization is credited to P. M. Senge, *The Fifth Discipline: The Art and Practice* (New York: Doubleday, 1990).
42. L. Mallak, "Understanding and Changing Your Organization's culture," *Industrial Management* (March/April 2001), pp. 18–24.
43. W. W. Jones and N. Macris, "Where Am I and Where Do I Go from Here? *Planning* (June 2000), pp. 18–21.
44. See S. P. Robbins, *Business Today: The New World of Business* (New York: Harcourt, 2001), pp. 317–8.
45. M. Boyle, "Just Right," *Fortune* (June 10, 2002), pp. 207–8; and T. Davis and M. Landa, "The Story of Mary? How 'Organization Culture' Can Erode Bottom-Line Profitability," *The Canadian Manager* (Winter 2000), pp. 14–17.
46. Based on G. Hofstede, B. Neuijen, D. D. Ohayv, and G. Sanders, "Measuring Organizational Culture: A Qualitative and Quantitative Study across Twenty Cases," *Administrative Science Quarterly* (June 1990), pp. 286–316; and C. A. O'Reilly III, J. Chatman, and D. F. Caldwell, "People and Organizational Culture: A Profile Comparison Approach to Assessing Person Organization Fit," *Academy of Management Journal* (September 1991), pp. 487–516. See also, M. Robinson, "The Ten Commandments of Intrapreneurs," *New Zealand Management* (December 2001), pp. 95–98.
47. "IBM Through the Years," <www-1.ibm.com/ibm/history/history/decade_1990.htm> (2002).
48. "We Weren't Just Airborne Yesterday," <www.southwest.com/about_swa/airborne.htm> (March 11, 2002).
49. G. Johnson, "Strategy Through a Cultural Lens: Learning for a Manger's Experience," *Management Learning* (December 2000), pp. 403–426.
50. A counterargument to this can be seen in G. Taninecz, "Healing the Corporate Soul," *Chief Executive* (Summer 2002), pp. 8–11.
51. M. French, "Practicity Drops Weight, Moves To Hub," *mass High Tech, (*August 28, 2000), p. 7.

52. L. Stavens, "Ota Moment's Notice," *Knowledge Management Magazine*, March 2001.
53. P. L. Hunsaker, *Training in Management Skills* (Upper Saddle River, NJ: Prentice Hall, 2001), ch. 14. Case based on information found in D. Pringle, "Investors Cheer Nokia Margins Amid Expected Drop in Sales," *Wall Street Journal* (June 12, 2002), p. B7; J. Eisinger, "Ahead of the Tape," *Wall Street Journal* (June 10, 2002), p. C1; Nokia's company Web site <www.press.nokia.com/pressreleases.htm>; J. Guyon, "Nokia Rocks Its Rivals, "*Fortune* (March 4, 2002), pp. 115–8; S. Baker and S. Prasso, "And Now, the $21,000 Cell Phone," *Business week* (February 18, 2002), p. 14; J. S. McClenahen, "CEO of the Year," *Industry Week* (November 20, 2000), pp. 38–44, J. Fox, "Nokia's Secret Code," *Fortune* (May 1, 2000), pp. 160–74, and "Nokia Steps Up Corporate Venturing," *European Venture Capital Journal (*February 1, 2002), p. 18.

Chapter 6

1. Vignette based on "Starbucks Celebrates Its First Decade as a Public Company," *Starbucks Coffee Company* (June 26, 2002), p. 1; Karyn Strauss, "Howard Schultz: Starbucks' CEO Serves a Blend of Community, Employee Commitment," *Nation's Restaurant News* (January 2000), pp. 162–163.
2. Material for this chapter is drawn from D. A. DeCenzo and S. P. Robbins, *Human Resources management*, 7th ed. (New York, John Wiley & Sons, 2002).
3. I. T. Robertson and M. Smith, "Personnel Selection," *Journal of Occupational and Organizational Psychology* (November 2001), pp. 441–72.
4. H. Palmer and W. Valet, "Job Analysis: Targeting Needed Skills," *Employment Relations Today* (Autumn 2001), pp. 85–92.
5. L. Greenhalgh, A. T. Lawrence, and R. I. Sutton, "Determinants of Work Force Reduction Strategies in Declining Organizations," *Academy of Management Review* (April 1988), pp. 241–54; "Even Non-Recruiting Companies Must Maintain Hiring Networks," *HR Focus* (November 2001), p. 8; and M. N. Martinez, "The Headhunter Within," *HR Magazine* (August 2001), pp. 48–55.
6. "Employee Referral Programs: Highly Qualified New Hires Who Stick Around," *Canadian HR Reporter* (June 4, 2001), p. 21; and C. Lachnit, "Employee Referral Saves Time, Saves Money, Delivers Quality," *Workforce* (June 2001), pp. 66–72.
7. J. Mooney, "Pre-Employment Testing on the Internet: Put Candidates a Click Away and Hire a Modem Speed," *Public Personnel Management* (Spring 2002), pp. 41–52.
8. See, for instance, R. D. Arvey and J. E. Campion, "The Employment Interview: A Summary and Review of Recent Research," *Personnel Psychology* (Summer 1982), pp. 281–322; and M. M. Harris, "Reconsidering the Employment Interview: A Review of Recent Literature and Suggestions for Future Research," *Personnel Psychology* (Winter 1989), pp. 691–726; J. H. Prager, "Nasty or Nice: 56–Question Quiz," *Wall Street Journal* (February 22, 2000), p. A4; and M. K. Zachary, "Labor Law for Supervisors," *Supervision* (March 2001), pp. 23–26.
9. See, for instance, G. Nicholsen, "Screen and Glean: Good Screening and Background Checks Help Make the Right Match for Every Open Position," *Workforce* (October 2000), p. 70.
10. R. A. Posthuma, F. P. Morgeson, and M. A. Campion, "Beyond Employment Interview Validity: A Comprehensive Narrative Review of Recent Research and Trends Over Time," *Personnel Psychology* (Spring 2002), pp. 1–81.
11. A. I. Huffcutt, J. M. Conway, P. L. Roth, and N. J. Stone, "Identification and Meta-Analysis Assessment of Psychological Constructs Measured in Employment Interviews," *Journal of Applied Psychology* (October 2001), pp. 897–913; and A. I. Huffcutt, J. A. Weekley, W. H. Wiesner, T. G. Degroot, and C. Jones, "Comparison of Situational and Behavioral Description Interview Questions for Higher-Level Positions," *Personnel Psychology* (Autumn 2001), pp. 619–44.
12. See E. Hermelin and I. T. Robertson, "A Critique and Standardization of Meta-Analytic Coefficients in Personnel Selection," *Journal of Occupational and Organizational Psychology* (September 2001), pp. 253–77; C. H. Middendorf and T. H. Macan, "Note-Taking in the Employment Interview: Effects on Recall and Judgments," *Journal of Applied Psychology* (April 2002), pp. 293–303; D. Butcher, "The Interview Rights and Wrongs," *Management Today* (April 2002), p. 4; and P. L. Roth, C. H. Can Iddekinge, A. I. Huffcutt, C. E. Eidson, and P. Bobko, "Corrections for Range Restriction in Structured Interview Ethnic Group Differences: The Value May Be Larger than Researchers Thought," *Journal of Applied Psychology* (April 2002), pp. 369–76.
13. S. H. Applebaum and M. Donia, "The Realistic Downizing Preview: A Management Intervention in the Prevention of Survivor Syndrome (Part II)," *Career Development International* (January 2001), pp. 5–19.
14. S. L. Premack and J. P. Wanous, "A Meta Analysis of Realistic Job Preview Experiments," *Journal of Applied Psychology* (November 1985), pp. 706–20.
15. C. Garvey, "The Whirlwind of a New Job," *HR Magazine* (June 2001), pp. 110–18.
16. B. P. Sunoo, "Results-Oriented Customer Service Training," *Workforce* (May 2001), pp. 84–90.
17. See, for instance, E. G. Tripp, "Aging Aircraft and Coming Regulations: Political and Media Pressures Have Encouraged the FAA to Expand Its Pursuit of Real and Perceived Problems of Older Aircraft and their Systems. Operators Will Pay," *Business and Commercial Aviation* (March 2001), pp. 68–75.
18. C. S. Duncan, J. D. Selby-Lucas, and W. Swart, "Linking Organizational Goals and Objectives to Employee Performance: A Quantitative Perspective," *Journal of American Academy of Business* (March 2002), pp. 314–18.
19. T. Galvin, "The 2002 Training Top 100," *Training* (March 2002), pp. 20–29.
20. R. Langlois, "Fairmont Hotels: Business Strategy Starts with People," *Canadian HR Reporter* (November 5, 2001), p. 19.
21. M. Dalahoussaye, "Show Me the Results," *Training* (March 2002), p. 28.
22. See, for example, R. E. Catalano and D. L. Kirkpatrick, "Evaluating Training Programs—The State of the Art," *Training and Development Journal* (May 1968), pp. 2–9.
23. A. Tziner, C. Joanis, and K. R. Murphy, "A Comparison of Three Methods of Performance Appraisal with Regard to Goal Properties, Goal Perception, and Rate Satisfaction," *Group and Organization Management* (June 2000), pp. 175–90; and T. W. Kent and T. J. Davis, "Using Re-translation to Develop Operational Anchored Scales to Assess the Motivational Context of Jobs," *International Journal of Management* (March 2002), pp. 10–16.
24. See also, C. A Ramus and U. Steger, "The Roles of Supervisory Support Behaviors and Environmental Policy in Employee 'Ecoinitiatives' at Leading-Edge European Companies," *Academy of Management Journal* (August 2000), pp. 605–26.
25. J. F. Brett and L. E. Atwater, "360 Degree Feedback: Accuracy, Reactions, and Perceptions of Usefulness," *Journal of Applied Psychology* (October 2001), pp. 930–42.
26. See also, "Performance Appraisals," *Business Europe* (April 3, 2002), p. 3.
27. M. A. Peiperl, "Getting 360 Feedback Right," *Harvard Business Review*, January 2001, pp. 142–47.
28. T. J. Maurer, D. R. D. Mitchell, and F. G. Barbeite, "Predictors of Attitudes Toward a 360-Degree Feedback System and Involvement in Post-Feedback Management Development Activity," *Journal of Occupational and Organizational Psychology* (March 2002), pp. 87–107.
29. A. Evans, "From Every Angle," *Training* (September 2001), p. 22.
30. M. Kennett, "First Class Coach," *Management Today* (December 2001), p. 84; and T. A. Beehr, L. Ivanitsjaya, C. P. Hansen, D. Erofeev, and D. M. Gudanowski, "Evaluation of 360 Degree Feedback Ratings: Relationships with Each Other and with Performance and Selection Predictors," *Journal of Organizational Behavior* (November 2001), pp. 775–88.

31. J. S. Miller, P. W. Hom, and L. R. Gomez-Mejia, "The High Cost of Low Wages: Does Maquiladora Compensation Reduce Turnover?" *Journal of International Business Studies* (Third Quarter 2001), pp. 585–95.
32. "Mandated Benefits: 2002 Compliance Guide," *Employee Benefits Journal* (June 2002), p. 64; and J. J. Kim, "Smaller Firms Augment Benefits, Survey Shows," *Wall Street Journal* (June 6, 2002), p. D2.
33. A. Joshi, "Managing the Organizational Melting Pot: Dilemmas of Workplace Diversity," *Administrative Science Quarterly* (December 2001), pp. 783–84.
34. "Generations at Work: Managing the Class of Veterans, Boomers, Xers, and Nexters in Your Workplace," *Diversity Factor* (Spring 2000), p. 3.
35. See, for instance, K. Iverson, Managing for Effective Workforce Diversity," *Cornell Hotel and Restaurant Administration Quarterly* (April 2000), pp. 31–38.
36. United States. Equal Employment Opportunity Commission, "Sexual Harassment Charges EEOC and FEPAs Combines: FY 1992–FY 2001," EEOC (February 22, 2002) <www.eeoc.gov/stats/harass.html.>
37. "One-Fifth of Women Are Harassed Sexually," *HR Focus* (April 2002), p. 2.
38. Norman F. Foy, "Sexual Harassment Can Threaten Your Bottom Line," *Strategic Finance* (August 2000), pp. 56–57.
39. "Federal Monitors Find Illinois Mitsubishi Unit Eradicating Harassment," *Wall Street Journal* (September 7, 2000), p. A8.
40. Liberty J. Munson, Charles Hulin, and Fritz Drasgow, Longitudinal Analysis of Dispositional Influences and Sexual Harassment: Effects on Job and Psychological Outcomes," *Personnel Psychology* (Spring 2000), p. 21.
41. See, for instance, Gerald L. Maatman Jr., "A Global View of Sexual Harassment," *HR Magazine* (July 2000), pp. 151–58.
42. "Nichols v. Azteca Restaurant Enterprises," *Harvard Law Review* (May 2002), p. 2074; Adam Jack Morrell, "Non-Employee Harassment," *Legal Report* (January-February 2000), p. 1.
43. While the male gender was referred to here, it is important to note that sexual harassment may involve people of either sex or the same sex. (See, for instance, *Oncale v. Sundowner Offshore Service, Inc.*, 118 S. Ct. 998.)
44. See also, M. Rotundo, D. H. Nguyen, and P. R. Sackett, "A Meta-Analytic Review of Gender Differences in Perceptions of Sexual Harassment," *Journal of Applied Psychology* (October 2001), pp. 914–22.
45. Richard L. Wiener and Linda E. Hurt, "How Do People Evaluate Social Sexual Conduct at Work? A Psychological Model," *Journal of Applied Psychology* (February 2000), p. 75.
46. *Meritor Savings Bank v. Vinson*, United States. Supreme Court 106, Docket No. 2399 (1986).
47. Robert D. Lee and Paul S. Greenlaw, "Employer Liability for Employee Sexual Harassment: A Judicial Policy-Making Study," *Public Administration Review* (March/April 2000), p. 127.
48. Ibid.
49. "You and DuPont: Diversity," DuPont Company Documents (1999–2000); <www.dupont.com/careers/you/diverse.html>; and "DuPont Announces 2000 Dr. Martin Luther King, Days of Celebration, DuPont Company Documents (January 11, 2000), <www.dupont.com/corp/whats-news/releases/00/001111.html>.
50. It should be noted here that under the Title VII and the Civil Rights Act of 1991, the maximum award that can be given, under the Federal Act, is $300,000. However, many cases are tried under state laws which permit unlimited punitive damages.
51. J. W. Janove, "Sexual Harassment and the Big Three Surprises," *HR Magazine* (November 2001), pp. 123–30.
52. W. L. Kosanovich, J. L. Rosenberg, and L. Swanson, "Preventing and Correcting Sexual Harassment: A Guide to the Ellerth/Faragher Affirmative Defense," *Employee Relations Law Journal* (Summer 2002), pp. 79–99; Milton Zall, "Workplace Harassment and Employer Liability," *Fleet Equipment* (January 2000), p. B1.
53. See, for instance, Peter W. Dorfman, Anthony T. Cobb, and Roxanne Cox, "Investigations of Sexual Harassment Allegations: Legal Means Fair—Or Does It?" *Human Resources management* (Spring 2000), pp. 33–39.
54. K. Hae-Ok, "CEO Charts a Course Toward a Prosperous Rebirth," *Business Korea* (January 2002), p. 34.
55. Daniel Costello, "Stressed Out: Can Workplace Stress Get Worse?—Incidents of 'Desk Rage' Disrupt America's Offices—Long Hours, Cramped Quarters Produce Some Short Fuses; Flinging Phones at the Wall," *Wall Street Journal* (January 16, 2001), p. B–1.
56. "Study: Lights, Nosolo Workers Help Reduce Homicides," *Occupational Hazards* (April 2002), p. 17; and United States. Department of Labor, Occupational Safety and Health Administration, *Workplace Violence* (Washington, DC: Government Printing Office, 2000), p. 1; and Lynn Miller, Karen Caldwell, and Laura C. Lawson, "When Work Equals Life: The Next State of Workplace Violence," *HR Magazine* (December 2000), pp. 178–80.
57. Michael Lynch, "Go Ask Alice," *Security Management* (December 2000), pp. 68–73.
58. T. Anderson, "Training for Tense Times," *Security Management* (March 2002), pp. 68–75.
59. Paul Temple, "Real Danger and 'Postal' Myth," *Workforce* (October 2000), p. 8.
60. P. P. Shah, "Network Destruction: The Structural Implications of Downsizing," *Academy of Management Journal* (February 2000), pp. 101–12.
61. See, for instance, K. A. Mollica and B. Gray, "When Layoff Survivors Become Layoff Victims: Propensity to Litigate," *Human Resource Planning* (January 2001), pp. 22–32.
62. S. Koudsi, "You're Stuck," *Fortune* (December 10, 2001), pp. 271–74.
63. See, for example, Robert J. Grossman, "Robbing the Cradle?" *HR Magazine* (September 2000), pp. 41–45.
64. Based on Kevin Ferguson, "Cisco High," *Business Week E-Biz* (June 5, 2000), pp. EB102–EB104; Joan O. C. Hamilton, "The Panic Over Hiring" *Business Week E-Biz* (April 3, 2000), pp. EB130–EB132; and "Book It," *Entrepreneur* (May 2000), p. 44.

Career Module

1. See, for example, T.J. Maurer, H.R. Pierce, and L.M. Shore, "Perceived Beneficiary of Employee Development Activity: A Three-Dimensional Social Exchange Model," *Academy of Management Review* (July 2002), pp. 432–44.
2. I.R. Schwartz, "Self Assessment and Career Planning: Matching Individuals and Organizational Goals," *Personnel* (January-February 1979), p. 48.
3. Michelle Neely Martinez, "Get Job Seekers to Come to You," *HR Magazine* (August 2000), pp. 42–52.
4. Ibid., p. 50.
5. See, for example, Bill Leonard, "Online and Overwhelmed," *HR Magazine* (August 2000), pp. 37–42; Pat Curry, "Log on for Recruits," *Industry Week* (October 16, 2000), pp. 46–54; Rachel Emma Silverman, "Your Career Matters: Raiding Talent Via the Web—Personal Pages, Firms' Sites Are Troves of Information for Shrewd Headhunters," *Wall Street Journal* (October 3, 2000), p. B1; and Michelle Neely Martinez, "Get Job Seekers to Come to You," *HR Magazine* (August 2000), pp 45–52.
6. Michael A. O'Neil, "How to Implement Relationship Management Strategies," *Supervision* (July 2000), p. 3.
7. A.Kristof-Brown, M.R. Barrick, and M. Franke, "Applicant Impression Management: Dispositional Influences and Consequences for Recruiter Perceptions of Fit and Similarity," *Journal of Management* (January 2002), pp. 27–46.
8. See, for example, K.J. Dunham, "Career Journal: The Jungle," *Wall Street Journal* (May 21, 2002), p. B10.

Chapter 7

1. Information from company Web Site <www.panamco.com>, July 2, 2002; and S. Van Yoder, "Thirst for Success," *Industry Week* (May 15, 2000), pp. 34–39.
2. I. M. Jawahar and G. L. McLaughlin, "Toward a Descriptive Stakeholder Theory: An Organizational Life Cycle Approach," *Academy of Management Review* (July 2001), pp. 397–415.
3. D. Rocks, "Reinventing Herman Miller," *Business Week E.Biz* (April 3, 2000), pp. EB89–EB96.
4. E. Shannon, "Agent of Change," *Time* (March 4, 2002), p. 17; B. Kenney, "SLA Head Shaffer Resigns Abruptly: Did 'Change Agent' Move too Fast in Aggressive Restructuring," *Library Journal* (March 15, 2002), pp. 17–19; and T. Mudd, "Rescue Mission," *Industry Week* (May 1, 2000), pp. 30–37.
5. The idea for these metaphors came from P. Vaill, *Managing As a Performing Art: New Ideas for a World of Chaotic Change* (San Francisco: Jossey Bass, 1989).
6. K. Lewin, *Field Theory in Social Science* (New York: Harper & Row, 1951).
7. R. E. Levasseur, "People Skills: Change Management Tools—Lewin's Change Model," *Interfaces* (August 2001), pp. 71–74.
8. See, for instance, C. R. Leana and B. Barry, "Stability and Change As Simultaneous Experiences in Organizational Life," *Academy of Management Review* (October 2000), pp. 753–59.
9. A. Mudio, "GM Has a New Model for Change," *Fast Company* (December 2000), pp. 62–64.
10. R. B. Reich, "Your Job Is Change," *Fast Company* (October 2000), pp. 140–68.
11. W. H. Bovey and A. Hede, "Resistance to Organizational Change: The Role of Cognitive and Affective Processes," *Leadership and Organizational Development Journal* (July–August 2001), pp. 372–83; W. H. Bovey and A. Hede, "Resistance to Organizational Change: The Role of Defense Mechanisms," *Journal of Managerial Psychology* (September–October 2001), pp. 488–503; and K. J. Jansen, "The Emerging Dynamics of Change: Resistance, Readiness, and Momentum," *Human Resource Planning* (June 2000), p. 53.
12. See, for example, P. de Jager, "Resistance to Change," *The Futurist* (May 2001), p. 24; and R. Maurer, "What Blocks Support?" *Journal for Quality and Participation* (May–June 2000), p. 47.
13. L. Coch and J. R. P. French Jr., "Overcoming Resistance to Change," *Human Relations* (November 1948), pp. 512–532.
14. J. P. Kotler and L. A. Schlesinger, "Choosing Strategies for Change," *Harvard Business Review*, March–April 1979, pp. 106–14; S. K. Piderit, "Rethinking Resistance and Recognizing Ambivalence: A Multidimensional View of Attitude Toward an Organizational Change," *Academy of Management Review* (October 2000), pp. 783–94; and R. Maurer, "What Blocks Support?" *Journal for Quality and Participation* (May–June 2000), p. 47.
15. J. L. Bennett, "Change Happens," *HR Magazine* (September 2001), pp. 149–56.
16. D. Rocks, "Reinventing Herman Miller," *Business Week E.Biz* (April 3, 2000), p. EB96.
17. Sabrina Hicks, "What Is Organization Development?" *Training and Development* (August 2000), p. 65; and H. Hornstein, "Organizational Development and Change Management: Don't Throw the Baby Out with the Bath Water," *Journal of Applied Behavioral Science* (June 2001), pp. 223–27.
18. M. J. Austin, "Introducing Organizational Development (OD) Practices into a Country Human Service Agency," *Administration in Social Work* (Winter 2001), p. 63.
19. See, for instance, H. B. Jones, "Magic, Meaning, and Leadership: Weber's Model and the Empirical Literature," *Human Relations* (June 2001), p. 753.
20. Gib Akin and Ian Palmer, "Putting Metaphors to Work for a Change in Organizations," *Organizational Dynamics* (Winter 2000), pp. 67–79.
21. J. Grieves, "Skills, Values or Impression Management? Organizational Change and the Social Processes of Leadership, Change Agent Practice, and Process Consultation," *Journal of Management Development* (May 2000), p. 407.
22. M. McMaster, "Team Building Tips," *Sales & Marketing Management* (January 2002), p. 140; and "How To: Executive Team Building," *Training and Development* (January 2002), p. 16.
23. "HR Execs Polled About Stress," *Work and Family Newsbrief* (May 2002), pp. 2–4.
24. William Atkinson, "When Stress Won't Go Away," *HR Magazine* (December 2000), p. 104.
25. "Japan Asks if It Works Too Hard," *Christian Science Monitor* (Tokyo) (April 6, 2000), p. 4. See also, "When Heartache May Bring on a Heart Attack," *BusinessWeek* (May 6, 2002), p. 97.
26. "Managers Fail to Tackle Rising Stress," *Personnel Today* (June 25, 2002), p. 10; and "Downtime the Workers' Reaction to Workplace Stress," *Australasian Business Intelligence* (June 27, 2002), p. 1008.
27. For some interesting reading on organizational stress, see Elaine Wethington, "Theories of Organizational Stress," *Administrative Science Quarterly* (September 2000), p. 640.
28. See, for example, "Stressed Out: Extreme Job Stress: Survivors' Tales," *Wall Street Journal* (January 17, 2001), p. B1.
29. N. Merrick, "Boxing Clever: Reducing Stress," *Employee Benefits* (March 2000), p. 34.
30. Fay Hansen, "Employee Assistance Programs (EAPs) Grow and Expand Their Reach," *Compensation and Benefits Review* (March/April 2000), p. 13.
31. William Atkinson, "Wellness, Employee Assistance Programs: Investments, Not Costs," *Bobbin* (May 2000), pp. 42–48.
32. J. Useem, "The New Company Town," *Fortune* (January 10, 2000), pp. 62–70.
33. See, for instance, P. Petesch, "Workplace Fitness or Workplace Fits?" *HR Magazine* (July 2001), pp. 137–40.
34. Carolyn Petersen, "Value of Complementary Care Rises, But Poses Challenges," *Managed HealthCare* (November 2000), pp. 47–48.
35. C. Vogel and J. Cagan, *Creating Breakthrough Products: Innovation from Product Planning to Program Approval* (Upper Saddle River, NJ: Prentice Hall, 2002).
36. J. Benditt, "Lessons from Innovation," *Technology Review* (July–August 2002), p. 9.
37. K. H. Hammonds, "How to Design the Perfect Product Start with Craig Vogel and Jonathan Cagan: Integrate Style and Technology with a Dash of Fantasy. Apply Everything from Toasters to Cars," *Fast Company* (July 2002), pp. 122–27.
38. "The House That Mice Build: Strong Brand Identity Comes from Products Known for Innovation, Quality, and Catchy Design," *BusinessWeek* (June 17, 2002), p. 74.
39. Ibid., p. 126.
40. "Aspirin Man Hoffman Recognized," *Chemical Week* (June 26, 2002), p. 30.
41. L. Bannon, "Think Tank in Toyland," *Wall Street Journal* (June 6, 2002), pp. B1; B3.
42. "Learning from Leading Innovators," *The Futurist* (May 2002), p. 62.
43. See, for example, L. P. Livinstone, L. E. Palicyh, and G. R. Carini, "Promotion Creativity Through the Logic of Contradiction," *Journal of Organizational Behavior* (May 2002), pp. 321–27; and Intel company information <www.intel.com>, July 4, 2002.
44. C. Vogel and J. Cagan, *Creating breakthrough Products: Innovation from Product Planning to Program Approval* (Upper Saddle River, NJ: Prentice Hall, 2002).
45. R. T. Frambac and N. Schillewaert, "Organizational Innovation Adoption: A Multi-Level Framework of Determinants and Opportunities for Future Research," *Journal of Business Research* (February 2002), pp. 63–77.
46. See, for instance, H. H. Meyer and P. C. Mugge, "Make Platform Innovation Drive Enterprise Growth," *Research-Technology Management* (January 2001), p. 25.
47. "Creating the Innovation Culture: Leveraging Visionaries, Dissenters, and Other Useful Troublemakers in Your Organization," *Indianapolis Business Journal* (February 4, 2002), p. 63.

48. G. Hamel, "Innovation's New Math," *Fortune* (July 9, 2001), p. 131.
49. A. Mudio, "GM Has a New Model for Change," *Fast Company* (December 2000), pp. 62–64.
50. See also, "Ten Ways to...Create an Innovative Culture," *Management Today* (February 2002), p. 20.
51. A. Genus and M. Kaplani, "Managing Operations with People and Technology," *International Journal of Technology and Management* (January–March 2002), p. 89; and K. Laursen, "The Importance of Sectoral Differences in the Application of Complementary HRM Practices for Innovative Performance," *International Journal of the Economics of Business* (February 2002), pp. 139–47.
52. See, for example, "Make Your Company an Idea Factory," *FSB* (May/June 2000), pp. 120–25.
53. M. J. McDermott, "Listening with a Purpose," *Chief Executive* (February 2001), p. 35.
54. G. N. Chandler, C. Keller, and D. W. Lyon, "Unraveling the Determinants and Consequences of an Innovation-Supportive Organizational Culture," *Entrepreneurship Theory and Practice* (Fall 2000), pp. 59–76.
55. Ibid.
56. J. Jusko, "Turning Ideas into Action," *Industry Week* (October 16, 2000), pp. 105–6.
57. See also, T. Pollock, "Mind Your Own Business: The Gentle Art of Selling Change," *Supervision* (December 2000), p. 11; and R. M. Kanter, "The Enduring Skills of Change Leaders," *Ivey Business Journal* (May 2000), p. 31.
58. Material for this case comes from "Royal Caribbean Cruise Line Parent Lays Off 400," *Knight-Ridder/Tribune Business News* (October 13, 2001), p. 1; "Royal Caribbean Cruises Ltd., Promotes Capt. William Wright to Senior VP of Safety and Environment," <www.royalcaribbean.com> (September 28, 2001), p. 1; "Save the Waves," <www.royalcaribbean.com/environment2000/save-waves/index.html> (2001), p. 1; and "One Big Problem—Save the Waves," *Fast Company* (March 2000), p. 188.

Chapter 8

1. This vignette is based on "In a Former Life: Anne Beiler," *Inc.* (September 2000), p. 107; "Gap, PA-Based Food Company Opens Store Offering Frozen Custard Fruit-Ice," *Knight-ridder/Tribune Business News* (May 16, 2002), p. 2; "Auntie Anne's Inc.," *Nations Restaurant News Daily News Fax* (May 6, 2002), p. 1; and company Web Site, <www.auntieannes.com> (July 2002).
2. See S. P. Robbins, *Essentials of Organizational Behavior,* 7th ed. (Upper Saddle River, NJ: Prentice Hall, 2003), p. 2.
3. J. A. Lepine and L. Van Dyne, "Peer Response to Low Performers: An Attributional Model of Helping in the Context of Groups," *Academy of Management Review* (January 2001), pp. 67–84.
4. S. J. Becker, "Empirical Validation of Affect, Behavior, and Cognition as Distinct Components of Behavior," *Journal of Personality and Social Psychology* (May 1984), pp. 1191–1205.
5. "A Case of Cognitive Dissonance," *U. S. News and World Report* (November 26, 2001), p. 10.
6. S. P. Robbins, *Essentials of Organizational Behavior,* p. 19.
7. L. Festinger, *A Theory of Cognitive Dissonance* (Stanford, CA: Stanford University Press, 1957).
8. H. C. Koh and E. H. Y. Boo, "The Link Between Organizational Ethics and Job Satisfaction: A Study of Managers in Singapore," *Journal of Business Ethics* (February 15, 2001), p. 309.
9. See, for example, J. Jermias, "Cognitive Dissonance and Resistance to Change: The Influence of Commitment Confirmation and Feedback on Judgment Usefulness of Accounting Systems," *Accounting, Organizations, and Society* (March 2001), p. 141.
10. J. B. Rotter, "Generalized Expectancies for Internal versus External Control of Reinforcement," *Psychological Monographs* 80, no. 609 (1966); and T. E. Becker, R. S. Billings, D. M. Eveleth, and N. L. Gilbert, "Foci and Bases of Employee Commitment: Implications for Job Performance," *Academy of Management Journal* (February 1996), pp. 464–82.
11. See, for example, J. B. Herman, "Are Situational Contingencies Limiting the Job Attitude–Job Performance Relationship?" *Organizational Behavior and Human Performance* (October 1973), pp. 208–24; M. M. Petty, G. W. McGee, and J. W. Cavender, A Meta Analysis of the Relationships between Individual Job Satisfaction and Individual Performance, *Academy of Management Review* (October 1984), pp. 712–21; C. N. Greene, "The Satisfaction-Performance Controversy," *Business Horizons* (February 1972), pp. 31–41; E. E. Lawler III, *Motivation and Organizations* (Monterey, CA: Brooks/Cole, 1973); A. H. Brayfield and W. H. Crockett, "Employee Attitudes and Employee Performance," *Psychological Bulletin* (September 1955), pp. 396–428; F. Herzberg, B. Mausner, R. O. Peterson, and D. F. Capwell, *Job Attitudes: Review of Research and Opinion* (Pittsburgh, PA: Psychological Service of Pittsburgh, 1957); V. H. Vroom, *Work and Motivation* (New York: John Wiley & Sons, 1964); and G. P. Fournet, M. K. Distefano Jr., and M. W. Pryer, "Job Satisfaction: Issues and Problems," *Personnel Psychology* (Summer 1966), pp. 165–83.
12. C. N. Greene, "The Satisfaction-Performance Controversy"; Lawler, *Motivation and Organizations*; and Petty, McGee, and Cavender, "A Meta Analysis of the Relationships between Individual Job Satisfaction and Individual Performance."
13. J. B. Rotter, "Generalized Expectancies for Internal versus External Control of Reinforcement"; Becker, Billings, and Gilbert, "Foci and Bases of Employee Commitment: Implications for Job Performance."
14. "Survey Reveals Three Things to Keep Workers Happy," *Knight Ridder/Tribune Business News* (May 13, 2001), p. 1.
15. Consulting Psychologists Press, Inc., *Myers-Briggs Type Indicator® (MBTI®)*, <www1.cpp.com/products/mbti/index.asp> (2000).
16. P. Moran, "Personality Characteristics and Growth-Orientation of the Small Business Owner Manger," *Journal of Managerial Psychology* (July 2000), p. 651; and M. Higgs, "Is There a Relationship Between the Myers-Briggs Type Indicator and Emotional Intelligence?" *Journal of Managerial Psychology* (September–October, 2001), pp. 488–513.
17. J. M. Digman, "Personality Structure: Emergence of the Five Factor Model," in M. R. Rosenweig and L. W. Porter, eds., *Annual Review of Psychology* 41 (Palo Alto, CA: Annual Reviews, 1990), pp. 417–40; O. P. John, "The Big Five Factor Taxonomy: Dimensions of Personality in the Natural Language and in Questionnaires," in L. A. Pervin, ed., *Handbook of Personality Theory and Research* (New York: Guilford Press, 1990), pp. 66–100; and M. K. Mount, M. R. Barrick, and J. P. Strauss, "Validity of Observer Ratings of the Big Five Personality Factors," *Journal of Applied Psychology* (April 1996), pp. 272–80.
18. See G. Vittorio, C. Barbaranelli, and G. Guido, "Brand Personality: How to Make the Metaphor Fit," *Journal of Economic Psychology* (June 2001), p. 377; G. M. Hurtz and J. J. Donovan, "Personality and Job Performance: The Big Five Revisited," *Journal of Applied Psychology* (December 2000), p. 869; and W. A. Hochwarter, L. A. Witt, and K. M. Kacmar, "Perceptions of Organizational Politics as a Moderator of the Relationship Between Conscientiousness and Job Performance," *Journal of Applied Psychology* (June 2000), p. 472.
19. Barrick and Mount, "Autonomy as a Moderator of the Relationship between the Big Five Personality Dimensions and Job Performance."
20. See also, I. T. Robertson, H. Baron, P. Gibbons, R. MacIver, and G. Nyfield, "Conscientiousness and Managerial Performance," *Journal of Occupational and Organizational Psychology* (June 2000), pp. 171–78.
21. R. Barrick, M. Piotrowski, and G. L. Stewart, "Personality and Job Performance: Test of the Mediating Effects of Motivation Among Sales Representatives," *Journal of Applied Psychology* (February 2002), pp. 43–52.
22. This section is based on R. Bar-On and J. D. A. Parker, *The Handbook of Emotional Intelligence: Theory, Development, Assessment, and Application at Home, School, and in the Work Place* (San Francisco, CA: Jossey-Bass, 2000); B. E. Ashforth, "The Handbook of Emotional Intelligence: Theory, Development, Assessment, and Application at Home, School, and in the Work Place: A Review)" *Personnel Psychology* (Autumn 2001), pp. 721–24; and S. Fox, "Promoting Emotional

Intelligence in Organizations: Make Training in Emotional Intelligence Effective," *Personnel Psychology* (Spring 2002), pp. 236–40.

23. For an interesting perspective on the application of emotional intelligence, see P. J. Jordan, N. M. Ashkanasy, and C. E. J. Hartel, "Emotional Intelligence as a Moderator of Emotional and Behavioral Reactions to Job Insecurity," *Academy of Management Review* (July 2002), pp. 361–72.
24. C. Cherniss and R. D. Caplan, "A Case Study of Implementing Emotional Intelligence Programs in Organizations," *Journal of Organizational Excellence* (Winter 2001), pp. 763–86; and S. B. Vanessa-Urch and W. Deuskat, "Building the Emotional Intelligence of Groups," *Harvard Business Review*, March 2001, pp. 81–91.
25. "Can't We All Just Get Along," *BusinessWeek* (October 9, 2000), p. 18.
26. C. Moller and S. Powell, "Emotional Intelligence and the Challenges of Quality Management," *Leadership and Organizational Development Journal* (July–August 2001), pp. 341–45.
27. See, for instance, J. Silvester, F. M. Anderson-Gough, N. R. Anderson, and A. R. Mohamed, "Locus of Control, Attributions and Impression Management in the Selection Interview, *Journal of Occupational and Organizational Psychology* (March 2002), pp. 59–77; D. W. Organ and C. N. Greene, "Role Ambiguity, Locus of Control, and Work Satisfaction," *Journal of Applied Psychology* (February 1974), pp. 101–102; and T. R. Mitchell, C. M. Smyser and S. E. Weed, "Locus of Control: Supervision and Work Satisfaction," *Academy of Management Journal* (September 1975), pp. 623–31.
28. R. G. Vleeming, "Machiavellianism: A Preliminary Review," *Psychology Reports* (February 1979), pp. 295–310.
29. P. Van Kenhove, I. Vermeir, and S. Verniers, "An Empirical Investigation of the Relationship Between Ethical Beliefs, Ethical Ideology, Political Preference and Need for Closure," *Journal of Business Ethics* (August 15, 2001), p. 347.
30. Based on J. Brockner, *Self Esteem at Work* (Lexington, MA: Lexington Books, 1988), Chs. 1–4.
31. See, for instance, R. Vermunt, D. van Knippenberg, B. van Knippenberg, and E. Blaauw, "Self-Esteem and Outcome Fairness: Differential Importance of Procedural and Outcome Considerations," *Journal of Applied Psychology* (August 2001), p. 621; T. A. Judge and J. E. Bono, "Relationship of Core Self-Evaluation Traits—Self-Esteem, Generalized Self-Efficacy, Locus of Control, and Emotional Stability—With Job Satisfaction and Job Performance," *Journal of Applied Psychology* (February 2001), p. 80; and D. B. Fedor, J. M. Maslyn, W. D. Davis, and K. Mathieson, "Performance Improvement Efforts in Response to Negative Feedback: The Roles of Source Power and Recipient Self-Esteem," *Journal of Management* (January–February 2001), pp. 79–97.
32. M. Snyder, *Public Appearances/Private Realities: The Psychology of Self Monitoring* (New York: W. H. Freeman, 1987).
33. See, for example, P. M. Fandt, "Managing Impressions with Information: A Field Study of Organizational Realities," *Journal of Applied Behavioral Science* (June 2001), pp. 180–205.
34. D. V. Day, A. L. Unckless, D. J. Schleicher, and N. J. Hiller, "Self-Monitoring Personality at Work: A Meta-Analytic Investigation of Construct Validity," *Journal of Applied Psychology* (April 2002), pp. 390–402; and J. S. Miller, "Self-Monitoring and Performance Appraisal Satisfaction: An Exploratory Field Study," *Human Resource Management* (Winter 2001), pp. 321–33.
35. R. N. Taylor and M. D. Dunnette, "Influence of Dogmatism, Risk Taking Propensity, and Intelligence on Decision Making Strategies for a Sample of Industrial Managers," *Journal of Applied Psychology* (August 1974), pp. 420–23.
36. I. L. Janis and L. Mann, *Decision Making: A Psychological Analysis of Conflict, Choice, and Commitment* (New York: Free Press, 1977).
37. N. Kogan and M. A. Wallach, "Group Risk Taking as a Function of Members' Anxiety and Defensiveness," *Journal of Personality* (March 1967), pp. 50–63.
38. K. Hyrshy, "Entrepreneurial Metaphors and Concepts: An Exploratory Study," *Journal of Managerial Psychology* (July 2000), p. 653; and B. McCarthy, "The Cult of Risk Taking and Social Learning: A Study of Irish Entrepreneurs," *Management Decision* (August 2000), pp. 563–75.
39. J. L. Holland, *Making Vocational Choices: A Theory of Vocational Personalities and Work Environments* (Upper Saddle River, NJ: Prentice Hall, 1982).
40. See, for example, A. R. Spokane, "A Review of Research on Person Environment Congruence in Holland's Theory of Careers," *Journal of Vocational Behavior* (June 1985), pp. 306–43; and D. Brown, "The Status of Holland's Theory of Career Choice," *Career Development Journal* (September 1987), pp. 13–23.
41. S. Bates, "Personality Counts: Psychological Tests Can Help Peg the Job Applicants Best Suited for Certain Jobs," *HR Magazine* (February 2002), pp. 28–38; and K. J. Jansen and A. K. Brown, "Toward a Multi Level Theory of Person Environment Fit," *Academy of Management Proceedings from the Fifty Eighth Annual Meeting of the Academy of Management* San Diego, CA, August 7–12, 1998, pp. HR: FR1–FR 8.
42. See M. R. Barrick, M. Piotrowski, and G. L. Stewart, "Personality and Job Performance: Test of the Mediating Effects of Motivation among Sales Representatives," *Journal of Applied Psychology* (February 2002), pp. 43–52.
43. P. B. Robinson, D. V. Simpson, J. C. Huefner, and H. K. Hunt, "An Attitude Approach to the Prediction of Entrepreneurship," *Entrepreneurship Theory and Practice* (Summer 1991), pp. 13–31.
44. B. M. Davis, "Role of Venture Capital in the Economic Renaissance of an Area," in R. D. Hisrich, ed. *Entrepreneurship, Intrapreneurship, and Venture Capital* (Lexington, MA: Lexington Books, 1086), pp. 107–18.
45. J. M. Crant, "The Proactive Personality Scale as a Predictor of Entrepreneurial Intentions," *Journal of Small Business Management* (July 1996), pp. 42–49.
46. H. H. Kelley, "Attribution in Social Interaction," in E. Jones et al., eds., *Behavior* (Morristown, NJ: General Learning Press, 1972).
47. G. Miller and T. Lawson, "The Effect of an Informational Option on the Fundamental Attribution Error," *Personality and Social Psychology Bulletin* (June 1989), pp. 194–204. See also, G. Charness and E. Haruvy, "Self-Serving Bias: Evidence from a Simulated Labour Relationship," *Journal of Managerial Psychology* (July 2000), p. 655; and T. J. Elkins, J. S. Phillips, and R. Konopaske, "Gender-Related Biases in Evaluations of Sex Discrimination Allegations: Is Perceived Threat a Key?" *Journal of Applied Psychology* (April 2002), pp. 280–93.
48. Z. Moukheiber and R. Langreth, "The Halo Effect," *Forbes* (December 10, 2001), p. 66.
49. See, for example, L. Jussim, "Self-fulfilling Prophecies: A Theoretical and Integrative Review," *Psychological Review* (October 1986), pp. 429–45; D. Eden, *Pygmalion in Management* (Lexington, MA: Lexington Books, 1990); and O. B. Davidson and D. Eden, "Remedial Self-Fulfilling Prophecy: Two Field Experiments to Prevent Golem Effects Among Disadvantaged Women," *Journal of Applied Psychology* (June 2000), p. 386.
50. J. C. Edwards, "Self-Fulfilling Prophecy and Escalating Commitment: Fuel for the Waco Fire," *Journal of Applied Behavioral Science* (September 2001), pp. 343–61.
51. B. F. Skinner, *Contingencies of Reinforcement* (East Norwalk, CT: Appleton-Century-Crofts, 1971).
52. A. Bandura, *Social Learning Theory* (Upper Saddle River, NJ: Prentice Hall, 1977).
53. S. E. Asch, "Effects of Group Pressure upon the Modification and Distortion of Judgements," in H. Guetzkow, ed., *Groups, Leadership, and Men* (Pittsburgh, PA: Carnegie Press, 1951), pp. 177–90.
54. Ibid.
55. See, for instance, E. J. Thomas and C. F. Fink, "Effects of Group Size," *Psychological Bulletin* (July 1963), pp. 371–84; and M. E. Shaw, *Group Dynamics: The Psychology of Small Group Behavior* (New York: McGraw-Hill, 1975).
56. R. Albanese and D. D. Van Fleet, "Rational Behavior in Groups: The Free Riding Tendency," *Academy of Management Review* (April 1985), pp. 244–55.

57. L. Berkowitz, "Group Standards, Cohesiveness, and Productivity," *Human Relations* (November 1954), pp. 509–19.
58. F.H. Ondorka Jr., "Tools in a Tight Market," *Hotel and Motel Management* (May 18, 1998), p. 30.
59. Ibid.
60. www.praendex.com
61. www.loperworks.com
62. www.praendex.com
63. Ibid.
64. Case is based on information from the Company's Web Site <www.plumtree.com>, July 2002; and L. Kroll, "The Plumtree Software Soap Opera," *Forbes* (May 29, 2000), pp. 96–100.

Chapter 9

1. The opening vignette is based on company information from its Web Site <www.strawberryfrog.com>, July 25 2002; and S. Ellison, "Ad Firm StrawberryFrog in Amsterdam Thinks Big but Wants to Stay Small," *Wall Street Journal* (April 3, 2000), p. A43.
2. L. Chaney and J. Lyden, "Making U.S. Teams Work," *Supervision* (January 2000), p. 6.
3. See, for example, A. Edmondson, "Psychological Safety and Learning Behavior in Work Teams," *Administrative Science Quarterly* (June 1999), p. 350: D. W. Tjosvold, *Working Together to Get Things Done: Managing for Organizational Productivity* (Lexington, MA: Lexington Books, 1986); Tjosvold, *Organization: An Enduring Competitive Advantage* (New York: John Wiley & Sons, 1991).
4. L. D. Fredendall, M. D. Crino, G. Curtain, S. Kittel, K. M. Elliott, and C. M. Hydrick, "Assigning Human Resource Responsibilities to Self-Directed Work Teams," *Production and Inventory Management Journal* (Summer 2000), p. 5.
5. See also, L. Chaney and J. Lyden, "Making U.S. Teams Work," *Supervision* (January 2000), p. 6.
6. "What Makes Team Work?" *HR Focus* (April 2002), pp. S1–S4. See also, B. L. Kirkman and D. L. Shapiro, "The Impact of Cultural Values on Job Satisfaction and Organizational Commitment in Self-Managing Work Teams: The Mediating Role of Employee Resistance, *Academy of Management Journal* (June 2001), pp. 557–70.
7. B. W. Tuckman and M. A. C. Jensen, "Stages of Small Group Development Revisited," *Group and Organizational Studies* 2, no. 3 (1977), pp. 419–27
8. T. Bragg, "Turn Around an Ineffective Team," *IIE Solutions* (May 1999), pp. 49–51: and L. N. Jewell and H. J. Reitz, *Group Effectiveness in Organizations* (Glenview, IL: Scott, Foresman, 1981).
9. F. M. J. LaFasto and C. E. Larson, *When Teams Work Best* (Thousands Oaks, CA: Sage Publications, 2001)
10. Information for this section is based on J. R. Katzenbach and D. K. Smith, *The Wisdom of Teams* (Boston: Harvard Business School Press, 1993), pp. 21, 45, 85; and D. C. Kinlaw, *Developing Superior Work Teams* (Lexington, MA: Lexington Books, 1991), pp. 3–21.
11. See, for example, J. D. Osborn, *The New Self-Directed Work Teams* (New York: McGraw-Hill, 2000).
12. S. Adams and L. Kydoniefs, "Making Teams Work: Bureau of Labor Statistics Learns What Works and What Doesn't," *Quality Progress* (January 2000), pp. 43–49.
13. D. Hoffman, "At Wachovia, Fund Teams Work: Bank's Buddy System Improves performance," *Investment News* (February 2001), p. 8.
14. T. Capozzoli, "How to Succeed with Self-Directed Work Teams," *Supervision* (February 2002), pp. 25–27.
15. P. Strozniak, "Teams at Work," *Industry Week* (September 18, 2000), p. 47.
16. H. F. Hullender, "It's All about Improving Performance: Teams Work Better with Expanded Problem-Solving and Decision-Making Skills," *Quality Progress* (February 2000), pp. 47–53; J. Barnard, "The Empowerment of Problem-Solving Teams: Is It an Effective Management Tool?" *Journal of Applied Management Studies* (June 1999), p. 73.
17. Ibid., p. 48.
18. See, for example, B. Carroll, "Using Focus Activities to Drive a Self-Managed Team to High Performance," *National Productivity Review* (Spring 2000), pp. 43–51.
19. G. L. Stewart and M. R. Barrick." Team Structure and Performance: Assessing the Mediating Role of Intrateam Process and the Moderating Role of Task," *Academy of Management Journal* (April 2000), p. 135.
20. For an interesting review of self-managed team behavior when evaluating one another, see C. P. Neck, M. L. Connely, C. A. Zuniga, and S. Goel, "Family Therapy Meets Self-Managing Teams: Explaining Self-Managing Team Performance Through Team Member Perception," *Journal of Applied Behavioral Science* (June 1999), pp. 245–59; G. A. Neuman, S. H, Wagner, and N. D. Christiansen, "The Relationship Between Work Team Personality Composition and the Job Performance of Teams," *Group and Organization Management* (March 1999), pp. 28–45; and V. U. Druskat and S. B. Wolff," Effects and Timing of Developmental Peer Appraisals in Self-Managing Work Groups," *Journal of Applied Psychology* (February 1999), pp. 58–74.
21. H. Simkovits, "Succession Problems? Build a More Self-Managed Team," *Boston Business Journal* (May 18, 2001), p. 24.
22. S. S. Webber, "Leadership and Trust Facilitating Cross-Functional Team Success," *Journal of Management Development* (March–April 2002), pp. 201–15.
23. T. L. Legare, "How Hewlett-Packard Used Virtual Cross-Functional Teams to Deliver HealthCare Industry Solutions," *Journal of Organizational Excellence* (Autumn 2001), pp. 29–39.
24. E. Berns, "Cross-Functional Teams Spawn Excellence," *Design News* (October 16, 2000), p. 53.
25. L. A. Witt, T. F. Hilton, and W. A. Hochwarter, "Addressing Politics in Matrix Teams," *Group and Organization Management* (June 2001), pp. 230–48.
26. See, for instance, H. E. Joy, D. Joyendu, and M. Bhadury, "Maximizing Workforce Diversity in Project Teams: A Network Flow Approach," *Omega* (April 2000), pp. 143–55.
27. See, for example, "How Do I Know You're Working When I Can't See You? Top Entrepreneur Offers Key Factors for Successfully Managing a Virtual Team," *Internet Wire* (June 26, 2002), p. 1.
28. D. Robb," Virtual Workplace," *HR Magazine* (June 2002), pp. 105–13.
29. J. Koranteng, "Heineken Puts Together Virtual Marketing Team," *Advertising Age International* (February 2000), p. 30.
30. P. Strozniak, "Teams at Work," *Industry Week* (September 18, 2000), pp. 47–50.
31. See, for example, H. W. Head, "How culture Helped Dow AgroSciences Succeed in Achieving Business Objectives of an Acquisition," *Journal of Organizational Excellence* (Winter 2001), pp. 17–26.
32. Ibid.
33. See T. L. Stanley, "The Challenge of Managing a High-Performance Team," *Supervision* (July 2001), pp. 10–13; M. A. Huselid and B. E. Becker, "The Impact of High Performance Work Systems, Implementation Effectiveness, and Alignment with Strategy on Shareholder Wealth," *Academy of Management Best Paper Proceedings*, L. N. Dosier and J. B. Keys, eds. (Boston: August 8–13, 1997), pp. 144–47; C. E. Larson and F. M. J. LaFasto, *Teamwork* (Newbury Park, CA: Sage Publications, 1992); J. R. Hackman, ed., *Groups That Work (and Those That Don't)* (San Francisco: Jossey Bass, 1990); and D. W. Tjosvold and M. M. Bass, *Leading the Team Organization* (Lexington, MA: Lexington Books, 1991).
34. K. T. Dirks, "The Effects of Interpersonal Trust on Work Group Performance," *Journal of Applied psychology* (June 1999), pp. 445–55.
35. Larson and LaFasto, *Teamwork*, p. 75.
36. See, for instance, G. Van Der Vegt, B. Emans, and E. Van DeVliert, "Motivating Effects of Task and Outcome Interdependence in Work Teams," *Journal of Managerial Psychology* (July 2000), p. 829.
37. M. Conley, "Self-Directed Work Teams," *Safety and Health* (April 2000), pp. 54–59.

38. D. Harrington Mackin, *The Team Building Tool Kit* (New York: AMACOM, 1994), p. 53.
39. See, for instance, J. E. Salk and M. Y. Brannien, "National Culture, Networks, and Individual Influence in a Multinational Management Team," *Academy of Management Journal* (April 2000), p. 191; B. L. Kirkman, C. B. Gibson, and D. L. Shapiro, "Enhanching the Implementation and Effectiveness of Work Teams in Global Affiliates," *Organizational Dynamics* (Summer 2001), pp. 12–30; and B. L. Kirkman and D. L. Shapiro, "The Impact of Cultural Values on Employee Resistance to Teams: Towards a Model of Globalized Self-Managing Work Team Effectiveness," *Academy of Management Review* (July 1997), pp. 730–57.
40. S. Stern, "Teams that Work," *Management Today* (June 2001), p. 48.
41. Based on C. Margerison and D. McCann, *Team Management: Practical New Approaches* (London, England: Mercury Books, 1990).
42. R. M. Yandrick, "A Team Effort," *HR Magazine* (June 2001), pp. 136–41.
43. Ibid.
44. M. A. Marks, C. S. Burke, M. J. Sabella, and S. J. Zaccaro, "The Impact of Cross-Training on Team Effectiveness," *Journal of Applied Psychology* (February 2002), pp. 3–14; and M. A. Marks, S. J. Zaccaro, and J. E. Mathieu, "Performance Implications of Leader Briefings and Team Interaction for Team Adaptation to Novel Environments," *Journal of Applied Psychology* (December 2000), p. 971.
45. C. Garvey, "Steer Teams with the Right Pay: Team-Based Pay Is a Success When It Fits Corporate Goals and Culture, and Rewards the Right Behavior," *HR Magazine* (May 2002), pp. 71–77.
46. D. C. Kinlaw, *Developing Superior Work Teams* (Lexington, MA: Lexington Books, 1991), p. 43.
47. L. Yu, "Does Diversity Drive Productivity? Different Experiences and points of View Don't, by Themselves, Make Work Groups More Productive. The Important Factor is How People Interrelate," *MIT Sloan Management Review* (Winter 2002), p. 17.
48. See, for example, C. K. DeDreu and M. A. West, "Minority Dissent and Team Innovation: The Importance of Participation in Decision Making," *Journal of Applied Psychology* (December 2001), pp. 1191–1202.
49. "Diversity Enhances Decision-making," *Industry Week* (April 2, 2001), p. 9.
50. See S. G. Barsade, A. J. Ward, J. D. F.Turner, and J. A. Sonnenfeld, "To Your Heart's Content: A Model of Affective Diversity in Top Management Teams," *Administrative Science Quarterly* (December 2000), p. 802.
51. L. H. Pelled, K. M. Eisenhardt, and K. R. Xin, "Exploring the Black Box: An Analysis of Work Group Diversity, Conflict, and Performance, "*Administrative Science Quarterly (* (March 1999), p. 128
52. H. E. Joy, D. Joyendu, and M. Bhadury, "Maximizing Workforce Diversity in Project Teams: A Network Flow Approach," *Omega* (April 2000), pp. 143–55.
53. J. Anders, "Software Brings Unity to Company functions," *Wall Street Journal-Eastern Edition,* (September 21, 2000), p. B10
54. www.engenia.com
55. A. Crowley, "Surviving the Rocky Recruiting Road," *PC Week* (June 7, 1999), p. 72.
56. Case information based company Web Site materials <www.taperesources.com>, July 24, 2002; "Legacies," *Inc.* (October 17, 2001), p, 177; and Now That We're Not a Start-Up, How Do I Promote Teamwork?" *Inc.* (October 20, 1998), pp. 154–56.

Chapter 10

1. C. Dahle, "The New Fabric of Success," *Fast Company* (June 2000), pp. 252–54.
2. R. Katerberg and G. J. Blau, "An Examination of Level and Direction of Effort and Job Performance," *Academy of Management Journal* (June 1983), pp. 249–57.
3. A. Maslow, *Motivation and Personality* (New York: Harper & Row, 1954).
4. See, for example, R. L. Payne, "Eupsychian Management and the Millennium," *Journal of Managerial Psychology* (March 2000), pp. 219–27; "Dialogue–Discussion of Abraham H. Maslow's Management Theory," *Academy of Management Review* (October 2000), p. 696; and S. Coles, "Satisfying Basic Needs: Professor Don Harper Tells Sarah Coles about the Profound Impact of Maslow's Hierarchy of Needs." He contends that if you want to motivate your staff, then finding the right reward and offering it for the right behavior doesn't have to be complicated, *Employee Benefits* (October 2001), pp. S3–S7.
5. N. K. Austin, "The Power of the Pyramid: The Foundation of Human Psychology and, Thereby, of Motivation, Maslow's Hierarchy Is One Powerful Pyramid," *Incentive* (July 2002), p. 10.
6. See, for instance, E. E. Lawler III and J. L. Suttle, "A Causal Correlational Test of the Need Hierarchy Concept," *Organizational Behavior and Human Performance* (April 1972), pp. 265–87; and D. T. Hall and K. E. Nongaim, "An Examination of Maslow's Need Hierarchy in an Organizational Setting," *Organizational Behavior and Human Performance* (February 1968), pp. 12–35.
7. D. McGregor, *The Human Side of Enterprise* (New York: McGraw-Hill, 1960).
8. L. Clifford, "Watch Out for Sudden Reputation Death Syndrome," *Fortune* (January 7, 2002), <www.fortune.com.>
9. F. Herzberg, B. Mausner, and B. Snyderman, *The Motivation to Work* (New York: John Wiley & Sons, 1959); and F. Herzberg, *The Managerial Choice: To Be Effective or To Be Human*, rev. ed. (Salt Lake City: Olympus, 1982).
10. See, for example, L. K. Savery and J. A. Luks, "The Relationship Between Empowerment, Job Satisfaction and Reported Stress Levels: Some Australian Evidence," *Leadership and Organization Development Journal* (March 2001), p 97.
11. See, for instance, M. F. Gordon, N. M. Pryor, and B. V. Harris, "An Examination of Scaling Bias in Herzberg's Theory of Job Satisfaction," *Organizational Behavior and Human Performance* (February 1974), pp. 106–21; E. A. Locke and R. J. Whiting, "Sources of Satisfaction and Dissatisfaction among Solid Waste Management Employees," *Journal of Applied Psychology* (April 1974), pp. 145–56; and J. B. Miner, *Theories of Organizational Behavior* (Hinsdale, IL: Dryden Press, 1980), pp. 76–105.
12. D. C. McClelland, *The Achieving Society* (New York: Van Nostrand Reinhold, 1961); J. W. Atkinson and J. O. Raynor, *Motivation and Achievement* (Washington, DC: Winston, 1974); and D. C. McClelland, *Power: The Inner Experience* (New York: Free Press, 1969).
13. McClelland, The Achieving Society.
14. Vignette based on D. C. McClelland and D. G. Winter, *Motivating Economic Achievement* (New York: Free Press, 1969); D. C. McClelland and D. H. Burnham, "Power Is the Great Motivator," *Harvard Business Review,* March–April 1976, pp. 100–10; D. C. McClelland," An Advocate of Power," *International Management* (July 1975), pp. 27–29; and D. Miron and D. C. McClelland, "The Impact of Achievement Motivation Training on Small Businesses," *California Management Review* (Summer 1979), pp. 13–28.
15. J. S. Adams, "Inequity in Social Exchanges," in L. Berkowitz, ed., *Advances in Experimental Social Psychology*, vol. 2 (New York: Academic Press, 1965), pp. 267–300.
16. P. S. Goodman, "An Examination of Referents Used in the Evaluation of Pay," *Organizational Behavior and Human Performance* (October 1974), pp. 170–95; S. Ronen, "Equity Perception in Multiple Comparisons: A Field Study," *Human Relations* (April 1986), pp. 333–46; R. W. School, E. A. Cooper, and J. F. McKenna, "Referent Effects on Behavioral and Attitudinal Outcomes," *Personnel Psychology* (Spring 1987), pp. 113–27; and C. T. Kulik and M. L. Ambrose, "Personal and Situational Determinants of Referent Choice," *Academy of Management Review* (April 1992), pp. 212–37.
17. P. Bordia and G. Blau, "Pay Referent Comparison and Pay Level Satisfaction in Private versus Public Sector Organizations in India," *International Journal of Human Resource Management* (February 1998), pp. 155–68.

18. P. S. Goodman and A. Friedman, "An Examination of Adams' Theory of Inequity," *Administrative Science Quarterly* (September 1971), pp. 271–88.
19. See, for example, M. R. Carrell, "A Longitudinal Field Assessment of Employee Perceptions of Equitable Treatment," *Organizational Behavior and Human Performance* (February 1978), pp. 108–18; R. G. Lord and J. A. Hohenfeld, "Longitudinal Field Assessment of Equity Effects on the Performance of Major League Baseball Players," *Journal of Applied Psychology* (February 1979), pp. 19–26; and J. E. Dittrich and M. R. Carrell, "Organizational Equity Perceptions, Employee Job Satisfaction, and Department Absence and Turnover Rates," *Organizational Behavior and Human Performance* (August 1979), pp. 97–132.
20. P. S. Goodman, "Social Comparison Process in Organizations," in B. M. Staw and G. R. Salancik, eds., *New Directions in Organizational Behavior* (Chicago: St. Clair, 1977), pp. 97–132.
21. See J. R. Hackman and G. R. Oldham, "Motivation Through the Design of Work: Test of a Theory," *Organizational Behavior and Human Performance* (August 1976), pp. 250–79; Y. Fried and G. R. Ferris, "The Validity of the Job Characteristics Model: A Review and Meta Analysis," *Personnel Psychology* (Summer 1987), pp. 287–322; S. J. Zaccaro and E. F. Stone, "Incremental Validity of an Empirically Based Measure of Job Characteristics," *Journal of Applied Psychology* (May 1988), pp. 245–52; and R. W. Renn and R. J. Vandenberg, "The Critical Psychological States: An Underrepresented Component in Job Characteristics Model Research," *Journal of Management* (February 1995), pp. 279–303.
22. G. Van Der Vegt, B. Emans, and E. Van Der Vliert, "Motivating Effects of Task and Outcome Interdependence in Work Teams," *Journal of Managerial Psychology* (July 2000), p. 829; and B. Bemmels, "Local Union Leaders' Satisfaction with Grievance Procedures," *Journal of Labor Research* (Summer 2001), pp. 653–69.
23. V. H. Vroom, *Work and Motivation* (New York: John Wiley & Sons, 1964).
24. See, for example, H. G. Henneman III and D. P. Schwab, "Evaluation of Research on Expectancy Theory Prediction of Employee Performance," *Psychological Bulletin* (July 1972), pp. 1–9; and L. Reinharth and M. Wahba, "Expectancy Theory As a Predictor of Work Motivation, Effort Expenditure, and Job Performance," *Academy of Management Journal* (September 1975), pp. 502–37.
25. See, for example, V. H. Vroom, "Organizational Choice: A Study of Pre- and Post-Decision Processes," *Organizational Behavior and Human Performance* (April 1966), pp. 212–25; L. W. Porter and E. E. Lawler III, *Managerial Attitudes and Performance* (Homewood, IL: Richard D. Irwin, 1968); M. L. Ambrose and C. T. Kulik, "Old Friends, New Faces: Motivation Research of the 1990s," *Journal of Management* (May-June 1999), pp. 231–42.
26. Among academicians these three variables are typically referred to as valence, instrumentality, and expectancy, respectively.
27. See, for example, K. Smith, E. Jones, and E. Blain, "Managing Salesperson Motivation in a Territory Realignment," *Journal of Personal Selling and Sales Management* (Fall 2000), p. 215; and R. G. Isaac, W. J. Zerbe, and D. C. Pitt, "Leadership and Motivation: The Effective Application of Expectancy Theory," *Journal of Managerial Issues* (Summer 2001), pp. 212–20.
28. This four-step discussion was adapted from K. F. Taylor, "A Valence-Expectancy Approach to Work Motivation," *Personnel Practice Bulletin* (June 1974), pp. 142–48.
29. See, for instance, M. Siegall, "The Simplistic Five: An Integrative Framework for Teaching Motivation," *Organizational Behavior Teaching Review* 12, no. 4 (1987–1988), pp. 141–43.
30. See G. M. Combs, "Meeting the Leadership Challenge of a Diverse and Pluralistic Workplace: Implications of Self-Efficacy for Diversity Training," *Journal of Leadership Studies* (Spring 2002), pp. 1–17.
31. J. R. Billings and D. L. Sharpe, "Factors Influencing Flextime Usage Among Employed Married Women," *Consumer Interests Annual* (1999), pp. 89–94; and I. Harpaz, "The Importance of Work Goals: An International Perspective," *Journal of International Business Studies* (First Quarter 1990), pp. 75–93.
32. G. Hofstede, "Motivation, Leadership, and Organizations: Do American Theories Apply Abroad?" *Organizational Dynamics* (Summer 1980), p. 55.
33. J. K. Giacobbe-Miller, D. J. Miller, and V. I. Victorov, "A Comparison of Russian and U. S. Pay Allocation Decisions, Distributive Justice Judgements, and Productivity Under Different Payment Conditions," *Personnel Psychology* (Spring 1998), pp. 137–63.
34. S. L Mueller and L. D. Clarke, "Political-Economic Context and Sensitivity to Equity: Differences Between the United States and the Transition Economies of Central and Eastern Europe," *Academy of Management Journal* (June 1998), pp. 319–29
35. P. d'Iribarne, "Motivating Workers in Emerging Countries: Universal Tools and Local Adoptions," *Journal of Organizational Behavior* (May 2002), pp. 243–57; D. H. B. Walsh, F. Luthens, and S. M. Sommer, "Organizational Behavior Modification Goes to Russia: Replicating an Experimental Analysis across Cultures and Tasks," *Journal of Organizational Behavior Management* (Fall 1993), pp. 15–35; and J. R. Baum, J. D. Olian, M. Erez, and E. R. Schnell, "Nationality and Work Role Interactions: A Cultural Contrast of Israel and U.S. Entrepreneurs' versus Managers' Needs," *Journal of Business Venturing* (November 1993), pp. 499–512.
36. "Pay for Performance Pays Off, According to Senior Executives," *HR Focus* (July 2002), p. 9.
37. "Exclusive PFP Survey: Latest Data–What's Hot and What's Not in PFP," *Pay for Performance Report* (May 2002), p. 1.
38. "Exclusive PFP Survey: Respondents' Insights into Why Some PFP Plans Work," *Pay for Performance Report* (June 2002), p. 1.
39. "BT's High Performers Get More Home time," *Personnel Today* (April 2, 2002), p. 1.
40. J. Wiscombe, "Can Pay for Performance Really Work?" *Workforce* (August 2001), p. 28.
41. "Exclusive PFP Survey: Latest Data–What's Hot and What's Not in PFP," *Pay for Performance Report* (May 2002), p. 1.
42. See D. A. DeCenzo and S. P. Robbins, *Human Resource Management*, 7th ed. (New York: John Wiley & Sons, 2002), p. 314.
43. "Pay for Performance Back in Vogue for CEOs." *Report on Salary Surveys* (April 2002), p. 9.
44. M. A. Carpenter and W. G. Sanders, "Top Management Team Compensation: The Missing Link Between CEO Pay and Firm Performance," *Strategic Management Journal* (April 2002), pp. 367–76.
45. See, M. T. Frank and J. M. Ocker, "New SEC Equity Compensation Plan Disclosure Rules and Changing Shareholder Approval Requirements Affect Public Company Compensation Planning and Reporting," *Tax Management Compensation Planning Journal* (July 5, 2002), pp. 210–13.
46. See, for example, "Anger at Executives' Profits Fuels Support for Stock Curb," *New York Times* (July 9, 2002), p. A1
47. "Exposed: Enron's Excesses: The Energy Giant's Lavish Culture was Encouraged at Expense of Employees," *Incentive* (April 2002), p. 9.
48. J. C. Cooper and K. Madigan, "Corporate Crime Isn't Fazing Consumers, Yet." *BusinessWeek* (July 22, 2002), p. 23.
49. L. Walczak, R. S. Dunham, P. Dwyer, R. Cohn, W. Zellner, G. Smith, and C. Scotti, "Let the Reforms Begin," *BusinessWeek* (July 22, 2002), pp. 26–31.
50. P. Falcone, "Motivating Staff Without Money," *HR Magazine* (August 2002), pp. 105–8.
51. Ibid., p. 106
52. See, for instance, G. Cheetham and G. Chivers, "The Reflective (and Competent) Practitioner: A Mode of Professional Competence Which Seeks to Harmonize the Reflective Practitioner and Competence-Based Approaches," *Journal of Managerial Psychology* (July 2000), p. 713.
53. R. Fournier, "Teamwork is the Key to Remote Development—Inspiring Trust and Maintaining Motivation Are Critical for a Distributive Development Team," *InfoWorld* (March 5, 2001), p. 48.

54. See, for example, M. Arndt, "How Does Harry Do It?" *BusinessWeek* (July 22, 2002), pp. 66–68; C. S. Meyer, S. Mukerjee, and A. Sestero, "Work-Family Benefits: Which Ones Maximize Profits?" *Journal of Managerial Issues* (Spring 2001), pp. 28–44; and P. W. Tam, "Silicon Valley Boots Up Quality of Life Programs," *Wall Street Journal* (Europe) (August 30, 2000), p. 14.
55. J. Wiscombe, "Flex Appeal–Not Just for Moms," *Workforce* (March 2002), p. 18.
56. S. Roberts, "Companies Slow to Employ Alternative Work Options; Use of Arrangements Such As Flextime Is Up Slightly, If at All," *Business Insurance* (April 8, 2002), p. T3.
57. S. F. Gale, "Formalized Flextime: The Perk That Brings Productivity," *Workforce* (February 2001), p. 38; and B.S. Gariety and S.Shaffer, "Wage Differentials Associated with Flestime," *Monthly Labor Review* (March 2001), pp. 68–75.
58. D. Fandray, "Eight Days a Week: Meeting the Challenges of the 24/7 Economy," *Workforce* (September 2000), pp. 35–42.
59. D. Sandford, "Wanting It All," *Management Today* (December 2001), p. 30.
60. D. Cadrain, "Cutting Hours, Saving Jobs," *Workforce* (June 2002), p. 16.
61. J. W. Gibson, C. W. Blackwell, P. Dominicis, and N. Demerath, "Telecommuting in the 21st Century: Benefits, Issues, and a Leadership Model Which Will Work," *Journal of Leadership Studies* (Spring 2002), pp. 75–87; "Time to Take Another Look at Telecommuting," *HR Focus* (May 2002), pp. 6–9; and "What You Need to Know about Web Collaboration," *HR Focus* (June 2002), pp. 1–3.
62. Gibson, Blackwell, Dominicis, and Demerath, "Telecommuting in the 21st Century," p. 78.
63. "Telecommunications on the Rise," *EuropeMedia* (June 7, 2002), p. 1.
64. Commerce Clearing House, "Work at Home Increasingly Appealing to Employers, but Legal Pitfalls Abound," *Human Resources Management: Ideas and Trends* (February 16, 1994), pp. 25–26.
65. "Time to Take Another Look at Telecommuting," *HR Focus* (May 2002), p. 8.
66. Information from company's Web site <www.sapient.com>, August 2, 2002; "America's Fastest-Growing Companies," *Fortune* (September 4, 2000), p. 164.
67. "Saluting the Global Awards Recipients of Arthur Andersen's Best Practices Awards 2000," *Fortune Online* <www.fortune.com>, January 16, 2001.
68. T. Purdum, "Winning with Empowerment," *Industry Week* (October 16, 2000), pp. 109–10.
69. P. Strozniak, "Rescue Operation," *Industry Week* (October 16, 2000), pp. 103–4.
70. L. Moriz, "Employees Are Precious assets," *Business News New Jersey* (May 23,2000), pp. 6–7.
71. S. Eads and R. Mcnott, "The Carrot-and-Rolex approach," *Business Week* (July 3,2000), p. 10.
72. "Novasoft Modeled Itself After Microsoft," *Business News New Jersey* (August 15, 2000), p. 30.
73. I. Mochari, "It's All in the Details," *Inc.* (March 2002), pp. 121–22.

Chapter 11

1. Vignette based on "Busy Being an Icon, Giuliani Keeps Political Future Alive," *New York Times* (September 5, 2002), p. A1; "Giuliani Reflects on 9/11, Shares Leadership Formula with HR," *HR Briefing* (August 1, 2002), pp. 1–2; "The Secret Skill of Leaders," *U.S. News &World Report* (January 14, 2002) p. 8; and J. Freed, "Real Leadership Shines in Tough Times: Leaders Demonstrate Compassion and Empathy in Times of Crisis," *Business Record* (April 1, 2002), p. 20.
2. See, for instance, R. A Barker, "The Nature of Leadership," *Human Relations* (April 2001), p. 469.
3. T. L. Gessner, M. S. Connelly, J. A. O'Connor, and T. C. Clifton, "Leadership and Destructive Acts: Individual and Situational Influences," *Leadership Quarterly* 4, no. 2 (1993), pp. 115–47.
4. B. Pfau and I. Kay, "HR: Playing the Training Game and Losing," *HR Magazine* (August 2002), pp. 49–54. See also, L. Lavelle, "For UPS Managers, A School of Hard Knocks," *BusinessWeek* (July 22, 2002), pp. 58–59.
5. K. Lewin and R. Lippitt, "An Experimental Approach to the Study of Autocracy and Democracy: A Preliminary Note," *Sociometry* 1 (1938), pp. 292–300; K. Lewin, "Field Theory and Experiment in Social Psychology: Concepts and Methods," *American Journal of Sociology* 44 (1939), pp. 868–96; K. Lewin, R. Lippitt, and R. K. White, "Patterns of Aggressive Behavior in Experimentally Created Social Climates," *Journal of Social Psychology* 10 (1939), pp. 271–301; and R. Lippitt, "An Experimental Study of the Effect of Democratic and Authoritarian Group Atmospheres," *University of Iowa Studies in Child Welfare* 16 (1940), pp. 43–95.
6. B. M. Bass, *Stodgills Handbook of Leadership* (New York: Free Press, 1981), pp. 298–99.
7. R. Tannenbaum and W. H. Schmidt, "How to Choose a Leadership Pattern," *Harvard Business Review,* (May–June 1973), pp. 162–80.
8. R. M. Stodgill and A. E. Coons, eds., *Leader Behavior: Its Description and Measurement, Research Monograph,* No. 88 (Columbus: Ohio State University, Bureau of Business Research, 1951). See also, S. Kerr, C. A. Schriesheim, C. J. Murphy, and R. M. Stodgill, "Toward a Contingency Theory of Leadership Based upon the Consideration and Initiating Structure Literature," *Organizational Behavior and Human Performance* (August 1974), pp. 62–82; and B. M. Fisher, "Consideration and Initiating Structure and Their Relationships with Leader Effectiveness: A Meta Analysis," in F. Hoy, ed., *Proceedings of the 48th Annual Academy of Management Conference* (Anaheim, CA, 1988), pp. 201–05.
9. R. Kahn and D. Katz, "Leadership Practices in Relation to Productivity and Morale," in D. Cartwright and A. Zander, eds., *Group Dynamics: Research and Theory,* 2nd ed. (Elmsford, NY: Pow, Paterson, 1960).
10. R. R. Blake and J. S. Mouton, *The Managerial Grid III* (Houston, TX: Gulf Publishing, 1984).
11. L. L. Larson, J. G. Hunt, and R. N. Osborn, "The Great Hi-Hi Leader Behavior Myth: A Lesson from Occams Razor," *Academy of Management Journal* (December 1976), pp. 628–41; and P. C. Nystrom, "Managers and the Hi-Hi Leader Myth," *Academy of Management Journal* (June 1978), pp. 325–31. See also, "Robert R. Blake and Jane S. Mouton: The Managerial Grid," *Thinkers* (March 2002), pp. 1–4.
12. See, for example, "The 3-D Theory of Leadership," in W. J. Reddin, *Managerial Effectiveness* (New York: McGraw-Hill, 1967).
13. F. E. Fiedler, *A Theory of Leadership Effectiveness* (New York: McGraw-Hill, 1967).
14. L. H. Peters, D. D. Hartke, and T. J. Pholman, "Fiedler's Contingency Theory of Leadership: An Application of the Meta Analysis Procedures of Schmidt and Hunter," *Psychological Bulletin* (March 1985), pp. 274–85.
15. See F. E. Fiedler, "When IQ + Experience [is not equal to] Performance," *Leadership and Organization Development Journal* (March 2001), p. 132.
16. R. J. House, "A Path Goal Theory of Leader Effectiveness," *Administrative Science Quarterly* (September 1971), pp. 321–38; R. J. House and T. R. Mitchell, "Path Goal Theory of Leadership," *Journal of Contemporary Business* (Autumn 1974), p. 86; and R. J. House, "Retrospective Comment," in L. E. Boone and D. D. Bowen, eds., *The Great Writings in Management and Organizational Behavior,* 2nd ed. (New York: Random House, 1987), pp. 354–64.
17. J. Seltzer and J. W. Smither, "A Role Play Exercise to Introduce Students to Path Goal Leadership," *Journal of Management Education* (August 1995), p. 381.
18. C. Silverthorne, "A Test of the Path-Goal Leadership Theory in Taiwan," *Leadership and Organization Development Journal* (March 2001), p. 151. See also, A. W. Joshi and S. Randall, "The Indirect

Effects of Organizational Controls on Salesperson Performance and Customer Orientation," *Journal of Business Research* (October 1, 2001), pp. 1–10; R. T. Keller, "A Test of the Path Goal Theory of Leadership with Need for Clarity as a Moderator in Research and Development Organizations," *Journal of Applied Psychology* (April 1989), pp. 208–12; J. C. Wofford and L. Z. Liska, "Path Goal Theories of Leadership: A Meta Analysis," *Journal of Management* (Winter 1993), pp. 857–76; and S. Sagie and M. Koslowsky, "Organizational Attitudes and Behaviors as a Function of Participation in Strategic and Tactical Change Decisions: An Application of Path Goal Theory," *Journal of Organizational Behavior* (January 1994), pp. 37–47.

19. V. H. Vroom and P. W. Yetton, *Leadership and Decision Making* (Pittsburgh: University of Pittsburgh Press, 1973).
20. V. H. Vroom and A. G. Yago, *The New Leadership: Managing Participation in Organizations* (Upper Saddle River, NJ: Prentice Hall, 1988). See especially, Chapter 8.
21. See, for example, R. H. G. Field, "A Test of the Vroom Yetton Normative Model of Leadership," *Journal of Applied Psychology* (October 1982), pp. 523–32; C. R. Leana, "Power Relinquishment versus Power Sharing: Theoretical Clarification and Empirical Comparison of Delegation and Participation," *Journal of Applied Psychology* (May 1987), pp. 228–33; J. T. Ettling and A. G. Yago, "Participation under Conditions of Conflict: More on the Validity of the Vroom Yetton Model," *Journal of Management Studies* (January 1988), pp. 73–83; and R. H. G. Field and R. J. House, "A Test of the Vroom Yetton Model Using Manager and Subordinate Reports," *Journal of Applied Psychology* (June 1990), pp. 362–66.
22. For additional information about the exchanges that occur between the leader and the follower, see A. S. Phillips and A. G. Bedeian, "Leader Follower Exchange Quality: The Role of Personal and Interpersonal Attributes," *Academy of Management Journal* 37, no. 4 (1994), pp. 990–1001; and T. A. Scandura and C. A. Schriesheim, "Leader Member Exchange and Supervisor Career Mentoring as Complementary Constructs in Leadership Research," *Academy of Management Journal* 37, no. 6 (1994), pp. 1588–1602.
23. P. Hersey and K. H. Blanchard, "So You Want to Know Your Leadership Style?" *Training and Development Journal* (February 1974), pp. 1–15; and P. Hersey and K. H. Blanchard, *Management of Organizational Behavior: Utilizing Human Resources*, 5th ed. (Upper Saddle River, NJ: Prentice Hall, 1988).
24. See the Ken Blanchard Companies home page, <www.animal–tv.ch/specialties/perfsys/performance/index.cfm> (August 23, 2002).
25. Readers may find an interview with Paul Hersey enlightening regarding the terms used in the SLT model. See "Paul Hersey Defines Situational Leadership Terms," *Journal of Leadership Studies* (Spring 2002), p. 87.
26. K. Carrier, "Situational Leadership," *Nation's Cities Weekly* (January 22, 2001), p. 5.
27. C. F. Hernandez and R. P. Vecchio, "Situational Leadership Theory Revisited: A Test of an Across-Jobs Perspective," *Leadership Quarterly* (January 1997), p. 67; and C. L. Graeff, "Evolution of Situational Leadership Theory: A Critical Review," *Leadership Quarterly* (February 1997), pp. 153–70. For another perspective, see G. C. Avery, "Situational Leadership Preferences in Australia: Congruity, Flexibility and Effectiveness," *Leadership and Organization Development Journal* (January 2001), p. 11; and C. Cranford, "Analysis of the Communication Components Found within the Situational Leadership Model: Toward Integration of Communication and the Model," *Technical Communication* (February 2002), p. 123.
28. J. A. Conger and R. N. Kanungo, *Charismatic Leadership in Organizations* (Thousand Oaks, CA: Sage, 1998). See also, A. M. O'Roark, *The Quest for Executive Effectiveness: Turning Inside-Out Charismatic-Participatory Leadership* (Nevada City, CA: Symposium, 2000); C. G. Emrich, H. H. Brower, J. M. Feldman, and H. Garland, "Images in Words: Presidential Rhetoric, Charisma, and Greatness," *Administrative Science Quarterly* (September 2001), pp. 527–61; and J. J. Sosik, "The Role of Personal Meaning in Charismatic Leadership," *Journal of Leadership Studies* (Spring 2000), pp. 60–75.
29. J. A. Conger, R. N. Kanungo, and S. T. Menon, "Charismatic Leadership and Follower Effects," *Journal of Organizational Behavior* (November 2000), p. 747; and J. M. Grant and T. S. Bateman, "Charismatic Leadership Viewed from Above: The Impact of Proactive Leadership," *Journal of Organizational Behavior* (February 2000), p. 63.
30. R. J. House, "A 1976 Theory of Charismatic Leadership," in J. G. Hunt and L. L. Larson, eds., *Leadership: The Cutting Edge* (Carbondale, IL: Southern Illinois University Press, 1977), pp. 189–207.
31. W. Bennis, "The Four Competencies of Leadership," *Training and Development Journal* (August 1984), pp. 15–19.
32. J. A. Conger and R. N. Kanungo, *Charismatic Leadership in Organizations.*
33. B. Shamir, R. J. House, and M. B. Authur, "The Motivational Effects of Charismatic Leadership: A Self-Concept Theory," *Organizational Science* (November 1993), pp. 577–94.
34. See, for example, R. F. Russell, "The Roles of Values in Servant Leadership," *Leadership and Organization Development Journal* (January 2001), p. 76.
35. R. W. Roden, "The Relationship Between Charismatic Leadership Behaviors and Organizational Commitment," *Leadership and Organization Development Journal* (January 2000), p. 30; D. A. Walman and F. J. Yammarino, "CEO Charismatic Leadership: Levels of Management and Levels of Analysis Effects," *Academy of Management Review* (April 1999), pp. 266–68; and C. Romm and N. Pliskin, "The Role of Charismatic Leadership in Defusion and Implementation of e-Mail," *Journal of Management Development* (March 1999), p. 273.
36. J. A. Conger and R. N. Kanungo, *Charismatic Leadership in Organizations.*
37. R. J. House, "A 1976 Theory of Charismatic Leadership;" and R. J. House and R. N. Aditya, "The Social Scientific Study of Leadership: Quo Vadis?" *Journal of Management* (Fall 1997), p. 441.
38. This definition is based on M. Sashkin, "The Visionary Leader," in J. A. Conger and R. N. Kanungo eds., *Charismatic Leadership*, pp. 124–25; B. Nanus, *Visionary Leadership* (New York: Free Press, 1992), p. 8; N. H. Snyder and M. Graves, "Leadership and Vision," *Business Horizons* (January/February 1994), p. 1; J. R. Lucas, "Anatomy of a Vision Statement," *Management Review* (February 1998), pp. 22–26; and S. Marino, "Where There Is No Visionary, Companies Falter," *Industry Week* (March 15, 1999), p. 20.
39. B. Nanus, *Visionary Leadership*, p. 8.
40. P. C. Nutt and R. W. Backoff, "Crafting Vision," *Journal of Management Inquiry* (December 1997), p. 309.
41. Ibid., pp. 312–14.
42. Based on M. Sashkin, "The Visionary Leader," pp. 128–30; and J. R. Baum, E. A. Locke, and S. A. Kirkpatrick, "A Longitudinal Study of the Relation of Vision and Vision Communication to Venture Growth in Entrepreneurial Firms," *Journal of Applied Psychology* (February 1998), pp. 43–54.
43. M. DePree, *Leadership Jazz* (New York: Currency Doubleday, 1992), pp. 8–9.
44. See, for instance, B. M. Bass, *Leadership and Performance Beyond Expectations* (New York: Free Press, 1985); B. M. Bass, "From Transactional to Transformational Leadership: Learning to Share the Vision," *Organizational Dynamics* (Winter 1990), pp. 19–31; F. J. Yammarino, W. D. Spangler, and B. M. Bass, "Transformational Leadership and Performance: A Longitudinal Investigation," *Leadership Quarterly* (Spring 1993), pp. 81–102; and J. C. Wofford, V. L. Goodwin, and J. L. Whittington, "A Field Study of a Cognitive Approach to Understanding Transformational and Transactional Leadership," *Leadership Quarterly* (Winter 1998), pp. 55–84.
45. H. H. Friedman and M. Langbert, "Abraham as a Transformational Leader," *Journal of Leadership Studies* (Spring 2000), p. 88.
46. B. M. Bass, "Leadership: Good, Better, Best," *Organizational Dynamics* (Winter 1985), pp. 26–40; J. Seltzer and B. M. Bass, "Transformational Leadership: Beyond Initiation and Consideration," *Journal of Management* (December 1990), pp. 693–703; and C. P. Egri and S.

Herman, "Leadership in the North American Environmental Sector: Values, Leadership Styles, and Contexts of Environmental Leaders and Their Organizations," *Academy of Management Journal* (August 2000), pp. 571–604.

47. R. L. Ackoff, "Transformational Leadership," *Strategy and Leadership* (January–February 1999), pp. 20–26. See also, D. I. Dung and B. J. Avolio, "Opening the Black Box: An Experimental Investigation of the Mediating Effect of Trust and Value Congruence on Transformational and Transactional Leadership," *Journal of Organizational Behavior* (December 2000), p. 949.
48. B. J. Avolio and B. M. Bass, "Transformational Leadership, Charisma and Beyond," working paper, School of Management, State University of New York, Binghamton, NY, 1985, p. 14.
49. Cited in B. M. Bass and B. J. Avolio, "Developing Transformational Leadership: 1992 and Beyond," *Journal of European Industrial Training* (January 1990), p. 23.
50. J. J. Hater and B. M. Bass, "Supervisors Evaluation and Subordinates Perceptions of Transformational and Transactional Leadership," *Journal of Applied Psychology* (November 1988), pp. 695–702.
51. K. A. Arnold, J. Barling, and E. K. Kelloway, "Transformational Leadership or the Iron Cage: Which Predicts Trust, Commitment, and Team Efficacy?" *Leadership and Organization Development Journal* (July–August 2001), pp. 315–21.
52. Bass and Avolio, "Developing Transformational Leadership."
53. See for instance, J. H. Zenger, E. Musslewhite, K. Hurson, and C. Perrin, *Leading Teams: Mastering the New Role* (Homewood, IL: Business One Irwin, 1994); and M. Frohman, "Nothing Kills Teams Like Ill-Prepared Leaders," *Industry Week* (October 2, 1995), pp. 72–76.
54. S. Caminiti, "What Team Leaders Need to Know," *Fortune* (February 20, 1995), pp. 93–100.
55. For instance, see M. L. Van Engen, R. Van Der Leeden, and T M. Willemsen, "Gender, Context and Leadership Styles: A Field Study," *Journal of Occupational and Organizational Psychology* (December 2001), pp. 581–99; R. F. Martell and A. L. DeSmet, "A Diagnostic-Ratio Approach to Measuring Beliefs about the Leadership Abilities of Male and Female Managers," *Journal of Applied Psychology* (December 2001), pp. 1223–32; "Are Women Better Leaders?" *U.S. News and World Report* (January 29, 2001), p. 10; R. Sharpe, "As Leaders, Women Rule," *BusinessWeek* (November 20, 2000), pp. 75–84
56. J. K. Winter, J. C. Neal, and K. K. Waner, "How Male, Female, and Mixed-Gender Groups Regard Interaction and Leadership Differences in the Business Communication Course," *Business Communication Quarterly* (September 2001), p. 43; and N. Z. Stelter, "Gender Differences in Leadership: Current Social Issues and Future Organizational Implications," *Journal of Leadership Studies* (Spring 2002), pp. 88–100.
57. W. H. Decker and D. M. Rotondo, "Relationships Among Gender, Types of Humor, and Perceived Leader Effectiveness," *Journal of Managerial Issues* (Winter 2001), pp. 450–66.
58. Ibid., p. 93
59. Ibid., p. 100.
60. B. Wise, "The Five Dysfunctions of a Team: A Leadership Fable," *Library Journal* (April 15, 2002), p. 102.
61. R. Renson-Armer and D. Stickel, "Successful Team Leadership Is Built on Trust," *Ivey Business Journal* (May 2000), p. 20.
62. N. Steckler and N. Fondas, "Building Team Leader Effectiveness: A Diagnostic Tool," *Organizational Dynamics* (Winter 1995), p. 20. See also, P. Kelly, "Lose the Boss," *Inc.* (December 1997), pp. 45–46; and J. Pfeffer and J. P. Veiga, "Putting People First for Organizational Success," *Academy of Management Executive* (May 1999), pp. 37–48.
63. R. S. Wellins, W. C. Byham, and G. R. Dixon, *Inside Teams* (San Francisco: Jossey Bass, 1994), p. 318.
64. N. Steckler and N. Fondas, "Building Team Leader Effectiveness," p. 21.
65. See T. Rickards, M. H. Chen, and S. Moger, "Development of a Self-Report Instrument for Exploring Team Factor, Leadership, and Performance Relationships," *British Journal of Management* (September 2001), pp. 243–51.
66. See K. T. Dirks, "Trust in Leadership and Team Performance: Evidence from NCA Basketball," *Journal of Applied Psychology* (December 2000), p. 1004.
67. For a review of the cross-cultural applicability of the leadership literature, see R. S. Bhagat, B. L. Kedia, S. E. Crawford, and M. R. Kaplan, "Cross Cultural Issues in Organizational Psychology: Emergent Trends and Directions for Research in the 1990s," in C. L. Cooper and I. T. Robertson, eds. *International Review of Industrial and Organizational Psychology*, vol. 5 (New York: John Wiley &Sons, 1990), pp. 79–89; and M. F. Peterson and J. G. Hunt, "International Perspectives on International Leadership," *Leadership Quarterly* (Fall 1997), pp. 203–31.
68. "Military Style Management in China," *Asia Inc.* (March 1995), p. 70.
69. Cited in R. J. House and R. N. Aditya, "The Social Scientific Study of Leadership," p. 463.
70. R. J. House, "Leadership in the Twenty-First Century," in A. Howard, ed., *The Changing Nature of Work* (San Francisco: Jossey Bass, 1995), p. 442.
71. Ibid.
72. R. J. House and R. N. Aditya, "The Social Scientific Study of Leadership," p. 463.
73. R. J. House, "Leadership in the Twenty-First Century," p. 443.
74. See, for instance, D. A. Yousef, "Organizational Commitment: A Mediator of the Relationships of Leadership Behavior with Job Satisfaction and Performance in a Non-Western Country," *Journal of Managerial Psychology* (January–February 2000), pp. 6–26.
75. This section is based on D. Coleman, *Working with Emotional Intelligence* (New York: Bantam, 1998); D. Goleman, "What Makes a Leader?" *Harvard Business Review*, November–December 1998, pp. 93–102; J. M. George, "Emotions and Leadership: The Role of Emotional Intelligence," *Human Relations*, (August 2000), pp. 1027–55; D. R. Caruso, J. D. Mayer, and P. Salovey, "Emotional Intelligence and Emotional Leadership," in R. E. Riggio, S. E. Murphy, and F. J. Pirozzolo eds., *Multiple Intelligences and Leadership* (Mahwah, NJ: Lawrence Erlbaum, 2002), pp. 55–74; and D. Coleman, R. E. Boyatzis, and A. McKee, *Primal Leadership: Realizing the Power of Emotional Intelligence* (Boston: Harvard Business School Press, 2002).
76. "The Secret Skill of Leaders," *U.S. News & World Report* (January 14, 2002) p. 8. See also, L. Gardner and C. Stough, "Examining the Relationship Between Leadership and Emotional Intelligence in Senior Level Managers," *Leadership and Organization Development Journal* (January–February 2002), pp. 68–79.
77. Ibid.
78. S. Kerr and J. M. Jermier, "Substitutes for Leadership: Their Meaning and Measurement," *Organization Behavior and Human Performance* (December 1978), pp. 375–403; J. P. Howell and P. W. Dorfman, "Substitutes for Leadership: Test of a Construct," *Academy of Management Journal* (December 1981), pp. 714–28; J. P. Howell, P. W. Dorfman, and S. Kerr, "Leadership and Substitutes for Leadership," *Journal of Applied Behavioral Science* 22, no. 1 (1986), pp. 29–46; and J. P. Howell, D. E. Bowen, P. W. Dorfman, S. Kerr, and P. M. Podsakoff, "Substitutes for Leadership: Effective Alternatives to Ineffective Leadership," *Organizational Dynamics* (Summer 1990), pp. 21–38; P. M. Podsakoff, S. B. MacKenzie, and W. H. Bommer, "Meta-Analysis of the Relationships between Kerr and Jermier's Substitutes for Leadership and Employee Attitudes, Role perceptions, and Performance," *Journal of Applied Psychology* (August 1996), pp. 380–99; and J. M. Jermier and S. Kerr, "Substitutes for Leadership: Their Meaning and Measurement—Contextual Recollections and Current Observations," *Leadership Quarterly*, vol 8, no. 2 (1997), pp. 95–101.
79. S. Simsarian, "Leadership and Trust Facilitating Cross-Functional Team Success," *Journal of Management Development* (March–April 2002), pp. 201–15.

80. For an interesting application of trust in academic institutions, see W. A. Jones, "A Study of the Relationship of Butler's Conditions of Trust to Birnbaum's Organizational Models: Implications for Leaders in Higher Education," *Journal of Leadership Studies* (Winter 2002), pp. 110–17.
81. This definition is based on S. D. Boon and J. G. Holmes, "The Dynamics of Interpersonal Trust: Resolving Uncertainty in the Face of Risk," in R. A. Hinde and J. Groebel, eds., *Cooperation and Pro-Social Behavior* (Cambridge, UK: Cambridge University Press, 1991), p. 194; D. J. McAllister, "Affect and Cognition Based Trust as Foundations for Interpersonal Cooperation in Organizations," *Academy of Management Journal* (February 1995), p. 25; and D. M. Rousseau, S. B. Sitkin, R. S. Burt, and C. Camerer, "Not So Different After All: A Cross Discipline View of Trust," *Academy of Management Review* (July 1998), pp. 393–404.
82. J. B. Rotter, "Interpersonal Trust, Trustworthiness, and Gullibility," *American Psychologist* (May 1980), p. 17.
83. J. D. Lewis and A. Weigert, "Trust as a Social Reality," *Social Forces* (June 1985), p. 970.
84. J. K. Rempel, J. G. Holmes, and M. P. Zanna, "Trust in Close Relationships," *Journal of Personality and Social Psychology* (July 1985), p. 96.
85. M. Granovetter, "Economic Action and Social Structure: The Problem of Embeddedness," *American Journal of Sociology* (November 1985), p. 491.
86. R. C. Mayer, J. H. Davis, and F. D. Schoorman, "An Integrative Model of Organizational Trust," *Academy of Management Review* (July 1995), p. 712.
87. C. Johnson George and W. Swap, "Measurement of Specific Interpersonal Trust: Construction and Validation of a Scale to Assess Trust in a Specific Other," *Journal of Personality and Social Psychology* (May 1982), p. 1306.
88. P. L. Schindler and C. C. Thomas, "The Structure of Interpersonal Trust in the Workplace," *Psychological Reports* (October 1993), pp. 563–73.
89. T. E. Becker, "Integrity in Organizations: Beyond Honesty and Conscientiousness," *Academy of Management Review* (January 1998), pp. 154–61. For a debate on Becker's article, see B. Barry and C. U. Stephens, "Objections to an Objectivist Approach to Integrity," *Academy of Management Review* (January 1998), pp. 162–69; and E. A. Locke and T. E. Becker, "Rebuttal to a Subjectivist Critique of an Objectivist Approach to Integrity in Organizations," *Academy of Management Review* (January 1998), pp. 170–75.
90. A. C. Wicks, S. L. Berman, and T. M. Jones, "The Structure of Optimal Trust: Moral and Strategic Implications," *Academy of Management Review* (January 1999), pp. 96–116; C. Braun, "Organizational Infidelity: How Violations of Trust Affect the Employee–Employer Relationship," *Academy of Management Executive* (November 1997), pp. 94–96; and J. K. Butler Jr. and R. S. Cantrell, "A Behavioral Decision Theory Approach to Modeling Dyadic Trust in Superiors and Subordinates," *Psychological Reports* (August 1984), pp. 19–28.
91. D. McGregor, *The Professional Manager* (New York, McGraw-Hill, 1967), p. 164.
92. B. Nanus, *The Leaders Edge: The Seven Keys to Leadership in a Turbulent World* (Chicago: Contemporary Books, 1989), p. 102.
93. J. P. Donlon, "Trust Is the Issue," *Chief Executive* (March 2001), p. 6.
94. D. E. Zand, *The Leadership Triad: Knowledge, Trust, and Power* (New York: Oxford University Press, 1997), p. 89.
95. Based on L. T. Hosmer, "Trust: The Connecting Link between Organizational Theory and Philosophical Ethics,"*Academy of Management Review* (April 1995), p. 393; and R. C. Mayer, J. H. Davis, and F. D. Schoorman, "An Integrative Model of Organizational Trust," *Academy of Management Review* (July 1995), p. 712.
96. M. Kouzes and B. Z. Posner, *Credibility: How Leaders Gain and Lose It, and Why People Demand It* (San Francisco: Jossey Bass, 1993), p. 14.
97. J. Brockner, P. A. Siegel, J. P. Daly, T. Tyler, and C. Martin, "When Trust Matters: The Moderating Effect of Outcome Favorability," *Administrative Science Quarterly* (September 1997), pp. 558–84.
98. K. T. Dirks, "Trust in Leadership and Team Performance: Evidence from NCAA Basketball," *Journal of Applied Psychology* (December 2000), p. 1004.
99. Cited in C. Lee, "Trust Me," *Training* (January 1997), p. 32.
100. R. A. Eckeert, "Where Leadership Starts," *Harvard Business Review,* (November 2001), p. 53.
101. This section is based on D. Shapiro, B. H. Sheppard, and L. Cheraskin, "Business on a Handshake," *Negotiation Journal* (October 1992), pp. 365–77; and R. J. Lewicki and B. B. Bunker, "Developing and Maintaining Trust in Work Relationships," in R. M. Kramer and T. R. Tyler, eds., *Trust in Organizations* (Thousand Oaks, CA: Sage, 1996), pp. 119–24.
102. A. Sacharow, "News Flash," Adweek Eastern Edition (March 31, 1997).
103. Ibid.
104. Based on F. Bartolome, "Nobody Trust the Boss Completely—Now What?" *Harvard Business Review* (March–April 1989), pp. 135–42; and J. K. Butler Jr., "Toward Understanding and Measuring Conditions of Trust: Evolution of a Condition of Trust Inventory," *Journal of Management* (September 1991), pp. 643–63.
105. "D. L. Rogers Corporation, Company Profile," *Hospitality Jobs Online* <profiles.hospitalityonline.com/201068> (August 12, 2002); R. Ruggless, "D. L. Rogers Group," *Nations Restaurant News* (January 1998), pp. 66–68; M. Ballon, "Extreme Managing," *Inc.* (July 1998), pp. 60–72; and "Jacks Recipe," *Inc.* (July 1998), p. 63.

Chapter 12

1. This opening vignette is based on J. Morgan, "Contract Clinched, but Sport Still Losing Fans," *Baltimore Sun* (August 31, 2002), p. A1; J. Reid, R. Newhan, and M. Landsberg, "Baseball Strike Averted," *Los Angeles Times* (August 31, 2002), p. A1; M. Chass, "Agreement Reached in Baseball's Contract Negotiations," *New York Times* (August 30, 2002), p. A1; and B. M. Bloom, "Bargaining Time Dwindles; Issues Narrow Slightly," (August 27, 2002).
2. D. K. Berlo, *The Process of Communication* (New York: Holt, Rinehart & Winston, 1960), pp. 30–32.
3. Ibid., p. 54.
4. See, for instance, "Get the Message: Communication Is Key in Managing Change within Organizations—Yet Ensuring Its Effectiveness at Times of High Concerns Can Be Tricky," *Employee Benefits* (February 2002), pp. 58–60.
5. Ibid., p. 103.
6. L. R. Birkner and R. K. Birkner, "Communication Feedback: Putting It All Together," *Occupational Hazards* (August 2001), p. 9.
7. L. Hilton, "They Heard It Through the Grapevine," *South Florida Business Journal* (August 18, 2000), p. 53.
8. M. Fulfer, "Nonverbal Communication: How to Read What's Plain as the Nose...Or Eyelid...Or chin...On Their Faces," *Journal of Occupational Excellence* (Spring 2001), pp. 19–38.
9. Ibid.
10. P. Mornell, "The Sounds of Silence," *Inc.* (February 2001), p. 117.
11. A. Warfield, "Do You Speak Body Language?" *Training and Development* (April 2001), p. 60.
12. "Information Overload," *Australian Business Intelligence* (April 16, 2002).
13. S. I. Hayakawa, *Language in Thought and Action* (New York: Harcourt Brace Jovanovich, 1949), p. 292.
14. "Jargon Leaves Us Lost for Words," *Australian Business Intelligence* (August 23, 2002); and W. S. Mossberg, "A Guide to the Lingo You'll Want to Learn for Wireless Technology," *The Wall Street Journal* (March 28, 2002), p. B1.
15. "Gobbledygook Begone," *Workforce* (February 2002), p. 12; and "Business-Speak," *Training and Development* (January 2002), pp. 50–52.
16. This section on gender differences in communications is based on D. Tannen, *You Just Don't Understand: Women and Men in Conversation* (New York: Ballantine Books, 1991); D. Tannen, *Talking from 9 to 5*

(New York: Morrow, 1994); and J. C. Tingley, *Genderflex: Men & Women Speak Others Language at Work* (New York: American Management Association, 1994).

17. See, for example, M. K. Kozan, "Subcultures and Conflict Management Styles," *Management International Review* (January 2002), pp. 89–106.
18. A. Mehrabian, "Communication Without Words," *Psychology Today* (September 1968), pp. 53–55.
19. Information for one incident comes from "Martha Stewart Could Be Charged as 'Tippee,' Court Papers in Guilty Plea by a Merrill Employee Say She Based Sales on Inside Information," *Wall Street Journal* (October 3, 2002), p. C1; and M. Roman, "A Fresh Stew for Martha," *BusinessWeek* (September 23, 2002), p. 50.
20. See also, W. L. Adair, T. Okumura, and J. M. Brett, "Negotiation Behavior When Cultures Collide: The United States and Japan," *Journal of Applied Psychology* (June 2001), p. 371.
21. C. H. Tinsley, "How Negotiators Get to Yes: Predicting the Constellation of Strategies Used across Cultures to Negotiate Conflict," *Journal of Applied Psychology* (August 2001), p. 583.
22. See S. P. Robbins and P. L. Hunsaker, *Training in Interpersonal Skills*, 3rd ed.(Upper Saddle River, NJ: Prentice Hall, Inc., 2003), Ch. 4.
23. See, for example, R. R. Panko, *Business Data Networks and Communications*, 4th ed. (Upper Saddle River, NJ: Prentice Hall, 2003).
24. "Virtual Paper Cuts," *Workforce* (July 2000), pp. 16–8.
25. J. Rohwer, "Today, Tokyo, Tomorrow the World," *Fortune* (September 18, 2000), pp. 140–152; and S. Rosenbush and E. Einhorn, "The Talking Internet," *BusinessWeek* (May 1, 2000), pp. 174–188.
26. See, for instance, A. Cohen, "Wireless Summer," *Time* (May 29, 2000), pp. 58–65; and K. Hafner, "For the Well Connected, All the World's an Office," *New York Times* (March 30, 2000), p. D1.
27. J. S. Brown and P. Duguid, "Balancing Act: How to Capture Knowledge Without Killing It," *Harvard Business Review*, (May–June 2000), pp. 73–80; and J. Torsilieri and C. Lucier, "How to Change the World," *Strategy and Business* (October 2000), pp. 17–20.
28. See J. Lloyd, "Derailing Your Career," *Baltimore Business Journal* (October 19, 2001), p. 3; H. Johnson, "Soften Up," *Training* (February 2002), p. 20; and M. Langbert, "Professors, Managers, and Human Resource Education," *Human Resource Management* (Spring 2000), pp. 65–78.
29. "Executive Update," *Training and Development* (March 2002), p. 19.
30. "More Than One-Third of People Surveyed Identified Communication Skills or Interpersonal Relationship Skills as the Most Important Quality in a Good Boss," *Training and Development* (February 2000), p. 16.
31. This material is adapted from S. P. Robbins and P. L. Hunsaker, *Training in Interpersonal Skills*. (Upper Saddle River, NJ: Prentice Hall, 1996), p. 3.
32. R. B. Cousins, "Active Listening Is More Than Just Hearing," *Supervision* (September 2000), p. 14.
33. D. Flack, "Active Listening Is [a] Skill that Needs Undivided Attention," *San Antonio Business Journal* (September 28, 2001), p. 33.
34. C. R. Rogers and R. E. Farson, *Active Listening* (Chicago: Industrial Relations Center of the University of Chicago, 1976).
35. See, for example, K. Leung, S. Su, and M. W. Morris, "When Is Criticism Not Constructive? The Roles of Fairness Perceptions and Dispositional Attributions in Employee Acceptance of Critical Supervisory Feedback," *Human Relations* (September 2001);1155; and C. A. Walker, "Saving Your Rookie Managers from Themselves," *Harvard Business Review*, April 2002, pp. 97–103.
36. D. Ilgen, C. D. Fisher, and M. S. Taylor, "Consequences of Individual Feedback on Behavior in Organizations," *Journal of Applied Psychology* (August 1979), pp. 349–71.
37. F. Bartolome, "Teaching about Whether to Give Negative Feedback," *The Organizational Behavior Teaching Review* 9, no. 2 (1986/1987), pp. 95–104.
38. K. Halperin, C. R. Snyder, R. J. Schenkel, and B. K. Houston, "Effect of Source Status and Message Favorability on Acceptance of Personality Feedback," *Journal of Applied Psychology* (February 1976), pp. 85–88.
39. Based on P. L. Hunsaker, *Training in Management Skills* (Upper Saddle River, NJ: Prentice Hall, 2001), pp. 60–61.
40. S. Gazda, "The Art of Delegating: Effective Delegation Enhances Employee Morale, Manager Productivity, and Organizational Success," *HR Magazine* (January 2002), pp. 75–79.
41. L. L. Steinmetz, *The Art and Skill of Delegation* (Boston: Addison-Wesley, 1976).
42. Based on P. L. Hunsaker, *Training in Management Skills*, pp. 135–36, and pp. 430–32; R. T. Noel, "What You Say to Your Employees When You Delegate, *Supervisory Management* (December 1993), p. 13; and S. Caudron, "Delegate for Results," *Industry Week* (February 6, 1995), pp. 27–30.
43. M. Delahoussaye, "Don't Get Mad, Get Promoted," *Training* (June 2002), p. 20; and C. Tinsley and J. Brett, "Managing Workplace Conflict in the United States and Hong Kong," *Organizational Behavior and Human Decision Processes* (July 2001), pp. 360–62.
44. K. W. Thomas and W. H. Schmidt, "A Survey of Managerial Interests with Respect to Conflict," *Academy of Management Journal* (June 1976), pp. 315–18.
45. Ibid.
46. This section is adapted from S. P. Robbins, *Managing Organizational Conflict: A Nontraditional Approach* (Upper Saddle River, NJ: Prentice Hall, 1977), pp. 11–14.
47. This section is drawn from K. W. Thomas, "Toward Multidimensional Values in Teaching: The Example of Conflict Behaviors," *Academy of Management Review* (July 1977), p. 487.
48. See also, J. R. Darling, and W. E. Walker, "Effective Conflict Management: Use of the Behavioral Style Model," *Leadership and Organization Development Journal* (May 2001), p. 230.
49. L. Greenhalgh, "Managing Conflict," *Sloan Management Review* (Summer 1986), pp. 45–51.
50. Robbins, *Managing Organizational Conflict*, pp. 31–55.
51. C. O. Kursh, "The Benefits of Poor Communication," *Psychoanalytic Review* (Summer–Fall, 1971), pp. 189–208
52. See M. M. Montoya-Weiss, A. P. Massey, and M. Song, "Getting It Together: Temporal Coordination and Conflict Management in Global Virtual Teams," *Academy of Management Journal* (December 2001), pp. 251–63.
53. See, for instance, D. Tjosvold and D. W. Johnson, *Productive Conflict Management Perspectives for Organizations* (New York: Irvington Publishers, 1983).
54. S. P. Robbins, "Conflict Management and Conflict Resolution Are Not Synonymous Terms," *California Management Review* (Winter 1978), p. 71.
55. See E. Van de Vliert, A. Nauta, E. Giebels, and O. Janssen, "Constructive Conflict at Work," in L. N. Dosier and J. B. Keys, eds., *Academy of Management Best Paper Proceedings*, (August 8–13, 1997), pp. 92–96; Robbins, *Managing Organizational Conflict*, pp. 78–89; and S. Berglas, "Innovate: Harmony Is Death. Let Conflict Reign," *Inc.* (May 1997), pp. 56–58.
56. R. E. Walton and R. B. McKersie, *A Behavioral Theory of Labor Negotiations: An Analysis of a Social Interaction System* (New York: McGraw Hill, 1965).
57. "Negotiation Skills Invaluable in Workplace," *Knight-Ridder/Tribune Business News* (June 23, 2002), p. 1.
58. K. W. Thomas, "Conflict and Negotiation Processes in Organizations," in M. D. Dunnette and L. M. Hough, eds. *Handbook of Industrial and Organizational Psychology*, vol. 3, 2nd ed. (Palo Alto, CA: Consulting Psychologists Press, 1992), pp. 651–717.
59. Based on R. Fisher and W. Ury, *Getting to Yes: Negotiating Agreement without Giving In* (Boston: Houghton Mifflin, 1981); J. A. Wall Jr. and M. W. Blum, "Negotiations," *Journal of Management* (June 1991), pp. 295–296; and M. H. Bazerman and M. A. Neale, *Negotiating Rationally* (New York: Free Press, 1992).

60. R. A. Posthuma, J. B. Dworkin, and M. S. Swift, "Mediator Tactics and Sources of Conflict: Facilitating and Inhibiting Effects," *Industrial Relations* (January 2002), pp. 94–109.
61. "Survey Shows Fundamental Managerial Skills Lacking," *Management Services* (January 1999), pp. 3.
62. This material is based on Larry Laufer, *Presenting for Results Program* (Ellicott City, MD: Applied Human Resource Systems, Inc., 2002); and K. Daley, "Presentation Skills: How to Be Focused, Forceful, Passionate, and Persuasive," *Information Executive* (September 1998).
63. J. Gately, "A Physician's Real-Time solution for Unified Communications, Health Management Technology (September 1999), pp. 50–51.
64. See R. B. Cousins, "Active Listening Is More Than Just Hearing," *Supervision* (September 2000), pp. 14–16.
65. M. Hofman, "Lost in the Translation," *Inc.* (May 2000), pp. 161–62.

Chapter 13

1. This vignette is based on K. Eichenwald, "Enron Panel Finds Inflated Profits and Self-Dealing; Harsh Internal Review Describes Failed Control and Ethics," *New York Times* (February 3, 2002), p. 1; J. R. Peterson, "Enron: What Went Wrong with the Accounting," *The Accountant* (February 2002), p. 2; M. France, D. Carney, M. McNamee, and A. Borrus, "Why Corporate Crooks Are Tough to nail," *BusinessWeek* (July 2, 2002), p. 34; P. Elkind and B. McLean, "The Feds Close in on Enron: After a Summer Lull, the Feds Are Widening Their Roundup with Subpoenas and a New Grand Jury," *Fortune* (September 2, 2002), p. 36; and P. C. Fusaro and R. M. Miller, *What Went Wrong at Enron: Everyone's Guide to the Largest Bankruptcy in U.S. History* (Hoboken, NJ: John Wiley & Sons, 2002).
2. E. Flamholtz, "Organizational Control Systems as a Managerial Tool," *California Management Review* (Winter 1979), p. 55.
3. W. G. Ouchi, "A Conceptual Framework for the Design of Organizational Control Mechanisms," *Management Science* (August 1979), pp. 833–838; and W. G. Ouchi, "Markets, Bureaucracies, and Clans," *Administrative Science Quarterly* (March 1980), pp. 129–141.
4. See SAS Institute Web site, <www.sasinstitute.com> (SAS Institute, Inc., 2002).
5. B. Nelson, "Long-Distance Recognition," *Workforce* (August 2000), pp. 50–52.
6. S. Kerr, "On the Folly of Rewarding A, While Hoping for B," *Academy of Management Journal* (December 1975), pp. 769–83.
7. See, for instance, "Closing the Loop on Corrective Action," *Quality* (March 2002), pp. 44–46.
8. H. Koontz and R. W. Bradspies, "Managing Through Feedforward Control," *Business Horizons* (June 1972), pp. 25–36.
9. W. H. Newman, *Constructive Control: Design and Use of Control Systems* (Upper Saddle River, NJ: Prentice Hall, 1975), p. 33.
10. Information on Marriott International and Lightbridge from Hoover's Online, <www.hoovers.com< (September 8, 2002); and A. Murr, "Final Answer: It Crashed," *Newsweek* (April 10, 2000), p. 46.
11. See, for instance, W. H. Newman, *Constructive Control: Design and Use of Control Systems.*
12. Information on Hoovers Online <www.hoovers.com> (September 8, 2002); and N. Shirouzu and J. Bigness, "7-Eleven Operators Resist System to Monitor Managers," *Wall Street Journal* (June 16, 1997), p. B1.
13. K. Gerringer, "Facing Goliath: Association CEO Kim Kenney Caught the Centers for Disease Control and Prevention Misspending Funds. Here's What She Learned from the Experience," *Association Management* (July 2002), pp. 54–58.
14. E. E. Lawler III and J. G. Rhode, *Information and Control in Organizations* (Santa Monica, CA: Goodyear, 1976), p. 108.
15. J. D. Thompson, *Organizations in Action* (New York: McGraw-Hill, 1967), p. 124.
16. See C. Morton, "Monitoring Communications...: At a Glance," *Personnel Today* (September 3, 2002), p. 1; "All the Changes to the Code on Employee Monitoring: What HR Needs to Know," *Personnel Today* (July 16, 2002), p. 2; and J. B. Lewis, "I Know What You E-Mailed Last Summer," *Security Management* (January 2002), pp. 93–98.
17. J. Jusko, "A Watchful Eye," *Industry Week* (May 7, 2001), p. 9; and "Big Brother Boss," *U.S. News and World Report* (April 30, 2001), p. 12.
18. For an interesting perspective on this issue, see D. Zweig and J. Webster, "Where is the Line Between Benign and Invasive? An Examination of Psychological Barriers to the Acceptance of Awareness Monitoring Systems, *Journal of Organizational Behavior* (August 2002), pp. 602–34.
19. L. Guernsey, "You've Got Inappropriate E-mail," *New York Times* (April 5, 2000), pp. C1+.
20. Ibid, p. 51.
21. Ibid.
22. E. Bott, "Are You Safe? Privacy Special Report," *PC Computing* (March 2000), pp. 87–88.
23. See <http://www4.law.cornell.edu/uscode/18/2510.html>
24. R. Brimelow, "Letter of the Law," *Personnel Today* (May 7, 2002), p. 2.
25. "Employers Watching Computer Use for Legal Liability, AMA Survey Finds," *BNA Daily Labor Report* (August 9, 2001), p. 1; and S. Boehle, "They're Watching You: Workplace Privacy is going ... Going ...," *Training* (August 2000), p. 50.
26. L. Yu, "Rational Cheaters vs. Intrinsic Motivators: Monitoring Employee Behavior May Not Always Have the Desired Effect," *MIT Sloan Management Review* (Summer 2002), p. 10.
27. See R. W. Thompson, "Corporate Security Plans to Focus on Surveillance, Experts Say," *HR News* (November 2001), pp. 2, 4; M. France, H. Green, J. Kerstetter, J. Black, and A. Salkever, "Privacy in an Age of Terror," *BusinessWeek* (November 5, 2001), pp. 83–87; and A. Stuart, "Creating a Cyberdefense," *Inc.* (January 1, 2002), pp. 90–92.
28. A. M. Bell and D. M. Smith, "Theft and Fraud May Be an Inside Job," *Workforce Online*, <www.workforce.com>, May 15, 2000.
29. See, for example, "Theft: Retails Real Grinch," *About Inc.* (September 2002), <retailindustry.about.com/library/weekly/aa001122a.htm>, and J. Rhine, "Study Sees Spike in Employment Theft," *San Francisco Business Times* (April 13, 2001), p. 14.
30. J. Greenberg, "The STEAL Motive: Managing the Social Determinants of Employee Theft," in R. Giacalone and J. Greenberg, eds., *Antisocial Behavior in Organizations* (Newbury park, CA: Sage, 1997), pp. 85–108.
31. "Cutting Your Losses: Employee Theft Under the Microscope," *Australian Business Intelligence* (July 12, 2002), p. 1008.
32. S. Phillips, "Parting Shot," *Personnel Today* (January 15, 2002), p. 2; and M. Cronin and A. Salkever, "Revenge of the Downsized Nerds," *BusinessWeek* (July 30, 2001), p. 40.
33. B. P. Niehoff and R. J. Paul, "Causes of Employee Theft and Strategies that HR Managers Can Use for Prevention," *Human Resource Management* (Spring 2000), pp. 51–64; and G. Winter, "Taking at the Office Reaches New Heights: Employee Larceny Is Bigger and Bolder," *New York Times* (July 12, 2000), pp. C1+.
34. This section is based on J. Greenberg, *Behavior in Organizations*, 7th ed. (Upper Saddle River, NJ: Prentice Hall, 2000), pp. 396–97.
35. A. H. Bell and D. M. Smith, "Why Some Employees Bite the Hand That Feeds Them," *Workforce Online*, <www.workforce.com>, May 16, 2000.
36. "Was Polygraph Tester Really an Employer?" *Fair Employment Practices Guidelines* (June 15, 2002), pp. 3–5.
37. Information from company's Web site <www.gloryfoods.com>, September 12, 2002; and C. Shock, "Making Haste Slowly," *Forbes* (September 22, 1997), pp. 220–22.
38. G. R. Merz, P. B. Weber, and V. B. Laetz, "Linking Small Business Management with Entrepreneurial Growth," *Journal of Small Business Management* (October 1994), pp. 48–60.
39. L. Beresford, "Growing Up," *Entrepreneur* (July 1995), pp. 124–28.
40. J. Summer, "More, Please!" *Business Finance* (July 2000), pp. 57–61.
41. T. Stevens, "Pedal Pushers," *Industry Week* (July 17, 2000), pp. 46–52.

42. P. Lorange and R. T. Nelson, "How To Recognize—and Avoid—Organizational Decline," *Sloan Management Review* (Spring 1987), pp. 41–48.
43. S. D. Chowdhury and J. R. Lange, "Crisis, Decline, and Turnaround: A Test of Competing Hypothesis for Short-Term Performance Improvement in Small Firms," *Journal of Small Business Management* (October 1993), pp. 8–17.
44. M. Henricks, "Out of Control," *Entrepreneur* (September 2001), p. 63.
45. C. Farrell, "How To survive a Downturn," *BusinessWeek* (April 28, 1997), pp. ENT4–ENT6.
46. R. W. Pricer and A. C. Johnson, "The Accuracy of Valuation Methods in Predicting the Selling Price of Small Firms," *Journal of Small Business Management* (October 1997), pp. 24–35.
47. P. Hernan, "Finding the Exit," *Industry Week* (July 7, 2000), pp. 55–61; D. Rodkin, "For Sale by Owner," *Entrepreneur* (January 1998), pp. 148–53; A. Livingston, "Avoiding the Pitfalls When Selling a Business," *Nation's Business* (July 1998), pp. 25–26; and G. G. Marullo, "Selling Your Business: A Preview of the Process," *Nation's Business* (August 1998), pp. 25–26.
48. B. Tedeschi, "E-Comerce Report," *The New York Times,* (January 27, 2003), p. C4.
49. Case based on company Web site information, "SiloCaf;" "Quality;" "Technology;" and "History," <www.silocaf.com> (August 14, 2002); and *Small Business 2000*, Show 109.

Chapter 14

1. "Best Plant Winners," *Industry Week* (October 1, 2002), available online at <www.industryweek.com>.
2. For a complete perspective on operations management, see R. S. Russell and B. W. Taylor III, *Operations Management*, 4th ed. (Upper Saddle River, NJ: Prentice Hall, 2003).
3. C. M. Wright and G. Mechling, "The Importance of Operations Management Problems in Service Organizations," *Omega* (April 2002), pp. 77–88.
4. U.S. Department of Labor, Bureau of Labor Statistics, "The Employment Situation," (August 2002), pp. 1–2.
5. See *The World Fact Book 2001*, available online, <www.odci.gov/cia/ publications/factbook/index.html>, 2002.
6. W.Royal, "Leading the Charge," *Industry Week* (March 20, 2000), p. 32.
7. D. Meyers, "Cutting Costs with Diamond Coatings: Carbide Tolls with CVD Diamond Coatings Can Help Manufacturers Increase Both Productivity and Product Quality in Machining Green Ceramics, Making Them Well Worth the Extra Investment," *Ceramic Industry* (July 2002), pp. 21–24.
8. "Integrated AutoCAD Routines Help Increase Productivity," *Process Heating* (April 2002), p. 11. see also <www.dispatch.com>.
9. J. Ordonez, "McDonald's to Cut the Cooking Time of Its French Fries," *Wall Street Journal* (May 19, 2000), p. B2.
10. T. Mudd, "The Last Laugh," *Industry Week* (September 2000), pp. 38–44.
11. G. Bylinksy, "The E-Factory Catches On: Huge Increases in Productivity Result When Customers Can Design the Products They Want and Send Orders Straight to the Plant Floor Via the Internet," *Fortune* (July 23, 2001), p. 200.
12. See "Industry Weeks Best Plants," *Industry Week* (October 2002), available online at <www.industryweek.com>; and J. H. Sheridan, "Managing the Value Chain," *Industry Week* (September 6, 1999), available online at <www.industryweek.com>.
13. J. S. McCleanahen, "The Future," *Industry Week* (April 17, 2000), pp 45–50.
14. D. Drickamer, "Getting Down to Brass Tacks: Value-Chain Management Moves from Dream to Reality," *Industry Week* (April 2002), pp. 53–55; and "Networked Value Chain: Seizing the Competitive Edge Supply Chain Management," *Chief Executive* (March 2002), pp. D1–D13.
15. J. H. Sheridan, "Managing the Value Chain,"
16. Ibid. p. 1.
17. M. E. Porter, *Competitive Advantage: Creating and Sustaining Superior Performance* (New York, Simon and Schuster, 1998).
18. R. Karkgaard, "ASAP Interview: Mike Hammer," *Forbes ASAP* (September 13, 1993), p. 70.
19. See, for instance, K.P. O'Brien, "Value Chain Report; Supply Chain Success in the Aftermarket," *Industry Week* (July 15, 2002). Available online at <www.industryweek.com>.
20. S. Leibs, "Getting Ready: Your Suppliers," *Industry Week* (September 6, 1999), available online at <www.industryweek.com>.
21. See, for example, J. Jusko, "Procurement-Not all Dollars and Cents," *Industry Week* (April 4, 2002), available online at <www.industryweek.com>.
22. See "News Item Future Challenges for the Aromatics Supply Chain," speech given by Nancy Sullivan, Vice President Aromatics & Phenol, to the First European Aromatics and Derivatives Conference, London, UK, (May 29, 2002). Available online at <www.shellchemicals.com/newstroom/1,1098.71.00.html>.
23. D. Bartholomew, "The Infrastructure," *Industry Week* (September 6, 1999), p. 1.
24. G. Taninecz, "Forging the Chain," Industry Week (May 15, 2000), pp. 40–46.
25. See J. H. Sheridan, Now It's a Job for the CEO," *Industry Week* (March 20, 2000), pp. 22–30.
26. R. Norman and R. Ramirez, "From Value Chain to Value Constellation," *Harvard Business Review on Managing The Value Chain* (Boston: Harvard Business School Press, 2000), pp. 185–219.
27. S. Leibs, "Getting Ready: Your Customers," *Industry Week* (September 6, 1999), p. 4.
28. See, for example, C. Lunan, "Workers Doing More in Less Time," *The Charlotte Observer* (June 1, 2002), p. D1.
29. S. Leibs, "Getting Ready: Your Customers," p. 3.
30. See, for instance, L. Harrington, "The Accelerated Value Chain: Supply Chain Management Just Got Smarter, Faster, and More Cost-Effective, Thanks to a Groundbreaking Alliance Between Intel and Technologies," *Industry Week*(April 2002), pp. 45–51.
31. Ibid. p. 2.
32. Ibid., and J. H Sheridan, "Managing the Value Chain."
33. J. H. Sheriden, "Managing the Value Chain," p. 3.
34. S. Leibs, "Getting Ready: Your Customers," p. 4.
35. J. H. Sheriden, "Managing the Value Chain," pp. 2–3; S. Leibs, "Getting ready: Your Customers," pp. 1 and 4; D. Bartholomew, "The Infrastructure," p. 6.
36. See D. Bartholomew, "E-commerce Bullies," *Industry Week* (September 4, 2002), pp. 48–54.
37. G. Taninecz, "Forging the Chain."
38. S. Leibs, "Getting Ready: Your Customers," p. 1.
39. Ibid.
40. Ibid.
41. D. Drickhamer, "On target," *Industry Week* (October 16, 2000), pp. 111–112.
42. S. Leibs, "Getting Ready: Your Customers," p. 2.
43. Ibid.
44. G. Taninecz, "Forging the Chain," p. 44.
45. "Straightline Provides Real-Time Visibility to the Supply Chain with New Online Service: StraightEdge™ Enables Customers to Increase Inventory Turns, Enhance Operational Efficiency and Improve Cash flow," *PR Newswire* (October 8, 2002), p. 1.
46. D. Bartholomew, "The Infrastructure," p. 3.
47. W. Royal, "Too Much Trust?" *Industry Week* (November 2, 1998), available online <www.industryweek.com>.
48. J. Sheridan, "Managing the Value Chain," p. 4.
49. W. Echikson, "Taking Hungary on a High-Tech Ride," *Business Week* (October 23, 2000), p. 148D.
50. H. Filman, "You Order It, They'll Make It," *Business Week* (May 29, 2000), pp. 218D–218J.

51. D. Bartholomew, "Supply Chain Moves Online," *Industry Week* (March 20, 2000), pp. 52–56.
52. J. Teresko, "The Dawn of E-Manufacturing," *Industry Week* (October 2, 2000), pp. 455–60.
53. See J. Cauhorn, "The Journey to World Class," *Industry Week* (April 6, 2001), available online at <www.industryweek.com>.
54. D. Bartholomew, "One Product, One Customer," *Industry Week* (September 12, 2002), available on line at <www.industryweek.com>.
55. S. Chausse, S. Landry, F. Paisn, and S. Fortier, "Anatomy of a Kanban: A Case Study," *Production and Inventory Management Journal* (Fall 2000) 4–15.
56. For a thorough overview of project management, see J. M. Nicholas, *Project Management for Business and Technology: Principles and practice,* 2nd ed. (Upper Saddle River, NJ: Prentice Hall, 2001).
57. H. Maylor, "Beyond the Gantt Chart: Project Management Moving On," *European Management Journal* (February 2001), pp. 92–101.
58. www.photondynamics.com.
59. R. ColinJohnson," AI Techniques Automate PC Bond Prospection," Electronic Engineering Times. (October 8, 2001) p. 67.
60. C. Hymourtz, "How One Each Chief fed through a Crisis and into the future," Wall tired Journal (August 29, 2000) p. B1.
61. These skills steps are adapted from The Prep Center, "Collaboration Skills Checklist," (2002), available online at <www.prepcenter.org>.
62. J. Millman, "The World's New Tiger on the Export scene Isn't Asia, It's Mexico," *Wall Street Journal* (May 9, 2000), p. A1.

Photo Credits

Chapter 1
2, 14, Beth Perkins/Renee Rhyner and Company
2, 13, James Ray; used with permission
3, AP/WideWorld Photos
4, Michael Macor/San Francisco Chronicle/Corbis/SABA Press Photos, Inc.
5, Venator Group, Inc.
6, AP/WideWorld Photos
9, Robbie McClaran
11, Courtesy of Earth Trek's Climbing Centers
17, Alex Wong/Getty Images, Inc.
19, Matthew Salacuse
27, CORBIS
28, Frederick Winslow Taylor Collection, Stevens Institute of Technology, Hoboken, NJ.
33, © Ariel Skelley/CORBIS
37, Hulton Archives/Getty Images Inc.
40, AFP Photos/Stephen JAFFE/CORBIS

Chapter 2
42, 69, AP/WideWorld Photos
42, 58, D.J. Hanlon; used with permission
43, Joe McDonald/*The Westchester Journal News*
44, Lester Lefkowitz/CORBIS
46, Thomas Sandberg/tomsand.com
48, AP/WideWorld Photos
49, Merillat Industries, LLC
64, Stew Leonard
67, Scott Thode Photography

Chapter 3
76, 91, PhotoEdit
76, 121, James Ray; used with permission
77, Evan Kafka
80, Random House, Inc.
81, Photo by Alan Dejecacion/Newsmakers/Getty Images, Inc.
83, AP/WideWorld Photos
86, Jon Feingersh/CORBIS
89, Susan Van Etten/PhotoEdit
94, Ford Motor Company
93, Canadian Tire Corporation, Limited

Chapter 4
104, 111, Quinn/Getty Images, Inc.-Liaison
105, C.R. Photo
107, Lonnie Duka/Index Stock Imagery, Inc.
113, AP/WideWorld Photos
114, AP/WideWorld Photos
115, Getty-Digital Vision
116, Advanced Cell Technology, Inc./CORBIS
120, Bonnie Kamin/PhotoEdit
123, Larry Ford Foto

Chapter 5
140, 154, Getty Images Inc.
141, Trufresh, LLC
142, © 1993 Seth Resnick
144, Penn State University
149, Getty Images Inc.
150, AP/WideWorld Photos
152, Getty Images, Inc.
160, David Woo

Chapter 6
166, 176, Michael Newman/PhotoEdit
167, AP/WideWorld Photos
174, David Stoecklein/CORBIS
178, Corbis/Sygma
182, Joel W. Rogers/CORBIS
185, David Urbina/PhotoEdit
186, Willie Hill, Jr./The Image Works
187, AP/WideWorld Photos
188, AP/WideWorld Photos

Chapter 7
200, 205, © Art Underground/CORBIS
201, © Galen Rowell/CORBIS
203, Michael L. Abramson Photography
208, Jose Luis Pelaez, Inc./CORBIS
211, © PBNJ Productions/CORBIS
212, Miles Schuster/SuperStock, Inc.
214, Dennis MacDonald/PhotoEdit
215, Robert Wright Photography
217, Terex Corporarion

Chapter 8
226, 247, Getty Images, Inc.
226, 237, Brian McGinty; used with permission
227, Auntie Anne's, Inc.
229, PhotoEdit
230, Steven Rubin/The Image Works
232, Michael Newman/PhotoEdit
234, Richard Lord/The Image Works
235, Men's Wearhouse.
240, AP/WideWorld Photos
241, David Barry/Corbis/Outline
241, © Bill Varie/CORBIS
244, AP/WideWorld Photos

Chapter 9
256, 269, Courtesy Seph Barnard/Tape Resources, Inc.
256, 264, Steve Peters; used with permission
257, StrawberryFrog
258, Deere & Company.
260, Wachovia Corporation
262, Getty Images, Inc.
263, Kevin Horan
270, AP/WideWorld Photos

Chapter 10
278, 282, Sal Skog Photography
278, 296, Mark Boice; used with permission
279, Mary Ellen Mark
287, Jason Glow/CORBIS/SABA Press Photos, Inc.
290, Bill Bachmann/PhotoEdit
294, Dennis MacDonald/PhotoEdit
295, Lorenzo Ciniglio/Corbis/Sygma
297, © Ted Horowitz/CORBIS
299, © 2001 Indianapolis Business Journal
300, Butler International

Chapter 11
308, 310, AP/WideWorld Photos
308, 327, Adele Sacarelli; used with permission
309, AP/Wide World Photos
315, AP/WideWorld Photos
318, AP/Wide World Photos
319, AP/WideWorld Photos
322, Courtesy of Wal-Mart Corporation
323, Photo courtesy of Mary Kay Inc.
324, Zurich Financial Services
328, Mark Segal/Getty Images Inc.
332, Mattel, Inc.

Chapter 12
338, 351, Amy Etra/PhotoEdit
338, 355, Lori DeGasso; used with permission
339, AP/WideWorld Photos
341, Spencer Ainsley/The Image Works
342, Bob Daemmrich
344, Larry Dale Gordon/Getty Images Inc.
350, Jay Reed
359, David Young-Wolff/PhotoEdit
364, © Mitchell Gerber/CORBIS

Chapter 13
372, 377, Andy Sacks/Getty Images, Inc.
373, James Nielsen/Getty Images Inc.
375, AP/WideWorld Photos
378, CVS Corporation
381, AP/WideWorld Photos
382, AFP Photo-Courtesy of Lockheed Martin Astronautics/NASA © AFP/CORBIS
387, Remi Benali/Getty Images, Inc./Liaison
392, © Tim Pannell/CORBIS

Chapter 14
400, 406, AP/WideWorld Photos
401, Medtronic Xomed
403, AP/WideWorld Photos
404, Wainwright Industries, Inc.
405, Deere & Company.
412, AFP/CORBIS
413, Michael Appelt/Regina Maria Anzenberger
414, Roger Ball/CORBiS

Name/Organization Index

C

I

J

K

N

O

P

T

U

V

Glindex

D

E

Q

R

Class Notes

Class Notes

Class Notes

Class Notes

Class Notes